Rick Steves'

GREECE
ATHENS & THE
PELOPONNESE

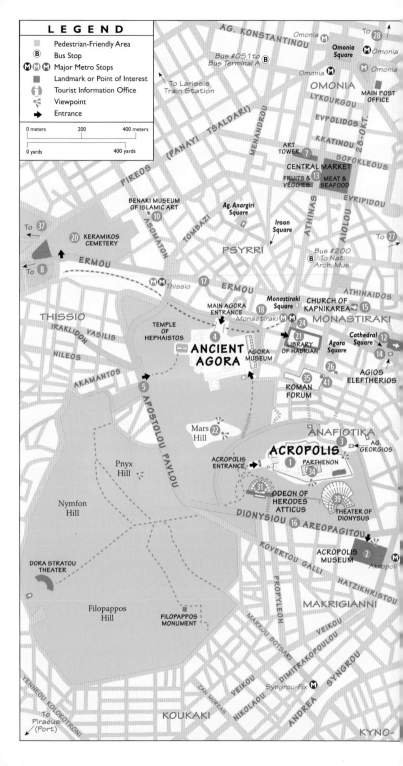

LEGEND

- Pedestrian-Friendly Area
- Ⓑ Bus Stop
- ⓂⓂⓂ Major Metro Stops
- Landmark or Point of Interest
- Tourist Information Office
- Viewpoint
- → Entrance

0 meters 200 400 meters
0 yards 400 yards

AG. KONSTANTINOU
Omonia Ⓜ Omonia Square
To 28

Bus #051 to Bus Terminal A Ⓑ
Omonia Ⓜ *Omonia*
OMONIA
Ⓜ *Omonia*
MAIN POST OFFICE

To Larissis Train Station
LYKOURGOU
EVPOLIDOS
KRATINOU
SOFOKLEOUS
28-OKT.

PIREOS (PANAYI TSALDARI)
MENANDROU
ATHINAS
AIOLOU
ART TOWER 7
CENTRAL MARKET
FRUITS & VEGGIES
MEAT & SEAFOOD
EVRIPIDOU

BENAKI MUSEUM OF ISLAMIC ART 10
ASOMATON
TOMBAZI
Ag. Anargiri Square
Iroon Square
To 27

To 37
20 KERAMIKOS CEMETERY
ERMOU
PSYRRI
Bus #200 To Nat. Arch. Mus. Ⓑ

To 8
ⓂⓂ *Thissio* 17
ERMOU
ATHINAIDOS

THISSIO
IRAKLIDON
VASILIS
NILEOS
AKAMANTOS

MAIN AGORA ENTRANCE
TEMPLE OF HEPHAISTOS
ANCIENT AGORA
4
AGORA MUSEUM
5

18 Monastiraki Square
Monastiraki ⓂⓂ 24
21 LIBRARY OF HADRIAN
Agora Square
CHURCH OF KAPNIKAREA 15
MONASTIRAKI
Cathedral Square 12
14
26
41
ROMAN FORUM 35
AGIOS ELEFTHERIOS

APOSTOLOU PAVLOU
Pnyx Hill
Nymfon Hill

Mars Hill 22
ACROPOLIS ENTRANCE →
ACROPOLIS 1
PARTHENON
34
ANAFIOTIKA
3 AG. GEORGIOS

31 ODEON OF HERODES ATTICUS
39 THEATER OF DIONYSUS
DIONYSIOU AREOPAGITOU
16

DORA STRATOU THEATER
Filopappos Hill
FILOPAPPOS MONUMENT

ACROPOLIS MUSEUM 2
Akropoli Ⓜ
MAKRIGIANNI
ROVERTOU GALLI
PROPYLEON
MARKOU BOTSARI
HATZIKHRISTOU
VEIKOU

YENNEOU KOLOKOTRONI
To Piraeus (Port)
ZAN MOREAS
VEIKOU
NIKOLAOU
DIMITRAKOPOULOU
ANDREA
SYNGROU

Syngrou-Fix Ⓜ
KOUKAKI
KYNO-

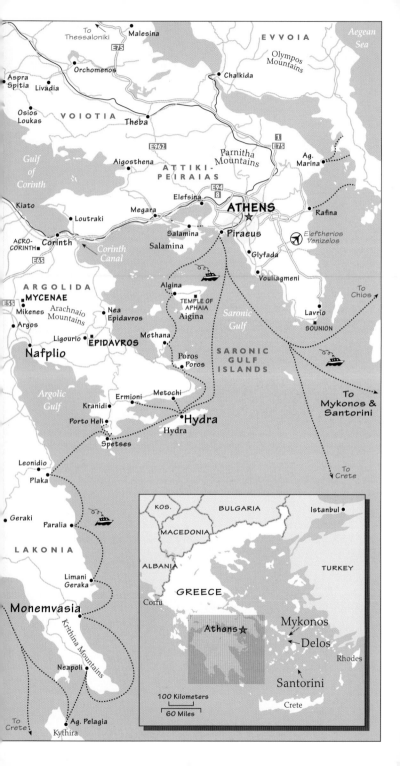

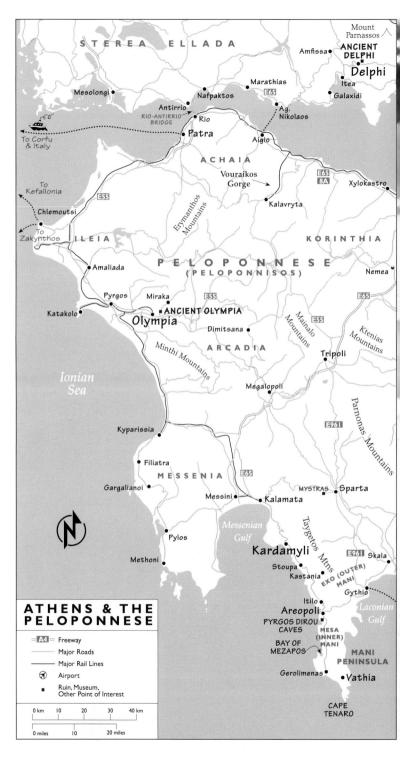

ATHENS

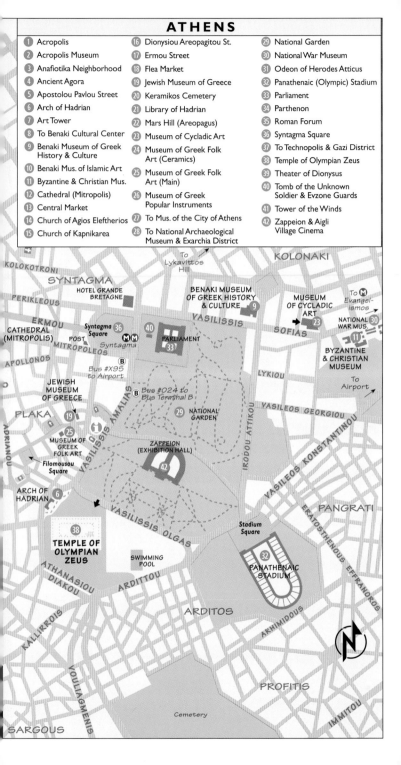

GREECE
ATHENS & THE
PELOPONNESE

AVALON
TRAVEL

CONTENTS

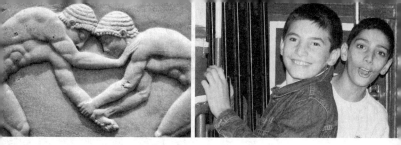

INTRODUCTION

Democracy and mathematics. Medicine and literature. Theater and astronomy. Mythology and philosophy. All of these, and more, were first thought up by a bunch of tunic-clad Greeks in a small village huddled at the base of the Acropolis. The ancient Greeks—who reached their apex in the city of Athens—have had an unmatched impact on European and American culture. For many travelers, coming to Athens is like a pilgrimage to the cradle of our civilization.

A century and a half ago, Athens was a humble, forgotten city of about 8,000 people. Today it's the teeming home of nearly four million Greeks. The city is famous for its sprawl, noise, and pollution. The best advice to tourists has long been to see the big sights, then get out. But over the last decade or so, the city has made a concerted effort to curb pollution, clean up and pedestrianize the streets, spiff up the museums, and invest in one of Europe's better public transit systems. All of these urban upgrades reached a peak as Athens hosted the 2004 Olympic Games.

And yet, the conventional wisdom still holds true: Athens is a great city to see...but not to linger in. This book also includes the best Greek destinations outside the capital, including the highlights of the Peloponnese—Greece's heartland peninsula, the site of the ancient oracle at Delphi, and the castaway islands of Hydra, Mykonos, and Santorini.

I'll give you all the information and opinions necessary to wring the maximum value out of your limited time and money. If you plan two weeks or less in this part of Greece and have a normal appetite for information, this book is all you need. If you're a travel-info fiend, this book sorts through all the superlatives and provides a handy rack upon which to hang your supplemental information.

Map Legend

⚏ View Point	✈ Airport		▋	Tunnel
↑ Entry Arrow	ⓣ Taxi Stand		▬	Pedestrian Zone
✪ Tourist Info	▥ Tram Stop		- - - -	Railway
⊞ Restroom	⑧ Bus Stop		··········	Ferry/Boat Route
⬛ Castle	ⓟ Parking		├──┼──┤	Tram
⬚ Church	)(Mtn. Pass		▥▥▥▥	Stairs
▪ Statue/Point of Interest	▨ Park		· · · · ·	Walk/Tour Route
			- - - - -	Trail

Use this legend to help you navigate the maps in this book.

Experiencing Europe's culture, people, and natural wonders economically and hassle-free has been my goal for three decades of traveling, tour guiding, and travel writing. With this new book, I pass on to you the lessons I've learned.

The destinations covered in this book are balanced to include a comfortable mix of cities and villages, ancient sites and Byzantine churches, great museums and relaxing beaches. While you'll find the predictable biggies (such as the Acropolis and ancient Olympia), I've also mixed in a healthy dose of Back Door intimacy (workaday towns such as Kardamyli, rustic seaside viewpoints, and neighborhood tavernas where you'll enjoy a warm welcome).

The best is, of course, only my opinion. But after spending a third of my adult life exploring and researching Europe, I've developed a sixth sense for what travelers enjoy. The places featured in this book will make anyone want to shout, *"Opa!"*

About This Book

Rick Steves' Greece: Athens & the Peloponnese is a tour guide in your pocket. Each destination is a mini-vacation on its own, filled with exciting sights, homey, affordable places to stay, and memorable places to eat.

The first half of this book focuses on Athens and contains the following chapters:

Greece offers an introduction to this mesmerizing land, including a crash course in the Greek alphabet.

Orientation to Athens includes specifics on public transportation, helpful hints, local tour options, tourist information, and an easy-to-read map. The "Planning Your Time" section suggests a schedule for how to best use your limited time.

Sights in Athens describes the top attractions and includes their cost and hours.

The **Self-Guided Walks** and **Tours** take you through interest-

Key to This Book

Updates

This book is updated regularly, but things change. For the latest, visit www.ricksteves.com/update, and for a valuable list of reports and experiences—good and bad—from fellow travelers, check www.ricksteves.com/feedback.

Abbreviations and Times

I use the following symbols and abbreviations in this book: Sights are rated:

▲▲▲	**Don't miss**
▲▲	**Try hard to see**
▲	**Worthwhile if you can make it**
No rating	**Worth knowing about**

When you see a ✪ in a sight listing, it means that the sight is covered in much more detail in one of the tour chapters.

Tourist information offices are abbreviated as **TI,** and bathrooms are **WC**s. To categorize accommodations, I use a **Sleep Code** (described on page 21).

Like Greece, this book uses the **24-hour clock** for schedules. It's the same through 12:00 noon, then keep going: 13:00, 14:00, and so on. For anything over 12, subtract 12 and add p.m. (14:00 is 2:00 p.m.).

When giving **opening times,** I include both peak season and off-season hours if they differ. So, if a museum is listed as "May-Oct daily 9:00-16:00," it should be open from 9 a.m. until 4 p.m. from the first day of May until the last day of October (but expect exceptions).

For **transit** or **tour departures,** I first list the frequency, then the duration. So, a bus connection listed as "2/hour, 1.5 hours" departs twice each hour, and the journey lasts an hour and a half.

ing neighborhoods and must-see sights. In Athens, these include a city walk, the Acropolis, the Ancient Agora, the Acropolis Museum, and the National Archaeological Museum.

Sleeping in Athens describes my favorite accommodations, from good-value *dhomatia* to cushy splurges.

Eating in Athens serves up a range of options, from inexpensive tavernas to fancy restaurants.

Shopping in Athens gives you tips for shopping painlessly and enjoyably, without letting it overwhelm your vacation or ruin your budget.

Nightlife in Athens is your guide to evening fun, including music, folk dances, outdoor movies, and bustling nighttime neighborhoods.

Athens Connections covers how to get to nearby destinations

Greece at a Glance

These attractions are listed (as in this book) starting with Athens, moving to the Peloponnese, and then covering other regions.

▲▲▲**Athens** Greece's capital, featuring the ancient world's most magnificent sight—the Acropolis—a pair of world-class museums, an atmospheric Old Town, and funky neighborhoods bursting with avant-garde nightlife.

▲▲**Nafplio** Greece's first capital and finest mid-sized town, with a cozy port, elegant Old Town, cliff-topping fortress, and energetic street life; handy to nearby ancient sites (Mycenae and Epidavros).

▲**Epidavros** Best-preserved theater of the ancient world, with unbelievable acoustics.

▲**Mycenae** Legendary mountaintop palace/fortress with iconic Lion Gate, massive beehive tomb, and mythic links to the Trojan War.

▲▲**Olympia** Birthplace of the Olympic Games, with stunning temple ruins, a still-functional stadium, and an intimate museum of ancient masterpieces.

▲**Kardamyli and the Mani Peninsula** Cozy, unspoiled beach town, providing a handy jumping-off point for a remote, rus-

by car or bus, and includes information on getting to and from Athens' airport.

The **Peloponnese** section includes in-depth chapters on that historic peninsula's top sights: **Nafplio, Epidavros, Mycenae, Olympia, Kardamyli and the Mani Peninsula,** and **Monemvasia.**

The **Beyond Athens & the Peloponnese** section covers the ancient oracle site at **Delphi** and the idyllic islands of **Hydra, Mykonos,** and **Santorini.**

The **Greek History and Mythology** chapter gives you a quick overview of the country's past.

The **appendix** is a traveler's tool kit, with telephone tips, useful phone numbers, recommended books and films, a festival list, climate chart, handy packing checklist, hotel reservation form, and Greek survival phrases.

Browse through this book and choose your favorite sights. Then have a great trip! Traveling like a temporary local and taking advantage of the information here, you'll enjoy the absolute most tic region with dramatic hill towns, spectacular caves (Pyrgos Dirou), and breathtaking jagged coastlines.

▲**Monemvasia** Greece's Gibraltar-like fortress on an imposing rock peninsula jutting out into the sea, blending Venetian and Byzantine charm, traffic-free cobbled lanes, and million-dollar views.

▲▲**Delphi** Mountainside draped with the Sanctuary of Apollo and other once-grandiose structures, where ancients came to consult the oracle.

▲▲▲**Hydra** Idyllic island getaway, convenient to Athens and the Peloponnese, with picturesque harbor, casual beaches, enticing coastal hikes, and no cars (but plenty of donkeys).

▲▲**Mykonos** Quintessential (and very popular) Greek isle with postcard-perfect whitewashed village, old-fashioned windmills, and pulsating nightlife; ruins on nearby Delos mark the birthplace of Apollo and a once-mighty shipping center.

▲▲**Santorini** Romantic island destination built on the remains of a volcano crater, renowned for cliff-clinging white villages punctuated by blue-domed churches, volcanic black-sand beaches, and spectacular sunsets.

of every mile, minute, and euro. I'm happy that you'll be visiting places I know and love, and meeting some of my favorite Greek people.

Planning

This section will help you get started on planning your trip—with advice on trip costs, when to go, and what you should know before you take off.

Travel Smart

Your trip to Greece is like a complex play—easier to follow and really appreciate on a second viewing. While no one does the same trip twice to gain that advantage, reading this book before your trip accomplishes much the same thing.

Design an itinerary that enables you to visit the various sights at the best possible times. Make note of festival weekends and days when sights are closed. For example, many museums are either closed or open limited hours on Mondays. Sundays have the same pros and cons as they do for travelers in the US (special events, limited hours, banks and many shops closed, limited public transportation, no rush hours). Saturdays are virtually weekdays with earlier closing hours and no rush hour (though transportation connections can be less frequent than on weekdays).

Mix intense and relaxed periods in your itinerary. To maximize rootedness, minimize one-night stands. It's worth a post-dinner drive or bus ride to be settled into a town for two nights. Small hotels and *dhomatia* (rooms in private homes) are also more likely to give a better price to someone staying more than one night.

Every trip (and every traveler) needs at least a few slack days (for picnics, laundry, people-watching, and so on). Pace yourself. Assume you will return.

If traveling beyond Athens, visit local TIs as you go. Upon arrival in a new town, lay the groundwork for a smooth departure; write down the schedule for the bus or boat you'll take when you depart. Drivers can study the best route to their next destination.

Get online at Internet cafés or at your hotel, and buy a phone card or carry a mobile phone: You can get tourist information, learn the latest on sights (special events, English tour schedules, etc.), book tickets and tours, make reservations, reconfirm hotels, research transportation connections, check weather, and keep in touch with your loved ones.

Connect with the culture. Set up your own quest to find the best baklava, Byzantine church, or secluded beach. Be open to unexpected experiences. Slow down and enjoy the hospitality of the Greek people. Ask questions—most locals are eager to point you in their idea of the right direction. Keep a notepad in your pocket for organizing your thoughts. Wear your money belt, get used to the local currency, and learn how to estimate prices in dollars. Those who expect to travel smart, do.

Trip Costs

Five components make up your trip costs: airfare, surface transportation, room and board, sightseeing and entertainment, and shopping and miscellany.

Airfare: A basic, round-trip, US-to-Athens flight costs $750-1,400, depending on where you fly from and when (cheaper in winter). If your trip extends beyond Greece, consider saving time and money by flying into one city and out of another (for example, into Paris and out of Athens). Note that if you're visiting only Greece, the airport at Athens is your most convenient way in and out of the country.

Surface Transportation: If you're just touring Athens, you can get around easily on the Metro (plan on $30 for three full days in Athens and a round-trip ticket to/from the airport). If you're venturing beyond the capital—say, doing a two-week loop of this book's destinations—figure per-person costs of $150 by public transit (boat to Hydra, bus to everything else) or $500 by car (based on two people sharing a rental car; includes gas and insurance).

Room and Board: You can thrive in Athens on $100 a day per person for room and board (less on the Peloponnese). That allows $15 for lunch, $20 for dinner, and $65 for lodging (based on two people splitting the cost of a $130 double room that includes breakfast). Students and tightwads eat and sleep for as little as $60 a day ($30 per bed, $30 for meals and snacks).

Sightseeing and Entertainment: In Athens, figure $7-17 per major sight (Acropolis, National Archaeological Museum); $5-10 for minor ones (Benaki Museum of Greek History and Culture, Museum of Cycladic Art); and $30-60 for splurge experiences such as concerts, special art exhibits, big-bus tours, and guided walking tours. An overall average of $25 a day works for most people. Don't skimp here. After all, this category is the driving force behind your trip—you came to sightsee, enjoy, and experience Greece.

Shopping and Miscellany: Figure $1-2 per postcard, coffee, or ice-cream cone. Shopping can vary in cost from nearly nothing to a small fortune. Good budget travelers find that this category has little to do with assembling a trip full of lifelong and wonderful memories.

Sightseeing Priorities

Depending on the length of your trip, and taking geographic proximity into account, here are my recommended priorities.

2-3 days:	Athens
5 days, add:	Hydra
7 days, add:	Delphi
10 days, add:	Nafplio, Epidavros, Mycenae
12 days, add:	Olympia, Monemvasia
14 days, add:	Kardamyli and the Mani Peninsula, and slow down

While this book focuses on Athens and the Peloponnese, I've also included Mykonos and Santorini—two of Greece's best islands—for travelers with more time.

For a suggested itinerary, see the next page.

When to Go

The "summer" and "winter" seasons can vary, but summer is roughly Easter through October, when Athens can be crowded.

Peak Season: In summer, Athens is packed with tourists and hotel prices can be correspondingly high. July and August are the

Athens and the Peloponnese in Two Weeks

Once you're outside of Athens, this region is best to visit by car. If you'd rather get around by bus, you'll see less in virtually the same amount of time. In general, avoid trains, which have more limited routes, are slower, and run less frequently than buses.

Best Trip by Car

Day	Plan	Sleep
1	Arrive Athens	Athens
2	Athens	Athens
3	Athens	Athens
4	Boat to Hydra	Hydra
5	Hydra	Hydra
6	Boat back to Athens, pick up rental car, drive to Delphi	Delphi
7	Sightsee Delphi, drive to Olympia	Olympia
8	Sightsee Olympia, drive to Kardamyli	Kardamyli
9	Relax in Kardamyli	Kardamyli
10	Mani Peninsula loop drive, on to Monemvasia	Monemvasia
11	Monemvasia	Monemvasia
12	See Mycenae en route to Nafplio	Nafplio
13	Nafplio, side-trip to Epidavros	Nafplio
14	Return to Athens, drop off rental car	Athens
15	Fly home, or continue to Mykonos and/or Santorini by plane or boat	

Best Trip by Bus

Day	Plan	Sleep
1	Arrive Athens	Athens
2	Athens	Athens
3	Athens	Athens
4	Morning in Athens, afternoon bus to Delphi	Delphi
5	Sightsee Delphi	Delphi
6	Morning bus to Athens, then boat to Hydra	Hydra
7	Hydra	Hydra
8	Morning boat back to Athens, then bus to Olympia	Olympia
9	Sightsee Olympia	Olympia
10	Morning bus to Nafplio	Nafplio
11	Day trip to Mycenae	Nafplio
12	Day trip to Epidavros	Nafplio
13	Bus to Athens	Athens
14	Fly home, or continue to Mykonos and/or Santorini by plane or boat	

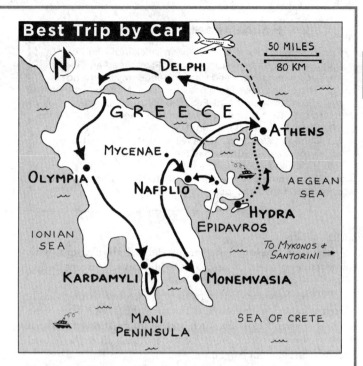

Bus Notes: The bus itinerary can be modified depending on your interests. Remember to take care with your bus connections, which can be limited and complicated, especially on the Peloponnese.

Two nights in Delphi offers a fine escape from big-city Athens, but if you have limited time, you can see Delphi either as a day trip on Day 4 (return to Athens to spend the night) or as a single overnight (bus from Athens to Delphi on the morning of Day 4, afternoon sightseeing and overnight in Delphi, then bus to Athens and boat to Hydra on Day 5).

The bus itinerary leaves out the hardest-to-reach destinations: Kardamyli/Mani Peninsula (best by car or with a hired local driver) and Monemvasia.

If you've seen enough ancient sites, you could skip Olympia (which is time-consuming to reach by bus), or visit Monemvasia instead (reachable by bus, with an extra transfer and more travel time than Olympia). Beach-lovers might prefer to skip both for more time on Hydra.

The easiest connection from Hydra to the Peloponnese is via Athens, but adventurous travelers might want to tackle the shorter, though more complicated, boat-taxi-bus connection via Nafplio instead; for tips see page 251.

With an extra week and a bunch of patience, you could include all of the recommended destinations.

Holidays and Weekends

Popular places are even busier on weekends...and can be inundated on three-day weekends. Plan ahead and reserve your accommodations and transportation well in advance.

The big holidays in Greece are "Clean Monday" (the first day of Lent: March 7 in 2011, Feb 27 in 2012), Independence Day (March 25), Orthodox Easter weekend (Fri-Mon: April 22-25 in 2011, April 13-16 in 2012), Labor Day (May 1), Assumption (Aug 15), Ohi Day (World War II anniversary, Oct 28), and a string of winter holidays: Christmas (celebrated Dec 25-26), New Year's Day, and Epiphany (Jan 6).

For a more complete list of festivals and holidays, see page 486 in the appendix.

hottest months.

Shoulder Season: Late spring and fall are pleasant, with comfortable weather, no rain, and lighter crowds (except during holiday weekends).

Winter Season: Travel from late October through mid-March is colder. Though rain is rare in Athens, this is the time for it. Some sights close for lunch, tourist information offices keep shorter hours, and some tourist activities vanish altogether. Hotel rates are soft; look for bargains.

Know Before You Go

Your trip is more likely to go smoothly if you plan ahead. Check this list of things to arrange while you're still at home.

You need a **passport,** but no visa or shots, to travel in Greece. You may be denied entry into certain European countries if your passport is due to expire within three to six months of your ticketed date of return. Get it renewed if you'll be cutting it close. It can take up to six weeks to get or renew a passport (for more on passports, see www.travel.state.gov). Pack a photocopy of your passport in your luggage in case the original is lost or stolen.

Book rooms in advance, especially if you'll be traveling during peak season or around any major **holidays.**

Call your **debit- and credit-card companies** to let them know the countries you'll be visiting, to ask about fees, and more (see page 14).

Do your homework if you want to buy **travel insurance.** Compare the cost of the insurance to the likelihood of your using it and your potential loss if something goes wrong. For more information, see www.ricksteves.com/insurance.

If you're bringing an MP3 player, you can download free information from **Rick Steves Audio Europe,** featuring hours of travel interviews on Greece, audio tours of major sights in Athens, and more (at www.ricksteves.com/audioeurope and in iTunes; for details, see page 481).

If you're planning on **renting a car** in Greece, you'll need your driver's license and an International Driving Permit (see page 471).

Because **airline carry-on restrictions** are always changing, visit the Transportation Security Administration's website (www .tsa.gov/travelers) for an up-to-date list of what you can bring on the plane with you...and what you have to check.

Practicalities

Emergency and Medical Help: Dial 171 for the Tourist Police or a medical emergency. The Tourist Police serves as a contact point between tourists and other branches of the police and is also responsible for handling problems such as disputes with hotels, restaurants, and other tourist services (available daily 24 hours, office located south of the Acropolis in Koukaki at Veikou 43-45, office tel. 210-920-0724). If you get sick, do as the Greeks do and go to a pharmacist for advice. Or ask at your hotel for help—they'll know the nearest medical and emergency services.

Lost or Stolen Passport: To replace a passport, you'll need to go in person to a US embassy (see page 469). While not required, having a backup form of ID—ideally a photocopy of your passport and driver's license—speeds up a replacement. For more info, see www.ricksteves.com/help.

Borders: You'll go through customs if arriving on a direct flight from the US. If you're coming from Europe, you may or may not have to go through customs, depending on which country you're coming from. Greece is part of Europe's open-borders Schengen Agreement, so if you fly in from another Schengen country (including all those in Western Europe and some in Eastern Europe) or take a boat from Italy, there are no passport checks. Since Greece's neighbors are not part of the pact, you'll go through customs coming from Turkey, Macedonia, Albania, and Bulgaria (although Bulgaria may join the pact in 2011). Even as borders fade, when you change countries, you must still change telephone cards, postage stamps, and underpants.

Time Zones: Greece is generally one hour ahead of continental Europe and seven/ten hours ahead of the East/West Coasts of the US. The exceptions are the beginning and end of Daylight Saving Time: Europe "springs forward" the last Sunday in March (two weeks after most of North America) and "falls back" the last Sunday in October (one week before North America). For a handy online time converter, try www.timeanddate.com/worldclock.

Business Hours: Most shops catering to tourists are open long hours daily. Those that cater to locals are more likely open these somewhat predictable hours: Monday, Wednesday, and Saturday from 8:30 or 9:00 until early afternoon (between 14:30 and 16:00); Tuesday, Thursday, and Friday from 8:30 or 9:00 until late (roughly 20:00 or 21:00), but often with an afternoon break (around 14:00-17:00 or 18:00); and closed Sunday. Some museums and sights are closed on Monday.

Watt's Up? Europe's electrical system is different from North America's in two ways: the shape of the plug (two round prongs) and the voltage of the current (220 volts instead of 110 volts). For your North American plug to work in Europe, you'll need an adapter, sold inexpensively at travel stores in the US and Canada. As for the voltage, most newer electronics (including hair dryers, laptops, and battery chargers) convert it automatically—if you see a range of voltages printed on the item or its plug (such as "110-220"), it'll work in Europe. It's not worth trying to make older appliances work overseas—while you can buy a voltage converter in the US ($20), they're heavy and unreliable. Either go without or buy a cheap replacement appliance in Europe. Travel hairdryers and other small appliances are sold at Public and Radio Korasidis stores (ask your hotelier for the closest branch).

Discounts: Discounts aren't listed in this book. However, many sights offer discounts for seniors (loosely defined as those who are retired or willing to call themselves a senior), groups of 10 or more, families, and students or teachers with proper identification cards (www.isic.org). Always ask. Children under 18 get in free at some museums and archaeological sites, including the Acropolis and Acropolis Museum. Some discounts are available only for EU citizens.

News: Americans keep in touch via the *International Herald Tribune* (published almost daily throughout Europe and online at www.iht.com). Another newsy site is http://news.bbc.co.uk. Every Tuesday, the European editions of *Time* and *Newsweek* hit the stands with articles of particular interest to travelers in Europe. Sports addicts can get their daily fix at www.espn.com or from *USA Today*. English-language periodicals in Athens include *Athens News* (www.athensnews.gr), *Athens Plus* (www.athensplus.gr), and the Greek lifestyle magazine *Odyssey* (www.odyssey.gr). Many hotels have CNN or BBC News channels.

Money

This section offers advice on how to pay for purchases on your trip (including getting cash from ATMs and paying with plastic), dealing with lost or stolen cards, VAT (sales tax) refunds, and tipping.

Exchange Rate

1 euro (€) = about $1.40

To convert prices in euros to dollars, add about 40 percent: €20 = about $28, €50 = about $70. Just like the dollar, the euro is broken down into 100 cents. You'll find coins ranging from 1 cent to 2 euros, and bills from 5 euros to 500 euros. (To get the latest rates and print a cheat sheet, see www.oanda .com.)

So those €65 amber worry beads are about $100, and the €90 taxi ride through Athens is...uh-oh.

What to Bring

Bring both a credit card and a debit card. You'll use the debit card at cash machines (ATMs) to withdraw euros for most purchases, and the credit card to pay for larger items. Some travelers carry a third card as a backup, in case one gets demagnetized or eaten by a temperamental machine.

As an emergency backup, I also carry a few hundred dollars in hard cash (in easy-to-exchange $20 bills). Don't bother changing cash before you leave home—ATMs in Greece are easy to find and easy to use. Avoid using currency exchange booths (lousy rates and/or outrageous fees); if you have foreign currency to exchange, take it to a bank. And skip traveler's checks—they're a waste of time (long waits at slow banks) and a waste of money in fees.

Cash

Cash is just as desirable in Greece as it is at home. Small businesses (hotels, restaurants, and shops) prefer that you pay your bills with cash. Some vendors will charge you extra for using a credit card, and some won't take credit cards at all.

Throughout Greece, cash machines (ATMs) are the standard way for travelers to get cash. To withdraw money from an ATM, you'll need a debit card (ideally with a Visa or MasterCard logo for maximum usability), plus a PIN code. Know your PIN code in numbers—there are no letters on European keypads. You could use a credit card for ATM transactions, but it's generally more expensive (since it's considered a "cash advance" rather than a "withdrawal"). For security, it's best to shield the keypad when entering your PIN at the ATM.

When using an ATM, taking out large sums of money can reduce the number of per-transaction bank fees you'll pay. If the machine refuses your request, try again and select a smaller amount (some cash machines limit the amount you can withdraw—don't take it personally). If that doesn't work, try a different machine.

Most ATMs in Greece are located outside of a bank. Try to use the ATM when the branch is open; if your card is eaten by the machine, you can immediately go inside for help. If the ATM dispenses big bills, try to break them at a bank or larger store, since it's easier to pay for purchases at small businesses using smaller bills.

To keep your cash safe, use a money belt—a pouch with a strap that you buckle around your waist like a belt and wear under your clothes. Pickpockets target tourists. A money belt provides peace of mind, allowing you to carry lots of cash safely. Don't waste time every few days tracking down a cash machine—withdraw a week's worth of money, stuff it in your money belt, and travel!

Credit and Debit Cards

For purchases, Visa and MasterCard are more commonly accepted than American Express. While you can use either a credit or a debit card for most transactions, using a credit card offers a greater degree of fraud protection (since debit cards draw funds directly from your account).

Just like at home, credit or debit cards are accepted by larger hotels and shops. I typically use my credit card only in a few specific situations: to book hotel reservations by phone, to make major purchases (such as car rentals, plane tickets, and long hotel stays), and to pay for things near the end of my trip (to avoid another visit to the ATM).

Ask Your Credit- or Debit-Card Company: Before your trip, contact the company that issued your debit or credit cards.

• Confirm your card will work overseas, and alert them that you'll be using it in Europe; otherwise, they may deny transactions if they perceive unusual spending patterns.

• Ask for the specifics on transaction **fees.** When you use your credit or debit card—either for purchases or ATM withdrawals— you'll often be charged additional "international transaction" fees of up to 3 percent (1 percent is normal) plus $5 per transaction. Some banks have agreements with European partners that reduce or eliminate the $5 transaction fee. If your fees are too high, consider getting a card just for your trip: Capital One (www.capitalone.com) and most credit unions have low-to-no international fees.

• If you plan to withdraw cash from ATMs, confirm your **daily withdrawal limit** (€300 is usually about the maximum). Some travelers prefer a high limit that allows them to take out more cash at each ATM stop, while others prefer to set a lower limit in case their card is stolen.

• Ask for your credit card's **PIN** in case you encounter Europe's chip-and-PIN system. For security reasons, most banks will only mail a PIN, so give yourself plenty of time to get the code if you don't already know it.

Chip and PIN: If your card is declined for a purchase in Europe, it may be because of chip and PIN, which requires cardholders to punch in a PIN instead of signing a receipt. Much of Europe—including Great Britain, Ireland, France, the Netherlands, and Scandinavia—is adopting this system. Chip and PIN is used by some merchants and also at automated payment machines—such as those at train stations, parking garages, luggage lockers, and self-serve pumps at gas stations. If you're prompted to enter your PIN (but don't know it), ask if the cashier can print a receipt for you to sign instead, or just pay cash. If you're dealing with an automated machine that won't take your card, look for a cashier nearby who can make your card work. The easiest solution is to carry sufficient cash.

Dynamic Currency Conversion: If merchants offer to convert your purchase price into dollars (called dynamic currency conversion, or DCC), refuse this "service." You'll pay even more in fees for the expensive convenience of seeing your charge in dollars.

Damage Control for Lost Cards

If you lose your credit, debit, or ATM card, you can stop people from using it by reporting the loss immediately to the respective global customer-assistance centers. Call these 24-hour US numbers collect: Visa (410/581-9994), MasterCard (636/722-7111), and American Express (623/492-8427).

At a minimum, you'll need to know the name of the financial institution that issued you the card, along with the type of card (classic, platinum, or whatever). Providing the following information will allow for a quicker cancellation of your missing card: full card number, whether you are the primary or secondary cardholder, the name exactly as printed on the card, billing address, home phone number, circumstances of the loss or theft, and identification verification (your birth date, your mother's maiden name, or your Social Security number—memorize this, don't carry a copy). If you are the secondary cardholder, you'll also need to provide the primary cardholder's identification-verification details. You can generally receive a temporary card within two or three business days.

If you promptly report your card lost or stolen, you typically won't be responsible for any unauthorized transactions on your account, although many banks charge a liability fee of $50.

Tipping

Tipping in Europe isn't as automatic and generous as it is in the US, but for special service, tips are appreciated, if not expected. As in the US, the proper amount depends on your resources, tipping philosophy, and the circumstances, but some general guidelines apply.

Restaurants: Tipping is an issue only at restaurants that have table service. If you order your food at a counter, don't tip.

At Greek restaurants that have waitstaff, service is generally included, although it's common to round up the bill after a good meal (usually 5-10 percent; so, for an €18.50 meal, pay €20).

Taxis: To tip the cabbie, round up about 5-10 percent (to pay a €4.50 fare, give €5; or for a €28 fare, give €30). If the cabbie hauls your bags and zips you to the airport to help you catch your flight, you might want to toss in a little more. But if you feel like you're being driven in circles or otherwise ripped off, skip the tip.

Special Services: Tour guides at public sites sometimes hold out their hands for tips after they give their spiel. If I've already paid for the tour, I don't tip extra unless they've really impressed me. At hotels, if you let porters carry your luggage, it's polite to give them a euro for each bag (another reason to pack light). I don't tip the maid, but if you do, you can leave a couple of euros in your room at the end of your stay.

In general, if someone in the service industry does a super job for you, a small tip of a euro or two is appropriate, but not required.

When in doubt, ask. If you're not sure whether (or how much) to tip for a service, ask your hotelier or the tourist information office; they'll fill you in on how it's done on their turf.

Getting a VAT Refund

Wrapped into the purchase price of your souvenirs is a Value-Added Tax (VAT) of 25 percent in Greece. If you make a purchase of more than €120 (about $170) at a store that participates in the VAT-refund scheme, you're entitled to get most of that tax back. Getting your refund is usually straightforward and, if you buy a substantial amount of souvenirs, well worth the hassle. If you're lucky, the merchant will subtract the tax when you make your purchase. (This is more likely to occur if the store ships the goods to your home.) Otherwise, you'll need to:

Get the paperwork. Have the merchant completely fill out the necessary refund document, called a "Tax-Free Shopping Cheque." You'll have to present your passport at the store.

Get your stamp at the border or airport. Process your cheque(s) at your last stop in the EU (e.g., at the airport) with the customs agent who deals with VAT refunds. It's best to keep your purchases in your carry-on for viewing, but if they're too large or dangerous (such as knives) to carry on, track down the proper customs agent to inspect them before you check your bag. You're not supposed to use your purchased goods before you leave. If you show up at customs wearing your chic Greek shirt, officials might look the other way—or deny you a refund.

Collect your refund. You'll need to return your stamped document to the retailer or its representative. Many merchants work with a service, such as Global Refund (www.globalrefund.com) or Premier Tax Free (www.premiertaxfree.com), which have offices at major airports, ports, or border crossings. These services, which extract a 4 percent fee, can refund your money immediately in your currency of choice or credit your card (within two billing cycles). If the retailer handles VAT refunds directly, it's up to you to contact the merchant for your refund. You can also mail the documents from your point of departure (using a stamped, addressed envelope you've prepared or one that's been provided by the merchant). You'll then have to wait—it can take months.

Customs for American Shoppers

You are allowed to take home $800 worth of items per person duty-free, once every 30 days. The next $1,000 is taxed at a flat 3 percent. After that, you pay the individual item's duty rate. You can also bring in duty-free a liter of alcohol (slightly more than a standard-size bottle of wine; you must be at least 21), 200 cigarettes, and up to 100 non-Cuban cigars.

As for food, you can take home vacuum-packed cheeses; dried herbs, spices, or mushrooms; and canned fruits or vegetables, including jams and vegetable spreads. Baked goods, candy, chocolate, oil, vinegar, mustard, and honey are OK. Fresh fruits or vegetables (even that banana from your airplane breakfast) are not permitted. Meats are generally not allowed. Just because a duty-free shop in an airport sells a food product doesn't mean it will automatically pass US customs. Be prepared to lose your investment.

Note that you'll need to carefully pack any bottles of wine, jam, honey, oil, and other liquid-containing items in your checked luggage, due to the three-ounce limit on liquids in carry-on baggage. To check customs rules and duty rates before you go, visit www.cbp.gov, and click on "Travel," then "Know Before You Go."

Sightseeing

Sightseeing can be hard work. Use these tips to make your visits to Greece's finest sights meaningful, fun, fast, and painless.

For online information (such as hours, contact info, and location) on virtually all of the major sites—including Athens' Acropolis, Ancient Agora, Acropolis Museum, National Archaeological Museum, and others, along with the attractions

INTRODUCTION

at Delphi, Olympia, Epidavros, Mycenae, and more—check www
.culture.gr. The website and the listed sites are managed by the
Ministry of Greek Culture. But be aware that the website might
not reflect unexpected changes (for example, closures at Delphi
due to rockslides). If you're traveling to a faraway sight and want to
be absolutely sure it's open, ask your hotelier or call ahead.

Plan Ahead

Set up an itinerary that allows you to fit in all your must-see sights.
For a one-stop look at opening hours in Athens, see the sidebar
on pages 68-69. Most sights keep stable hours, but you can easily
confirm the latest by asking the local TI.

Don't put off visiting a must-see sight—you never know when
a place will close because of a strike, budget cut, or restoration
project. On holidays (see list on page 486), expect shorter hours or
closures.

When possible, visit major sights first thing (when your
energy is best) and save other activities for the afternoon. Hit a
sight's highlights first, then see the rest if you have the stamina
and time. Going at the right time can also help you avoid crowds.
This book offers tips on specific sights. Try visiting very early, at
lunch, or—in summer—very late. Evening visits (when possible)
are usually peaceful, with fewer crowds and cooler temperatures.

Note that ancient sites managed by the Ministry of Greek
Culture can abruptly switch between longer "summer" hours and
shorter "winter" hours. If you're traveling from mid-September
to late April, visit these sights in the morning, when they're more
likely to be open. Confirm hours carefully to avoid unexpected
early closures.

Study up. To get the most out of the self-guided tours and
sight descriptions in this book, reread them the night before your
visit. The Acropolis is much more entertaining if you've polished
up on Pheidias and marble the night before. When you arrive at a
sight, use the overview map to get the lay of the land and the basic
tour route.

At Sights

Here's what you can typically expect:

Many major ancient sights (including Athens' Agora and
Acropolis, Delphi, Mycenae, and Olympia) have both an archaeological site and a nearby museum. You can choose between visiting
the museum first (to mentally reconstruct the ruins before seeing
them) or the site first (to get the lay of the ancient land before seeing the items found there). In most cases, I prefer to see the site
first, then the museum. However, crowds and weather can also
help determine your plan. If it's a blistering hot afternoon, tour

the air-conditioned museum first, then hit the ruins in the cool of evening. Or, if rain clouds are on the horizon, do the archaeological site first, then duck into the museum when the rain hits.

Some important sights may have metal detectors or conduct bag searches that will slow your entry, while others may require you to check daypacks and coats. They'll be kept safely. If you have something you can't bear to part with, stash it in a pocket or purse. To avoid checking a small backpack, carry it under your arm like a purse as you enter. From a guard's point of view, a backpack is generally a problem, while a purse is not.

Ancient sites are meticulously monitored. The Greeks take their ancient artifacts very seriously. Don't cross any barriers or climb on the ruins. (If you do, you might hear a jarring whistle and look up to see an attendant waving you off.)

Flash photography is sometimes banned, but taking photos without a flash is usually OK. Look for signs or ask. Flashes damage ancient works and distract others in the room. Even without a flash, a handheld camera will take a decent picture (or buy postcards or posters at the museum bookstore). If photos are permitted, video cameras are generally OK, too. Posing with ancient statues—or even standing next to them for a photo—is strictly forbidden.

Museums have special exhibits in addition to their permanent collection. Some exhibits are included in the entry price; others come at an extra cost (which you may have to pay even if you don't want to see the exhibit).

In Greece, audioguides are rare, but good guidebooks are available. Or download my free Athens audio tours—covering the Acropolis, Agora, and National Archaeological Museum, and the Athens city walk—onto your MP3 player and bring them along (see page 481).

You can usually hire a live local guide at the entrance to major ancient sites or museums at a reasonable cost (prices are soft and negotiable; save money by splitting the guide fee with other travelers). I list recommended guides in the "Helpful Hints" section of many chapters.

Some sights run short films featuring their highlights and history. These are generally well worth your time. I make it standard operating procedure to ask when I arrive at a sight if there is a film.

Expect changes—items can be on tour, on loan, out sick, or shifted at the whim of the curator. To adapt, pick up any available free floor plans as you enter. Ask the museum staff if you can't find a particular urn or statue.

Most important sights have an on-site café or cafeteria (usually a good place to rest and have a snack or light meal). Museum WCs are generally free and clean (it's smart to carry tissues in case a WC runs out of TP). Many places sell postcards that highlight their attractions. Before you leave, scan the postcards and thumb through the biggest guidebook (or skim its index) to be sure you haven't overlooked something that you'd like to see.

Most sights stop admitting people 30-60 minutes before closing time, and some rooms shut down early (often 45 minutes before the actual closing time). Guards usher people out, so don't save the best for last.

Every sight or museum offers more than what is covered in this book. Use the information in this book as an introduction— not the final word.

Sleeping

I favor accommodations (and restaurants) handy to your sightseeing activities. Rather than list hotels scattered throughout a city, I choose two or three favorite neighborhoods and recommend the best accommodations values in each, from $25 bunk beds to fancy $500 doubles at Athens' grand hotels.

I look for places that are friendly; clean; a good value; located in a central, safe, quiet neighborhood; English-speaking; and not mentioned in other guidebooks. I'm more impressed by a handy location and a fun-loving philosophy than flat-screen TVs and shoeshine machines. I also like local character and simple facilities that don't cater to American "needs." Obviously, a place meeting every criterion is rare, and all of my recommendations fall short of perfection—sometimes miserably. But I've listed the best values for each price category, given the above criteria. I've also thrown in a few hostels, private rooms, and other cheap options for budget travelers.

I've described my recommended accommodations using a Sleep Code. Prices listed are for one-night stays in peak season but may go up during major holidays and festivals (see page 486), and generally include breakfast.

As you look over the listings, you'll notice that some accommodations promise special prices to my readers who book direct (without using a room-finding service or hotel-booking website, which take a commission). To get these rates, mention this book when you reserve, then show the book upon arrival.

Given the economic downturn, hoteliers are willing and eager to make a deal. I'd suggest emailing several hotels to ask for their best price. Comparison-shop and make your choice.

In general, prices can soften up if you do any of the following: offer to pay cash, stay at least three nights, or mention this book. You can also try asking for a cheaper room or a discount, or offer to

Sleep Code

(€1 = about $1.40, country code: 30)
To help you sort easily through these listings, I've divided the accommodations into three categories based on the price for a standard double room with bath:

> **$$$** **Higher Priced**
> **$$** **Moderately Priced**
> **$** **Lower Priced**

I always rate hostels as $, whether or not they have double rooms, because they have the cheapest beds in town.

To give maximum information in a minimum of space, I use the following code to describe the accommodations. Prices listed are per room, not per person. When a price range is given for a type of room (such as "Db-€80-120"), it means the price fluctuates with the season, size of room, or length of stay.

- **S** = Single room (or price for one person in a double).
- **D** = Double or twin. Double beds are usually big enough for nonromantic couples.
- **T** = Triple (generally a double bed with a single).
- **Q** = Quad (usually two double beds).
- **b** = Private bathroom with toilet and shower or tub.
- **s** = Private shower or tub only (the toilet is down the hall).

According to this code, a couple staying at a "Db-€85" hotel would pay a total of €85 (about $120) for a double room with a private bathroom. Unless otherwise noted, English is spoken, breakfast is included, and credit cards are accepted.

If I mention "Internet access" in a hotel description, there's a public terminal in the lobby for guests to use. If I list "Wi-Fi" or "cable Internet," you can access it in your room, but only if you have your own laptop.

---

skip breakfast. To save money off-season, consider arriving without a reservation and dropping in at the last minute.

Before accepting a room, confirm your understanding of the complete price. The only tip my recommended hotels would like is a friendly, easygoing guest.

Hoteliers can be a great help and source of advice; they're experts on their cities. But remember, even at the best hotels, mechanical breakdowns occur: Air-conditioning malfunctions, sinks leak, hot water turns cold, and toilets gurgle and smell. Report your concerns clearly and calmly (not angrily) at the front desk. For more complicated problems, don't expect instant results.

If you suspect night noise will be a problem, ask for a quiet room in the back or on an upper floor.

To guard against theft in your room, keep valuables out of sight. Some rooms come with a safe, and other hotels have safes at the front desk. Use them if you're concerned.

Checkout can pose problems if surprise charges pop up on your bill. If you settle up your bill the night before you leave, you'll have time to discuss and address any points of contention.

Above all, keep a positive attitude. After all, you're on vacation. If your hotel is a disappointment, spend more time out enjoying the city you came to see.

Types of Accommodations

Greece's hotels differ from American-style hotels in several ways. Most bathrooms come with just a shower—if you want a bathtub, ask for one when you reserve. Also, there's a reason every bathroom has a small wastebasket next to the toilet—bad plumbing. Don't flush toilet paper; use the wastebasket instead.

If visiting areas with mosquitoes (such as Kardamyli and Monemvasia), avoid opening your windows, especially at night. If your hotel lacks air-conditioning, request a fan. Many hotels furnish a small plug-in bulb that helps keep the bloodsuckers at bay. If not already plugged into the electric socket, it may be in or near the ashtray. Some may have a separate scented packet that you have to unwrap and insert into the device.

Hotels in Greece are required to set aside only 10 percent of their rooms for non-smokers—and often it's the least desirable rooms that are designated as non-smoking. Thankfully, hoteliers are obsessive about cleaning out any odors. When I'm in Greece, I never bother asking for a non-smoking room, and so far, I have found all my accommodations acceptable. If your room smells like the Marlboro man slept there, ask to be moved.

Hotels

You'll usually see the word "hotel," but you might also see the traditional Greek word *Xenonas* (ΞΕΝΩΝΑΣ/Ξενώνασ). In some places, especially Nafplio, small hotels are called *pensions*.

In this book, the price for a double room ranges from about $75 (very simple, toilet and shower down the hall) to $500 (maximum plumbing and more), with most clustering at about $120. You'll pay more at hotels in Athens and on the islands, less on the Peloponnese.

Most hotels have lots of doubles and a few singles, triples, and quads. While groups sleep cheap, traveling alone can be expensive.

Singles (except for the rare closet-type rooms that fit only a twin bed) are simply doubles used by one person—so they often cost nearly the same as a double.

A satisfying Greek breakfast with cheese, ham, yogurt, fresh bread, honey, jam, fruit, juice, and coffee or tea is standard and included in hotel prices. More expensive hotels sometimes also serve hard-boiled eggs and cereal.

Dhomatia (Rooms)

Rooms in private homes (similar to B&Bs, called *dhomatia/* ΔΩΜΑΤΙΑ/Δωματια in Greece) offer double the cultural intimacy for a good deal less than most hotel rooms. You get what you pay for—expect simple, stripped-down accommodations, but you'll usually have your own bathroom. Hosts generally speak English and are interesting conversationalists. Your stay probably won't include breakfast, but you'll have access to a kitchen.

Local tourist information offices may have lists of *dhomatia* and can book a room for you, but you'll save money by booking direct with the *dhomatia* listed in this book.

Hostels

For about $30 a night, you can stay at a youth hostel. Travelers of any age are welcome, if they don't mind dorm-style accommodations or meeting other travelers. Cheap meals are sometimes available, and kitchen facilities are usually provided. Hostels are also a tremendous source of local and budget travel information. Expect crowds in the summer, snoring, and lots of youth groups giggling and making rude noises while you try to sleep.

If you're serious about traveling cheaply, get a membership card (www.hihostels.com), carry your own sheets, and cook in the members' kitchens. Travelers without a hostel card can generally spend the night for a small, extra "one-night membership" fee. In official IYHF-member hostels, family rooms are sometimes available on request, but it's basically boys' dorms and girls' dorms. You usually can't check in before 17:00 and must be out by 10:00. There's often a 23:00 curfew.

Athens also has private hostels, where you'll find no midday lockout, no curfew, no membership requirement, co-ed dorms, simple double rooms, a more easygoing staff, and a rowdy atmosphere.

Phoning

To call Greece, you'll need to know its country code: 30. To call from the US or Canada, dial 011-30-local number. If calling Greece from another European country, dial 00-30-local number. For more tips on calling, see page 464.

Making Reservations

Given the quality of the places I've found for this book, I'd recommend that you reserve your rooms in advance, particularly if
you'll be traveling during peak season. Book several weeks ahead,
or as soon as you've pinned down your travel dates. Note that some
holidays merit your making reservations far in advance (see sidebar on page 10). Just like at home, holidays that fall on a Monday,
Thursday, or Friday can turn the weekend into a long holiday, so
book ahead for the entire weekend.

Requesting a Reservation: To make a reservation, contact
hotels directly by email, phone, or fax. Email is the clearest and
most economical way to make a reservation. Or you can go straight
to the hotel website: Many have secure online reservation forms
and can instantly inform you of availability and any special deals.
But be sure you use the hotel's official site and not a booking
agency's site—otherwise you may pay higher rates than you should.
If phoning from the US, be mindful of time zones (see page 11).
Most hotels listed are accustomed to English-only speakers.

The hotelier wants to know these key pieces of information
(also included in the sample request form in the appendix):

- number and type of rooms
- number of nights
- date of arrival
- date of departure
- any special needs (e.g., bathroom in the room or down the
  hall, twin beds vs. double bed, air-conditioning, quiet, view,
  ground floor, etc.)

When you request a room, use the European style for writing dates: day/month/year. For example, for a two-night stay in
July, I would request: "2 nights, arrive 16/07/12, depart 18/07/12."
Consider carefully how long you'll stay; don't just assume you
can tack on extra days once you arrive. Mention any discounts
offered—for Rick Steves readers or otherwise—when you make
the reservation.

If you don't get a reply to your email or fax, it usually means
the hotel is already fully booked (but you can try sending the message again, or call to follow up).

Confirming a Reservation: If the hotel's response includes
its room availability and rates, it's not a confirmation. You must
tell them that you want that room at the given rate. Most hoteliers
will request your credit-card number for a one-night deposit to
hold the room. While you can email your credit-card information (I do), it's safer to share that confidential info via phone call,
fax, two successive emails, or secure online reservation form (if the
hotel has one on its website).

Canceling a Reservation: If you must cancel your reservation, it's courteous to do so with as much advance notice as possible—at least three days. Simply make a quick phone call or send an email. Hotels and *dhomatia* lose money if they turn away customers while holding a room for someone who doesn't show up. Understandably, many places bill no-shows for one night.

Hotels in larger cities such as Athens sometimes have strict cancellation policies. For example, you might lose a deposit if you cancel within two weeks of your reserved stay, or you might be billed for the entire visit if you leave early. Internet deals may require prepayment, with no refunds for cancellations. If concerned, ask about cancellation policies before you book.

If canceling via email, request confirmation that your cancellation was received to avoid being accidentally billed.

Reconfirm Your Reservation: Always call to reconfirm your room reservation a day or two in advance from the road. Smaller hotels and *dhomatia* appreciate knowing your time of arrival. If arriving after 17:00, be sure to let your hotelier know. On the small chance that a hotel loses track of your reservation, bring along a hard copy of your emailed or faxed confirmation. Don't have the TI reconfirm rooms for you; they'll take a commission.

Reserving Rooms as You Travel: It's possible to make reservations as you travel, calling hotels or *dhomatia* a few days to a week before your arrival. If everything's full, don't despair. Call a day or two in advance and fill in a cancellation. If you'd rather travel without any reservations at all, you'll have greater success snaring rooms if you arrive at your destination early in the day. If you anticipate crowds, call hotels at about 9:00 or 10:00 on the day you plan to arrive, when the hotel clerk knows who'll be checking out and just which rooms will be available. If you encounter a language barrier, ask the fluent receptionist at your current hotel to call for you.

Eating

Greek food is simple...and simply delicious. Unlike the French or the Italians, who are forever experimenting to perfect an intricate cuisine, the Greeks found an easy formula and stick with it—and

it rarely misses. The four Greek food groups are olives (and olive oil), salty feta cheese, tasty tomatoes, and crispy phyllo dough. Virtually every dish you'll have here is built on a foundation of these four tasty building blocks.

Menus are usually written in both Greek and English, but it's acceptable to go into the kitchen and point to the dish you want. This is a good way to make some friends, sample from each kettle, get what you want (or at least know what you're getting), and have a truly memorable meal. Be brave. For convenience, the day's specials are sometimes arranged in a display case for your perusal.

Smoking is banned in enclosed spaces, such as restaurants and bars. As a result, many smokers occupy outdoor tables—often that's where you'll want to sit too.

If a tourist complains about Greek food, they'll usually say something like, "It was fish with heads and the same salads every day." Remember that eating in Europe is sightseeing for your taste buds. Greece has local specialties that are good, memorable, or both. At least once, seek out and eat or drink the notorious "gross" specialties: ouzo, eggplant, fish eggs, octopus, and so on. You've heard references to them all your life—now's your chance to actually experience what everyone's talking about. *Kali orexi! (Bon appétit!)*

Types of Restaurants

Greeks like to eat late, especially in Athens. When you sit down, you'll be given a basket of (generally fresh, good) bread, often with your napkins and flatware tucked inside. You'll pay a bread and cover charge of about €0.50-1 (usually noted clearly on the menu). You are welcome to linger as late as you want—don't feel pressured to eat quickly and turn over the table.

In addition to the traditional Greek restaurant *(estiatorio)*, you'll also find:

Taverna: Common, rustic neighborhood restaurant with a smaller menu, slinging the Greek favorites.

Mezedopolio: Eatery specializing in small plates/appetizers/*mezedes.*

Ouzerie: Bar that makes ouzo, often selling basic pub grub to go along with it.

If you're looking for fast food, in addition to the usual international chains (McDonald's and Starbucks), there are some Greek versions. Coffee Right is the local version of Starbucks, and Goody's is the Greek take on McDonald's. Everest is open 24/7, selling sandwiches and savory pies to go.

Greek Cuisine

While the Greeks don't like to admit it, their cuisine has a lot in common with Turkish food, including many of the same dishes. (This is partly because they share a similar climate, and partly because Greece was under the Ottoman Empire for nearly 400 years.) Some names—such as moussaka—come directly from Turkish. You'll find traces of Italian influences as well, such as *pastitsio,* the "Greek lasagna."

My favorite Greek snack is souvlaki pita, a tasty shish kebab wrapped in flat bread. Souvlaki stands are all over Greece. On the islands, eat fresh seafood. Don't miss the creamy yogurt with honey. Feta cheese salads and flaky, nut-and-honey baklava are two other tasty treats. Dunk your bread into *tzatziki* (TZAHT-zee-kee), the ubiquitous and refreshing cucumber-and-yogurt dip. (Tourists often call it *tzitziki*, which sounds like the Greek word for crickets—a mispronunciation which endlessly amuses local waiters).

Here are more flavors to seek out during your time in Greece.

Olives

As you'll quickly gather when you pass endless tranquil olive groves on your drive through the countryside, olives are a major staple of Greek food—both the olives themselves and the oil they produce. Connoisseurs can distinguish as many varieties of olives as there are grapes for wine, but they fall into two general categories: those for eating and those for making oil.

Greeks are justly proud of their olive oil: Their country is the third-largest producer in the EU, and they consume more olive oil per capita than any other Mediterranean nation—almost seven gallons per person a year. Locals say that the taste is shaped both by the variety and the terrain where the olives are grown. Olive oils from the Peloponnese, for example, are supposed to be robust with grassy or herbaceous overtones. See if you can tell the difference as you travel. Common, edible Greek olives include:

Kalamata: Purple and almond-shaped, the best-known variety. These come from the southern Peloponnese and are cured in a red-wine vinegar brine.

Throubes: Black, wrinkled olives, usually from the island of Thassos, that stay on the tree until fully ripe. Dry-cured, they have an intense, salty taste and chewy texture.

Amfissa: Found in both black and green varieties, grown near Delphi. They are rounder and mellower than other varieties.

Halkithiki: Large green olives from northern Greece, often stuffed with pimento, sun-dried tomato, feta cheese, or other delicacies.

Tsakistes: Green olives grown mainly in Attica (near Athens) that are cracked with a mallet or cut with a knife before being steeped in water and then brine. After curing, they are marinated in garlic and lemon wedges or herbs.

Cheese

Feta: Protected by EU regulations, it's made with sheep's milk, although a small percentage of goat's milk can be added (but never cow's milk). Feta comes in many variations—some are soft, moist, and rather mild; others are sour, hard, and crumbly.

Kasseri: The most popular Greek cheese after feta, it's a mild, yellow cheese made from either sheep's or goat's milk.

Graviera: A hard cheese usually made in Crete from sheep's milk, it tastes sweet and nutty, almost like a fine Swiss cheese.

Savory Pastries

Savory, flaky phyllo-dough pastries called "pies" (*pita*, not to be confused with pita bread) are another staple of Greek cuisine. These can be ordered as a starter in a restaurant or purchased from a bakery for a tasty bite on the run. They make pies out of just about anything, but the most common are *spanakopita* (spinach), *tiropita* (cheese), *kreatopita* (lamb), and *meletzanitopita* (eggplant).

Salads and Starters *(Mezedes)*

Mezedes (meh-ZEH-dehs), known internationally as *meze*, are a great way to sample several tasty Greek dishes. This "small plates" approach is common and easy—instead of ordering a starter and a main dish per person, get two or three starters and one main dish to split.

Almost anything in Greece can be served as a small-plate "starter" (including several items listed in other sections here—olives, cheeses, and main dishes), but these are most common:

Greek salad (a.k.a. *horiatiki*, "village" salad): Ripe tomatoes chopped up just so, rich feta cheese (sometimes in a long, thick slab that you break apart with your fork), olives, and onions, all drenched with olive oil. You'll find yourself eating this combination again and again—yet somehow, it's hard to tire of its delicious simplicity.

Tzatziki: A pungent and thick sauce of yogurt, cucumber, and garlic. It seems like a condiment but is often ordered as a starter, then eaten as a salad or used to complement other foods.

Pantzarosalata: Beet salad dressed with olive oil and vinegar.

Bekri meze: Literally "drunkard's snack"—chunks of chicken, pork, or beef cooked slowly with wine, cloves, cinnamon, bay leaves, and olive oil.

Dolmathes: Stuffed grape leaves filled with either meat or rice and served hot or cold.

Taramosalata: Smoky, pink, fish-roe mixture with the consistency of mashed potatoes, used as a dip for bread or vegetables.

Melitzanosalata: Cooked eggplant with the consistency of mashed potatoes, usually well-seasoned and delicious.

Roasted red peppers: Soft and flavorful, often drizzled with olive oil.

Tirokafteri: Feta cheese that's been softened and mixed with white pepper to give it some kick, served either as a spread or stuffed inside roasted red peppers.

Saganaki: Cooked cheese, often breaded, sometimes grilled and sometimes fried, occasionally flambéed.

Soutzoukakia: Meatballs with spicy tomato sauce.

Keftedes: Small meatballs, often seasoned with mint, onion, parsley, and sometimes ouzo.

Papoutsaki: Eggplant "slippers" filled with ground beef and cheese.

Soups

Summertime visitors might be disappointed not to find much soup on the menu (including *avgolemono,* the delicious egg, lemon, and rice soup). Soup is considered a winter dish and almost impossible to find in warm weather. If available, Greek chicken soup *(koto-soupa)* is very tasty. *Kremithosoupa* is the Greek version of French onion soup, and *kakavia* is a famous fish soup often compared to bouillabaisse.

Main Dishes

Here are some popular meat and seafood dishes you'll likely see.

Meat

Gyros: Literally "turn," this is not a type of meat but a way of preparing it—stacked on a metal skewer and vertically slow-roasted on a rotisserie. In Greece, it's usually made from chicken or pork.

Souvlaki: Pork or chicken cooked on a skewer, often eaten with pita bread or a rice pilaf.

Moussaka: A classic casserole, with layers of minced meat, eggplant, and tomatoes, and a topping of cheesy Béchamel sauce or egg custard.

Pastitsio: A layered, baked dish called the "Greek lasagna." Ground meat is sandwiched between two layers of pasta, with an egg-custard or Béchamel topping.

Arnaki kleftiko: Slow-cooked lamb, usually wrapped in phyllo dough or parchment paper. Legend says it was created by bandits who needed to cook without the telltale signs of smoke or fire.

Stifado: Beef stew with onions, tomatoes, and spices such as cinnamon and cloves. It was traditionally made with rabbit *(kouneli).*

Fish and Seafood

Gavros: An appetizer similar to anchovies. Squeeze lemon luxuriously all over them, and eat everything but the wispy little tails.

Htapothi: Octopus, often marinated and grilled, then drizzled with olive oil and lemon juice.

Barbounia: Red mullet that is usually grilled or fried and is always expensive. These small fish are bony, but the flesh melts in your mouth.

Psari plaki: Fish baked with tomatoes and onions.

Dessert

Baklava: Phyllo dough layered with nuts and honey.

Kataifi: Thin fibers of phyllo (like shredded wheat) layered with nuts and honey.

Ekmek: A cake made of thin phyllo fibers soaked in honey, then topped with custard and a layer of whipped cream.

Loukoumades: The Greek doughnut, soaked in honey or sugar syrup.

Meli pita: Honey-cheese pie, traditionally served at Easter.

Karydopita: Honey-walnut cake made without flour.

Drinks

Wine: This is a rough land with simple wines. A local vintner told me there's no fine $50 bottle of Greek wine. I asked him, "What if you want to spend $30?" He said, "Fine, you can buy three $10 bottles."

There are two basic types of Greek wines: *retsina* (resin-fla-vored) and non-resinated wines. With dinner, I generally order the infamous resin-flavored **retsina wine.** It makes you want to sling a patch over one eye and say, "Arghh." The first glass is like drink-ing wood. The third glass is dangerous: It starts to taste good. If you drink any more, you'll smell like it the entire next day. Why resin? Way back when, Greek winemakers used pine resin to seal the amphoras that held the wine—protecting the wine from the air. Discovering that they liked the taste, the winemakers began adding resin to the wine itself. *Retsina* is also sold in bottles, but in traditional tavernas it comes from a barrel. Give it a try.

If pine sap is not your cup of tea, there are plenty of other **wine options.** With its new generation of winemakers (many of them trained abroad), Greece is getting better at wine. More than 300 native varietals are now grown in Greece's wine regions. About two-thirds of the wine produced in Greece is white. The best known are Savatiano (the most widely grown grape used for *retsina* and other wines), Assyrtiko (a crisp white mostly from the islands), and Moschofilero (a dry white from the Peloponnese). Red wines include Agiorgitiko (a medium red also from the Peloponnese; one carries the name "Blood of Hercules") and Xynomavro (an intense red from Naoussa in Macedonia). Greeks also grow Cabernet Sauvignon, Merlot, Chardonnay, and other familiar varieties.

Here are a few wine terms that you may find useful: *inos* (οίνος—term for "wine" printed on bottles), *krasi* (spoken term for

---

How Was Your Trip?

Were your travels fun, smooth, and meaningful? If you'd like to share your tips, concerns, and discoveries, please fill out the survey at www.ricksteves.com/feedback. I value your feedback. Thanks in advance—it helps a lot.

"wine"), *ktima* (winery or estate), *inopolio* (wine bar), *lefko* (white), *erithro* or *kokkino* (red), *xiros* (dry), *agouro* (young), *me poli soma* (full-bodied), *epitrapezio* (table wine), and O.P.A.P. (an indication of quality that tells you the wine came from one of Greece's designated wine regions).

Beer: These days, like many locals, I often skip the wine and go for a cold beer. Much of the beer here is either imported or a Greek-brewed version of foreign beers such as Amstel and Heineken. You'll also find a few local brands including Alpha, Athenian, Marathon, and Mythos.

Spirits: Beyond wine and beer, consider special Greek spirits such as ouzo or Metaxa. Cloudy, anise-flavored **ouzo,** supposedly invented by monks on Mount Athos, is worth a try even if you don't like the taste (black licorice). Similar to its Mediterranean cousins, French *pastis* and Turkish *raki,* ouzo turns from clear to milky white when you add ice or water (don't drink it straight). Greeks drink it both as an aperitif and with food. I like to sip it slowly in the early evening while sharing several *mezedes* with my travel partner. Some of the bestselling brands are Ouzo 12, Plomari Ouzo, and Sans Rival Ouzo. **Metaxa** is to be savored after dinner. This rich, sweet, golden-colored liqueur has a brandy base blended with aged wine and a "secret" herbal mixture.

If you're traveling on the Peloponnese, try **Tentura,** a regional liqueur flavored with cloves, nutmeg, cinnamon, and citrus. It packs a spicy kick.

Coffee: All over Greece, Starbucks-style coffee houses have invaded Main Street. But in tavernas you can still find traditional **Greek coffee,** made with loose grounds and similar to Turkish coffee. Let the grounds settle to the bottom of the cup, and avoid this highly caffeinated "mud" unless you want a jolt. It's usually served with a glass of water.

You can order your coffee *pikro/sketos* (bitter/plain), *metrio* (semi-sweet), or *gliko* (sweet). Most people take theirs *metrio*.

Especially in the summer, cafés are filled with Greeks sipping **iced coffee** drinks. First it was iced Nescafé, called a frappé (order it black or white—with milk). Now cafés offer an entire array of iced coffees: *freddo espresso* (iced espresso), *freddo-cino* (iced cappuccino), and even *freddo Mokka*.

Water: Water is served in bottles. It's generally cheap and rarely carbonated.

Traveling as a Temporary Local

We travel all the way to Europe to enjoy differences—to become temporary locals. You'll experience frustrations. Certain truths that we find "God-given" or "self-evident," such as cold beer, ice in drinks, bottomless cups of coffee, hot showers, and bigger being better, are suddenly not so true. One of the benefits of travel is the eye-opening realization that there are logical, civil, and even better alternatives.

Europeans generally like Americans. But if there is a negative aspect to their image of us, it's that we are loud, aggressive, impolite, rich, superficially friendly, and a bit naive.

While Europeans look bemusedly at some of our Yankee excesses—and worriedly at others—they nearly always afford us individual travelers all the warmth we deserve. Judging from all the happy feedback I receive from travelers who have used this book, it's safe to assume you'll enjoy a great, affordable vacation—with the finesse of an independent, experienced traveler.

Happy travels! *Kalo taxidi!*

Back Door Travel Philosophy
From *Rick Steves' Europe Through the Back Door*

Travel is intensified living—maximum thrills per minute and one of the last great sources of legal adventure. Travel is freedom. It's recess, and we need it.

Experiencing the real Europe requires catching it by surprise, going casual..."Through the Back Door."

Affording travel is a matter of priorities. (Make do with the old car.) You can travel—simply, safely, and comfortably—anywhere in Europe for $120 a day plus transportation costs (allow more in big cities). In many ways, spending more money only builds a thicker wall between you and what you came to see. Europe is a cultural carnival, and, time after time, you'll find that its best acts are free and the best seats are the cheap ones.

A tight budget forces you to travel close to the ground, meeting and communicating with the people, not relying on service with a purchased smile. Never sacrifice sleep, nutrition, safety, or cleanliness in the name of budget. Simply enjoy the local-style alternatives to expensive hotels and restaurants.

Connecting with people carbonates your experience. Extroverts have more fun. If your trip is low on magic moments, kick yourself and make things happen. If you don't enjoy a place, maybe you don't know enough about it. Seek the truth. Recognize tourist traps. Give a culture the benefit of your open mind. See things as different but not better or worse. Any culture has much to share.

Of course, travel, like the world, is a series of hills and valleys. Be fanatically positive and militantly optimistic. If something's not to your liking, change your liking.

Travel can make you a happier American as well as a citizen of the world. Our Earth is home to six and a half billion equally important people. It's humbling to travel and find that people don't have the "American Dream"—they have their own dreams. Europeans like us, but, with all due respect, they wouldn't trade passports.

Thoughtful travel engages us with the world. In tough economic times, it reminds us what is truly important. By broadening perspectives, travel teaches new ways to measure quality of life.

Globe-trotting destroys ethnocentricity, helping you understand and appreciate different cultures. Rather than fear the diversity on this planet, celebrate it. Among your prized souvenirs will be the strands of different cultures you choose to knit into your own character. The world is a cultural yarn shop, and Back Door travelers are weaving the ultimate tapestry. Join in!

GREECE

Hellas / Ελλάς

Slip that coaster under the rickety table leg, take a sip of wine, and watch the sun extinguish itself in the sea. You've arrived in Greece.

Greece offers sunshine, seafood, whitewashed houses with bright-blue shutters, and a relaxed, Zorba-the-Greek lifestyle. As the cradle of Western civilization, it has some of the world's greatest ancient monuments. As a late bloomer in the modern age, it also retains echoes of a simpler, time-passed world. And contemporary Greece has one of Europe's fastest-changing cultural landscapes. With its classical past, hang-loose present, and edgy future, Greece offers something for every traveler.

Start in Athens, a microcosm of the country. By day, tour the Acropolis, the Agora, and the history-packed museums. Light a candle alongside an old lady in black at an icon-filled church. Haggle with a sandal maker at the busy market stalls, or have coffee with the locals in a Plaka café. At night, Athens becomes a pan-European party of Greeks, Germans, Brits, and Swedes eating, drinking, and dancing in open-air tavernas. In the colorful Thissio or rickety-chic Psyrri neighborhoods, rub elbows with a trendy new breed of Athenians to get a taste of today's urban Greece.

With its central location, Athens is the perfect launch pad for farther-flung Greek destinations. Commune with ancient spirits at the center of the world: the oracle near the picturesque mountain hamlet of Delphi. Take a vacation from your busy vacation on one of the best and

easiest-to-reach Greek isles, traffic-free Hydra. For longer island getaways, the picture-perfect, whitewashed village of Mykonos and the dramatically situated towns overlooking the flooded volcano crater at Santorini are tops.

An hour's drive west of Athens, the Peloponnese is the large peninsula that hangs from the rest of the Greek mainland by the narrow Isthmus of Corinth. Its name, which means "the Island of Pelops," derives from the mythical hero Pelops. This wild, mountainous landscape is dotted with the ruins of Mycenaean palaces, ancient temples, frescoed churches, and countless medieval hilltop castles built by the Crusaders and the Venetians. At Mycenae, visit the hub of a civilization that dominated Greece from 1600-1200 B.C. Hike up the stone rows of the world's best-preserved ancient theater, at Epidavros. Run a lap at Olympia, site of the first Olympic Games. To round things out, enjoy the stunning landscapes of the wild Mani Peninsula and the charming old Venetian towns of Monemvasia (a fortified, village-topped giant rock hovering just offshore) and Nafplio (the first capital of independent Greece). As you hop from town to town, compare Greek salads and mountains-and-olive-grove views.

Greece possesses a huge hunk of human history. It's the place that birthed the Olympics; the mischievous gods (Zeus, Hermes,

Greece Almanac

Official Name: It's the Hellenic Republic (*Elliniki Dhimokratia* in Greek). In shorthand, that's Hellas—or Greece in English.

Population: Greece is home to 11.2 million people (similar to the state of Ohio). About 93 percent are Greek citizens, and 7 percent are citizens of other countries—mainly Albanian, Bulgarians, and Romanians. Greece does not collect ethnic data. More than 95 percent are Greek Orthodox, the state religion. A little more than 1 percent are Muslim. The dominant language is Greek.

Latitude and Longitude: 39°N and 22°E. The latitude is the same as Maryland.

Area: With 51,485 square miles, Greece is a bit smaller than Alabama.

Geography: Greece is a mountainous peninsula that extends into the Mediterranean Sea between Albania and Turkey in southern Europe. It includes the Peloponnesian Peninsula—separated from the mainland by a canal—and 6,000 rugged islands (227 are inhabited). Nearly four-fifths of the country's landscape is covered by mountains, the highest of which is Mount Olympus (9,570 feet). About 30 percent of the land is forested. Flat, arable plains are centered in Macedonia, Thrace, and Thessaly. Greece's coastline is the 10th longest in the world at 9,246 miles.

Biggest Cities: One in three Greeks lives in the capital of Athens (about 750,000 in the city, 3.7 million including the greater metropolitan area). Thessaloniki has 365,000 (one million in its urban area).

Economy: Greece has a GDP of $331 billion, with a GDP per capita of $31,000. A European Union member, Greece has used

Dionysius); the tall tales of Achilles, Odysseus, and the Trojan War; the rational philosophies of Socrates, Plato, and Aristotle; democracy, theater, mathematics...and the gyros sandwich.

Besides impressive remnants of its Golden Age (450-400 B.C.), you'll see Byzantine churches, Ottoman mosques, and Neoclassical buildings marking the War of Independence—all part of Greece's 3,000-year history.

Greece is easy on travelers. Tourism makes up 15 percent of the gross domestic product, and the people are welcoming and accommodating. Greeks pride themselves on a concept called *filotimo* ("love of honor"), roughly translated as openness, friendliness, and hospitality. Social faux pas by unwary foreigners are easily overlooked by Greeks. The food is uncomplicated, the weather is good, and the transportation infrastructure is sufficient.

Greece's geography of mountains, peninsulas, and 6,000

the euro as its currency since 2002. At first, its economy—based heavily on tourism, shipping, and agriculture—benefited from an infusion of EU cash. But a spending spree resulted in a severe recession, and the country's national debt—nearly $400 billion—now exceeds its gross domestic product, prompting credit rating agencies to rate Greece's bonds as junk. The prime minister has launched a major austerity program of spending cuts and tax increases totaling $40 billion over three years.

Government: Greece is a parliamentary republic, headed by a largely ceremonial president elected by the parliament. Power resides with the prime minister, chosen from the majority political party. American-born George Papandreou became prime minister in October of 2009.

Flag: A blue square bears a white cross (the symbol of Greek Orthodoxy) in the upper-left corner, against a field of horizontal blue-and-white stripes. Blue stands for the sky and seas, while white represents the purity of the push for Greek independence. Each of the nine stripes symbolizes a syllable in the Greek motto, *Eleutheria e Thanatos,* which translates as "Freedom or Death."

The Average Zorba: The average Greek is 41.5 years old, will live to be 79.5, and has 1.3 children. About 80 percent of Greeks have mobile phones. A typical local eats 55 pounds of cheese a year (mostly feta)—the highest per capita cheese consumption in the world.

islands divides the Greek people into many regions, each with its distinct cultural differences. "Where are you from?" is a common conversation-starter among Greeks.

Greece is also divided by a severe generation gap. Up until late 1974 (when the military junta was ousted), Greek society was traditional, economically backward, and politically repressed. Then the floodgates opened, and Greece has gone overboard trying to catch up with the modern world.

You'll find two Greeces: the traditional/old/rural Greece, and the modern/young/urban one. In the countryside, you'll still see men on donkeys, women at the well, and people whose career choice was to herd goats across a busy highway. In the bigger cities, it's a concrete world of honking horns and buzzing mobile phones. Well-dressed, educated Greeks listen to hip-hop music, surf the Internet, and thumb text messages. As the rural exodus continues, the urban environment is now home to a majority of Greeks. Social observers point out that young Greeks seem to overcompensate for their country's conservative past with excessive consumerism, trendiness, and anti-authoritarianism.

Still, Greece is unified by language and religion. The Greek Orthodox Church—a rallying point for Greeks during centuries of foreign occupation—remains part of everyday life. Ninety-five percent of all Greeks declare themselves Orthodox, even if they rarely go to church. The constitution gives the Orthodox Church special privileges, blurring church-state separation.

Orthodox elements appear everywhere. Icon shrines dot the highways. Orthodox priests—with their Old Testament beards, black robes, necklaces, cake-shaped hats, and families in tow—mingle with parishioners on street corners and

chat on their mobile phones. During the course of the day, Greeks routinely pop into churches to light a candle, asking for favors. Men clack their worry beads on a string—an old custom that's become a fashion statement. Even the young celebrate feast days with their families and make the sign of the cross when passing a church. Greek lives are marked by the age-old rituals of baptism, marriage, and funeral.

It seems like every man in Greece shares the same few names: Georgios, Kostas, Nikos, Constantinos, and Yiannis. That's because many still follow the custom of naming boys after their grandfathers using the names of Orthodox saints. Most surnames seem to have the same endings: -polous, -aikis, or -idis; all mean "son of." Names ending in -ous or -os are usually male, while -ou names are female.

Despite modern changes, men and women live in somewhat different spheres. Women rule the home and socialize at open-air marketplaces. Fewer women join the workforce than in other European countries.

Men rule the public arena. You'll see them hanging out endlessly at coffee shops, playing backgammon, watching soccer games on TV (basketball is also popular), and arguing politics with loud voices and dramatic gestures.

Greeks are family-oriented, with large extended families. Kids live at home until they're married, and then they might just move into a flat upstairs in the same apartment building. The "family" extends to the large diaspora of emigrants. Three million Greek-Americans (including TV journalist George Stephanopoulos, tennis player Pete Sampras, and 1988 presidential candidate Michael Dukakis) keep ties to the home country through their Orthodox faith and their Big Fat Greek Weddings.

The pace of life in Greece remains relaxed. People work in the mornings, then take a mid-afternoon "siesta," when they gather with their families to eat the main meal of the day. On warm summer nights, they stay up very late, even kids. Families spill into the streets to greet their neighbors on the evening stroll. For entertainment, they go out to eat (even poor people), where they order large amounts and share it family-style.

Later, they might gather to hear folk songs sung to a bouzouki, a long-necked mandolin. These days, the music is often amplified, fleshed out with a synthesizer, and tinged with pop influences. People still form a circle to dance the traditional dances, with arms outstretched or thrown across each other's shoulders. A few might get carried away, "applaud" by throwing plates or flowers, and dance on the tables into the wee hours.

While pollution still plagues traffic-choked cities and dirty beaches, there are signs of change. The country's capital has newly traffic-free pedestrian zones, modern public transport, a state-of-the-art airport, and the Acropolis Museum. Greeks everywhere took great pride in the 2004 Olympics. And most of the people realize that they have to reform their bloated civil service system and pay for their profligate past (see next section). They seem anxious to prove themselves as a modern state and regain their place as an enlightened people.

It's easy to surrender to the Greek way of living. With its long history and simple lifestyle, Greece has a timeless appeal.

Greece's Economic Crisis and Other Challenges

This is a particularly rocky time for the Greeks. Sharing a beer or an iced coffee with a talkative native can provide you with a lesson in contemporary Greece that's every bit as fascinating as the Classical stuff. Here's a quick run-down of the issues you might hear about:

Visiting Greece Despite Riots and Rumors of Riots

Travelers to Greece are sometimes concerned about the effect the country's "economic meltdown" might have on their trip. (A magazine I write for didn't want to run my article on Greece, fearing that it would inspire its traveling readers to venture into trouble.) But, as with most high-profile crises, visitors who experience the situation firsthand learn that many problems have simply been played up by both Greek and international media outlets.

While there have been many demonstrations and the occasional riot—which have sometimes turned violent—these are isolated and unlikely to affect travelers who have their wits about them. Strikes have long been a way of life in Greece. Most Greeks see a general strike as an excuse for an impromptu holiday. But there is a tiny anarchist fringe element that sees a peaceful demonstration or rally by teachers or doctors at Athens' Parliament building as an opportunity to get media coverage. A handful of troublemakers will "come out to play with their friends" (as locals term it), and things can become violent. Like back home, when it comes to TV news, "If it bleeds, it leads." People who don't get out much overreact, offering anarchists huge rewards.

These destructive attempts to grab headlines and express anger and frustration at corporations and the government will likely continue. (After two Starbucks stores in Athens were burned, some other branches, realizing they were targets, closed up shop.) But the violence is relatively easy to avoid. As of late

In recent years, Greece has become infamous as one of the world's most troubled economies. Embarrassingly high national debt figures prompted foreign investors to abandon Greek bonds; now, after a hefty EU/International Monetary Fund bailout, the country is struggling to put its economy back together.

In the view of many observers (and many Greeks), the Greeks have lived beyond their means, worked too short, retired too early, consumed too much, produced too little, enjoyed too much job security, created a real-estate bubble with overvalued properties, and funded too much on a growing deficit. The black market has thrived, and many Greeks practice tax evasion as if it were a fine art (with the effect of limiting legitimate tax revenue).

The government itself has been notoriously corrupt and nepotistic. Government employees, with cushy jobs, 100 percent job security, and great benefits, are seen as luxuriating away their work lives in worry-free comfort. Stories of fiscal scandal and fraud fill the news almost daily, sparking public anger. Over the past couple of years, Greece's young people have taken to the streets in violent

2010, virtually all demonstrations and acts of violence have taken place within a single, small, high-profile area of central Athens, and have not affected the main tourist attractions (ancient sites and islands) elsewhere in Greece. Protest rallies are scheduled in advance: Your hotelier can tell you which areas to avoid. Unlike random marketplace bombings in more volatile countries, violence here generally occurs with notice and at off-times (for instance, anarchists might call a newspaper at 4:00 in the morning, just before bombing an empty building).

On my last trip here (in 2010), I found Greece to be the same old wonderful place...with, perhaps, a few more minor headaches. Strikes are a nuisance, but generally not prolonged—just a day or two here and there. If the Metro isn't running, taxis or buses can fill the gaps. People still need to get to and from the islands, and they still need services. And museums generally remain open. When I asked a Greek friend about this, she responded, "Why would we close the Acropolis? It would make no sense. Tourism is an important part of our economy. People pay to see it. That's why they are here." As a bonus, major sights may have fewer crowds, and hotel prices have dropped from a few years ago.

In my mind, the biggest impact of the crisis on anyone visiting Greece is the satisfaction you'll get from contributing to the economy of a nation dealing with tough times, and the joy that comes with a tourist industry that really appreciates your presence.

demonstrations challenging every public institution.

Now the Greek government is scrambling to salvage the economy by raising taxes and getting more serious about tax collection. From the beginning to the end of 2010, the Greek national sales tax, or VAT (Value Added Tax), rose from 19 percent to 25 percent. This means everything people consume costs more, with a significant chunk of people's income going to the government to rescue the economy. Many businesses have gone bankrupt during the crisis, so there's less competition—which also means higher consumer prices.

The Greek people are also feeling the pinch of cuts to social benefits. For example, Greeks who turned 60 in 2009 are comfortably retired; those who turned 60 in 2010 will need to work seven more years. These austerity measures have triggered strikes and more civil unrest.

Many other countries—including the US—are plagued by similar problems, but Greece is an extreme case, with extreme consequences. If there's a positive outcome from all of this, it's that Greece's economic irresponsibility has sparked a sweeping realization among politicians and political movements across Europe that government pork, corporate corruption, and personal production relative to consumption all need to be recalibrated.

Greece is also grappling with other, somewhat related issues. Young, well-educated, multilingual Greeks feel that they're over-qualified for what their country has to offer and are tempted to go abroad for employment. This potential "brain drain" of bright young people—which has only been exacerbated by the recent economic woes—is a threat to Greece's future.

At the same time, Greece's until-now-homogeneous populace is threatened by recently arrived immigrants happy to take the low-paying jobs—the woman cleaning your hotel room is likely from Albania or Romania. The culture that gave us the word "xeno-phobic" is suspicious of threats from abroad. Like other European countries, Greece must figure out how to keep its own cultural identity even as it becomes more of a melting pot.

Greece has, it seems, more than its share of troubles right now. Still, Greeks are optimistic by nature. Most believe that they'll get through these "tough economic times" and other worries. And they understand that a reality check—which will come with some brutal belt-tightening—is necessary.

Greek Language

Even though the Greek alphabet presents challenges to foreign visitors, communication is not hard. You'll find that everybody in the tourist industry—and virtually all young people—speak fine English. Many signs and menus (especially in Athens and major tourist spots) use both the Greek and our more familiar Latin alphabet. Greeks realize that it's unreasonable to expect visitors to learn Greek (which has only 14 million speakers worldwide). It's essential for them to find a common language with the rest of the world—especially their European neighbors to the west—so they learn English early and well.

Of course, not everyone speaks English. You'll run into the most substantial language bar-rier when traveling in rural areas and/or dealing with folks over 60, who are more likely to have learned French as a second lan-guage. Because signs and maps aren't always transliterated into

our alphabet (i.e., spelled out using a Latin-letter equivalent), a passing familiarity with the basics of the Greek alphabet is help-ful for navigating—especially for drivers (see "Greek Alphabet," later).

There are certain universal English words all Greeks know: hello, please, thank you, OK, pardon, stop, menu, problem, and no problem. While Greeks don't expect you to be fluent in their tongue, they definitely appreciate it when they can tell you're making an effort to pronounce Greek words correctly and use the local pleasantries.

It's nice to learn "Hello" (*"Gia sas,"* pronounced "yah sahs"), "Please" (*"Parakalo,"* pronounced "pah-rah-kah-LOH"), and "Thank you" (*"Efharisto,"* pronounced "ehf-hah-ree-STOH"). Watch out for this tricky point: The Greek word for "yes" is *ne* (pronounced "neh"), which sounds a lot like "no" to us. What's more, the word for "no" is *ohi* (pronounced "OH-hee"), which sounds enough like "OK" to also be potentially confusing. For more Greek words, see the Greek Survival Phrases on page 491.

Don't be afraid to interact with locals. You'll find that doors open a little more quickly when you know a few words of the language. Give it your best shot.

Greek Alphabet

Most visitors find the Greek alphabet daunting, if not indecipherable. At first, all the signs look like...well, Greek to us. However,

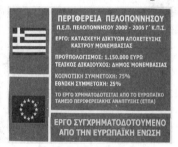

Greek has more in common with English than may be immediately apparent. Technically the world's oldest complete alphabet (Phoenician, its predecessor, had no vowel symbols), Greek is the parent of our own Latin alphabet—itself named for the first two Greek letters (alpha and beta). Since it's used worldwide among mathematicians and scientists (not to mention frat guys), you may recognize some letters from your student days—but that doesn't help much when you're trying to read a map or menu.

Fortunately, with a little effort the alphabet becomes a lot less baffling. Many uppercase Greek letters look just like their Latin counterparts (such as A, B, and M), and a few more look similar with a little imagination (Δ, Ξ, and Σ look a little like D, X, and S, if you squint). A few look nothing like anything in our alphabet, and a couple are particularly confusing (Greek's P is our R, and Greek's H is our I.)

Getting comfortable with the lowercase letters is more challenging. Just like in our alphabet, most lowercase letters are similar to their uppercase versions, but a few bear no resemblance at all.

Once you're familiar with the letters, it's less of a challenge to learn how each is said. Nearly every letter (except P and H) is

GREECE

Greek from A to Ω

Transliterating Greek to English is an inexact science, but here is the Greek alphabet, with the most common English counterparts for the Greek letters and letter combinations.

Greek	English Name	Common Transliteration	Pronounced
Α α	alpha	a	A as in father
Β β	beta	b or v	V as in volt
Γ γ	gamma	y or g	Y as in yes or G as in go*
Δ δ	delta	d or dh	TH as in then
Ε ε	epsilon	e	E as in get
Ζ ζ	zeta	z	Z as in zoo
Η η	eta	i	I as in ski
Θ θ	theta	th	TH as in theme
Ι ι	iota	i	I as in ski
Κ κ	kappa	k	K as in king
Λ λ	lambda	l	L as in lime
Μ μ	mu	m	M as in mom
Ν ν	nu	n	N as in net
Ξ ξ	xi	x	X as in ox
Ο ο	omicron	o	O as in ocean
Π π	pi	p	P as in pie
Ρ ρ	rho	r	R as in rich (slightly rolled)
Σ σ,ς	sigma	s or c	S as in sun
Τ τ	tau	t	T as in tip
Υ υ	upsilon	y	Y as in happy
Φ φ	phi	f or ph	F as in file
Χ χ	chi	ch, h, or kh	CH as in loch (gutturally)
Ψ ψ	psi	ps	PS as in lapse
Ω ω	omega	o or w	O as in ocean

*Gamma is pronounced, roughly speaking, like the English "hard" G only when it comes before consonants, or before the letters a, o, and ou.

pronounced roughly like the Latin letter it most resembles. As for the handful of utterly unfamiliar characters, you'll just have to memorize those.

Most Greek words have one acute accent that marks the stressed vowel (such as ά rather than α, έ rather than ε, ί rather than ι, ό rather than ο, and ύ rather than υ). These accents are worth paying attention to, as a change in emphasis can bring a change in meaning. Also, note the list of letter combinations below—pairs of letters that, when together, sound a little different than expected (similar to our own "th" or "ch" combinations).

Learn to recognize and pronounce each letter, and you'll be able to sound out the words you see around you: Μάνη = M-a-n-i, Mani (the peninsula, pronounced MAH-nee). Greek is phonetic—it has rules of pronunciation, and it sticks to them. As you stroll the streets, practice reading aloud—you may be surprised how quickly you'll be able to sound out words.

Certain Greek letter combinations create specific sounds. These include:

Greek		Transliteration	Pronounced
AI	αι	e	E as in get
AY	αυ	av/af	AV as in have, or AF as in after
EI	ει	i	I as in ski
EY	ευ	ev/ef	EV as in never, or EF as in left
OI	οι	i	I as in ski
OY	ου	ou/u	OU as in you
ΓΓ	γγ	ng	NG as in angle
ΓΚ	γκ	ng/g	NG as in angle, or G as in go (at start of word)
ΜΠ	μπ	mb/b	MB as in amber, or B as in bet (at start of word)
ΝΔ	νδ	nd/nt/d	ND as in land, or D as in dog (at start of word)
ΤΣ	τσ	ts	TS as in hats
ΤΖ	τζ	dz	DS as in lands, or DG as in judge

Greek Place Names

One Greek word can be transliterated into English in many different ways. For example, the town of Nafplio may appear on a map or road sign as Navplio, Naufplio, or Nauvplio. Even more confusingly, there are actually two different versions of Greek: proper Greek, which was used until the 1950s (and now sounds affected to most Greeks); and popular Greek, a simplified version that is the norm today. This means that even Greeks might use different names for the same thing (for example, the city names Nafplio and Patra are popular Greek, while Nafplion and Patras are formal Greek).

The following list includes the most common English spelling and pronunciation for Greek places. If the Greeks use their own, differently spelled transliteration, it's noted in parentheses.

English	Pronounced	Greek Transliteration
Greece (Ellada or Hellas)	eh-LAH-thah, eh-LAHS	Ελλάδα or Ελλάς
Athens (Athina)	ah-THEE-nah	Αθήνα
Delphi	dell-FEE	Δελφοί
Epidavros	eh-pee-DAH-vrohs	Επίδαυρος
Hydra	EE-drah	Ύδρα
Kardamyli	kar-dah-MEE-lee	Καρδαμύλη
Mani	MAH-nee	Μάνη
Monemvasia	moh-nehm-VAH-see-ah	Μονεμβασιά
Mycenae (Mikenes)	my-SEE-nee (mee-KEE-nehs)	Μυκήνες
Mykonos	MEE-koh-nohs	Μυκονοσ
Nafplio	NAF-plee-oh	Ναύπλιο
Olympia	oh-LEEM-pee-ah	Ολυμπία
Peloponnese (Peloponnisos)	PEL-oh-poh-neez (pel-oh-POH-nee-sohs)	Πελοπόννησος
Piraeus	pee-reh-AHS	Πειραιάς
Santorini (Thira)	sahn-toh-REE-nee (THEE-rah)	Θηρα

Note that these are the pronunciations most commonly used in English. Greeks might put the emphasis on a different syllable— for example, English-speakers call the Olympics birthplace oh-LEEM-pee-ah, while Greeks say oh-leem-PEE-ah.

ATHENS

ΑΘΗΝΑ / Αθήνα

ORIENTATION TO ATHENS

Athens, while sprawling and congested, has a compact, pleasant tourist zone capped by the famous Acropolis—the world's top ancient site. In this historic town, you'll walk in the footsteps of the great minds who created democracy, philosophy, theater, and more...even when you're dodging motorcycles on "pedestrianized" streets. Romantics can't help but get goose bumps as they kick around the same pebbles that once stuck in Socrates' sandals, with the floodlit Parthenon forever floating ethereally overhead.

Many tourists visit Athens without ever venturing beyond the Plaka (Old Town) and ancient zone. With limited time, this is not a bad plan, as greater Athens offers few sights (other than the excellent National Archaeological Museum). But for a more authentic taste of the city, visit the fun, thriving districts of Thissio, Psyrri, and Gazi.

Because of its prominent position on the tourist trail, and the irrepressible Greek spirit of hospitality, the city is user-friendly. It seems that virtually all Athenians speak English, major landmarks are well-signed, and most street signs are in Greek followed by a transliteration in English.

Athens: A Verbal Map

Ninety-five percent of Athens is noisy, polluted modern sprawl, jammed with characterless concrete suburbs—poorly planned and hastily erected to house the area's rapidly expanding population. The construction of the Metro for the 2004 Olympics was, in many ways, the first time urban

Athens Neighborhoods

NATIONAL ARCHAEOLOGICAL MUSEUM

OMONIA SQUARE

EXARCHIA

LYKAVITTOS HILL

NAT'L. LIBRARY

PANEPISTIMOU

← GAZI

KOLONAKI

PSYRRI

ERMOU

SYNTAGMA

ATHINAS

VASILISSIS SOFIAS

MONASTIRAKI

AGORA

THISSIO

SYNTAGMA SQUARE

PARLIAMENT

PLAKA

ADRIANOU

NAT'L. GARDEN

ACROPOLIS

APOSTOLOU PAVLOU

DIONYSIOU AREOPAGITOU

VASILISSIS AMALIAS

FILOPAPPOS HILL

ACROPOLIS MUSEUM

TEMPLE OF OLYMPIAN ZEUS

MAKRIGIANNI

SYNGROU

KOUKAKI

NOT TO SCALE

DCH

↙ TO PIRAEUS

ORIENTATION

planners had ever attempted to tie the city together and treat it as a united entity.

But most visitors never see that part of Athens. In fact, you can pretend that Athens is the same small, atmospheric village at the foot of the Acropolis as it was a century ago. Almost everything of importance to tourists is within a few blocks of the Acropolis. As you explore this city-within-a-city on foot, you'll realize just how small it is.

A good map is a necessity for enjoying Athens on foot. The fine map the TI gives out works great. Get a good map and use it.

Athens by Neighborhood

The Athens you'll be spending your time in includes the following districts:

The Plaka (PLAH-kah, Πλάκα in Greek): This neighborhood at the foot of the Acropolis is the core of the tourist's Athens. One of the only parts of town that's atmospheric and Old World–feeling, it's also the most crassly touristic. Its streets are lined with souvenir shops, tacky tavernas, a smattering of small museums, ancient Greek and Roman ruins, and pooped tourists. The Plaka's narrow, winding streets can be confusing at first, but you can't get too lost with a monument the size of the Acropolis looming

Athens Landmarks

Area (Greek Name)	Description	Pronounced
Syntagma	Main square	seen-DOG-mah
Plaka	Old town	PLAH-kah
Adrianou	Old town's main street	ah-DREE-ah-noo
Monastiraki	Market district	mah-nah-stee-RAHee-kee
Psyrri	Nightlife district	psee-REE
Thissio	Western dining district	thee-SEE-oh
Gazi	Artsy district	GAH-zee
Makrigianni/ Koukaki	Southern residential and hotel districts	mah-kree-YAH-nee/ koo-KAH-kee
Kolonaki	Wealthy museum area	koh-loh-NAH-kee
Exarchia	Edgy student district	ex-AR-kee-yah
Dionysiou Areopagitou/ Apostolou Pavlou	Pedestrian walkways near Acropolis	dee-oo-NEE-see-oo ah-reh-oh-PAH-gee-too/ah-PAH-stoh-loo PAW-loo
Akropoli	Acropolis	ah-KROH-poh-lee
Agora	Ancient market	ah-GOH-rah
Piraeus	Athens' port	pee-reh-AHS

overhead to keep you oriented. Think of the Plaka as Athens with training wheels for tourists. While some visitors are mesmerized by the Plaka, others find it obnoxious and enjoy venturing outside it for a change of scenery.

Monastiraki (mah-nah-stee-RAHee-kee, Μοναστηρακι): This area ("Little Monastery") borders the Plaka to the northwest, surrounding the square of the same name. It's known for its handy Metro stop (where line 1/green meets line 3/blue), seedy flea market, and souvlaki stands. The Ancient Agora is nearby (roughly between Monastiraki and Thissio).

Psyrri (psee-REE, Ψυρή): Formerly a dumpy ghetto just north of Monastiraki, Psyrri is emerging as a cutting-edge nightlife and dining district. Don't be put off by the crumbling, graffiti-slathered buildings...this is one of central Athens' most appealing areas to explore after dark, and for now, locals still outnumber tourists here.

Syntagma (seen-DOG-mah, Σύνταγμα): Centered on Athens' main square, Syntagma ("Constitution") Square, this urban-feeling zone melts into the Plaka to the north and east. While the Plaka is dominated by tourist shops, Syntagma is where

---

Greek Words and English Spellings

Any given Greek name—for streets, sights, businesses, and more—can be transliterated many different ways in English. Throughout this book, I've used the English spelling you're most likely to see locally, but you will definitely notice variations. If you see a name that looks (or sounds) similar to one in this book, it's likely the same place. For example, the Ψυρή district might appear as Psyrri, Psyrrí, Psyri, Psirri, Psiri, and so on.

Most major streets in Athens are labeled in Greek in signs and on maps, followed by the transliteration in English. The word ΟΔΟΣ *(odos)* means "street," ΛΕΩΦΌΡΟΣ *(leoforos)* is "avenue," and ΠΛΑΤΕΙΑ *(plateia)* is "square."

If a name used in this book appears locally only in Greek, I've included that spelling to aid with your navigation.

---

local urbanites do their shopping. Syntagma is bounded to the east by the Parliament building and the vast National Garden.

Thissio (thee-SEE-oh, Θησείο): West of the Ancient Agora, Thissio is an upscale, local-feeling residential neighborhood with piles of outdoor cafés and restaurants. It's easily accessible thanks to the handy pedestrian walkway around the Acropolis.

Gazi (GAH-zee, Γκάζι): At the western edge of the tourist's Athens (just beyond Thissio and Psyrri), Gazi is trendy, artsy, and gay-friendly. Its centerpiece is a former gasworks-turned-events center called Technopolis.

Makrigianni (mah-kree-YAH-nee, Μακρυγιάννη) and **Koukaki** (koo-KAH-kee, Κουκάκι): Tucked just behind (south of) the Acropolis, these overlapping, nondescript urban neighborhoods have a lived-in charm of their own. If you want to escape the crowds of the Plaka, this area makes a good home base—with fine hotels and restaurants within easy walking distance of the ancient sites and the Plaka.

Kolonaki (koh-loh-NAH-kee, Κολωνάκι): Just north and east of the Parliament/Syntagma Square area, this upscale diplomatic quarter is home to several good museums and a yuppie dining zone. It's huddled under the tall, pointy Lykavittos Hill, which challenges the Acropolis for domination of the skyline.

Exarchia (ex-AR-kee-yah, Εξάρχεια): Just beyond Kolonaki is a rough-and-funky student zone. The origin of many of the protests that grabbed Greek headlines in 2010, it's a fascinating but not-for-everyone glimpse into an Athens that few tourists experience.

Major Streets: Various major streets define the tourist's Athens. The Acropolis is ringed by a broad traffic-free walkway, named **Dionysiou Areopagitou** (Διονυσιου Αρεοπαγιτου) to the south and **Apostolou Pavlou** (Αποστολου Παυλου) to the west; for simplicity, I call these the **"Acropolis Loop."** Touristy **Adrianou** street (Αδριανου) curves through the Plaka a few blocks away from the Acropolis' base. Partly pedestrianized **Ermou** street (Ερμου) runs west from Syntagma Square, defining the Plaka, Monastiraki, and Thissio to the south and Psyrri to the north. Where Ermou meets Monastiraki, **Athinas** street (Αθηνας) heads north to Omonia Square. The tourist zone is hemmed in to the east by a series of major highways: The north–south **Vasilissis Amalias** avenue (Βασιλισσης Αμαλιας) runs between the National Garden and the Plaka/Syntagma area. To the south, it jogs around the Temple of Olympian Zeus and becomes **Syngrou** avenue (Συγγρου). To the north, at the Parliament, it forks: the eastward branch, **Vasilissis Sofias** (Βασιλισσης Σοφιας), heads past some fine museums to Kolonaki; the northbound branch, **Panepistimiou** (Πανεπιστιμίου), angles northwest past the library and university buildings to Omonia Square.

Planning Your Time

Although Athens is a big city, its sights can be seen quickly. The three top sights—the Acropolis/Ancient Agora, the Acropolis Museum, and the National Archaeological Museum—deserve a half-day each. Two days total is plenty of time for the casual tourist to see the city's main attractions. When setting up your itinerary, keep in mind that the Acropolis Museum is closed on Monday. To enhance your experience, consider downloading my free audio versions of the Athens City Walk and tours of the major sights (see page 481).

Day 1: In the morning, follow my Athens City Walk. Grab a souvlaki lunch near Monastiraki, and spend midday in the markets (shopping in the Plaka, browsing in the Central Market, and wandering through the flea market—best on Sun). After lunch, as the crowds (and heat) subside, visit the ancient biggies: First tour the Ancient Agora, then hike up to the Acropolis (confirming carefully how late the Acropolis is open—it closes at 15:00 Oct-April). Be the last person off the Acropolis. Stroll down the Dionysiou Areopagitou pedestrian boulevard, then promenade to dinner—in Thissio, Monastiraki, Psyrri, or the Plaka.

Day 2: Spend the morning visiting the Acropolis Museum and exploring the Plaka. After lunch, head to the National Archaeological Museum.

Day 3: Museum-lovers will want more time to visit other archaeological sites, museums, and galleries. The city has many "also-ran" museums that reward patient sightseers. I'd suggest heading out toward Kolonaki to take in the Benaki Museum

Daily Reminder

Sunday: Most sights are open, but the Art Tower and Central Market are closed. The Monastiraki flea market is best to visit today. An elaborate changing of the guard—including a marching band—sometimes takes place at 11:00 in front of the Parliament building. Off-season (Nov-March), the Acropolis is free.

Monday: Many museums and galleries are closed, including the Acropolis Museum, Benaki Museum of Islamic Art, Museum of Greek Folk Art, Museum of Greek Popular Instruments, Art Tower, and National War Museum. The National Archaeological Museum opens at 13:30, and the Agora Museum opens at 13:00. Off-season (Nov-March), the Byzantine and Christian Museum is closed.

Tuesday: These sights are closed today: the Museum of Cycladic Art, Museum of Greek Folk Art Ceramics Collection, Museum of the City of Athens, Art Tower, and Benaki Museum of Greek History and Culture.

Wednesday: All major sights are open.

Thursday: All major sights are open.

Friday: All major sights are open.

Saturday: All major sights are open, except the Jewish Museum, which is closed.

Evening Sightseeing: In summer, these places stay open daily until 20:00: the Acropolis, Ancient Agora, National Archaeological Museum, Temple of Olympian Zeus, Byzantine and Christian Museum, and Keramikos Cemetery. Some sights are open until 20:00 year-round, including the cathedral (daily), Acropolis Museum (Tue-Sun), Art Tower (Wed-Fri), and Museum of Cycladic Art (Thu only). The Benaki Museum of Islamic Art is open Wednesday until 21:00, and the Benaki Museum of Greek History and Culture is open Thursday until 24:00.

of Greek History and Culture, Museum of Cycladic Art, and Byzantine and Christian Museum (and the nearby National War Museum, if you're interested).

Note that a third (or fourth) day could also be used for the long but satisfying side-trip by bus to Delphi or a quick getaway by boat to the isle of Hydra—each more interesting than a third or fourth day in Athens. But these sights—and many others—are better as an overnight stop. For suggestions on an itinerary that gets you out of Athens, see page 8.

Tourist Information

The Greek National Tourist Organization (EOT), with its main branch near Syntagma Square, covers Athens and the rest of the

ORIENTATION

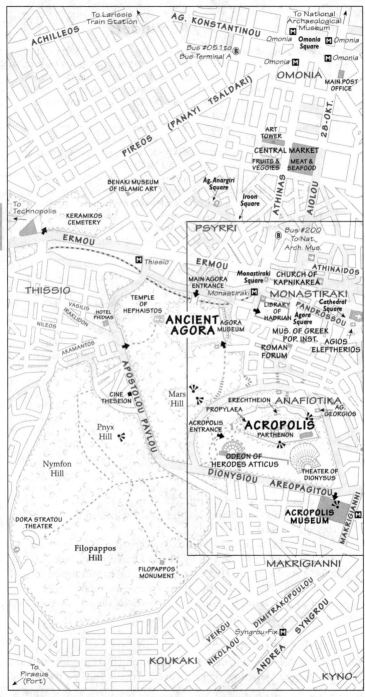

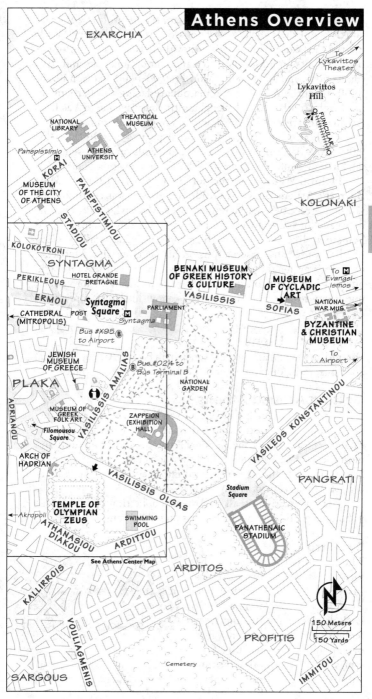

Athens Overview

EXARCHIA

To Lykavittos Theater

Lykavittos Hill

FUNICULAR

NATIONAL LIBRARY

THEATRICAL MUSEUM

Panepistimio M

KORAI

ATHENS UNIVERSITY

PANEPISTIMIOU

MUSEUM OF THE CITY OF ATHENS

KOLONAKI

STADIOU

KOLOKOTRONI

SYNTAGMA

PERIKLEOUS

HOTEL GRANDE BRETAGNE

ERMOU

CATHEDRAL (MITROPOLIS)

POST

Syntagma Square M

Syntagma

PARLIAMENT

Bus #X95 B to Airport

JEWISH MUSEUM OF GREECE

PLAKA

ADRIANOU

MUSEUM OF GREEK FOLK ART

Filomousou Square

ARCH OF HADRIAN

Akropoli

VASILISSIS AMALIAS

Bus #024 to B Bus Terminal B

BENAKI MUSEUM OF GREEK HISTORY & CULTURE

VASILISSIS

MUSEUM OF CYCLADIC ART

To M Evangel-ismos

SOFIAS

NATIONAL WAR MUS.

BYZANTINE & CHRISTIAN MUSEUM

To Airport

NATIONAL GARDEN

ZAPPEION (EXHIBITION HALL)

VASILISSIS OLGAS

TEMPLE OF OLYMPIAN ZEUS

SWIMMING POOL

ATHANASIOU DIAKOU

ARDITTOU

See Athens Center Map

VASILEOS KONSTANTINOU

PANGRATI

Stadium Square

PANATHENAIC STADIUM

ARDITOS

KALLIRROIS

VOULIAGMENIS

Cemetery

PROFITIS

IMMITOU

SARGOUS

N

150 Meters
150 Yards

ORIENTATION

country. Pick up their handy city map, the helpful *Athens Guide* booklet, and their slick, glossy book on Athens (all free). While their advice can be hit-or-miss, they do have stacks of informative handouts on museums, entertainment options, bus and train connections, and much more (Mon-Fri 9:00-19:00, Sat-Sun 10:00-16:00; from the top of Syntagma Square facing the Parliament, head right/south a few blocks along the busy avenue to Vasilissis Amalias 26; tel. 210-331-0392, www.gnto.gr, info@gnto.gr).

EOT also has an office at the airport (generally Mon-Fri 9:00-18:00, Sat-Sun 10:00-16:00 but depends on flight schedule, tel. 210-353-0448), plus a seasonal kiosk on Syntagma Square.

Helpful Website: While not officially part of the TI, **Matt Barrett's Athens Survival Guide** is a great resource for anyone visiting Greece (www.athensguide.com). Matt, who splits his time between North Carolina and Greece, splashes through his adopted hometown like a kid in a wading pool, enthusiastically sharing his discoveries and observations on his generous site. Matt covers emerging neighborhoods that few visitors venture into, and offers offbeat angles on the city and recommendations for vibrant, untouristy restaurants. He also blogs about his latest impressions on the city.

Arrival in Athens

For information on arriving in (or departing from) Athens by plane, boat, bus, train, or car, see the Athens Connections chapter.

Getting Around Athens

Because Athens is such a huge city, you'll likely use public transportation to reach farther-flung destinations (such as the port of Piraeus, the airport, or the National Archaeological Museum). But most travelers on a short visit find they don't need to take any public transit at all, once they're settled into their hotel—the tourists' core of Athens is surprisingly walkable.

For information on all of Athens' public transportation, see www.oasa.gr. Beware of pickpockets on public transportation.

By Metro

The Metro is the most straightforward way to get around Athens. Just look for signs with a blue M in a green circle. The Metro is slick, user-friendly, and new-feeling—mostly built, renovated, or expanded for the 2004 Olympics. Signs are in both Greek and English, as are announcements

Athens Transit

— METRO LINE 1 (GREEN)
— METRO LINE 2 (RED)
--- METRO LINE 3 (BLUE)
--- BUS LINE w/#
+++ RAIL
— COASTAL TRAM w/#

TRAINS TO ALL OVER GREECE

Kifissia
Irini
LINE 1 (GREEN)
BUS TERMINAL B LIOSSION
#024
TO AIRPORT
Agios Antonios
Attiki
Victoria
LINE 3 (BLUE)
Larissa (TRAIN STN.)
NATIONAL ARCHAEOLOGICAL MUSEUM
Egaleo
Keramikos
Omonia
LYKAVITTOS HILL
TO AIRPORT
BUS TERMINAL KIFISSOU A
#051
Evangelismos
#X95
TO AIRPORT X1 #1
Monastiraki
Thissio
ACRO-POLIS
Syntagma
Neo Faliro
Akropoli
Syngrou-Fix
Neos Kosmos
Piraeus
Nea Smyrni
LINE 2 (RED)
Agios Dimitrios
SARONIC GULF
FERRIES & HYDROFOILS TO ISLANDS
1&2
1
2
DCH
NOT TO SCALE
TO VOULA

ORIENTATION

inside subway cars. Trains run about every five minutes (Sun-Thu 5:00-24:20, Fri-Sat 5:00-2:20 in the morning, www.amel.gr).

There are various types of tickets, which you can buy at machines or from ticket windows. The **basic ticket** (€1.40) is good for 1.5 hours, including transfers. If planning more than three rides in a day, consider the **24-hour ticket** (€4). For a longer visit with lots of travel, you might get your money's worth with a **one-week ticket** (€14). Be sure to stamp your ticket in a validation machine, located near the ticket booth (24-hour and one-week tickets only need to be stamped the first time). Those riding without a ticket (or with an unstamped ticket) are subject to stiff fines. Note that even though the airport is on the Metro system, it's not covered by any of these tickets (you have to buy a separate €8 ticket—see page 209).

The three Metro lines are color-coded and numbered. Use the end-of-the-line stops to figure out which direction you need to go.

Line 1 (green) runs from the port of Piraeus in the southwest to Kifissia in the northern suburbs. Since this is an older line (officially called ISAP or "subway" rather than "Metro"), it's slower than the other two lines. Key stops include **Piraeus** (boats to the islands), **Thissio** (enjoyable neighborhood with good restaurants and nightlife), **Monastiraki** (city center), **Victoria** (10-minute

walk from National Archaeological Museum), and **Irini** (Olympic Stadium). You can transfer to line 2 at Omonia, and to line 3 at Monastiraki. (Confusingly, on line 1, the Monastiraki stop is labeled "Monastirion.")

Line 2 (red) runs from Agios Antonios in the northwest to Agios Dimitrios in the southeast. Important stops include **Larissa** (train station), **Syntagma** (city center), **Akropoli** (Acropolis and Makrigianni/Koukaki hotel neighborhood), and **Syngrou-Fix** (Makrigianni/Koukaki hotels). Transfer to line 1 at Omonia and to line 3 at Syntagma. Be aware that construction is currently underway to extend line 2 at both ends. When the work is completed (possibly in 2011), the end stations will be Anthoupoli in the northwest and Helliniko in the southeast.

Line 3 (blue) runs from Egaleo in the west to the airport in the east. Important stops are **Keramikos** (near Keramikos Cemetery and the lively Gazi district), **Monastiraki** (city center), **Syntagma** (city center), **Evangelismos** (Kolonaki neighborhood, with Byzantine and Christian Museum and National War Museum), and the **Airport** (requires a separate ticket). Transfer to line 1 at Monastiraki and to line 2 at Syntagma.

By Bus and Tram

Athens has many forms of public transit, but their usefulness is limited for visitors sticking to the city-center sightseeing zone.

Public **buses** help connect the dots between Metro stops. Buy the €1.20 tickets in advance, either from a special ticket kiosk or from one of the many regular newsstands that dot the streets. Tickets must be validated in the orange machines as you board. In general, I'd avoid buses—which are slow and overcrowded—with these exceptions: Bus **#200** whisks you from Athinas street near Monastiraki to the National Archaeological Museum. Bus **#X95** zips between the airport and Syntagma Square (bus **#X96** connects the airport with Piraeus). And local buses are crucial for getting to Athens' two major intercity bus terminals (bus **#051** from near Omonia Square to Terminal A/Kifissou, and bus **#024** from Syntagma Square to Terminal B/Liossion; for more on reaching these two bus terminals, see page 216).

The **Athens Coastal Tram**—essentially worthless to tourists—starts at Syntagma and runs 18 miles through the neighborhoods of Neos Kosmos and Nea Smyrni, emerging at the sea near Paleo Faliro. From there, it splits: One branch heads north, to the modern stadium and Olympic coastal complex in Neo Faliro; the other runs south, past the marinas and beaches to the Voula neighborhood. The price depends on how many stops you're going (www.tramsa.gr).

The city also has various **suburban rail lines,** but you're unlikely to need them. If you need details, talk to the TI or your hotelier.

By Taxi

Despite the vulgar penchant cabbies here have for ripping off tourists, Athens is a great taxi town. Its yellow taxis are cheap and handy (€3 minimum charge covers most short rides in town; after that, it's €0.66/km, plus surcharges: €1 from Piraeus passenger ports and train and bus stations, €3.10 from the airport, €5.20 from cruise terminal at Piraeus). The €0.66 per kilometer day rate (tariff 1 on the meter) doubles between midnight and 5:00 in the morning (tariff 2). You'll also pay the double rate outside the city limits, and you're responsible for any tolls incurred by the driver (such as on the speedy road to the airport). Baggage costs €0.40 for each item over 10 kilograms (about 22 pounds).

In a semi-legal local custom, Athens' cabbies double up, picking up additional passengers headed the same way. Unfortunately, sharing the cab with strangers doesn't mean sharing the fare. The cabbie makes more and the passengers save nothing. Still, this makes it easier to find an available cab. You can simply hail any taxi, empty or not, and if your destination works for the cabbie, he'll welcome you in.

Hotels and restaurants can order you a cab, but there's a €2 surcharge to call for a taxi ("radio-taxi"). Note that cabbies may try to cheat you by saying the surcharge is €5. Hold firm, and they will docilely take the €2.

Helpful Hints

Theft Alert: Be wary of pickpockets, particularly in crowds, at the Monastiraki flea market, on major public transit routes (such as the Metro between the city and Piraeus), and at the port. The main streets through the Plaka—such as Adrianou and Pandrossou—attract as many pickpockets as tourists.

Bar Alert: Single male travelers are strongly advised to stay away from bars recommended by strangers encountered on the street. Multilingual con men prowl Syntagma Square and the Plaka looking for likely dupes. They pretend that they, too, are strangers in town who just happen to have stumbled upon a "great little bar." You'll end up at a sleazy bar and be coerced into paying for bottles of overpriced champagne for your new "friend" and the improbably attractive women who inevitably appear.

Traffic Alert: Streets that appear to be "traffic-free" often are shared by motorcycles or moped drivers gingerly easing their machines through crowds. Keep your wits about you, and don't step into a street—even those that feel pedestrian-friendly—without looking both ways.

Slippery Streets Alert: Athens (and other Greek towns) have some marble-like streets and red pavement tiles that become very slick when it rains. Watch your step.

Emergency Help: The tourist police have a 24-hour help-line in English and other languages for emergencies (tel. 171). Their office, south of the Acropolis in the Makrigianni/Koukaki district, is also open 24 hours daily (Veikou 43-45, tel. 210-920-0724). The American Embassy may also be able to help (tel. 210-721-2951 during office hours; 210-729-4301 or 210-729-4444 at other times).

Free Sights: The Museum of Greek Popular Instruments, Art Tower contemporary gallery, National Garden, cathedral, Church of Kapnikarea, and Church of Agios Eleftherios are always free. The Acropolis is free on all national holidays and on Sundays off-season (Nov-March).

Internet Access: Bits and Bytes, in the heart of the Plaka, has plenty of terminals, a peaceful folk/jazz ambience, and air-conditioning (€2 minimum, €2.50/hour, can burn your digital photos to a CD or DVD, open 24 hours daily, just off Agora Square at Kapnikareas 19, tel. 210-325-3142). At Syntagma Square, **Ivis Travel** has several Internet terminals (€2/30 minutes, €3/hour, €2 minimum, daily 8:00-22:00, upstairs at Mitropoleos 3—look for signs, tel. 210-324-3365). See the map on page 181 for both locations.

Post Offices: The most convenient post office for travelers is at Syntagma Square (Mon-Fri 7:30-20:00, Sat 7:30-14:00, Sun 9:00-13:30, bottom of the square, at corner with Mitropoleos). Smaller neighborhood offices with shorter hours (generally Mon-Fri 7:30-14:00 or 14:30, closed Sat-Sun) are in Monastiraki (Mitropoleos 58) and Makrigianni (Dionysiou Areopagitou 7).

Bookshops: Compendium Bookstore stocks mostly English-language books and has a secondhand section (Mon-Sat 9:00-17:00, until 20:30 on Tue and Thu-Fri, closed Sun; just southwest of Syntagma Square at the corner of Nikis and Nikodimou, Nikodimou 5, tel. 210-322-1248). **Eleftheroudakis (ΕΛΕΥΘΕΡΟΥΔΑΚΗΣ)** is Greece's answer to Barnes & Noble. Their main branch has a floor for travel guides and maps, and an entire floor for English books (Mon-Fri 9:00-21:00, Sat 9:00-18:00, closed Sun, 3 blocks north of Syntagma Square at Panepistimiou 17, tel. 210-325-

8440, www.books.gr). Their smaller branch is in the tight streets southwest of Syntagma Square, near Compendium (same hours, Nikis 20, tel. 210-322-9388). For locations, see the map on page 198.

Laundry: A full-service **launderette,** on Apollonos Street in the heart of the Plaka, will wash, dry, and fold your clothes (€4.50/kilogram—about 2.2 pounds, typical load about 10 pounds or €18, same-day service if you drop off by noon; Mon and Wed 8:00-20:00, Tue and Thu-Fri 8:00-17:00, closed Sat-Sun; Apollonos 17, tel. 210-323-2226). **Athens Studios,** near the Acropolis Museum in the Makrigianni neighborhood, operates a self-service launderette (wash-€5/load, dry-€2/load, daily 8:00-22:00, Veikou 3A, tel. 210-922-4044).

Tours in Athens

On Wheels

Bus Tours—Various companies offer half-day, bus-plus-walking tours of Athens for €52-54 (about 4 hours, including a guided visit to the Acropolis). Add a guided tour of the Acropolis Museum, and the price goes up to €67.

Some companies also offer a night city tour that finishes with dinner and folk dancing at a taverna (€62) and a 90-mile round-trip evening drive down the coast to Cape Sounion for the sunset at the Temple of Poseidon (€42, 4 hours—not worth the time if visiting ancient sites elsewhere in Greece). The buses pick up at various points around town and near most hotels.

The most established operations include the well-regarded **Hop In** (modern comfy buses, narration usually English only, tel. 210-428-5500, www.hopin.com), **CHAT Tours** (tel. 210-323-0827, www.chatours.gr), **Key Tours** (tel. 210-923-3166, www.keytours .gr), and **GO Tours** (tel. 210-921-9555, www.gotours.com.gr). It's convenient to book tours through your hotel; most act as a booking agent for at least one tour company. While hotels do snare a commission, some offer discounts to their guests.

Beyond Athens: Some of these companies also offer day-long tours to Delphi and to Mycenae, Nafplio, and Epidavros (either tour €99 with lunch, €89 without), two-day tours to the monasteries of Meteora (€175), and more.

Hop-on, Hop-off Bus Tours—Two companies compete for the usual hop-on, hop-off bus tour business: **CitySightseeing Athens** (€18/24 hours, tel. 210-922-0604, www.citysightseeing .gr) and **Athens City Tour** (€15/24 hours, tel. 210-881-5207, www .athensopenbus.com). The main stop for both buses is on Syntagma Square, though you can hop on and buy your ticket at any stop— look for signs around town. Since most of the major sights in

Athens are within easy walking distance of the Plaka, I'd use this only if I wanted an overview of the city or had extra time to get to the outlying sights.

Tourist Trains—Two different trains do a sightseeing circuit through Athens' tourist zone. As these goofy little trains can go where big buses can't, they can be useful for people with limited mobility. The **Sunshine Express** train runs about hourly; catch it on Aiolou street along the Hadrian's Library fence at Agora Square (€5, 40-minute loop, departs hourly; May-Sept Mon-Fri 11:30-14:30 & 17:00-24:00, Sat-Sun 11:00-24:00; Oct-April Sat-Sun only; www.sunshine-express.gr). The **Athens Happy Train** is similar, but offers hop-on, hop-off privileges at a few strategic stops (€6, full loop takes 1 hour, 2/hour, daily 9:00-24:00; catch it at the bottom of Syntagma Square, at Monastiraki Square, or just below the Acropolis; www.athenshappytrain.com).

By Foot

Rick Steves Free Audio Tours—I've produced free, self-guided audio versions of my tours of the major sights in Athens (available spring 2011; download from www.ricksteves.com/audio europe or from iTunes). These user-friendly, easy-to-follow, fun, and enlightening audio tours are available for the Acropolis, the Agora, the National Archaeological Museum, and my Athens City Walk. I created these tours because none of these sights offers good information on the spot, and quality local guides can be expensive, unreliable, and elusive. If you don't mind me in your ear, these audio tours are hard to beat: Nobody will stand you up, the quality is reliable, you can take the tour exactly when you like, and they're free.

Walking Tours—Athens Walking Tours offers two basic walks: the Acropolis and City Tour (€36 plus entry fees, daily at 9:30, 3 hours, departs from Syntagma Metro station, under hanging clock one level down) and Acropolis Museum tour (€29 plus entry fee, Tue-Sun at 13:45, 1.5 hours, meet inside museum, in front of cash desk). Those with energy can sign up for a combo version of these tours (€53, Tue-Sun at 9:30, 5.5 hours, reserve in advance, tel. 210-884-7269, mobile 694-585-9662, www.athenswalkingtours.gr, Despina).

Local Guide—A good private guide can bring Athens' sights to life. **Effie Perperi** is a fine choice (€50/hour, tel. 210-951-2566, mobile 697-739-6659, effieperperi@gmail.com).

SIGHTS IN ATHENS

The sights listed in this chapter are arranged by neighborhood for handy sightseeing. When you see a ✪ in a listing, it means the sight is covered in much more depth in my Athens City Walk or one of my self-guided tours. This is why Athens' most important attractions get the least coverage in this chapter—we'll explore them later in the book.

For tips on sightseeing, see page 17. For a self-guided walk connecting many of central Athens' top sights, ✪ see the Athens City Walk.

Note that most of Athens' top ancient sites are covered by the Acropolis ticket (see page 66).

Acropolis and Nearby

A broad pedestrian boulevard that I call the "Acropolis Loop" strings together the Acropolis, Mars Hill, Theater of Dionysus, Acropolis Museum, and more. The ✪ Acropolis and the ✪ Acropolis Museum are each covered in more detail in their respective tour chapters.

▲▲▲**Acropolis**—The most important ancient site in the Western world, the Acropolis (which means "high city" in Greek) rises gleaming like a beacon above the gray concrete drudgery of

modern Athens. This is where the Greeks built the mighty Parthenon—the most famous temple on the planet and an enduring symbol of ancient Athens' glorious Golden Age from nearly 2,500 years ago.

This icon of Western

SIGHTS

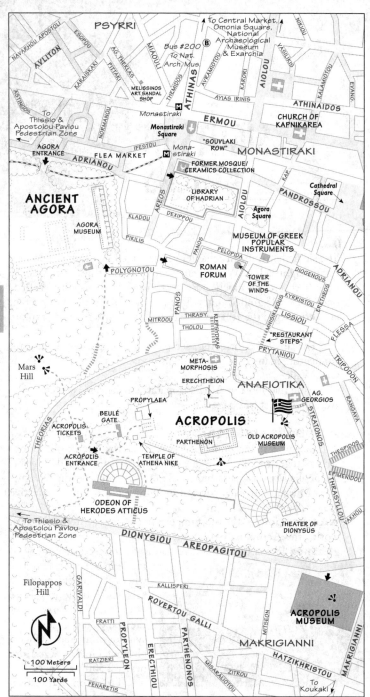

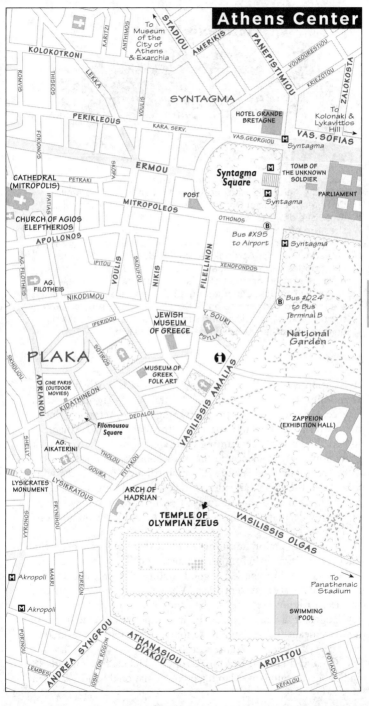

Athens Center

SIGHTS

SIGHTS

Acropolis Ticket

Your €12 Acropolis ticket gives you entry to six major ancient sites: the Acropolis, Ancient Agora, Roman Forum, Keramikos Cemetery, Temple of Olympian Zeus, and Theater of Dionysus. If you see only the Acropolis, you'll still pay €12—so the other sites are effectively free add-ons. (The other attractions do sell cheaper individual tickets—but as you're virtually guaranteed to visit the Acropolis sometime during your trip, these are pointless.) It's technically valid for four days, but there's no date printed on the ticket, so in practice you can use it anytime. The ticket is one long strip; perforated "coupons" are removed and used to enter the smaller sites. You can buy the ticket at any participating site. Only the Acropolis ticket is unique—the other stubs can be used as you like.

civilization was built after a war with Persia. The Athenians had abandoned their city when the Persian king's troops invaded Greece; his soldiers destroyed everything on the Acropolis. But in the naval Battle of Salamis (480 B.C.), the outnumbered Athenians routed the Persians, reclaiming their city. Now at the very peak of its power, Athens became the most popular kid on the block. Other city-states and islands paid cash tributes to be on the winning side. The Athenian ruler, Pericles, spared no expense as he set about rebuilding the Acropolis, transforming it into a complex of lavishly decorated temples to honor the city's patron goddess, Athena.

The four major monuments built during this time—the Parthenon, Erechtheion, Propylaea, and Temple of Athena Nike—survive in remarkably good condition given the battering they've taken over the centuries. While the Persians, Ottomans, and Lord Elgin were cruel to the Acropolis in the past, the greatest dangers it faces now are acid rain and pollution. Ongoing restoration means that you might see some scaffolding—but even that can't detract from the greatness of this site.

Cost and Hours: €12 for Acropolis Ticket; free for kids 18 and under, on Sun Nov-March, and on all national holidays. Open daily May-Sept 8:00-20:00, Oct-April 8:00-15:00, last entry 30 minutes before closing. The main entrance is at the western end of the Acropolis. From the Ancient Agora in the Plaka, signs point uphill. Tel. 210-321-4172, www.culture.gr.

○ See the Acropolis Tour chapter.

▲▲**"Acropolis Loop" (a.k.a. Dionysiou Areopagitou and Apostolou Pavlou)**—One of Athens' best attractions, this

wide, well-manicured, delight-fully traffic-free pedestrian boulevard circles the Acropolis. It's composed of two streets with tongue-twisting names—Dionysiou Areopagitou and Apostolou Pavlou (think of them as Dionysus Street and Apostle Paul's Street); for simplicity, I refer to them collectively as the "Acropolis Loop." One of the city's many big improvements made in preparation for its 2004 Olympics-hosting bid, this walkway immediately became a favorite local hangout, with vendors, al fresco cafés, and frequent special events enlivening its cobbles.

Dionysiou Areopagitou, wide and touristy, runs along the southern base of the Acropolis. It was named for Dionysus the Areopagite, a member of the ancient Roman-era senate that met atop Mars Hill (described next). The other section, **Apostolou Pavlou**—quieter, narrower, and tree-lined—curls around the western end of the Acropolis and the Ancient Agora. It feels more local and has the best concentration of outdoor eateries (in the Thissio neighborhood; see page 205 for recommendations). This section was named for the Apostle Paul, who presented himself before Dionysus the Areopagite at Mars Hill.

Where Apostolou Pavlou meets the Thissio Metro stop, it flows into **Ermou** street—a similarly enjoyable, recently pedestrianized boulevard that continues westward to Keramikos Cemetery and the Gazi district's Technopolis (both described later).

Stray cats are common in this warm part of Europe, but Athens also has a huge population of stray dogs. Many of them—including some who hang out along the Dionysiou Areopagitou—are cared for (but not housed) by local animal-rights organizations. Even if a dog has a collar, it might be a stray.

▲**Mars Hill (Areopagus)**—The knobby, windswept hill crawling with tourists in front of the Acropolis is Mars Hill, also known as Areopagus (from *Areios Pagos,* "Ares Hill," referring to the Greek version of Mars). While the views from the Acropolis are more striking, rugged Mars Hill (near the Acropolis' main entrance, at the western end) makes a pleasant perch. As you're climbing

Athens at a Glance

▲▲▲**Acropolis** The most important ancient site in the Western world, where Athenians built their architectural masterpiece—the Parthenon. **Hours:** Daily May-Sept 8:00-20:00, Oct-April 8:00-15:00. See page 63.

▲▲▲**Acropolis Museum** Glassy modern temple for ancient art. **Hours:** Tue-Sun 8:00-20:00, closed Mon. See page 71.

▲▲▲**Ancient Agora** Social and commercial center of ancient Athens, with a well-preserved temple and intimate museum. **Hours:** Daily May-Sept 8:00-20:00, Oct-April 8:00-15:00, museum opens Mon at 13:00. See page 71.

▲▲▲**National Archaeological Museum** World's best collection of ancient Greek art, displayed chronologically from 7000 B.C. to A.D. 500. **Hours:** May-Sept Tue-Sun 8:00-20:00, Mon 13:30-20:00; Oct-April Tue-Sun 8:30-15:00, Mon 13:30-19:30. See page 79.

▲▲**"Acropolis Loop"** Traffic-free pedestrian walkways ringing the Acropolis with vendors, cafés, and special events. **Hours:** Always open. See page 67.

▲▲**Thissio and Psyrri** Vibrant nightlife neighborhoods near the center, great for eating, exploring, and escaping other tourists. **Hours:** Always open. See page 72.

▲▲**Anafiotika** Delightful, village-like neighborhood draped across the hillside north of the Acropolis. **Hours:** Always open. See page 73.

▲▲**Temple of Olympian Zeus** Remains of the largest temple in ancient Greece. **Hours:** Daily 8:00-20:00, off-season until 17:00. See page 77.

▲▲**Benaki Museum of Greek History and Culture** Exquisite collection of artifacts from the ancient, Byzantine, Ottoman, and modern eras. **Hours:** Wed-Mon 9:00-17:00 except Thu until 24:00 and Sun until 15:00, closed Tue. See page 81.

▲▲**Museum of Cycladic Art** World's largest compilation of Cycladic art, which looks surprisingly modern even though it's 4,000 years old. **Hours:** Mon and Wed-Sat 10:00-17:00, Thu until 20:00, Sun 11:00-17:00, closed Tue. See page 82.

▲▲**Byzantine and Christian Museum** Fascinating look at the Byzantines, who borrowed from ancient Greece and Rome, then put their own stamp on a flourishing culture. **Hours:** April-Oct

Tue-Sun 8:00-20:00, Mon 13:30-20:00; Nov-March Tue-Sun 8:30-15:00, closed Mon. See page 83.

▲**Mars Hill** Historic spot—with a classic view of the Acropolis—where the Apostle Paul preached to the Athenians. **Hours:** Always open. See page 67.

▲**Gazi** Former depressed industrial zone, now the colorful and kinetic heart of Athens' gay community. **Hours:** Always open. See page 73.

▲**Roman Forum and Tower of the Winds** Ancient Roman marketplace with wondrously intact tower. **Hours:** Daily 8:00-19:00, until 15:00 off-season. See page 74.

▲**Museum of Greek Popular Instruments** Musical instruments from the 18th century to today. **Hours:** Tue and Thu-Sun 10:00-14:00, Wed 12:00-18:00, closed Mon. See page 74.

▲**Jewish Museum of Greece** Triumphs—and persecutions—of Greek Jews since the second century B.C. **Hours:** Mon-Fri 9:00-14:30, Sun 10:00-14:00, closed Sat. See page 75.

SIGHTS

▲**Syntagma Square** Athens' most famous public space with a popular changing-of-the-guard ceremony. **Hours:** Always open, guards change five minutes before the top of each hour. See page 75.

▲**Church of Kapnikarea** Small 11th-century Byzantine church with symbols of Greek Orthodox faith. **Hours:** Likely open daily 8:30-13:30 & 17:00-19:30. See page 76.

▲**Cathedral (Mitropolis)** Large, underwhelming head church of the Greek Orthodox faith. **Hours:** Generally open daily 8:00-13:00 & 16:30-20:00, no afternoon closure in summer. See page 76.

▲**Church of Agios Eleftherios** Tiny Byzantine church decorated with a millennia of Christian bric-a-brac. **Hours:** Likely open daily 8:30-13:30 & 17:00-19:30. See page 76.

▲**Panathenaic (a.k.a. "Olympic") Stadium** Gleaming marble stadium restored to its second-century A.D. condition. **Hours:** Daily 8:00-19:30. See page 78.

▲**Museum of the City of Athens** Models and exhibits about Athenian history, housed in a former royal residence. **Hours:** Mon and Wed-Fri 9:00-16:00, Sat-Sun 10:00-15:00, closed Tue. See page 85.

Mars Hill, be warned: The stone stairs (and the top of the rock) have been polished to a slippery shine by history, and can be treacherous even when dry. Watch your step and use the metal staircase.

This hill has an interesting history. After Rome conquered Athens in 86 B.C., the Roman overlords wisely decided to extend citizenship to any free man born here. (The feisty Greeks were less likely to rise up against a state that had made them citizens.) While Rome called the shots on major issues, minor matters of local governance were determined on this hill by a gathering of leaders. During this time, the Apostle Paul—the first great Christian missionary and author of about half of the New Testament—preached to the Athenians here on Mars Hill. Paul looked out over the Agora and started talking about an altar he'd seen—presumably in the Agora (though archaeologists can't confirm)—to the "Unknown God." (A plaque embedded in the rock near the stairs contains the Greek text of Paul's speech.) Although the Athenians were famously open-minded, Paul encountered a skeptical audience and only netted a couple of converts (including Dionysus the Areopagite, a local judge and the namesake of the pedestrian drag behind the Acropolis). Paul moved on to Corinth and a better reception.

Theater of Dionysus—The very scant remains of this theater are scattered southeast of the Acropolis, just above the Diony-

siou Areopagitou walkway. During Roman times, the theater was connected to the Odeon of Herodes Atticus (see page 115) by a long, covered stoa, creating an ensemble of inviting venues. But its illustrious history dates back well before that: It's fair to say that this is where our culture's great tradition of theater was born. During Athens' Golden Age, Sophocles and others watched their plays performed here. Originally just grass, with a circular dirt area as the stage, the theater was eventually expanded to accommodate 17,000—and stone seating was added—in 342-326 B.C., during the time of Alexander the Great. Later the Romans added a raised stage. Because the theater is included in your Acropolis ticket, consider an evocative stroll through its rubble. Plans are afoot to restore the theater to its former greatness.

Cost and Hours: €2, included in Acropolis ticket, same hours as Acropolis, main gate across from Acropolis Museum, tel. 210-322-4625.

▲▲▲**Acropolis Museum**—This museum is a modern-day temple to the Acropolis. Located at the foot of Athens' famous ancient

hill, it contains relics from the Acropolis, including statues of gods and goddesses, reliefs that once adorned the hilltop temples, and four of the six original caryatids (lady-columns) that once held up the roof of the prestigious Erechtheion temple. But the highlight is a life-size re-creation of the frieze that once wound all the way around the outside of the Parthenon, blending original pieces with copies of panels housed in the British Museum and other collections.

The stunning glass building—completed in 2009—is a work of art in itself. The top floor sits slightly askew, like a graduation cap, mimicking the orientation of the Parthenon. The glass walls are designed not only to flood the place with natural light, but also to disappear into the background so that the architecture plays second fiddle to the real stars: the statues and the views of the Acropolis.

Cost and Hours: €5, free for kids 18 and under; open Tue-Sun 8:00-20:00, closed Mon, last entry 30 minutes before closing. The museum faces the south side of the Acropolis from across the broad Dionysus Areopagitou pedestrian drag, and is right at the Akropoli Metro stop (line 2/red). Tel. 210-924-1043, www.the acropolismuseum.gr.

✪ See the Acropolis Museum Tour chapter.

Ancient Agora and Beyond

These sights are listed in geographic order, starting with the Agora and fanning out from there (mostly to the west—see the map on page 54). You can walk to the last three sights—the cemetery, Technopolis, and the Gazi district—via the wide, recently pedestrianized Ermou street.

▲▲▲**Ancient Agora: Athens' Market**—If the Acropolis was Golden Age Athens' "uptown," then the Ancient Agora was "downtown." Although literally and figuratively overshadowed by the impressive Acropolis, the Agora was for eight centuries the true meeting place of the city—a hive of commerce, politics, and everyday bustle. Everybody who was anybody in ancient Athens spent time here, from Socrates and Plato to a visiting missionary named

Paul. Built upon, forgotten, and ignored for centuries, the Agora was excavated in the 1930s. Now it's a center of archaeological study and one of the city's top tourist attractions. A visit here lets you ponder its sparse remains, wander through a modest museum in a rebuilt stoa (the Agora Museum), admire its beautifully preserved Temple of Hephaistos, and imagine sharing this hallowed space with the great minds of the ancient world.

Cost and Hours: Don't pay the €4 admission if you're also going to the Acropolis, as the Ancient Agora is included in the Acropolis ticket (see sidebar, earlier). Open daily May-Sept 8:00-20:00, Oct-April 8:00-15:00, last entry 30 minutes before closing, Agora Museum opens at 13:00 on Mon, main entrance on Adrianou. From Monastiraki (Metro line 1/green or line 3/blue), walk a block south (uphill, toward the Acropolis). Tel. 210-321-0180, www.culture.gr.

○ See the Ancient Agora Tour chapter.

▲▲**Thissio and Psyrri**—These two neighborhoods, just west and north (respectively) of the Ancient Agora, offer a real-world alternative to the tourist-clogged, artificial-feeling Plaka. **Thissio,** around the far side of the Acropolis (just follow the main pedestrian drag) has a trendy, yuppie vibe and a thriving passel of cafés and restaurants with point-blank Acropolis views. **Psyrri**—the yang to Thissio's yin—is grungy and run-down, but increasingly populated by a wide range of eateries, cafés, and clubs, with everything from dives to exclusive dance halls to crank-'em-out chain restaurants. While enjoyable any time of day, both neighborhoods are ideal in the evening—either for dinner or for a stroll afterwards. Both also have appealing open-air cinemas. For more details on Thissio and Psyrri, see the Nightlife in Athens chapter.

Benaki Museum of Islamic Art—Sometimes it seems the Greeks would rather just forget the Ottoman chapter of their past...but when you're talking about nearly 400 years, that's difficult to do. If you're intrigued by what Greeks consider a low point in their history, pay a visit to this branch of the prominent, private Benaki Museum (see listing for main branch on page 81). The 8,000-piece collection, displayed in two renovated Neoclassical buildings, includes beautifully painted ceramics, a 10th-century golden belt, a rare 14th-century astrolabe, and an entire marble room from a 17th-century Cairo mansion.

Cost and Hours: €5, Tue-Sun 9:00-15:00, until 21:00 on

Wed, closed Mon, northeast of Keramikos Cemetery at Agion Asomaton 22, on the corner with Dipilou, Metro line 1/green: Thissio. Tel. 210-325-1311, www.benaki.gr.

Keramikos Cemetery—Named for the ceramics workshops that used to surround it, this is a vast place to wander among marble tombstones from the seventh century B.C. onward. While the sprawling cemetery provides more exercise than excitement—and requires a good imagination to take on much meaning—the small, modern museum (air-con, great English descriptions) is a delight. With a wealth of artifacts found right here, it explains the evolution of ancient burial rituals one age at a time.

Cost and Hours: €2, covered by Acropolis ticket; open daily in summer 8:00-20:00, off-season 8:30-16:00, museum doesn't open until 13:30 on Mon; Ermou 148, Metro line 1/green: Thissio or line 3/blue: Keramikos.

Technopolis—This events center, built from the remains of a 19th-century gasworks, hosts an eclectic assortment of cultural happenings, including art exhibits, rock concerts, and experimental theater. The still-standing smokestacks are illuminated in red after dark, giving an eerie impression of its former industrial activity. The only permanent exhibit within Technopolis is a free museum dedicated to Greek-American diva Maria Callas, who had her heart broken when Ari left her for Jackie O. Technopolis is located in the up-and-coming Gazi district (described next), across a busy street from Keramikos Cemetery (free entry, Pireos 100, Metro line 3/blue: Keramikos—as you exit, walk to the square brick smokestacks, tel. 210-346-1589).

▲**Gazi**—Huddled around the Technopolis complex just beyond Keramikos Cemetery, this former industrial zone is now the center of the city's gay community. Recent gentrification is transforming it into one of central Athens' most interesting neighborhoods (for more details, see the Nightlife in Athens chapter).

In the Plaka and Monastiraki

These sights are scattered around the super-central Plaka neighborhood. The first two sights are covered in more detail in the ✪ Athens City Walk chapter.

▲▲**Anafiotika**—Clinging to the northern slope of the Acropolis (just above the Plaka), this improbable Greek-island-on-a-hillside feels a world apart from the endless sprawl of concrete and moped-choked streets

that stretch from its base. For a break from the big city, escape here for an enjoyable stroll.

▲Roman Forum (a.k.a. "Roman Agora") and Tower of the Winds—After the Romans conquered Athens in 86 B.C., they built their version of an agora—the forum—on this spot. Today it's a pile of ruins, watched over by the marvelously intact Tower of the Winds. Panels circling the top of the tower depict the various winds that shape Greek weather. Nearby, a separate, fenced area of Roman ruins contains what's left of the Library of Hadrian.

Cost and Hours: €2, covered by Acropolis ticket, daily 8:00-19:00, until 15:00 off-season, corner of Pelopida and Aiolou streets, Metro lines 1/green and 3/blue: Monastiraki.

▲Museum of Greek Popular Instruments—Small but well-presented, this charming old place is one of the most entertaining museums in Athens. On its three floors, you can wander around listening (on headphones) to different instruments and styles of music. Examine instruments dating from the 18th century to today, including flutes, clarinets, bagpipes, drums, fiddles, violins, mandolins, bells, and even water whistles. Photos and paintings illustrate the instruments being played, and everything is described in English. This easily digestible collection is an enjoyable change of pace from more of the same old artifacts.

Cost and Hours: Free, Tue and Thu-Sun 10:00-14:00, Wed 12:00-18:00, closed Mon, near Roman Forum at Diogenous 1-3, Metro lines 1/green and 3/blue: Monastiraki. Tel. 210-325-0198, www.culture.gr.

Museum of Greek Folk Art (Ceramics Collection)—Housed in the old mosque overlooking Monastiraki Square, this contains mostly pieces from the early 20th century, with an emphasis on traditional Greek and Cypriot workshops. Each item is accompanied by a brief description of the artist who crafted it. The mosque interior—with a rainbow-painted niche—is more interesting than the collection (€2, Wed-Mon 9:00-14:30, closed Tue, entrance along fence to right of mosque, Metro lines 1/green and 3/blue: Monastiraki, tel. 210-322-9031, www.culture.gr).

Museum of Greek Folk Art (Main Collection)—This dusty but well-presented little museum offers a classy break from the folk kitsch on sale throughout the Plaka. Five small floors display four centuries (17th-20th) of traditional artwork, all well-described in English. From the entry, turn right to find the elevator and head to the top floor. Then work your way down through each part of the collection. Wonderful folk costumes from each region fill the top floor, followed by jewelry and other silver and gold items. On the next floor down is a photo essay about Karpathos Island, called "Ethnographic Images of the Present." These vivid photos give you a fun trip to one of the country's most remote and traditional corners, with poetic descriptions: "In the coffee shop, there is room for everybody and everything: wise political words, incredible nautical tales, and memories." Continue down to the mezzanine, displaying Greek shadow puppets and ceramics. The ground floor holds a series of tapestries. While the collection can be a little difficult to appreciate, it offers a good look at Greek folk art.

Cost and Hours: €2, Tue-Sun 9:00-14:30, closed Mon, across from the Church of Metamorphosis at Kidathineon 17, Metro line 2/red: Akropoli or lines 2/red and 3/blue: Syntagma. Tel. 210-322-9031, www.culture.gr.

▲**Jewish Museum of Greece**—Many Jewish communities trace their roots back to medieval Spain's Sephardic diaspora and, before that, to classical Greece. (Before the Nazis invaded, Greece had 78,000 Jews; more than 85 percent of them perished in the Holocaust.) This impressive collection of more than 8,000 Jewish artifacts—thoughtfully displayed on four floors of a modern building—traces the history of Greek Jews since the second century B.C. Downstairs from the entry, you can visit a replica synagogue with worship items. Then spiral up through the split-level space to see exhibits on Jewish holidays, history, Zionism, the Nazi occupation and Holocaust, traditional dress, everyday life, and the recollections of Greek Jews.

Cost and Hours: €6, borrow English descriptions in each room, Mon-Fri 9:00-14:30, Sun 10:00-14:00, closed Sat; Nikis 39, at the corner with Kidathineon, behind the Hard Rock Café—ring bell to get inside; Metro lines 2/red and 3/blue: Syntagma. Tel. 210-322-5582, www.jewishmuseum.gr.

In Syntagma

The Syntagma area borders the Plaka to the north and east. All of these sights are covered in detail in the ❂ Athens City Walk chapter. I've listed only the essentials here.

▲**Syntagma Square (Plateia Syntagmatos)**—The "Times Square" of Athens is named for Greece's historic 1843 constitution, prompted by demonstrations right on this square. A major transit hub, the square is watched over by Neoclassical masterpieces such as the Hotel Grande Bretagne and the Parliament building.

Parliament—The former palace of King Otto, this is now a house of democracy. In front, colorfully costumed evzone guards stand at attention at the Tomb of the Unknown Soldier and periodically

do a ceremonial changing of the guard to the delight of tourists (guards change five minutes before the top of each hour, less elaborate crossing of the guard on the half-hour, full ceremony with marching band most Sundays at 11:00).

Ermou Street—This pedestrianized thoroughfare, connecting Syntagma Square with Monastiraki (and on to Thissio and Keramikos Cemetery), is packed with top-quality international shops. While most Athenians can't afford to shop here, it's enjoyable for people-watching and is refreshingly traffic-free in an otherwise congested area.

Churches in the Plaka and Syntagma Area

All of these sights are covered in detail in the ✪ Athens City Walk chapter. Only the basics are listed here.

▲Church of Kapnikarea—Sitting unassumingly in the middle of Ermou street, this small, typical, 11th-century Byzantine church offers a convenient look at the Greek Orthodox faith (free, likely open daily 8:30-13:30 & 17:00-19:30).

▲Cathedral (Mitropolis)—Dating from the mid-19th century, this big but stark head church of Athens— and therefore of all of Greece—is covered in scaffolding inside and out (free, generally open daily 8:00-13:00 & 16:30-20:00, no afternoon closure in summer, Plateia Mitropoleos). The cathedral is the centerpiece of a reverent neighborhood, with a pair of statues out front honoring great heroes of the Church, surrounding streets lined with religious paraphernalia shops (and black-cloaked, long-bearded priests), and the cute little...

▲Church of Agios Eleftherios— This tiny church, huddled in the shadow of the cathedral, has a delightful hodgepodge of ancient and early Christian monuments embedded in its facade. Like so many Byzantine churches, it was partly built (in the 13th century) with fragments of earlier buildings, monuments, and even tombstones. Today it's a giant *Da Vinci Code*–style puzzle of millennia-old bits and pieces (free, likely open daily 8:30-13:30 & 17:00-19:30, Plateia Mitropoleos).

At the Edge of the Plaka, Along Vasilissis Amalias Avenue

These two sights, dating from Athens' Roman period, overlook a busy highway at the edge of the tourist zone (just a few steps up Dionysiou Areopagitou from the Acropolis Museum and Metro line 2/red: Akropoli, or a 10-minute walk south of Syntagma Square). Both are described in greater detail in the ☻ Athens City Walk chapter.

▲**Arch of Hadrian**—This stoic triumphal arch marks the entrance to what was once the proud "Hadrianopolis" development—a new suburb of ancient Athens built by the Roman Emperor Hadrian in the second century A.D. (free, always viewable). Just beyond the arch is the...

▲▲**Temple of Olympian Zeus**—Started by an overambitious tyrant in the sixth century B.C., this giant temple was not completed until Hadrian took over, seven centuries later. Now 15 (of the original 104) Corinthian columns stand evocatively over a

ruined base in a field. You can get a good view of the temple ruins through the fence by the Arch of Hadrian, but since the site is covered by the Acropolis ticket, you can easily drop in for a closer look (otherwise €2, daily 8:00-20:00, off-season until 17:00, tel. 210-922-6330, www.culture.gr).

The National Garden: South and East of the Parliament and Syntagma Square

The busy avenue called Vasilissis Amalias rumbles south of Syntagma Square, where you'll find the following sights. Note that the Arch of Hadrian and the Temple of Olympian Zeus

(both described earlier) are just south of the National Garden and Zappeion.

National Garden— Extending south from the Parliament, the National Garden is a wonderfully cool retreat from the traffic-clogged streets of central Athens. Covering an area of around 40 acres, it was planted in 1839 as the palace garden, created for the pleasure of Queen Amalia. The garden was opened to the public in 1923 (free, open daily from dawn to dusk).

Zappeion—At the southern end of the National Garden stands the grand mansion called the Zappeion, surrounded by formal gardens of its own. To most Athenians, the Zappeion is best known as the site of the Aigli Village outdoor cinema in summer (behind the building, on the right as you face the colonnaded main entry; for details, see page 203). But the building is more than just a backdrop. During Ottoman rule, much of the Greek elite, intelligentsia, and aristocracy fled the country. They returned after independence and built grand mansions such as this. Finished in 1888, it was designed by the Danish architect Theophilus Hansen, who was known (along with his brother Christian) for his Neoclassical designs. The financing was provided by the Zappas brothers, Evangelos and Konstantinos, two of the prime movers in the campaign to revive the Olympic Games. This mansion housed the International Olympic Committee during the first modern Olympics in 1896 and served as a media center during the 2004 Olympics. Today the Zappeion is a conference and exhibition center.

Cost and Hours: Gardens free and always open, building only open during exhibitions for a fee, Vasilissis Amalias, Metro line 2/red: Akropoli or line 3/blue: Evangelismos. Tel. 210-323-7830.

▲Panathenaic (a.k.a. "Olympic") Stadium—In your travels through Greece, you'll see some ruined ancient stadiums (including the ones in Olympia and Delphi). Here's your chance to see one intact. This gleaming marble stadium has many names. Officially it's the Panathenaic Stadium, built in the fourth century B.C. to host the Panathenaic Games. Sometimes it's referred to as the Roman Stadium, because it was rebuilt by the great Roman benefactor Herodes Atticus in  the second century A.D., using the same prized Pentelic marble that was used in the Parthenon. This magnificent white marble gives the place its most popular name: Kalimarmara ("Beautiful Marble") Stadium. It was restored to its Roman condition in preparation for the first modern Olympics in 1896. It saw Olympic action again in 2004, when it provided a grand finish for the marathon. In ancient times, 50,000 filled the stadium; today, 80,000 people can pack the stands.

Cost and Hours: €3, daily 8:00-19:30, located southeast of the Zappeion off Vasilissis Konstantinou, Metro line 2/red: Akropoli or line 3/blue: Evangelismos. Tel. 210-325-1744.

North of Monastiraki

Athinas street leads north from Monastiraki Square to Omonia Square. Walking this grand street offers a great chance to feel the pulse of modern, workaday Athens, with shops tumbling onto broad sidewalks, striking squares, nine-to-fivers out having a smoke, and lots of urban energy. The first two sights are on the way to Omonia Square (see map on page 54). Farther up Athinas street, past Omonia Square, is the superb National Archaeological Museum.

Central Market—Take a vibrant, fragrant stroll through the modern-day version of the Ancient Agora. It's a living, breathing, smelly, and (for some) nauseating barrage on all the senses. You'll see dripping-fresh meat, livestock in all stages of dismemberment, still-wriggling fish, exotic nuts, and sticky figs. While it's not Europe's most colorful or appealing market, it offers a lively contrast to Athens' ancient sites.

The entire market square is a delight to explore, with colorful and dirt-cheap souvlaki shops and a carnival of people-watching. The best and cheapest selection of whatever's in season is at the fruit and vegetable stalls, which spread across Athinas street downhill to the west, flanked by shops selling feta from the barrel and a dozen different kinds of olives. Meat and fish markets are housed in the Neoclassical building to the east, behind a row of shops facing Athinas street that specialize in dried fruit and nuts. Try the roasted almonds and the delicious white figs from the island of Evia.

Cost and Hours: Free to enter, Mon-Sat 7:00-15:00, closed Sun, on Athinas between Sofokleous and Evripidou, between Metro lines 1/green and 2/red: Omonia and Metro lines 1/green and 3/blue: Monastiraki.

Art Tower—This contemporary gallery is worth seeking out for fans of cutting-edge art. Various temporary exhibits fill some of this skyscraper's eight stimulating floors; if it's open, just poke around. Located near the Central Market action, it's squeezed between produce stalls, overlooking the big, open square with the underground parking garage (free, Wed-Fri 15:00-20:00, Sat 12:00-16:00, closed Sun-Tue, Armodiou 10—look for ΑΡΜΟΔΙΟΥ 10, tel. 210-324-6100, www.artower.gr).

▲▲▲**National Archaeological Museum**—This museum is the single best place on earth to see ancient Greek artifacts. Strolling through the chronologically displayed collection—from 7,000 B.C. to A.D. 500—is like watching a time-lapse movie of the evolution of art. You'll go from the stylized figurines of the Cycladic Islands, to the golden artifacts of the Mycenaeans (including the so-called Mask of Agamemnon), to the stiff, stoic kouros statues of the Archaic age. Then, with the arrival of the Severe style (epitomized

by the *Artemision Bronze*), the art loosens up and comes to life. As Greece enters the Classical Period, the *Bronze Statue of a Youth* is balanced and lifelike. The dramatic *Statue of a Horse and Jockey* hints at the unbridled exuberance of Hellenism, which is taken to its extreme in the *Statue of a Fighting Gaul*. Rounding out the collection are Roman statuary, colorful wall paintings from Thira (today's Santorini), and room upon room of ceramics.

Cost and Hours: €7; free for kids 18 and under, on the first Sun of each month, and all Sun Nov-March; May-Sept Tue-Sun 8:00-20:00, Mon 13:30-20:00; Oct-April Tue-Sun 8:30-15:00, Mon 13:30-19:30. While there are no audioguides, live guides hang out in the lobby waiting to give you a €50, hour-long tour. It's at 28 Oktovriou (a.k.a. Patission) #44, a 10-minute walk from the Omonia Metro station. Tel. 210-821-7717, www.namuseum.gr.

○ See National Archaeological Museum Tour chapter.

Exarchia—For an edgier taste of Athens, wander into Exarchia, just a short walk behind the National Archaeological Museum. Wedged between the National Technical University, Omonia Square, and Lykavittos Hill, Exarchia is nicknamed the city's

"New Berlin." As you roam its colorful streets, you'll begin to understand why.

Populated mostly by students, immigrants, and counterculture idealists, Exarchia is defiant, artsy, coated in graffiti, and full of life. According to locals, many of the anarchists who are the firepower behind Athens' recent riots call this area home. While Exarchia sounds intimidating—and is a bit farther afield than other areas described in this book—with a sense of adventure and an extra helping of common sense, it can be a fascinating and worthwhile area to wander.

From the small Exarchia Square, side-streets spin off into grungy neighborhoods. Mainstream businesses tend to steer clear of this area; instead, streets are lined with alternative boutiques, record stores, and cafés. About two blocks south of the main square—at the corner of Mesolongiou and Tzabella streets—is a memorial to Alexandros Grigoropoulos, a local teen who was shot and killed here in December 2008 when police fired into a

crowd of protestors. The incident sparked an attention-grabbing wave of riots across Greece, and ever since, frustrated neighbors keep the cops out and do their own policing. The juxtaposition between Exarchia and the adjacent, very ritzy Kolonaki district makes the tragedy even more poignant. (You might notice that Exarchia's border with Kolonaki is marked by Athens police vans.)

With its penchant for riots and protests, Exarchia feels less safe than other Athens neighborhoods. (In fact, during riots in 2010, the US government warned travelers to avoid Exarchia.) For some people, this is the seedy underbelly of Athens they came to see; others can't wait to get back to the predictable souvlaki stands and leather salesmen of the Plaka. If you do venture here, exercise caution, try to avoid conflict, and, unless you're street-smart and comfortable in gritty urban neighborhoods, think twice before wandering around after dark.

SIGHTS

In Kolonaki, East of Syntagma Square

The district called Kolonaki, once the terrain of high-society bigwigs eager to live close to the Royal Palace (now the Parliament), is today's diplomatic quarter. Lining the major boulevard called Vasilissis Sofias are many embassies, a thriving local yuppie scene, and some of Athens' top museums outside the old center. These are listed in the order you'd reach them, heading east from the Parliament (see map on page 55).

▲▲**Benaki Museum of Greek History and Culture**—This exquisite collection takes you on a fascinating walk through the ages. The mind-boggling array of artifacts—which could keep a museum-lover busy for hours—is crammed into 36 galleries on four floors, covering seemingly every era of history: antiquity, Byzantine, Ottoman, and modern. The private collection nicely complements the many state-run museums in town. Each item is labeled in English, and it's all air-conditioned. The Benaki gift shop is a fine place to buy jewelry (replicas of museum pieces).

The first exhibit kicks things off by saying, "Around 7000 B.C., the greatest 'revolution' in human experience took place: the change from the hunting-and-gathering economy of the Paleolithic Age to the farming economy of the Neolithic Age..." You'll see fine painted vases, gold wreaths of myrtle leaves worn on heads 2,300 years ago, and evocative Byzantine icons and jewelry. Upstairs, the first floor picks up where most Athens museums leave off:

the period of Ottoman occupation. Here you'll find traditional costumes, furniture, household items, farm implements, musical instruments, and entire rooms finely carved from wood and lovingly transplanted. In rooms 22 and 23, a fascinating exhibit shows Greece through the eyes of foreign visitors, who came here in the 18th and 19th centuries (back when Athens was still a village, spiny with Ottoman minarets) to see the same ruins you're enjoying today. Then you'll climb up through smaller rooms to the café and exhibit hall (which has good temporary exhibits). On the top floor, Romantic art depicts Greece's stirring and successful 19th-century struggle for independence. Finally, one long hall brings us up to the 20th century.

Cost and Hours: €6, Wed-Mon 9:00-17:00 except Thu until 24:00 and Sun until 15:00, closed Tue, classy rooftop café, across from back corner of National Garden at Koumbari 1, Metro lines 2/red and 3/blue: Syntagma. Tel. 210-367-1000, www.benaki.gr.

Other Branches: Note that other branches of the Benaki are scattered around Athens, including the **Benaki Museum of Islamic Art** (see page 72) and the **Benaki Cultural Center** (a.k.a. "Pireos Street Annex"), which hosts temporary exhibits with a more modern/contemporary flavor (€4-6 depending on exhibits, Wed-Sun 10:00-18:00, Fri-Sat until 22:00, closed Mon-Tue, about seven blocks southwest of Keramikos Cemetery and Technopolis at Pireos 138, Metro line 3/blue: Keramikos, tel. 210-345-3111, www.benaki.gr).

▲▲**Museum of Cycladic Art**—This modern, cozy, enjoyable museum shows off the largest exhibit of Cycladic art anywhere, collected by one of Greece's richest shipping families (the Goulandris clan). You'll get a good first taste of Cycladic art in the National Archaeological Museum (see page 79); if you're intrigued, come here for more. The exhibition rooms are small, but everything is well-described in English.

Cost and Hours: €7, Mon and Wed-Sat 10:00-17:00, Thu until 20:00, Sun 11:00-17:00, closed Tue and many religious holidays; Neophytou Douka 4, Metro line 3/blue: Evangelismos. Note that the museum's entrance is a few steps up the side street (Neophytou Douka), while the more prominent corner building, fronting Vasilissis Sofias, is their larger annex (or "New Wing"), hosting special exhibits. Tel. 210-722-8321, www.cycladic.gr.

⬤ **Self-Guided Tour:** The **first floor** up focuses on art from the Cycladic Islands, which surround the isle of Delos, off the coast southeast of Athens. The Aegean city-states here—predating Athens' Golden Age by 2,000 years—were populated by a mysterious people who left no written record. But they did leave behind an ample collection of fertility figurines. These come in all different sizes but follow the same general pattern: skinny, standing ramrod-straight, with large alien-like heads. Some have exaggerated breasts and hips, giving them a violin-like silhouette. Others (likely symbolizing pregnancy) appear to be clutching their midsections with both arms. These items give an insight into the matriarchal cultures of the Cycladic Islands. With their astonishing simplicity, the figurines appear almost abstract, as if Modigliani or Picasso had sculpted them.

While that first floor is the headliner, don't miss three more floors of exhibits upstairs: ancient Greek art, Cypriot antiquities, and scenes from daily life in antiquity. The highlight—for some, even better than the Cycladic art itself—is the engrossing **top-floor exhibit** that explains ancient Greek lifestyles. The engaging illustrations, vivid English descriptions, and actual artifacts resurrect a fun cross-section of the fascinating and sometimes bizarre practices of the ancients: weddings, athletics, agora routine, warfare, and various female- and male-only activities (such as the male-bonding/dining ritual called the symposium). A movie uses actors and colorful sets to dramatize events in the life of "Leon," a fictional young man of ancient Greece. Another movie demonstrates burial rituals (for the dearly departed Leon), many of which are still practiced by Orthodox Christians in Greece today.

▲▲Byzantine and Christian Museum—While Athens (like all of Greece) is dominated by its ancient sites, this excellent museum traces a different chapter of the Greek story: the Byzantine Empire, from Emperor Constantine's move from Rome to Byzantium (which he renamed Constantinople, now known as Istanbul) in A.D. 324 until the fall of Constantinople to the Ottomans in 1453. While the rest of Europe fell into the Dark Ages, Byzantium shone brightly. And, as its dominant language was Greek, today's Greeks proudly consider the Byzantine Empire "theirs." Outside of the Golden Age of antiquity, the Byzantine era is considered the high-water mark for Greek culture. This recently restored museum displays and thoughtfully describes key artifacts from this time.

Cost and Hours: €4; April-Oct Tue-Sun 8:00-20:00, Mon 13:30-20:00; Nov-March Tue-Sun 8:30-15:00, closed Mon; Vasilissis Sofias 22, Metro line 3/blue: Evangalismos. Tel. 210-721-1027, www.byzantinemuseum.gr.

◑ Self-Guided Tour: The museum consists of two buildings flanking an entry courtyard. The building on the right holds temporary exhibits, while the one on the left features the permanent collection, which sprawls underground through the complex and is well-described in English.

The permanent exhibit—organized both chronologically and thematically—traces the story of the Byzantine Empire, from the waning days of antiquity, to the fledgling days of early Christianity, and on to the glory days of Byzantium. It's divided into two sections.

The **first section,** "From the Ancient World to Byzantium," explains how the earliest Byzantine Christians borrowed artistic forms from the Greek and Roman past, and adapted them to fit their emerging beliefs. For example, the classical Greek motif of the calf-bearer became the "good shepherd" of Byzantine Christianity, while early depictions of Jesus are strikingly similar to the Greek "philosopher" prototype. You'll also view mosaics and capitals from the earliest "temples" of Christianity and see how existing ancient temples were "Christianized" for new use. Other topics include Coptic art (from Egyptian Christians), and graves and burial customs.

The **second section,** "The Byzantine World," delves into various facets of Byzantium: the administration of a vast empire; the use of art in early Christian worship; wall paintings transplanted from a Byzantine church; the role of Athens (and the surrounding region of Attica) in the Byzantine Empire; the introduction of Western European artistic elements by Frankish and Latin Crusaders during the 13th century; everyday countryside lifestyles (to balance out all that stuffy ecclesiastical art); the final artistic flourishing of the 13th and 14th centuries; and the fall of Constantinople (and the Byzantine emperor) to Ottoman Sultan Mehmet the Conqueror. All together, it's a fascinating place to learn about a rich and often-overlooked chapter of Greek history.

National War Museum—This imposing three-story museum documents the history of Greek warfare, from Alexander the Great to today. The rabble-rousing exhibit, staffed by members

of the Greek armed forces, stirs the soul of a Greek patriot. Pick up the free booklet as you enter, then ride the elevator upstairs to the first floor. Here you'll get a quick chronological review of Greek military history, including replicas of ancient artifacts you'll see for real in other museums. The mezzanine level focuses on the Greek experience in World War II, including the Nazi occupation, resistance, and liberation. Back on the ground floor, you'll parade past

SIGHTS

military uniforms, browse an armory of old weapons, and (outside) ogle modern military machines—tanks, fighter jets, and more.

Cost and Hours: €2, Tue-Sat 9:00-14:00, Sun 9:30-14:00, closed Mon, scant English descriptions but audioguide available, Rizari 2-4 at Vasilissis Sofias, Metro line 3/blue: Evangelismos. Tel. 210-725-2975.

North of Syntagma Square

A few blocks up from Syntagma Square and the traffic-free Ermou street thoroughfare are more museums, including the National History Museum and the Numismatic Museum (i.e., coins). This one is the best of the bunch:

▲**Museum of the City of Athens**—Housed in the former residence of King Otto and Queen Amalia (where they lived from 1836-1843), this museum combines an elegant interior with a charming overview of the history of Athens. The highlight (on the ground floor) is a giant panoramic late 17th-century painting of Louis XIV's ambassador and his party, with Athens in the background. The work shows a small village occupied by Ottomans (with prickly minarets rising from the rooftops), before the Parthenon was partially destroyed. In another room, an interesting model shows Athens circa 1842, just as it was emerging as the capital of Greece. Upstairs are lavishly decorated rooms and exhibits that emphasize King Otto's role in the fledgling new Greek state following the Ottoman defeat. Throughout the place, you'll see idyllic paintings of Athens as it was a century and a half ago: a red-roofed village at the foot of the Acropolis, populated by Greek shepherds in traditional costume. Stepping back outside into the smog and noise, you'll wish you had a time machine.

Cost and Hours: €3, audioguide-€0.50, Mon and Wed-Fri 9:00-16:00, Sat-Sun 10:00-15:00, closed Tue, Paparigopoulou 5-7, Metro line 2/red: Panepistimio. Tel. 210-323-1397, www.athens citymuseum.gr.

ATHENS CITY WALK

From Syntagma Square to Monastiraki Square

Athens is a bustling metropolis of nearly four million people, home to one out of every three Greeks. Much of the city is unappealing, cheaply built, poorly zoned, 20th-century sprawl. But the heart and soul of Athens is engaging and refreshingly compact. This walk takes you through the striking contrasts of the city center, from chaotic, traffic-clogged urban zones; to sleepy streets packed with bearded priests shopping for a new robe or chalice; to peaceful back lanes—barely wide enough for a donkey—that twist their way up toward the Acropolis. Along the way, we'll learn about Athens' rich history, the intriguing tapestry of Orthodox churches that dot the city, and the way that locals live and shop.

The walk begins at Syntagma Square, meanders through the fascinating old Plaka district, and finishes at lively Monastiraki Square (near the Ancient Agora, markets, good restaurants, and a handy Metro stop). This sightseeing spine will help you get a once-over-lightly look at Athens, which you can use as a springboard for diving into the city's various colorful sights and neighborhoods.

Orientation

Churches: Athens' churches keep irregular hours, but they're generally open daily 8:30-13:30 & 17:00-19:30. If you want to buy candles at churches (as the locals do), be sure to have a few small coins.

Cathedral: Generally open daily 8:00-13:00 & 16:30-20:00, no afternoon closure in summer.

Temple of Olympian Zeus: €2, covered by Acropolis ticket, daily 8:00-20:00, until 17:00 off-season, Vasilissis Olgas 1, Metro line 2/red: Akropoli, tel. 210-922-6330, www.culture.gr.

Roman Forum: €2, covered by Acropolis ticket, daily 8:00-19:00, until 15:00 off-season, corner of Pelopida and Aiolou streets, Metro line 1/green or 3/blue: Monastiraki.

When to Go: Do this walk early in your visit, as it can help you get your bearings in this potentially confusing city. I'd suggest doing it on your first morning here, while all the churches are open (since many close for an afternoon break) and other sights—such as the Acropolis—are too crowded to enjoy.

Dress Code: Wearing shorts inside churches (especially the cathedral) is frowned upon, though usually tolerated.

Getting There: The walk begins at Syntagma Square, just northeast of the Plaka tourist zone. It's a short walk from the recommended Plaka hotels; if you're staying away from the city center, get here by Metro (line 2/red or line 3/blue to Syntagma stop).

Audioguide Tours: A free audio version of this walk is available at www.ricksteves.com/audioeurope and from iTunes.

Length of This Walk: Allow plenty of time. This three-part walk takes two hours without stops or detours. But if you explore and dip into sights here and there—pausing to ponder a dimly lit Orthodox church, or doing some window- (or actual) shopping—it can enjoyably eat up a half-day or more. If you find this walk too long, it's easy to break up—stop after Part 2 and return for Part 3 at a different time or on another day.

Starring: Athens' top squares, churches, and Roman ruins, connected by bustling urban streets that are alternately choked with cars and mopeds, or thronged by pedestrians, vendors... and fellow tourists.

The Walk Begins

This lengthy walk is thematically divided into three parts: The first part focuses on modern Athens, centered on Syntagma Square and the Ermou shopping street. The second part focuses on Athens' Greek Orthodox faith, with visits to three different but equally interesting churches. And the third part is a wander through the charming old core of Athens, including the touristy Plaka and the mellow Greek-village-on-a-hillside of Anafiotika.

ATHENS CITY WALK

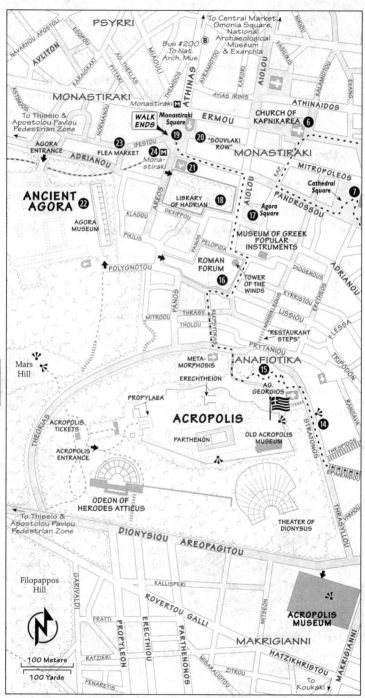

Athens City Walk

1. Syntagma Square
2. Tomb of the Unknown Soldier & Evzone Guards
3. Parliament
4. Hotel Grande Bretagne
5. Ermou Street
6. Church of Kapnikarea
7. Cathedral & Square
8. Church of Agios Eleftherios
9. Agia Filotheis Street
10. Church of Agia Filotheis
11. Adrianou Street
12. Arch of Hadrian & Temple of Olympian Zeus
13. Lysicrates Monument & Square
14. View of Lykavittos Hill
15. Anafiotika
16. Roman Forum & Tower of the Winds
17. Agora Square
18. Library of Hadrian
19. Monastiraki Square
20. "Souvlaki Row"
21. Former Mosque & Ceramics Museum
22. Ancient Agora
23. Flea Market
23. Monastiraki Metro Stn.

Part 1: Modern Athens

This part of our walk lets you feel the pulse of a European capital.

• *Start at Syntagma Square. From the leafy park at the center of the square, climb to the top of the stairs (in the middle of the square) and stand across the street from the big, Neoclassical Greek Parliament building.*

❶ Syntagma Square (Plateia Syntagmatos)

As you look at posh hotels and major banks, you are standing atop the city's central Metro stop, surrounded by buses, cars, and taxis.

Facing the Parliament building (east), get oriented to the square named for Greece's constitution (*syntagma;* seen-DOG-mah). From this point, sightseeing options spin off through the city like spokes on a wheel.

Fronting the square on the left (north) side are high-end hotels, including the opulent Hotel Grande Bretagne (with its swanky rooftop garden restaurant—see page 194).

Directly to the left of the Parliament building is the head of Vasilissis Sofias avenue, lined with embassies and museums, including the Benaki Museum of Greek History and Culture, Museum of Cycladic Art, Byzantine and Christian Museum, and National War Museum. This boulevard leads to the ritzy Kolonaki quarter, with its funicular up to the top of Lykavittos Hill. Extending to the right of the Parliament building is the National Garden, Athens' "Central Park." Here you'll find the Zappeion mansion-turned-conference-hall (with a fine summer outdoor cinema nearby) and, beyond the greenery, the evocative, ancient Panathenaic Stadium.

On your right (south) is one of Athens' prime transit hubs, with stops for bus #X95 to the airport, bus #024 to Bus Terminal B/Liossion, and the Athens Coastal Tram. Beneath your feet is the Syntagma Metro station, the city's busiest. The TI is a few blocks away down busy Vasilissis Amalias street (beyond the tram terminus, not visible from here).

Behind you, at the west end of the square, stretches the traffic-free shopping street called Ermou, which heads to the Plaka neighborhood and Monastiraki Square. (We'll be heading that way soon.) Nearby is the terminus for one of Athens' two tourist trains (see page 62).

Take a moment to look at the square and modern Athens: People buzz about on their way to work, handing out leaflets, feeding pigeons, or just enjoying a park bench (and, perhaps, the free Wi-Fi the city provides here), shaded by a variety of trees. Plane trees (chosen for their resilience against pollution and the generous shade they provide) make Syntagma a breezy and restful spot. Breathe deep and ponder the fact that until 1990, Athens was the most polluted city in Europe. People advertising facial creams would put a mannequin outside on the street for three hours and film it turning black. The moral: You need our cream.

But over the last two decades, "green" policies have systematically cleaned up the air. Traffic, while still pretty extreme, is limited: Even- and odd-numbered license plates are prohibited in the center on alternate days. Check the license plates of passing cars (not taxis or motorcycles): The majority end with either an even or odd number, depending on the day of the week. Wealthy locals get around this restriction by owning two cars—one with even plates, the other with odd. While car traffic is down, motorcycle usage is up (since bikes are exempt). Central-heating fuel is more expensive and much cleaner these days (as required by European Union regulations), more of the city center is pedestrianized, and the city's public transport is top-notch.

• *Using the crosswalk (one on either side of Syntagma Square), cross the busy street. Directly in front of the Parliament you'll see the...*

❷ Tomb of the Unknown Soldier and the Evzone Guards

Standing amid pigeons and tourists in front of the imposing Parliament building, overlooking Syntagma Square, you're at the center of Athens' modern history. Above the simple marble-slab tomb—marked only with a cross—is a carved image of the Unknown Soldier, inspired by statues of ancient Greek warriors. Etched into the stone on each side of the tomb are the names of great battles in Greek military history from 1821 forward (practice your Greek alphabet by trying to read them: Cyprus, Korea, Rimini, Crete, and so on.)

The tomb is guarded by the much-photographed evzone, an elite infantry unit of the Greek army. The guard changes five minutes before the top of each hour, with a less elaborate crossing of the guard on the half-hour. They march with a slow-motion, high-stepping march to their new positions, then stand ramrod straight, where you can pose alongside them. A full changing-of-the-guard ceremony, complete with marching band, takes place most Sundays at 11:00.

These colorful characters are clad in traditional pleated kilts *(fustanella),* white britches, and pom-pom shoes. (The outfits may look a little goofy to a non-Greek, but their mothers and girlfriends are very proud.) The uniforms were made famous by the Klephts, ragtag bands of mountain guerrilla fighters. After nearly four centuries under the thumb of the Ottoman Empire (from today's Turkey, starting in 1453), the Greeks rose up. The Greek War of Independence (1821-1829) pitted the powerful Ottoman army against the lowly but wily Klephts. The Klephts reached back to their illustrious history, modeling their uniforms after those worn by soldiers from ancient Athens (the pom-poms date all the way back to the ancient Mycenaeans). The soldiers' winter skirts have 400 pleats...one for each year of Ottoman occupation (and don't you forget it). While considered heroes today for their courage and outrageous guerrilla tactics, the Klephts were once regarded as warlike bandits (their name shares a root with the English word "kleptomania").

As the Klephts and other Greeks fought for their independence, a number of farsighted Europeans (including the English poet Lord Byron)—inspired by the French Revolution and their own love of ancient Greek culture—came to their aid. In 1829, the rebels finally succeeded in driving their Ottoman rulers out of central Greece, and there was a movement to establish a modern democracy. However, the Greeks were unprepared to rule themselves, and so, after the Ottomans came...Otto.

• *For the rest of the story, take a step back for a view of the...*

❸ Parliament

The origins of this "palace of democracy" couldn't have been less democratic. The first independent Greek government, which had its capital in Nafplio, was too weak to be viable. As was standard operating procedure at that time, the great European powers forced Greece to accept a king from established European royalty.

In 1832, Prince Otto of Bavaria became King Otto of Greece. A decade later, after the capital shifted to Athens, this royal palace was built to house King Otto and his wife, Queen Amalia. The atmosphere was tense. After fighting so fiercely for its independence from the Ottomans, the Greeks now chafed under royal rule from a dictatorial Bavarian monarch. The palace's over-the-top luxury only angered impoverished locals.

On September 3, 1843, angry rioters gathered in the square to protest, demanding a democratic constitution. King Otto stepped onto the balcony of this building, quieted the mob, and gave them what they wanted. The square was dubbed Syntagma (Constitution), and modern Athens was born. The former royal palace has been the home of the Greek parliament since 1935. Today this is where 300 Greek parliamentarians (elected to four-year terms) tend to the business of the state—or, as more cynical locals would say, become corrupt and busily get themselves set up for their cushy, post-political lives.

• *Cross back to the heart of Syntagma Square, and focus on the grand building fronting its north side.*

❹ Hotel Grande Bretagne and Neoclassical Syntagma

Imagine the original Syntagma Square (which was on the outskirts of town in the early 19th century): a big front yard for the new royal palace, with the country's influential families building mansions

around it. Surviving examples include Hotel Grande Bretagne, the adjacent Hotel King George Palace, the Zappeion in the National Garden (not visible from here), and the stately architecture lining Vasilissis Sofias avenue behind the palace (now embassies and museums).

These grand buildings date from Athens' Otto-driven Neoclassical makeover. Eager to create a worthy capital for Greece, Otto imported teams of Bavarian architects to draft a plan of broad avenues and grand buildings in what they imagined to be the classical style. This "Neoclassical" look is symmetrical and geometrical, with pastel-colored buildings highlighted in white trim. The windows are rectangular, flanked by white Greek half-columns (pilasters), fronted by balconies, and topped with cornices. Many of the buildings themselves are also framed at the top with cornices. When you continue on this walk, notice not only the many Neoclassical buildings, but also the more modern buildings that try to match the same geometric lines.

Syntagma Square is also worth a footnote in American Cold War history. In December of 1944, Greek communists demonstrated here, inducing the US to come to the aid of the Greek government. This became the basis (in 1947) for the Truman Doctrine, which pledged US aid to countries fighting communism and helped shape American foreign policy for the next 50 years.

The Story of Modern Athens

By the time of the Greek War of Independence (1821-1829), Athens had declined to become little more than a rural backwater on the fringes of the Ottoman Empire. Its population had shrunk to about 2,000 people occupying a cluster of red-tiled Turkish houses on the northern side of the Acropolis (the area now known as the Plaka).

When it came to choosing a capital for the new nation, Athens wasn't even considered. The first choice was Nafplio on the Peloponnese, which the Ottomans had also favored as a seat of government. It would probably have stayed that way, if it weren't for the assassination of Greece's first president, Ioannis Kapodistrias, in 1831. His death led to international pressure to install an outsider, 17-year-old Prince Otto of Bavaria, as the first king of Greece.

Otto was as wet behind the ears as any teenager, and was heavily influenced by his forceful father, King Ludwig I of Bavaria (grandfather of "Mad" King Ludwig, of Neuschwanstein Castle fame). These Bavarians—great admirers of classical Athens—insisted that the city become the capital in 1834. They were also responsible for the shape of the new Athens, ferrying in teams of Bavarian architects to create a plan of broad avenues and grand Neoclassical buildings—much as they had done in Munich.

The character of Athens changed once more after 1922, when the defeat of the occupying Greek army in Turkey resulted in a forced population exchange between the two rivals. Athens' population doubled almost overnight, and any thought of town planning went out the window as authorities scrambled to build cheap apartment blocks to house the newcomers.

Greece's belated industrialization in the 1950s, coupled with the hard times of the Nazi occupation and civil war (when villagers, who no longer could afford to feed themselves, flocked to the city), sparked a wave of migration from rural areas. It's amazing to think that the city with less then a million inhabitants in 1950 now has about four million. The trend continues to this day: More than a third of Greece's population now lives in greater Athens.

When they hosted the Olympic Games in 2004, the Greeks turned over a new leaf and showed a passion for city planning. Improvements in infrastructure, public transportation, and an overall beautification program quickly pulled the city up to snuff. These enhancements seem poised to continue, making the city an increasingly attractive tourist destination. It's always had great museums and ancient sites...but now Athens itself is becoming a more pleasant place to visit.

• *Head down to the bottom of Syntagma (directly across from the Parliament). Stroll down the traffic-free street near the McDonald's.*

❺ Ermou Street

The pedestrian mall called Ermou (AIR-moo) leads from Syntagma down through the Plaka to Monastiraki, then continues westward to the ancient Keramikos Cemetery and the Gazi district. Not long ago, this street epitomized all that was terrible about Athens: lousy building codes, tacky neon signs, double-parked trucks, and noisy traffic. When Ermou was first pedestrianized in 2000, merchants were upset. Now they love the ambience created as countless locals stroll through what has become a people-friendly shopping zone.

This has traditionally been the street of women's shops. However, these days Ermou is dominated by high-class international chain stores, which appeal to young Athenians but turn off older natives, who lament the lack of local flavor. For authentic, hole-in-the-wall shopping, many Athenians prefer the streets just to the north, such as Perikleous, Lekka, and Kolokotroni. (For a self-guided shopping stroll in that area, see page 200.)

Even so, this people-crammed boulevard is a pleasant place for a wander. Do just that, proceeding gradually downhill and straight ahead for seven blocks. As you window-shop, notice that many of Ermou's department stores are housed in impressive Neoclassical mansions. Talented street performers (many of them former music professionals from Eastern Europe) provide an entertaining soundtrack. All of Athens walks along here: businesspeople, teen-age girls with iPods, Orthodox priests, men twirling worry beads, activists gathering signatures, illegal vendors who sweep up their wares and scurry when they see police, cell phone–toting shoppers, and, of course, tourists. Keep an eye out for vendors selling various snacks—including pretzel-like sesame rings called *koulouri* and slices of fresh coconut.

After six short blocks, on the right (at the intersection with Evangelistrias/Ευαγγελιστριασ), look for the little **book wagon** selling cheap lit. You'll likely see colorful, old-fashioned alphabet books (labeled ΑΛΦΑΒΗΤΑΡΙΟ, *Alphabetario*), which have been reprinted for nostalgic older Greeks. Remember that the English word "alphabet" comes from the first two Greek letters (alpha, beta).

Reaching the little church in the middle of the street (we'll visit it next, in Part 2 of this walk), look around you for **recycling bins.** Athens—long notorious for its grime and pollution—is striving to catch up to the green 21st century. While slow to adapt, Athenians are warming up to this new ethic.

Cap this first part of your walk (20 yards past the little church) by popping into the **shopping mall** on the right at Ermou 54. Enjoy the cool air along with the cool architecture. This slice of 19th-century Athenian elegance has been nicely preserved and earns its keep today as a place to shop.

Part 2: The Greek Orthodox Church

This part of our walk introduces you to the Orthodox faith of Greece, including stops at three different churches. Before beginning, read the sidebar on pages 98-99.
• *Stranded in the middle of both Ermou street and the commercial bustle of the 21st century is a little medieval church.*

❻ Church of Kapnikarea

After the ancient Golden Age, but before Otto and the Ottomans, Athens was part of the Byzantine Empire (A.D. 323-1453). In the

11th and 12th centuries, Athens boomed, and several Eastern Orthodox churches like this one were constructed.

The Church of Kapnikarea—named for the tax on the cloth merchants that once lined this square—is a classic 11th-century Byzantine church. Notice that Kapnikarea is square and topped

with a central dome. Telltale signs of a Byzantine church include tall arches over the windows, stones surrounded by a frame of brick and mortar, and a domed cupola with a cross on top. The large white blocks are scavenged from other, earlier monuments (also typical of Byzantine churches from this era). Over the door is a mosaic of glass and gold leaf, which, though modern, is made in the traditional Byzantine style.

If the church is open, step inside. (If it's closed, don't fret—we'll be visiting a couple of similar churches later.) The church has no nave, just an entrance hall. Notice the symmetrical Greek-cross floor plan. It's decorated with standing candelabras, hanging lamps, tall arches, a wooden pulpit, and a few chairs. If you wish, you can do as the Greeks do and follow the standard candle-buying, icon-kissing ritual (see sidebar on page 98). The icon displayed closest to the door gets changed with the church calendar. You may notice lipstick smudges on the protective glass and a candle-recycling box behind the candelabra.

Look up into the central dome, lit with windows, which symbolizes heaven. Looking back down is the face of Jesus, the omnipotent *Pantocrator* God blessing us on Earth. He holds a Bible in one hand and blesses us with the other. On the walls are iconic murals of saints. Notice the focus on the eyes, which are considered a mirror of the soul and a symbol of its purity.

• *When you leave the church, turn south toward the Acropolis and proceed downhill on Kapnikareas street. Up ahead, catch a glimpse of the Acropolis. Go two blocks, to the traffic-free Pandrossou shopping street. Turn left and walk (passing the recommended Restaurant Hermion) up the pedestrian street to the cathedral.*

❼ Cathedral (Mitropolis) and Cathedral Square (Plateia Mitropoleos)

Built in 1842, this "metropolitan church" (as the Greek Orthodox call their cathedrals) is the most important in Athens, which makes

it the head church of the Greek Orthodox faith. Unfortunately, it's unremarkable and oddly ramshackle inside and out...and has been decorated by scaffolding since the earthquake of 1989.

If it's open, head inside. Looking up (likely through more scaffolding), you'll notice balconies. Traditionally, women worshipped apart from men in the balconies upstairs. Women got the vote in Greece in 1954, and since about that time, they've been able to worship in the prime, ground-floor real estate alongside the men.

When you're back outside on the square, notice the statue facing the cathedral. This was erected by Athens' Jewish community as thanks to **Archbishop Damaskinos** (1891-1949), the rare Christian leader who stood up to the Nazis during the occupation of Greece. At great personal risk, Damaskinos formally spoke out against the Nazi occupiers on behalf of the Greek Jews he saw being deported to concentration camps. When a Nazi commander threatened to put Damaskinos before a firing squad, the archbishop defiantly countered that he should be hanged instead, in good

The Eastern Orthodox Church

In the fourth century A.D., the Roman Empire split in half, dividing Eastern Europe and the Balkan Peninsula down the middle. Seven centuries later, with the Great Schism, the Christian faith diverged along similar lines, into two separate branches: Roman Catholicism in the west (based in Rome and including most of Western and Central Europe), and Eastern or Byzantine Orthodoxy in the east (based in Constantinople—today's Istanbul—and prevalent in far-eastern Europe, Russia, the eastern half of the Balkan Peninsula, and Greece). The root *orthos* is Greek for "right belief"—and it seems logical that if you've already got it right, you're more conservative and resistant to change.

Over the centuries, the Catholic Church shed old traditions and developed new ones. Meanwhile, the Eastern Orthodox Church—which remained consolidated under the stable and wealthy Byzantine Empire—stayed true to the earliest traditions of the Christian faith. Today, rather than having one centralized headquarters (such as the Vatican for Catholicism), the Eastern Orthodox Church is divided into about a dozen regional branches that remain administratively independent even as they share many of the same rituals. These include the Russian Orthodox Church, the Serbian Orthodox Church, and the Greek Orthodox Church—which is based at Athens' cathedral. The Greek constitution recognizes Orthodox Christianity as the "prevailing" religion of Greece. The Archbishop of Athens is Greece's "pope."

The doctrine of Catholic and Orthodox churches remains very similar, but many of the rituals are different. As you enter any Greek Orthodox church, you can join in the standard routine: Drop a coin in the wooden box, pick up a candle, say a prayer, light the candle, and place it in the candelabra. Make the sign of the cross and kiss the icon.

Where's the altar? Orthodox churches come with an altar screen covered with curtains and icons (the "iconostasis"). The standard design of the iconostasis calls for four icons flanking the central door, with Jesus to the right, John the Baptist to Jesus' right, Mary and the baby Jesus on the left, and an icon featuring the saint or event that the church is dedicated to on the far left.

This iconostasis divides the lay community from the priests—the material world from the spiritual one. Following Old Testament Judeo-Christian tradition, the Bible is kept on the altar behind the iconostasis. The spiritual heavy lifting takes place behind the iconostasis, where the priests symbolically turn bread and wine into the body and blood of Jesus. Then they open the doors or curtains and serve the Eucharist to their faithful flock—spooning the wine from a challis while holding a cloth under each chin so as not to drop any on the floor.

Notice that there are few (if any) pews. Worshippers stand through the service as a sign of respect (though some older parishioners sit on the seats along the walls). Traditionally, women stand on the left side, men on the right (equal distance from the altar—to represent that all are equal before God).

The Orthodox faith tends to use a Greek cross, with four equal arms (like a plus sign, sometimes inside a circle), which focuses on God's perfection. The longer Latin cross, more typically used by Catholics, more literally evokes the Crucifixion, emphasizing Jesus' death and sacrifice. This also extends to the floor plans of church buildings: Many Orthodox churches have Greek-cross floor plans rather than the elongated nave-and-transept designs that are common in Western Europe.

Unlike many Catholic church decorations, Orthodox icons (golden paintings of saints) are not intended to be lifelike. Packed with intricate symbolism and cast against a shimmering golden background, they're meant to remind viewers of the metaphysical nature of Jesus and the saints rather than their physical form, which is considered irrelevant. You'll almost never see statues, which are thought to overemphasize the physical world—and, to Orthodox people, feel a little too close to the forbidden worship of graven images.

Most Eastern Orthodox churches have at least one mosaic or painting of Christ in a standard pose—as *Pantocrator,* a Greek

word meaning "Ruler of All." The image, so familiar to Orthodox Christians, shows Christ as King of the Universe, facing directly out, with penetrating eyes. Behind him is a halo divided by a cross, with only three visible arms—an Orthodox symbol for the Trinity (the fourth arm is hidden behind Christ).

Orthodox services generally involve chanting (a dialogue that goes back and forth between the priest and the congregation), and the church is filled with the evocative aroma of incense, combining to heighten the experience for the worshippers. While many Catholic and Protestant services tend to be more of a theoretical and rote covering of basic religious tenets (come on—don't tell me you understand every phrase in the Nicene Creed), Orthodox services are about creating a religious experience. Each of these elements does its part to help the worshipper transcend the physical world and enter communion with the spiritual one.

Orthodox tradition. After the occupation, Damaskinos served as regent and then prime minister of Greece until the king returned from exile.

Here Damaskinos is depicted wearing the distinctive hat of an archbishop (a kind of fez with cloth hanging down the sides). He carries a staff and blesses with his right hand, making a traditional Orthodox sign of the cross, touching his thumb to his ring finger. This gesture forms the letters ICXC, the first and last letters of the Greek name for Jesus Christ (ΙΗΣΟΥΣ ΧΡΙΣΤΟΣ— traditionally C was substituted for Σ). Make the gesture yourself with your right hand. Touch the tip of your thumb to the tip of your ring finger and check it out: Your pinkie forms the I, your slightly crossed index and middle fingers are the X, and your thumb and ring finger make a double-C. Jesus Christ, that's clever. If you were a priest, you'd make the sign of the cross three times, to symbolize the Father, the Son, and the Holy Spirit.

The double-headed eagle that hangs around Damaskinos' neck is an important symbol of the Orthodox faith. It evokes the Byzantine Empire, during which Orthodox Christianity was at its peak as the state religion. Appropriately, the eagle's twin heads have a double meaning: The Byzantine Emperor was both the secular and spiritual leader of his realm, which exerted its influence over both East and West. (Coincidentally, a similar symbol has been used by many other kingdoms and empires, including the Holy Roman Empire and the Austro-Hungarian Empire.)

At the far end of the square from the cathedral is another statue, of a warrior holding a sword. This is **Emperor Constantine XI Palaeologus** (1404-1453), the final ruler of the Byzantine Empire. He was killed defending Constantinople from the invading Ottomans, led by Mehmet the Conqueror. Considered the "last Greek king" and an unofficial saint, Constantine XI's death marked the ascension of the Ottomans as overlords of the Greeks for nearly four centuries. On his boots and above his head, you'll see the double-headed eagle again.

• *The small church tucked behind the right side of the cathedral is the...*

❽ Church of Agios Eleftherios

A favorite of local church connoisseurs, the 13th-century Church of Agios Eleftherios (St. Eleutherius) is sometimes referred to as "the old cathedral" and was used by the archbishops of Athens after the Ottomans evicted them from the church within the Parthenon.

It's a jigsaw-puzzle hodgepodge of B.C. and A.D. adornments (and even tombstones) from earlier buildings. For example, the carved marble reliefs above the door were scavenged from the Ancient Agora in the 12th century. They are part of a calendar of ancient Athenian festivals, thought to have been carved in the second century A.D. The frieze running along the top of the building depicts a B.C. procession.

Later, Christians added their own symbols to the same panels—making the church a treasure trove of medieval symbolism. There are different kinds of crosses (Maltese, Latin, double) as well as carved rosettes, stars, flowers, and griffins feeding on plants and snakes. Walk around the entire exterior. Then, step inside to sample unadorned 12th-century Orthodox simplicity.

• *Exit the church, go around its right side, then turn right. Look for a street sign that reads* ΑΓΙΛΣ ΦΙΛΟΘΕΗΣ, *and start up...*

❾ Agia Filotheis Street

This neighborhood is a hive of activity for Orthodox clerics. The priests dress all in black, wear beards, and don those fez-like hats. Despite their hermetic look, most priests are husbands, fathers, and well-educated pillars of the community, serving as counselors and spiritual guides to Athens' cosmopolitan populace.

Notice the stores. Just behind and facing the little church is the shop of the **Theodoropoulos** family—whose name strives to use every Greek character available (ΘΕΟΔΟΡΟΠΟΥΛΟΣ). They've been tailoring priestly robes since 1907.

This is just the first of many **religious objects stores** that line the street (most are open Mon, Wed, and Fri 8:30-15:00; Tue and Thu 8:30-14:00 & 17:30-20:30; closed Sat-Sun). Cross the busy Apollonos street and continue exploring the shops of Agia Filotheis street. The Orthodox religion comes with unique religious paraphernalia: icons, gold candelabras, hanging lamps, incense burners, oil lamps, chalices, various crosses, and gold objects worked in elaborate repoussé design.

Pop into the **stoas** (arcades) at #15 and #17 (on the left) to see workshops of local artisans who make these objects—painters creating or restoring icons in the traditional style, tailors making bishops' hats and robes, carvers making little devotional statuettes.

A few more steps up on the left, the ❿ **Church of Agia Filotheis** (named, like the street, for a patron of Athens—St.

Philothei) is adjacent to an office building (at #19) that serves as the headquarters for the Greek Orthodox Church. Athenians come here to file the paperwork to make their marriages (and divorces) official.

Part 3: Athens' "Old Town" (The Plaka and Anafiotika)

This part of our walk explores the atmospheric, twisty lanes of old Athens. Remember, back before Athens became Greece's capital in the early 1800s, the city was a small town consisting of little more than what we'll see here.

• *Continue up Agia Filotheis street until you reach a tight five-way intersection. The street that runs ahead and to your right (labeled ΑΔΡΙΑΝΟΥ)—choked with souvenir stands and tourists—is our next destination. Look uphill and downhill along...*

⓫ Adrianou Street

This intersection may be the geographical (if not atmospheric) center of the neighborhood called the Plaka. Touristy Adrianou street is a main pedestrian drag that cuts through the Plaka, running roughly east–west from Monastiraki to here. Adrianou offers the full gauntlet of Greek souvenirs: worry beads, sea sponges, olive products, icons, carpets, jewelry, sandals, faux vases and Greek statues, profane and tacky T-shirts, and on and on. It also offers plenty of cafés for tourists seeking a place to sit and rest their weary feet.

• *Bear left onto Adrianou and walk uphill several blocks, following it as it curves to the right (south). Finally, the street dead-ends at a T-intersection with Lysikratous street. (There's a small square ahead on the left, with palm trees, the Byzantine church of Agia Aikaterini, and an excavated area showing the street level 2,000 years ago.)*

From here, you can turn right and take a few steps uphill to the Lysicrates Monument and Square (and skip ahead to the section on the Lysicrates Monument). But if you've got more time and stamina, it's worth a two-block walk to the left down Lysikratous street to reach the remains of the Arch of Hadrian.

⓬ "Hadrianopolis": Arch of Hadrian and Temple of Olympian Zeus

After the Romans conquered the Greeks, Roman emperor Hadrian (or Adrianou) became a major benefactor of the city of Athens. He

ATHENS CITY WALK

built a triumphal arch, completed a temple beyond it (now ruined), and founded a library we'll see later. The area beyond the arch was known as Hadrianopolis, a planned neighborhood built by the emperor. The grand archway overlooks the bustling, modern Vasilissis Amalias avenue, facing the Plaka and Acropolis. (If you turned left and followed this road for 10 minutes, you'd pass the TI, then end up back on Syntagma Square—where we began this walk.)

Arch of Hadrian

The arch's once-brilliant-white Pentelic marble is stained by the exhaust fumes from some of Athens' worst traffic. The arch

is topped with Corinthian columns, the Greek style preferred by the Romans. Hadrian built it in A.D. 132 to celebrate the completion of the Temple of Olympian Zeus (which lies just beyond—described next). Like a big *paifang* gate marking the entrance to a modern Chinatown, this arch represented the dividing line between the ancient city and Hadrian's new "Roman" city. An inscription on the west side informs the reader, "This is Athens, ancient city of Theseus," while the opposite frieze carries the message, "This is the city of Hadrian, and not of Theseus." This must have been a big deal for Hadrian, as the emperor himself came here to celebrate the inauguration.

• *Look past the arch to see the huge (and I mean huge) Corinthian columns remaining from what was once a temple dedicated to the Olympian Zeus. For a closer look, cross the busy boulevard (crosswalk to the right). You can pretty much get the gist by looking through the fence. But if you want to get close to those giant columns and wander the ruins, enter the site (covered by Acropolis ticket). To reach the entrance (a five-minute walk), curl around the left side of the arch, then turn right (following the fence) up the intersecting street called Vasilissis Olgas. The entrance to the temple is a few minutes' walk up, on the right-hand side.*

Temple of Olympian Zeus (Olympieion)

This largest temple in ancient Greece took almost 700 years to finish. It was begun late in the sixth century B.C. during the rule of the tyrant Peisistratos. But the task proved beyond him. The temple lay abandoned, half-built, for centuries until the Roman emperor Hadrian arrived to finish the job in A.D. 131. When completed, it was 360 feet by 145 feet, consisting of two rows of 20 columns on each of the long sides and three rows of eight columns along each end. Although only 15 of the original 104 Corinthian

columns remain standing, their sheer size (a towering 56 feet high) is enough to create a powerful impression of the temple's scale. The fallen column—which resembles a tipped-over stack of bottle caps—was toppled by a storm in 1852. The temple once housed a suitably oversized statue of Zeus, head of the Greek gods who lived on Mount Olympus, and an equally colossal statue of Hadrian.

• *Return to Lysikratous street and backtrack two blocks, continuing past the small square with the church you passed earlier. After another block, you'll run into another small, leafy square with the Acropolis rising behind it. In the square is an elegant, round, white, columned monument.*

⓭ Lysicrates Monument and Square

This elegant marble monument has Corinthian columns that support a dome with a (damaged) statue on top. A frieze runs along

the top, representing Dionysus turning pirates into dolphins. The monument is the sole survivor of many such monuments that once lined this ancient "Street of the Tripods." It was so called because the monuments came with bronze tripods that displayed grand ornamental pottery vases and cauldrons (like those you'll see in the museums) as trophies. These ancient "Oscars" were awarded to winners of choral and theatrical competitions staged at the Theater of

Dionysus on the southern side of the Acropolis. This now-lonely monument was erected in 334 B.C. by "Lysicrates of Kykyna, son of Lysitheides"—proud sponsor of the winning choral team that year. Excavations around the monument have uncovered the foundations of other monuments, which are now reburied under a layer of red sand and awaiting further study.

The square itself, shaded by trees, is a pleasant place to take a break before climbing the hill. Have a frappé or coffee at the café tables (€3.50), grab a cheap cold drink from the cooler in the hole-in-the-wall grocery store to the left, or just sit for free on the benches under the trees.

• *Passing the monument on its left-hand side, head uphill toward the Acropolis, climbing the staircase called Epimenidou street. At the top of the stairs, turn right onto Stratonos street, which leads around the base of the Acropolis. As you walk along, the Acropolis and a row of olive trees are on your left. The sound of the crickets evokes for Athenians the black-and-white movies that were filmed in this area in the 1950s and '60s. To your right, you'll catch glimpses of another hill off in the distance.*

⑭ View of Lykavittos Hill

This cone-shaped hill (sometimes spelled "Lycabettus") topped with a tiny white church is the highest in Athens, at just over 900 feet above sea level. The hill can be reached by a funicular, which leads up from the Kolonaki neighborhood to a restaurant and view terrace at the top. Although it looms high over the cityscape, Lykavittos Hill will always be overshadowed by the hill you're climbing now.

• *At the small Church of St. George of the Rock (Agios Georgios), go uphill, along the left fork. As you immerse yourself in a maze of tiny, whitewashed houses, follow signs that point to the Acropolis (even if the path seems impossibly narrow). This charming "village" is a neighborhood called...*

⑮ Anafiotika

These lanes and homes were built by people from the tiny Cycladic island of Anafi, who came to Athens looking for work after Greece gained its independence from the Ottomans. In this delightful spot, nestled beneath the walls of the Acropolis, the big city seems miles away. Keep following the *Acropolis* signs as you weave through narrow paths, lined with flowers and dotted with cats dozing peacefully in the sunshine (or slithering luxuriously past your legs). Though ancestors of the original islanders still live here, Anafiotika (literally "little Anafi") is slowly becoming a place for wealthy

locals to keep an "island cottage" in the city. As you wander through the oleanders, notice the male fig trees—no fruit—that keep away flies and mosquitoes. Smell the chicken-manure fertilizer, peek into delicate little yards, and enjoy the blue doors and maroon shutters...it's a transplanted Cycladic world. Posters of Anafi hang here and there, evoking the sandy beaches of the ancestral home island.

• *You'll know you're on the right track when you see a religious building with the date 1874 on a wall plaque. Follow the narrow walkway a few more steps. Emerging from the maze of houses, you'll hit a fork at a wider, cobbled lane. Turn right (downhill) and continue down the steep incline. When you hit a wider road (Theorias), turn left and walk toward the small, Byzantine-style Church of the Metamorphosis. (Note: To walk to the Acropolis entry from here, you would continue along this road as it bends left around the hill. For more on the Acropolis, ✪ see the Acropolis Tour chapter. For now, though, let's continue our walk.) Just before this church, turn right and go down the steep, narrow staircase (a lane called Klepsydras, labeled ΚΛΕΨΥΔΡΑΣ). Cross the street called Tholou and continue down Klepsydras. The lane gets even narrower (yes, keep going between the plants). Eventually you'll run into a railing overlooking some ruins.*

⑯ The Roman Forum and the Tower of the Winds

The rows of columns framing this rectangular former piazza were built by the Romans, who conquered Greece around 150 B.C. and stayed for centuries. This square—sometimes called the "Roman Agora"—was the commercial center, or forum, of Roman Athens, with a colonnade providing shade for shoppers browsing the many stores that fronted it. Centuries later, the Ottomans made this their grand bazaar. The mosque survives (although its minaret,

like all minarets in town, was torn down by the Greeks when they won their independence from the Ottomans in the 19th century).

Take a few steps to the right to see the octagonal, domed

Tower of the Winds (a.k.a. "Bath-House of the Winds"). The carved reliefs depict winds as winged humans who fly in, bringing the weather. Built in the first century B.C., this building was an ingenious combination of clock, weathervane, and guide to the planets. The beautifully carved reliefs are believed to represent the ancient Greek symbols for the eight winds. Even local guides don't know which is which, but the reliefs are still beautiful. As you walk down the hill (curving right, then left around the fence, always going downhill), you'll see reliefs depicting a boy with a harp, a boy with a basket of flowers (summer wind), a relief with a circle, and a guy blowing a conch shell—he's imitating Boreas, the howling winter wind from the north. The tower was once capped with a weathervane in the form of a bronze Triton (half-man, half-fish) that spun to indicate which wind was blessing or cursing the city at the moment. Bronze rods (no longer visible) protruded from the walls and acted as sundials to indicate the time. And when the sun wasn't shining, people told time using the tower's sophisticated water clock, powered by water piped in from springs on the Acropolis. Much later, under Ottoman rule, dervishes used the tower as a place for their whirling worship and prayer.

• *It's possible but unnecessary to enter the ruins: You've seen just about everything from this vantage point. If you do decide to enter the ruins, follow the spike-topped fence below the tower down Pelopida street and through an outdoor dining zone (where it curves and becomes Epameinonda) to reach the ticket office and entry gate, near the tallest standing colonnade (tower explained on a plaque inside; entry covered by Acropolis ticket). Don't confuse the Roman Forum with the older, more interesting Ancient Agora, which is near the end of this walk (see page 71).*

Otherwise, from just below the Tower of the Winds, head down Aiolou street to...

⑰ Agora Square (Plateia Agoras)

This leafy, restaurant-filled square is the touristy epicenter of the Plaka. A handy Internet café is nearby (Bits and Bytes, see page

60), as well as a stop for one of the city's tourist trains (see page 62).

On the left side of the square, you'll see the second-century A.D. ruins of the ⑱ **Library of Hadrian.** Four lone columns sit atop the apse-like foundations of what was once a cultural center (library, lecture halls, garden, and art gallery), built by the Greek-loving Roman emperor for the Athenian citizens.

• *Continue downhill alongside the ruins to the next block, where Aiolou intersects with the claustrophobic Pandrossou market street (which we walked along earlier). Remember that this crowded lane is worked by expert pickpockets—be careful. Look to the right up Pandrossou: You may see merchants sitting in folding chairs with their backs to each other,*

competition having soured their personal relationships. Turn left on
Pandrossou and wade through the knee-deep tacky tourist souvenirs.
The second shop is dedicated to "The Round Goddess"—soccer. ("Soccer
widows" are as prevalent in Greece as "football widows" in the US.)
Continue until you spill out into Monastiraki Square.

⑲ Monastiraki Square Spin-Tour

We've made it from Syntagma Square—the center of urban
Athens—to the city's *other* main square, Monastiraki Square, the
gateway to the touristy Old Town. To get oriented to Monastiraki
Square, stand in the center, face the small church with the cross on
top (which is north), and pan clockwise.

The name Monastiraki ("Little Monastery") refers to this
square, the surrounding neighborhood, the flea-market action
nearby...and the cute **Church of the Virgin** in the square's center
(12th-century Byzantine, mostly restored with a much more modern bell tower).

Beyond that (straight ahead from the end of the square),
Athinas street heads north to the Central Market, Omonia
Square, and (after about a mile) the National Archaeological
Museum.

Just to the right (behind the little church) is the head of
Ermou street—the bustling shopping drag we walked down earlier (though no longer traffic-free here). If you turned right and
walked straight up Ermou, you'd be back at Syntagma Square in
10 minutes.

Next (on the right, in front of the little church) comes Mitropoleos street—Athens' ⑳ **"Souvlaki Row."** Clogged with outdoor
tables, this atmospheric lane is home to a string of restaurants that
serve sausage-shaped, skewered meat—grilled up spicy and tasty.
The place on the corner—Bairaktaris (ΜΠΑΪΡΑΚΤΑΡΗΣ)—is
the best-known, its walls lined with photos of famous politicians
and artists who come here for souvlaki and pose with the owner.

But the other two joints along here—
Thanasis and Savas—have a better reputation for their souvlaki. You can sit at
the tables, or, for a really cheap meal,
order a souvlaki to go for less than €2.
(For details, see the Eating in Athens
chapter.) A few blocks farther down
Mitropoleos is the cathedral we visited
earlier.

Continue spinning clockwise.
Just past Pandrossou street (where you
entered the square), you'll see a ㉑ **former mosque** (look for the Arabic script

under the portico and over the wooden door). Known as the Tzami (from the Turkish word for "mosque"), this was a place of worship from the 15th to 19th centuries. Today, it houses the Museum of Greek Folk Art's **ceramics collection** (see page 74). The mosque's front balcony (no ticket required) offers fine views over Monastiraki Square.

To the right of the mosque, behind the fence along Areos street, you might glimpse some huge Corinthian columns. This is the opposite end of the **Library of Hadrian** complex we saw earlier. Areos street stretches up toward the Acropolis. If you were to walk a block up this street, then turn right on Adrianou, you'd reach the ❷ **Ancient Agora**—one of Athens' top ancient attractions (✪ see Ancient Agora Tour). Beyond the Agora are the delightful Thissio neighborhood, ancient Keramikos Cemetery, and Gazi district.

As you continue panning clockwise, next comes the pretty yellow building that houses the **Monastiraki Metro station**. This was Athens' original, British-built, 19th-century train station— Neoclassical with a dash of Byzantium. This bustling Metro stop is the intersection of two lines: the old line 1 (green, with connections to the port of Piraeus, the Thissio neighborhood, and Victoria—near the National Archaeological Museum) and the modern line 3 (blue, with connections to Syntagma Square and the airport). The stands in front of the station sell seasonal fruit and are popular with local commuters.

Just past the station, Ifestou street leads downhill into the ❷ **flea market** (antiques, jewelry, cheap clothing, and so on—for more details, see page 197). If locals need a screw for an old lamp, they know they'll find it here.

Keep panning clockwise. Just beyond busy Ermou street (to the left of Athinas street) is the happening **Psyrri** district. For years a run-down slum, this zone is being gentrified by twenty-somethings with a grungy sense of style. Packed with cutting-edge bars, restaurants, cafés, and nightclubs, it may seem foreboding and ramshackle, but is actually fun to explore. (Wander through by day to get your bearings, then head back at night when it's buzzing with activity.) For more on Psyrri, see page 195 and page 206.

❷ Monastiraki Metro Station

Finish your walk by stepping into the Monastiraki Metro station and riding the escalator down to see an exposed bit of ancient Athens. Excavations for the Metro revealed an ancient aqueduct, which confined Athens' Eridanos River to a canal. The river had been a main axis of the town since the eighth century B.C. In the second century A.D., Hadrian and his engineers put a roof over it, turning it into a more efficient sewer. You're looking at Roman brick and classic Roman engineering. A cool mural shows the treasure trove archaeologists uncovered with the excavations.

This walk has taken us from ancient ruins to the Roman era, from medieval churches and mosques to the guerrilla fighters of Greek Independence, through the bustling bric-a-brac of the modern city, and finally to a place where Athens' infrastructure—both ancient and modern—mingles.

• *Our walk is over. If you're ready for a break, savor a spicy souvlaki on "Souvlaki Row."*

ACROPOLIS
TOUR

ΑΚΡΟΠΟΛΗ / Ακρόπολη

Even in this age of superlatives, it's hard to overstate the historic and artistic importance of the Acropolis. Crowned by the mighty Parthenon, the Acropolis ("high city") rises above the sprawl of modern Athens, a lasting testament to ancient Athens' glorious Golden Age in the fifth century B.C.

The Acropolis has been the heart of Athens since the beginning of recorded time (Neolithic era, 6800 B.C.). This limestone plateau, faced with sheer, 100-foot cliffs and fed by permanent springs, was a natural fortress. The Mycenaeans (c. 1400 B.C.) ruled the area from their palace on this hilltop, and Athena—the patron goddess of the city—was worshipped here from around 800 B.C. on.

But everything changed in 480 B.C., when Persia invaded Greece for the second time. As the Persians approached, the

Athenians evacuated the city, abandoning it to be looted and vandalized. All of the temples atop the Acropolis were burned to the ground. The Athenians fought back at sea, winning an improbable naval victory at the Battle of Salamis. The Persians were driven out of Greece, and Athens found itself suddenly victorious. Cash poured into Athens from the other Greek city-states, which were eager to be allied with the winning side.

By 450 B.C., Athens was at the peak of its power and the treasury was flush with money...but in the city center, the Acropolis still lay empty, a vast blank canvas. Athens' leader at the time, Pericles, was ambitious and farsighted. He funneled Athens'

newfound wealth into a massive rebuilding program. Led by the visionary architect/sculptor Pheidias, the Athenians transformed the Acropolis into a complex of supersized, ornate temples worthy of the city's protector, Athena.

The four major monuments—the Parthenon, Erechtheion, Propylaea, and Temple of Athena Nike—were built as a coherent ensemble (c. 450-400 B.C.). Unlike most ancient sites, which have layer upon layer of ruins from different periods, the Acropolis we see today was started and finished within two generations—a snapshot of the Golden Age set in stone.

For visitors with more time, this tour of the Acropolis can easily be preceded by the Ancient Agora Tour (see the next chapter).

Orientation

Cost: €12 for Acropolis ticket (which also covers Ancient Agora, Roman Forum, Keramikos Cemetery, Temple of Olympian Zeus, and Theater of Dionysus—see sidebar on page 66); free for kids 18 and under, on Sun Nov-March, and on national holidays.

Hours: Daily May-Sept 8:00-20:00, Oct-April 8:00-15:00, last entry 30 minutes before closing.

When to Go: Get there early or late to avoid the crowds and midday heat. The place is miserably packed with tour groups from 10:00 to about 12:30 (when you might have to wait up to 45 minutes to get inside). On some days, as many as 6,000 cruise passengers converge on the Acropolis in a single morning. It's not the ticket-buying line that holds you up; instead, the worst lines are caused by the bottleneck of people trying to squeeze into the site through the Propylaea gate (so buying your ticket elsewhere doesn't ensure a speedy entry). Late in the day, as the sun goes down, the white Parthenon stone gleams a creamy golden brown, and what had been a tourist war zone is suddenly peaceful. On my last visit, I showed up late and had the place to myself in the cool of early evening.

Getting There: There's no way to reach the Acropolis without a lot of climbing (though people with disabilities can use an elevator—see below). Figure a 10- to 20-minute hike from the base of the Acropolis up to the hilltop archaeological site. There are multiple paths up to the Acropolis, but the only ticket office and site entrance are at the western end of the hill (to the right as you face the Acropolis from the Plaka).

If you're touring the Ancient Agora, you can hike directly up to the Acropolis entrance along the Panathenaic Way. The approach from the Dionysiou Areopagitou pedestrian zone behind (south of) the Acropolis is a bit less steep. From this walkway, various well-marked paths funnel visitors up to the entrance; the least steep one climbs up from the parking lot at the western end of the pedestrian zone. You can reach this path either by taxi or by tourist train (the Athens Happy Train—see page 62), but note that it still involves quite a bit of uphill hiking.

If you use a **wheelchair,** you can take the elevator that ascends the Acropolis (from the ticket booth, go around the left side of the hilltop). However, once up top, the site is not particularly level or well-paved, so you may need help navigating the steep inclines and uneven terrain.

Information: Supplement this tour with the free information brochure (you may have to ask for it when you buy your ticket) and info plaques posted throughout. Tel. 210-321-4172, www.culture.gr.

Tours: At the entrance, you can hire your own tour guide, generally a professional archaeologist (around €90). My free audio

version of this tour is available at www.ricksteves.com/audio
europe and from iTunes. The Acropolis is particularly suited
to an audio tour, as it allows your eyes to enjoy the wonders of
this sight while your ears learn its story.

Length of This Tour: Allow two hours.

Baggage Check: Backpacks are allowed. Baby strollers are not.
There's a checkroom just below the ticket booth near Mars
Hill.

Services: There are WCs at the Acropolis ticket booth and more
WCs and drinking fountains atop the Acropolis, in the former museum building (behind the Parthenon). Picnicking is
not allowed on the premises. A post office and museum shop
are near the ticket booth. A vending machine sells bottled
water (just inside the ticket-check turnstile and to the right,
€0.50, coins only).

Plan Ahead: Wear sensible shoes—Acropolis paths are steep and
uneven. In summer, it gets very hot on top, so take a hat, sunscreen, sunglasses, and a bottle of water. Inside the turnstiles,
there are no services except WCs and drinking fountains;
pack whatever else you'll need (little snacks, guidebooks,
camera batteries).

Starring: The Parthenon and other monuments from the Golden
Age, plus great views of Athens and beyond.

The Tour Begins

• *Climb up to the Acropolis ticket booth and the site entrance, located at
the west end of the hill.*

Near this entrance (below and
toward the Ancient Agora) is the
huge, craggy boulder of **Mars
Hill** (a.k.a. Areopagus). Consider
climbing this rock for great views
of the Acropolis' ancient entry
gate (the Propylaea, described
later) and the Ancient Agora.
Mars Hill's bare, polished rock is
extremely slippery—a metal stair-
case to the left helps somewhat. (For more on Mars Hill and its
role in Christian history, see page 67.)

Before you show your ticket and enter the Acropolis site, make
sure you have everything you'll need for your visit. Remember,
after you enter the site, there are no services except WCs and water
fountains.

• *Enter the site, and start climbing the paths that switchback up the hill, following signs on this one-way tourist route (bearing to the right). Before you reach the summit, peel off to the right for a bird's-eye view of the...*

Odeon of Herodes Atticus

This grand venue huddles under the Acropolis' majestic Propylaea entrance gate. While tourists call it a "theater," Greeks know it's technically an *odeon,* as it was used for musical rather than theatrical performances. (*Odeon* comes from the same root as the English "ode," from the Greek word for "song.")

A large 5,000-seat amphitheater built during Roman times, it's still used today for performances. From this perch you get a good look at the stage set-up: a three-quarter-circle orchestra (where musicians and actors performed in Greek-style theater), the overgrown remnants of a raised stage (for actors in the Roman tradition), and an intact stage wall for the backdrop. Originally, it had a wood-and-tile roof as well.

The *odeon* was built in A.D. 161 by Herodes Atticus, a wealthy landowner, in memory of his wife. Herodes Atticus was a Greek with Roman citizenship, a legendary orator, and a friend of Emperor Hadrian. This amphitheater is the most famous of the many impressive buildings he financed around the country.

Destroyed by the invading Herulians a century after it was built, the "Herodion" (as it's also called) was reconstructed in the

1950s to the spectacular state it's still in today. It's open to the public only during performances, such as the annual Athens & Epidavros Festival, which features an international line-up of dance, music, and theater performed beneath the stars. If there's something on tonight, you may see a rehearsal from here. Athenians shudder when visitors—recalling the famous "Yanni Live at the Acropolis" concert—call this stately place "Yanni's Theater."

• *After climbing a few steps, you'll see two gates: On the right, steps lead down to the Theater of Dionysus (described on page 70); on the left is the actual entry uphill into the Acropolis. Stay left and continue up to reach the grand entrance gate of the Acropolis: the Propylaea. Stand at the*

ACROPOLIS

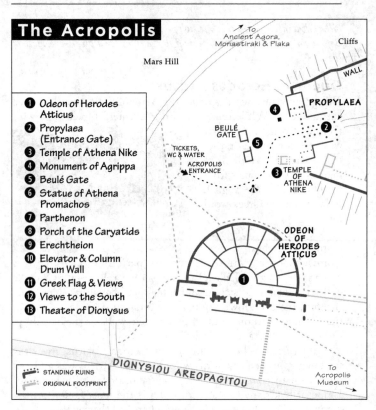

The Acropolis

1. Odeon of Herodes Atticus
2. Propylaea (Entrance Gate)
3. Temple of Athena Nike
4. Monument of Agrippa
5. Beulé Gate
6. Statue of Athena Promachos
7. Parthenon
8. Porch of the Caryatids
9. Erechtheion
10. Elevator & Column Drum Wall
11. Greek Flag & Views
12. Views to the South
13. Theater of Dionysus

To Ancient Agora, Monastiraki & Plaka

Cliffs

Mars Hill

WALL

PROPYLAEA

BEULÉ GATE

TICKETS, WC & WATER

ACROPOLIS ENTRANCE

TEMPLE OF ATHENA NIKE

ODEON OF HERODES ATTICUS

STANDING RUINS
ORIGINAL FOOTPRINT

DIONYSIOU AREOPAGITOU

To Acropolis Museum

ACROPOLIS

foot of the (very) steep marble staircase, facing up toward the big Doric columns.

As you face the Propylaea, to your left is a tall, gray stone pedestal with nothing on it: the Monument of Agrippa. On your right, atop the wall, is the Temple of Athena Nike. Behind you stands a doorway in a wall, known as the Beulé Gate.

The Propylaea

The entrance to the Acropolis couldn't be through just any old gate; it had to be the grandest gate ever built. Ancient visitors would stand here, catching their breath before the final push to the summit, and admire these gleaming columns and steep steps that almost fill your entire field of vision. Imagine the psychological impact this awe-inspiring, colonnaded entryway to the sacred rock must have had on

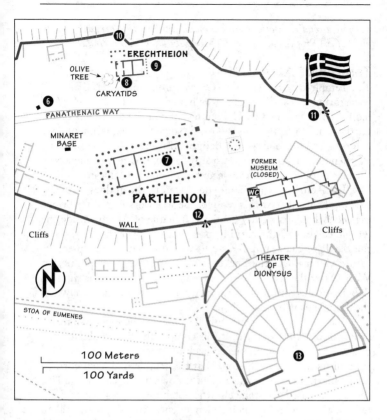

ancient Athenians. Unlike today's path, the grand marble staircase didn't zigzag, but instead headed straight up. (A few original stairs survive under the wooden ramp.)

The Propylaea (pro-puh-LEE-ah) is U-shaped, with a large central hallway (the six Doric columns), flanked by side wings that reach out to embrace the visitor. The central building looked like a mini-Parthenon, with Doric columns topped by a triangular pediment. Originally, the Propylaea was painted bright colors and decorated with statues.

The left wing of the Propylaea was the Pinacoteca, or "painting gallery." In ancient times, this space contained artwork and housed visiting dignitaries and VIPs.

The buildings of the Acropolis were all built to complement each other. The Propylaea, constructed in five short years (437-432 B.C., just after the Parthenon was finished) was designed by Mnesicles, who also did the Erechtheion. The Propylaea gave the visitor a taste of the Parthenon to come. Both buildings are Doric (with Ionic touches) and are aligned east–west, with columns of similar width-to-height ratios.

• Before ascending, notice the monuments flanking the entryway. To the right of the Propylaea, look up high atop the block wall to find the...

Temple of Athena Nike

The Temple of Athena Nike (Greeks pronounce it "NEEK-ee") was started as the Propylaea was being finished (c. 427-421/415 B.C.). It was designed by Callicrates, one of the architects of the Parthenon. This little temple—nearly square, 11 feet tall, with four columns at both ends—had delightful proportions. Where the Parthenon and Propylaea are sturdy Doric, this temple pioneered the new style of Ionic, with elegant scroll-topped columns.

The Acropolis was mainly dedicated to the goddess Athena, patron of the city. At this temple, she was worshipped for bringing the Athenians victory ("Nike"). A statue of Athena inside the temple celebrated the turning-point victory over the Persians at the Battle of Plataea in 479 B.C. It was also meant to help ensure future victory over the Spartans in the ongoing Peloponnesian Wars. After the statue's wings were broken by Athenians wanting Athena to stay and protect their city, the place became known as the Temple of Wingless Athena.

The Temple of Athena Nike has undergone extensive restoration. From 2001 to 2010, it was completely disassembled, then cleaned, shored up, and pieced back together. This was the third time in its 2,500-year history that the temple had been entirely taken apart. The Ottomans pulled it down at the end of the 17th century and used the stone elsewhere, but Greeks reassembled the temple after regaining their independence. In 1935, it was taken apart for renovation and put back together in 1939. Unfortunately, that shoddy work did more harm than good—prompting the most recent restoration. Now it's been done the right way and should hold for another 2,500 years.

• To the left (as you face the Propylaea) is the...

Monument of Agrippa

This 25-foot-high pedestal, made of big blocks of gray marble with yellow veins, reaches as high up as the Temple of Athena Nike. The (now-empty) pedestal once held a bronze statue of the four-horse chariot driven by the winner of the race at the 178 B.C. Olympics.

Over the centuries, each ruler of Athens wanted to put his mark on the mighty Acropolis. When Rome occupied the city, Marc Antony placed a statue of himself and his girlfriend Cleopatra atop the pedestal.

After their defeat, the Roman general Agrippa (son-in-law of Augustus) replaced it with a statue of himself (in 27 B.C.).

• *Before entering, look downhill. Behind you is the...*

Beulé Gate

This ceremonial doorway was built by the Romans, who used the rubble from buildings that had recently been destroyed in the barbarian Herulian invasion of A.D. 267. (The gate's French name comes from the archaeologist who discovered it in 1852.) During Roman times, this gate was the official entrance to the Acropolis, making the Propylaea entry even grander.

• *Now climb the steps (or today's switchback ramps for tourists) and go...*

Inside the Propylaea

Imagine being part of the grand parade of the Panathenaic Festival, held every year (see page 146). The procession started at Athens' city gate (near the Keramikos Cemetery), passed through the Agora, then went around Mars Hill, through the central hall of the Propylaea, and up to the glorious buildings atop the summit of the Acropolis. Ancient Greeks approached the Propylaea by proceeding straight up a ramp in the middle, which narrowed as they ascended, funneling them into the central passageway. There were five doorways into the Propylaea, one between each of the six columns.

The Propylaea's central hall was once a roofed passageway.

The marble-tile ceiling, now partially restored, was painted sky blue and studded with stars. Floral designs decorated other parts of the building. The interior columns are Ionic, a bit thinner than the Doric columns of the exterior. You'll pass by some big column drums with square holes in the center, where iron pins once held the drums in place. (Greek columns were not usually made from a single piece of stone, but from sections—"column drums"—stacked on top of each other.)

• *Pass through the Propylaea. As you emerge out the other end, you're on top of the Acropolis. There it is—the Parthenon! Just like in the books. Stand and take it all in.*

ACROPOLIS

The Acropolis

The "Acropolis rock" is a flat, slightly sloping limestone ridge covering seven acres, scattered with ruins. There's the Parthenon ahead to the right. To the left of that, with the six lady pillars (caryatids), is the Erechtheion. The Panathenaic Way ran between them. The processional street and the buildings were aligned east–west, like the hill.

Ancient visitors here would have come face-to-face with a welcoming 30-foot **Statue of Athena Promachos,** which stood

between the Propylaea and the Erechtheion. (Today there's just a field of rubble, with the statue's former location marked by three stones forming a low wall.) This was one of three statues of Athena on the Acropolis. The patron of the city was worshipped for her wisdom, purity, and strength; here she appeared in her role as "Frontline Soldier" *(promachos),* carrying a shield and spear. The statue was cast by Pheidias, the visionary sculptor/architect most responsible for the design of the Acropolis complex. The bronze statue was so tall that the shining tip of Athena's spear was visible from ships at Cape Sounion, 30 miles south. The statue disappeared in ancient times, and no one knows its fate.

Two important buildings, now entirely gone, flanked this statue and the Panathenaic Way. On the right was the Chalkotheke, a practical storage area for the most precious gifts brought to the temple—those made of copper and bronze. On the left stood the Arrephorion, a house where young virgins called *ergastinai* worked at looms to weave the *peplos,* the sacred dress given to Athena on her birthday.

• *Move a little closer for the classic view of the...*

Parthenon—The West End

The Parthenon is the hill's showstopper—the finest temple in the ancient world, standing on the highest point of the Acropolis, 490 feet above sea level. The Parthenon is now largely in ruins, partly from the ravages of time, but mostly from a freak accident in 1687, when it suffered bomb damage during a war.

It's impressive enough today, but imagine how awesome the Parthenon must have looked when it was completed nearly 2,500 years ago. This largest Doric temple in Greece is 228 feet long and 101 feet wide. At each end were eight fluted Doric columns, with 17 columns along each side (46 total), plus 19 inner columns in the Ionic style. The columns are 34 feet high and six feet in diameter.

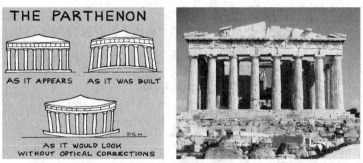

THE PARTHENON

AS IT APPEARS   AS IT WAS BUILT

AS IT WOULD LOOK
WITHOUT OPTICAL CORRECTIONS

In its heyday, the temple was decorated with statues and carved reliefs, all painted in vivid colors. It's considered Greece's greatest Doric temple (though not its purest textbook example because it incorporates Ionic columns and sculpture).

The Parthenon served the cult of Virgin Athena, and functioned as both a temple (with a cult statue inside) and as the treasury of Athens (safeguarding the city's funds, which included the treasury of the Athenian League). You're looking at the west end—the classic view that greets visitors—but the building's main entrance was at the other end.

This large temple was completed in less than a decade (c. 450-440 B.C.), though the sculptural decoration took a few years more (finished c. 432). The project's overall "look" was supervised by the master sculptor-architect Pheidias; built by well-known architects Ictinus and Callicrates; and decorated with carved scenes from Greek mythology by sculptors Agoracritos and Alcamenes.

It's big, sure. But what makes the Parthenon truly exceptional is that the architects used a whole bagful of optical illusions to give the building an ever-so-subtle feeling of balance, strength, and harmonious beauty. Architects know that a long, flat baseline on a building looks to the human eye like it's sagging, and that parallel columns appear to bend away from each other. To create a building that looked harmonious, the Parthenon's ancient architects calculated bends in the construction. The base of the Parthenon actually arches several inches upward in the middle to counteract the "sagging" illusion (and to drain rainwater). Its columns tilt ever so slightly inward (one of the reasons why the Parthenon has withstood earthquakes so well). If you extended all the columns upward several miles, they'd eventually touch. The corner columns are thicker to make them appear the same size as the rest; they're also spaced more closely. And the columns bulge imperceptibly halfway up ("entasis"), giving the subconscious impression of stout, barrel-chested men bearing the weight of the roof. For a building that seems at first to be all about right angles, the Parthenon is amazingly short on straight, structural lines.

ACROPOLIS

All these clever refinements form a powerful subconscious impression on the viewer that brings an otherwise boring architectural box to life. It's amazing to think that all this was planned and implemented in stone so long ago.

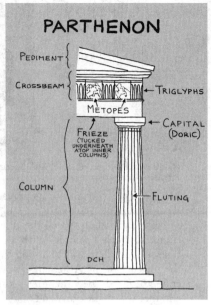

The statues and carved reliefs that once decorated the outside of the Parthenon are now mostly fading or missing, but a few remain. Look up at the crossbeam atop the eight columns, decorated with panels of relief carvings called "metopes," depicting Athenians battling Amazons. Originally, there were 92 Doric-style metopes in high relief, mostly designed by Pheidias himself.

The crossbeams once supported a triangular pediment (now gone). This area was once filled in with statues, showing Athena with her olive tree competing with Poseidon and his trident to be Athens' patron god. Today just one statue remains (and it's a reconstruction).

Approach closer and look between the eight columns. Inside, there's another row of eight columns, supporting a covered entrance porch. Look up above the inner eight columns. Decorating those crossbeams are more relief carvings—the "frieze." Originally, a 525-foot-long frieze of panels circled the entire building. It showed the Panathenaic parade—dancing girls, men on horseback, sacrificial animals being led to the slaughter—while the gods looked on.

All of these sculptures—metopes, pediment, and frieze—were originally painted in bright colors. Today, most of the originals are

in museums across Europe. In the early 1800s, the cream of the crop, the famous "Elgin Marbles," were taken by Lord Elgin to England, where they now sit in the British Museum. The Acropolis Museum (which stands at the base of the hill—you'll see it from a distance later on this tour) was built to house the fragments of the Parthenon sculpture that Athens still owns...and to try to entice the rest back from London.

• *Continue along the Panathenaic Way, walking along the long left (north) side of the Parthenon.*

Parthenon—The North Side

This view of the Parthenon gives a glimpse into how the temple was constructed and how it is being reconstructed today by modern archaeologists.

Looking between the columns, you can see remnants of the interior walls, built with thousands of rectangular blocks. The columns formed an open-air porch around the main building, which had an entry hall and *cella* (inner sanctum). Large roof tiles were fitted together atop wooden beams. These tiles were made of ultra-white, translucent Parian marble, and the interior glowed with the light that shone through it.

The Parthenon's columns are in the Doric style—stout, lightly fluted, with no base. The simple capital on top consists of a convex plate topped with a square slab. The capitals alone weigh 12 tons. The crossbeams consist of a lower half ("architrave") and upper half, its metopes interspersed with a pattern of grooves (called triglyphs).

The Parthenon (along with the other Acropolis buildings) was constructed from the very finest materials, including high-quality, white Pentelic marble from Penteliko Mountain, 16 miles away. Unlike the grand structures of the Egyptians (pyramids) and the Romans (Colosseum), the Parthenon was built not by slaves but by free men who drew a salary (though it's possible that slaves worked at the quarries).

Imagine the engineering problems of quarrying and transporting more than 100,000 tons of marble. Most likely, the column drums were cut at the quarry and rolled here. To hoist the drums in place, they used four-poster cranes (and Greek mathematics), centering the drums with a cedar peg in the middle. The drums were held together by metal pins that were coated in lead to prevent corrosion, then fitted into a square hole cut in the center of the drum. (The Ottomans scavenged much of this lead to make bullets, contributing to the destruction of the temple over the ages.) Because the Parthenon's dimensions are not mathematically precise (intentionally so), each piece had to be individually cut and sized to fit its exact place. The Parthenon's stones are so well-crafted that they fit together within a thousandth of an inch. The total cost to build the Parthenon (in today's dollars) has been estimated at over a billion dollars.

• *Continue on to the...*

Parthenon—The East End (Entrance) and Interior

This end was the original entrance to the temple. Over the doorway, the triangular pediment depicted the central event in Athenian

history—the Birth of Athena, their patron goddess. Today, the pediment barely survives, and the original statues of the gods are in the British Museum. Originally, the gods were gathered at a banquet (see a copy of the reclining Dionysus at the far left—looking so drunk he's afraid to come down). Zeus got a headache and asked Hephaistos to relieve it. As the other gods looked on in astonishment, Hephaistos split Zeus' head open, and—at the peak of the pediment—out rose Athena. The now-missing statues were surprisingly realistic and three-dimensional, with perfect anatomy and bulging muscles showing through transparent robes.

Imagine this spot during the age of Pericles and Socrates. Stand back far enough to take it all in, mentally replace the 40-foot statue inside, and picture the place in all its glory, on the day of the Panathenaic parade. The parade has traveled through the Agora, ascended the Acropolis, passed through the Propylaea, and arrived here at the entrance of the Parthenon. People gather on the surrounding grass (the hard stone that you see today was once covered with earth and plants). Musicians play flutes and tambourines, girls dance, and men on horseback rein in their restless animals. On open-air altars, the priests offer a sacrifice of 100 oxen (a hecatomb—the ultimate sacrificial gift) to the goddess Athena.

Here at the Parthenon entrance, a select few are chosen to go inside. They proceed up the steps, entering through the majestic columns. First they enter a foyer called the *pronaos,* then continue into the main hall, the *cella*—100 feet long, 60 feet wide, and four stories tall. At the far end of the room is an enormous statue of Athena Parthenos ("Athena the Virgin"), standing 40 feet tall. The

ACROPOLIS

Acropolis Now: The Renovation Project

The scaffolding, cranes, and modern construction materials you see here are part of an ongoing renovation project. The challenge is to save what's left of the Parthenon from the modern menaces of acid rain and pollution, which have already caused irreversible damage. Funded by Greece and the EU, the project began in 1984, which means that they've been at it more than twice as long as it took to build the Parthenon in the first place.

The project first involves cataloging every single stone of the Parthenon—blocks, drums, capitals, bits of rock, and pieces lying on the ground or in museums around the world. Next, archaeologists hope to put it back together, like a giant 70,000-piece jigsaw puzzle. Along the way, they're fixing previous restorations that were either inaccurate or problematic. For example, earlier restorers used uncoated iron and steel rods to hold things together. As weather fluctuations caused the metal to expand, the stone was damaged. This time around, restorers are using titanium instead of steel.

Whenever possible, the restorers use original materials. But you'll see big blocks of new marble lying on the ground—freshly cut from the same Pentelic quarries. The new marble is being used to replace damaged and missing marble. Many of the columns have lighter-colored "patches" where the restorers have added material. This looks like concrete or plaster, but it's actually new marble, cut to fit the exact hole. Though this newly cut marble looks much whiter, in time, it will age to the same color as the rest of the Parthenon.

When complete, the renovated Parthenon won't look like the pre-1687, undestroyed building—just a shored-up version of the ruin we see today. If you want to see the Parthenon temple in its heyday, there's a full-scale replica open to visitors...in Nashville, Tennessee.

wooden core of the *chryselephantine* statue (from the Greek *chrysos,* "gold," and *elephantinos,* "ivory") was plated with ivory to represent her skin, and a ton of pure gold (a third of an inch thick) for her garments (or so say local guides). She was dressed as a warrior, wearing a helmet with her shield resting at her side. Her image was reflected in a pool in the center of the room. (The pool also served a practical purpose—the humidity helped preserve the ivory treasures.) In Athena's left hand was a spear propped on the ground. In her upturned right hand was a statuette of Nike—that is, she literally held Victory in the palm of her hand.

The statue was the work of the master Pheidias himself (447-438 B.C.). The statue was carried off to Constantinople in A.D. 426, where it subsequently vanished. A small-scale Roman copy is on display in Athens' National Archaeological Museum (see the photo of *Athena Varvakeion* on page 168). Another famous *chryselephantine* statue by Pheidias—of a seated Zeus—was considered one of the Seven Wonders of the Ancient World (see sidebar on page 285).

The culmination of the Panathenaic parade was the presentation of a newly woven *peplos* to Athena, the patron of the city. Generally, the dress was intended for the life-size wooden statue of Athena kept at the Erechtheion (described later). But during the Grand Panathenaia (every four years), the Athenians presented a huge robe—big enough to cover a basketball court—to the 40-foot Virgin Athena in the Parthenon.

• *Behind you, the modern brown-brick building once housed the **former Acropolis museum**—its collection has been painstakingly moved into the modern Acropolis Museum down the hill. The old museum building may reopen someday as a coffee shop, but for now, it has just WCs and a drinking fountain alongside.*

Across the street from the Parthenon stands the Erechtheion, where the Panathenaic parade ended. There were three entrances to this building: the famous Porch of the Caryatids (the six ladies), the north porch (behind the Erechtheion), and the east end (to the right of the caryatids). Start by enjoying the...

Porch of the Caryatids

An inspired piece of architecture, this balcony has six beautiful maidens functioning as columns that support the roof. Each of the lady-columns has a base beneath her feet, pleated robes as the fluting, and a fruit-basket hat as the capital. Both feminine and functional, they pose gracefully,

ACROPOLIS

exposing a hint of leg. It was the first time that the Greeks combined architectural elements and sculpture.

These are faithful copies of the originals, four of which are on display in the Acropolis Museum. The fifth was removed (c. 1805) by the sticky-fingered Lord Elgin, who shipped it to London. The sixth statue is in France. The caryatids were supposedly modeled on *Karyatides*—women from Karyai (modern Karyes, near Sparta on the Peloponnese), famous for their upright posture and noble character.

The Erechtheion was built by Mnesicles (c. 421-406 B.C.), the man who also did the Propylaea. Whereas the Propylaea and Parthenon are both sturdy Doric, the Erechtheion is elegant Ionic. In its day, it was a stunning white building (of Pentelic marble) with black trim and painted columns.

Near the porch (below, to the left) is an **olive tree,** a replacement for the one Athena planted here in her face-off with Poseidon (described later). Olive trees have been called "the gift of Athena to Athens." Greece has more than 100 million of these trees.

• *Walk around to the right and view the Erechtheion from the east end, with its six Ionic columns in a row.*

Erechtheion

Though overshadowed by the more impressive Parthenon, the Erechtheion (a.k.a. Erechtheum) was perhaps more prestigious.

It stood on one of the oldest sites on the hill, where the Mycenaeans had built their palace. (The huge ruined stones scattered on the south side, facing the Parthenon, are all that's left of the Mycenaean palace.) Inside the Erechtheion was a life-size, olive-wood statue of Athena in her role of Athena Polias ("Protector of the City"). Pericles took the statue with him when the Athenians evacuated their city to avoid the invading Persians. Dating from about 900 B.C., this statue was much older and more venerable than either of Pheidias' colos-sal statues, supposedly having dropped from the sky as a gift from Athena.

This unique, two-story structure fits nicely into the slope of the hill. The east end (with the six Ionic columns) was the upper-level entrance. The lower entrance was on

After the Golden Age: The Acropolis Through History

Classical: The Parthenon and the rest of the Acropolis' buildings survived through classical times largely intact, despite Herulian looting (A.D. 267). As the Roman Empire declined, precious items were carried off, including the 40-foot Athena statue.

Christian: The Christian Emperor Theodosius II (a.k.a. Theodosius the Great) labored to outlaw pagan worship and close temples and other religious sites. After nearly a thousand years as Athena's temple, the Parthenon became a Christian church (fifth century A.D.). It remained Christian for the next thousand years, first as the Byzantine Orthodox Church of Holy Wisdom, then as a Roman Catholic cathedral (dedicated to Mary in 1204 by Frankish Crusaders). Throughout medieval times it was an important stop on the pilgrimage circuit.

After the Parthenon was converted into a church, the exterior was preserved, but pagan sculptures and decorations were removed (or renamed), and the interior was decorated with colorful Christian frescoes. The west end of the building became the main entrance, and the interior was reconfigured with an apse at the east end.

Muslim: In 1456, the Turks arrived, and converted the Parthenon into a mosque, adding a minaret. The Propylaea entry gate was used as a palace for the Turkish ruler of Athens. The Turks had no respect for the sacred history of the Acropolis—they even tore down stones just to get the lead clamps that held them in place, in order to make bullets. (The exasperated Greeks even offered them bullets to stop destroying the temple.) The Turks also used the Parthenon to store gunpowder, unfortunately

the north side (on the right), 10 feet lower, where you see six more Ionic columns. (These columns are the "face of the Acropolis" that Athenians see from the Plaka.) The Porch of the Caryatids (on the south side of the building, to the left) was yet another entrance. Looking inside the temple, you can make out that the inner worship hall, the *cella*, is divided in two by walls.

This complex layout accommodated the worship of various gods who had been venerated here since the beginning of time. Legend says this was the spot where Athena and Poseidon fought for naming rights to the city. Poseidon threw his trident, which opened a gash in the earth to bring forth water. It left a diagonal crack that you can still see in the pavement of the entrance leading to the greatest catastrophe in the Acropolis' long history. It happened in…

1687: A Venetian army laid siege to the Acropolis. The Venetians didn't care about ancient architecture. As far as they were concerned, it was a lucky hit of mortar fire that triggered the massive explosion that ripped the center out of the Parthenon, rattled the Propylaea and the other buildings, and wiped out the Turkish defenders. Pieces of the Parthenon lay scattered on the ground, many of them gathered up as souvenirs by soldiers.

Lord Elgin: In 1801, Lord Elgin, the British Ambassador to the Ottomans in Constantinople, got "permission" from the  sultan to gather sculptures from the Parthenon, buy them from locals, and even saw them off the building (Greeks scoff at the idea that "permission" granted by an occupying power should carry any weight). He carted half of them to London, and the "Elgin Marbles" are displayed in the British Museum to this day, despite repeated requests for their return. Although a few original frieze, metope, and pediment carvings still adorn the Parthenon, most of the sculptures are on display in museums, including the Acropolis Museum.

From Independence to the Present: In the 19th century, newly independent Greece tore down the Parthenon's minaret and the other post-Classical buildings atop the Acropolis, turning it into an archaeological zone. Since then, the place has been excavated and there have been several renovation efforts. Today, the Acropolis still strikes wonder in the hearts of visitors, just as it has for centuries.

farthest from the Parthenon (although lightning is a more likely culprit). But Athena won the contest by stabbing a rock with her spear, sprouting an olive tree near the Porch of the Caryatids. The twin *cellas* of the Erechtheion allowed the worship of both gods— Athena and Poseidon—side by side to show that they were still friends.

• *Look to the right (beyond the Plaka-facing porch). The modern* **elevator,** *useful during the Paralympics in 2004, carries people with disabilities up to the Acropolis. The north wall of the Acropolis has a retaining wall built from* **column drums.** *This is about all that remains of an earlier Parthenon that was destroyed after the Persian invasion of 480 B.C. The Persians razed the entire Acropolis, including an* *unfinished temple then under construction. When the Athenians rebuilt, this column from the old temple helped preserve the bitter memory of the Acropolis' destruction.*

Walk to the far end of the Acropolis. There you'll find an observation platform with a giant...

Greek Flag

The blue-and-white Greek flag's nine stripes symbolize (according to popular myth) the nine syllables of the Greek phrase for "Freedom or Death." That phrase took on new meaning when the Nazis entered Athens in April of 1941. The evzone (elite member of a select infantry unit) who was guarding this flag was ordered by the Nazis to remove it. He calmly took it down, wrapped himself in it...and jumped to his death. About a month

later, two heroic teenagers, Manolis Glezos and Apostolis Santas, scaled the wall, took down the Nazi flag, and raised the Greek flag. This was one of the first well-known acts of resistance against the Nazis, and the boys' bravery is honored by a plaque near the base of the steps. To this day, Greeks can see this flag from just about anywhere in Athens and think of their hard-won independence.

• *Walk out to the end of the rectangular promontory to see the...*

View of Athens

The Ancient Agora spreads below the Acropolis, and the sprawl of modern Athens whitewashes the surrounding hills. In 1830, Athens' population was about 5,000. By 1900, it was 600,000, and during the 1920s, with the influx of Greeks from Turkey, the population surged to 1.5 million. The city's expansion could barely keep up with its exploding population. With the boom times in the 1950s and 1980s, the city grew to nearly four million. Pan around. From this perch, you're looking at the homes of one out of every three Greeks.

Looking down on the **Plaka,** find (looking left to right) the Ancient Agora, with the Temple of Hephaistos. Next comes the Roman Forum (the four columns and palm trees) with its round, white, domed Temple of the Winds monument. The Anafiotika neighborhood clings to the Acropolis hillside directly below us. Beyond that, find the green and red dome of the cathedral.

Lykavittos Hill, Athens' highest point (see photo on next page), is crowned with the Chapel of St. George (and an expensive view restaurant; cable car up the hill). Looking farther in the distance, you'll see white bits on the mountains behind—these are

ACROPOLIS

the **Pentelic quarries,** the source of the marble used to build (and now restore) the monuments of the Acropolis.

As you continue panning to the right, you'll spot the beige Neoclassical **Parliament** building, marking Syntagma Square; the **National Garden** is behind and to the right of it. In the garden is the yellow **Zappeion,** an exhibition hall. The green area in the far distance contains the 80,000-seat, marble **Panathenaic Stadium**—an ancient venue (on the site where Golden Age Athens held its games), which was rehabbed in 1896 to help revive the modern Olympics.

• *Complete your visual tour of Athens at the south edge of the Acropolis. To reach the viewpoint, walk back toward the Parthenon, then circle along its left side, by the cliff-top wall. Belly up to that wall for a....*

View from the South Side of the Acropolis

Look to the left. In the near distance are the huge columns of the **Temple of Olympian Zeus.** Begun in the sixth century B.C., it

wasn't finished until the time of the Roman emperor Hadrian, 700 years later. It was the biggest temple in all of Greece, with 104 Corinthian pillars, housing a 40-foot seated statue of Zeus, a replica of the famous one created by Pheidias in Olympia. This was part of "Hadrianopolis," a planned community in his day, complete with the triumphal **Arch of Hadrian** near the temple.

The **Theater of Dionysus**—which hosted great productions (including works by Sophocles) during the Golden Age—lies in ruins at your feet (a visit to these ruins is covered by your Acropolis ticket). For some background on Greek theater, see the sidebar on page 256.

Beyond the theater is the wonderful **Acropolis Museum,** a black-and-gray modern glass building, with three rectangular floors stacked at irregular angles atop each other. The top floor—which houses replicas and some originals of the Parthenon's art—is angled to match the orientation of that great temple.

Looking right, you see **Filopappos Hill**—the green, tree-dotted hill topped with a marble monument to a popular Roman

ACROPOLIS

general in ancient times. This hill is where the Venetians launched the infamous mortar attack of 1687 that destroyed the Parthenon. Today, a theater here hosts popular folk-music performances (described in the Nightlife in Athens chapter).

Farther in the distance, you get a glimpse of the turquoise waters of the **Aegean** (the only island visible is Aegina). While the Persians were burning the Acropolis to the ground, the Athenians watched from their ships as they prepared to defeat them in the history-changing Battle of Salamis. In the distance, far to the right, is the port of Piraeus (the main departure point for boats to the islands).

• *Our tour is finished. Enjoy a few final moments with the Acropolis before you leave. If you're not yet ready to return to modern Athens, you can continue your sightseeing at several nearby sights.*

To reach the Theater of Dionysus ruins and the Acropolis Museum: Head left when you exit the Acropolis site, and walk down to the Dionysiou Areopagitou pedestrian boulevard. Turn left and follow this walkway along the base of the Acropolis. First you'll pass (on the left) the entrance to the Theater of Dionysus ruins, then (on the right) the Acropolis Museum (see the ✪ Acropolis Museum Tour chapter).

To reach the Ancient Agora: Turn right as you exit the Acropolis site, pass Mars Hill, and follow the Panathenaic Way down to the Ancient Agora (possible to enter through the "back door," facing the Acropolis). You'll find the ✪ Ancient Agora Tour in the next chapter.

ACROPOLIS

ANCIENT AGORA TOUR

ΑΡΧΑΙΑ ΑΓΟΡΑ / Αρχαία Αγορά

While the Acropolis was the ceremonial showpiece, it was the Agora that was the real heart of ancient Athens. For some 800 years, from its founding in the sixth century B.C. to its destruction by barbarians in A.D. 267, it was the hub of all commercial, political, and social life in Athens, as well as home to much of its religious life.

Agora means "gathering place," but you could call this space by any of the names we typically give to the busiest part of a city—downtown, main square, forum, piazza, marketplace, commons, and so on. It was a lively place where the pace never let up—much like modern Athens.

Little survives from the classical Agora. Other than one very well-preserved temple and a rebuilt stoa, it's a field of humble ruins. But that makes it a quiet, uncrowded spot—nestled in the shadow of the Acropolis—to wander and get a feel for the ancients.

Orientation

Cost: €4 or covered by €12 Acropolis ticket (which you can buy here; see page 66).

Hours: Daily May-Sept 8:00-20:00, Oct-April 8:00-15:00, last entry 30 minutes before closing. The Agora Museum inside has the same hours, except on Mon when it opens at 13:00.

Getting There: From Monastiraki (Metro line 1/green or line 3/blue), walk a block south (uphill, toward the Acropolis). Turn right on Adrianou street, and follow the pedestrian-only, café-lined street along the railroad tracks for about 200 yards. The Agora entrance is on your left, across from a small yellow church. The entrance can be hard to spot: It's where a path crosses over the railroad tracks (look for a small, pale-yellow sign that says *Ministry of Culture—Ancient Agora*).

Compass Points: The Agora entrance is north; the Acropolis is south.

Information: Panels with printed descriptions of the ruins are scattered helpfully throughout the site. Tel. 210-321-0180, www.culture.gr.

Audioguide Tours: A free audio version of this tour is available at www.ricksteves.com/audioeurope and from iTunes.

Cuisine Art: Picnicking is not allowed in the Agora. Plenty of cafés and tavernas line busy Adrianou street near the Agora entrance, and more good eateries front the Apostolou Pavlou pedestrian walkway that hems in the western edge of the Agora, in the district called Thissio (see the Eating in Athens chapter).

Starring: A well-preserved temple, a rebuilt stoa, three monumental statues, and the ruins of the civilization that built the Western world.

The Tour Begins

Entering the site from the Adrianou street entrance, belly up to the illustration at the top of the ramp that shows Athens at its peak.

Face the Acropolis (to the south), look out over the expanse of ruins and trees, and get oriented.

The long column-lined building to the left is the reconstructed Stoa of Attalos (#13 on the illustration). To your right, atop a hill (the view is likely blocked by trees) is the well-preserved Temple of Hephaistos (#20). The pathway called the Panathenaic Way (#21) runs from the Agora's entrance up to the Acropolis. Directly ahead of you are three tall statue-columns—part of what was once the Odeon of Agrippa (#12).

In the distance, the Agora's far end is bordered by hills. From left to right are the Acropolis (#1), the Areopagus ("Hill of Ares," or Mars Hill, #2), and Pnyx Hill (#3).

Although the illustration implies that you're standing somewhere behind the Stoa Poikile ("Painted Stoa," #28), in fact you are located closer to the heart of the Agora, near the Altar of the Twelve Gods (#26). In ancient times, that altar was considered the geographical center of Athens, from which distances were measured. Today, the area north of the altar (and north of today's illustration) remains largely unexcavated and inaccessible to tourists, taken over by the railroad tracks and Adrianou street. The

The Agora at Its Peak

ACROPOLIS

MARS HILL

DCH

A Stoa of Attalos
B Temple of Hephaistos
C Panathenaic Way
D Odeon of Agrippa
E Current Entrance

computer terminal (just to your right) is an impractical boondoggle that has never really worked—the result of corrupt cronyism that is so frustrating to Athenians. Someone made a fortune setting these things up.

This self-guided tour starts at the Stoa of Attalos (with its museum), then crosses the Agora to the Temple of Hephaistos, returning to the Panathenaic Way via three giant statues. Finally, we'll head up the Panathenaic Way toward the Acropolis.

• *Walk to the bottom of the ramp at your left for a better view. Find a shady spot to ponder...*

❶ The Agora at Its Peak, circa A.D. 150

What lies before you now is a maze of ruins—the remains of many centuries of buildings.

A millennium before the time of Socrates, during the Mycenaean Period (around 1400 B.C.), this area held the oldest cemetery in Athens. Later, the Agora was developed into an open marketplace—a rectangular area (about 100 yards by 200 yards), bordered by hills. Over time, that central square became surrounded by buildings, then filled in by more buildings. There were stoas like the (reconstructed) Stoa of Attalos (above on the left), used for shops and offices; temples such as the Temple of

ANCIENT AGORA

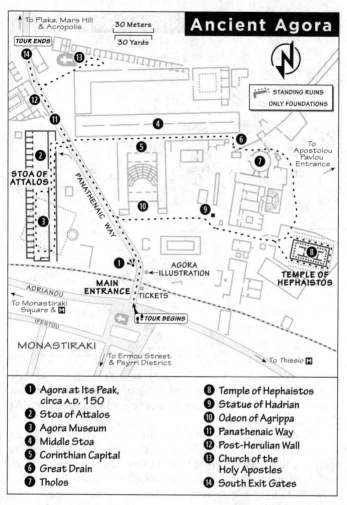

Ancient Agora

To Plaka, Mars Hill & Acropolis

TOUR ENDS

30 Meters
30 Yards

STANDING RUINS
ONLY FOUNDATIONS

STOA OF ATTALOS

PANATHENAIC WAY

To Apostolou Pavlou Entrance

AGORA ILLUSTRATION

MAIN ENTRANCE
TICKETS

TOUR BEGINS

TEMPLE OF HEPHAISTOS

ADRIANOU
To Monastiraki Square & M

IFESTOU

MONASTIRAKI

To Ermou Street & Psyrri District

To Thissio M

1. Agora at Its Peak, circa A.D. 150
2. Stoa of Attalos
3. Agora Museum
4. Middle Stoa
5. Corinthian Capital
6. Great Drain
7. Tholos
8. Temple of Hephaistos
9. Statue of Hadrian
10. Odeon of Agrippa
11. Panathenaic Way
12. Post-Herulian Wall
13. Church of the Holy Apostles
14. South Exit Gates

ANCIENT AGORA

Hephaistos; and government buildings. Imagine the square framed by these buildings—made of gleaming white marble, fronted with columns, topped with red-tile roofs. The square itself was studded with trees and dotted with statues, fountains, and altars. Merchants sold goods from wooden market stalls.

The square buzzed with people—mostly men and lower-class working women, as the place was considered a bit vulgar for gen- teel matrons. Both men and women would be dressed in simple tunics (men's were knee-length, women's to the ankle). The Agora was the place to shop—to buy groceries, clothes, dishes, or to get your wagon wheel fixed. If you needed a zoning permit for your business, you came to the courthouse. You could make an offering to the gods at a number of temples and altars. At night, people attended plays and concerts, and the tavernas hummed with excited drinkers. Many people passed through here on their way to somewhere else, as this was the main intersection in town (and ancient Athens probably had a population of at least 100,000). The Agora was the center for speeches, political announcements, and demonstrations. On holidays, the parade ran down main street, the Panathenaic Way. At any time, this was the place to come to run into your friends, to engage in high-minded discussion with philosophers such as Socrates or Diogenes, or just to chat and hang out.

• *Now go to the long, intact, colonnaded building on your left (entrance at the south/far end), which is the...*

❷ Stoa of Attalos

This stoa—an ancient shopping mall—was originally built by the Greek-loving King Attalos II of Pergamon (in modern-day

Turkey, 159-138 B.C.) as a thank-you gift for the education he'd received in Athens. However, that structure is long gone, and the building we see today is a faithful reconstruction built in the 1950s by the American School of Classical Studies.

This is a typical two-story stoa. Like many of the Agora's buildings, it's made of white Pentelic marble. The portico is 381 feet by 64 feet, supported on the ground floor by 45 Doric columns (outer layer) and 22 Ionic columns (inner layer). The upper story uses Ionic columns. This mix of Doric and Ionic was typical of buildings from the period.

Stoas, with their covered walkways, provided protection from sun and rain for shoppers and businesspeople. This one likely served as a commercial mall. The ground floor was divided by walls into 21 rooms that served as shops (it's now the museum). Upstairs were offices (which today house the American School of Classical Studies).

Like malls of today, the Agora's stoas were also social magnets. Imagine ancient Greeks (their hard labor being done by slaves) lounging here, enjoying the shade of the portico. The pillars were designed to encourage people

to lean against them (just as you may be doing right now)—with fluting starting only above six feet—for the comfort of philosophers.

• *The Stoa of Attalos houses the...*

❸ Agora Museum

The Agora is mostly ruins, but the excellent little museum displays some choice rubble that helps bring the place to life. Before entering, enjoy the arcade. Near the fifth column, find the impressive sculpted head of a bearded man with a full head of hair. This **Head of a Triton** (c. A.D. 150) comes from one of the statues that decorated the Odeon of Agrippa. Three of his fellow statues are still standing (we'll see them soon).

Walk halfway down the arcade and step inside the museum (included with your Agora ticket). The museum's modest but engaging collection fills a single long hall. Look in the corner for the 1952 photo showing this spot before the reconstruction. This well-described chronological stroll through art from 3200 B.C. gives you a glimpse of life in ancient Athens. Along the hall on the left, big panels show the Agora and Acropolis during each age, allowing you to follow their physical evolution.

The first few cases show off **jars** from various eras, including Neolithic (from the era when the Agora was first inhabited) and Geometric (with hash-mark designs). Much of this exhibit shows how pottery evolved over time. Usually painted red and black,

pottery was a popular export product for the sea-trading Greeks. The earliest featured geometric patterns (eighth century B.C.), then a painted black silhouette on the natural orange clay, then a red figure on a black background.

In case 26 (on the right), look for the cute little baby's **commode,** with a photo showing how it was used. Nearby (case 69, on left) are Archaic-era statues with smiling faces.

Cases 30-32 (on right), with items from **early democracy,** are especially interesting. The "voting machine" (*kleroterion,* case 31) was used to choose council members. Citizens put their name in the slots, then black and white balls went into the tube to randomly select who would serve (much like your turn in jury duty). Below the machine are bronze

ballots from the fourth century. The pottery shards with names painted on them (*ostrakan,* case 30) were used as ballots in voting to ostracize someone accused of corruption or tyranny. Find the ones marked **ΘEMISΘOKLES NEOKLEOS** (item #37) and **ARISSTEIΔES** (item #17, see photo on previous page). During the Golden Age, Themistocles and Aristides were rivals (in both politics and romance) who served Athens honorably but were also exiled in political power struggles.

In case 32, see the *klepsydra* ("water thief")—a water clock used to time speeches at Council meetings. It took six minutes for the 1.7 gallons to drain out. A gifted orator truly was good to the last drop...but not a second longer.

Across the hall (under the banner, between cases 68 and 67) is the so-called **"Stele of Democracy"** (c. 336 B.C.). This stone monument is inscribed with a decree outlawing tyranny. Above, a relief carving shows Lady Democracy crowning a man representing the Athenian people.

Next to that (in case 67) is a **bronze shield** captured from defeated Spartans in the tide-turning Battle of Sphacteria, which gave Athens the upper hand in the first phase of the Peloponnesian War. The next case over (case 66) displays herm heads. With news and directions attached, these functioned as signposts along roads.

In the middle of the room, find the case of **coins.** These drachms and tetradrachms feature Athena with her helmet. In Golden Age times, a drachm was roughly a day's wage. The ancients put coins like these in the mouth of a deceased person as payment for the underworld ferryman Charon to carry the soul safely across the River Styx. Coin #7, with the owl, was a fourdrachm piece; that same owl is on Greece's €1 coin today.

For a reminder that the ancients weren't so different from us, look for the two **barbecue grills** (case 61, left; and case 42, right).

The exhibit winds up with **Roman sculpture heads** (cases 58 and 56, left), which show how the Romans were more honest than the Greeks when it came to portraying people with less-than-ideal features, and even more pottery items—including various toys (case 48, right).

• *Exiting the museum at the far end of the arcade (where there's a WC and a water fountain), backtrack to the southern end of the stoa (where you entered), then cross the main road and continue straight (west) along the lane, across the middle of the Agora. You're walking alongside the vast ruins (on your left) of what once was the...*

The Agora in Action

Think of thousands of angry Athenian citizens assembled here, listening to speeches as they voted to ostracize a corrupt or tyrannical leader. Other than ostracisms, general assemblies were usually not held here, but rather on Pnyx Hill, which rises southwest of the Agora.

The roving philosopher **Socrates** (469-399 B.C.) spent much of his life simply hanging out in the Agora, questioning passersby, and urging people to "know thyself." Socrates discussed the meaning of piety, as recorded by Plato in the dialogue called the *Euthyphro*. "The lover of inquiry," said Socrates, "must follow his beloved wherever it may lead him." Shortly after, Socrates was tried and condemned to death here for "corrupting the youth"...by encouraging them to question Athenian piety.

Plato, Socrates' disciple and chronicler of his words, spent time teaching in the Agora, as did Plato's disciple **Aristotle.** (Their schools—Plato's Academy and Aristotle's Lyceum—were located elsewhere in Athens.)

The great statesman **Pericles** must have spent time here, since he oversaw the rebuilding program after the Persian invasion. (His famous Funeral Oration, however, was not given here.)

When Athens triumphed over Sparta in one battle during the Peloponnesian War (425 B.C.), **General Cleon** displayed the shields of captured prisoners in the Agora. This action mocked the Spartans for their surrender, since brave Spartans were

❹ Middle Stoa

Stretching clear across the Agora, this was part of a large complex of buildings that likely served as a big mall of shops and offices. It was a long, narrow rectangle (about 500 feet by 60 feet), similar to the reconstructed Stoa of Attalos you just left. You can still see the two lines of stubby column fragments that once supported the roof, a few stone steps, and (at the far end) some of the reddish foundation blocks. Constructed around 180 B.C., this stoa occupied what had been open space in the center of the Agora.

• *Midway down the lane (just before the wooden ramp), you'll come across a huge and frilly upper cap, or capital, of a column.*

❺ Corinthian Capital: The Center of the Agora

This capital (dating from the fourth century B.C.) once stood here atop a colossal column, one of a dozen columns that lined the monumental entrance to the Odeon of Agrippa, a theater that extended northward from the Middle Stoa. (We'll learn more about the Odeon later on this tour.) The capital's elaborate acanthus-leaf always supposed to die with their shields on.

Diogenes the Cynic lived as a homeless person in the Agora and shocked the Athenians with his anti-materialist and free life-style. He lived in a wooden tub (in disregard for material comfort), masturbated openly (to prove how simply one's desires could be satisfied), and wandered the Agora with a lighted lamp in daylight (looking for one honest man in the corrupt city). According to legend, Alexander the Great was intrigued by this humble philosopher who shunned materialism. One day he stood before him and said, "Diogenes, I will give you whatever you want. What would you like?" History's first hippie looked at the most powerful man on earth and replied, "Please get out of my sunshine."

The earliest Greek plays and concerts were performed here in the open air and, later, in theaters (including the Odeon of Agrippa). The playwright **Aristophanes** set scenes in the Agora, **Sophocles** spent time here, and all the major Greek plays would most likely have been performed here.

Imagine the buzz in the Agora at key points in Athens' history—as Athenians awaited the onslaught of the Persians and debated what to do, or as they greeted the coming of Alexander the Great, the conquering Romans, and the invasions of the Herulians and Slavs.

The **Apostle Paul** likely talked religion here in the Agora on his way to Corinth in A.D. 49 (Acts 17:17). He would have seen the various altars dedicated to pagan gods, which he decried from Mars Hill, overlooking the Agora.

decoration is an early example of the Corinthian order. The style was rarely used in Greek buildings but became wildly popular with the Romans.

From here, look back toward the entrance, overlooking what was once the vacant expanse at the center of the Agora. In 400 B.C., there was no Middle Stoa and no Odeon—this was all open space. As Athens grew, the space was increasingly filled in with shops and monuments. Now, imagine the place in its heyday (see sidebar).

• *Continue westward (over a wooden bridge) across the Agora. Near the end of the Middle Stoa, you'll pass a gray well—still in its original spot and worn by the grooves of ropes. From here, look up at the Acropolis, where the towering but empty pedestal once sported the Monument of Agrippa, a grand statue with four horses. Mars Hill, likely lined with tourists, is where the Apostle Paul famously preached the Gospel (described on page 67). Below the Erechtheion are broken columns shoring up the side of the hill. These were rubble from the Mycenaean temples that were destroyed by the Persians. Past the well, jog to the right and cross the ditch over the wooden bridge. This ditch is part of the waterworks system known as the...*

❻ Great Drain

Dug in the fifth century B.C. and still functioning today, these ditches channel rainwater run-off from the southern hills through the Agora. Here at the southwest corner of the Agora, two main collection ditches meet and join. You can see exposed parts of the stone-lined ditch. The well we just passed was also part of this system.

• *Just over the wooden bridge is a 60-foot-across round footprint with a stubby column in its center. This is the...*

❼ *Tholos*

This rotunda-shaped building housed Athens' rulers. Built around 465 B.C., it was originally ringed with six Ionic columns that held up a conical roof. In the middle was an altar (marked today by the broken column).

The fundamental unit of Athenian democracy was the Assembly, made up of the thousands of adult male citizens who could vote. Athenian citizens were organized into 10 tribes; in order to prevent the people living in any one geographical area from becoming dominant, each tribe was composed of citizens from the city, the coast, and inland areas. Each man in the Assembly was considered to be from one of these tribes.

All of Athens' governing bodies met in the Agora. Though some Assembly meetings were held in the Agora's main square, the main assemblies were just uphill, on the slope of Pnyx Hill. The City Council also met in the Agora. The Council consisted of 500 men (50 from each of the 10 tribes) who were chosen from the Assembly by lottery to serve a one-year term. The Council proposed and debated legislation, but since Athens practiced direct (not representational) democracy, all laws eventually had to be approved by the whole Assembly. The Council chose 50 ministers who ran the day-to-day affairs.

As part of the civic center complex, the *tholos* served several functions. It was the headquarters, offices, and meeting hall for the 50 ministers. Many also lived and ate here, since the law required that at least a third of these ministers be on the premises at all times. The *tholos* housed the official weights and measures. Any shopper in the Agora could use these to check whether a butcher or tailor was shortchanging them. As the center of government, the *tholos* was also a kind of temple to the city. The altar in the middle held an eternal flame, representing the hearth of the extended "family" that was Athens.

• *Beyond and above the* tholos *is the hill-capping Temple of Hephaistos. To reach it, climb the stairs to the left and go through the trees, pausing along the way at a viewpoint with a chart.*

❽ Temple of Hephaistos (a.k.a. the Theseion or Theseum)

One of the best-preserved and most typical of all temples, this is textbook Golden Age architecture. Started in 450 B.C., it was built

at Athens' peak as part of the massive reconstruction of the Agora after invading Persians destroyed the city (480 B.C.). But the temple wasn't completed and dedicated until 415 B.C., as work stalled when the Greeks started erecting the great buildings of the Acropolis. Notice how the frieze around the outside of the building was only finished on the side facing the Agora (it's blank elsewhere).

As a classic "peripteral" or "peristyle" temple (like the Parthenon), the building is surrounded by columns—6 on each end, 13 on the long sides (counting the corners twice). Also like the Parthenon, it's made of Pentelic marble in the Doric style, part of Pericles' vision of harking back to Athens' austere, solid roots. But the Temple of Hephaistos is only about half the size of the grand Parthenon and with fewer refinements (compared to the Parthenon's elaborate carvings and fancy math).

The temple's entrance was on the east end (the one facing the Agora). Priests would enter through the six columns here, into a covered portico (note the coffered ceiling). Next came a three-sided alcove called the *pronaos,* or "pre-temple." From there, you'd continue into the central hall *(cella),* which once housed large bronze statues of Hephaistos, the blacksmith god, and Athena, patroness of Athens and of pottery. In ancient times, the temple was surrounded by metal-working and pottery shops, before the Romans replaced them with gardens, similar to today's. Behind the *cella* (the west end) is another three-sided alcove, matching the *pronaos.*

The carved reliefs (frieze and metopes) that run around the upper part of the building are only partly done. Some panels may have been left unfinished, others may have once been decorated with painted (not sculpted) scenes, and a few panels have been removed and put in the Agora Museum.

At the end overlooking the Agora, look between the six columns and up at the frieze above the *pronaos* to find scenes of Theseus battling his enemies, trying to unite Athens. Theseus would go on to free Athens from the dominance of Crete by slaying the bull-headed Minotaur. To this day, Athenians call the temple the "Theseion" because the frieze decorations led them to mistakenly believe that it once held the remains of the mythical hero Theseus.

Walk around behind the temple, to the far (west) end. The frieze above the three-sided alcove depicts the mythological battle between the Lapith tribe and centaurs during a wedding feast. Other scenes you'll see around the building (there are many interpretations) include Hercules (his labors and deification) and the birth of Erichthonios (one of Athens' first kings, who was born when spurned Hephaistos tried to rape Athena, spilled semen, and instead impregnated Gaia, the earth).

In A.D. 1300, the temple was converted into the Church of Agios Georgios, dedicated to Greece's patron saint, George, and given the vaulted ceiling that survives today. During the Ottoman occupation, the Turks kept the church open but permitted services to be held only once each year (on St. George's Day). Because it was continually in use, the temple-turned-church is remarkably well-preserved.

• *Note that there's a "back door" exit nearby for those wanting to take the smooth, paved walkway up to the Acropolis, rather than the rough climb above the Agora. (To find the exit, face the back of the temple, turn right, and follow the path to the green gate, which deposits you on the inviting, café-lined Apostolou Pavlou pedestrian drag. From here, you can turn left and walk up toward the Acropolis. ❍ See the Acropolis Tour chapter.)*

But there's still more to see in the Agora. Wind your way down the hill (east) and find the headless...

❾ Statue of Hadrian (second century A.D.)

The first Roman emperor to wear a beard (previously a Greek fashion), Hadrian (r. A.D. 117-138) was a Grecophile and benefactor of Athens. Get close to the statue and notice the insignia on the breastplate. There's Romulus and Remus, being suckled by the she-wolf who supports Athena on her back. This was Hadrian's vision—that by conquering Greece, Rome actually saved it. Hadrian was nicknamed Graecula ("The Little Greek") for his

love of Greek philosophy, literature, and a handsome Greek teenager named Antinous (see the story on page 367). Hadrian personally visited Athens, where he financed new construction, including Hadrian's Arch, the Library of Hadrian, the Temple of Olympian Zeus (which had been started by the Greeks), and a whole planned neighborhood called Hadrianopolis. (For more on these sights, see the ❷ Athens City Walk chapter.) Hadrian's legacy endures. The main street through the Plaka is now called Adrianou—"Hadrian's" street.

• *Farther along, the lane passes three giants on four pedestals, which once guarded the...*

❿ Odeon of Agrippa (a.k.a. the "Palace of the Giants")

This theater/concert hall, once fronted by a line of six fierce Triton statues (of which just three survived), was the centerpiece of the Agora during the Roman era.

A plaque explains the history of this building: During the Golden Age, this site was simply open space in the very center of the Agora. The *odeon* (a venue designed for musical performances) was built by the Roman general and governor Marcus Agrippa in the time of Caesar Augustus (around 15 B.C.), when Greece was a Roman-controlled province. For the theater-loving Greeks and their Greek-culture-loving masters, the *odeon* was a popular place. Two stories tall and built into the natural slope of the hill, it could seat more than a thousand people.

Back then, the entrance was on the south side (near the Middle Stoa), and these Triton statues didn't exist yet. Patrons entered from the south, walking through two rows of monumental columns, topped by Corinthian capitals. After the lobby, they emerged at the top row of a 20-tier, bowl-shaped auditorium, looking down on an orchestra and stage paved with multicolored marble and decorated with statues. The sightlines were great because the roof, spanning 82 feet, had no internal support columns. One can only assume that, in its heyday, the *odeon* hosted plays by Aristophanes, Euripides, and Sophocles, plus lute concerts, poetry readings, and more lowbrow Roman-oriented entertainment.

Around A.D. 150, the famously unsupported roof collapsed. By then, Athens had a bigger, better performance venue (the Odeon of Herodes Atticus, on the other side of the Acropolis—described on page 115), so the Odeon of Agrippa was rebuilt at half the size as a 500-seat lecture hall. The new entrance was here on the north side, fronted by six colossal statues serving as pillars. Only two tritons (with fish tails), a giant (snake's tail), and an empty pedestal remain.

The building was burned to the ground in the Herulian invasion of A.D. 267 (explained later, under "Post-Herulian Wall"). Around A.D. 400, a large palace was built here, which also served as the university (or "gymnasium," which comes from the Greek word for "naked"—young men exercised in the buff during PE here). It lasted until the Constantinople-based Emperor Justinian closed all the pagan schools in A.D. 529. A plaque under the first statue gives more information.

• *Continue to the main road, where you'll see we've made a loop. Now turn right and start up toward the Acropolis on the...*

⓫ Panathenaic Way

The Panathenaic Way was Athens' main street. It started at the main city gate (the Dipylon Gate, near the Keramikos Cemetery),

cut diagonally through the Agora's main square, and wound up to the Acropolis—two-thirds of a mile in all. The Panathenaic Way was the primary north–south road, and here in the Agora it intersected with the main east–west road to the port of Piraeus. Though some stretches were paved, most of it (then as now) was just packed gravel. It was lined with important temples, businesses, and legal buildings.

During the Panathenaic Festival (July-Aug), this was the main parade route. Every year on Athena's birthday, Greeks celebrated by giving her statue a new dress, called a *peplos*. A wheeled float carrying the *peplos* was pushed up this street. Thousands participated—some dancing, some on horseback, others just walking—while spectators watched from wooden grandstands erected along the way. When the parade reached the Acropolis, the new dress was ceremonially presented to Athena and used to adorn her life-size statue at the Erechtheion. Every fourth year was a special celebration, when Athenians created an enormous *peplos* for the 40-foot statue in the Parthenon. Today's tourists use the same path to connect the Agora and the Acropolis.

• *Continue up the Panathenaic Way, past the Stoa of Attalos. Along the left-hand side of the Panathenaic Way are several crude walls and column fragments.*

⑫ Post-Herulian Wall

This wall marks the beginning of the end of classical Athens.

In A.D. 267, the barbarian Herulians sailed down from the Black Sea and utterly devastated Athens. (The crumbling Roman Empire was helpless to protect its provinces.) The Herulians burned most of the Agora's buildings to the ground, leaving it in ashes.

As soon as the Herulians left, the surviving Athenians began hastily throwing up this wall—cobbled together from rubble— to keep future invaders at bay. They used anything they could find: rocks, broken columns, statues, frieze fragments, all thrown together without mortar to make a wall 30 feet high and 10 feet thick. Archaeologists recognize pieces scavenged from destroyed buildings, such as the Stoa of Attalos and the Odeon of Agrippa.

Up until this point, the Agora had always been rebuilt after invasions (such as the Persians in 480 B.C. and Romans in 89 B.C.); but after the Herulian invasion, the Agora never recovered as a public space. What remained suffered through a Slavic invasion in A.D. 580. By A.D. 700, it was a virtual ghost town, located outside the city walls, exposed to bandits and invaders. Only the hardiest of souls used it as a residence. (Looking up at the sheer face of the Acropolis, you may be able to make out other crude medieval dwellings—caves that pockmark the hillside.) Considering how accessible the Agora was over the centuries as a quarry for pre-cut stones, it's no wonder that so little of it survives today.

• *Next came the Christians. On the right is the...*

⑬ Church of the Holy Apostles

This charming little church with the lantern-like dome marks the Agora's revival. Built around A.D. 1000, it commemorates St. Paul's teaching in the Agora (see information about Mars Hill on page 67). Under protection from the Christian rulers of Byzantium (in Constantinople, modern-day Istanbul), Athens—and the Agora—slowly recovered from centuries of invasions and neglect. The

ANCIENT AGORA

church was built on the ruins of an ancient nymphaeum, or temple atop a sacred spring, and became one of many Christian churches that served the booming populace of Byzantine Athens.

This church was the prototype for later Athenian churches: a Greek-cross floor plan with four equal arms, topped by a dome and featuring windows with tall horseshoe-shaped arches. (The narthex, or entrance, was added later, spoiling the four equal arms.) The church was built of large, rectangular dressed stone (ashlar) blocks, rather than small bricks. Ringing the eaves is a decorative pattern of bricks shaped into Arabic letters (Kufic script) added later, during the Ottoman occupation, when Christian churches like this were tolerated (but taxed) by the Muslim rulers.

Enter around the far side. It contains some interesting 18th-century Byzantine-style frescoes. The windows are in flower and

diamond shapes. From the center, look up at Jesus as *Pantocrator* at the top of the dome, and see the icon on the altar and the faded frescoes on the walls. The uniform chipping on the surface of the frescoes was part of a process designed to rough it up so a new coat of whitewashing could adhere. Notice the remains of the marble altar screen with wide-open spaces—frames that once held icons.

• *End your tour by continuing up the Panathenaic Way to the south exit gates and looking back over the Agora and modern Athens.*

Legacy of the Agora

By the 18th century, the Agora had become a flourishing Turkish residential district. The Church of the Holy Apostles was only one of many churches serving the populace. In the early 20th century, outdoor movies were shown in the Agora. In the 1930s, the American School of Classical Studies arrived, forced everyone out of their houses and businesses, and demolished buildings that had stood for centuries—all so they could dig here. The

Church of the Holy Apostles was the only structure left standing, and it was heavily renovated by the American School to return it to its original state. Excavation in the Agora has continued nearly without pause for the past 70-some years.

Now that the ancient Agora has become a museum, the role of city center has shifted to Athens' many modern neighborhoods. Produce is bought and sold at the Central Market. The government center is at Syntagma Square. Multiple neighborhoods, like the Plaka, Psyrri, Thissio, and Gazi harbor nightlife. Monastiraki and a dozen other squares have become the new social-center "agoras." And the Metro has replaced the Panathenaic Way as the main arterial.

• *Your tour is finished. There are three exits from the Agora: the gate you used to enter, at Adrianou street; the "back door" gate behind the Temple of Hephaistos; and the gate next to the Church of the Holy Apostles (⑭; where you are now). Keep your ticket if you want to return to the Agora later (note that the Acropolis ticket has one designated stub for the Acropolis, but all the others are interchangeable—so you can visit each covered sight once, or the same one several times).*

To head straight up to the Acropolis (to complete your own Panathenaic Festival), exit through the gate by the church, head straight up the hill, and turn to the ✪ *Acropolis Tour chapter.*

ACROPOLIS MUSEUM TOUR

ΜΟΥΣΕΊΟ ΑΚΡΌΠΟΛΗΣ /
Μουσείο Ακρόπολης

Athens' Acropolis Museum, opened in 2009, was custom-built to showcase artifacts from the Acropolis—the Parthenon sculptures, the original caryatids from the Erechtheion, and much more—complemented by modern exhibits about the Acropolis. The state-of-the-art building that houses the collection is the boldest symbol yet of today's Athens.

The museum also serves as a sort of 21st-century Trojan horse, intended to lure the famous Parthenon sculptures (the Elgin Marbles) away from London's British Museum and back to Athens. For years, the Greeks have asked for the Marbles back, and for years, the Brits have claimed that Greece can't give them a suitable home. Even now, with this ultramodern facility ready and waiting, Britain is reluctant to give in, for fear of setting a precedent...and getting "me, too" notices from Italy, Egypt, Iran, Iraq, and all the other nations who'd like to reclaim the missing pieces of their cultural heritage.

With or without the Elgin Marbles, this new museum has trumped the National Archaeological Museum as the most exciting museum in town, and is definitely worth your time.

Orientation

Cost: €5, free for kids 18 and under.

Hours: Tue-Sun 8:00-20:00, closed Mon, last entry 30 minutes before closing.

Getting There: It's the giant, can't-miss-it modern building facing the south side of the Acropolis from across the broad Dionysiou Areopagitou pedestrian drag. The museum is next to the Akropoli Metro stop (line 2/red).

Information: Museum archaeologists (with red badges) can answer questions, and a 13-minute video plays continuously in the atrium on Level Three. Tel. 210-924-1043, www.the acropolismuseum.gr.

Length of This Tour: Allow 1.5 hours.

Photography: Not allowed inside.

Services: A café and gift shop are on the ground floor (Level Zero); Level Two has a pricey but well-regarded restaurant, a bookstore, and great views.

Starring: Marble masterpieces from one of the most influential works of art in human history.

The Tour Begins

The striking, glassy building—designed by Swiss-born, New York-based architect Bernard Tschumi—gives a postmodern jolt

to Athens' otherwise staid, mid-century-concrete cityscape, even as it echoes the ancient history all around it. Its two lower levels are aligned with the foundations of ancient ruins discovered beneath the building (which are exposed and still being excavated). The top floor sits askew, imitating the orientation of the Parthenon. A long terrace extends over the main entry, with café tables stretching toward panoramic views of the Acropolis. The glass walls of the museum not only maximize the amount of natural light inside, but are also designed to "disappear," focusing attention away from the building and onto the statuary and views of the Acropolis itself.

Visitors enter into a grand lobby. The ground floor (Level Zero) has the ticket office, WCs, museum shop, and temporary exhibits. To proceed chronologically through the exhibits, you'd start with the Archaic collection on Level One, then go upstairs (to the top floor—Level Three) for the Parthenon section, then back down to Level One for Hellenistic and Roman sculpture. But for this tour, we'll do the small Hellenistic and Roman section as an out-of-chronological-sequence side-trip from the Archaic and Classical sections, and let the top-floor Parthenon sculptures be our finale.

• *After going through the turnstiles, head up the long, glass...*

Ramp

Pause to look through the glass floor at the ancient ruins being excavated beneath the museum. While the major buildings of ancient Athens were at the Acropolis and Agora, this was a neighborhood of everyday houses and shops. Appropriately, the ramp is lined with artifacts that were found in the sanctuaries on the slopes leading up to the Parthenon. Many of these fifth-century B.C. artifacts owe their well-preserved state to having been buried with their owners.

Among the ramp's highlights is case #5, which takes you step by step through marriage rituals in ancient Athens. Freestanding cases mid-ramp give insight into the similarities between ancient Greek pagan worship rituals and later Christian styles. One has Christian-looking votives thanking the gods for prayers answered. On the right, just below the stairs, is an offering box (like you see in churches today); this one stood at the Sanctuary of Aphrodite. To assure a good marriage, you'd have been wise to pop in a silver drachma.

Level One

• *Climb the stairs at the top of the ramp toward a collection of statues.*

Pediment of the Hekatompedon (570 B.C.)

Throughout the centuries, three temples of Athena have occupied the spot where the Parthenon stands today. These statues once adorned the Hekatompedon, the first of those temples. On the left, Hercules fights a sea monster (Triton). In the center are the scant remains of two lions killing a bull. To the right, looking like the Three Musketeers, is a three-headed demon with a snake tail holding the three elements (air, water, fire). They look more goofy then demonic. These so-called "Bluebeards" still have traces of the original paint.

• *Turn right and enter a gallery flooded with daylight.*

Kore and Kouros Statues

In this column-lined gallery stand several kore (female) and kouros (male) statues. They sport the characteristic stiff poses, braided hair, generic faces, and mysterious smiles of the Archaic era (c. 650-480 B.C.). For more on Archaic statues, see page 164.

The men are generally naked, showing off buff and toned bodies. The bearded dudes are adults, while boys are beardless. Women are modestly clothed—except for Aphrodite. If you can find one naked breast in this gal-

Acropolis Museum Level One

ESCALATORS TO LEVELS 2 & 3

POST-PARTHENON GALLERY

ROMAN PERIOD GALLERY

ELEVATORS

ERECHTHEION

Open to below

Open to below   STAIRS

ARCHAIC GALLERY

1 Pediment of the Hekatompedon

2 Kore & Kouros Statues

3 Pediment of the Old Temple

4 Pensive Athena Relief

5 Nike Adjusting Her Sandal Relief

6 Side-Trip to Hellen- istic & Roman Art

7 Caryatids from the Erechtheion

8 Up to Parthenon Gallery

lery, it belongs to the goddess of love. The women pull up their robes as if readying to take a step. Before the coming of Golden Age realism, this was a crude way to suggest motion. These figures are almost always holding something. That's because the Greeks believed you shouldn't approach the gods without a gift of some kind. The equestrian statues represent the upper class, those wealthy elites who owned horses.

• *Halfway down the gallery, on the right against the interior wall, is the...*

Pediment of the Old Temple (Archaios Naos)

This decorated the short-lived temple to Athena that succeeded the Hekatompedon. The still-under-construction building was leveled by invading Persians in 480 B.C., paving the way for the Parthenon to be built. In the center, a large statue of Athena, dressed in an ankle-length cloak, strides forward, brandishing a snake as she attacks a giant, who sprawls backward onto his bum. These figures were part of a scene depicting the "Gods Versus Giants" battle atop the temple.

The glass case nearby displays fragments with burn marks, traces of the fire set by the Persians. The pesky Persians invaded Greece several times over a 50-year period (c. 499-449 B.C.).

On the plus side, the wars forced Greeks to band together, and Athens emerged as a dominant naval power. Athenians rebuilt the Acropolis as a symbol of rebirth, with the Parthenon as its centerpiece. In just a few short decades, Greek society—and art—evolved rapidly and remarkably.

• Continue down the gallery. Near the end, look for a well-preserved marble relief placed in front of a concrete pillar.

Pensive Athena Relief (460 B.C.)

The goddess, dressed in a helmet and belted peplos, rests her forehead thoughtfully on her spear. While called "pensive," some think she was actually meant to be mourning the deaths of her citizens in the Persian War.

Enjoying the statuary in this hall, you can trace the evolution of Greek art from the static Archaic period to the mastery of the body as a living thing, free and full of movement, that we see in the Golden Age. In the Classical style of fifth-century B.C. Greece, the spine moves with the hips realistically.

• Turn right and walk past a bank of elevators. Continue past an open gallery with some statuesque women (we'll visit them in a minute). After the second bank of elevators, look for a series of four squarish marble slabs on your left.

Nike Adjusting Her Sandal Relief (c. 410 B.C.)

This relief originally decorated the Temple of Athena Nike (which stands near the entrance to the Acropolis). Nike figures had a better chance of survival through the ages than other statues, because anti-pagan Christian vandals mistook the winged Nikes for angels. Nearby is a display containing more chunks of the Temple of Athena Nike. You'll see toes gripping rocks, windblown robes, and realistically twisted bodies—exuberant, life-filled carvings signaling Athens' emergence from the Persian War.

• Turn right and go up the long gallery for a...

Side-Trip to Hellenistic and Roman Art

Before heading upstairs for the highlight of the collection, continue around on this floor to the small stretch of statues from the Hellenistic and Roman period. The head of Alexander the Great, on a square pillar in the center of the gallery, is a rare original, likely sculpted from life (336 B.C.). Alexander's upper lip curls, and his thick hair sprouts from the center of his forehead—immediately identifying this remarkable man. When he died in 323 B.C., this Macedonian had conquered Greece, embraced its customs, and spread Greek culture throughout the Mediterranean world and as far east as India.

Nearby, find a model that shows the Acropolis as it looked

in Roman times. The room also holds something that resembles a dirty soccer ball covered with graffiti. It's actually a spooky marble sphere etched with mysterious magic symbols (Roman, second or third century A.D.).

• *Now turn around, retracing your steps, and turn left at the bank of elevators. Around the corner, on their own, as if starring in their own revue on a beautifully lit stage, are the...*

Caryatids from the Erechtheion

Here stand four of the original six lady-columns that once supported the roof of the prestigious Erechtheion temple. (The six on the Acropolis today are copies; another original is in London's British Museum, and the last one is in France.) Despite their graceful appearance, these sculptures were fully functional structurally. Each has a fluted column for a leg, a capital-like hat, and buttressing locks of hair in the back. The caryatids were modeled on and named after the famously upright women of Karyai, near Sparta.

Time and the elements have ravaged these maidens. As recently as the 17th century (see the engravings), they had fragile arms holding baskets of flowers and jugs for ritual wine. Until the 1950s (before modern smog), their worn-down faces had crisp noses and mouths. In a half-century of Industrial Age pollution, they experienced more destruction than in the previous 2,000 years. But their future looks brighter now that they've been brought indoors out of the acidic air, cleaned up with a laser, and safely preserved for future generations. (For more on the caryatids in their original location, see page 126.)

There's a glass floor overhead, but you may not want to look up, out of respect for any female visitors wearing dresses above you.

• *Walk out of the Caryatid Gallery to the end of the building and ride the escalators up. Keep going up past Level Two, which has a restaurant and awesome view terrace. Head for the top floor—it's the reason you're here.*

Level Three

• *Before entering the actual Parthenon Gallery, sit in the atrium and enjoy the video on the Parthenon, which covers the temple's 2,500-year history, including a not-so-subtle jab at how Lord Elgin got the Marbles and made off with them to England. For more on Lord Elgin, see page 129.*

Parthenon Models

Two models show how the west and east pediment statues (which are mostly fragments today) would have looked in their prime.

The east pediment (the model on the right) features Nike crowning newly born Athena with a wreath of olive branches. Zeus' head is split open, allowing Athena, the goddess of wisdom, to rise from his brain fully grown and fully armed, inaugurating the Golden Age of Athens. The other gods at this Olympian banquet—naked men and clothed women—are astounded by the amazing event. At the far left, Helios' four horses are doing their morning chore, dragging the sun out of the sea. And on the far right, the sun follows the horses back as it sets into the sea again.

The west pediment model (on the left) shows Athena and Poseidon competing for Athens' favor by giving gifts to the city. Poseidon spurts water (beneath him) and Athena presents an olive tree (behind). A big, heavenly audience looks on. Had Poseidon bested Athena, you'd be in Poseidonia today instead of Athens. Among the bystanders—tucked into the left corner of the pediment—are the mythical king of Athens and his daughters (Kekrops and Pandrosos). Passed over by Lord Elgin, their now headless and limbless statues are on display in the next room.

• *Leave the atrium and enter the huge gallery.*

The Parthenon Frieze

In the center of the room stands the museum's highlight—a life-size mock-up of the 525-foot frieze that once wrapped all the way around the outside of the Parthenon. The relief panels depict the annual parade, the Panathenaic procession, in which citizens climbed up the Acropolis to celebrate the birth of the city. Circle the perimeter and watch the parade unfold.

Men on horseback, chariots, musicians, children, and animals for sacrifice are all part of the grand parade, all heading in the same direction—uphill. Prance on. At the heart of the procession are maidens dressed in pleated robes. They shuffle along, carrying gifts for the gods, including incense burners, along with jugs of wine and bowls to pour out offerings. The procession culminates in the presentation of the *peplos* to Athena, as the gods look on.

Notice the details—for example, the muscles and veins in the horses' legs and the intricate folds in the cloaks and dresses. Some panels have holes drilled in them, where accessories such as gleaming bronze reins were fitted to heighten the festive look. Of course, all of these panels were originally painted in realistic colors. As you move along, notice that, despite the bustle of figures posed every which way, the frieze has one unifying element—all of the people's heads are at the same level, creating a single ribbon around the Parthenon.

Of the 525-foot-long frieze, the museum owns only 32 feet of original panels. These parts were already so acid-worn in 1801 that Lord Elgin didn't bother taking them. Filling in the gaps in this jigsaw puzzle are white plaster replicas of panels still in London's British Museum (marked BM), in Paris' Louvre, and in Copenhagen. Blank spaces represent the panels that were lost forever. Small 17th-century engravings show how the frieze looked before the 1687 explosion that devastated the Parthenon.

• *Now stroll through the gallery and look out the windows. Take a moment to...*

Ponder the Parthenon

There's the Parthenon itself, perched on the adjacent hilltop. The museum "disappears" around you, leaving you to enjoy the art and the temple it once decorated. The Parthenon is one of the most influential works humankind has ever created. For 2,500 years, it's inspired generations of architects, sculptors, painters, engineers, and visitors from around the globe. Here in the Acropolis Museum, you can experience the power of this cultural landmark. The people of Athens relish the Acropolis Museum. Local guides grow taller with every visit, knowing that Greece finally has a suit-

able place to preserve and share the best of its artistic heritage.

• *On your way down, stop by the restaurant on Level Two for its exterior terrace and the awesome view of the Acropolis. You're allowed to take photos here—and why not pay homage to Athena, too, while you're at it?*

NATIONAL ARCHAEOLOGICAL MUSEUM TOUR

ΕΘΝΙΚΟ ΑΡΧΑΙΟΛΟΓΙΚΟ ΜΟΥΣΕΙΟ /
Εθνικό Αρχαιολογικό Μουσείο

The National Archaeological Museum is far and away the top ancient Greek art collection anywhere. Ancient Greece set the tone for all Western art that followed, and this museum lets you trace its evolution—taking you in air-conditioned comfort from 7000 B.C. to A.D. 500 through beautifully displayed and described exhibits on one floor. You'll see the rise and fall of Greece's various civilizations: the Minoans, Mycenaeans, those of Archaic Greece, the Classical Age, and Alexander the Great, and the Romans who came from the west. You can also watch Greek sculpture evolve: from prehistoric Barbie dolls; to stiff Egyptian-style; to the *David*-like balance of the Golden Age; to wet T-shirt, buckin'-bronco Hellenistic; and finally, to the influence of the Romans. Walk once around fast for a time-lapse effect, then go around again for a closer look.

This museum is a great way to either start or finish off your sightseeing through Greece. It's especially helpful for those travel-ing beyond Athens because it displays artifacts found else-where in Greece, including Mycenae, Epidavros, Santo-rini, and Olympia. In fact, the treasures displayed here are generally better than those remaining at the sites them-selves. The sheer beauty of the statues, vases, and paintings helps bring the country's dusty ruins to life.

Orientation

Cost: €7; free for kids 18 and under, on the first Sun of the month, and every Sun Nov-March.

Hours: May-Sept Tue-Sun 8:00-20:00, Mon 13:30-20:00; Oct-April Tue-Sun 8:30-15:00, Mon 13:30-19:30.

Getting There: The only major Athens sight outside the city center, the museum is a mile north of the Plaka at 28 Oktovriou (a.k.a. Patission) #44. A **taxi** between the Plaka and the museum is a steal at €4. The nearest **Metro** stop is Omonia (as you exit, follow signs to *28 Oktovriou/28 October Street*, and walk seven blocks to the museum). Or you can catch **bus** #200 or #400 from along Athinas street (just north of Monastiraki, right side of street) and go straight to the museum.

Information: Tel. 210-821-7717, www.namuseum.gr.

Tours: While there are no audioguides, live guides hang out in the lobby waiting to give you a €50, hour-long tour. My free audio version of this tour is available at www.ricksteves.com/audioeurope and from iTunes.

Length of This Tour: Allow two hours for this tour; more if you want to dig deeper into this world-class museum.

Baggage Check: Free and required, except for small purses.

Services: A museum shop, WCs, and an inviting café surround a shady and restful courtyard in the lower level (to access from the main entrance lobby, take the stairs down behind ticket desk); these are easiest to access at the beginning or end of your museum tour.

Photography: Photos are allowed, but no flash or goofy poses in front of statues. The Greek museum board considers this disrespectful of the ancient culture and is very serious about it—you'll hear, "No posing!" from stern guards if someone stands in front of the Zeus/Poseidon statue and tries to match his trident-throwing pose.

Starring: The gold Mask of Agamemnon, stately kouros and kore statues, the perfectly posed *Artemision Bronze*, the Horse and Jockey of Artemision, and the whole range of Greek art.

The Tour Begins

The collection is delightfully chronological. To sweep through Greek history, simply visit the numbered rooms in order. From the entrance lobby (Rooms 1-2), start with the rooms directly in front of you (Rooms 3-6), containing prehistoric and Mycenaean artifacts. Then circle clockwise around the building's perimeter on the ground floor (Rooms 7-33) to see the evolution of classical Greek statuary. Breeze through the rooms at the back of the building,

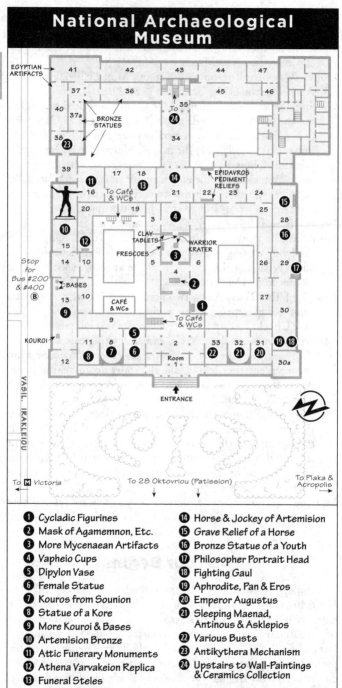

National Archaeological Museum

EGYPTIAN ARTIFACTS

BRONZE STATUES

EPIDAVROS PEDIMENT RELIEFS

To Café & WCs

CLAY TABLETS

WARRIOR KRATER

FRESCOES

Stop for Bus #200 & #400 B

BASES

CAFÉ & WCs

To Café & WCs

KOUROI

Room 1

ENTRANCE

VASIL. IRAKLEIOU

To M Victoria

To 28 Oktovriou (Patission)

To Plaka & Acropolis

① Cycladic Figurines
② Mask of Agamemnon, Etc.
③ More Mycenaean Artifacts
④ Vapheio Cups
⑤ Dipylon Vase
⑥ Female Statue
⑦ Kouros from Sounion
⑧ Statue of a Kore
⑨ More Kouroi & Bases
⑩ Artemision Bronze
⑪ Attic Funerary Monuments
⑫ Athena Varvakeion Replica
⑬ Funeral Steles
⑭ Horse & Jockey of Artemision
⑮ Grave Relief of a Horse
⑯ Bronze Statue of a Youth
⑰ Philosopher Portrait Head
⑱ Fighting Gaul
⑲ Aphrodite, Pan & Eros
⑳ Emperor Augustus
㉑ Sleeping Maenad, Antinous & Asklepios
㉒ Various Busts
㉓ Antikythera Mechanism
㉔ Upstairs to Wall-Paintings & Ceramics Collection

then go upstairs to see several more exhibits. Keep track of your ticket—you'll need to show it again to enter some of the exhibits.

The following self-guided tour zeroes in on a few choice pieces (out of many) that give an overview of the collection. See these items, then browse to your heart's content. Note that my descriptions here are brief—for more detail, read the excellent posted English information in each room.

• *From the entrance lobby, go straight ahead into the large central hall (Room 4). This first area—Rooms 3-6—is dedicated to prehistory (7000-1050 B.C.), including the treasures of the Mycenaeans. Start in the small side room to the right, Room 6. In several of this room's cases—including the one directly to the right as you enter—you'll find stiff marble figures with large heads. Look closely into that first case, filled with...*

❶ Cycladic Figurines

Goddess, corpse, fertility figure, good-luck amulet, spirit guide, beloved ancestor, or Neolithic porn? No one knows for sure the

purpose of these female figurines, which are older than the Egyptian pyramids. These statuettes were found all over Greece, particularly in the Cycladic Islands. The earliest Greeks may have worshipped a Great Mother earth goddess long before Zeus and company (variously called Gaia, Ge, Rhea, and other names), but it's not clear what connection she had, if any, with these statuettes. The ladies are always naked, usually with folded arms. The figures evolved over the years from flat-chested (c. 5000 B.C.), to violin-shaped, to skinny supermodels (c. 3000 B.C.). There is evidence that the eyes, lips, and ears were originally painted on.

The map on the wall (straight across from the entry) demarcates the Cycladic region, showing how the sacred island of Delos (described on page 416) marks the center of the circle, or cycle, formed by the Cycladic Islands. As these islands were in close proximity, there was plenty of trade and contact between them.

Before returning to the main room, stroll the long, dead-end Cycladic Hall. You'll see more figurines, painted vases, and tools such as knives and spears made of worked obsidian—a hard, shiny, black volcanic glass. Obsidian objects like these were probably exportable treasures, as the Cycladic society was a relatively peaceful culture with an artistic sense of style. Notice the finely painted bathtub on the left. You'll see carved marble bowls so thin and delicate that light shines through, along with bronze blades, tweezers, and needles. All of these artifacts are from around 2500 B.C., roughly 1,000 years before Mycenae and 2,000 years before Greece's Golden Age.

• *Return to the long central hall (Room 4), divided into four sections. Here you'll find...*

❷ Mycenaean Treasures, Including the Mask of Agamemnon (#624), c. 1550 B.C.

Room 4 displays artifacts found in the ruins of the ancient fortress-city of Mycenae, 80 miles west of Athens. Besides the famous Mask of Agamemnon, you'll see finely decorated swords, daggers, body armor, and jewelry, all found buried alongside bodies in Mycenaean graves. Many items were discovered in the cemetery that archaeologists call "Grave Circle A." (For more on the history of this site, see the Mycenae chapter.) The objects' intricately hammered detail and the elaborate funeral arrangements point to the

sophistication of this early culture.

In a glass case in the middle of the second section is the so-called Mask of Agamemnon. Made of gold and showing a man's bearded face, this mask was tied over the face of a dead man—note the tiny ear-holes for the string.

The Mycenaeans dominated southern Greece a thousand years before the Golden Age (1600-1200 B.C.). Their (real) history was lost in the misty era of Homer's (fanciful) legends of the Trojan War. Then Mycenae was unearthed in the 19th century by the German archaeologist Heinrich Schliemann (the Indiana Johannes of his era). Schliemann had recently discovered the real-life ruins of Troy (in western Turkey), and he was convinced that Mycenae was the city of the Greeks who'd conquered Troy. That much, at least, may be historically true. Schliemann went on to declare this funeral mask to be that of the legendary King Agamemnon, which *isn't* true, since the mask (c. 1550 B.C.) predates the fall of Troy (c. 1200 B.C.).

You're surrounded by 14 kilos (30 pounds) of gold pounded into decorative funerary objects, excavated from the coffins of 19 bodies found in a circular tomb. Notice the baby whose entire body was covered in a gold-leaf blanket when buried.

On the back side of the Mask of Agamemnon case, look closely at the knife and sheath with a warrior-versus-lions scene. Compared with the Minoan and Cycladic civilizations, Mycenaean society was warlike, and their weapons were artfully rendered. Note the light and flexible bone helmet nearby. The colorful wall

frescoes show a Minoan influence and feature scenes such as men with dogs hunting wild boar, and men ritually leaping over bulls.
• *In the next section of Room 4, you'll find...*

❸ More Mycenaean Artifacts

A **model of the Acropolis of Mycenae** (left side) shows the dramatic hilltop citadel where many of these objects were unearthed. Find the famous Lion Gate entrance (#1 on the model), the round cemetery known as "Grave Circle A" (#2), and the king's royal palace crowning the hill (#8). Also in Room 4 are **frescoes** from the royal palace, done in bright colors in the Minoan style. **Clay tablets** show the Mycenaean written language known as "Linear B," whose syllabic script (in which marks stand for syllables, as in Japanese) was cracked only 50 years ago.
• *Look at the back side of the display case in the center of this section.*

The painted, two-handled vase known as the **Warrior Krater (#1426)** was Schliemann's favorite find. A woman (far left) waves

goodbye to a line of warriors heading off to war, with their fancy armor and duffle bags hanging from their spears. While this provided the world with its first glimpse of a Mycenaean soldier, it's a timeless scene with countless echoes across the generations.
• *In the center of the last section of Room 4 is a glass case displaying the...*

❹ Vapheio Cups (#1758 and #1759), c. 1600-1550 B.C.

The intricate metal-worked detail on #1758 shows a charging bull sending a guy head over heels. On #1759, you'll see a bull and a

cow making eyes at each other, while the hind leg of another bull gets tied up by one good-looking cowboy. These realistic, joyous scenes are the product of the two civilizations that made 15th-century B.C. Greece the wonder of Europe—the

Mycenaeans and the Minoan culture of Crete.

But around 1450 B.C., the Minoan society collapsed, and Minoan artisans had to find work painting frescoes and making cups for the rising Mycenaean culture. Then around 1200 B.C., the Mycenaeans disappeared from history's radar screen. Whether from invasion, famine, internal strife, or natural disaster, these sudden disappearances plunged Greece into 400 years of Dark Ages (c. 1200-800 B.C.). Little survives from that chaotic time, so let's pick up the thread of history as Greece began to recover a few centuries later.

• *Backtrack to the entrance lobby and begin circling right (clockwise) around the perimeter of the building, starting in Room 7. After showing your ticket again to enter this room, look for the tall vase on your right.*

❺ Dipylon Vase (Monumental Attic Grave Amphora, #804), c. 750 B.C.

This ochre-and-black vase, nearly four feet tall, is painted with a funeral scene. In the center, a dead man lies on a funeral bier,

flanked by a line of mourners, who pull their hair in grief. It's far from realistic. The triangular torsos, square arms, circular heads, and bands of geometric patterns epitomize what's known as the Geometric Period (760-750 B.C.). A few realistic notes pop through, such as the raw emotions of the mourners and some grazing antelope (near the top). Note the one little child in attendance. Discovered in Athens' Keramikos Cemetery, the vase gets its name from the nearby Dipylon Gate, the ancient city's renowned main entrance.

After four centuries of Dark Ages and war, the Greeks of the eighth century B.C. were finally settling down, establishing cities, and expanding abroad (as seen on the map behind the big vase), with colonies in Western Turkey (Ionia), southern Italy (Magna Graecia), and Sicily. They were developing a written language and achieving the social stability that could afford to generate art. This vase is a baby step in that progression. Next, large-scale statues in stone were developed.

• *In Rooms 7-14, you'll get a look at some of these giant statues, including...*

Early Greek Statues: Kore and Kouros, c. 700-500 B.C.

Some of the earliest surviving examples of post-Mycenaean Greek art are these life-size and larger-than-life statues of clothed young women (called kore) and naked young men (called kouros). Influenced by ancient statues of Egyptian pharaohs, the earliest of these are big and stiff, with triangular faces and arms at their sides. As you walk through the next few rooms, you'll see the statues become more realistic and natural in their movements, with more personality than we see in these earlier rigid shells.

• *Take a closer look at a few particular statues. First, facing the vase in the middle of Room 7 is a...*

❻ Female Statue (#1), c. 650 B.C.

With hands at her sides, a skinny figure, a rectangular shape, and dressed in a full-length robe (called a chiton), this kore looks as much like a pillar as a woman. Her lion-mane hairstyle resembles an Egyptian headdress. The writing down her left leg says she's dedicated to Apollo. Stroll around. The Egyptian influence is clear.

• *In the next room (Room 8), your eyes go right to a very nice pair of knees that belong to a...*

❼ Kouros from Sounion (#2720), c. 600 B.C.

A typical kouros from the Archaic Period (c. 800-500 B.C.), this young naked man has braided dreadlocks and a stable forward-facing pose, and is stepping forward slightly with his left leg. His fists are clenched at his sides, and his scarred face obscures an Archaic smile—a placid smile that suggests the inner secret of happiness. His anatomy is strongly geometrical and stylized, with almond-shaped eyes, oval pecs, an arched ribcage, cylindrical thighs, and a too-perfect symmetry. The overdeveloped muscles (look at those quads!) and his narrow waist resemble those of an athletic teenager.

Rather than strict realism, kouros statues capture a geometric ideal. The proportions of the body parts follow strict rules—for example, most statues are precisely seven "heads" tall. Although this kouros steps forward slightly, his hips remain even (think about it—the hips of a real person would shift forward on one side). The Greeks were obsessed with the human body, and remember, these statues were of humans, not gods. Standing naked and alone, these statues represented a microcosm of the rational order of nature.

Statues were painted in vivid, lifelike colors. Notice that the rough surface of the marble lacks the translucent sheen of Classical Age statues (Archaic chisels were not yet strong or efficient enough to avoid shattering the crystalline marble).

Kouros statues were everywhere, presented as gifts to a god at a temple or to honor the dead in a cemetery. This one was dedicated to Poseidon at the entrance to the temple at Sounion. As a funeral figure, a kouros represented the deceased in his prime of youth and happiness, forever young.

• *Continue into the next room (Room 11). On the left, holding a flower, is a...*

❽ Statue of a Kore (#4889), c. 550 B.C.

Where a male kouros was either life-size or larger than life and naked (emphasizing masculine power), a female kore was often

slightly smaller than life and modestly clothed, capturing feminine grace. This petite kore stands with feet together, wearing a pleated chiton belted at the waist. Her hair is braided and held in place with a wreath, and she wears a necklace. Her right hand tugs at her dress, indicating motion (a nice trick if the artist lacks the skill to actually show it), while her left hand holds a flower. Like most ancient statues, she was painted in lifelike colors, including her skin. Her dress was red—you can still see traces of the paint—adorned with flower designs and a band of swastikas down the front. (In ancient times—before German archaeologist Schliemann's writings popularized it and Hitler appropriated it—the swastika was a harmless good-luck symbol representing the rays of the sun.) This kore, like all the statues in the room, has that distinct Archaic smile (or smirk, as the Greeks describe it). Browse around. Study the body types—the graceful, Avatar-like builds, those mysterious smirks, and the rigid hairdos.

• *The next room—a long hall labeled Room 13—has...*

❾ More Kouroi and Bases for Funerary Kouroi (#3476 and #3477)

These statues, from the late Archaic Period (around 500 B.C.), once decorated the tombs of hero athletes— perhaps famous Olympians. (The map just inside the door shows the continued expansion of

Greek civilization in the sixth century B.C.) Notice that these young men are slightly more relaxed and realistic, with better-formed thighs and bent elbows. Some kouros statues stood on pedestals, like the two square marble bases located farther down Room 13 (left side). The indentations atop each base held a kouros statue that represented an idealized version of the deceased. On the first base, the carved relief shows wrestlers and other athletes. Perhaps this was an excuse for the artist to show off a new ability to depict the body in a twisting pose. Notice the cute dog-and-cat fight. The second base features a game of field hockey— each scene reflecting the vigor of the deceased

The Four Stages of Greek Sculpture

Archaic (c. 800-500 B.C.): Rigid statues with stylized anatomy, facing forward, with braided hair and mysterious smiles (see photo at right).

Severe (c. 500-450 B.C.): More realistic and balanced statues (with no smiles), capturing a serious nobility.

Classical (c. 450-338 B.C.): Realistic statues whose poses strike a balance between movement and stillness, with understated emotion. (Within this period, the Golden Age was roughly 450-400 B.C.)

Hellenistic (c. 338-331 B.C.): Photorealistic (even ugly) humans engaged in dramatic, emotional struggles, captured in snapshot poses that can be wildly unbalanced.

man in his prime.

During the Archaic Period, Greece was prospering, growing, expanding, trading, and colonizing the Mediterranean. The smiles on the statues capture the bliss of a people settling down and living at peace. But in 480 B.C., Persia invaded, and those smiles suddenly vanished.

• *Pass through Room 14 and into Room 15, which is dominated by one of the jewels of the collection, the...*

❿ Bronze Statue of Zeus or Poseidon, Called the *Artemision Bronze* (#X. 15161), c. 460 B.C.

The god steps forward, raises his arm, sights along his other arm at the distant target, and prepares to hurl his thunderbolt (if it's

Zeus) or trident (if Poseidon). This statue was discovered amid a shipwreck off Cape Artemision in 1928. The weapon was never found, so no one knows for sure if this is Zeus or Poseidon.

The god stands 6'10" and has a physique like mine. His hair is curly and tied at the back, and his now-hollow eyes once shone white with inset bone. He plants his left foot and pushes off with the right. Even though every limb moves in a different direction, the whole effect is one of balance. The statue's dimensions are a study in Greek geometry. His head is one Greek foot high, and he's six heads tall (or one Greek fathom). The whole figure has an "X" shape that would fit into a perfect circle, with his navel at the center and his fingertips touching the rim. Although the bronze statue—cast with the "lost wax" technique (explained later, on page 170)—is fully three-dimensional, it's most impressive from the front. Later Greek statues seem fully alive from every angle, including the three-quarter view.

Zeus/Poseidon is an example of the so-called Severe style (500-450 B.C.). Historically, the Severe period covers the time when Greece battled the Persians and emerged victorious—the era when ordinary men shook off tyrants and controlled their own destiny through democracy. The Greeks were entering the dawn of the Golden Age. During this time of horrific war, the Greeks made art that was serious (no more Archaic smiles), unadorned, and expressed the noble strength and heroism of the individuals who had carried them through tough times. The statues are anatomically realistic, celebrating the human form.

With this statue of Zeus/Poseidon, his movements frozen in time, we can examine the wonder of the physical body. He's natural yet ideal, twisting yet balanced, moving while at rest. With his geometrical perfection and godlike air, the figure sums up all that is best about the art of the ancient world.

• *Browse the rest of the art in this room from this generation, including a mini-Zeus with a thunderbolt and a sacred eagle (just to the right of Poseidon), painted vases, and funeral monuments. Next, we enter the Golden Age. Room 16 is filled with big tall vases made of marble, labeled ⓫ Attic Funerary Monuments. These gravestones are in the shape of actual ceramic urns used as coffins to bury people in ancient times. (The Greeks also burned their dead on open biers.)*

Continue through Room 16 and into Room 17. The WCs and café are out the door and downstairs, in the courtyard. From Room 17, turn right into Rooms 19 and 20 (then right again, then left). At the dead-end is a small glass case containing the...

⓬ Statuette of Athena (#129), Called the *Athena Varvakeion,* c. A.D. 250, Original from 438 B.C.

This is the most famous copy of the statue of *Athena Varvakeion* by Pheidias—a one-twelfth-size replica of the 40-foot statue that once stood in the Parthenon (c. 438 B.C.). While this is just a miniature copy of the glorious original, it provides a good look at Greek art at its Golden Age pinnacle. Athena stands dressed in flowing robes, holding a small figure of Nike (goddess of victory) in her right hand and a shield in her left. Athena's helmet sprouts plumes with winged horses and a sphinx. To give a sense of scale of the original, the tiny Nike in Athena's hand was six feet tall in the Parthenon statue. Athena loved snakes, which shed their skin, representing renewal. There's a big one next to her shield, she wears a snake belt and bracelet, coiled snakes decorate her breastplate, and the snake-headed Medusa (whom Athena helped Perseus slay) adorns the center of her chest. (For more on the statue's original location, ✪ see the Acropolis Tour chapter.)

• *Backtrack to Room 17, turn right, and continue circling the museum clockwise into room 18, which has....*

⓭ Funeral Steles

The tombstones that fill this room, all from the fifth century B.C., are more good examples of Golden Age Greek art. With a mastery of the body, artists show poignant scenes of farewell, as loved ones bid a sad goodbye to the dead, who are seated. While the dead are often just shaking hands, there's usually a personal meaning with each scene. For example, on the tombstone opposite the window, a woman who died in childbirth looks at her baby, held by a servant as it reaches for its dead mother. Other scenes include a beautiful young woman who died in her prime, narcissistically gazing into a mirror. Servants are shown taking part in the sad event, as if considered part of the family. In the center of the room, a rich and powerful woman ponders which treasure from her jewel box to take with her into eternity. While shallow reliefs, these works are effectively three-dimensional. There's a timeless melancholy in the room, a sense that no matter who you are—or how powerful or affluent your family is—when you go, you go alone...and shrouds have no pockets.

• *Pass into Room 21, a large central hall. We'll take a temporary break from the chronological sequence to see statues dating from the second century B.C., when Greece was ruled by Rome. The hall is dominated by the...*

⓮ Bronze Statue of a Horse and Jockey of Artemision (#X.15177), c. 140 B.C.

The horse is in full stride, and the young jockey looks over his shoulder to see if anyone's gaining on them. In his left hand he holds the (missing) reins, while with his right he whips the horse to go even faster—maybe too fast, judging by the look on his face.

Greeks loved their horse races, and this statue may celebrate a victory at one of the Panhellenic Games. The jockey (who has the features of a non-Greek) is dressed in a traditional short tunic, has inlaid eyes, and was originally painted black—probably depicting a mixed-race Ethiopian.

The statue, like other ancient bronzes done by Greeks in Roman times, was made not by hammering sheets of metal, but with the classic "lost wax" technique. The artist would first make a rough version of the statue out of clay, cover it with a layer of wax, and then cover that with another layer of clay to make a form-fitting mold. When heated in a furnace to harden the mold, the wax would melt—or be "lost"—leaving a narrow space between the clay model and the mold. The artist would then pour molten bronze into the space, let it cool, break the mold, and—*voilà!*—end up with a hollow bronze statue. This particular statue was cast in pieces, which were then welded together. After the cast was removed, the artist added a few surface details and polished it smooth. Notice the delightful detail on the rider's spurs, which were lashed to his bare feet.

Stylistically, we've gone from stiff Archaic, to restrained Severe, to balanced Classical...to this preview of the unbridled emotion of Hellenism.

The other statues in the room are second-century B.C. Roman copies of fifth-century B.C. Greek originals. While the Romans were great warriors, engineers, and administrators, they had an inferiority complex when it came to art and high culture. For high-class Romans, Greek culture was the ideal, which created a huge demand for Greek statues. As demand exceeded supply, making copies of Greek originals became a big industry, and the Romans excelled at it. In fact, throughout Europe today, when you see a "Greek" statue, it's likely a Roman copy of a Greek original. Thanks to excellent copies like the ones in this room, we know what many (otherwise lost) Golden Age Greek masterpieces looked like.

By the way, while the Greeks could cast a freestanding bronze statue with no problem, when the Romans tried to re-create it in marble, the statue needed extra support. Here's a tip: When you see a tree trunk buttressing some statue...it's a Roman copy.

• *To return to our chronological tour (picking up back before the Romans arrived), head into Room 22, with pediment reliefs (Sack of Troy on the right, Greeks vs. Amazons on the left) that once decorated the Temple of Asklepios at Epidavros (see page 260). Pass through a couple of rooms displaying funeral monuments with progressively higher relief and more monumental scale until you reach the long Room 28, where you'll come face-to-face with a large...*

⓯ Grave Relief of a Horse (#4464), Late Fourth Century B.C.

The spirited horse steps lively and whinnies while an Ethiopian boy struggles with the bridle and tries to calm him with food. The

realistic detail of the horse's muscles and veins is astonishing, offset by the panther-skin blanket. The horse's head pops out of the relief, becoming fully three-dimensional. The boy's pose is slightly off-balance, anticipating the "un-posed poses" of later Hellenism. We sense the emotions of both the overmatched boy and the nervous horse. We also see a balance between the horse and boy, with the two figures creating a natural scene together rather than standing alone.

• *Farther down Room 28 stands the impressive, slightly-larger-than-life-size...*

⓰ Bronze Statue of a Youth (#X.13396), c. 340-330 B.C.

Scholars can't decide if this statue is reaching out to give someone an apple or demonstrating a split-finger fastball. He's most

likely the mythical Paris, awarding a golden apple to the winner of a beauty contest between goddesses (sparking jealousies that started the Trojan War).

The statue is caught in mid-step as he reaches out, gazing intently at the person he's giving the object to. Split this youth vertically down the middle to see the *contrapposto* (or "counter-poise") stance of so many Classical statues. His left foot is stable, while the right moves slightly, causing his hips to shift. Meanwhile, his right arm is tense while the left hangs loose. These subtle, contrary motions are in perfect balance around the statue's vertical axis.

In the Classical Age, statues reached their peak of natural realism and balanced grace. During the following Hellenistic Period, sculptors added to that realism, injecting motion and drama. Statues are fully three-dimensional, interesting from every angle. Their poses are less rigid than those in the Archaic Period and less overtly heroic than those of the Severe. The beauty of the face, the perfection of the muscles, the balance of elegant grace and brute power—these represent the full ripeness of the art of this age.

• *Continue into the small Room 29. To the left of the following door, find a black bronze head in a glass case. Look into the wild and cynical inlaid eyes of this...*

⓱ Portrait Head from a Statue of a Philosopher (#X.13400), c. 240 B.C.

This philosopher was a Cynic, part of a movement of non-materialist nonconformists founded in the fourth century B.C. by Diogenes. The term "cynic" aptly describes these dislikable, arrogant guys with unkempt hair. The statue's aged, bearded face captures the personality of a distinct individual. It's typical of the Hellenistic Period, the time after the Macedonian Alexander the Great conquered Greece and proceeded to spread Greek values across much of the Mediterranean and beyond. Hellenistic Greek society promoted a Me-Generation individualism, and artists celebrated every-day people like this. Rather than Photoshop out their eccentricities, they presented their subjects warts and all. For the first time in history, we see human beings in all their gritty human glory: with wrinkles, male-pattern baldness, saggy boobs, and middle-age spread, all captured in less-than-noble poses.

This head, like a number of the museum's statues, was found by archaeologists on the seabed off the coast of Greece. Two separate shipwrecks in ancient times have yielded treasures now in this museum: At the wreck off Cape Artemision (north of Athens), Zeus/Poseidon and the *Horse and Jockey* were found. Another wreck, off the tiny island of Antikythira (near the southern tip of the Peloponnesian Peninsula), is the source of this statue, as well as the *Bronze Statue of a Youth* and the Antikythira Mechanism (which we'll see later).

• *Continue into the long Room 30 and head to the far end to find the...*

⓲ Statue of a Fighting Gaul (#247), c. 100 B.C.

Having been wounded in the thigh (note the hole), this soldier has fallen to one knee and reaches up to fend off the next blow. The helmet indicates that he's not a Greek, but a Gaul from Galatia (western Turkey). The artist catches the exact moment when the tide of battle is about to turn. The face of this Fighting Gaul says he's afraid he may become the Dying Gaul.

The statue sums up many of the features of Hellenistic art: He's frozen in motion, in a wild, unbalanced pose that dramatizes his inner thoughts. The diagonal pose runs up his left leg and out his head and outstretched arm. Rather than a noble, idealized god, this is an ordinary soldier caught in an extreme moment. His arms flail, his muscles strain, his eyes bulge, and he cries out in pain. This statue may have been paired with others, creating a theatrical mini-drama that heightens the emotion. Hellenism shows us the thrill of victory, and—in this case—the agony of defeat.

• *Directly to the right is a...*

⓳ Statue of Aphrodite, Pan, and Eros (#3335)

In this playful ensemble from the sacred island of Delos, Aphrodite—seen here in a rare total nude of a female—is about

to whack Pan with her sandal. Striking a classic *contrapposto* pose (with most of her weight on one foot), Aphrodite is more revealing than modest, her voluptuous body polished smooth. There's a bit of whimsy here, as Aphrodite seems to be saying, "Don't! Stop!"...but may instead be saying, "Don't stop." The actions of the (literally) horny Pan can also be interpreted in two ways: His left arm is forceful, but his right is gentle—holding her more like a dance partner. Eros, like an omnipresent Tinkerbell, comes to Aphrodite's aid—or does he? He has the power to save her if she wants help, but with a hand on Pan's horn and a wink, Eros seems to say, "OK, Pan, this is your chance. Come on, man, go for it." Pan can't believe his luck. This marble is finer than those used in earlier statues, and it has been polished to a sheen with an emery stone. As you walk around this delightful statue, enjoy the detail, from the pudgy baby feet and the remnants of red paint on the sandal to the way the figures all work together in a cohesive vignette.

Across the room, another sculpture shows the ability of the artists of this age to capture action and tell a story. Find the carved relief showing two hairy men stomping grapes in big stone bins. Between them, like wrestlers dancing, two other brutes are toting a giant two-handled vase (krater) filled with grape juice, hauling it off to the next step in the process of becoming wine.

• *Now, enter Room 31 to see a...*

⓴ Statue of the Emperor Augustus (#X.23322), c. 12-10 B.C.

The Roman emperor rides commandingly atop a (missing) horse, holding the (missing) reins in his left hand. Although Greece was conquered by the Romans (146 B.C.), Greek culture ultimately "conquered" the Romans, as the Grecophile Romans imported Greek statues to Italy to beautify their villas. They preserved Greece's monuments and cranked out high-quality copies of Greek art. When the Roman Emperor Augustus began remaking the city of Rome, he used Greek-style Corinthian columns—a veneer of sophistication on buildings erected with no-nonsense, brick-and-concrete Roman-arch engineering. It's largely thanks to

the Romans and their respect for Greek culture that so much of this ancient art survives today.

• *Step into room 32 and find a beautiful woman asleep on a rock.*

㉑ Coffin Lid with a Sleeping Maenad, c. A.D. 120

In the center of the room is the lid of a coffin featuring a sleeping Maenad, a female follower of the god Dionysus. This Roman copy was made during the reign of Emperor Hadrian. Like a sleeping beauty, this slumbering Maenad lies exposed atop a rock on a soft skin of a panther. As if being mooned by the Maenad, a bust of the emperor himself stands on the nearby wall.

Hadrian was a Grecophile in two senses—he not only loved Greek culture, but he also had a hunky young Greek boyfriend named Antinous. Just to Hadrian's left is a fine portrait bust of **Antinous**—look into his disarmingly beautiful eyes. After the young man drowned in the Nile in A.D. 130, the depressed Hadrian had him deified and commissioned statues of him throughout the empire.

At the (missing) feet of the Maenad stands a statue of the Greek god of medicine, **Asklepios,** from the renowned ancient Sanctuary of Epidavros. Asklepios is portrayed with his snake and stick—back then, a snake's venom was considered to have mysterious healing powers. This statue is a Roman copy (A.D. 160) of a fourth-century Greek original.

• *Continue into Room 33 to see...*

㉒ Various Busts from the Late Empire, A.D. 300-500

These busts capture the generic features and somber expressions of the late Roman Empire. As Rome decayed and fell to barbarians,

the empire shifted its capital eastward to Constantinople (modern Istanbul). For the next thousand years, the Byzantine Empire—which included Greece—lived on as an enlightened, Christian, Greek-speaking enclave, while Western Europe fell into poverty and ignorance. During that time, Greek culture was mostly lost to the West, and lay hidden until it was rediscovered during Europe's Renaissance (c. 1500). Gradually, Greek sites were unearthed, its statues cleaned up and repaired, and Greek culture once again was revived in all its inspirational glory.

• *Exit into the entrance lobby and take a breath. You've seen the core of this museum and its highlights. If you have an appetite for more, stay on the ground level, and pass straight to the back-left corner of the building (passing through Rooms 4, 21, and 34). You'll find bronze statues in Rooms 36-39, and devotional offerings—statuettes and intricate artifacts—from the Sanctuary of Olympia. Egyptian artifacts are in Rooms 40 and 41.*

Room 38 has one of the most amazing items in the entire museum. It's the...

㉓ Antikythera Mechanism

This crude computer from the first century B.C. was recovered from the same shipwreck as the *Bronze Statue of a Youth*. While pretty corroded after 20 centuries underwater, its scant remains (along with X-rays of its gears) show an eerily advanced proto-computer. It was calibrated to show the positions of the sun and the moon, so astrologers could determine the exact date for telling fortunes. A modern reconstruction shows what the working mechanism may have looked like.

• *The museum's upper level holds one more major set of works that you should muster up the energy for: Minoan-age wall paintings. Find the ㉔ staircase in Room 35. At the top of the stairs, continue straight into Room 48, and go to the far end of the room to see the...*

Wall Paintings from Akrotiri, Thira (Santorini)

These magnificent frescoes were uncovered on the walls of homes at the ancient settlement of Akrotiri on the island of Thira (better known today as Santorini). When the island's volcano blew in a massive, bigger-than-Krakatoa eruption (c. 1630 B.C.), it preserved these frescoes in a thick blanket of ash. (Luckily, the town's inhabitants escaped, probably having been encouraged by a large earthquake and previous minor eruption to pack up their more-portable treasures in bubble wrap and find a less-cranky island.) For more about Akrotiri and the eruption, see the Santorini chapter.

Akrotiri was part of the Minoan culture, which was centered on the isle of Crete. Unlike most early peoples, the Minoans were

not fighters but traders, and their work made them prosperous. Their unfortified homes and palaces were decorated with colorful frescoes like these, which celebrate life in landscapes and everyday scenes. Swallows soar over hillsides of lilies. An antelope buck turns to make eyes at a doe. Two boys box. The frescoes are vivid, featuring primary colors of red, yellow, and blue, with thick black outlines. These are true frescoes, created by laying a coat of wet plaster on the walls and painting them before the plaster dried. The pigments interacted with the plaster, creating a glowing translucent effect. Remember that most early cultures used art only as propaganda for a king, to commemorate a famous battle, or to represent a god. But the Minoans were among the first to love beauty for its own sake. That love of beauty became part of the legacy of ancient Greece.

• As long as you're upstairs, you might as well enter Room 49 (turn left as you exit) to browse a world-class...

Ceramics Collection

Starting in this room, you can walk clockwise through eight rooms showing the evolution of pottery from the Bronze Age, to Geometric/Archaic, to Severe, to Classical. In the sixth century B.C., artists painted black figures on a red background. During the Classical Age, the trend was red-on-black (with the occasional red-and-black on white). It's amazing to see how these ancient potters mastered the art of creating three-dimensional scenes on a two-dimensional surface. Along the way, you can also see two well-preserved skeletons from the Keramikos Cemetery.

• Whew! Our tour is over.

SLEEPING IN ATHENS

Because of the economic situation in Greece, you'll find good values in Athens hotels. Prices are soft; and if you show up without a reservation, you'll often get a deep discount. Still, small, inexpensive hotels in the Plaka and Syntagma area are relatively scarce, listed in all the guidebooks, and filled with other tourists. For this reason, be willing to expand your search beyond the old center. I've found several gems in the Makrigianni and Koukaki neighborhoods, behind the Acropolis and a short walk from the Plaka action. These typically offer better value and a more sedate and authentic (rather than bustling and touristy) experience. Reserve ahead, especially in the summer months.

Check the hotel's website for special deals, and try asking for a lower price. Local travel agencies also have access to discount rates for many hotels (including some listed here). But don't be sucked in by some of the *very* cheap, too-good-to-be-true deals: Most of those are located in sleazy districts around Omonia Square, or down in the coastal suburbs of Glyfada and Voula—far from the places you've come to see. You'll pay a premium to stay near the Acropolis...and it's worth it. Many hotels have Acropolis-view rooms—some for no extra charge, but usually for a higher rate.

In general, lower your expectations. In ramshackle Athens, any room less than €85 will likely come with very well-worn bathrooms and furnishings. At least they're clean...or as clean as an old hotel room can be.

Some hotels include breakfast in their rates; others serve it for an extra per-person charge; and still others (usually the budget places) don't offer it at all—but can direct you to a nearby café or restaurant that serves a €5-6 breakfast. In my listings, you can assume that the prices include breakfast unless I note otherwise.

SLEEPING

Sleep Code

(€1 = about $1.40, country code: 30)
To help you sort easily through the listings, I've divided the rooms into three categories based on the price for a standard double room with bath in high season:

   $$$ Higher Priced—Most rooms €100 or more.
    $$ Moderately Priced—Most rooms between €70-100.
     $ Lower Priced—Most rooms €70 or less.

   Prices can change without notice; verify the hotel's current rates online or by email. For other updates, see www.ricksteves.com/update.

If you want a bathtub, ask for one when you reserve, as most hotel bathrooms have just a shower. While we're on the topic of bathrooms, note that Athens has ancient plumbing that clogs very easily. Rather than flushing toilet paper, dispose of it in the wastebasket next to the toilet. This may seem unusual, but it keeps the sewer system working and prevents you from getting cozy with your hotel janitor.

One final word: Athens is a noisy city, and Athenians like to stay out late. This, combined with the abundance of heavy traffic on city streets, can make things challenging for light sleepers. I've tried to recommend places in quieter areas, but that's not always possible. Many hotels were renovated for the Olympics, adding "soundproof" doors and windows that can be successful at blocking out noise. Still, be ready to use earplugs.

In the Plaka and Syntagma
Business-Class Hotels

These interchangeable places, scattered between the Plaka and Syntagma Square, were spiffed up for the 2004 Olympics. Today they offer predictable business-class comfort and fairly new-feeling rooms (though some can be a bit rough around the edges, especially the bathrooms). All have smart public spaces, air-conditioning, and elevators. Prices at these places tend to be soft; check their websites for special rates, and try to snare a discount during slow times.

$$$ Hotel Plaka and **Hotel Hermes** are owned by the same company and have rooms at the same price. Hotel Plaka has a rooftop bar/terrace and 67 modern rooms (some with Acropolis views) with updated bathrooms. The better-value Hotel Hermes has 45 even newer, nicer rooms on a quiet street closer to Syntagma and a little less convenient to the ancient sights (Sb-€69-99, Db-€89-135, Tb-€99-145, cheapest Nov-March, 10 percent discount when you reserve direct and show this book at check-in, check website for deals—mostly for longer stays, pay Wi-Fi). Hotel Plaka is at the corner of Mitropoleos and Kapnikarea (tel. 210-322-2096, fax 210-321-1800, www.plakahotel.gr, plaka@tourhotel.gr); Hotel Hermes is at Apollonos 19 (tel. 210-323-5514, fax 210-321-1800, www.hermeshotel.gr, hermes@tourhotel.gr).

$$$ **Central Hotel** has 84 sleek, mod rooms and an anonymous business-class vibe. There are several classes of rooms (determined by size and amenities, such as balconies and views). If you stick with the cheaper rooms, it's a good value (Sb-€93, standard Sb-€116, superior Sb-€124, superior-plus Sb-€137, Db-€114, standard Db-€138, superior Db-€145, superior-plus Db-€155, pay Internet access and cable Internet in rooms, elevator, air-con, rooftop terrace, Apollonos 21, tel. 210-323-4357, fax 210-322-5244, www.centralhotel.gr, reservation@centralhotel.gr).

$$$ **Athens Cypria Hotel** sits in the middle of a very local-feeling shopping zone, just above the Ermou pedestrian street. Its 115 rooms, designed for tour groups, have little character or personality, but do offer predictable comfort (April-June and Sept-Oct: Db-€130, July-Aug: Db-€120, Nov-March: Db-€98, €15 more for bigger and newer "superior" rooms, check website for deals, pay Internet access, free Wi-Fi in rooms, Diomias 5, tel. 210-323-8034, www.athenscypria.com, info@athenscypria.com).

Budget Hotels

$$ **Hotel Acropolis House** was once a wealthy lawyer's villa, and it still feels homey. You'll find antiques scattered amid the dark-wood furnishings in its lobby and 23 rooms. All rooms have mini-fridges and many have balconies—ask about one when you reserve. Rooms without a bath have a private bathroom across the hall (S-€55, Sb-€73, D-€68, Db-€83, 20 percent less off-season, reserve with credit card but pay in cash, air-con, no elevator, free Wi-Fi, Kodrou 6-8, tel. 210-322-2344, fax 210-322-6241, www.acropolishouse.gr, htlarchs@otenet.gr, charming Jasmine and Andreas).

$$ **Niki Hotel** has plenty of artistic flair. With New Age decor, 23 tight-but-trendy rooms, and reasonable rates, this popular place books up early (peak season: Sb/Db-€89-99 depending on demand, off-season: Sb/Db-€60-65, free Internet access and Wi-Fi, café, Nikis 27, tel. 210-322-0913, fax 210-322-0886, www.nikihotel.gr, info@nikihotel.gr).

$$ **Hotel Adonis,** with 26 slightly overpriced, retro-simple rooms, stands on the quiet, traffic-free upper reaches of Kodrou, right in the heart of the Plaka. The rooms on the fourth floor have

SLEEPING

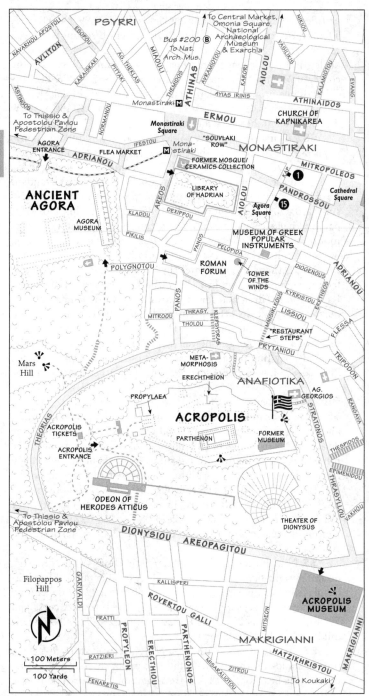

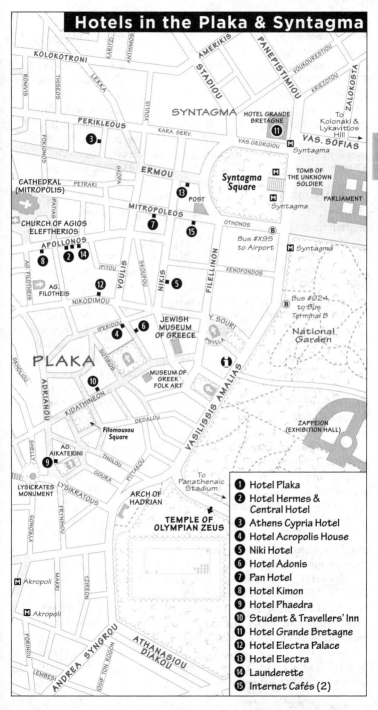

Hotels in the Plaka & Syntagma

SLEEPING

1. Hotel Plaka
2. Hotel Hermes & Central Hotel
3. Athens Cypria Hotel
4. Hotel Acropolis House
5. Niki Hotel
6. Hotel Adonis
7. Pan Hotel
8. Hotel Kimon
9. Hotel Phaedra
10. Student & Travellers' Inn
11. Hotel Grande Bretagne
12. Hotel Electra Palace
13. Hotel Electra
14. Launderette
15. Internet Cafés (2)

good views of the Acropolis, as does the rooftop bar. As it's popular, book ahead (Sb-€65, Db-€88, Tb-€103, cheaper for 3 nights or more, 40 percent cheaper Nov-March, roof-terrace breakfast, air-con, elevator, public areas can be smoky, Kodrou 3, tel. 210-324-9737, fax 210-323-1602, www.hotel-adonis.gr, info@hotel-adonis .gr, owner Spiros).

$$ Pan Hotel is an old-school business hotel centrally located just below Syntagma Square. The 33 rooms are ancient but well-maintained (Sb-€70, Db-€90, €10 cheaper Nov-March, skip breakfast to save some euros, air-con, elevator, pay Wi-Fi, Mitropoleos 11, tel. 210-323-7816, fax 210-323-7819, www.pan hotel.gr, reservations@panhotel.gr).

$ Hotel Kimon is a crank-'em-out hotel with little character. However, the 16 well-maintained, nicely appointed rooms have modern flair; the location—in the Plaka, near the cathedral—is handy; and the prices are affordable (Sb-€55, Db-€70, 10-20 percent less off-season, no breakfast, air-con, no elevator, Internet access and free Wi-Fi, rooftop garden overlooking the Acropolis, Apollonos 27, tel. 210-331-4658, fax 210-321-4203, www.kimon hotelathens.com, hotel_kimon@yahoo.gr).

$ Hotel Phaedra is simple but wonderfully located, over-looking a peaceful Plaka square with ancient ruins and a Byzantine church. The very institutional hallways lead to 21 nicely appointed rooms (Sb-€60, D-€65, twin Db-€70, Db with balcony-€80, T-€75, Tb-€90, 10 percent less off-season, breakfast-€5 extra, air-con, elevator, free Wi-Fi in lobby, 2 blocks from Hadrian's Arch at Cherefondos 16, at intersection with Adrianou, tel. 210-323-8461, fax 210-322-7795, www.hotelphaedra.com, info@hotelphaedra .com).

$ Student & Travellers' Inn, an HI hostel, is the best back-packer place in the Plaka, and the perfect spot to meet up with other young travelers. The 33 recently renovated rooms come in all shapes and sizes, from dorms with communal bathrooms to private rooms. An in-house travel agency specializes in trips to the Greek islands (dorm beds-€20-25 depending on size of room, S-€50, Sb-€55, D-€55, Db-€60, T-€70, Tb-€80, €1 less for hostel members, prices 30 percent cheaper Nov-March, breakfast-€3-5, open 24 hours, air-con, elevator, free Internet access and Wi-Fi, laundry service-€8, courtyard bar, kitchen, Kidathineon 16, tel. 210-324-4808, fax 210-321-0065, www.studenttravellersinn.com, info@studenttravellersinn.com, managed by Pericles, a.k.a. Perry). More beds at a cheaper price are available at the **Athens International Youth Hostel** (a.k.a. "Hotel Victor Hugo"), a high-rise hostel just outside the tourist zone near the Metaxourghio Metro stop (16 Victor Hugo, see map on page 184, tel. 210-523-2540, www.athens-international.com).

Cream of the Crop
$$$ Hotel Grande Bretagne, a five-star splurge with 320 sprawl-ing and elegantly furnished rooms, is considered the best hotel in Greece and ranks among the grand hotels of the world. It's *the* place to stay if you have royal blood—or wish you did and feel like being treated like royalty for a few days. Built in 1862 to accom-modate visiting heads of state, it became a hotel in 1874 and still retains its 19th-century elegance. No other hotel in Athens can boast such a rich history (Sb/Db-generally around €350, can vary based on demand, American-style breakfast-€35, air-con, elevator, free Wi-Fi, overlooking Syntagma Square at Vassileos Georgiou 1, tel. 210-333-0000, fax 210-322-8034, www.grandebretagne.gr, info@grandebretagne.gr). If you'd rather just eat here, consider their recommended rooftop restaurant.

$$$ Hotel Electra Palace is a luxury five-star hotel with 150 rooms in a nondescript urban zone where the Plaka meets Syntagma. It's pricey but plush, if a bit snooty, with top-notch ser-vice and elegance (Db-€230-300, "superior" Db with Acropolis view-€275-360; in slow times rates can drop to Db-€190, superior Db-€240; check website for deals, air-con, elevator, free cable Internet in rooms, free Wi-Fi in lobby, indoor pool, Acropolis-view outdoor pool, Nikodimou 18-20, tel. 210-337-0000, fax 210-324-1875, www.electrahotels.gr, salesepath@electrahotels.gr). Their second hotel—**Hotel Electra,** at #5 on the busy pedestrian Ermou street—has four stars and lower rates.

In and near Psyrri
$$$ Athens Center Square Hotel is part of the Plaka and Hermes Hotel chain but is much less expensive. Its 54 modern rooms are fresh, minimalist, and painted in colorful pastel hues, offering a comfortable base in the middle of the insane market scene. The wonderful roof garden has commanding Acropolis views (Sb-€59-99, Db-€70-125, 10 percent discount when you reserve direct and show this book at check-in, air-con, pay Wi-Fi, across from market hall just off Athinas street at Aristogitonos 15, reservation tel. 210-322-2706, reception tel. 210-321-1770, www.athenscenter squarehotel.gr, acs@athenshotelsgroup.com).

$$ Hotel Cecil has 36 rooms in a formerly grand, then faded, and now lightly updated old building. The rooms can be a bit worn, but the price is decent, the breakfast is generous, and the loca-tion—between Monastiraki and the Central Market, on the edge of the Psyrri neighborhood—is convenient. Its antique, iron-cage elevator is so rare that the manufacturer wanted it for the company museum and offered to replace it for free—but the owners declined (Sb-€55-70, Db-€75-105, about 20 percent less off-season, prices fluctuate with demand, air-con, free Wi-Fi, ask for quieter back

SLEEPING

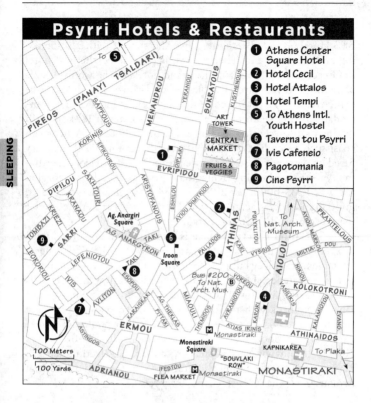

Psyrri Hotels & Restaurants

1. Athens Center Square Hotel
2. Hotel Cecil
3. Hotel Attalos
4. Hotel Tempi
5. To Athens Intl. Youth Hostel
6. Taverna tou Psyrri
7. Ivis Cafeneio
8. Pagotomania
9. Cine Psyrri

room, Athinas 39, tel. 210-321-7079, fax 210-321-8005, www.cecil .gr, info@cecil.gr, Trevlakis family).

$$ Hotel Attalos, an 80-room budget standby, is a bit tired but peaceful, friendly, and well-run. Their roof garden offers commanding Acropolis views and a great bar (Sb-€76, Db-€94, Tb-€110, Qb-€134, cheaper Nov-March, breakfast-€8, air-con, elevator, free Internet access and Wi-Fi, Athinas 29, tel. 210-321-2801, fax 210-324-3124, www.attaloshotel.com, info@attaloshotel .com).

$ Hotel Phidias, in the Thissio neighborhood behind the Ancient Agora, has a charming location right on the delightful Apostolou Pavlou pedestrian drag. The 15 rooms are dated and faded, but reasonably priced for this location. Streetside rooms get some noise from nearby cafés—especially on weekends—so ask for a quieter back room (Db-€70 but prices very soft, air-con, elevator, free Wi-Fi, Apostolou Pavlou 39—for location see map on page 205, tel. 210-345-9511, fax 210-345-9082, www.phidias .gr, phidiasa@otenet.gr, Vassilis).

$ Hotel Tempi, run by friendly Yiannis and Katerina, offers traditional hospitality at prices that won't break the bank. The 24

Makrigianni & Koukaki
Hotels & Restaurants

150 Meters
150 Yards

Filopappos Hill

FILOPAPPOS MONUMENT

MAKRIGIANNI

ACROPOLIS MUSEUM

Akropoli

KOUKAKI

Syngrou-Fix

KYNO-SARGOUS

1 Hotel Hera
2 Hotel Acropolis Select
3 Art Gallery Hotel
4 Athens Studios & Launderette
5 Marble House Pension
6 Tony's Hotel
7 Athens Backpackers Hostel
8 Mani Mani Restaurant
9 Strofi Athenian Restaurant
10 To Kati Allo Restaurant
11 Swift/Avanti Car Rental

spartan rooms are on a quiet, pedestrian-only section of Aiolou street, roughly between Syntagma Square and Monastiraki. The shared bathrooms are cramped and minimal—spring for a private bath unless you're on a tight budget. Ask for a room at the front—they come with balconies that overlook the flower markets on Plateia Agia Irini and have views of the Acropolis (S-€40, Sb-€50, D-€57, Db-€64, Tb-€75, cheaper Nov-March, air-con, no elevator, free Wi-Fi, lots of stairs, kitchen/breakfast room but no breakfast provided, Aiolou 29, tel. 210-321-3175, fax 210-325-4179, www.tempihotel.gr, info@tempihotel.gr).

In Makrigianni and Koukaki, Behind the Acropolis

The Plaka has all of the charm...and all of the noise, crowds, and higher prices. Instead, consider making the adjoining residential Makrigianni and Koukaki neighborhoods, just south of the Acropolis, your home base in Athens. With the Acropolis Museum standing boldly as its gateway, this typically Athenian urban area—full of six-story concrete apartment buildings, colorful grocery stores, and corner cafés—offers the chance to become a temporary Athenian. Most importantly, it allows easy access to the sights (all of the following hotels are within a 10-minute walk of the Dionysiou Areopagitou pedestrian boulevard under the Acropolis, and the edge of the Plaka). These hotels are all located between the Akropoli and Syngrou-Fix Metro stops on line 2/red.

$$$ Hotel Hera is a tempting splurge, with 38 plush rooms above a classy lobby. With helpful service, lots of thoughtful little touches, an air of elegance, and a handy location near the Acropolis end of this neighborhood, it's a great value for this price range (Sb-€135, Db-€155, €15 extra for Acropolis-view room on fourth floor, cheaper Nov-March, check website for deals, air-con, elevator, free Internet access and cable Internet in rooms, rooftop Acropolis-view restaurant open for dinner only, Falirou 9, tel. 210-923-6682, fax 210-923-8269, www.herahotel.gr, info@herahotel.gr).

$$$ Hotel Acropolis Select has 72 rooms over a stylish lobby. Well-run by Kyriaki, it features a can-do staff and a generous breakfast. Their service ethic goes way beyond the norm—they've been known to send a guide on a motorbike to lead lost drivers to the hotel (Db-€80-120 depending on size and season, air-con, elevator, pay Internet access and pay Wi-Fi, Falirou 37-39, tel. 210-921-1611, fax 210-921-6938, www.acropoliselect.gr, selective@ath.forthnet.gr).

$$ Art Gallery Hotel is a comfy, cozy, well-run small hotel with 22 rooms near the top of a pleasant, pedestrian stair-step lane. The original artwork in the halls and rooms adds boutique-hotel charm (Sb-€40-70, Db-€60-90, Tb-€80-110, breakfast-€7, air-con, elevator, free Internet access and Wi-Fi, Erecthiou 5, tel. 210-923-8376, fax 210-923-3025, www.artgalleryhotel.gr, art galleryhotel@gmail.com). Say hello to the hotel's cats—Nelly, Sugar, and Artie.

$$ Athens Studios, run by the gang at Athens Backpackers (described later), rents nicely appointed, good-value apartments with retro-mod decor, kitchens, and other nice touches (Db-€80, Tb-€90, Qb-€120, 5b-€130, 6b-€150, check website for deals, includes breakfast, air-con, elevator, pay Internet access, free Wi-Fi, ground-floor sports bar and launderette, long-term luggage storage available, Veikou 3A, tel. 210-923-5811, www.athens studios.gr, info@athensstudios.gr, Edward).

$ Marble House Pension is a small, family-run place hiding at the end of a little cul-de-sac, a few minutes' walk past my other listings in this area. The 16 cozy rooms are simple but well-cared for, and (true to its name) it's decorated with real marble. If you don't mind the dreary urban location, it's an excellent deal (Sb-€39, D-€45, Db-€49, Tb-€59, Qb-€65, cheaper late Oct-mid-March, breakfast-€5; air-con in some rooms-€9, ceiling fans in others; no elevator, free Internet access and Wi-Fi, 5-minute walk from Syngrou-Fix Metro at Zini 35a—from Zini street take the alley to the left of the tidy Catholic church, tel. 210-923-4058 or 210-922-8294, fax 210-922-6461, www.marblehouse.gr, info@marble house.gr).

$ Tony's Hotel is another budget option, renting 24 rooms in two adjacent buildings. The deluxe rooms in the newer building are smartly remodeled and come with mini-fridges and electric tea kettles (Sb-€55, deluxe Sb-€60, Db-€65, deluxe Db-€80-85, Tb-€75, deluxe Tb-€85-95, breakfast extra, cash only, air-con, free Internet access and Wi-Fi, Zaharitsa 26, tel. 210-923-0561, tel. & fax 210-923-6370, www.hoteltony.gr, tony@hoteltony.gr).

$ Athens Backpackers is the best place in town for back-packer bonding. Youthful and fun-loving (with two different bars on the premises), and well-run by gregarious Aussies, it offers good bunks and an opportunity to meet up with other travelers (€18-22/ bunk depending on season, all rooms have 6 beds and bathroom, includes breakfast, air-con, free Wi-Fi, launderette at Athens Studios, runs day trips from Athens, Makri 12, tel. 210-922-4044, www.backpackers.gr, info@backpackers.gr).

EATING IN ATHENS

Greek food is simple but delicious. Even here in the capital, there's little point in seeking out trendy, non-Greek eateries. Locals and tourists alike fill endless tavernas, *mezedopolio*s (eateries selling small plates called *mezedes*), *ouzeries* (bars selling ouzo liquor and pub grub), and other traditional eateries dishing up the basics. For tips on Greek cuisine, see page 25.

I've listed these restaurants by neighborhood. You probably won't be able to resist dining in the Plaka one night, but in that very touristy area, the prices are high and the quality is mixed. Don't be afraid to venture elsewhere. Thissio and Psyrri—very different but equally worthwhile dining zones—lie just beyond the Plaka, a short walk away. If you're staying in Makrigianni or Koukaki (or even if you aren't), I've listed a couple of good options there for your convenience. At some eateries, credit cards are not accepted, so bring cash.

In the Plaka

Diners—Greeks and tourists alike—flock to the Plaka. Frankly, in this neighborhood, the ambience is better than the food. I've avoided the obvious, touristy joints on the main pedestrian drag—with obnoxious touts out front trying to lure in diners with a desperate spiel—in favor of more authentic-feeling eateries huddled on the quieter hillside just above. Eat at one of my recommendations, or simply choose the place with your favorite view of the ancient monument, on a square that appeals to you, or with live music.

Traditional Greek Sit-Down Tavernas

Taverna O Thespis is a rarity that feels like the good old days in the Plaka. It's tucked away above the crowds along the sleepy, stepped Thespidos lane, with tables cascading down a series of breezy terraces and the floodlit walls of the Acropolis towering overhead. Inside, two dining rooms feature murals of old Athens and Greek gods. Dine affordably on traditional specialties, such as the €12 *bekri meze* (pork with flavorful sauce). The menu is limited to the same old Greek standards you'll find elsewhere...but here, everything seems particularly well-executed (€5 starters, most main dishes €8-10, some seafood splurges, handy fixed-price meals for €14 or €17 including wine, daily 11:00-24:00, Thespidos 18, tel. 210-323-8242, Vlahos family).

Palia Taverna tou Psara ("The Old Tavern of Psaras") is a big, slick, pricey eatery that enjoys bragging about the many illustrious guests they've hosted since opening in 1898. It's the kind of place where a rowdy, rollicking group of a hundred can slam down a dish-'em-up Greek meal. If you don't want a main course (€10-23), you can order a good selection of their *mezedes* (€3-14). There's seating in two kitty-corner buildings, plus tables on the atmospheric street between them. The lower building features live folk music and an outdoor terrace with views over Athens' rooftops (daily 11:00-24:00, music generally Thu-Sat from 21:00, signposted off Tripodon at Eretheos 16, tel. 210-321-8734).

Restaurant Hermion is a dressy wicker indulgence in a quiet arcade off traffic-free (and loaded-with-tourists) Pandrossou. Choose between outdoor seating in an inviting courtyard and a cool air-conditioned interior. Under a canvas canopy surrounded by potted plants, you forget you're in a big city. The menu offers a wide range of €6-11 salads and lots of fish (€6-13 starters, €10-25 grilled meats, €17-30 fish dishes, daily 11:30-24:00; with your back to cathedral, leave the square downhill to the left, going 50 yards down Pandrossou to *Hermion* sign, then follow arcade passageway to Pandrossou 15; tel. 210-324-7148).

Mezedes

Sholarhio Ouzeri Kouklis, at the intersection of Tripodon and Epicharmou streets, serves only the small plates called *mezedes* (*meh-ZEH-dehs;* known internationally as *mezes*). While you could assemble a meal of these Greek "tapas" at nearly any restaurant, this one makes it their specialty. It's fun, inexpensive, and ideal for small groups wanting to try a variety of traditional *mezedes* and drink good, homemade booze on an airy perch at the top of the Plaka. Since 1935, the Kouklis family has been making ouzo liquor and running their restaurant—

EATING

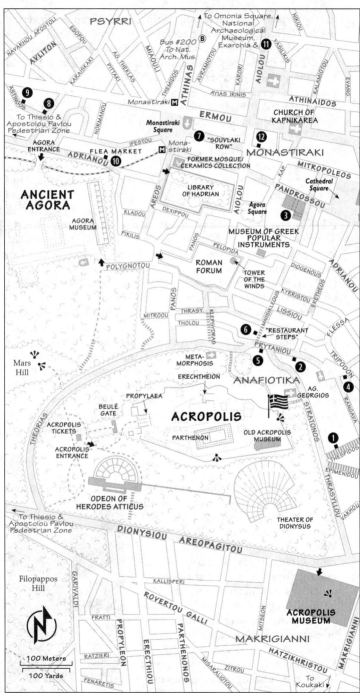

PSYRRI

To Omonia Square,
National
Archaeological
Museum,
Exarchia & ❶❶

Bus #200
To Nat.
Arch. Mus.

❾

❽

To Thissio &
Apostolou Pavlou
Pedestrian Zone

Monastiraki Ⓜ

ERMOU

CHURCH OF
KAPNIKAREA

ATHINAIDOS

AGORA
ENTRANCE

ADRIANOU

FLEA MARKET

❿

Monastiraki
Square

❼ "SOUVLAKI
ROW"

Monastiraki Ⓜ

❶❷ MONASTIRAKI

MITROPOLEOS

ANCIENT
AGORA

FORMER MOSQUE/
CERAMICS COLLECTION

LIBRARY
OF HADRIAN

Cathedral
Square

PANDROSSOU

AGORA
MUSEUM

KLADOU

DEXIPPOU

Agora
Square

❸

CATHEDRAL
SQUARE

PIKILIS

PELOPIDA

MUSEUM OF GREEK
POPULAR
INSTRUMENTS

ADRIANOU

POLYGNOTOU

ROMAN
FORUM

TOWER
OF THE
WINDS

DIOGENOUS

KYRRISTOU

EPETHEOS

FLESSA

MITROOU

THRASY.

THOLOU

LISSIOU

❻ "RESTAURANT
STEPS"

TRIPODON

Mars
Hill

PRYTANIOU

❺

META-
MORPHOSIS

❷

ANAFIOTIKA

❹

ERECHTHEION

AG.
GEORGIOS

RANGAVA

PROPYLAEA

THEORIAS

BEULÉ
GATE

ACROPOLIS
TICKETS

ACROPOLIS

STRATONOS

ACROPOLIS
ENTRANCE

PARTHENON

OLD ACROPOLIS
MUSEUM

❶

THESPIDOS

EPIMENIDOU

THRASYLLOU

VAKHOU

ODEON OF
HERODES ATTICUS

THEATER OF
DIONYSUS

To Thissio &
Apostolou Pavlou
Pedestrian Zone

DIONYSIOU   AREOPAGITOU

Filopappos
Hill

KALLISPERI

ACROPOLIS
MUSEUM

GARIVALDI

ROVERTOU GALLI

PROPYLEON

PARTHENONOS

ERECHTHIOU

MITSEON

MAKRIGIANNI

FRATTI

MAKRIGIANNI

RATZIERI

HATZIKHRISTOU

100 Meters

100 Yards

FENARETIS

ZITROU

MISARALIOTOU

To
Koukaki

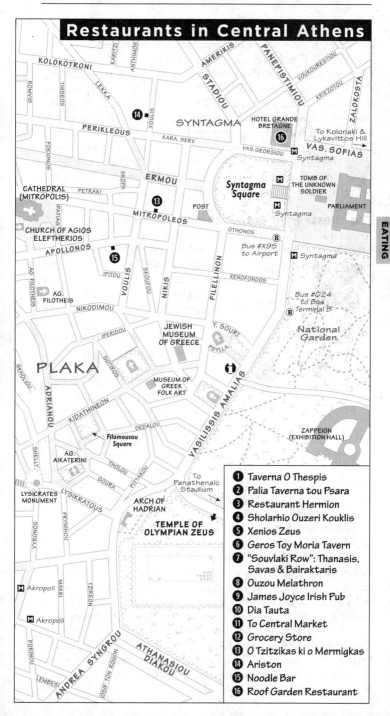

Restaurants in Central Athens

EATING

1. Taverna O Thespis
2. Palia Taverna tou Psara
3. Restaurant Hermion
4. Sholarhio Ouzeri Kouklis
5. Xenios Zeus
6. Geros Toy Moria Tavern
7. "Souvlaki Row": Thanasis, Savas & Bairaktaris
8. Ouzou Melathron
9. James Joyce Irish Pub
10. Dia Tauta
11. To Central Market
12. Grocery Store
13. O Tzitzikas ki o Mermigkas
14. Ariston
15. Noodle Bar
16. Roof Garden Restaurant

which maintains a 1930s atmosphere to this day. The waiter comes around with a big platter of dishes, and you choose what you like (€3-6/plate). Drinks are cheap, dessert is free, and the stress-free €14 meal deals are worth considering. As the plates are pretty big, this is most fun with a group of four or more. Many people sit on the street, waiting for a spot to open up on their lively front terrace, but you can also climb the spiral staircase to the often-empty upstairs area with its tiny romantic balconies for two. This place is in all the guidebooks—hardly a local scene, but still enjoyable (daily 11:00-2:00 in the morning, Tripodon 14, tel. 210-324-7605). Upon request, Nikos and his gang welcome anyone with this book with a free taste of homemade ouzo.

The "Restaurant Steps" at Mnisikleous Street

At the top of the Plaka, the stepped lane called Mnisikleous (stretching up toward the Acropolis) is lined with eateries featuring interchangeable food and delightful outdoor seating. It's enjoyable to climb the stairs and window-shop along this dreamy drag. Note that most of these places have live music and/or rooftop gardens. Don't limit your search to just these two eateries; seek out the music and setting you like best.

Xenios Zeus (ΞΕΝΙΟΣ ΖΕΥΣ), sitting proudly at the top of the Mnisikleous steps, is in every sense a step above the others. Exuberant Eleni and her husband Yiannis offer good, traditional Greek food inside or out on a terrace overlooking Athens' rooftops. Eleni prides herself on using only fresh ingredients... and it shows. Your meal starts with a €1.50 piece of toasted village bread with garlic and olive oil. Consider their "special menu," a €12 *mezedes* sampler plate (€3-8 appetizers, €9-20 main dishes, €15-18 fixed-price meals, daily 10:00-24:00, closed Nov-Feb, Mnisikleous 37, tel. 210-324-9514).

Geros Toy Moria Tavern is probably the best-regarded of the eateries that line the steps. It has three eating areas: the "oldest tavern in the Plaka"—a group-friendly, powerfully air-conditioned indoor dining hall featuring a more-formal menu and live Greek music and dance (no cover, nightly from 20:15); the more intimate Palio Tetradio ("Old Notebook"), with a terrace, nostalgic/cozy-in-the-winter indoor seating, and more *mezedes;* and, maybe best of all, tables along the steps under grapevines (€4-9 starters and salads, €9-20 main dishes, daily 9:00-3:00 in the morning, Mnisikleous 27, tel. 210-322-1753).

In Monastiraki
Eating Cheap on "Souvlaki Row"

Monastiraki Square (where it meets Mitropoleos street) is a popular place to head for fast food. This is souvlaki heaven, with several frantic restaurants—Thanasis, Savas, and Bairaktaris—spilling into the street and keeping hordes of hungry eaters happy. Souvlaki is grilled meat on a skewer, served on a plate or wrapped in pita bread to make a sandwich. These places also sell meat shaved from gyros, hearty Greek salads, wine, beer, and ouzo. Souvlaki goes well with *tzatziki*, the thick, garlicky yogurt-and-cucumber sauce. First decide whether you want your meal "to go" or at a table.

Take-Out: Gyros or a single souvlaki sandwich wrapped in a pita "to go" cost about €1.70—these places can fill and wrap a pita before you can blink. For these cheap carry-out prices, order and pay at the cashier, then take your receipt to the counter to claim your meal. It can be tricky to find a comfortable bench or other suitable perch in this crowded neighborhood—plan to munch as you walk (and watch out for the inevitable dribbles of souvlaki juice).

Table Service: The joints here on "Souvlaki Row" offer a good value if you're getting your food "to go." But you'll pay substantially more to sit and be waited on. Still, the ambience is lively, especially at the outdoor tables. A big plate of four souvlaki (plus pita bread, onions, and tomatoes) costs €9-10; a smaller helping of two souvlaki—plenty for most eaters—runs about €5-6.

Two popular options face each other across the street: **Thanasis** is famous for its special kebab, made from a traditional recipe that combines ground beef and lamb with Thanasis' secret blend of seasonings (daily 10:00-2:00 in the morning, Mitropoleos 69, tel. 210-324-4705). **Savas** is another old favorite with a similar menu and a little less character (daily 10:00-3:00 in the morning, Mitropoleos 86, tel. 210-324-5048). The dominant operation, **Bairaktaris,** offers lesser value.

Elsewhere in Monastiraki

Ouzou Melathron is a Greek T.G.I. Friday's, with a huge menu of fun food including *mezedes* (€5-8 appetizers, €8-10 salads, open daily, corner of Filippou and Astiggos, tel. 210-324-0716).

The **James Joyce Irish Pub** offers an escape from Greece. Stepping inside, the complete Irish-pub menu (€8-12 main dishes), top Irish beers on tap, air-conditioned freshness, and rock 'n' roll ambience combine to transport you to Ireland (between the Thissio temple and Ermou street at Astiggos 12, tel. 210-323-5055, Tom Cameron).

An enticing stretch of traditional restaurants sits along Adrianou across from the Ancient Agora. I ate well at **Dia Tauta** (a.k.a. Dai Tafta), which offers the usual Greek standards and makes a yummy *bouyiourdi*—vegetables baked with feta cheese and chili pepper. The free olives and carafes of tap water are nice touches (€4-7 starters, €8-15 main dishes, daily 9:30-1:30 in the morning, 37 Adrianou, tel. 210-321-2347).

Picnics

To assemble a cheap meal of your own, head 500 yards north of Monastiraki (on Athinas) to the **Central Market.** For details, see page 79. There are no big supermarkets nearby, but the **Soros grocery store** stays open long hours and stocks enough for you to throw together a decent picnic (daily 8:00-22:00, near "Souvlaki Row" at Mitropoleos 78, tel. 210-322-6677).

For other inexpensive alternatives, check out "Souvlaki Row" (described earlier) or the pies at Ariston (described later).

Around Syntagma Square

O Tzitzikas ki o Mermigkas ("The Ant and the Cricket") serves up pricey, updated, regional Greek cuisine. Choose between the two levels of indoor seating in a fun, mod, retro-grocery-store atmosphere, or grab a sidewalk table. It's named for the beloved folktale about an ant who works hard all summer to prepare for the winter, while the lazy cricket goofs off...only to come asking for help when winter arrives (€6-11 starters, €10-14 main dishes, Mon-Sat 13:00-1:00 in the morning, Sun 13:00-23:00, Mitropoleos 12-14, tel. 210-324-7607).

Cheap and Tasty Pies: **Ariston** (ΑΡΙΣΤΟΝ), in business for nearly a century, is one of Athens' top spots for a wide range of savory and sweet pastries (less than €2 apiece). Choose between *spanakopita* (spinach pie), *tiropita* (cheese pie), *kreatopita* (lamb pie), *meletzanitopita* (eggplant pie), and lots more (leek, shrimp, olives and feta, and so on...all labeled in English). They also have lovely sweet desserts made with flaky phyllo pastry. This is perhaps the cheapest hot meal in town (Mon-Sat 7:30-18:00, until 21:00 on Tue-Wed and Fri, closed Sun, 2 blocks from Syntagma toward the Plaka at Voulis 10, tel. 210-322-7626).

Asian: **Noodle Bar** offers a break from Greek fare, with tasty pan-Asian dishes in a small, informal, indoor-outdoor setting in an urban zone, a few blocks from Syntagma Square (salads, soups, wok dishes, rice dishes, most meals €5-9, also carry-out, daily 12:00-24:00, Apollonos 11, tel. 210-331-8585).

Splurge: **Hotel Grande Bretagne's Roof Garden Restaurant** is considered by many the finest place in town to dine on Greek and Mediterranean cuisine in pure elegance—in a rooftop garden with spectacular Acropolis and city views (€15-30 pastas, €30-40 main dishes, plan on spending €60 for dinner, daily 13:00-1:00 in the morning, reservations required for meals, "smart casual" dress code, north side of Syntagma Square, tel. 210-333-0766). If you don't want such an expensive meal, drop by their bar for a €10 beer or a €16 cocktail.

In Psyrri

The thriving Psyrri nightlife district, just north of Monastiraki, is one of Athens' most enjoyable areas to explore. To locate the following restaurants, see the map on page 184. Most eateries are concentrated near the squares called Iroon and Agii Anargiri, and a couple of reliable local options offer unpretentious decor and food at reasonable prices.

Taverna tou Psyrri, right in the heart of the restaurant action, is older and more authentic-feeling than other nearby Psyrri eateries, with red-and-white-checkerboard tablecloths, a straightforward menu, and good prices (€3-6 starters, €7-10 main dishes, daily 13:00-24:00, Eshilou 12—look for the drunk clinging to the lamppost out front, tel. 210-321-4923).

Ivis Cafeneio is a tiny corner ouzo pub run with a passion for tradition. The owner plays traditional Greek music and offers a Greek-only menu featuring a tiny selection of modern Mediterranean dishes. While splashier eateries abound, this joint is a classic. The calamari is good here (€3-5 plates, daily 13:00-24:00, corner of Ivis and Navarhou Apostoli just off Ermou, tel. 210-323-2554).

Ice Cream: It's hard to miss—or resist—**Pagotomania,** in the heart of Psyrri, with its display case bursting with colorful mounds of tasty ice cream (€2 for a small cone, open long hours daily, corner of Taki and Esopou, tel. 210-323-0001).

In Thissio

Filistro (Φίλιστρο), on a tranquil stretch of the Apostolou Pavlou promenade just beyond the heart of the outdoor café zone, offers one of the best dining experiences in Athens. They serve great regional dishes from around Greece at fair prices, and their delightful rooftop terrace makes a memorable perch, with panoramic views of the Acropolis, Lykavittos Hill, and Athens receding to the horizon. Ask your waiter about daily specials— four starters make a good meal for two (€5-11 starters, €8-15 main dishes, Tue-Sun 12:00-24:00, July-Aug from 18:00, closed Mon, cozy country interior, Apostolou Pavlou 23—see map on page 205, tel. 210-342-2897).

In Makrigianni and Koukaki, Near the Acropolis Museum

New development in this area, including the Akropoli Metro stop, has brought with it a trendy and touristy row of restaurants, cafés, and ice-cream shops along pedestrian Makrigianni street facing the Acropolis Museum. The other pedestrian street, Dionysiou Areopagitou, also has plenty of tourist-friendly options between the museum and the Arch of Hadrian. The Makrigianni and Koukaki neighborhoods are also home to several recommended hotels. If you're staying here and would rather not venture to other parts of town for a meal, consider these options. For locations, see the map on page 185.

Mani Mani offers a touch of class for reasonable prices. The focus is on cuisine from the Mani Peninsula (see Kardamyli and the Mani Peninsula chapter), so you'll find some pleasantly atypical options here—a nice change of pace from the same old standards. The decor, like the food, is thoughtfully updated Greek, with a soothing green-and-white color scheme. As it's all indoor seating, this is an especially good bad-weather option (€5-9 starters, €9-13 main dishes, Tue-Sat 13:00-17:30 & 20:00-24:00, Sun 13:00-17:30, closed Mon, reservations smart, look for low-profile green *MANH MANH* banner at Falirou 10 and go upstairs, tel. 210-921-8180).

Strofi Athenian Restaurant is my favorite place in town for white-tablecloth, elegantly modern, rooftop-Acropolis-view dining. A five-minute walk from the tourist crush, Niko Bletsos and his staff need to be as good as they are. Once you're seated on their rooftop enjoying classic Greek cuisine—especially lamb—under a floodlit Acropolis, you'll be glad you made dinner reservations here. While they have a fine air-conditioned interior, the breeze makes the rooftop comfortable even on hot evenings (€5-9 starters, €10-14 main dishes, daily 12:00-24:00, about 100 yards down Propyleon street off Dionysiou Areopagitou at Rovertou Galli 25, tel. 210-921-4130).

To Kati Allo Restaurant, under the far side of the Acropolis Museum, lacks tourists and is the quintessential neighborhood hole-in-the-wall. Run by English-speaking Kostas Bakatelos and his family, this place offers both sidewalk seating and (cooled-by-a-fan) inside tables. The menu, written on a blackboard, features a short list of cheap, fresh, and tasty local options (€6-8 main dishes, open daily, just off Makrigianni street at Hatzichristou 12, tel. 210-922-3071).

EATING

SHOPPING IN ATHENS

While not quite a top shopping destination, Athens offers plenty of opportunities for visitors who want to pick up some good Greek souvenirs.

The main streets of the Plaka—especially **Adrianou** and **Pandrossou**—are crammed with crass tourist-trap shops, selling cheap plaster replicas of ancient artifacts, along with calendars, playing cards, postcards, and shockingly profane T-shirts. Competition is fierce between shops, so there's room to bargain, especially if you're buying several items.

The famous **Monastiraki flea market** stretches west of Monastiraki Square, along Ifestou street and its side streets. It's a

fun place for tourists and pickpockets to browse, but it's not ideal for buying gifts for friends back home—unless they like junk. You'll see fake designer clothes, antiques, dusty books, and lots of stuff that might raise eyebrows at the airport (something going on every day, but best Sun 8:00-15:00, Metro line 1/green and line 3/blue: Monastiraki or line 1/green: Thissio).

For upscale shopping at mostly international chain stores, stroll the pedestrianized **Ermou street** between Syntagma Square and Monastiraki. Even fancier boutiques are in the swanky **Kolonaki** area.

For a self-guided walk of a more down-to-earth shopping area (which, thanks to its local flavor, might interest non-shoppers even more than shoppers), see the "Shop Like an Athenian" walk at the end of this chapter.

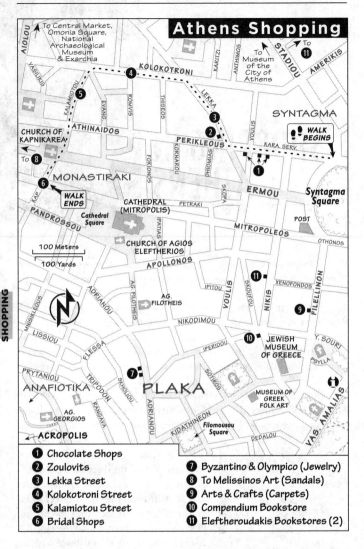

Athens Shopping

1 Chocolate Shops
2 Zoulovits
3 Lekka Street
4 Kolokotroni Street
5 Kalamiotou Street
6 Bridal Shops
7 Byzantino & Olympico (Jewelry)
8 To Melissinos Art (Sandals)
9 Arts & Crafts (Carpets)
10 Compendium Bookstore
11 Eleftheroudakis Bookstores (2)

Most shops catering to tourists are open long hours daily. Those serving locals are more likely open Monday, Wednesday, and Saturday from 8:30 or 9:00 until early afternoon (between 14:30 and 16:00); Tuesday, Thursday, and Friday from 8:30 or 9:00 until late (roughly 20:00 or 21:00), but often with an afternoon break (around 14:00-17:00 or 18:00); and closed Sunday.

To find out how to get a VAT (Value-Added Tax) refund on your purchases, see page 16.

What and Where to Buy

Here are some of the more authentic items you can buy, along with good places to find them.

Jewelry—Serious buyers tell me that Athens is the best place in Greece to purchase jewelry, particularly at the shops along Adrianou. The choices are much better than you'll find elsewhere, and—if you know how to haggle—so are the prices. The best advice is to take your time, and don't be afraid to walk away. The sales staff gets paid on commission, and they hate to lose a potential customer. Most stores have similar selections, which they buy from factory wholesalers.

For something a bit more specialized (with very high prices), visit the sister shops of Byzantino and Olympico (both open daily 10:00-21:00, sometimes later in summer, tel. 210-324-6605, www.byzantino.com, run by Kosta). **Byzantino,** which made the jewelry worn by Greek dancers in the closing ceremonies of the 2000 Sydney Olympics, creates pricey handmade replicas of museum pieces (most cost hundreds of euros; Adrianou 120, plus another location nearby at the corner of Pandrossou and Eolou). **Olympico,** nearly next door, creates modern pieces in the Greek style, including some more affordable options (Adrianou 122).

The gift shop at the **Benaki Museum of Greek History and Culture** (described on page 81) is also popular for its jewelry.

Sandals—The place to buy real leather sandals is **Melissinos Art,** the famous "poet sandal-maker" of Athens. You'll find an assortment of styles for about €25 per pair. Prices depend on size and style: The more leather they use, the more you pay (daily 10:00-22:00, just off Monastiraki Square at the edge of Psyrri, Ag. Theklas 2—see map on page 64, tel. 210-321-9247, www.melissinos-art.com). Stavros Melissinos—who's also a poet—ran this shop for decades. Now that he's retired, his son Pantelis (also a painter and playwright) has taken over the family business. When the Beatles came to his shop in 1968, Stavos was asked why he didn't ask for their autographs. He replied, "Why did they not ask for mine? I will be around long after the Beatles." He was right.

Carpets—The shops around the Plaka sell Persian-style carpets, but generally don't stock Greek ones. For Greek carpets, visit the **Institute of Social Protection and Solidarity Arts & Crafts Shop** (run by the Ministry of Health and Welfare). It has a good selection of colorful hand-knotted carpets, hand-woven kilims, needlepoint rugs, tablecloths, and cushion covers embroidered with folk designs. What's more, the profits go toward preservation of traditional handicrafts. The work is done by women who live in rural Greece and depend on this shop as their sole source of income (Tue-Fri 8:00-20:00, Mon and Sat 8:00-14:30, closed Sun, a block from the TI near Syntagma Square at Filellinon 14, tel. 210-325-0240).

Religious Items—For Greek Orthodox items, visit the shops near the cathedral, along Agia Filotheis street (described on page 101).

Worry Beads—Attentive travelers will notice Greeks (mostly men) constantly fidgeting with these strings of beads—endlessly flipping, spinning, and counting them. Loosely based on prayer beads, but today a secular hobby, worry beads make for a fun Greek souvenir. You'll see them sold all over central Athens. For more on worry beads—and how to shop for them—see the sidebar on page 233.

Shop Like an Athenian: A Self-Guided Walk

While tourists and big-money Athenians strut their stuff on the upscale Ermou shopping street (described in the Athens City

Walk), many locals prefer the streets just to the north—including Perikleous, Lekka, and Kolokotroni—for authentic, hole-in-the-wall shopping. Let's join them for this brief walk through some of central Athens' more colorful and totally untouristy neighborhoods.

Begin on Syntagma Square. At the bottom of the square, face the McDonald's. Exit the square on the street to the right, Karageorgi Servias (parallel to Ermou). About a block down this street, on the left, spot the several

chocolate shops. Leonidas is a famous Belgian chocolatier with a Greek name (and origin). Beyond that are a pair of favorites: Aristokratikon (at #9, Mon-Fri 8:00-21:00, Sat 8:00-16:00, closed Sun) and Le Chocolat (at #3, daily 8:00-22:00). At Aristokratikon, you can point one-by-one at various treats to assemble a collection of top-notch candies: pistachio clusters, chocolate-dipped fruit, almond paste in white chocolate, and more (€35/kilogram, or about €4 for five pieces). Le Chocolat is a bit more genteel and stuffy-feeling. Notice the case of fancy desserts. Greeks bring these to a home when they're invited for a visit (instead of, say, a bottle of wine).

Passing Nikis street, continue along Karageorgi Servias. Notice that, while shopping malls are becoming as popular here as anywhere in Europe, many Greeks still prefer to do their shopping in more specialized, **hole-in-the-wall shops.** They explain that the items they can buy here are unique, with more personality than the cookie-cutter stuff sold at malls and department stores. For example, check out the make-your-own-jewelry shop on the left, at #11.

After another block, around Voulis street, the road's name changes to Perikleous. Keep walking along it. Ahead on the right, watch for the shop called ΖΟΥΛΟΒΙΤΣ (**Zoulovits**)—the Greek answer to Tiffany's (since 1948). Well-heeled Athenians buy high-class silver gifts here for weddings and christenings (for a baby, a silver cup with a blue or pink ribbon is a must; Mon-Fri 9:00-20:30, Sat 9:00-15:30, closed Sun, Perikleous 10, tel. 210-322-7694).

Turn right down **Lekka street,** in front of Zoulovits. Before Ermou was pedestrianized, Lekka was the main shopping drag. Along here are more silver and jewelry gift shops (cheaper alternatives to the "big Z" mentioned above). On the left, watch for some shopping galleries that burrow into the city block.

Soon Lekka hits **Kolokotroni street,** which is lined with more small shops (including some that specialize in engravings, old maps, and books). The traffic and noise along here will give you a new appreciation for the traffic-free shopping zones in the city center. Turn left and walk down Kolokotroni, watching (on the left) for a worry-bead shop—supplying the means of this very Greek nervous habit. Consider dropping in to peruse the many variations.

After a few blocks, turn left on traffic-free **Kalamiotou street,** and bear right at the fork. Soon after, cross Ermou street at the Byzantine Church of Kapnikarea. (This will look familiar if you've done the Athens City Walk.) Continue straight ahead past the church and one block down Kapnikareas.

When you reach the busy cross-street (Mitropoleos), you're near three other favorite shops. Across Mitropoleos, notice the two shops flanking Kapnikareas. On the left corner, **Το Κεντημα** (To Kentema) sells linens—specializing in white pieces that are given as a gift to a daughter or niece for her marriage. On the right corner, at #49, is **Selections** ΧΥΤΗΡΟΓΛΟΥ (Hitiroglou), selling Athens' best-quality fabric. And a few steps down the street to the right, at #74 (on the right-hand side), the shop called **Home Sweet Home** specializes in wedding gifts. Traditionally, weddings are held on the weekend. Three days beforehand, family and friends gather to make the couple's bed with brand-new bedding, then scatter cash across the top of it—sort of like a big, fat, Greek wedding shower.

Our shopping walk is finished. For more shopping, backtrack a block up to the Ermou pedestrian mall, or continue ahead one block (across Mitropoleos) to the tourist-trinket-heavy Pandrossou drag. Turn right on Pandrossou to head straight for Monastiraki Square, epicenter of the flea-market action.

SHOPPING

NIGHTLIFE IN ATHENS

Athens is a thriving, vibrant city...and the Athenians know how to have a good time after hours. While I've recommended some specific tips, consider simply strolling through a lively neighborhood and finding a scene that appeals to you. Your best bet is to get out of the touristy Plaka/Monastiraki rut, and head for the trendy (and very nearby) Psyrri, Thissio, and Gazi neighborhoods.

Athens is most inviting from May through October (but not in miserably hot August), when al fresco activities such as outdoor cinema, festivals (including the Athens & Epidavros Festival), and folk-dancing shows at Dora Stratou Theater are in full swing. In the winter, your options are limited to indoor venues (concerts and other performances). However, folk musicians who spend their summers in small towns and islands hibernate in Athens—offering ample opportunities to hear traditional music in winter.

Athens' biggest party is the **Athens & Epidavros Festival,** in June and July. Performances at the Odeon of Herodes Atticus are the highlight of the festival, and outdoor performances at other venues enliven an already hopping city. For a run-down of other festivals in Athens throughout the year, see page 486.

If you're **club-hopping,** you'll find that things don't really get rolling until after midnight. Thursdays, Fridays, and Saturdays are busiest, while Mondays are quietest. In the heat of summer, some clubs close down to relocate to outdoor venues on the coast.

Event Listings: Athens has a constantly rotating schedule of cultural activities, such as concerts to suit every audience. For local events, ask the TI for a pair of free brochures: *Life in Capital A* (specializes in festivals and events listings) and *Athens Today* (broader focus, but includes some events). The weekly, English-language *Athens News* lists events (www.athensnews.gr). Also, look

The Athens & Epidavros Festival

The Athens & Epidavros Festival—every June and July in Athens—offers the opportunity to watch world-class performances of dance, music, and theater at the ancient Odeon of Herodes Atticus, nestled spectacularly below the floodlit Acropolis. A few events are held elsewhere in the city, while other performances take place at the famous Theater of Epidavros on the Peloponnese (these extend into August; see www.greekfestival.gr).

Tickets generally go on sale three weeks in advance. You can buy them online, over the phone, and at the festival box office (Mon-Fri 8:30-16:00, Sat 9:00-14:30, closed Sun, in the arcade at Panepistimiou 39, opposite the National Library, tel. 210-327-2000). Same-day tickets are also sold at the theater box office.

for the *Athens Plus* newspaper (www.athensplus.gr) and the Greek lifestyle magazine *Odyssey* (www.odyssey.gr).

Nightlife Activities

Strolling—The place to be for people who enjoy an evening stroll is the pedestrian boulevard arcing around the base of the Acropolis—what I call the "Acropolis Loop" (consisting of Dionysiou Areopagitou to the south and Apostolou Pavlou to the west). As the sun goes down, it's busy with locals (lovers, families, seniors, children at play) and visitors alike. For more details about this main drag, see page 67.

Outdoor Cinema—Athens has a wonderful tradition of outdoor movies. Screenings take place most nights in summer (€8, roughly June-Sept, sometimes in May and Oct depending on weather, shows start around 20:00 or 21:00, depending on when the sun sets). The "theaters" are actually compact open-air courtyards with folding chairs and small tables for your drinks. Movies are typically shown in their original language, with Greek subtitles (though children's movies might be dubbed in Greek). While Athens has many such venues, the four that I list are particularly well-known, convenient, and atmospheric. Call or look them up online to see what's playing.

The **Aigli Village Cinema** is a cool, classic outdoor theater in the National Garden (at the Zappeion), playing the latest blockbusters with a great sound system (tel. 210-336-9369).

Cine Paris, in the Plaka, is another large outdoor movie venue, and comes with Acropolis views (overlooking Filomousou Square on the roof of Kidathineon 22—see map on page 65, tel. 210-324-8057, www.cineparis.gr).

Cine Psyrri, buried deep in the trendy Psyrri district, has cute seating in an ivy-draped lot with a great bar. Movies play nightly and change weekly (Sarri 44, near intersection with Ogigou—see map on page 184, tel. 210-324-7234).

Cine Theseion, along the Apostolou Pavlou pedestrian drag in the Thissio neighborhood, enjoys grand floodlit Acropolis views from some of its seats. It shows mostly classic movies rather than today's blockbusters (Apostolou Pavlou 7—see map on page 205, tel. 210-347-0980 or 210-342-0864, www.cine-thisio.gr).

Folk Dancing—The **Dora Stratou Theater** on Filopappos Hill is *the* place to go to see authentic folk dancing. The company—the best in Greece—was originally formed to record and preserve the country's many traditional dances. Their repertoire includes such favorites as the graceful *kalamatianos* circle dance, the *syrtaki* (famously immortalized by Anthony Quinn in *Zorba the Greek*), and the dramatic solo *zimbetikos* (€15, late May-late Sept Tue-Sat at 21:30, Sun 20:15, no show Mon, 80 minutes, Dora Stratou Theater, on southern side of Filopappos Hill, tel. 210-324-4395, after 19:30 call 210-921-4650, www.grdance.org).

If you're taking the Metro, get off at Petralona (on line 1/green, plus 10-minute walk) rather than the farther Akropoli stop (on line 2/red, 20-minute walk). To walk to the theater from below the Acropolis, figure at least 20 minutes (entirely around the base of Filopappos Hill, signposted from western end of Dionysiou Areopagitou).

Other Outdoor Venues—The rebuilt ancient theater at the foot of the Acropolis, the **Odeon of Herodes Atticus,** occasionally hosts concerts under the stars. The theater atop **Lykavittos Hill** is another outdoor favorite. Both of these are used in summer for the Athens & Epidavros Festival.

Nightlife Neighborhoods

If you're looking for after-dark fun, don't miss a trio of engaging districts just north and west of the Plaka/Monastiraki area: Thissio, Psyrri, and Gazi. Just a few minutes' walk away from the tourist-clogged Plaka streets, these neighborhoods feel more local and authentically lively. Travelers of all ages will enjoy all three areas; however, older travelers may feel a bit more comfortable in Thissio, while younger travelers gravitate to Psyrri and Gazi. Because they're so close, you can wander through all three in a single evening—but if you're in town for multiple nights, delve into one each night.

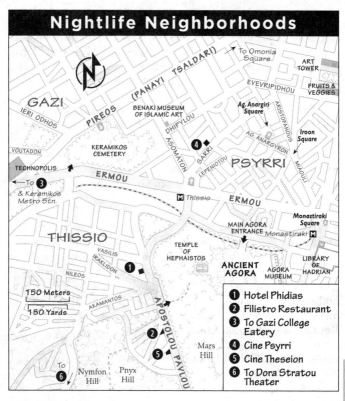

Nightlife Neighborhoods

Map legend:
1. Hotel Phidias
2. Filistro Restaurant
3. To Gazi College Eatery
4. Cine Psyrri
5. Cine Theseion
6. To Dora Stratou Theater

NIGHTLIFE

Thissio

In the Thissio district, just beyond the Agora, the tables and couches of trendy clubs and cocktail bars clog the pedestrian lanes under the Acropolis. More upscale than the Plaka, Thissio gives you an easy escape from the tired tourism of that zone. Thissio is basically composed of three or four streets running into Apostolou Pavlou (part of the "Acropolis Loop"). Iraklidon street is a tight lane with people socializing furiously at café tables squeezed under trees. Akamantos street, while still colorful, is a bit more sedate. Backgammon boards chatter, TVs blare the latest sporting events, and young Athenians sip their iced coffees en masse. As the sun sets and the floodlit temples of the Acropolis ornament the horizon, you understand why this quiet and breezy corner is such a hit with locals enjoying an evening out.

Come here just to stroll through the hippest café scene in town, to enjoy a drink and some great people-watching, to see a movie under the stars (at Cine Theseion, listed earlier), or to eat on the rooftop of one of my favorite Athens restaurants (Filistro—see page 195).

To reach Thissio, walk the pedestrian lane around the Acropolis from either end. It makes a wonderful destination after the more peaceful stretch from the Acropolis Museum (Metro: Akropoli, line 2/red). Or ride the Metro (line 1/green) to Thissio, then follow the crowds uphill along the broad Apostolou Pavlou walkway toward the Acropolis.

For a better selection of restaurants and a great Irish pub, drop into the neighboring **Monastiraki** district (between the Thissio and Monastiraki Metro stops, along the wall of the Ancient Agora). Adrianou street has a line of inviting restaurants and cafés with outdoor seating—some with spectacular Acropolis views. If you're in the mood for a break from Greece, stop into the James Joyce Irish Pub (see page 193).

Psyrri

The Psyrri district, immediately north of Thissio, is downscale and more cutting-edge...seedy-chic. Until recently, it was a grimy area of workshops and cottage indus-
tries, famous locally as a onetime hotbed of poets, musicians, revo-
lutionaries, and troublemakers. But now it's taking off as one of central Athens' top after-hours zones. The crumbling buildings are slathered with graffiti, and the streets are crammed with dump-

sters, broken-down cars, and pungent odors. The mix of trendy and crusty gives the area a unique charm. The options include slick, touristy tavernas with live traditional music (many are painted in the same Greek saloon style—these places are fresh, formulaic, and part of a chain); highly conceptual café/bars catering to cool young Athenians; and clubs with DJs or live music for partying the night away.

The epicenter of the restaurant area is between two squares, **Iroon** and **Agii Anargiri** (with St. Anargiri Church), and along the street that connects them, **Agion Anargyron.** This is where you'll find the most comfortable, tourist-friendly, all-ages eateries, serving traditional Greek dishes and often featuring live music at dinnertime. For more on dining here, see the Eating in Athens chapter.

If you're seeking nightlife, explore the streets spinning off from this central axis. **Lepeniotou street** has the most creatively themed café/bars—most of them mellow and colorful, and great spots to relax with a drink and appreciate the decor. Each one has its own personality and idiosyncratic sense of style (from Lebanese to Buenos Aires)...wander around a bit looking for the place that

NIGHTLIFE

suits you. **Aristofanous street** has more clubs than bars or restaurants—some of them with DJs or live music. And **Miaouli street,** extending toward Monastiraki, is jam-packed with outdoor tables of unpretentious, local-feeling, crank-'em-out pubs and tavernas— a striking contrast to the upscale/touristy eateries just a block or two away.

A great way to enjoy an evening here is by watching a movie under the stars with the gang at Cine Psyrri (described earlier).

Gazi

Residents here must be dizzy at the rapid change sweeping through what was just recently a depressed industrial zone. Towering overhead are the square, brick smokestacks of Technopolis, a complex of warehouses and brick factory buildings that now host galleries and theaters with a world of cutting-edge culture. As a center of Athens' gay community, the area has a special flamboyance and style. You can't miss the Gazi energy.

And it's easy to reach: Simply ride the Metro to Keramikos. You'll emerge in a delightful park surrounded by streets lined with super-stylish restaurants, clubs, bars, and cafés. Maps at the Metro station show the lay of the land. I'd just browse the main streets (Dekeleon, Persefonis, Voutadon, Triptolemou) that radiate out from the station, enjoy the scene, and pick a place to eat a meal or sip a drink. **Gazi College Eatery** is a fresh, modern, and inviting place for a light meal or drink in the company of a student crowd that's typical of the area. It offers a fun and affordable menu all day and evening (Persefonis 53, tel. 210-342-2112).

Other Areas

The **Kolonaki** district, at the foot of Lykavittos Hill, is Athens' top area for yuppie nightlife—upscale and stylish.

Exarchia, the very grungy student/anarchist zone that stretches north of Kolonaki, is rougher around the edges than the other places I describe here. But adventurous travelers might enjoy exploring the area...with care. (First, read the description of Exarchia on page 80.)

Although the old stand-by, the **Plaka,** is jammed full of tourists, it couldn't be more central or user-friendly, with live traditional music spilling out of seemingly every other taverna. One particularly pleasant area to explore is the "Restaurant Steps" at Mnisikleous street (described in the Eating in Athens chapter).

ATHENS CONNECTIONS

Athens is the transportation hub for all of Greece. This chapter covers arrivals and departures by plane, boat, bus, train, and car.

Because Athens has a good public transportation system, don't rent a car until you are ready to leave the city—you absolutely do *not* want to drive in Athens traffic. If you're venturing to landlocked destinations beyond Athens, the best option for the rest of your trip is to travel by car. The Greek train system is slated to be privatized (if anyone wants to buy it), and it will take years before it is up to Western European standards. Most recommended sights beyond Athens do not have train service. Buses can get you just about anywhere for a reasonable fare, but connections to remote areas can be long and complicated, and straightforward schedule information is hard to come by. For specifics on transportation beyond Athens, see the "Connections" sections in each of the following chapters and page 470 in the appendix.

For more extensive travels beyond Greece, you can study your railpass options at www.ricksteves.com/rail.

By Plane

Eleftherios Venizelos International Airport

Athens' airport is at Spata, 17 miles east of downtown (tel. 210-353-0000, www.aia.gr). This impressively slick, user-friendly airport has two sections: B gates (serving European/Schengen countries—no passport control) and A gates (serving other destinations, including the US). Both sections feed into the same main terminal building (with a common baggage claim, ATMs, shops, car-rental counters, information desks, and additional services). Upstairs, on the second floor (above entrance/exit #3), is a minimuseum of Greek artifacts.

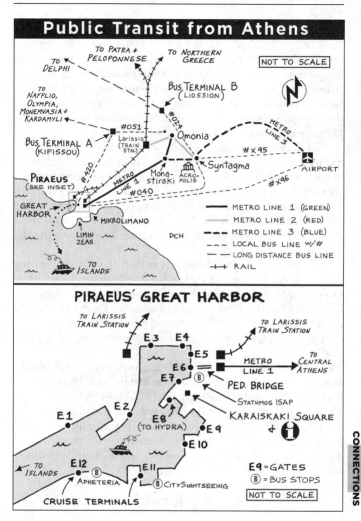

Public Transit from Athens

TO DELPHI

TO PATRA & PELOPONNESE

TO NORTHERN GREECE

TO NAFPLIO, OLYMPIA, MONEMVASIA & KARDAMYLI

NOT TO SCALE

BUS TERMINAL B (LIOSSION)

#051

BUS TERMINAL A (KIFISSOU)

#024

Larissis (TRAIN STN.)

Omonia

METRO LINE 3

#420

PIRAEUS (SEE INSET)

METRO LINE 1

Mona-stiraki

ACRO-POLIS

Syntagma

#X95

AIRPORT

#040

#X96

GREAT HARBOR

MIKROLIMANO

DCH

LIMIN ZEAS

TO ISLANDS

- ▬▬▬ METRO LINE 1 (GREEN)
- ▬▬▬ METRO LINE 2 (RED)
- ▬ ▬ ▬ METRO LINE 3 (BLUE)
- - - - LOCAL BUS LINE w/#
- – – LONG DISTANCE BUS LINE
- +++ RAIL

PIRAEUS' GREAT HARBOR

TO LARISSIS TRAIN STATION

TO LARISSIS TRAIN STATION

E3 E4

E5

E6

METRO LINE 1

TO CENTRAL ATHENS

E7

Ⓑ

PED. BRIDGE

STATHMOS ISAP

KARAISKAKI SQUARE & ⓘ

E1

E2

E8 (TO HYDRA)

E9

E10

TO ISLANDS

E12 Ⓑ APHETERIA

E11 Ⓑ CITYSIGHTSEEING

CRUISE TERMINALS

E9 = GATES
Ⓑ = BUS STOPS
NOT TO SCALE

CONNECTIONS

Getting from the Airport to Downtown

By Metro: Line 3/blue zips you downtown in 45 minutes for €8 (2/hour, usually departs at :05 and :35 after the hour, daily 6:00-23:30; half-price for people under 18 or over 65, ticket good for 1.5 hours on other Athens transit). To catch this train from the airport arrivals hall, go through exit #3, cross the street, escalate to the skybridge, walk to the terminal to buy tickets, and follow signs down to the platforms (look for signs to *Metro*, not *suburban trains*). In downtown Athens, this train stops at Syntagma (transfer to line 2/red) and Monastiraki (transfer to line 1/green).

By Bus: Buses wait outside exit #5. Express bus #X95 operates

24 hours daily between the airport and Syntagma Square (3-5/hour, 3/hour at night, trip takes 1-1.5 hours depending on traffic). The downtown bus stop is on Othonos street, along the side of Syntagma Square. Bus #X96 operates between the airport and Athens' port of Piraeus (also runs 24 hours daily, 3-4/hour, 1-1.5 hours depending on traffic; stops at Piraeus' Karaiskaki Square, then at the Metro station—marked by the pedestrian bridge). A ticket for either bus costs €5 (tel. 185, www.oasa.gr).

By Taxi: A well-marked taxi stand outside exit #3 offers fixed-price transfers that include all fees (€40 to central Athens or to the port of Piraeus). If you arrange your own taxi (to or from the airport), figure around €30-40 total. Note that the cabbie will tack on several legitimate fees beyond what's on the meter, including the tolls to take the fast road, per-piece baggage charges, and a special airport fee (for details, see "Getting Around Athens—By Taxi" on page 59).

People on package trips are met at the airport by sign-waving cabbies who take them to their hotel and help get them settled in for about €75. Recently, private English-speaking cabbies have been providing this same service to anyone for about €55—though its value over simply catching a normal cab is questionable.

Airlines

Two major Greek carriers offer daily flights to many Greek islands, as well as to cities throughout Europe and beyond: **Olympic Airlines** (tel. 210-356-9111, toll-free tel. 801-114-4444, www.olympic airlines.com) and **Aegean Airlines** (tel. 210-626-1000, toll-free tel. 801-112-0000, www.aegeanair.com). If you're headed to far-flung islands such as Mykonos or Santorini—which have small airports—check flights on these airlines, which can be surprisingly affordable (and save you the long boat journey).

By Boat

Piraeus

Piraeus, a city six miles southwest of central Athens, has been the port of Athens since ancient times. Today it's also the main port for services to the Greek islands, making it the busiest passenger port in the Mediterranean. A staggering 13 million journeys begin or end here each year.

CONNECTIONS

Orientation to Piraeus

All ferries, hydrofoils, catamarans, and cruise ships use Piraeus' Great Harbor (Megas Limin). To the east are two smaller harbors used for private yachts: Limin Zeas and the picturesque Mikrolimano, or "Small Harbor."

The vast Great Harbor area is ringed by busy streets. At the northeast corner is the hub of most activity: the Metro station, a big yellow Neoclassical building with white trim, sometimes labeled "Electric Railway Station" on maps. There's a free and good little electric-railway museum inside, which might entertain trainspotters with time to kill (daily 9:00-14:00). Next door to the Metro station is the suburban train station. A modern pedestrian bridge connects the Metro station to the harbor and serves as a handy landmark.

Just down the street is Karaiskaki Square, which juts out into the harbor. Cheap eateries, flophouse hotels, and dozens of travel agencies round out the scene. The port's dreary appearance aside, Piraeus' Port Authority has recently invested in several air-conditioned waiting areas, free Wi-Fi around the port, and big electronic display boards showing gate numbers and times for upcoming departures.

Gates: Twelve "gates" (docks) stretch for about three miles around the harbor, numbered in clockwise order. Gate assignments depend on both the destination and the company operating the line, but very roughly, you can expect the following:

- **E1:** Dodecanese Islands
- **E2:** Crete; North Aegean Islands (Samos, Ikaria, Chios, Mytilene/Lesbos)
- **E3:** Crete and Kithira (vehicle entrance)
- **E4:** Kithira (vehicle exit)
- **E5:** Bus Terminal
- **E6:** Cyclades (including **Mykonos** and **Santorini**), pedestrian walkway to Metro
- **E7:** Cyclades (including high-speed boats to **Mykonos** and **Santorini**)
- **E8:** Saronic Gulf Islands (Argosaronikos in Greek, including **Hydra,** Spetses, Paros, and Ermioni)
- **E9:** Cyclades (including **Mykonos** and **Santorini**), Samos, Ikaria
- **E10:** Vehicle exit from E9
- **E11:** Cruise Terminal A
- **E12:** Cruise Terminal B

These departure gates are prone to change—carefully check your ticket for the gate number, and ask locally (any travel agent, port worker, or taxi driver) if you're unsure.

Information: Frustratingly, official tourist information is in short supply here. Both the cities of Athens and Piraeus sometimes run seasonal TI kiosks near the docks, but these tend to come and go. Your best sources of information are the many travel agencies scattered around the area; all have a line on current boats, where they leave from, and how to get tickets. The port police (with several offices clearly marked in English) can also be helpful. You can also call the Piraeus Port Authority ship-schedule line at tel. 14541 (€0.89/call); hear recorded weekly itineraries at tel. 210-414-7800; or contact the port police at tel. 210-417-2675. The port authority website is www.olp.gr.

Baggage Storage: Luggage lockers (€3) are at both the Metro and the suburban train stations; if the Metro station lockers are full, there's generally room next door at the train station (go out the front door of the Metro station, turn right, and cross the street; once inside the train station, the lockers are to the left of the tracks). If you're in a pinch, various travel agencies closer to the port might be willing to store your bags for a fee.

Getting from Piraeus to Downtown Athens, the Airport, and More

To Downtown Athens: To take the **Metro,** use the pedestrian bridge near gates E6 and E7 to reach the Metro station (the big yellow building across the street from the port). Metro line 1/ green conveniently links Piraeus with downtown Athens (covered by €1.40 basic transit ticket, good for 1.5 hours including transfers, train departs about every 10 minutes between 6:00-24:00). In about 20 minutes, the train reaches the city-center Monastiraki stop, near the Plaka and many recommended hotels and sights. (For Syntagma, Akropoli, and Syngrou-Fix Metro stops, ride the train one more stop to Omonia to transfer to line 2/red.) Warning: The Metro line between Piraeus and downtown Athens teems with pickpockets—watch your valuables and wear a money belt.

A suburban **train** connects Piraeus' Great Harbor train station (next door to Metro station) with Athens' Larissis train station in 20 minutes (covered by €1.40 basic transit ticket). It runs less frequently (every 40 minutes) than the Metro and is less convenient (at Larissis station, you need to change to line 2/red Metro to get into central Athens).

A **taxi** between Piraeus and downtown Athens costs €10-20 and can take anywhere from 20 minutes to an hour, depending on traffic and on your starting/ending point at Piraeus (€1 surcharge from gates E1-E10; €5.20 surcharge from gates E11-E12).

To the Airport: Bus #X96 connects Piraeus directly to the airport. In Piraeus, it stops along the top of Karaiskaki Square (Plateia Karaiskaki/ΠΛ. ΚΑΡΑΪΣΚΑΚΗ stop, between gates E7 and E8), and also in front of the Metro station (Stathmos ISAP/

ΣΤΑΘΜΟΣ ΗΣΑΠ stop; €3.20, runs 24 hours daily, 2-6/hour depending on time of day, 1-1.5 hours depending on traffic).

To Other Points in Greece: For **long-distance buses,** you'll have to connect through Athens. To reach Athens' Bus Terminal A (Kifissou), you can take bus #420 (catch it in Piraeus at the corner of Thermopilon and Akti Kondili, straight ahead along the top of the harbor from the Metro station, near gate E3). For **trains** to Patra on the Peloponnese, take the train directly from Piraeus to Kiato, and transfer there.

Getting from Piraeus to the Islands

Greek ferry services are operated by several different companies, without a single office to keep track of all the options. This can make it frustrating to get a clear rundown of the possibilities for trips to the different islands. You can research schedules online— good websites include www.openseas.gr, www.danae.gr/ferries -Greece.asp, and www.greekferries.gr.

Buying Boat Tickets

If you're already in Greece, the easiest solution is to simply go to any travel agency. They're experts on the various ferries, and can sell you a ticket for no extra fee (prices are the same from any agency and cost no more than buying direct from the boat company). However, agencies will sometimes tell you only about the boats for which they sell tickets, and at some places it's standard practice to try to upsell you on a package trip. Still, a good agency can provide the easiest way to understand your options and get tickets.

In the busy summer season (especially July-August), some popular connections can sell out early. (For example, for summer weekends—especially late in the day—it's smart to book tickets for the Piraeus–Hydra catamaran/hydrofoil a week in advance.) If you'll be setting sail very soon after your arrival in Greece, do your research online from home, and book a ticket on the Internet. Or you can call a travel agent in Athens, give them your credit-card number over the phone, and they'll print a ticket for you to pick up later (though, some agencies might be reluctant to do this for you unless you're also booking a package with them).

Departing Piraeus by Boat

If you're taking a boat to the islands, begin by riding the Metro (line 1/green) from downtown Athens to Piraeus. Arriving at the Piraeus Metro station (end of the line), walk out the side door (with your back to the tracks, it's to the left) and into a chaotic little square filled with vendors slinging knock-off designer bags. Head up the escalator and walk to the far end of the pedestrian bridge, overlooking the water. You're standing above gates E6 and E7. Gates with higher numbers are to your left; those with lower numbers are to your right. (For example, Hydra-bound boats usually depart from gate E8, to your left on the far side of the tree-filled park.) Once you have your bearings, descend to the port and walk to your gate. If you boat leaves from gates E1 or E2 on the north side of the port (the Dodecanese Islands, plus some boats to Crete or the North Aegean Islands), turn right and walk to gate E5 (near the end of the pedestrian bridge) to catch a free shuttle bus.

Piraeus Boat Connections

It's risky to give specifics when it comes to boat connections, which can change from day to day. But here's a rough sense of your options to get you started. While the Piraeus gates listed earlier are somewhat reliable, always confirm locally which gate your boat leaves from.

To the Saronic Gulf Islands: Aegina, Poros, Hydra, and **Spetses** are served by conventional ferries and high-speed boats, operated by Hellenic Seaways (tel. 210-419-9000, www.hsw.gr). For more details on connections to Hydra, see page 400.

To the Cyclades: Blue Star Ferries serves **Mykonos, Santorini,** and other Cycladic Islands (tel. 210-891-9010, www .bluestarferries.com). Their comfortable and modern boats are fitted with stabilizers that provide a smooth ride and enable them to keep sailing even in intense winds. Other regular ferry service is provided by Hellenic Seaways (listed earlier) and ANEK Lines (tel. 210-419-7420, www.anek.gr). Faster—and more expensive—hydrofoils, catamarans, and high-speed ferries are operated by Hellenic Seaways, Aegean Speed Lines (tel. 210-969-0950, www .aegeanspeedlines.gr), and SeaJets (tel. 210-412-1800, www.seajets .gr). For more details on connections to Mykonos, see page 415; for Santorini, see page 424.

To Crete: To reach **Iraklio,** the capital of Crete, the sleek Minoan Lines fleet (tel. 210-337-6910, www.minoan.gr) is better than ANEK Lines (tel. 210-419-7420, www.anek.gr).

To the North Aegean Islands: To get to **Samos,** try Hellenic Seaways (listed earlier) or Kallisti Ferries (tel. 210-422-2971 or toll-free tel. 801-117-7700, www.ferries.gr/kallisti-ferries).

Piraeus' Cruise-Ship Terminals

Piraeus has two adjacent cruise-ship terminals, at the far-south end of the port: Gate E11 is Cruise Terminal A, and gate E12 is Cruise Terminal B. Each terminal has basic café and gift-shop facilities, and ATMs.

Getting from the Cruise-Ship Terminals to Downtown

Your basic options for getting from the terminals into central Athens are a taxi (fast but expensive); public bus (a bit slower, but cheap and handy); the Metro (fast and cheap, though you'll first have to walk or take a public bus to Piraeus' Metro station); or a hop-on, hop-off bus tour (expensive and infrequent, but with sightseeing commentary).

By Taxi: Cabbies wait in front of each cruise terminal. The fair metered rate from either terminal into downtown is about €15-20, depending on traffic (includes legitimate €5.20 cruise terminal surcharge—you can try to avoid this by walking up to the main road and finding a taxi there). Some drivers offer a three-hour tour around the city center, including basic commentary and waiting time at the Acropolis (about €120). If this appeals to you, find a driver who speaks good English and would be fun to chat with.

By Bus: Bus #040 goes from Piraeus' cruise-terminal area to Athens' main Syntagma Square (€1.20, 6-8/hour, 30-60 minutes depending on traffic). The bus leaves from the stop called Apheteria (ΑΦΕΤΗΡΙΑ, "starting point"), which is on the main road between the two cruise terminals. Several different bus lines stop here, so make sure you get on the right bus. To reach the bus stop from **Cruise Terminal A,** exit the building, bear left, and walk along the road up the low hill. When you reach the main road, turn right and walk along it to reach the Apheteria bus stop. From **Cruise Terminal B,** exit the building, follow the road to the left of the pretty yellow church. You'll see the row of buses ahead.

By Metro: The Metro speedily connects Piraeus with downtown Athens' Monastiraki stop (every 10 minutes, 20-minute trip). The catch is that the Metro station is between gates E6 and E7, a 15- to 20-minute walk from Cruise Terminal A (5-10 minutes more from Cruise Terminal B). If you don't want to walk, you can take a taxi there (about €5), or catch public bus #843 from the Apheteria bus stop between the two terminals (buy €1.40 ticket from a kiosk to cover both the bus and the Metro ride, 6-10/hour Mon-Sat, 3-5/hour Sun). The Metro station is a big yellow building with white trim, marked by a pedestrian bridge over the busy street (it's the only such bridge at Piraeus; the bus stop in front is named Stathmos ISAP/ΣΤΑΘΜΟΣ ΗΣΑΠ). For more details on the Metro, see page 56.

To reach the Metro from **Cruise Terminal A,** exit the terminal building, keep left, and walk up the incline to the main road. At this road, head right to reach the Apheteria bus stop, and find bus #843; or, if you don't mind walking the whole way to the Metro (about 15-20 minutes), turn left onto the main road and simply follow it along the port.

To reach the Metro from **Cruise Terminal B,** exit the building and follow the road to the left of the yellow church to reach the Apheteria stop (for bus #843), or continue walking on the same road around the port to the Metro station (about 20-30 minutes total).

By Hop-On, Hop-Off Bus: CitySightseeing offers a hop-on, hop-off bus that includes a 70-minute itinerary around Piraeus, and links to a separate 1.5-hour bus route around Athens (€22 for all-day tour; bus departs Piraeus at 8:30, 9:00, 9:30, 10:00, 11:30, 13:00, and 14:30; returns to Piraeus in the afternoon from across from Athens' Temple of Olympian Zeus at "Melina Merkouri" stop at 10:45, 12:15, 13:45, 15:15, 16:45, and 20:00).

The low-profile bus stop (a sign on a post) is about 300 yards around the port past Cruise Terminal A on the main road, on the port side of the road.

By Bus

Athens has two major intercity bus stations. Frustratingly, both are far from downtown, and neither is conveniently reached by Metro. Buses serving the south, including the Peloponnese, use the bus station called Kifissou, or "Terminal A." Most buses serving the north, including Delphi, use the station called Liossion, or "Terminal B." (There has been some talk of combining these two stations, but progress is slow.)

Although most destinations in this book are served by at least one daily direct bus from Athens, connecting between destinations outside Athens can involve several changes (as noted in each chapter). Even though all Greek buses are operated by ΚΤΕΛ (KTEL), there's no useful general website or phone number (each regional bus station only keeps track of its own schedules). There is a list of local phone numbers at www.ktelbus.com, however you'll need to know the name of the province where you are traveling. You can get details for buses originating in Athens by phoning 14505. Matt Barrett's website has schedules for long-distance buses to and from Athens (www.athensguide.com), or try the helpful, unofficial website (in English) at http://livingingreece.gr/2008/06/13/ktel -buses-of-greece.

Terminal A (Kifissou)

This bus station is about three miles northwest of the city center. Getting here is a pain, involving a Metro-plus-bus connection or a taxi ride.

Orientation to Terminal A

In the vast ticket hall (signs to *ΕΚΔΟΤΗΡΙΑ*), the counters are divided by which region they serve; if you aren't sure which one you need, ask at the information desk near the main door. Beyond the ticket hall are a cafeteria, restaurant, and supermarket, and the door out to the buses. This immense bus barn is crammed with well-labeled bus stalls, which are organized—like the ticket windows—by region.

Getting from Central Athens to Terminal A

The easiest way is to take a **taxi** (pay no more than €12 from central Athens).

The **public transit** connection costs just €1.40 but involves both the Metro and bus—and walking down busy streets with your luggage. From central Athens, ride the Metro to Omonia (on line 1/green or 2/red). At Omonia, follow signs to exit for *Pireos/Ag. Konstantinou.* Escalate up to street level, exit to the left, then take your first right, down busy Panagi Tsaldari. Walk straight ahead, then take the second right onto traffic-free Zinonos street. Walk two blocks down this pedestrian zone. When you reach the cross-street with traffic, the bus stop is directly across the street (on the right-hand corner, at the corner of Zinonos and Menandrou, labeled *ΑΦΕΤΗΡΙΑ*). This is the start of the route for bus #051, which you'll ride about 15 minutes to the end of the line, at Terminal A (covered by the same ticket you used for the Metro ride, 3-9/hour depending on time of day, no buses 24:00-5:00). The bus station stop is labeled *ΤΕΡΜΑ* (ΣΤ. ΥΠΕΡ ΚΩΝ ΛΕΩΦ. ΚΗΦΙΣΟΥ).

Getting from Terminal A to Central Athens

To take **public transit** into town, look for the public bus stop between the bus stalls and the main terminal building/ticket office, and catch **bus** #051 (buy ticket at adjacent kiosk). While you could ride it all the way to the end of the line (ΑΦΕΤΗΡΙΑ stop, see directions above), it's faster to get off one stop before, at the ΕΦΕΤΕΙΟ stop (corner of Ag. Konstantinou and Sokratous). From here, continue by foot to the end of the block, turn left across the street, then walk straight ahead one block to the entrance of the Omonia Metro station.

At the bus station, **taxis** wait out in front of the ticket hall, as well as under the canopy between the ticket hall and the bus stalls. Note that if you arrive here between 24:00 and 5:00 (when bus #051 does not run), you'll have no choice but to take a taxi.

By Bus from Terminal A to: Nafplio (hourly direct, 2.5 hours, €12), **Epidavros** (3-4/day, 2.5 hours, €11), **Mycenae** (go to Nafplio, then 2/day, 45 minutes), **Olympia** (2/day direct, 5 hours, €27), **Monemvasia** (3/day, transfer in Sparta, 6 hours total, €27), **Kardamyli** (1/day direct, 5 hours, €24). Terminal A info: tel. 210-512-4910.

CONNECTIONS

Terminal B (Liossion)

Smaller, more manageable, and a bit closer to the city center, Liossion (lee-oh-SEE-yohn) is in northwest Athens, a 15-minute, €8 taxi ride from the Plaka. You can also take bus #024 from near Syntagma Square in central Athens (leaves from alongside the National Garden on Amalias street—facing the Parliament, walk along the busy street to your right).

By Bus from Terminal B to: Delphi (6/day, 3 hours, €13.60).

By Train

In Athens, most trains use **Larissis Station,** just north of downtown (on Metro line 2/red). Eventually, the Acharnes Railway Center (abbreviated SKA), currently under construction 13 miles north of the city center, will become a major hub for Athens rail traffic.

Greek trains are of limited usefulness to travelers—especially if you're sticking to the destinations described in this book. For most places, it's better to take buses or to drive. Complicating matters, the government is planning to privatize the system. As a result, many routes may be cut, especially on the Peloponnese.

However, one train connection might be useful for you to know about: A new line is being built to connect Athens to **Patra** (via Corinth, then along the northern coast of the Peloponnese); currently this line is open only until Kiato, where passengers transfer to a bus to reach Patra. In early 2011, international service to Istanbul, Sofia, and Belgrade was "temporarily" suspended. It is uncertain when it might resume.

Trains are operated by Greek Railways (abbreviated OSE, www.trainose.gr), but be aware that their unhelpful website may not have the most up-to-date information. It's best to call the customer service office, which has English-speaking staff (open 7:00-24:00, tel. 210-529-7777).

By Car

Renting a Car

Syngrou avenue is Athens' "rental car lane," with all the big companies (and piles of little ones) competing for your business. Syngrou is an easy walk from the Plaka and recommended hotels (it's especially near those in Makrigianni and Koukaki). Budget travelers can often negotiate great deals by visiting a few rental places and haggling. You could go with one of the established, predictable biggies. Or, for a friendly local car-rental company, consider **Swift/Avanti,** run by can-do Elias and Salvator. They'll pick you up at your hotel and drive you out of central Athens—so you can avoid the stress of Athens city-center driving (€40/day including tax, unlimited mileage, and insurance for three days or more; office open Mon-Sat 9:00-18:00, until 17:00 in winter, open Sun on demand; Syngrou 50, tel. 210-923-3919 or 210-924-7006, www.greektravel.com/swift or www.avanti.com.gr, swift@avanti .com.gr). You can drop off the car at locations outside downtown Athens for about €0.50 per kilometer (for example, €30 for Athens airport, €80 for Nafplio).

Route Tips for Drivers

Avoid driving in Athens as much as possible—traffic is stressful and parking is a headache. Before you leave Athens, get detailed directions from your rental agency on how to get back to their office and drop off your car.

Here's your strategy for getting out of the city: If you're heading north, such as to **Delphi,** aim for expressway 1 northbound (toward Lamia; see specific directions on page 371). To head for the **Peloponnese,** go westbound on expressway 6, which feeds into expressway 8 to Corinth (the gateway to the Peloponnese). The handy E-75 expressway (a.k.a. Kifissou avenue), which runs north–south just west of downtown Athens, offers an easy connection to either of these.

Assuming you pick up your car on or near Syngrou avenue, and traffic isn't that heavy, the best bet (with the fewest traffic lights and turns) is usually to simply head south on Syngrou. As you approach the water, the road forks; follow signs toward *Piraeus* on the left. After the merge, get into the right lane and be ready to hop on E-75 northbound. Then watch for your exit: for the Peloponnese, exit for expressway 6 (which merges into expressway 8 to Corinth); for Delphi, continue straight north to expressway 1.

THE PELOPONNESE

ΠΕΛΟΠΟΝΝΗΣΟΣ /
Πελοπόννησος

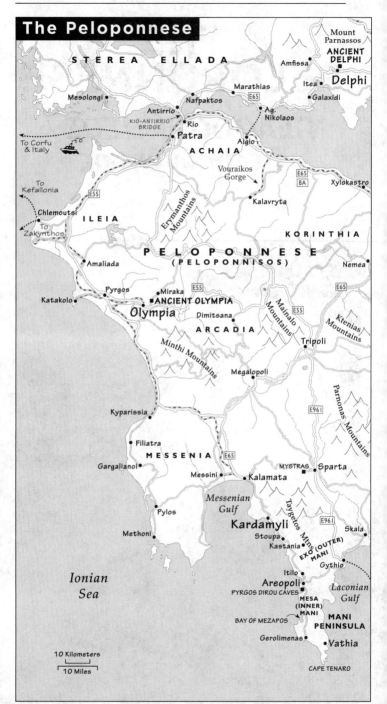

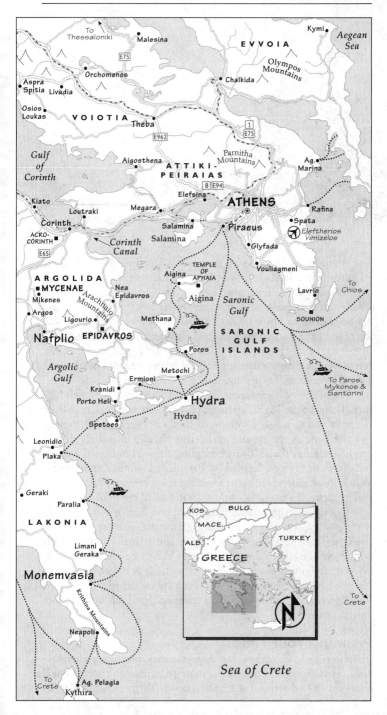

NAFPLIO

ΝΑΎΠΛΙΟ / Ναύπλιο

The charming Peloponnesian port town of Nafplio is small, cozy, and strollable. Though it has plenty of tourism, Nafplio is both elegant and proud. It's a must-see on any Greek visit because of its historical importance, its accessibility from Athens (an easy 2.5-hour drive or bus ride), and its handy location as a home base for touring the ancient sites of Epidavros and Mycenae (described in the next two chapters). Nafplio has great pensions, appealing restaurants, a thriving evening scene, inviting beaches nearby, and a good balance of real life and tourist convenience.

Nafplio loudly trumpets its special footnotes in Greek history. Thanks to its highly strategic position—nestled under cliffs at the apex of a vast bay—it changed hands between the Ottomans and the Venetians time and again. But Nafplio ultimately distinguished itself in the 1820s by becoming the first capital of a newly independent Greece, headed by President Ioannis Kapodistrias. While those glory days have faded, the town retains a certain genteel panache. It's as chic as Athens, without all the graffiti.

Owing to its prestigious past, Nafplio's harbor is guarded by three castles: one on a small island (Bourtzi), another just above the Old Town (ancient Akronafplia), and a third capping a tall cliff above the city (Palamidi Fortress). All three are wonderfully floodlit at night. If you're not up for the climb to Palamidi, explore Nafplio's narrow and atmospheric back streets, lined with elegant Venetian houses and Neoclassical mansions, and dip into its likeable museums.

Planning Your Time

Nafplio is light on sightseeing opportunities, but heavy on ambience. Two nights and one day is more than enough time to enjoy everything the town itself has to offer. With one full day in

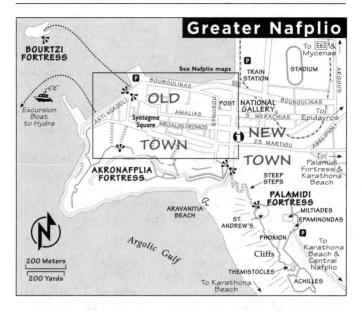

Nafplio, consider the arduous hike up to Palamidi Fortress first thing in the morning, before the worst heat of the day (bring water and wear good shoes; to save time and sweat, you can also drive or taxi there). Then get your bearings in the Old Town by following my self-guided walk, and visit any museums that appeal to you. In the afternoon, hit the beach.

Nafplio also serves as an ideal launch pad for visiting two of the Peloponnese's best ancient sites (each within a 45-minute drive or bus ride, and covered in the next two chapters): the best-preserved ancient theater anywhere, at **Epidavros;** and the older-than-old hilltop fortress of **Mycenae.** It's worth adding a day to your Nafplio stay to fit these in. If you have a **car,** you can see both of these (and drive up to the Palamidi Fortress) in one very full day; for an even more efficient plan, consider squeezing them in on your way into or out of town (for example, notice that Mycenae is between Nafplio and the major E-65 expressway to the north). These sites are also reachable by **bus,** but it might not be possible to do them both on the same day; instead, consider two full days in Nafplio, spending a half-day at each of the sites, and two half-days in the town.

Orientation to Nafplio

Because everything of interest is concentrated in the peninsular Old Town, Nafplio feels smaller than its population of 15,000. The mostly traffic-free Old Town is squeezed between the hilltop Akronafplia fortress and the broad seafront walkways of Bouboulinas and Akti Miaouli; the core of this area has atmospherically tight pedestrian lanes, bursting with restaurants and shops. Syntagma Square (Plateia Syntagmatos) is the centerpiece of the Old Town. From here, traffic-free Vasileos Konstantinou—called "Big Street" (Megalos Dromos) by locals—runs east to Syngrou street, which separates the Old Town from the New Town. The tranquil upper part of the Old Town, with some of my favorite accommodations, is connected by stepped lanes.

Note that the town's name can be spelled a staggering number of different ways in English: Nafplio(n), Nauplio(n), Navplio(n), Naufplio(n), Nauvplio(n), and so on. This makes it tricky to look for information online (e.g., weather reports or hotel-booking sites); try all the variations until you find one that works.

Tourist Information

Nafplio's clueless TI is just outside the New Town, a block away from the bus station (daily 9:00-13:00 & 16:00-20:00, in a dumpy building next to a fire station at 25 Martiou #4, tel. 27520-24444). Its guaranteed-job-security clerks are living proof that Greece needs to reform its civil-service system. If you visit, pick up the free town map and brochure...then get your questions answered at your hotel.

Arrival in Nafplio

By Car: Parking is free, easy, and central along the port, which runs in front of the Old Town (look for the big lots). If you're staying higher up, ask your hotel about more convenient parking (for example, there are several free spaces near the old, abandoned Hotel Xenia on the road up to the smaller Akronafplia fortress).

By Bus: The bus station is conveniently located right where the Old Town meets the New; from here, all my recommended accommodations are within a 10-minute walk.

Helpful Hints

Festivals: Nafplio hosts a classical music festival in late June. It features a mix of Greek and international performers playing at such venues as the Palamidi and Bourtzi fortresses (www.nafplionfestival.gr). The town is also a good base for seeing performances of drama and music at the famous Theater of Epidavros during the Athens & Epidavros Festival (weekends in July-Aug; see page 255). The local bus company operates special buses to the festival.

Store Hours: Businesses in Nafplio are very seasonal, keeping longer hours in peak times (summer and weekends) than at slower times. I've tried to list the correct hours, but if you're here outside of peak time (June-Aug), you may find some shops or restaurants taking an unexpected siesta (generally 15:00 or 16:00 until 18:00 or 19:00). To be sure to hit a place while it's open, get there in the morning.

Internet Access: Posto, overlooking the big park just outside the Old Town, is probably Nafplio's most user-friendly Internet café (€2/hour, daily 8:00-1:00 in the morning, next to Goody's at Sidiras Merarchias 4). Most accommodations in town offer free Wi-Fi to guests.

Post Office: The post office is at the corner of Syngrou and Sidiras Merarchias (Mon-Fri 7:30-14:00, closed Sat-Sun).

Bookshops: Conveniently located right on Syntagma Square, **Odyssey** sells international newspapers, maps, local guidebooks, and paperbacks in English (daily 8:00-24:00, on Syntagma Square next to the National Bank building, tel. 27520-23430).

Local Guide: Patti Staikou is a charming Nafplio native who enjoys sharing her town and nearby ancient sites with visitors (fair and negotiable prices for a 1-hour tour of Nafplio or 1.5-hour tours of Epidavros or Mycenae—she'll meet you there, mobile 697-778-3315, pstaikou@mail.gr).

Photo Services: Aris and Yiannis Karahalios at **Digital Photo Studio** can download your pictures to a CD (€5) or DVD (€8), and can even email a few of your favorites home (daily 9:00-22:30, Konstantinou 7, tel. 27520-28275).

Self-Guided Walk

Welcome to Nafplio

This walk—which takes about an hour and a half—will give you a feel for Nafplio's pleasant Old Town.

• *We'll begin on the harborfront square opposite the fortified island, marked by a sturdy obelisk.*

Square of the Friends of the Greeks (Plateia Filellinon)

This space is named for the French soldiers who fell fighting for Greek independence in 1821. On the memorial **obelisk,** a classical-style medallion shows brothers in arms: Hellas and Gallia (Greeks and French). On the other side is the French inscription.

Face the **waterfront.** Nafplio has a busy cruise-ship business. Since they deepened the port a few years back,

Nafplio Self-Guided Walk

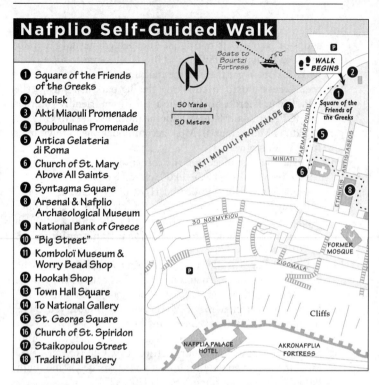

1. Square of the Friends of the Greeks
2. Obelisk
3. Akti Miaouli Promenade
4. Bouboulinas Promenade
5. Antica Gelateria di Roma
6. Church of St. Mary Above All Saints
7. Syntagma Square
8. Arsenal & Nafplio Archaeological Museum
9. National Bank of Greece
10. "Big Street"
11. Komboloï Museum & Worry Bead Shop
12. Hookah Shop
13. Town Hall Square
14. To National Gallery
15. St. George Square
16. Church of St. Spiridon
17. Staikopoulou Street
18. Traditional Bakery

small ships can actually dock here, while tenders for bigger ships drop their passengers here. A goofy tourist train leaves from this parking lot (pricey at €4 for a 20-minute tour, doesn't even go to the most charming center of town; departs every 30-45 minutes, sometimes with afternoon break).

Plenty of Nafplio bars, cafés, restaurants, and tavernas face the harbor. The embankment called **Akti Miaouli** (which covers all the vowels but one) promenades to the left with a long line of sedate al fresco tables filled by an older clientele. (Locals warn that these are the most expensive cafés in town, but well-heeled tourists don't mind shelling out an extra euro or two for the view.) The promenade continues along the shore entirely around the point to Arvanitia Beach, where a road returns to town up and over the saddle between the two fortresses (consider this route for an easy hike).

The **Bouboulinas** promenade heads in the other direction (to the right, as you face the water)—first passing fine fish tavernas (listed on page 249), and then trendy bars. Late at night, forget about the fish—this is Nafplio's meat market, where hormone-oozing young Greeks hit the town. (The better-for-families hang-out is the kid-friendly Syntagma Square, which we'll visit later.)

From the harbor, you can also see the three Venetian forts

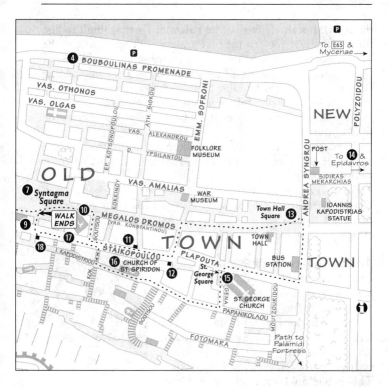

of Nafplio. (All of these are described in more detail later in this chapter.) First, the mighty little fortress island just offshore, called

Bourtzi, was built during the first Venetian occupation (15th century) to protect the harbor. Most of what you see today is an 18th-century reconstruction from the second Venetian occupation. A shuttle boat departs from here to visit the island. It's a fun little trip, but there's not much to see there beyond a pleasant city view (€4 round-trip, returns after 15 minutes, catch a later boat if you want to linger).

To see the other two forts, turn 180 degrees, putting your back to the water. Capping the hill high above is the **Palamidi Fortress** (highest, to the left); below it is Nafplio's ancient acropolis, the Akronafplia (lower, to

the right). Locals claim that the Palamidi Fortress, built in just three years (1711-1714), is the best-preserved Venetian fort in the Mediterranean. It can be reached by climbing nearly a thousand stone stairs...or by paying €7 for a taxi. While the commanding view is rewarding, the building itself is a bulky, impressive, empty shell. The lower **Akronafplia Fortress** is built upon the remains of an ancient fort. The big stones at the base of its wall date from the third century B.C.

On your left as you face the hilltop fortresses, the building to the left of the white church is Harvard University's Center for Hellenic Studies.

• *With your back to the water, walk up the street to the right of Hotel Grande Bretagne (Farmakopoulou). After a block, on the first corner (left), is a popular gelateria. Across the small square just beyond it (Komninou) is a church. First things first...*

Antica Gelateria di Roma

Greece has great honey-dripping desserts, but nobody does ice cream like the Italians. This popular, fun-loving, air-conditioned ice-cream parlor is run by Marcello and family, who offer a taste of Italy: gelato, fruit-based *sorbetto,* as well as other treats such as *biscotti, lemoncello,* and cappuccino. This is one holdover from the Venetian occupation that no local will complain about. (For more details, see page 250.)

• *Just across the square stands the...*

Church of St. Mary Above All Saints

This church has a proud history: It originally dates from the 15th century; today's building is from the 18th century; and just

a few years ago, they peeled back, then reapplied, all the plaster. The priest at this church is particularly active, keeping it open late into the evening (long after many other Nafplio churches have closed). Outside the door he posts a daily message—a thought to ponder or a suggested prayer.

Step inside—it's generally open. The flat ceiling with the painted Trinity in three circular panels shows a Venetian influence—most Greek Orthodox churches of this period are domed.

NAFPLIO

The more typical iconostasis, a wall of Greek Orthodox icons, separates worshippers from priests. If you're so moved, drop in a coin for a candle and light up a prayer. Next to one of the icons on the side, you might see a basket with individually wrapped cotton balls. These have been dipped in oil that was blessed by the priest; you can take one home to transfer the blessing to somebody (often used for children).

• *Leaving the church through the door you came in, go right (around the corner of the church), and walk down the street with the church on your right. Go past the imposing Venetian arsenal, then stop to take in the big square you've suddenly landed in. If it's sunny, stand under the shady tree in the corner nearest where you entered.*

Syntagma Square (Plateia Syntagmatos)

Like the main square in Athens, Nafplio's central plaza is "Constitution Square," celebrating the 1843 document that established a constitutional monarchy for Greece. Nafplio was one of the first towns liberated from the Ottoman Turks (1822), and became the new country's first capital. The square is a delightful mix of architecture revealing the many layers of local history.

Survey this scene in a counterclockwise spin-tour, starting on your immediate right. The big building flying the Greek flag at the bottom of the square (on your right as you look into the square) was the Venetian **arsenal.** Of course, wherever Venice ruled, you'll find its symbol: the winged lion of its patron saint, Mark. The building is stout with heavily barred windows because it once stored gunpowder and weapons. Today, it houses the town's **Archaeological Museum,** which has reopened after a six-year renovation (museum described on page 237).

Just to the left of the arsenal, a block farther inland, is a domed **mosque.** In 1825, with the Muslim Ottomans expelled, this building was taken over and renovated to house independent Greece's first parliament. Now it serves as a conference center.

The big **National Bank of Greece** (facing the long side of the square, opposite the cafés) could be described as "Neo-Minoan"—with its inverted Minoan-style columns (similar to those found in circa-1500 B.C. Minoan ruins on Crete) that taper toward the base, as if they were tree trunks stood on their heads. They are painted with the same color scheme found in Minoan frescoes.

Two small **monuments** stand in front of the bank: a Venetian winged lion from the old fortress (see photo on next page); and

NAFPLIO

a relief of an aristocratic woman waving from a balcony—in 1833, she welcomed the newly imported-from-Bavaria King Otto with his first waltz in Greece. (Otto spent just one year here before moving his capital to Athens.) The handy Odyssey bookshop is just beyond the bank (see "Helpful Hints," earlier). (From here, this walk does a loop through the Old Town, ending at the traditional pastry shop on the corner immediately behind the bookshop.)

The second former **mosque** fronting this square (at the far end) was converted after independence into Greece's first primary school. Today it's a gallery and theater. The main drag through the Old Town is immediately opposite the arsenal, at the far end of the square (we're headed there next). And a series of Neoclassical buildings (now popular cafés and restaurants, including the recommended Noufara) face the bank from the left side of the square.

• *Head across the square and walk down the pedestrian street opposite the arsenal.*

The "Big Street" (Megalos Dromos)

While Nafplio's main drag is named for King Constantine (Vasileos Konstantinou), locals know it as Megalos Dromos ("Big

Street"). Strolling along here, you'll soon pass the quirky (and recommended) Lathos Bar ("Mistake Bar," #1 on left), run by an eccentric character. As you walk, you might notice that this town is something of a shoppers' paradise. Streets like this one are crammed with shops selling everything from the usual tacky tourist trinkets to expensive jewelry, all aimed at the fat wallets of Athenian out-of-towners.

• *You could continue along this shop-lined street. But instead, we'll take a more colorful route: Head up one block to the right and walk down the parallel street (turn right at the first corner up the narrow alley, then turn left onto Staikopoulou).*

Along this stretch of Staikopoulou are a pair of...

Uniquely Greek Shops

After about a block, on the left (at #25), is the **Komboloï Museum.** Owner Aris Evangelinos has a real passion for worry beads. If

Worry Beads

The longer you're in Greece, the more you'll notice it: Greeks everywhere spinning, stroking, fondling, and generally fidgeting with their worry beads.

Greeks use these beaded strings to soothe themselves and get focused. (Traditionally, only men used worry beads, but they're becoming increasingly popular among Greek women, too.)

Many major world faiths—aware of the calming and concentration-focusing effects of beads—employ some version of stringed beads as a worship aid, typically to help keep track of prayers. Think of the Catholic rosary, Muslim prayer beads, and the long, knotted rope belts worn by medieval monks. Hindus and Buddhists also make use of beads. Today's Greeks—likely inspired by Muslims during the nearly 400 years of Ottoman rule—have adopted the habit, but stripped it of its religious overtones.

Technically, there are two different types of worry beads: Most typical is the *komboloï,* a loop with an odd number of beads (it can be any number, so long as it's odd). At the top of the loop, there can be a fixed bead (or two), which is called the "priest" or the "main bead." The relatively new *begleri*—popular only since the 1950s—is a single string with an even number of beads (so it can be comfortably balanced in the hand).

The beads can be made from a wide variety of materials. The basic tourist version is a cheap "starter set" made from synthetic materials, similar to marbles. You'll pay more for organic materials, which are considered more pleasant to touch: precious stones, bones, horn, wood, coral, mother-of-pearl, seeds, and more. The most prized worry beads are made of amber. Most valuable are the hand-cut amber beads, which are very soft and fragile; machine-cut amber is processed to be stronger.

If buying a set of worry beads, try several to find one that fits well in your hand. When test-driving beads, connoisseurs tune into the feel of the smooth beads and the sound they make when clacking together.

There is no "right" or "wrong" way to use your worry beads—everyone finds a routine that works for them. Some flip or spin the beads in their hands, while others sit quietly and count the beads over and over. There are as many ways to use worry beads as there are Greeks. Their seeming "nervous habit" seems to have the opposite effect—defusing stress and calming the nerves.

you're in the market for a set of beads, the ground-floor shop here features a remarkable selection—with beads from every material you can imagine (the cheapest, synthetic sets cost about €8; the priciest—which can cost hundreds of euros—are antique or made of amber). While you can buy cheap worry beads at practically every tourist shop in Greece, if you'd like to survey all your options and pick out something a little more special, you might as well do it here. The staff is helpful in explaining the varieties. The upstairs "museum"—overpriced at €3—shows off a few small rooms of the owner's favorites from his vast collection, while a handful of English labels explain how variations on worry beads are used by many different faiths (shop—free, museum—€3; both open April-Sept daily 9:30-22:00; Oct-March Wed-Mon 9:30-20:30, closed Tue; Staikopoulou 25, tel. 27520-21618).

At the end of the block, look for a shop on the right (at #56) with a sign reading *ΕΡΓΑΣΤΗΡΙΟ ΚΟΜΠΟΛΟΓΙΟΥ* (Worry Bead Workshop) and, in English, oddly, "Laboratory." More than just another bead shop, this store also sells **hookahs** (water pipes) and the apple-flavored tobacco that smokers burn in them.

• *At the intersection next to the hookah shop, turn left and walk one block back down to the "Big Street." Turn right onto the "Big Street" and follow it until you emerge into...*

Town Hall Square

A statue of **King Otto** (ΟΘΩΝ) marks the one-time location of his palace. Otto, who had come from Bavarian royalty to rule Greece, decided to move the capital to Athens after just a year here in Nafplio. (An enthusiastic student of clas-sical history, Otto was charmed by the idea of reviving the greatness of ancient Athens.) His palace here in Nafplio finally burned down in 1929.

Otto, looking plenty regal, gazes toward the New Town. Fifty yards in front of Otto (on the right) is the Neoclassical "first high school of Greece"—today's Town Hall. The monument in front celebrates a local hero from the war against the Ottomans. Until recently this square was named "Three Admirals Square"—remembering the three great European powers (France, Britain,

NAFPLIO

and Russia) that helped the Greeks overthrow their Ottoman rulers in 1821.

• *At the far end of Town Hall Square, you hit the busy...*

Syngrou Street and the New Town

This thoroughfare separates the Old Town from the New. Out of respect for the three-story-tall Old Town, no new building is allowed to exceed that height—even in the New Town.

In the square across the street, the statue honors **Ioannis Kapodistrias,** the first president of Greece (back when Nafplio was the capital). He faces the Old Town...and Otto, who stepped in when the president's reign was cut tragically short. (We'll get the whole story later.)

Just behind Kapodistrias is a family-friendly **park.** If you want a cheap and fast meal, consider grabbing a bite at one of the family-filled gyros and souvlaki eateries surrounding the park (cheap €3 meals: order and pay at the bar, then find a bench in the park). Goody's (on the left, by the post office) is the Greek McDonald's—the local kids' favorite hamburger joint, found in towns all over Greece. The good Posto Internet café is two doors down from Goody's (see "Helpful Hints," earlier).

A few minutes' walk straight ahead, past the end of the park,

is one of Nafplio's best museums: the **National Gallery,** which shows off evocative artwork from the Greek War of Independence (described later, under "Sights in Nafplio").

Without crossing Syngrou street, turn right. The commotion surrounds Nafplio's tiny but busy **bus station.** KTEL (or ΚΤΕΛ in Greek) is the national bus company; in the office here, you can buy tickets for bus trips, or use the ticket machine out front. The **TI**—which offers little help to visitors—is a block away from the bus station (see page 226).

• *At the first corner, turn right on Plapouta street. Walk a block to...*

St. George Square

The focal point of the square, Nafplio's metropolitan church (equivalent to a Catholic "cathedral"), is dedicated to St. George and was the neighborhood church for King Otto. (Otto's palace was a block away—you can see Town Hall Square by looking down

the small alley.) Step into the church's dark interior (noticing the clever system that prevents the doors from slamming) to see a gigantic chandelier hovering overhead.

Back outside, surveying St. George Square, you get a feel for an old Nafplio neighborhood. Well-worn Neoclassical buildings date—like most of the Old Town—from the boom that followed the city's rise to prominence when it was Greece's first capital. During the 1820s and 1830s, Nafplio became a haven to refugees from other lands still threatened by the Ottomans.

• *Walk a block uphill (toward the fortress) and turn right on Papanikolaou street.*

Upper Streets of the Old Town

Strolling this quiet lane, note that the Neoclassical grid-planned town is to your right, while the higgledy-piggledy Ottoman town climbs the hillside (with winding and evocative lanes and stepped alleys) on your left.

Straight ahead (100 yards away) stands the white bell tower marking the **Church of St. Spiridon** and its square. Facing the square (on the left, hiding in a niche in the wall, near the steps) is the first of several 18th-century Turkish fountains we'll see. When the Ottomans controlled Greece, they still used the squiggly Arabic script you see here. It's likely a verse from the Quran, a jaunty greeting, and/or a tribute to the person who paid for the fountain.

Continue straight along the side of the church to another Ottoman fountain (on the left)—with its characteristic cypress-tree-and-flowers decor.

Between here and the door of the church just ahead is the rough equivalent—to the Greeks—of Ford's Theater (where Lincoln was assassinated). Ioannis Kapodistrias was elected the first president of independent Greece in 1828. But just three years later, on October 9, 1831, he was shot and stabbed in this spot by Mani landowners who feared his promises of land reform. This led to chaos, less democratic idealism, and the arrival of Greece's imported Bavarian royalty (King Otto, whom we met earlier).

NAFPLIO

Pop into the church if it's open. Across from the church is a collapsing *hamam*, a Turkish bath from the 18th century.

• *At the next corner (Kokkinou street), turn right and climb down the slippery marble steps to Staikopoulou street (where we saw the hookah and worry bead shops earlier). This time we'll take it left, back to Syntagma Square.*

Staikopoulou Street

This bustling pedestrian drag is lined with grill restaurants (the harborfront is better for fish) and their happy hustlers, and another

 fine Ottoman fountain (on the right after a block). For a caloric finale, find the **traditional bakery** (on the left corner at #18, with the ΠΑΡΑΔΟΣΙΑΚΑ ΓΛΥΚΑ sign, 10 yards before the tall skinny tree and the back of the National Bank). This place has been delighting locals with its *baklava* and *ekmek* (roughly,

crème-topped *baklava*) since 1955. Choose a tasty Greek dessert from the display case, and enjoy it at the outdoor tables (for more details on this bakery, see page 250).

A few steps down on the right take you back to Syntagma Square. Find the tiny black cube in the center and sit on it. Apart from being a handy meeting point for the town's kids and a stand for the community Christmas tree, it means absolutely nothing.

• *Your walk is over. From here, you can enjoy the rest of the city. In addition to the museums we've already passed (which you can circle back to now), a few more sights—including a folklore museum and a war museum—are within a few blocks (described in the next section). Or you can head to any of Nafplio's three Venetian forts (see page 239). If you're ready to relax, hit the beach (all described later, under "Sights in Nafplio").*

Sights in Nafplio

In the Old Town

▲▲**Nafplio Archaeological Museum**—Nafplio's top museum gives a concise overview of prehistoric Greece and the Mycenaean civilization. Visit here for a great warm-up before you go to Mycenae.

Recently renovated, the museum occupies the top two floors of the grand Venetian arsenal on the main square. Before touring the exhibits, climb the stairs to the second floor and watch one of two videos covering what you're about to see. If you have a choice, avoid the long, overly scholarly slideshow about regional

NAFPLIO

archaeological digs; ask for the impressionistic video of school-children learning about the discovery of the museum's priceless set of bronze armor.

After the film, go back downstairs and tour the exhibits, which are well-described in English. The collection runs in chronological order, with Stone Age tools suddenly giving way to dolphin frescos inspired by the Minoan civilization on Crete. Eye-catching jewelry includes a bull-shaped crystal bead (look for the magnifying glass inside a glass case) and strings of gold beads.

The star of the museum stands in the center: the "Dendra Panoply," a 15th-century B.C. suit of bronze armor that was discovered in a Mycenaean chamber tomb. Also found at the site (and displayed here) is a helmet made from boar tusks. Experts consider this the oldest surviving suit of armor in all of Europe.

The second floor displays artifacts from the Age of Homer to the Roman occupation. Particularly striking are the ceremonial terra-cotta masks along one wall, which look as if they belong in a circus. Check out the display of rare glasswork from the first century A.D.—somehow these pieces have survived two millennia without getting smashed.

Cost and Hours: €2; May-Sept Tue-Sun 8:00-20:00, Mon 13:30-20:00; Oct-April Tue-Sun 8:30-13:00, closed Mon; at the bottom of Syntagma Square, tel. 27520-27502, www.culture.gr.

Peloponnese Folklore Foundation Museum—Dedicated to Peloponnesian culture, this modern exhibit fills two floors with clothing, furniture, and jewelry that trace the cultural history of Nafplio and the surrounding region. While not explained in a particularly engaging way, the interesting collection—which ranges from colorful and traditional costumes, to stiff urban suits, to formal gowns—is at least well-displayed.

Cost and Hours: €2; April-Oct Mon and Wed-Sat 9:00-14:30 & 18:00-21:00, Sun 9:30-15:00, Tue 18:00-21:00; Nov-March Mon and Wed-Sat 9:00-14:30 & 17:30-20:30, Sun 9:30-15:00, Tue 17:30-20:30; last entry 30 minutes before closing, Vasileos Alexandrou 1, tel. 27520-28947, www.pli.gr.

War Museum (Nafplio Branch)—This small exhibit, operated and staffed by the Greek armed forces, is best left to military buffs. It displays old illustrations and photos of various conflicts, plus weapons and uniforms (with some English descriptions). The top floor, dedicated to the modern era, displays some fascinating WWII-era political cartoons from the Greek perspective.

Cost and Hours: Free; Tue-Sat 9:00-14:00, Sun 9:30-14:00, closed Mon, on Amalias, tel. 27520-25591, www.warmuseum.gr.

In the New Town

This museum is a 10-minute walk into the New Town from the bus station, along the major road called Sidiras Merarchias.

▲**National Gallery (Alexandros Soutzos Museum, Nafplio Annex)**—Housed in a grandly restored Neoclassical mansion,

this museum features both temporary and permanent exhibits. The permanent collection, displayed upstairs, is devoted to Romantic artwork (mostly paintings) stemming from the inspirational Greek War of Independence (1821-1829), which led to Nafplio's status as the first capital of independent Greece. The small, manageable collection is arranged thematically. Thoughtful English descriptions explain the historical underpinnings for each piece of art, illuminating common themes such as the dying hero, naval battles, and the hardships of war. While the art itself might not be technically masterful, the patriotism shimmering beneath it is stirring even to non-Greeks.

Cost and Hours: €3, free on Mon; open Mon and Wed-Sat 10:00-15:00, Wed and Fri also 17:00-20:00, Sun 10:00-14:00, closed Tue; Sidiras Merarchias 23, tel. 27520-21915, www.culture.gr.

Nafplio's Three Venetian Fortresses

In the days when Venice was the economic ruler of Europe (15th-18th centuries), the Venetians fortified Nafplio with a trio of stout fortresses. These attempted—but ultimately failed—to fend off Ottoman invasion. Conquered by the Ottomans in 1715, Nafplio remained in Turkish hands until the Greeks retook the city in 1822.

Today all three parts of the Venetian fortifications are open to visitors. These are listed in order from lowest to highest.

Bourtzi—While this heavily fortified island—just offshore from Nafplio's waterfront—looks striking, there's not much to do here. Still, it's a pleasant vantage point, offering fine views back on the city (boats depart from the bottom of the square called Plateia Filellinon, €4 round-trip, 4-person minimum, on island it's free to enter the fortress).

Akronafplia—Nafplio's ancient acropolis, capping the low hill just behind the Old Town, is fairly easy to reach (a manageable  but sometimes-steep 10- to 15-minute uphill hike—from the Old Town, just find your way up on any of a number of narrow stepped lanes, then bear left to reach the main road that leads up into the eastern end of the fortress). The earliest surviving parts of this fortress date back to the third century B.C., but the Venetians brought it up to then-modern standards in the 15th century. Up top, there's little to see aside from a few ruins (free to enter and explore anytime). The top of the hill is flanked by two modern hotels: at the east end (toward Palamidi), the deserted and decaying Hotel Xenia; and at the west end, the top-of-the-top Nafplia Palace hotel (which is connected by elevator to the top of the Old Town).

▲▲Palamidi Fortress—This imposing hilltop fortress, built 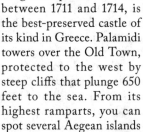 between 1711 and 1714, is the best-preserved castle of its kind in Greece. Palamidi towers over the Old Town, protected to the west by steep cliffs that plunge 650 feet to the sea. From its highest ramparts, you can spot several Aegean islands and look deep into the mountainous interior of the Peloponnesian Peninsula.

Cost and Hours: €4, daily April-Oct 8:30-19:15, Nov-March 8:30-15:00, tel. 27520-28036.

Getting There: If you're fit, you can reach  the fortress the old-fashioned way: by **climbing** the strenuous, loooong flight of steps that lead up from the road to Akronafplia fortress (near the top end of Polyzoidou street, just outside the Old Town, roughly behind the TI). A fun Nafplio pastime is asking locals exactly how many steps there are—most estimates are between 850 and 1,000, but you'll never hear the same answer twice. (One favorite legend says that there used to be exactly 1,000 steps, but Theodoros Kolokotronis—hero of the Greek War of Independence—broke the bottom one when he tried to ride his horse up the steps after defeating the Ottomans in 1822.) I lost count looking at the views, but whatever the number of stairs, it was plenty—get an early start (to avoid the midday heat), wear sturdy shoes, and bring along water. Alternatively, you can catch a **taxi** to the top for about €7 one-way. Or, if you have your own car, you can **drive** to the top for free: Follow signs east of town for the beach at Karathona/ Καραθωνα, and after ascending the hill, watch for the turn-off on the right up to *Palamidi/Παλαμηδη*.

❍ **Self-Guided Tour:** The mighty outer walls enclose a series of interconnected bastions. Spend some time just poking around this sprawling complex, playing king- or queen-of-the-castle. Everything is well-marked with directional signs. I've described each bastion from lowest to highest (in a roughly counterclockwise order), as you would approach them from the steps up from town. If you arrive by car, walk down to the St. Andrew's Bastion to begin this loop.

The most important and best-preserved is **St. Andrew's Bastion** (Agios Andreas), at the top of the steps from town. This

area also offers the fortress' best views over the rooftops of old Nafplio. Inside the bastion, scamper up the giant vaults, which form an angled approach up to the ramparts.

Following the outer wall of the complex farther uphill, you reach the **Phokion Bastion,** and beyond it the **Themistocles Bastion,** which crowns the hilltop. At the bastion's highest point, find the little door leading to the cliff. According to legend, in 1779 the occupying Ottomans hired hundreds of Albanian mercenaries to suppress a local rebellion. Unable to pay them for a job ruthlessly done, the Ottomans lured the mercenaries here, then hurled them to their deaths on the rocks of Arvanitia ("Treachery") Beach far below.

Just beyond the Themistocles Bastion— guarding Palamidi's remote southern flank—is the fortress' weakest point, the appropriately named **Achilles Bastion.** The low walls (less than 20 feet tall) proved easy to scale when

the Ottomans captured the fortress in 1715, less than a year after its completion. A century later, defenders still hadn't learned their lesson—this was also the route used in 1822 by Greek independence forces when they ousted the Ottomans.

To find the final two bastions, retrace your steps back up to the Themistocles Bastion, then downhill toward the parking lot. The largest of all is the notorious **Miltiades Bastion,** which was used as a prison from 1840 to 1920. Here you'll need to crouch and scramble to reach the miserable little Kolokotronis Prison, which once held the Greek leader Theodoros Kolokotronis (famous as a hero of Greek liberation, but later imprisoned here by his political opponents). The entry gate (at the parking lot) is the **Epaminondas Bastion.**

Beaches

When Nafplio residents (and visitors) want to hit the beach, they head behind the Old Town peninsula. A rocky pay beach called **Arvanitia** is on the back side of this peninsula (walk over the saddle between Palamidi and Akronafplia fortresses, or follow the pedestrian drag around the western end of the peninsula from the Old Town). For more serious beach-going, consider the one-hour walk (or 10-minute drive) to the **Karathona** beach, which huddles behind the Palamidi Fortress.

Sights near Nafplio

Each of these ancient attractions is within a 45-minute drive of Nafplio (in different directions).

▲▲▲**Epidavros**—This ancient site, 18 miles east of Nafplio, has an underwhelming museum, forgettable ruins...and the most magnificent theater of the ancient world. It was built nearly 2,500 years ago to seat 15,000. Today, it's kept busy reviving the greatest plays of antiquity. You can catch musical and dramatic performances from July through August. Try to see Epidavros either early or late in the day; the theater's marvelous acoustics are best enjoyed in near-solitude. Sitting in the most distant seat as your partner stands on the stage, you can practically hear the *retsina* wine rumbling in her stomach. For more on the theater and surrounding site, see the Epidavros chapter.

▲▲▲**Mycenae**—This was the capital of the Mycenaeans, who won the Trojan War and dominated Greece 1,000 years before the

Acropolis and other Golden Age Greek sights. The classical Greeks marveled at the huge stones and workmanship of the Mycenaean ruins. Visitors today can still gape at the Lion's Gate, peer into a cool, ancient cistern, and explore the giant *tholos* tomb called the Treasury of Atreus. The tomb, built in the 15th century B.C., stands like a huge stone igloo, with a smooth subterranean dome 47 feet wide and 42 feet tall. For more on this ancient site, see the Mycenae chapter.

Nightlife in Nafplio

Nafplio enjoys a thriving after-hours scene. Poke around to find the café or bar that appeals to you most for a pre- or post-dinner drink. A few zones to consider, by demographic:

Young people flock to the **Bouboulinas** promenade, where each café/bar tries to trump the last with trendy decor and throbbing soundtracks. Each place has both indoor and outdoor seating. Locals use the Italian word *pasarella* ("catwalk") to describe this scene, where sexy young Greeks (many of them Athenians on holiday) put on their most provocative outfits to parade for each other.

Everyone seems to enjoy the floodlit marble drawing-room vibe of **Syntagma Square.** Cafés and restaurants with ample, atmospheric al fresco seating surround a relaxed, open area with people at play. Kids happily run free in the square.

The upper crust enjoys the cafés lining the promenade **Akti Miaouli.** Prices are high, but the water views (with the illuminated island fortress) might be worth the expense.

Various other bars and cafés are scattered around the Old Town. Just find one with ambience, music, and people-watching you enjoy. For a unique experience, consider dropping by the **Lathos Bar** ("Mistake Bar"). The junk-shop decor is topped by the quirky owner, a town character who couldn't care less about business. If he doesn't like you, he won't serve you (nights only, closed Tue, a few steps off Syntagma Square on the "Big Street" at Konstantinou 1).

There are no true **dance clubs** in Nafplio (which has a strict noise ordinance—no loud music in the Old Town after 23:00, unless it's in a specially insulated room). In the summer, seasonal outdoor clubs sprout along the road toward Argos. Ask for advice about the latest scene.

Sleeping in Nafplio

Nafplio enjoys an abundance of excellent accommodations. Because this is a chic getaway for wealthy Athenians, many of the best beds are in well-run, boutique-ish little pensions. (Some of the smaller pensions are run by skeleton staffs, so don't expect 24-hour reception; let them know what time you'll arrive so they can greet you.) The many options allow hotel-seekers to be picky. After surveying the scene, I've listed my favorites here, but there are many other good choices.

It's boom or bust in Nafplio. At the busiest times (June, July, especially August, and weekends year-round), hotels are full and prices go up; outside these times, hoteliers are lean and hungry, and rates become very soft. Don't be afraid to ask for a deal, especially if you're staying more than a couple of nights. Unless otherwise noted, rates include breakfast; most cafés in town sell a basic breakfast for €5-6.

Most of these accommodations (except Ippoliti) are uphill from the heart of the Old Town—some higher up than others. The good news is that they provide a quiet retreat from the bustling old center; the bad news is that you might have to walk uphill, and probably climb a few flights of stairs, to reach your room.

$$$ Amfitriti Boutique Hotels has two locations at the top of the Old Town. Pension Amfitriti (Αμφι τρίτη), with five rooms, overlooks a pleasant small square along a pedestrian street (corner of Zigomala and Kokkinou); Amfitriti Belvedere rents seven rooms in a renovated old mansion, higher up along some stairs. The rooms at both locations are colorful and trendy (Db-€95-110, family room-€120, cheaper Oct-April, free Wi-Fi, tel. 27520-96250, fax 27520-96252, www.amfitritihotels-nafplio.com, info@amfitriti-pension.gr).

$$$ Amymone Pension and **Adiandi Hotel** are a pair of super-stylish, trendy boutique hotels a few doors apart along one of Nafplio's most inviting restaurant lanes. Each room is different, but all are hip and boldly decorated (both hotels have air-

---

Sleep Code

(€1 = about $1.40, country code: 30)
S = Single, **D** = Double/Twin, **T** = Triple, **Q** = Quad, **b** = bathroom,
s = shower only.

    To help you easily sort through these listings, I've divided the rooms into three categories, based on the price for a standard double room with bath:

  $$$ Higher Priced—Most rooms €100 or more.
   $$ Moderately Priced—Most rooms between €65-100.
    $ Lower Priced—Most rooms €65 or less.

    Prices can change without notice; verify the hotel's current rates online or by email. For other updates, see www.ricksteves.com/update.

---

con, lots of stairs with no elevator, free Wi-Fi, tel. 27520-99477 or 27520-22073, fax 27520-99478). The very central location can come with a bit more noise than my other listings. The Amymone (Αμυμώνη) has eight rooms, a lighter color scheme, and a country-mod aesthetic (Db-€75-125 depending on size, Othonos 39, www.amymone.gr, info@amymone.gr). The Adiandi (Αδιάντη), with seven rooms, comes with darker colors and seriously artsy decor (Db-€90-140 depending on size, Othonos 31, www.hotel-adiandi.com, info@hotel-adiandi.com).

$$$ Ippoliti Hotel (ΙΠΠΟΛΥΤΗ) is my choice for a classy business-hotel splurge, with all the little touches—including a small swimming pool and gym—and 19 elegantly decorated, hardwood-floor rooms—some furnished with antiques (Db-€120-180 depending on size, air-con, elevator, free Wi-Fi, Ilia Miniati 9, at corner with Aristidou, tel. 27520-96088, fax 27520-96087, www.ippoliti.gr, info@ippoliti.gr).

$$ Pension Marianna sets the bar for welcoming, good-value accommodations in Nafplio (and all of the Peloponnese). The friendly Zotos brothers—Petros, Panos, and Takis—have

earned their top billing in all the guidebooks by offering genuine hospitality, fair rates, and comfortable rooms. It's scenically situated just under the lower Akronafplia wall at the top of town, well worth the steep climb up the stairs from the Old Town. The 27 rooms—some with views

1. Amfitriti Boutique Hotels (2)
2. Amymone Pension; Adiandi Hotel
3. Ippoliti Hotel
4. Pension Marianna
5. Pension Filyra
6. Hotel Leto
7. Byron Hotel
8. Pension Rigas
9. Pension Anapli
10. Dimitris Bekas Rooms
11. Mezedopoleio O Noulis Rest.
12. Imarton Bistro
13. Taverna Paleo Arhontiko
14. Epi Skinis Restaurant
15. Olgas St. Tavernas
16. Bouboulinas St. Eateries
17. Noufara Restaurant
18. Karonis Wine Shop
19. Supermarket
20. Antica Gelateria di Roma
21. Pastry Shop
22. Lathos Bar
23. Odyssey Bookshop
24. Posto Internet Café
25. Digital Photo Studio

and/or little balconies, some with old-stone decor, all well cared for—are scattered throughout several levels, overlooked by an airy, glassed-in breakfast terrace. Regardless of your price range, try here first—but book early, as this understandably popular place can fill up (Sb-€75, Db-€85, Tb-€100, Qb-€110, same prices year-round, €5 less per person if you skip breakfast, air-con, free Wi-Fi, Potamianou 9, tel. 27520-24256, fax 27520-99365, www.pension marianna.gr, info@pensionmarianna.gr).

$$ Hotel Leto is a likeable family-run hotel with 20 forget-table but fine rooms in a residential quarter uphill from the Old Town. Ask for a balcony at no extra charge—and try to get the elusive and popular room #121 (Sb-€46, Db-€70, Tb-€90, prices soft in slow times, skip breakfast to save €6 per person, air-con, mini-fridge, free Wi-Fi, Zigomala 28, tel. 27520-28093, fax 27520-29588, www.leto-hotel.com, letoht@otenet.gr).

$$ Byron Hotel is a traditional, family-run standby with 18 simple, older-feeling rooms in a scenic setting up some stairs above the Old Town (Sb-€50, Db-€60, view Db-€70, bigger superior Db-€80, Tb-€90, breakfast-€7, air-con, pay Wi-Fi, Platonos 2, tel. 27520-22351, fax 27520-26338, www.byronhotel.gr, byronhotel @otenet.gr).

$ **Pension Rigas** is a gem with seven small, cozy rooms in a refurbished old building with exposed stone and beams, and lots of character. Its comfy central lobby provides a convivial place for guests to share travel stories. Your host, kindly Nicholas Vasiliou, is generous with travel tips (Db-€40-70 depending on size—the €40 Db is tiny but adequate, slightly cheaper for Sb, no breakfast, most rooms have an electric tea kettle and mini-fridge, air-con, free Wi-Fi, Kapodistriou 8, tel. 27520-23611, fax 27520-23566, www.pension-rigas.gr, reserve by phone).

$ **Pension Filyra** (Φιλύρα) has six tastefully decorated rooms at a nice price in a few buildings in the heart of the Old Town (Db-€50-60 depending on size, attic suite with kitchenette and low beams-€60, all rates €5 more on Sat, cheaper Sept-May, your mini-fridge is stocked with a basic continental breakfast, air-con, free Wi-Fi, Aggelou Terzaki 29, tel. 27520-96096, fax 27520-99093, www.pensionfilyra.gr, info@pensionfilyra.gr).

$ **Pension Anapli** has seven colorful rooms with iron-frame beds (Db-€50, or €60 with balcony, €10 extra on weekends, air-con, Fotomara 21, tel. 27520-24585, www.pension-anapli.gr, info@pension-anapli.gr).

$ Dimitris Bekas rents seven no-frills, clean, backpacker rooms sharing an incredible view terrace at the very top of town. Dimitris is a devotee of American sports—if you're falling behind on the scores, he'll fill you in (D-€29, Db-€45, no breakfast, no air-con but fans, look for signs off Potamiou, above the Catholic church at Efthimiopoulou 26, tel. & fax 27520-24594).

Eating in Nafplio

Nafplio is bursting with tempting eateries. Because most of them cater to Athenians on a weekend break, they aim to please return customers. This also means that prices can be a bit high. In two high-profile restaurant zones—the tavernas along Staikopoulou street (just above Syntagma Square) and the fish restaurants on Bouboulinas street (along the waterfront)—waiters compete desperately for the passing tourist trade. While I'd avoid the places on Staikopoulou (in favor of similar but better alternatives nearby), if you want seafood, the Bouboulinas fish joints are worth a look (described in this section). I've focused most of my coverage on the tight pedestrian lanes between these two areas, toward the water from Syntagma Square, where values are good and ambience is excellent. Note that hours can fluctuate between seasons; take the hours listed here as a rough guideline.

Mezedopoleio O Noulis—run by Noulis, the man with the mighty moustache shown on the sign—serves up a fabulous range of *mezedes* (appetizers). Three or four *mezedes* constitute a tasty meal for two people. This place offers a rare chance to sample *saganaki flambé* (fried cheese flambéed with Metaxa brandy, €7). As Noulis likes to do it all himself, don't come here if you're in a hurry (€4-7 starters, €7 appetizer plate, €8-12 seafood and meat dishes; mid-May-Sept Mon-Sat 11:00-15:00 & 19:00-23:00, Oct-mid-May Mon-Sat 12:00-16:00, closed Sun year-round, Moutzouridou 21, tel. 27520-25541).

Imarton (ήμαρτον, "God Forbid Me") is a bright, tiny bistro with appealing traditional decor mingled with mod flair. Because the place is so small, dishes are prepared in advance and heated up when you order. They specialize in small plates rather than big dishes—mostly cheeses and a staggering variety of sausages. Their *soutzoukakia*—meatballs with spicy tomato sauce—are delicious (€3-6 small plates, €6-8 main dishes, €8-12 seafood items, late May-late Sept Tue-Sun 11:00-15:00 & 19:00-23:00, off-season Tue-Sun 12:00-16:00, closed Mon year-round, Plapouta 33).

Taverna Paleo Arhontiko ("Old Mansion") is a favorite town hangout. That's partly because of the food, and partly because there's live music every night from 22:00 in summer, and on Friday and Saturday nights in winter. It gets packed on weekends, when reservations are recommended (€3-5 appetizers, €6-12 main dishes, daily 12:00-16:00 & 19:00-24:00, at corner of Ypsilandou and Siokou, tel. 27520-22449).

Epi Skinis ("On Stage") is a new stage for former theater director Kouros Zachos and his wife Evangalia. The cozy dining room, decorated with playbills and other theater paraphernalia, feels a bit classier than the tavernas nearby. Theater-lovers in town to visit Epidavros might enjoy capping their day here (€3-8 starters, €8-17 main dishes, daily 12:00-1:00 in the morning, Amalias 19A, tel. 27520-21331).

Tavernas on Olgas Street: The lane called Olgas, tucked away in a grid of streets just two blocks up from the waterfront, is filled

with charming, family-run tavernas serving Greek classics to happy tourists. At any of these, you can choose between a cozy, rustic interior or outdoor tables. Window-shop along here, or seek out these two good options: **Aiolos** (αιολος, €3-5 starters, €5-9 pastas, €7-11 main dishes, try the "drunken chicken," Mon-Fri 17:00-24:00, Sat-Sun 12:00-24:00, Olgas 30, tel. 27520-26828) and **To Omorfo Tavernaki** ("The Beautiful Little Tavern"; €3-5 starters, €7-12 main dishes, daily 17:00-24:00, Kotsonopoulou 1, at corner with Olgas, tel. 27520-25944, Tsioli family).

Fish Restaurants on Bouboulinas: As you stroll the harborfront, the throbbing dance beats of the trendy café/bars gradually give way to the fishy aromas and aggressive come-ons of a string of seafood eateries. As these places are fairly interchangeable, you could just browse for what looks best to you (all open daily 12:00-24:00). Seafood here is typically priced by the kilogram or half-kilogram (figure about 250-300 grams for a typical portion—around €10-20 for a seafood entrée, or about €6-15 for a meat dish). These three are well-regarded: **Savouras** (ΣΑΒΟΥΡΑΣ, at #79), **Taberna Tou Stelara** (ΤΑΒΕΡΝΑ του Στελάρα, at #73), and **Arapakos** (ο Αραπάκοσ, at #81).

Italian on Syntagma Square: For a break from Greek food, **Noufara** offers Italian cuisine in a classy two-level interior or at a sea of white tables out on classy Syntagma Square. Heaters and fans allow this place's delightful outdoor seating to stay open in all sorts of weather (€4-6 starters, €6-12 pizzas and pastas, €8-18 main dishes, daily 10:00-2:00 in the morning, Syntagma Square 3, tel. 27520-23648).

Wine-Tasting: Dimitri Karonis specializes in Greek wines and ouzo, and gives a thorough and informative wine-tasting in the **Karonis Wine Shop** near Syntagma Square (Mon-Sat 8:30-14:30 & 18:00-21:30, closed Sun, Amalias 5, tel. 27520-24446).

Picnics: The **Carrefour Express** supermarket is the most convenient of several supermarkets in town (Mon-Fri 8:00-21:00, Sat 8:00-20:00, closed Sun, 100 yards from the post office at corner of Syngrou and Flessa, tel. 27520-25631).

Dessert

Antica Gelateria di Roma is the place to go for a mouthwatering array of *gelati* (dairy-based ice cream) and *sorbetti* (fruit-based

sorbet) made fresh on the premises daily by Italian gelato master Marcello Raffo, his wife Monica, and his sister Claudia. According to their menu, gelato "is suggested for a balanced diet [for] children, athletes, pregnant women, and the elderly for a year round" (prices range from €1.50 to a small cone up to €4.50 for a big waffle cone). The Raffos also offer other Italian flavors, including *biscotti* cookies, the lemon liqueur *lemoncello,* the grape brandy *grappa,* and Italian-style cappuccino (daily 9:00-2:00 in the morning, Farmakopoulou 3, at corner with Kominou, tel. 27520-23520). Don't confuse this place with a different ice-cream parlor just up the street.

The best **sweets and pastries** in town are at the no-name shop at Staikopoulou 18 (with the ΠΑΡΑΔΟΣΙΑΚΑ ΓΛΥΚΑ sign). While English is limited, you can point to the dessert you'd like in the case inside, and they'll bring it out to you at a sidewalk table (treats for under €3, tel. 27520-26198).

Nafplio Connections

By Bus

Information given by the often-surly ticket sellers at the bus station can be incomplete. Fortunately, this is one of the few regional bus offices in Greece with an English option on its website; you can even buy tickets online (www.ktel-argolidas.gr). The printed bus schedule is also in English. But be sure to ask drivers and other passengers carefully if you'll be required to change buses. From Nafplio, direct buses go to **Athens** (hourly, 2.5 hours, €12), **Epidavros** (3/day, 45 minutes, €2.70), and **Mycenae** (2/day, no buses on Sun, 45 minutes, €2.70).

Journeys to other Peloponnesian destinations are possible but more complicated, requiring multiple transfers; get an early start, and be prepared for frustrations and delays: **Tripoli** (2/day, 1.5 hours—transfer point for many other destinations), **Monemvasia** (1/day, leaves around 8:30, 4.5 hours, change in Tripoli and Sparta), **Olympia** (1/day, leaves around 16:30, 5 hours, change in Tripoli).

By Taxi

To cut some time off the trip to the ancient sites, you can take a taxi to **Mycenae** (about €35 round-trip) or **Epidavros** (about €25-30 round-trip); arrange a pick-up time for the return trip in advance.

By Boat

In the past, Nafplio enjoyed convenient, direct hydrofoil connections to **Hydra** and to **Monemvasia;** unfortunately, these boats are no longer running. (If you're headed to these places, inquire locally in case the hydrofoils are running again.) You can still use a boat to connect to Hydra and Monemvasia, but you'll have to hitch a ride on a package day trip offered by Pegasus Tours (€30-34, boats depart from Tolo—7.5 miles away from central Nafplio, but served by a shuttle bus that departs Nafplio around 8:00). For Monemvasia, boats run only on summer Wednesdays. Boats to Hydra leave four times a week in summer, then sail on to Spetses. While you can easily take your bag and disembark in Hydra, you have to pay the whole cost of the ride to Spetses (2 hours to Hydra, 3-4 hours to Monemvasia, no boats off-season, tel. 27520-59430, www.pegasus-cruises.gr). Note that this is faster, simpler, and not much more expensive than the bus-plus-boat connection to Hydra described next.

To Hydra and Other Saronic Gulf Islands: Be warned that this connection is more complicated than it should be. Fast catamarans to Hydra, Spetses, and other Saronic Gulf Islands depart from **Ermioni** (a.k.a. Hermioni), about an hour's drive southeast of Nafplio (Ermioni to Hydra: 4/day in summer, 2-3/day in winter, 20 minutes, €10, www.hsw.gr). Buses that are supposedly going to Ermioni usually go instead to Kranidi, a larger town about six miles from Ermioni's port (3/day Mon-Sat, 2/day Sun, 2 hours, €7; this Nafplio–Kranidi bus connection often requires a transfer at the town of Ligourio—pay careful attention so as not to miss this change). From Kranidi, it's about a €10-15 taxi ride to the dock at Ermioni (try to split the fare with other Ermioni-bound travelers).

A new service—the slower Freedom Boat—connects Hydra to a parking lot immediately across the water on the Peloponnese at **Metochi,** about 10 miles east of Ermioni (€6.50, about 8/day in

summer, 4/day in winter, 12 minutes, mobile 694-424-2141, www
.hydralines.gr). As with Ermioni (described earlier), bus connections with Nafplio are difficult: You'll take the bus from Nafplio to
Kranidi, then pay for a taxi to Metochi.

For more on Hydra boat connections, see page 400.

By Train

Nafplio's cute but forlorn little train station along the side of the
harbor—with old train cars that have been converted into a ticket
office and café—is no longer operating.

EPIDAVROS

ΕΠΙΔΑΥΡΟΣ / Επιδαυρος

Nestled in a leafy valley some 18 miles east of Nafplio, Epidavros was once the most famous healing center in the ancient Greek world. It was like an ancient Lourdes, a place of hope where the sick came to be treated by doctor-priests acting on behalf of Asklepios, the god of medicine.

The site began as a temple to Apollo, god of light, who was worshipped here in Mycenaean times. By the fourth century B.C., Apollo had been replaced by his son, Asklepios, who was born here, according to legend. Since pilgrims prayed to Asklepios for health, a sanctuary was needed, with a temple, altars, and statues to the gods. The sanctuary reached the height of its popularity in the fourth and third centuries B.C., when it boasted medical facilities, housing for the sick, mineral baths, a stadium for athletic competitions, and a theater.

These days the famous theater is Epidavros' star attraction. It's the finest and best-preserved of all of Greece's ancient theaters—and that's saying something in a country with 132 of them. Epidavros also has some (far) less interesting sights. The once-great sanctuary is now just a lonely field of rubble. The small Archaeological Museum displays a few crumbled fragments of statuary. The stadium is under renovation and is closed to visitors. But the theater alone makes Epidavros worth the side-trip.

Orientation

Cost: €6 includes the theater, Archaeological Museum, and the rest of the Sanctuary of Epidavros archaeological site.

Hours: The sanctuary and theater are open late March-late Oct daily 8:00-20:00, off-season daily 8:00-17:00. The museum is open late March-late Oct Mon 12:00-20:00, Tue-Sun

8:00-20:00; off-season Mon 12:00-17:00, Tue-Sun 8:00-17:00.

Getting There: It's a 45-minute **drive** east of Nafplio, along winding roads. Head east out of Nafplio toward the town of Ligourio/Λυγουριό, then carry on along the main road to the archaeological site, just on Ligourio's outskirts. The site has plenty of free parking.

You can also reach the theater from Nafplio by **bus** (3/day, 45 minutes, €2.15; there are typically 3 return buses per day from Epidavros departing in the afternoon, last one typically departs Epidavros around 18:00—ask locally for times) or by **taxi** (round-trip about €25-30, arrange your return in advance).

From **Athens,** buses head to Nafplio, then continue on to Epidavros (3-4/day, 2.5 hours, might require a transfer in Nafplio—ask when you buy your ticket).

Name Variation: Epidavros can be spelled Epidaurus in English. Confusingly, many locations in this area carry the name Epidavros/Επιδαυρος. Don't be distracted by signs to Nea ("New") Epidavros/Νεα Επιδαυρος, or Palea ("Old") Epidavros/Παλαιά Επιδαυρος, which will route you to a modern coastal town far from the theater.

Length of This Tour: Unfortunately, Epidavros is not really "on the way" to anything else. Budget two to three hours for the round-trip excursion from Nafplio. You can see the entire site in an hour, but it's delightful to linger at the theater. Many tourists visit both Epidavros and Mycenae (each a short trip from Nafplio, but in different directions) on the same day; you might see some familiar faces at each site.

Services: There's not much here. A simple café/restaurant is along the lane between the parking and ticket office. WCs are near the parking lot (outside the site entry), and more are near the museum (inside the site).

Information: Tel. 27350-22009, www.culture.gr.

Performances: The theater is still used today for performances during the annual Athens & Epidavros Festival on summer weekends (generally July-Aug Fri-Sat at 21:00—arrive by 20:00; ideally buy your tickets the day before). A schedule is available online at www.greekfestival.gr. Special buses run from Athens and Nafplio on performance nights.

Starring: The most intact (and most spectacularly located) theater from ancient Greece.

EPIDAVROS

The Tour Begins

From the parking lot, follow signs up the long lane to the ticket desk. Buy your ticket and enter. The theater, sanctuary, and museum are all a couple minutes' walk from each other. You basically look at the stunning theater, climb the seats, take some photos, try out the acoustics—and that's it. The other sights are pretty skimpy.

• *From the entry gate, climb the stairs on the right up to the theater. Enter the theater, stand in the center of the circular "orchestra," look up at the seats, and take it all in. (I've marked your spot with a weathered marble stump, where fellow theatergoers might be posing, singing, or speaking.)*

Theater of Epidavros (c. 300 B.C.)

It's a magnificent sight, built into the side of a tree-covered hill. The perfect symmetry of its two tiers of seating stands as a tribute

to Greek mathematics. It's easy to locate the main elements of a typical Greek theater: the round **orchestra;** the smaller **stage** area, or *skene;* and the **seating,** or *kavea.*

The audience sat in bleacher seats that wrapped partially around the performers. The limestone blocks are set into the hillside. Together, the lower rows and 21 upper rows (added by the Romans, c. 50 B.C.) seated up to 15,000. The spectators looked down on the orchestra, a circular area 70 feet across where the group of actors known as the chorus sang and danced. Behind the orchestra are the rectangular foundations of a building called the *skene* that served as the stage. (These days, the *skene* is usually covered with a modern stage.) The *skene* had a raised stage where actors performed, a back wall for scenery, dressing rooms in the back, and various doorways and ramps where actors could make dramatic entrances and exits. The *skene* was not very tall (one or two stories at most), so spectators could look over it during the performance, taking in the view of the valley below.

The acoustics are superb. From the orchestra, whisper to your partner on the top row (higher frequencies carry better over the limestone seats). The ancient acoustical engineering is remarkable: The marble circle in the middle of the orchestra (in front of the *skene*...that is, pro-scenium) opens into a hollow underground space that projects voices up to the seats. Though it

Greek Theater

The Greeks invented modern theater, and many plays written 2,500 years ago are still performed today.

Greek drama began in prehistoric times with the songs, poems, and rituals performed to honor Dionysus, the god of wine and orgiastic revelry. By the sixth century B.C., these fertility rites developed into song competitions between choruses of men who sang hymns about Dionysus, heroes, and gods. The contests were held at religious festivals as a form of worship.

Later, Athenian playwrights (such as Thespis, the first "thespian") introduced actors who acted out the story through spoken monologues, alternating with the chorus's songs. Over time, these monologues became dialogues between several actors, and the spoken scenes became as important as the songs of the chorus. Plays evolved from Dionysian hymns to stories of Dionysus to stories of all sorts—myths of gods and heroes, and comedies about contemporary events. By the Golden Age (c. 450-400 B.C.), Athens was the center of a golden age of theater, premiering plays by Sophocles, Euripides, and Aristophanes.

Greek plays fall into three categories. Tragedies, the oldest and most prestigious, were super-serious plays about gods and legends that usually ended with the hero dying. Comedies, which emerged during the Golden Age, were witty satires about contemporary people and events. "Satyr plays" spoofed the seriousness of tragedies—things like Oedipus with a massive strap-on phallus.

Greek drama, like Greek art and philosophy, put human beings at center stage. The theaters were built into the natural slopes of hillsides, giving the audience a glimpse of human emotions against the awesome backdrop of nature. The plays showed mortals wrestling with how to find their place in a cosmos ruled by the gods and Fate.

EPIDAVROS

seems counter-intuitive, for the best effect, actors pointed their heads downward, toward this spot, rather than upward toward the spectators.

Picture a typical performance of a Greek tragedy here at this theater. Before the show began, spectators would file in the same way tourists do today, through the passageway between the seating and the *skene*. The performance began with a sober monologue by a lone actor, setting the scene. Next, the chorus members would enter in a solemn parade, singing as they took their place in the orchestra circle. Then the story would unfold through dialogue on the stage, interspersed with songs by the chorus members. At play's end, the chorus sang a song summing up the moral of the play, then paraded out the way they came.

The speaking actors performed on a raised stage, while the chorus members flitted about in the circular orchestra at the foot of the stage. Traditionally, there were only three actors in a play, each playing multiple roles. Actors wore masks with a hole for the mouth (such as the grinning mask of comedy or the drooping mouth of tragedy). Actors were always men; to play a woman they wore a female mask, women's clothes, and wooden breasts.

Actors could enter and exit by ramps on either side of the stage, through doorways at the back of the stage, or via the same passageways tourists enter today. For costume changes, they exited to the backstage dressing rooms. There was no curtain at the front of the stage.

The chorus—a group of three to fifty singers—was a unique part of Greek plays. They commented on the action through songs, accompanied by flute or lyre (small harp), and danced around in the circular orchestra (literally, "dancing space"). The lead chorus member often entered the onstage action and exchanged dialogue with characters.

During the course of the play, demons could pop up through a trap door in the stage, and gods could make their dramatic appearance atop the roof of the *skene*. The most famous stage gimmick was the cherry-picker crane that lowered an actor down from the heavens at the play's climax—the "god from a machine," or deus ex machina.

For about seven centuries (c. 300 B.C.-A.D. 400), the theater at Epidavros hosted song contests and plays, until the area was looted by invading Gauls. Over time, the theater became buried in dirt, preserving it until it was unearthed in almost original condition in 1881. Today, it is once again a working theater.

Even if you're not here for one of the theater's official performances, you can still enjoy the show: Tourists take turns performing monologues, jokes, arias, and more. If there's an actor inside

Greek Monologues

To get you into the theatrical mood, here are a few (condensed) passages from some famous Greek plays.

Oedipus Rex (or *Oedipus Tyrannus*), by Sophocles
A man unwittingly kills his father, sleeps with his mother, and watches his wife commit suicide. When he learns the truth, he blinds himself in shame and sorrow:

> "With what eyes could I ever behold again my honored
>   father or my unhappy mother, both destroyed by me?
> This punishment is worse than death, and so it should be.
> I wish I could be deaf as well as blind, to shut out all
>   sorrow.
> My friends, come bury me, hide me from every eye,
> cast me into the deepest ocean and let me die.
> Anything so I can shake off this hated life.
> Come friends, do not be afraid to touch me, polluted as
>   I am.
> For no one will suffer for my sins—no one but me."

Antigone, by Sophocles
The heroine Antigone defies the king in order to give her brother a proper burial. Here she faces her punishment:

> "O tomb, my bridal chamber, where I go most miserably,
> before my time on earth is spent!
> What law of heaven have I broken?!

you, speak up. Try out any of the ancient Greek passages (see sidebar). Or just clap your hands loudly to test the echo.

When you've finished your turn on stage, climb the stairs to the seats to join the spectators. Only from up here can you fully appreciate the incredible acoustics—not to mention the remarkable scale and intactness of the place. No matter how high you climb, you can hear every word of the naturally amplified performances down below...all while enjoying the backdrop of sweeping mountains and olive groves.

• *Walk down the stairs across from the theater, to find the...*

Archaeological Museum
The first room (of three) in this small museum displays various steles, or inscribed stone tablets. Some of these document successful cases

Why should I ever beseech the gods again,
if I am to be punished for doing nothing but good.
If I am guilty, I accept my sin.
But if it is my accusers that are wrong,
I pray that they do not suffer any more than the evils they
have inflicted upon me."

Plutus, by Aristophanes

In this comedy, a man befriends a blind beggar who is actually Plutus, the god of wealth, in disguise. He helps Plutus regain his sight by bringing him to Epidavros. (If the monologue lacks some of Aristophanes' famed side-splitting humor, maybe it's because I left out the bit about cutting a huge fart in the presence of the god Asklepios.)

"Having arrived at the Temple of Asklepios, we first led our patient to the sea to purify him. Back at the temple, we gave offerings of bread and wheat cake, then bedded down. During the night, the god Asklepios appeared, sitting on the bed. He took a clean rag and wiped Plutus' eyelids. He then whistled, and two huge snakes came rushing from the temple and licked the patient's eyelids. As quick as you could drain 10 shots of wine, Plutus stood up—he could see! Asklepios disappeared with the snakes, and, as dawn broke, we clapped our hands with joy and gave praise and thanks to the mighty god."

where patients were healed here by the god Asklepios. Others are rules governing the hospital. The only people to be excluded from the sanctuary were the terminally ill and pregnant women (both were considered too high-risk—their deaths would sully the sanctuary's reputation).

The second room has many (headless) statues of gods who were invoked in the healing process. The columns and cornice on display were part of the sanctuary's impressive entryway, or Propylaea.

The star of the final room is an extremely well-preserved capital from a Corinthian column. The builders of the temple buried it on the site, perhaps as an offering to the gods. Archaeologists who dug it up in the 19th century were astonished

at its condition; it may have been the prototype for all the capitals in the temple complex. The room also displays two replicas of small, square reliefs (left wall) showing the god Asklepios on his throne. Asklepios is often depicted as a kindly, bearded man, carrying a staff with a snake wound around it, the forerunner of today's medical symbol.

• *Up the stairs beyond the museum is the sprawling field of ruins called the...*

Sanctuary of Epidavros

The sanctuary—set in an open field just below the theater—once held Epidavros' mineral baths, health clubs, hostels, and temples.

Today the various ruins are well-described in English, but precious little survives. (While Epidavros' theater is stunning, the sanctuary is a distant also-ran to those at other great ancient sites, such as Delphi and Olympia.)

Ardent sightseers can kill time waiting for the bus back to Nafplio by seeking out the foundations of the sanctuary's main building, the Temple of Asklepios, or *asclepion* (undergoing restoration in the north part of the field). Here, patients spent the night in a large hall *(katagogion)* connected to the temple, hoping to be visited in a dream by Asklepios, who could give them the secret to their cure. In the morning, priests interpreted the dreams and told the patient what to do in order to be healed...by the grace of the god Asklepios.

Modern doctors still invoke Asklepios in the opening line of the Hippocratic oath: "I swear by Apollo, Asclepius, etc..." (While Hippocrates, the father of modern medicine, worked in an *asclepion*, it was at the temple at Kos, not Epidavros.)

• *One final part of the Epidavros site is worth knowing about.*

Stadium

Epidavros' 6,000-seat stadium is presently under reconstruction. It was used for the Festival of Asklepios every four years (like other ancient Greek athletic competitions). To ensure a good crowd, the festival was staged nine days after the Isthmian Games, at Isthmia near Corinth, which was one of the big events of the Panhellenic sporting calendar, along with the Olympic Games and the Pythian Games at Delphi.

MYCENAE

ΜΥΚΉΝΕΣ / Μυκήνες

Mycenae—a fortress city atop a hill—was the hub of a mighty civilization that dominated the Greek world between 1600 and 1200 B.C., a thousand years before Athens' Golden Age. The Mycenaeans were as distant and mysterious to the Golden Age Greeks as Plato and Socrates are to us today. Ancient Greek tourists visited the dramatic ruins of Mycenae and concluded that the Mycenaeans must have been the heroes who'd won the Trojan War, as related in Homer's epic poems, the *Iliad* and the *Odyssey*. They thought of the Mycenaeans as their ancestors, the first "Greeks."

Following the same ancient sandal-steps as the ancient Greeks, today's visitors continue to enjoy Mycenae's majestic setting of mountains, valleys, and the distant sea. Exploring this still-impressive hilltop, you'll discover the famous Lion Gate, a manageable museum, an enormous domed burial chamber... and distant echoes of the Trojan War.

When it comes to unraveling the mystery of the Mycenaeans, modern historians—armed with only the slimmest written record—are still trying to sort out fact from legend. They don't know exactly who the Mycenaeans were, where they came from, or what happened to them. Here are the sketchy (and oft-disputed) details:

Around 1600 B.C., a Bronze Age civilization originating in Asia Minor developed an empire of autonomous city-states that covered the southern half of mainland Greece and a few islands. Their capital was the city of Mycenae, which also gave its name to the people and the era. From contact with the sophisticated

Minoan people on the isle of Crete, the militaristic Mycenaeans borrowed elements of religion and the arts.

Sometime about the year 1200 B.C., the aggressive Mycenaeans likely launched an attack on Troy, a rich city on the northwest coast of Asia Minor (present-day Turkey). After a long siege, Troy fell, and the Mycenaeans became the undisputed rulers of the Aegean. Then, just as suddenly, the Mycenaeans mysteriously disappeared, and their empire crumbled. Whether the Mycenaeans fell victim to a sudden invasion by the Dorians (a Greek tribe), an attack of the mysterious tribes later dubbed the "Sea People," a drought, or internal rebellion—no one knows. Whatever the reason, by 1100 B.C., Mycenae was abandoned and burned, and Greece plunged into four centuries known as the Dark Ages.

Nearly three millennia later, in 1876, German archaeologist Heinrich Schliemann excavated this site and put it back on the archaeologists' (and tourists') map. Today, a visit to Mycenae is a trip back into prehistory to see some of the oldest remains of a complex civilization in all of Europe—a thousand years older than Athens' Acropolis.

Orientation

Cost: €8 ticket includes the archaeological site, the museum, and the Treasury of Atreus up the road.

Hours: The site is open daily late March-mid Sept 8:00-20:00, off-season daily 8:00-17:00—but off-season hours can change without notice. The museum is open late March-late Oct Tue-Sun 8:00-19:30, Mon 12:00-19:30, off-season Tue-Sun 8:00-17:00, Mon 12:00-17:00. Both can close daily at 15:00 in slow times.

Getting There: Mycenae is 18 miles north of Nafplio (on the way to the major E-65 expressway)—it's easiest to **drive** there. From the modern town of Mycenae/Μυκήνες (near the larger town of Fichti/Φιχτι), the ruins are about two miles north, dramatically obvious atop a hill.

Buses run from Nafplio directly to ancient Mycenae (2/day, 45 minutes, €2.60). Confirm that your bus goes to the archaeological site; other buses take you only as far as Fichti, two miles away.

You can also take a **taxi** to Mycenae from Nafplio (figure €35 round-trip, best to arrange your return in advance; or, if you need to arrange a return taxi from Mycenae on the spot, call mobile 694-643-1726).

Arrival in Mycenae: From the entrance, the acropolis is to the east. Drivers can use the free parking lot near the entrance to the ruins and museum; if it's full, it's OK to park along the

MYCENAE

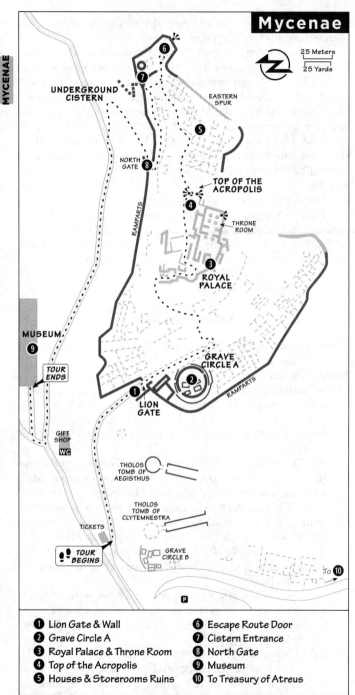

Mycenae

25 Meters
25 Yards

UNDERGROUND
CISTERN

EASTERN
SPUR

6

7

5

NORTH
GATE 8

TOP OF THE
ACROPOLIS

4

THRONE
ROOM

RAMPARTS

3

ROYAL
PALACE

MUSEUM

9

TOUR
ENDS

GRAVE
CIRCLE A

2

RAMPARTS

1

LION
GATE

GIFT
SHOP

WC

THOLOS
TOMB OF
AEGISTHUS

THOLOS
TOMB OF
CLYTEMNESTRA

TICKETS

TOUR
BEGINS

GRAVE
CIRCLE B

To 10

P

1 Lion Gate & Wall	**6** Escape Route Door
2 Grave Circle A	**7** Cistern Entrance
3 Royal Palace & Throne Room	**8** North Gate
4 Top of the Acropolis	**9** Museum
5 Houses & Storerooms Ruins	**10** To Treasury of Atreus

road leading to the lot.

Information: Tel. 27510-76802 (at Mycenae) or 27520-27502 (in Nafplio), www.culture.gr.

Services: Unmarked WCs are near the museum shop—as you face the ruins from the ticket booth, walk around the left side of the hill (toward the museum). A truck sells basic snacks in the parking lot.

Planning Your Time: As with most ancient sites with a museum, you can decide whether to see the museum first (to help reconstruct the ruins) or the site first (to get the lay of the land). If you want to explore the cistern, bring a flashlight. To complement the information in this self-guided tour, read the chapter on Athens' National Archaeological Museum, where many Mycenaean artifacts are now displayed (see page 158).

Length of This Tour: Allow an hour for the site, a half-hour for the museum, and a half-hour for the Treasury of Atreus. It makes for a handy half-day side-trip from Nafplio, and can be combined conveniently with the Theater of Epidavros for a full day of ancient sight-hopping (best by car).

Pronunciation: Mycenae is pronounced my-SEE-nee by English-speakers; Greeks call the town Mykenes/Μυκήνες (mee-KEE-nehs). The ancient people are known as the Mycenaeans (my-seh-NEE-uhns).

Starring: The hilltop fortress at the center of the most ancient, powerful, and enigmatic of ancient Greek civilizations.

The Tour Begins

The three main sightseeing areas at Mycenae are a few minutes' walk from each other. The **archaeological ruins** consist of the walled city of Mycenae atop the hill called the acropolis. Here you'll find the famous Lion Gate entrance, Grave Circle A that yielded precious artifacts, and the ruins of the palace. Below the site is the **museum,** housing artifacts that were found here. Finally, as impressive as anything here, is the **Treasury of Atreus**—a huge domed tomb, located about 300 yards away from the main site (along the main road). A handful of other ruins and tombs are scattered around the area, but stick to these three to start your visit.

Note that some of the ruins (confusingly) have two different names—for example, the Treasury of Atreus is also known as the Tomb of Agamemnon.

• *Buy your ticket for the archeological site and enter, climbing the ramp up the acropolis.*

Archaeological Site

• You'll enter the fortified complex through the...

Lion Gate and Wall

The grand Lion Gate (c. 1300 B.C.) guards the entrance to this fortress city on a hill. Above the doorway, two lionesses flank a col-

umn, symbolically protecting it the way the Mycenaean kings once protected the city. The lions' missing heads may have once turned outward, greeting the visitor. The heads were either made of stone or possibly of gold, and may have been attached with metal fasteners, as indicated by two red-brown rust stains on the right lion's neck.

The lions form a triangle above the massive lintel (or crossbeam above the door). Mycenaean architects used the weak corbelled arch, less sturdy than the rounded Roman arch developed later. A simple horizontal stone spans the door, while heavy stones above it inch in to bridge the gap. The triangle (featuring the twin lions) helps relieve the weight of the stones. Apart from its rather fragile technology, Mycenaean architecture is really massive. The lintel weighs 18 tons—as much as a B-17 bomber.

The exterior walls that girdle the base of the hill (c. 1300 B.C.) were about 40 feet high, 20 feet thick, and 3,000 feet long, enclosing 39,000 cubic yards. They were built with an estimated 14,000 boulders weighing five to ten tons each. Marveling at the enormous scale, classical-era Greeks figured the legendary Perseus (who slew the Medusa) must have built the city with the help of the giant one-eyed Cyclopes, and dubbed the style "cyclopean."

In reality, the Mycenaeans probably lifted these big stones into place the same way the Egyptians built the pyramids—by building ramps and rolling the stones up on logs drawn by oxen or horses.

Pass through the gate. Carved into the stone are **post-holes** that held the wooden door. Just as you emerge, look left to see a square **niche** in the wall—this is where statues of the gods who guarded the gates were displayed.

• Head up the ramp. About 30 yards ahead, you'll begin to see (below and on the right) a circular

Mycenae and Troy: Fact or Fiction?

Several sites at Mycenae bear legendary names—"Agamemnon's Palace," the "Tomb of Clytemnestra," the

"Tomb of Agamemnon," and so on. Although these names are fanciful with no basis in fact, real-life Mycenae does sound eerily similar to the legends found in writings attributed to the poet Homer (c. 850 B.C.) and other ancient scribes.

The tales of the Trojan War are set during the time when the Mycenaeans dominated the Greek world and had the power to conquer Troy. They tell of the abduction of the beautiful Helen (who had "the face that launched a thousand ships") by Paris, a prince of Troy. Outraged at the loss of his bride, Menelaus, king of Sparta, convinced his brother Agamemnon, king of Mycenae, to lead the Greeks in an attack on Troy. But the winds were not favorable for launching the fleet. An oracle told Agamemnon that he had to sacrifice his daughter to get underway, so he lied to his wife, Clytemnestra, and ordered the priests to kill their daughter.

After the sacrifice, the Greek ships finally made it to Troy. When a long siege failed to defeat the Trojans, Odysseus suggested tricking the enemy by building a wooden idol (the famous "Trojan horse"), leaving it outside the city walls, and pretending to withdraw. The Trojans took the bait, brought the horse inside, and were met with an unpleasant surprise: The greatest warriors of Greece emerging from inside the horse to complete the conquest of Troy. The famous heroes of the Trojan War include Achilles and Ajax on the Greek side, and Paris' brother Hector—all of whom died by the war's end.

Homer's *Odyssey* tells of the homeward journey of Odysseus, who survived the war, only to wander for 10 years, thwarted by the god Poseidon, before finally reaching home. Agamemnon's fate is also told in the epic. After sacking Troy, Agamemnon returned to Mycenae with his Trojan concubine, where he was murdered by his wife (who was still brooding over her daughter's sacrifice and not very happy about the new competition). Not that Clytemnestra was a dutiful spouse—her new lover helped her murder Agamemnon and the concubine.

Metaphorically, Agamemnon's tragic story matches that of the historical Mycenaeans—no sooner had they returned home victorious from Troy than their own homes were destroyed. These legends of ancient Mycenae were passed down via oral tradition for centuries until, long after the fall of both Troy and Mycenae, they were preserved for posterity in Homer's *Iliad* and *Odyssey* as well as other ancient epics.

wall that encloses rectangular graves. Walk a bit higher up the path and look down for the best view.

Grave Circle A (c. 1550 b.c.)

The name denotes the round cluster of graves where Mycenaean royalty were buried. The rectangular holes are called shaft graves,

which were cut into the rock up to 20 feet deep. There are six graves, each of which contained several bodies (19 total—9 women, 8 men, 2 children). The bodies were found embalmed and lying on their backs along with their most precious belongings, with their heads facing east—toward the rising sun—indicating a belief in an afterlife. Gravestones atop the graves (including one displayed in the museum—see later in this chapter) were decorated with a spiral, possibly a symbol of continuous existence.

In 1876, these graves were unearthed by the famed German archaeologist Heinrich Schliemann. Schliemann had recently discovered the long-lost city of Troy, finally giving some historical credibility to Homer's tales. He next turned his attention to Mycenae, the legendary home of Agamemnon. In Grave Circle A, he found a treasure trove of gold swords, spears, engraved cups, and ritual objects buried with the dead—30 pounds in all, confirming Homer's description of Mycenae as a city "rich in gold."

The prize discovery was a gold mask showing the face of a bearded man. Masks like this were tied onto the faces of the deceased. This one was obviously for an important warrior chieftain. Schliemann was convinced the mask proved that Homer's tales of the Trojan War were true, and he dubbed it the "Mask of Agamemnon." This mask and other artifacts are now in the National Archaeological Museum in Athens.

Could it really be the Mask of Agamemnon? No. Not only is it unlikely that Agamemnon ever really existed, but the mask is from the 16th century b.c.—at least 300 years before the legendary king supposedly burned Troy.

The Mycenaeans practiced several different types of burial: interred in pits (for the poorest), encased in ceramic jars called cist graves (for wealthier folks), laid in shaft graves (for royalty), or in elaborate domed chambers called a *tholos* (like the Treasury of Atreus, described at the end of this tour).

• *Continue to climb up the paths—zigzagging past the ruins of former houses and shops—to the top of the acropolis. On the right are the rectangular foundations of the former...*

Royal Palace and Throne Room *(Megaron)*

Kings ruled the Mycenaeans from this palace, which consisted of a line of several rectangular rooms (about all that remains today are the outlines of the rooms).

Imagine entering the palace and walking through a series of rooms from right to left. You'd start in an open-air courtyard—that's the biggest rectangle to the far right (west, toward the parking lot). Next, you'd enter the palace itself, passing between two columns (see the remaining bases) onto a covered porch. Next, at the far end of the porch, was a small anteroom. Finally, you'd spill into the main hall—the throne room—at the east end. This great hall, or *megaron,* contains the outlines of a round hearth, which is where a fire burned. Here you could make burnt offerings to the gods. The four remaining bases around the hearth once held four inverted columns that supported the roof, which had a sunroof-type hole to let out the smoke. (Be warned that all of this might be covered by a tarp when you visit.) Against the wall to the right (the south wall) sat the king on his throne—the very center of power of the Mycenaean empire. The walls and floors were brightly painted with a pattern of linked spirals.

The same type of palace was found in every Mycenaean city. Note the layout—entering from a courtyard, passing through a colonnade, into a small room, and then reaching the main hall where sacrificial offerings were made. This same series of rooms later became the standard layout of the Greek temple—courtyard, porch, *pronaos,* and *cella.*

• *While we're on the top of the acropolis, check out the view and imagine the city/fortress at its peak.*

The Top of the Acropolis: Mycenae the Fortress-City

Mycenae was a combination citadel, palace, residence, and administrative capital of the extended empire of Mycenaean cities. But first and foremost, it was a for-tress, occupying a superb natural defensive position guarding a major crossroads in Greece. The hill is flanked

by steep ravines. To the south, there are spacious views across the fertile plains of Argos to the Argolic Gulf, giving the inhabitants ample time to prepare for any attack by sea. The cone-shaped hill in the distance ringed with walls near the top was the fortress of Argos. The Argonauts (who, in legend, sailed with Jason to get the Golden Fleece) were allies of the Mycenaeans. Mycenae controlled trade on the road from Corinth to Nafplio, and sea trade from Nafplio to points beyond.

In case of siege, Mycenae could rely on natural springs located on the mountainside to the east (away from the entrance—near the eucalyptus tree, a little above acropolis level). The water was channeled through clay pipes underground to a cistern dug inside the acropolis (which we'll visit soon).

Though Mycenae was fundamentally a fortress, up to 60,000 people lived here, either within the walls or in surrounding villages. They lived in box-shaped buildings (much like today's museum building) on the steep, terraced hillside.

From this viewpoint, check out the long horizontal ridgeline to the south—not the farthest mountain range, but a little closer. It looks like a man lying on his back, with his Easter-Island-like nose at the left end. Locals call him "Sleeping Agamemnon."

• *Work your way eastward (farther away from the entrance, and a bit downhill), descending to...*

The Cistern and Other Sights at the East End

The ruins at this end were once mostly **houses and storerooms.** At the far eastern end, notice the doorway in the wall (now covered with a gate). This was an **escape route** out the back.

Find the gaping cave-like opening of the **cistern,** where 99  (slippery!) steps lead 50 feet down. Peering inside, you can see... absolutely nothing, unless you've packed a flashlight. (While the cistern has been open in the past for tourists to explore, you might only be able to descend a few steps before reaching a barrier.) The cistern stored water from springs within the hillside, in case of siege or drought.

• *Head back toward the entrance—but bear to the right, following the north (outer) wall. Look for a gate on the right.*

This **North Gate,** smaller than the Lion Gate, has a similar rectangular crossbeam shape and heavy lintel. The wooden door is a reconstruction similar to the original, fit into the original holes cut in the lintel stone. Compare the two side pillars of the entrance. They're both of the same type of local rock, but the one on the left was never finished during construction, while the right side is polished smooth, as most of the stones here would have been. Next to the North Gate is a niche in the wall (similar to the Lion Gate) to display guardian gods.

MYCENAE

• *Exit through the North Gate, and bear left/downhill along the serpentine path to the modern building on the hillside below. This holds the...*

Museum

While the ruins give a sense of the engineering sophistication of these people, the museum emphasizes their artistic, religious, literary, and cultural sides. You'll see various funeral objects from the graves, plus everyday objects that show influences from the Egyptian, Minoan, and Hittite cultures.

• *Follow the one-way, counterclockwise route through the collection, beginning in the...*

Entrance Hall

The model of the Mycenae acropolis in the center of the room helps

you visualize the city as it once was. The glass cases that surround it contain mostly dull artifacts, with a few colorful exceptions. In the first case toward the window, look for the teeny ceramic pitcher used as a baby "feeding bottle." In the case nearest the window, find an ancient barbecue (yes, that's exactly what it is).

Large illustrated boards in the room convey popular Mycenaean myths.

• *From the entrance hall, move into the next room, where you'll find...*

Religious Symbols

On the right about halfway down this room, look for the case labeled "The Temple." Not much is known of Mycenaean religion, so it's unclear what purpose the little E.T.-looking idols served (see photo on next page). The three clay coiled snakes are another theme. In the Mycenaean view, snakes were not bad—living both under and above the ground, the reptiles connected the two worlds. The Mycenaeans borrowed the (snake-handling) Minoan goddesses to serve their own all-powerful ruler of the skies, Zeus. These elements were passed down to the pantheon of classical-era Greeks.

Across the room (high up), the interconnected spiral pattern is common in Mycenaean art. At the end of the room, fresco fragments from the palace give an idea of how colorful the place must have been in its day.

• *Descend to the lower level to see...*

Funeral Objects

In the octagonal case, you'll see reproductions of the famous Mask of Agamemnon and other golden items (such as crowns and

medallions). These objects were discovered here in graves and at the Treasury of Atreus. (The originals are now in Athens' National Archaeological Museum.) The dead in Grave Circle A may have been buried in coffins, which are now long gone. Near the mask stands a funeral stele (gravestone) from Grave Circle A.

Displayed around the walls are many ceramic vases and cups. The cups that were found in graves may indicate that the dead were sent off with a goodbye toast by their loved ones.

• *As you continue into the next room, notice (on your left) a big clay urn used as a coffin for burial, with a band of spiral designs across the middle. Many funeral objects (such as this urn) were engraved with a spiral pattern—possibly a symbol of the never-ending path of life.*

Mycenaean Writing and Everyday Objects

In the case at the end of the partition, you'll see fragments of clay tablets inscribed in the Mycenaean written language known to scholars as Linear B. Each character represented a syllable. These fragments are about subjects, including "Religion," "Lists of Names," "Products," and so on. Very few written documents survived from the Mycenaean era—no literature or history or stories—so we know very little of the Mycenaeans' inner thoughts.

On the other side of the partition, a glass case displays sealstones, used to put a person's mark in wax or clay on a sealed document or box, to ensure it reached the intended recipient unopened. The Mycenaeans led an active trading life, and every businessman would have had one of these. The red one on

top, in the center (#14), has the Lion Gate on it.

To the left, a large map shows the vast Mycenaean trading world. The Mycenaeans were seafarers, bringing back gold from Egypt, lapis lazuli from Afghanistan, amber from Scandinavia, ivory from Syria, jewelry from Spain, and more.

Near the door, the display on "Women of the Mycenaean World" makes it clear they had plenty of toiletry and jewelry items: combs, tweezers, mirrors, beads, pendants, and so on. Apparently, packing light was a challenge even back then.

• *Leaving the museum, climb the long stairway back up to the parking lot, then continue to the last area, one of the highlights of Mycenae: the tomb known as the Treasury of Atreus. It's located about 300 yards south of the ruins, along the road back toward the modern town of Mycenae. You can walk there in less than 10 minutes. Or, if you have a car, stop at the Treasury on your way out of the site—there's a small parking lot there (often clogged with tour buses). Follow the crowds gradually uphill from the parking lot, and show your entry ticket once more to get to the...*

Treasury of Atreus
(a.k.a. Tomb of Agamemnon)

Tholos Tomb (13th century B.C.)

Mycenae's royalty were buried in massive beehive-shaped underground chambers like this one, which replaced shaft graves (like the ones at Grave Circle A) beginning in the 15th century B.C.

The entryway itself is on a grand "cyclopean" scale—110 feet long and 20 feet wide. Imagine entering in a funeral procession carrying the body of the king. The walls rise at a diagonal up to the entrance, giving the illusion of swallowing you up as you enter.

The lintel over the doorway is mind-bogglingly big—26 feet across by 16 feet by 3 feet—and weighs 120 tons. (For comparison, the biggest stones of the Egyptian pyramids were 30 tons.)

Step inside and hear the 3,300-year-old echoes of this domed

room. The round chamber (*tholos* means "round") is 47 feet in diameter and 42 feet tall, with an igloo-style dome made of 33 rings of corbelled (gradually projecting) stones, each weighing about five tons. The dome was decorated with bronze ornaments (you can see a few small nail holes where they were attached in the fifth row of stones up). The soot on the dome is from the campfires of fairly recent shepherds.

Kings were elaborately buried in the center of the room along with their swords, jewels, and personal possessions. There is also a side chamber (the door to the right) whose purpose can only be guessed at. After the funeral was over, the whole structure was covered with a mountain of dirt. But grave robbers got in anyway, and modern archaeologists have not found any bodies.

Notice that the "keystone" at the peak of the dome is missing (probably taken by grave robbers). So why didn't the dome collapse? The weight of the dome is actually borne by two triangular spaces, or niches—one over the main lintel, and one over the side doorway. Notice how the dome has collapsed a bit and the lintel has a crack in it. That crack is to the side of the doorway, right where the triangular niche spills all the weight of the dome onto it.

• *Our tour is nearing its end. But serious archaeologists could spend much more time exploring...*

The Rest of Mycenae

Only 10 percent of Mycenae has been excavated. Scattered in the surrounding hillsides are cave openings, where the Mycenaeans buried people in yet another way, in "chamber tombs." There are also some ruins of houses, several more *tholos* tombs (the Tomb of Clytemnestra and the Lion Tomb) and Grave Circle B.

As for me, I've Mycenae-n enough.

OLYMPIA

ΑΡΧΑΊΑ ΟΛΥΜΠΊΑ /
Αρχαία Ολυμπία

A visit to Olympia—most famous as the site of the original Olympic Games—offers one of your best opportunities for a hands-on antiquity experience. Line up at the original starting line in the 2,500-year-old Olympic Stadium. Visit the Temple of Zeus, former site of a gigantic statue of Zeus that was one of the Seven Wonders of the Ancient World. Ponder the temple's once-majestic columns—toppled like towers of checkers by an earthquake—which are as evocative as anything from ancient times. Take a close look at the Archaeological Museum's gold-medal-quality statues and artifacts. And don't forget to step back and enjoy the setting itself. Despite the crowds that pour through here, Olympia remains a magical place, with ruins nestled among lush, shady groves of pine trees.

The modern-day town of Olympia (pop. 11,000) is far less inspiring—a concrete community custom-built to cater to the needs of the thousands of tourists who flock here year-round to visit the site. For convenience while sightseeing, you might want to spend one night in town; more time isn't necessary (though limited bus connections might require a two-night stay). While not romantic, Olympia is tidy, straightforward, functional, and pleasant enough.

Orientation to Olympia

The Sanctuary of Olympia sits in the fertile valley of the Alphios River in the western Peloponnese, nine miles southeast of the regional capital of Pyrgos. The archaeological site curves along the southeastern edge of the tidy modern village of Archaia (Ancient) Olympia. The town's layout is basically a low-lying, easy-to-manage grid, five streets wide by eight streets long. The main road (called

Praxitelous Kondyli) runs from Pyrgos in the north and leads right into a parking lot (and bus stop) at the south end of town. From here, the museum and site are due east, over the Kladeos River.

Tourist Information

The TI, in the center of town on the main road next to the National Bank of Greece, is open only sporadically.

Arrival in Olympia

By Bus: The bus stop is just before the retail strip on the main street, near the large sign with the town map (Pyrgos bus station tel. 26210-20600).

By Train: The train station is on a side-street near the entrance to town, one block east (downhill) from the main street.

By Car: For driving directions into and out of Olympia, see "Route Tips for Drivers," page 301. Parking is free and easy in town and at the sights.

By Cruise Ship: To reach Olympia from the cruise-ship port of Katakolo, see "Tips for Cruise-Ship Passengers," page 302.

Helpful Hints

Services: Olympia's main street has wide sidewalks, countless gift shops, and ample hotels, eateries, ATMs, and other tourist services. You'll also find a small grocery store here.

Taxis: There's a taxi stand in town where the main street meets a shady, angled side-street called Georgiou Douma (tel. 26240-22555).

Local Guide: Consider hiring **Niki Vlachou** to show you around the ruins and museums (reasonable and negotiable rates, contact for exact price, mobile 697-242-6085, niki@olympic tours.gr).

Helpful Website: A good (but unofficial) website is www.olympia -greece.org. It has information on both the sights and the town itself, including a map of the city.

Sights in Olympia

There are three parts to an Olympia visit: The Sanctuary of Olympia archaeological site, the Archaeological Museum, and two smaller museums on a nearby hill (the Museum of the History of the Olympic Games in Antiquity, and the Museum of the History of Excavations). The Museum of the Modern Olympic Games, located in Olympia town, is currently closed.

Planning Your Time: While you can see Olympia's sights in any order, I recommend walking the archaeological site first (while your energy is high), then touring the Archaeological Museum to reconstruct what you've seen. If you have time left, hit the two smaller museums. Allow 1.5 hours for the site, an hour for the Archaeological Museum, and another hour for the two other museums.

Try to visit in the early morning or late afternoon (though the site can be very hot in the afternoon). It's most crowded between 10:00 and 13:00 (especially the Archaeological Museum). If you're coming in the off-season, it's best to visit in the morning, in case it closes at 15:00.

Getting There: By **car,** park for free at one of two lots: at the south end of town (closest to the site entrance), or at the east edge of town (closest to the Archaeological Museum). To reach the site from either parking lot, follow the signs, walking several hundred yards and crossing the Kladeos River. If staying in town, it's about a 10-minute **walk** from the center to either the site or the Archaeological Museum.

▲▲▲The Sanctuary of Olympia (The Site)

Olympia was the "Mecca" of ancient Greek religion—the location of its greatest sanctuary and one of its most important places of worship. In those times, people didn't live here—it was set aside as a monastery and pilgrimage site. The nearest city was 30 miles away. Ancient Greeks came here only every four years, during the religious festival that featured the Games. The heart of the sanctuary was a sacred enclosure called the Altis—a walled-off, rectangular area that housed two big temples, multiple altars, and statues to the gods.

Whereas Delphi served as a pilgrimage destination mostly for groups of wealthy people on a particular mission, every four years Olympia drew 40,000 ordinary folks for a Panhellenic party. As the site of the Olympic Games for more than a thousand years (c. 776 B.C.-A.D. 393), it was home to both temples and sports facilities.

Cost and Hours: €6, €9 combo-ticket includes Archaeological Museum; daily April-mid-Sept Tue-Sun 8:00-20:00, Mon 12:30-20:00; off-season hours vary but generally mid-Sept-March Tue-Sun 8:00-15:00, Mon 12:30-15:00; may stay open until 17:00 in early fall and late spring. Note that hours can change without warning, and could be shortened due to budget cuts. Tel. 26240-22517, www.culture.gr.

Compass Points: As you walk from the entrance of the site along the Sacred Way toward the ruins, you're heading south.

Services: The site itself has WCs just inside the entrance and near the far end of the Sacred Way. An open-air café is located between the site and the Archaeological Museum. No food is allowed inside the site.

OLYMPIA

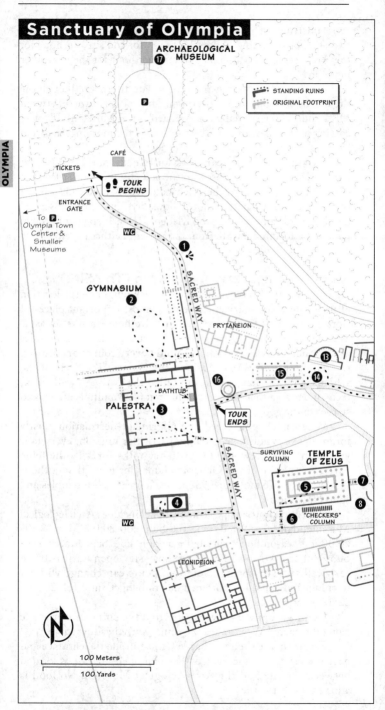

Sanctuary of Olympia

ARCHAEOLOGICAL MUSEUM 17

P

STANDING RUINS

ORIGINAL FOOTPRINT

CAFÉ

TICKETS

👣 *TOUR BEGINS*

ENTRANCE GATE

← To P
Olympia Town Center & Smaller Museums

WC

1

SACRED WAY

PRYTANEION

GYMNASIUM 2

13

15

14

16

BATHTUB

PALESTRA 3

TOUR ENDS

SURVIVING COLUMN

TEMPLE OF ZEUS

5

7

8

SACRED WAY

4

6 "CHECKERS" COLUMN

WC

LEONIDEION

N

100 Meters

100 Yards

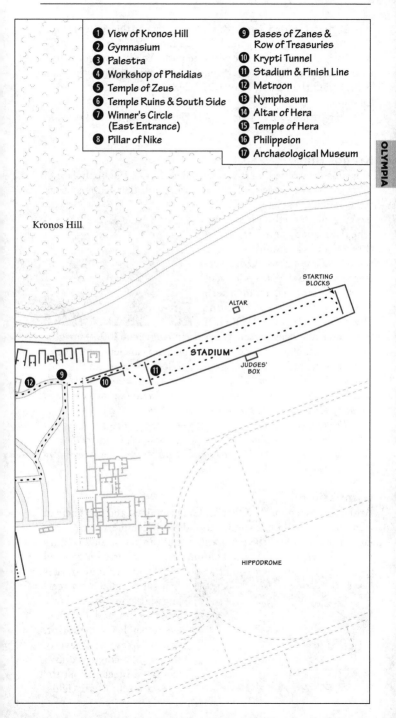

1. View of Kronos Hill
2. Gymnasium
3. Palestra
4. Workshop of Pheidias
5. Temple of Zeus
6. Temple Ruins & South Side
7. Winner's Circle (East Entrance)
8. Pillar of Nike
9. Bases of Zanes & Row of Treasuries
10. Krypti Tunnel
11. Stadium & Finish Line
12. Metroon
13. Nymphaeum
14. Altar of Hera
15. Temple of Hera
16. Philippeion
17. Archaeological Museum

OLYMPIA

Kronos Hill

STARTING BLOCKS

ALTAR

STADIUM

JUDGES' BOX

HIPPODROME

⊙ Self-Guided Tour: Buy your tickets at the site entrance, then head through the gate. Walk straight ahead (passing WCs on the right), then bear left with the path. You'll pass an orientation board, then head south through the sanctuary down the main path, called the Sacred Way, which leads to the ancient world of Olympia.

• *Walking south, look to your left (through the trees) to catch glimpses of....*

Kronos Hill

This area was sacred, as it was considered to be the birthplace of Zeus. According to legend, it was on this hill that Kronos, Zeus' father, tried to eat baby Zeus. But pesky Zeus (aided by his mom, Rhea) escaped, and later overthrew Kronos and went on to lead the pantheon of gods. (Other versions of the myth place this event on Mt. Olympus, in northern Greece, where the gods eventually made their home.) The hill

was scorched by devastating wildfires in August of 2007—imagine how close the flames came to enveloping this ancient site. Locals replanted the hill, and it is beginning to look green again.

• *As you descend gradually down the Sacred Way, you enter a wide field scattered with ruins. The area to the left of the Sacred Way was the sacred enclosure. To the right was the area for the athletes.*

The first set of ruins on your right—consisting of two long rows of stubby columns—was once part of the gymnasium. (To explore the area more closely, look for the stairs down the path on the right, which lead farther into the ruins.)

Gymnasium

Athletes arriving for the Olympic Games trained and lived here in a complex of buildings similar to today's "Olympic Village." The largest building was the gymnasium (built in the second century B.C.). The truncated Doric columns once supported a covered

arcade, one of four arcades that surrounded a big rectangular courtyard. Here athletes trained for field events such as the sprint, discus throw, and javelin throw. The courtyard (393 feet by 728 feet—about the size of six football fields, side-by-side) matched the length of the Olympic Stadium, so athletes could practice in a space similar to the one in which they would compete.

Because ancient Greeks believed that training the body was as important as training the mind, sports were a big part of every boy's education. Moreover, athletic training doubled as military training (a key element in citizenship)—so most towns had a gymnasium. The word "gymnasium" comes from the Greek *gymnos* ("naked"), which is how athletes trained and competed. Even today, the term "gymnasium" is used in many European countries (including Greece) to describe what Americans call high school.

Athletes arrived in Olympia a month early for the Games in order to practice and size up the competition. The Games were open to any free-born Greek male (both men and boys, who competed separately), but a good share of competitors were from aristocratic homes. Athletes trained hard. Beginning in childhood, they were given special diets and training regimens, often subsidized by their city. Many became professionals, touring the circuit of major festivals.

• *At the far end of the gymnasium ruins, you can walk directly into another twin row of (taller, more intact) columns. (You can also access this site from the Sacred Way, by taking the little wooden stairs farther down the path.) This is the...*

Palestra

Adjoining the gymnasium was this smaller but similar "wrestling school" (built around 300 B.C.). This square courtyard (216 feet

on each side—about one acre), also surrounded by arcades, was used by athletes to train for smaller-scale events: wrestling, boxing, long jump (performed while carrying weights, to build strength), and *pangration*, a kind of ancient "ultimate fighting" with only two rules: no biting and no eye-gouging.

Picture athletes in the courtyard working out. They were always naked, except for a layer of olive oil and dust for a bit of protection against scrapes and the sun. Sometimes they exercised in time with a flute player to coordinate their movements and to keep up the pace. Trainers and spectators could watch from the shade of the colonnades. Notice that the columns are smooth (missing their fluting) on the lower part of the inside face. This way, when it rained, athletes could exercise under the arcade (or take a breather by leaning up against a column) without scraping

OLYMPIA

The Ancient Olympic Games

The Olympic Games were athletic contests held every four years as a way of honoring Zeus, the king of the gods. They were the culmination of a pilgrimage, as Greeks gathered to worship Zeus, the Games' patron.

The exact origins of the Games are lost in the mists of time, but they likely grew from a local religious festival first held at the Sanctuary of Olympia in about 1150 B.C. According to one legend, the festival was founded by Pelops, namesake of the Peloponnese; a rival legend credits Hercules. Sporting events became part of the festivities. A harmonious, healthy body was a "temple" that celebrated its creator by performing at its peak.

The first Olympic Games at which results were recorded are traditionally dated at 776 B.C. The Games grew rapidly, attracting athletes from throughout the Greek world to compete in an ever-growing number of events (eventually taking up to five days in all). They reached their height of popularity around 400 B.C. Of the four major Greek games (including those at Delphi—see page 362, Corinth, and Nemea), Olympia was the first, biggest, and most prestigious.

Besides honoring Zeus and providing entertainment, the Games served a political purpose: to develop a Panhellenic ("all-Greek") identity among scattered city-states and far-flung colonies. Every four years, wars between bickering Greeks were halted with a one-month "sacred truce" so that athletes and fans could travel safely to Olympia. Leading citizens from all corners would assemble here, including many second- and third-generation Greeks who'd grown up in colonies in Italy, France, or Africa. Olympia was geographically central, and for the length of the festivities, it was also the symbolic heart of Greece.

This went on for 1,169 years, finally concluding in A.D. 393. Olympia today lives on in the spirit of the modern Olympic Games, revived in Athens in 1896. Every other year, athletes from around the world gather and—despite the politics that divide their countries—compete in contests that challenge the human spirit and foster a sense of common experience. Whether we're cheering on an American swimmer, a Chinese gymnast, or a Jamaican sprinter to go faster, longer, and better than any human has before, the Games still bring the world together...just as they did in this tranquil pine grove so many centuries ago.

themselves on the grooves.

In the area nearest the Sacred Way, notice the benches where athletes were taught and people gathered for conversation. You can still see the bathtubs that athletes used to wash off their oil-dust coating. (They also used a stick-like tool to scrape off the oil.)

Besides being training facilities, palestras (found in almost any city) were also a kind of health club where men gathered to chat. Plato set his dialogue *Charmides* at a palestra in Athens, where Socrates goes to find his old friends.

• *Before you leave, there's a nice photo-op. Look back through the columns, across the Sacred Way, to the three surviving columns of the Philippeion (which we'll circle back to later).*

Continue (south) down the Sacred Way. Ahead on the right (set back from the path) is a ruined brick building. Climb the stairs at the far end and peek into the...

Workshop of Pheidias

In this building, the great sculptor Pheidias (c. 490-430 B.C.) created the 40-foot statue of Zeus (c. 435 B.C.) that once stood in the

Temple of Zeus across the street. (It was later named one of the Seven Wonders of the Ancient World—see sidebar on page 285.) The workshop was built with the same dimensions as the temple's *cella* (inner room) so that Pheidias could create the statue with the setting in mind. Pheidias arrived here having recently completed his other masterpiece, the colossal Athena Parthenos for the Parthenon in Athens (see page 124). According to ancient accounts, his colossal Zeus outdid even that great work.

How do we know this building was Pheidias' place? Because archaeologists found sculptors' tools and molds for pouring metals, as well as a cup with Pheidias' name on it (all now displayed in the museum).

• *Farther south down the Sacred Way—but skippable—is a large, rubble-strewn, open field, with dozens of thigh-high Ionic capitals. This was the site of the massive* **Leonideion**, *a luxury, four-star hotel with 145 rooms (and private baths) built in the fourth century* B.C. *to house VIPs (dignitaries and famous athletes) during the Games.*

Now turn your attention to Olympia's main sight: the Temple of Zeus. It's located across the Sacred Way from Pheidias' workshop. All that remain are ruins, marked by a single standing column.

Temple of Zeus

The center of ancient Olympia—both physically and symboli-

cally—was the massive Temple of Zeus, the King of the Gods and patron of the Games. It was the first of the Golden Age temples, and one of the biggest (not much smaller than the Parthenon), and is the purest example of the Doric style.

The temple was built in the fifth century B.C. (470-457 B.C.), stood for a thousand years, and then crumbled into the evocative pile of ruins we see today, still lying where they fell in the sixth century A.D.

Mentally reconstruct the temple. It was huge—209 feet by 89 feet (about half an acre)—and stood six stories tall. The lone standing column is actually a reconstruction (of original pieces, cleaned and re-stacked), but it gives a sense of the scale: It's 34 feet tall, 7 feet thick, and weighs nine tons. This was one of 34 massive Doric columns that surrounded the temple (6 on each end, 13 along the sides)—making this a typical peripteral/peristyle temple, like Athens' Parthenon and Temple of Hephaistos (in the Ancient Agora).

The columns originally supported a triangular pediment at each end (now in the Archaeological Museum), carved with scenes of the *Battle of the Lapiths and Centaurs* (west end) and *Pelops and the Chariot Race* (east end, which was the main entrance).

• *Find the path that lets you get up close to the temple. As you approach the ruins, you're entering the Altis, or sacred enclosure. Wend your way through the...*

Temple Ruins: Walk between big gray blocks, two-ton column drums, and fallen 12-ton capitals. They're made not of marble

but from local limestone. Look closely and you can see the seashell fossils in this porous (and not terribly durable) sedimentary rock. Most of the temple was made of this cheaper local stone, then covered with a marble-powder stucco to make it glisten as brightly as if it were made of pure marble. The pediments and some other deco-

Statue of Zeus

Imagine yourself as a visitor to the Temple of Zeus in ancient times. You'd enter the temple from the east end (the end opposite the Sacred Way). Peering to the far side of the temple, you'd see the monumental statue of Zeus sitting 40 feet high on a golden throne. The statue gleamed gold and white, with colored highlights. In his right hand Zeus held a winged statue of Nike (goddess of victory), and in his left hand was a scepter topped with an eagle. Zeus completely filled the space.  His head almost touched the ceiling (which was higher than the exterior columns), and his arms almost touched the sides, making the colossal statue appear even bigger. A cistern of olive oil on the temple floor reflected golden hues onto the statue.

Pheidias made the statue with a core of wood. He covered that with plates of ivory (soaked, carved, and worked into shape) to make Zeus' skin, and 500 pounds of gold plates for the clothes and the throne. (Such statues, when decorated with gold and ivory—as many religious statues in ancient Greece were—are called "chryselephantine.") Pheidias' assistants painted the throne with scenes of the gods.

The statue was considered by ancient people as one of the Seven Wonders—a list of tourist musts that also included the Colossus of Rhodes and the pyramids of Egypt. We know the general outlines of the statue because it appeared on coins of the day.

We also know that the statue stood for 900 years, but no one knows what became of it. It may have been melted down by Christians or destroyed in the earthquakes that toppled the temple. Others think it was carried off to Constantinople and accidentally burned in that city's catastrophic fire of A.D. 476.

ration were made of expensive white marble from the isle of Paros.

The olive trees mark the spot of the original tree (planted by Hercules, legends say) from which the winners' wreaths were made. Then as now, olives were vital to Greece, providing food, preservatives, fuel, perfumes...and lubrication for athletes.

• *If open, ascend a set of stairs (in the southwest corner, at the opposite end from the standing column, to the right) up onto what was once the south porch of the temple—the edge facing away from Kronos Hill.*

South Side: From here, you can look inside and make out the temple's layout, including the rectangular shape of the *cella*. This was the most sacred part of the temple, where Pheidias' statue of Zeus stood. Looking down to the ground along the south side, see five huge fallen columns, with their drums lined up in a row like dominos—or the vertebrae of dinosaurs.

• *Continue to the east end of the temple. From atop the temple's main stairs, look down on the courtyard below, the...*

Winner's Circle (East End): Here at the main entrance to the temple, winners of the Olympic Games were announced and crowned. As thousands gathered in the courtyard below, priests called the name of the winner, who scaled the steps against a backdrop of cheers from the crowd. The winner was crowned with a wreath of olive (not laurel) branches, awarded a statue in his honor—and nothing more. There were no awards for second and third place, and no gold, silver, or bronze medals—those are inventions of the modern Olympics. However, winners were usually showered with gifts and perks from their proud hometowns: free food for life, theater tickets, naming rights for gymnasiums, statues, pictures on ancient Wheaties boxes, and so on.

In the courtyard below, you can see pedestals that once held statues of winners, who were considered to be demi-gods. The inscriptions listed the winner's name, the date, the event won, his hometown, and the names of his proud parents.

A bit to the right stands the 29-foot-tall, white-marble, triangular **Pillar of Nike.** It's empty now, but it once held a famous statue of the goddess Nike (now in the museum). Nike was, of course, the personification of "Victory" (this particular statue commemorated the Messenian defeat of the Spartans in 425 B.C.). Overlooking this place, where athletic victories were celebrated, the statue must have been an inspiring sight.

The ruined building directly east of here was the Echo Hall, a long hall where winners were also announced as if into a microphone—the sound echoed seven times.

• *Descend the steps and turn left when you can (passing several of the inscribed pedestals mentioned earlier). Make your way north, until you bump into the low wall at the base of Kronos Hill. The foot of that hill is lined with a row of 16 pedestals, the...*

Bases of Zanes (Cheater Statues) and Row of Treasuries

At the Olympic Games, there were no losers...except quitters and cheaters.

These 16 pedestals once held bronze statues of Zeus (plural "Zanes"). The statues were paid for with fines levied on cheaters, whose names and ill deeds were inscribed in the bases. As people entered the stadium, they'd spit on the statues. Offenses ranged from doping (using forbidden herbs) or taking bribes, to failing to train in advance of the Games or quitting out of cowardice. Drinking animal blood— the Red Bull of the day—was forbidden. Official urine drinkers tested for this ancient equivalent of steroids.

Athletes took an oath not to cheat (at the Bouleuterion, along the south side of the Temple of Zeus) by stepping on castrated bulls' balls. As this was a religious event, and because physical training was a part of moral education, the oaths and personal honor were held sacred.

Just behind the statues (and a few feet higher in elevation) is a terrace with a row of treasuries. These small buildings housed expensive offerings to the gods. Many were sponsored by colonies as a way for Greeks living abroad to stay in touch with their cultural roots.

• *Turn right and pass under the arch of the...*

Krypti

Built around 200 B.C., this 100-foot-long tunnel, which once had

a vaulted ceiling, was the athletes' entrance to the stadium. Along the walls are niches that functioned as equipment lockers. Just like today's NFL players, Olympia's athletes psyched themselves up for the big contest, shouting as they ran through this tunnel, then emerging into the stadium to the roar of the crowd.

• *On your mark, get set, go. Follow the Krypti as it leads into the...*

OLYMPIA

Stadium

Line up on that original marble-paved starting line from the ancient Olympic Games and imagine the scene. The place was filled with 45,000 spectators—men, boys, and girls—who sat on the manmade banks on either side. One lone adult woman was allowed in: a priestess of the goddess Demeter Chamyne, who rose above the sea of testosterone from an altar on the north (left) bank (still visible today).

The stadium (built in the sixth century B.C.) held no seats except those for the judges, who sat in a special box (visible on the south bank, to your right). These Hellanodikai ("Judges of the Greeks") kept things on track. Elected from local noble families and carefully trained over 10 months for just a few days of Games, these referees were widely respected for their impartiality.

The stadium track is 192 meters (640 feet) from start to finish line. In fact, the Greek word *stadion* literally means a course that is 600 traditional Olympic feet long, supposedly first stepped off by the legendary hero Hercules. The line at the near (west) end marked the finish, where all races ended. (Some started at this end as well, depending on how many laps in the race, but most started at the far end.) The racers ran straight up and back on a clay surface, not around the track. There were 20 starting blocks (all still visible today—count 'em), each with two grooves—one for each foot (athletes competed barefoot). They once had wooden starting gates (similar to those used in horse races today) to make sure no one could jump the gun.

The first Games featured just one event, a sprint race over one length of the stadium, or one *stadion*. (Imagine running this distance in 19.3 seconds, as Usain Bolt of Jamaica did at the 2008 Olympic Games.) Over time, more events were added. There were races of two *stadia* (that is, up and back, like today's 400-meter event), 24 *stadia* (similar to today's 5K race), and a race in which

athletes competed in full armor, including shields.

At the height of the Games (c. 400 B.C.), there were 13 events (most held here in the stadium) over five days. Besides footraces, you'd see events such as the discus, javelin, boxing, wrestling, long jump, *pangration* (a wrestling/boxing/martial arts event), and the pentathlon. (In ancient times, there was no decathlon—that event is a modern invention.) South of the stadium was the hippodrome, or horse-racing track, where riding and chariot races took place. During the 2004 Games in Athens, the shot put competition was held in this stadium.

• *Backtrack through the tunnel and continue straight past the Zeus statues. You'll bump into some rectangular foundations, the ruins of the...*

Metroon (Temple of Gaia) and Site of the Altar of Zeus

The Metroon (mid-fourth century B.C.) was dedicated to the mother of the gods, worshipped by many names (Gaia, Ge, Ghea, Rhea, Kybele, and others). From here, you get nice views up to Kronos Hill.

Somewhere near here once stood the Altar of Zeus, though no one knows exactly where— nothing remains today. At this altar the ancient Olympians slaughtered and burned animals in sacrifice to the gods. For special festivals, they'd sacrifice 100 cattle (a "hecatomb"), cook them on the altar, throw offerings into the flames, and feast on the flesh, leaving a pile of ashes 25 feet high.

In the middle of the wide path, under an olive tree, is a **sunken apse,** recently excavated by archaeologists. What you see are the foundations of a 4,000-year-old house, emphasizing that this site was important long before the Olympic Games and the Golden Age of ancient Greece.

• *Continuing on (westward), you'll find the ruins of a semi-circular structure built into the hillside, the...*

Nymphaeum

This was once a spectacular curved fountain, lined with two tiers of statues of emperors, some of which are now in the Archaeological Museum. The fountain provided an oasis in the heat and also functioned as an aqueduct, channeling water throughout the sanctuary. It was built around A.D. 150 by the wealthy Roman Herodes Atticus (who also financed construction of the famous theater at the base of the Acropolis in Athens—see page 115).

When the Romans conquered Greece in the second century B.C., they became fans of Greek culture, including the Olympics. The Romans repaired neglected buildings and built new structures, such as this one. But they also changed (some say perverted) the nature of the Games, transforming them from a Greek religious ritual to secular Roman spectacle. Rome opened up the Games to any citizen of the Empire, broadening their appeal at the cost of their Greek-ness.

Rome's notorious Emperor Nero—a big fan of the Olympics—attended the Games in the mid-first century A.D. He built a villa nearby, started music contests associated with the Games, and entered the competition himself as a charioteer. But when he fell off his chariot, Nero ordered the race stopped and proclaimed himself the winner.

• *In front of the Nymphaeum, between the Metroon and the Temple of Hera, are the rectangular foundations of what was once the...*

Altar of Hera

This humble site provides a bridge across millennia, linking the original Olympics to today's modern Games. Since 1936, this is where athletes have lit the cer-emonial Olympic torch (for both the summer and winter Games). A few months before the modern Games begin, local women dress up in priestess garb and parade here from the Temple of Hera. A curved, cauldron-shaped mirror is used to focus the rays of the sun, igniting a flame. The women then carry the flame into the stadium, where runners light a torch and begin the long relay to the next city to host the Games. From here, the relay will cover more than 1,500 miles to London for the 2012 Summer Games, and 1,000 miles to Sochi, Russia, for the 2014 Winter Games.

• *Continuing west, you'll come to the four standing Doric columns of the well-preserved...*

Temple of Hera

First built in 650 B.C., this is the oldest structure on the site and one of Greece's first monumental temples. The temple originally honored both Hera and her husband Zeus, before the Temple of Zeus was built.

The temple is long but not tall, giving it an intimate feel. It's

61.5 feet wide by 164 feet long and surrounded by columns (6 wide by 16 long)—both of which are a ratio of 3:8. That proportion was considered aesthetically harmonious as well as astronomically significant because the ancients synchronized the lunar and solar calendars by making the year three months longer every eight years.

The temple was originally made of wood. Over time, the wooden columns were replaced with stone columns, resulting in a virtual catalog of the various periods of the Doric style. The columns are made from the same shell-bearing limestone as most of the site's buildings, also originally covered in marble stucco.

Inside, a large statue of Hera once sat on a throne with Zeus standing beside her. Hera's priestesses wove a new dress for the statue every four years. The temple also housed a famous statue of Hermes and was topped with the Disk of the Sun (both are now in the museum).

Though women did not compete in the Olympics, girls and maidens competed in the Heraean Games, dedicated to Hera. The Heraean Games were also held every four years, though not in the same years as the Olympics. They were open only to unmarried virgins—no married women allowed—who raced on foot (running five-sixths of a *stadion,* or 160 meters/525 feet) and in chariots, wearing dresses with one breast exposed. Like the men, the winners received olive wreaths and fame, as well as a painted portrait displayed on a column of the Temple of Hera.

• *Continuing west, you'll reach a round-shaped temple with three Ionic columns (which we saw earlier), the...*

Philippeion

The construction of the Philippeion announced a new era in Greece—the Hellenistic era.

It was built by Philip of Macedon to mark his triumph over Greece. The Macedonians spoke Greek and had many similar customs, but they were a kingdom (not a democracy), and the Greeks viewed them as foreigners. Philip, the father of Alexander the Great, conquered Greece around 340 B.C., thus uniting the country—by force—while bringing its Classical Age to an end.

The temple—the first major building visitors saw upon entering the sacred site—originally had 18 Ionic columns of limestone and marble stucco (though today it appears dark, as the gleaming stucco is long gone). Inside stood statues of Philip and his family, including his son, the man who would bring Greece to its next phase of glory: Alexander the Great.

Just north of the Philippeion, bordering the Sacred Way and difficult to make out, are the scant remains of the Prytaneion, the building that once housed the eternal Olympic flame.

Olympia's Legacy

After the Classical Age, the Games continued, but not in their original form. First came Alexander and a new era of more secular values. Next came the Romans, who preserved the Games but also commercialized them and opened them up to non-Greeks. The Games went from being a somber celebration of Hellenic culture to being a bombastic spectacle. The lofty ideals for which the games were once known had evaporated—along with their prestige. As Rome/Greece's infrastructure decayed, so did the Games. A series of third-century earthquakes and the turmoil of the Herulian invasion (in A.D. 267) kept the crowds away. As Greece became Christian, the pagan sanctuary became politically incorrect.

The last ancient Games (the 293rd) were held in A.D. 393. A year later, they were abolished by the ultra-Christian emperor Theodosius I as part of a general purge of pagan festivals. The final blow was delivered in 426, when Theodosius II ordered the temples set ablaze. The remaining buildings were adopted by a small early Christian community, who turned Pheidias' workshop into their church. They were forced to abandon the area after a combination of earthquakes (in 522 and 551) and catastrophic floods and mudslides. Over the centuries, two rivers proceeded to bury the area under 25 feet of silt—thus preserving the remaining buildings until archaeologists rediscovered the site in 1766.

• *The Archaeological Museum is 200 yards to the north, and well-signed.*

▲▲▲Archaeological Museum

Many of Olympia's greatest works of art and artifacts have been removed from the site and are now displayed in this compact and manageable museum.

Cost and Hours: €6, €9 combo-ticket includes archaeological site, same hours as the Sanctuary of Olympia, tel. 26240-22517, www.culture.gr.

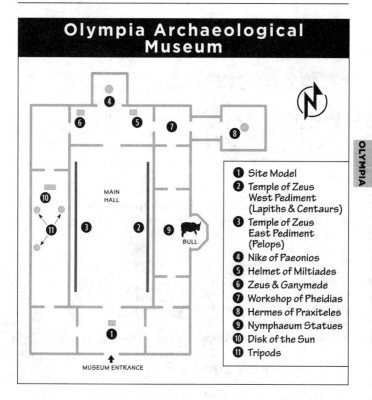

Olympia Archaeological Museum

- ❶ Site Model
- ❷ Temple of Zeus West Pediment (Lapiths & Centaurs)
- ❸ Temple of Zeus East Pediment (Pelops)
- ❹ Nike of Paeonios
- ❺ Helmet of Miltiades
- ❻ Zeus & Ganymede
- ❼ Workshop of Pheidias
- ❽ Hermes of Praxiteles
- ❾ Nymphaeum Statues
- ❿ Disk of the Sun
- ⓫ Tripods

Services: A museum shop, WCs, and café are to the right of the entrance.

➲ **Self-Guided Tour:** Everything is well-described in English. This tour takes you past the highlights, but there's much more to see if you have time. As you enter, ask for the free booklet that includes a map of the museum (and the site).

• *In the entrance lobby, you'll encounter a...*

Model of the Site, Reconstructed: Looking at Olympia as it appeared in its Golden Age glory, you can see some of the artifacts that once decorated the site (and which now fill this museum). On the Temple of Zeus, notice the pediments, topped with statues and tripods. Southeast of the temple is the Pillar of Nike, topped with the statue of Nike. Find Pheidias' workshop and the Temple of Hera, topped with the Disk of the Sun. We'll see all of these items on this tour.

• *Continue straight ahead into the main hall. On the right wall are...*

Statues of Lapiths and Centaurs from the West Pediment of the Temple of Zeus: This 85-foot-long pediment stood over the back side of the temple (facing the Sacred Way). Study the

scene: In the *Battle of the Lapiths and Centaurs,* the centaurs have crashed a human wedding party in order to carry off the women. See one dramatic scene of a woman and her horse-man abductor just left of center. The Lapith men fight back. In the center, a 10-foot-tall Apollo stands calmly looking on. He puts his arm around the king's shoulder to assure him that they will drive off the centaurs.

• *On the opposite side of the hall are...*

Statues of Pelops from the East Pediment of the Temple of Zeus: This is what you would've seen above the temple's main entrance. Olympic victors stood beneath this pediment as they

received their olive wreaths. The statues tell the story of King Pelops, the legendary founder of the Games. A 10-foot-tall Zeus in the center is flanked by two competing chariot teams. Pelops (at Zeus' left hand, with the fragmented legs) prepares to race King Oenomaus (at Zeus' right) for the hand of the king's daughter Hippodamia (standing beside Pelops). The king, aware of a prophecy predicting that he would be murdered by his son-in-law, killed 13 previous suitors after defeating them in chariot races. But Pelops wins this race by sabotaging the king's wheels (that may be what the crouching figure is up to behind the king's chariot), causing the king to be dragged to his death by his horses (just like that chariot race in *Ben-Hur*). Pelops becomes king and goes on to unify the Peloponnesian people with a festival: the Olympic Games.

As some of the first sculpture of the Golden Age (made after the Persian invasion of 480 B.C.), this shows the realism and relaxed poses of the new age (note that they're missing those telltale Archaic-era smiles). But it's still done in the Severe style—the sculptural counterpart to stoic Doric architecture—with impassive faces and understated emotion, quite different from the exuberant West Pediment.

• *Continue straight ahead, where you'll see a statue rising and floating on her pedestal. She's the...*

Nike of Paeonios: This statue of Victory (c. 421 B.C.) once stood atop the triangular Pillar of Nike next to the Temple of Zeus. Victory holds her billowing robe in her outstretched left

hand and a palm leaf in her right as she floats down from Mt. Olympus to proclaim the triumph of the Messenians (the Greek-speaking people from southwest Peloponnese) over Sparta.

The statue, made of flawless pure-white marble from the island of Paros, was damaged in the earthquakes of A.D. 522 and 551. Today, her wings are completely missing, but they once stretched behind and above her, making the statue 10 feet tall. (She's about seven feet today.) With its triangular base, the whole monument to Victory would have been an imposing 36 feet tall, rising above the courtyard where Olympic winners were crowned.

• *In the glass case to the right as you face Nike are two bronze helmets. The green, battered one (#2) is the...*

Bronze Helmet of Miltiades (Hero of the Battle of Marathon): In September of 490 B.C., a huge force of invading

Persians faced off against the outnumbered Greeks on the flat plain of Marathon, north of Athens. While most of the Athenian generals wanted to wait for reinforcements, Miltiades convinced them to attack. The Greeks sprinted across the plain, into the very heart of the Persians—a bold move that surprised and routed the enemy. According to legend, the good news was carried to Athens by a runner. He raced 26 miles from Marathon to Athens, announced "Hurray, we won!"...and dropped dead on the spot.

The legend inspired the 26-mile race called the marathon—but the marathon was not an Olympic event in ancient times. It was a creation for the first modern Games, revived in Athens in A.D. 1896.

• *A glass case to the left of Nike has the smaller-than-life-size...*

Statue of Zeus Carrying Off Ganymede: See Zeus' sly look as he carries off the beautiful Trojan boy Ganymede to be his cup-bearer and lover. The terra-cotta statue was likely the central roof decoration (called an *akroterion*—see the nearby diagram) atop the Temple of Zeus.

• *Enter the room to the right as you face Nike.*

Workshop of Pheidias Room: The poster shows Pheidias' great statue of Zeus, and a model reconstructs the workshop where he created it. In the display case directly to the left as you enter, find exhibit #10, the clay cup of Pheidias. The inscription on it reads: "I belong to Pheidias." The adjacent case holds clay molds that were likely used for making the folds of Zeus' robe. The case in the opposite corner contains lead and bronze tools that would have been used by ancient sculptors.

• *The room hiding behind the Zeus poster contains...*

Hermes of Praxiteles: This seven-foot-tall statue (340-330 B.C.), discovered in the Temple of Hera, is possibly a rare original by the great sculptor Praxiteles. Though little is known of this fourth-century

sculptor, Praxiteles was recognized in his day as the master of realistic anatomy and the first to sculpt nude women. His works influenced generations of Greek and Roman sculptors, who made countless copies.

Hermes leans against a tree, relaxed. He carries a baby—the recently orphaned Dionysus—who reaches for a (missing) object that Hermes is distracting him with.

Experts guess he was probably groping for a bunch of grapes, which would have hinted at Dionysus' future role as the debauched god of wine and hedonism.

Circle the statue and watch Hermes' face take on the many shades of thoughtfulness. From the front he appears serene. From the right (toward the baby), there's the hint of a smile, while from the left (toward his outstretched arm), he seems sad.

The statue has some of Praxiteles' textbook features. The body has the distinctive S-curve of Classical sculpture (head tilted one way, torso the other, legs another). He's leaning against a tree with his robe draped down. And the figure is interesting from all angles, not just the front. The famous Praxiteles could make hard, white, translucent marble appear as supple, sensual, and sexual as human flesh.

• *Consider detouring to see more statues, from the Roman Nymphaeum fountain. (If you're in a rush, skip this section and head for the Disk of the Sun.) To see the statues, backtrack into the Workshop of Pheidias Room, turn left, and proceed through the next room into the long hall.*

Nymphaeum Statues: The grand, semi-circular fountain near the Temple of Hera had two tiers of statues, including Roman emperors and the family of the statue's benefactor, Herodes

Atticus. Here you can see some of the surviving statues, as well as a sculpted bull (in the center of the room) that stood in the middle of the fountain. The bull's inscriptions explain the fountain's origins.

The next (smaller) room holds more Roman-era statues, from the Metroon and the Temple of Hera.

• *Head back to the Workshop of Pheidias Room, then backtrack past the helmets, Nike, and Zeus/Ganymede. Pass through the next room, and continue into the long hall with the large...*

Disk of the Sun: This terra-cotta disk—seven and a half feet across and once painted in bright colors—was the *akroterion* that perched atop the peak of the roof of the Temple of Hera. It stood as a symbol of how Hera's truth shines to earth.

• *The rest of this long room contains several...*

Tripods: These cauldrons-with-legs were used as gifts—to the gods and to victorious athletes. For religious rituals, tripods were used to pour liquid libations, to hold sacred objects, or to burn incense or sacrificial offerings. As ceremonial gifts to the gods, tripods were placed atop or around temples. And as gifts to athletes, they were a source of valuable bronze (which could easily be melted down into some other form), making for a nice "cash" prize.

Other Olympia Sights

The first two sights are perched on a low hill above the southern parking lot. These buildings started life as Olympia's original archaeological museum and the town's first hotel for antiquity-loving tourists. Today the core of Olympia's collection is displayed at the newer, modern museum described earlier, but this old museum building still houses a fine exhibit that nicely complements the other attractions here.

▲▲**Museum of the History of the Olympic Games in Antiquity**—This museum is dedicated to the games played by those

early Olympians. First the exhibit traces the history of the original Olympic Games. Then, in the main central hall, well-described artifacts explain the athletic events of the time—from track and field to wrestling to equestrian contests. You'll see ancient discuses, shots, javelin heads, and large shields that were carried by fully armor-clad runners in some particularly exhausting footraces. You'll also see the awards and honors for the victors, and a beautiful mosaic floor depicting some of these events (from the late second century or early third century B.C.). While the artifacts are nothing special, the collection offers a handy "Ancient Olympics 101" lesson that helps bring the events to life (free, open same hours as the Sanctuary of Olympia).

• *The small building just outside the museum (to the left as you face the entrance) houses WCs on one side, and on the other side, the tiny...*

Museum of the History of Excavations—This one-room exhibit explains the various waves of excavations that have taken place since the site of Olympia was re-identified in the mid-18th century. While early investigations were done by archaeologists from France (in the 1820s) and Germany (in the 1870s), most of the site was systematically uncovered to the point you see today by Germans between 1936 and 1966. (When Berlin hosted the 1936 Olympics, Germany took a special interest in the history of the original Games.) You'll see old maps, photos, and archaeologists' tools (free, open same hours as the Sanctuary of Olympia).

Museum of the Modern Olympic Games—This museum is currently closed, and it's unclear when it will reopen. Its dusty-but-cute collection gives an overview of the foundation of the modern Games, then launches into a chronological survey of each Olympiad, with photos, torches, medals, and other memorabilia (€2, 2 blocks uphill from the main drag on Kosmopoulou street, run by the Hellenic Olympic Committee in Athens: tel. 210-687-8888).

Sleeping in Olympia

Olympia's impressive archaeological site and museum—and the town's inconvenient location far from other attractions—make spending the night here almost obligatory. Fortunately, there are just enough good options to make it worthwhile, including one real gem (Hotel Pelops). If you have a car, consider sleeping above Olympia in the more charming village of Miraka.

Sleep Code

(€1 = about $1.40, country code: 30)
S = Single, **D** = Double/Twin, **T** = Triple, **Q** = Quad, **b** = bathroom, **s** = shower only. Unless otherwise noted, credit cards are accepted and breakfast is included.

To help you easily sort through these listings, I've divided the rooms into two categories, based on the price for a standard double room with bath:

$$ Higher Priced—Most rooms €55 or more.
$ Lower Priced—Most rooms less than €55.

Prices can change without notice; verify the hotel's current rates online or by email. For other updates, see www .ricksteves.com/update.

In Olympia

$$ Hotel Pelops is Olympia's top option, with 18 comfortable rooms—try this place first. Run by the Spiliopoulos clan—father Theodoros, Aussie mom Susanna, and children Alkis, Kris, and Sally—the hotel oozes hospitality. They're generous with travel advice and include free tea and coffee in each room. On the wall of the breakfast room, look for the three Olympic torches that family members have carried in the official relay: Tokyo 1964, Mexico City 1968, and Athens 2004 (Sb-€48, Db-€65, Tb-€85, non-smoking rooms, air-con, elevator, free Internet access and Wi-Fi, fee for cooking classes—arrange well in advance, Barela 2, tel. 26240-22543, fax 26240-22213, www.hotelpelops.gr, hotelpelops @gmail.com).

$$ Kronio Hotel, run by friendly Panagiotis Asteris, rents 23 straightforward rooms along the main street, some with balconies (Sb-€45, Db-€55, air-con, elevator, free Internet access and Wi-Fi, Tsoureka 1, tel. 26240-22188, fax 26240-22502, www.hotelkronio .gr, kronio@hol.gr).

$ Pension Posidon is a good budget option, with 10 simple but clean and affordable rooms in a homey house just two blocks above the main street, near the Museum of the Modern Olympic Games (Sb-€35, Db-€45, breakfast-€5, air-con, free Internet access and Wi-Fi, Stefanopoulou 9, tel. 26240-22567, mobile 69732-16726, www.pensionposidon.gr, info@pensionposidon.gr, Liagouras family).

$ Hotel Inomaos has 25 basic, crank-'em-out rooms on the main street (Sb-€45, Db-€53, air-con, elevator, free Internet access and Wi-Fi, tel. 26240-22056, fax 26240-22516, www.hotel inomaos.gr, inomaos@hol.gr).

Near Olympia, in Miraka

The village of Miraka, which sits on a hill above Olympia, is the site of the ancient settlement of Pissa (Archea Pissa/Αρχαια Πισα). Today it offers an authentic-feeling, Old-World village experience and a scenic perch with fine views over the fire-charred (but gradually reviving) olive groves in the valley below.

$$ Bacchus Tavern (also a recommended restaurant) rents six modern, comfortable rooms in a traditional village a 10-minute drive above Olympia. This is a luxurious-feeling retreat from the drabness of modern Olympia (Db-€75, Tb-€85, Qb-€95, off-site apartment with kitchen, air-con, free Wi-Fi, inviting terrace and swimming pool, tel. & fax 26240-22298, mobile 69371-44800, www.bacchustavern.gr, info@bacchustavern.gr, Costas).

Getting There: It's about a 10-minute drive from Olympia's town center: Take the main road out of town toward Pyrgos, then turn right toward Tripoli and twist uphill on the new, modern highway. After the fourth tunnel, exit to the left and curve around to reach Miraka. Bacchus Tavern is on the right as you enter town (look for the parking lot).

Eating in Olympia

Because its restaurants cater to one-nighters, Olympia has no interest in creating return visitors—making its cuisine scene uniformly dismal. A few functional places in town are decent and convenient, but if you have a car, it's worth the hike to the Europa Hotel or a short drive to Miraka for something more special.

In Olympia

As no place in town really has an edge, you could simply window-shop to find the setting you like best. Along the main road, **Taverna Dionysos** (ΤΑΒΕΡΝΑ ΔΙΟΝΥΣΟΣ) is cozier than most, with indoor and outdoor seating (€2-5 starters, €6-9 main dishes, daily 11:00-23:00, tel. 26240-22932). More places cluster along the shady, angled side-street called Georgiou Douma; along here, **Taverna Gefsis Melathron** has the most charm and a good reputation (€3-5 starters, €5-9 main dishes, daily 11:00-23:00, until 22:00 off-season, Douma 3, tel. 26240-22916). Just above the main street, near the Museum of the Modern Olympic Games, is the more local-feeling **Anesi,** which specializes in grilled meat (€3 starters, €5-7 main dishes, open daily, corner of Avgerinou and Spiliopoulou, tel. 26240-22644).

Europa Hotel restaurant, on the hills overlooking Olympia, is a 20-minute uphill hike, or a 5-minute taxi ride. Chef Alki practices his art on fresh products from the hotel's farm. His "farm dish" consists of layers of Talagani cheese and roasted vegetables—a refreshing break from traditional Greek salad. The grilled meats and fish are savory and satisfying. Try sitting outdoors on the terrace with grapevine arbors—in the fall, Alki will cut off clumps of grapes and bring them to your table for dessert (€3-7 starters, €5-7 salads, €7-14 main dishes, vegetarian options, 1 Drouva Street, tel. 26240-22650).

Near Olympia, in Miraka

Bacchus Tavern, with a striking setting and pleasant decor that mingles new and old, is the best eatery in the area. The Zapantis family is proud of their traditional, homemade Greek cuisine with creative flair. Olympians favor their lamb baked in oregano and olive oil. Ask owner Costas how he used water from the swimming pool to save his tavern from the 2007 wildfires (€3-6 starters, €7-12 grilled dishes, €11-15 fixed-price meals, good vegetarian options, daily 12:00-17:00 & 18:30-24:00, tel. 26240-22298). For driving directions, see the Bacchus Tavern hotel listing, earlier.

Olympia Connections

From Olympia by Bus: Two direct buses a day connect Olympia with **Athens** (5 hours, €27). For most other connections, you'll transfer in **Pyrgos** to the west (1-2/hour, less Sat-Sun, last bus at 22:15, 30 minutes) or in **Tripoli** to the east (1/day Mon-Fri, none Sat-Sun, 3.5 hours; buy ticket from bus driver). From Pyrgos, you can connect to **Athens, Patra** (with onward connections to **Delphi**), or **Kalamata** (with connections to **Kardamyli**). From Tripoli, you can reach **Nafplio, Gythio,** and **Sparta** (with connections to **Monemvasia**).

By Train: Privatization has resulted in drastic reduction of train routes. For the latest information, call Athens tel. 210-529-7777, www.trainose.gr.

Route Tips for Drivers

Olympia is situated in the hilly interior of the Peloponnese, connected to the outside world by one main highway, called E-55. You can take this west to **Pyrgos** (30 minutes), where E-55 forks: Take it north to **Patra** (2 hours from Olympia) and **Delphi** (3.5 hours from Olympia—see Delphi's "Route Tips for Drivers" on page 371); or south to **Kalamata** (2.5 hours from Olympia) and on to **Kardamyli** (3.5 hours from Olympia). Or, from Olympia, you can take E-55 east on its twisty route to **Tripoli** (2.5 hours), then get on the major E-65 expressway to zip to **Nafplio** (3.5 hours from Olympia) or **Athens** (4.5 hours from Olympia).

Tips for Cruise-Ship Passengers

Cruise ships stop at the village of Katakolo, about 18 miles west of Olympia. The TI at the dock only opens when a ship arrives.

Katakolon Express runs a private **bus** service for cruise-ship passengers. You must book in advance on their website (€20 round-trip, mobile 69772-57417, www.katakolon-express.com).

As many as 50 **taxis** descend upon the dock hoping to pick up passengers; the round-trip fare for a one-hour visit to Olympia runs €70-80, while a 2.5-hour visit costs €80-100 (to book in advance, consider friendly George Letsios, mobile 694-457-9917, www.taxikatakolon.gr, georgetaxitours@gmail.com).

If you want to **drive,** avoid the sleazy rental agency on the main street as you leave the dock. Try Avis (marked with a big red sign), just uphill from the main street (€45/day plus gas for air-conditioned Fiat with manual transmission, tel. 26210-42200, mobile 694-700-2290, www.katakolo-rentacar.com, helpful Kostas). The route is an easy 30-minute drive that bypasses any towns; ask the rental agent for directions.

Near Olympia: Patra

The big port city of Patra (Πάτρα, sometimes spelled "Patras" in English, pop. 170,000) is many visitors' first taste of Greece, as the hub for boats arriving from Italy (and from the Ionian Islands, including Corfu and Ithaca). While it's not a place to linger, Patra has rejuvenated its main thoroughfare to become a fairly enjoyable place to kill a little time waiting for your boat or bus.

Orientation to Patra

Patra sprawls along its harborfront, which is traced by the busy road called Othnos Amalias. Patra's transit points line up along here (from north to south, as you'll reach them with the sea on your right): slick, modern, new main boat terminal; ragtag main bus station; and low-profile train station. While everything is within about a 15-minute walk, it's not quite as simple as it sounds, as there are multiple smaller bus terminals (scattered along the street near the main station) and boat docks (seven "gates" that stretch along the seafront, numbered from south to north). Travel agencies are everywhere. If you're not able to check your bag at the train or bus station, try the boat terminal.

Tourist Information

Patra has an unusually well-organized TI, which can help you with transit information and advice on how to spend your time here

(Mon-Fri 7:30-21:00, Sat-Sun 10:00-17:00, Agiou Andreou 12-14, tel. 26104-61740, www.infocenterpatras.gr). They also offer free Internet access (up to 20 minutes) and free loaner bikes (3-hour max). The TI is behind the main bus station in a new building made of cream-colored stone. From the main boat terminal, it's a bit south (walk with the sea on your right, then turn uphill at the bus station). From the train station, it's a bit north (walk with the sea on your left, then turn uphill at the bus station).

Sights in Patra

Town Walk—Patra's most enjoyable stretch begins at the Agiou Nikolaou Wharf, extending into the sea from the middle of the port (near the train station). From this well-manicured wharf, a broad plaza faces an enticing traffic-free street that leads up through the middle of the drab concrete congestion to Patra's upper/old town. This pedestrian zone, also called **Agiou Nikolaou,** bustles with a lively, engaging chaos you'll only find in a Mediterranean port town. Lined with al fresco cafés, fancy restaurants, and hopping discos, it's a fine place to feel the pulse of urban Greece.

Other Sights—With more time, consider checking out the city's three major sights: The town **castle,** built by the Emperor Justinian in the sixth century, is reachable from a staircase at the top of Agiou Nikolaou. Near the castle, the impressively restored **ancient odeon** (theater) dates from Roman times. And along the waterfront south of the main transit zone, the vast **Church of Agios Andreas** is the city's metropolitan church (like a cathedral).

Sleeping in Patra

(€1 = about $1.40, country code: 30, area code: 261)
Patra is best avoided, and accommodations values are poor. But if you're stuck here overnight, these options are handy to the boats, buses, and trains.

   $$ Olympic Star Hotel has 34 rooms with luxurious touches on the main Agiou Nikolaou street, four blocks up from the port and just below the old town and castle (Sb-€65, Db-€90, skip breakfast and save €10, air-con, elevator, free Internet access and Wi-Fi, Agiou Nikolaou 46, tel. 26106-22939, fax 26102-43754, www.olympicstar.gr, info@olympicstar.gr).

   $$ Hotel Acropole, with 27 slightly faded business-class rooms, is wedged between busy streets across from the train station (Sb-€58, Db-€77, Db with balcony-€89, Tb-€100, air-con, elevator, free cable Internet, Agiou Andreou 32, tel. 26102-79809, fax 26102-21533, www.acropole.gr, info@acropole.gr).

Patra Connections

From Patra by Boat: You can sail from Patra to three towns in Italy: **Bari** (daily, 15.5 hours, Superfast Ferries, tel. 21089-19000, www.superfast.com), **Brindisi** (daily, 15 hours, Endeavor Lines, tel. 28103-46185, www.greekislands.gr/hml), and **Ancona** (daily, 20-21 hours, Superfast Ferries). There are also two non-direct ferry lines that run to Ancona via Igoumenotsa: Minoan Lines (tel. 21041-45700, www.minoan.gr) and ANEK Lines (tel. 21041-97420, www.anek.gr). Minoan and ANEK also both run to the Greek Ionian isle of **Corfu** (6/week, departs 24:00, 7 hours). Strintzis Ferries goes to **Kefalonia** and **Ithaki** islands (tel. 21042-25000, www.ferries.gr/strintzis-ferries). Other useful websites for Greek ferry schedules include www.ferries.gr, www.greece-ferries.com, and www.greekferries.gr.

If you have a Eurailpass, Superfast Ferries and Minoan Lines will either give you free deck-class passage or a discount (depends if your pass covers only Greece, or also Italy; verify details with ferries).

By Bus: Frequent buses connect Patra directly to **Athens** (1-2/hour, 3 hours). You can also take a bus to **Pyrgos** (with connections to **Olympia**) or **Kalamata** (with connections to **Kardamyli**). To reach **Delphi,** you'll change in Nafpakos and often also in Itea. Bus info: tel. 26106-23888.

By Train: From Patra, trains head east along the northern Peloponnesian coast all the way to **Athens**—but because of construction, you currently must take a bus to Kiato, then transfer to a train. Be aware that the government is planning to privatize the train system and routes may be cut, especially on the Peloponnese. Train info: Athens tel. 210-529-7777, www.trainose.gr.

KARDAMYLI AND THE MANI PENINSULA

ΚΑΡΔΑΜΎΛΗ / Καρδαμύλη •
ΜΆΝΗ / Μάνη

To discover the Back Door Peloponnese, head to its remotest frontier. The Mani Peninsula—the southern tip of mainland Greece (in fact, of the entire continent east of Spain)—feels like the end of the road. Sealed off from the rest of Greece by a thick ring of mountains, the peninsula has seen its population ebb and flow throughout history with tides of refugees, fleeing whatever crises were gripping the rest of Greece. The only part of Greece that never completely fell to the Ottoman invaders, the Mani became the cradle of the 1821 revolution that finally brought independence to the country.

In the Mani, travelers discover a timeless region of rustic villages and untrampled beaches. A day's drive around this desolate, rural peninsula offers dramatic mountain scenery and bloody history all tied up in an evocative package—making hedonism on the Mani coast feel all the more hedonistic. At the end of the day, you can retire to charming Kardamyli, an anti-resort that delicately mingles conscientious travelers with real-world Greece.

Planning Your Time

Two nights and a full day is a minimum for this area. To really be on vacation, add more nights. Sleep in Kardamyli. With one day, first take my self-guided walk of Kardamyli to get your bearings, then head up to Old Kardamyli. In the afternoon, go for a hike or hit the beach. With a second day and a car, do the self-guided driving tour of the Mani Peninsula. Those with three days here can do the driving tour at a more leisurely pace, saving the Pyrgos Dirou Caves (and possibly also the detour to Kastania) for a separate side-trip from Kardamyli.

If you're continuing on to Monemvasia, you can head from

the Mani loop directly to Monemvasia, but you'll likely need to cut a few stops off the loop to make it in one day.

Kardamyli

The village of Kardamyli (kar-dah-MEE-lee) is the gateway to the Mani Peninsula and its best home base. It's an ideal spot to relax and tune into the pace of Greek country life. On Kardamyli's humble but oddly fascinating main drag, locals-only mom-and-pop shops mingle with tourist stalls...and everyone's happy.

Little Kardamyli bears one of the oldest city names in the annals of Greek history. In the *Iliad*, Homer described "well-peopled" Kardamyli as one of seven cities presented to the Greek hero Achilles to persuade him to return to the siege of Troy. Achilles' son Pyrrhus sailed to Kardamyli, then walked to Sparta to claim the hand of Ermioni. And the legendary Gemini twins—Castor and Pollux—are said to be buried here.

Kardamyli is wedged between the sparkling pebble beaches of the Messenian Gulf and towering Mount Profitas Ilias (7,895 ft)—the Peloponnese's highest peak, which is snowcapped from November to early May. Between

the sea and the distant mountaintop, undulating hills and cliffs are topped with scenic villages, churches, and ruined towers. As throughout the rest of the Mani, in the sixth century A.D. Kardamyli's residents fled from pirates into these hills—returning to sea level only in the 18th century, after the construction of Old Kardamyli's defensive tower house (the Mourtzinos Tower) made it safe.

While visitors enjoy hiking into the hills, learning about the region's rough-and-tumble history at Old Kardamyli, swimming at the town's Ritsa Beach, and driving deeper into the Mani Peninsula, the real charm of Kardamyli is its low-key ambience—the place works like a stun gun on your momentum. On my last trip, I could have stayed here for days, just eating well and hanging out. It's the kind of place where travelers plan their day around the sunset.

Kardamyli

- SELF-GUIDED WALK
- **P** PARKING

To AGIA SOPHIA

To **4** & KALAMATA

OLD KARDAMYLI

RITSA BEACH

RIVERBED

P

BOTANA HERB SHOP

MESSENIAN

START

VILLAGE CHURCH

MAIN SQUARE

MONUMENT TO THE HEROES

P

B

NOT TO SCALE

FISHING SHOP

PYRRHUS LANDING

2

MAISTROS CAFÉ

BAKERY

LOTTERY

7

12

CLOTHES SHOP

OLD FACTORY

13

1

BUTCHER

Thanks to Lucy Stubbs

10

PHARMACY

BIO SHOP

11

6

15

NEWS SHOP

3

5

CITY HALL

TOWN PIER

END

HARDWARE STORE

TO **8**
PETROVOUNI & EXOHORI

GULF

HARBOR

TO **9**,
FONEAS BEACH,
DELFINIA BEACH,
STOUPA &
MANI PENINSULA
LOOP DRIVE

P

DCH

14

MAIN STREET

- **1** Hotel Anniska
- **2** Hotel Liakoto
- **3** Hotel Esperides
- **4** To Antonia's Apartments & Kastro Taverna
- **5** Gorgones Studios & Harilaos Restaurant
- **6** Olympia Koymanakou Rooms
- **7** Markeas Stavoros Rooms
- **8** To Vardia Hotel
- **9** To Kalamitsi Hotel
- **10** Lela's Taverna
- **11** Tikla Café
- **12** Tis Eftichias
- **13** Taverna Perivolis
- **14** Taverna Dioskouroi
- **15** To Kolonaki's Café
- **16** Grocery Stores

KARDAMYLI

Orientation to Kardamyli

Tiny Kardamyli (sometimes spelled Kardamili or Kardhamili in English)—with about 200 year-round residents—swells with far more visitors in the summer months. The town is compact, branching off from a convenient central spine (the main road running south from Kalamata). Kardamyli is small enough to feel like a cozy village (locals claim they can leave their wallet on the seat of their car with doors unlocked—and two months later still find it there), but big enough to serve the needs of its many visitors—with grocery stores, ATMs, a post office, and more (all described in my self-guided walk, next).

Because Kardamyli has no TI, hoteliers pick up the slack, sometimes offering free hiking maps and usually eager to direct visitors to the best restaurants and attractions. The very helpful official town website has lots of good information, including accommodations (www.kardamili-greece.com).

Arrival in Kardamyli: For specifics on driving into town, see page 320.

Local Guide: Elias Polimeneas is a soulful native who proudly introduces visitors to his town and region. If you'd like to explore Kardamyli with a Kardamylian, or see the Mani Peninsula without driving yourself, Elias is your man (reasonable and negotiable rates, tel. 27210-73453, mobile 69469-98416, antonias apartments@yahoo.gr).

Self-Guided Walk

Welcome to Kardamyli

You could walk from one end of Kardamyli to the other in five minutes, but you'd miss the point. Slow down, keeping an eye out for intriguing pockets of traditional Greek village culture. This take-your-time stroll lasts about an hour.

• *Begin at the beginning of town, by the...*

Village Church

The modern Church of St. Mary isn't a tourist attraction, but a real church with a thriving congregation. Notice the loudspeakers outside, which allow overflow congregations to take part in the Mass on very important days, such as Easter. Kardamyli takes its Easter celebration very seriously: On Good Friday, a processional passes through the town and the priest blesses each

house. At midnight on Holy Saturday, everyone in town turns off their lights and comes to this main square. The priest emerges from the church with a candle, which he spreads through the candle-carrying crowd, who then take the light home with them...gradually illuminating the entire town. And then the fireworks begin.

Near the Church: If you were to go down the stairs behind the church and head toward the water (crossing the old, dry river-bed), you'd find the first few pebbles of Kardamyli's **Ritsa Beach** (described later).

For a fragrant detour, walk down the main street toward the edge of the village, away from the main square. Look for a worn wooden fence on the right side of the street, across from two grocery stores. Behind the fence is the **Botana Herb Shop,** a celebration of what grows in the hills behind Kardamyli. Owner Yiannis Dimitreas offers free tastes of his organic produce—marinated olives, fresh olive oil, and local honey—and also sells homemade herbal teas, soaps, and skin creams (daily 8:00-13:30 & 17:00-20:00, tel. 27210-73367, mobile 69726-90170).

• *Extending toward town from the church is the leafy...*

Main Square

The square, a popular playground for Kardamylian kids, is lined with eucalyptus trees. The trunks are painted with a sanitizing

lime wash that keeps pests and disease at bay.

Walk to the end of the square. In the little park is the town water spigot and an oddball collection of **monuments.** Find the busts of two almost comically medal-laden generals who fought in the Macedonian War. The

modern sculpture between them, called *Unity,* evokes the many fortified towers that dot the Mani Peninsula. Despite the vendettas that frequently cropped up among the peninsula's inhabitants, called Maniots, today they generally feel united with each other.

Across the street, on the pedestal, is a **monument to the heroes** who have fought for Greek unity and independence since antiquity. Next to the palm branch is the Greek motto "Freedom or Death." While two wars are highlighted in the wreath below (the 1821 Greek War of Independence, and the 1912-1913 First Balkan War), the monument is a reminder that the ideals behind those conflicts date back to the ancients.

The cobbled path just behind this monument takes hikers (in about 10 minutes) to the restored ruins and museum of **Old Kardamyli** (described later).

Back across the street, in the small square with the fountain, notice the good **map** of Kardamyli (get your bearings here). To the right is a little glass display case with a notice board from the mayor's office, announcing town business.

When you reach the cross street at the end of the square, look right to the **waterfront.** According to a legend dating back to the Trojan War, Achilles' son Pyrrhus (a.k.a. Neoptolemus) arrived at this very pier to begin the long walk to Sparta (about 50 miles northeast of here). There he would claim the hand of his betrothed, Ermioni, in marriage. Supposedly, the sea nymphs living in Kardamyli's bay surfaced to appreciate the young warrior's good looks as he passed. (Strangely, no sea nymphs popped up when I walked by...)

Now look in the opposite direction, up at the **hillsides** above Kardamyli. From here, you can see two of the most popular nearby hiking destinations: On the left is the little hilltop church of Agia Sophia, and to the right is the village of Petrovouni. An enjoyable three-hour loop covers both of these sights (see "Hiking" on page 315).

• *Across from the end of the park begins the commercial zone of...*

Kardamyli's "Main Street"

The next few blocks reveal a fascinating blend of traditional Greek village lifestyles side-by-side with just the right kind of tourism.

In most Greek towns with such a fine seaside setting, the beach is lined with concrete high-rise hotels, and the main street is a cavalcade of tacky T-shirt shops. But the people of Kardamyli are determined to keep their town real—a hard-fought local law prohibits new construction over a certain height limit (ruling out big resorts), and the town has made long-term sustainability a priority over short-term profit. (It also helps that the beach has pebbles instead of sand—keeping away the party-hearty crowds.) Its residents have created a smart little self-sustaining circle: The town keeps its soul even as it profits from visitors...allowing it to attract the caliber of travelers who appreciate Kardamyli for what it is.

Take a walk down the main street for examples of both faces

of Kardamyli. Notice that (with the exception of the big, red, empty eyesore a half-block down) all of the buildings are traditionally built, using local stone. Even new buildings (such as the Maistros/Μαϊστρος café, right at the start of the street) match the old style.

Mom-and-pop shops sell necessities side-by-side with touristy stuff. Across from the café, on the right, notice the **"fishing suppliment"** shop, which sells fishing gear, paint, and a few postcards. Today's Kardamyli has only two professional fishermen—more on them later—but many locals (and some tourists) enjoy recreational fishing.

On the left is the town **bakery**—drop in here for a sweet treat (closed Sun). Peruse the case, and consider the Peloponnesian specialty of *dipla*—a pastry fried in olive oil, then topped with nuts and honey.

Next door, notice the **lottery shop** (with the ΛΟΤΤΟ/ΠΡΟΤΟ sign). People come here to buy lottery tickets, place bets on sporting events, and play keno. At the end of this block are a bike-rental shop (on the left) and the town's post office (on the right, Mon-Fri 7:30-14:00, closed Sat-Sun).

A half-block down on the right is the **Sotirula clothes shop.** Old, black-clad Mrs. Sotirula, one of Kardamyli's most loyal shopkeepers, is often sitting outside. While she mostly sells to tourists today, originally she and her husband clothed the locals. In the 1960s, they had one of the first VWs on the peninsula. They'd load it with clothes, fire up its roof-top loudspeaker, and drive to nearby villages to hawk their wares.

On the left is the **butcher shop** (ΚΡΕΟΠΩΛΕΙΟ). For a time-travel experience, peek inside to see a giant butcher block, a row of hooks with smocks and butchers' tools, and a sturdy cooler humming away in the back corner. The Mani's mountain shepherds produce lots of goat meat and some beef...and they can get you a rabbit with two days' notice.

Next door (also on the left) is a **real-estate office**—one of two on this street. Mani property is popular among foreigners (and some Athenians) seeking vacation homes.

A few more steps down, on the left, is the **Bio shop,** selling organic products. Christos is evangelical about his homegrown goodies, offering free tastes of his olive oils and honeys—he'll even show you photos of how he harvested his products. Though his English is non-existent, it's a pleasure to feel his passion. If you've tasted too much, help is nearby—the town's **pharmacy** (ΦΑΡΜΑΚΕΙΟ) is across the street.

Ahead on the left is the town **news shop,** selling international newspapers, English-language books, and maps and guidebooks about the Mani. Curmudgeonly owner Gregoris grumbles that he has to sell all the touristy stuff to stay in business, but his true love is the smell of the newsprint. Everyone finds their own bliss. Breathe deeply.

Look down the rest of the street, and you'll see the **dressmaker/tailor's shop** (on the right), the **City Hall** (on the left), and the **hardware store** (on the right). Why such a well-stocked hardware store for such a small town? Lots of expats buy their dream houses here on the Mani, and many of those properties are fixer-uppers.

• *Now head down the cobbled side-street next to the pharmacy (to the right), and find yourself among...*

Kardamyli's Backstreets

While the main drag is all business, it's amazing how quickly Kardamyli's backstreets turn into cobbles, then gravel, then red dirt. Civilization melts away in just a few steps.

On the right, at **To Kolonaki's Café** (ΤΟΚΟΛΟΝΑΚΙ), is the classic Greek coffeehouse experience. You might see weather-beaten locals huddled around tables out front, under a grape vine-strewn trellis. For Kardamyli's best time-warp experience, step inside (generally open after 16:00). Take a deep breath, and taste the residue of a half-century's worth of spilled wine. In Greece, a café (καφε) is

not just a place to drink coffee; it's also the neighborhood bar and watering hole.

Owner Michailis' father, who had emigrated to Chicago, returned home to Kardamyli and opened this place in 1967...but it feels more like 1867. Order a traditional Greek coffee (unfiltered... take your time and let the "mud" settle to the bottom of the cup, €1) and take a look around. Notice the antique radio, the ancient fridge, and the old-fashioned scales, from the time when this place sold olive oil by the weight. Take in all the little details: linoleum-topped tables, rough poured-concrete floor, chalkboard menu, bare fluorescent bulbs, and wimpy-looking ceiling fan set in the nicotine-stained ceiling. The adjoining building was once the town barbershop.

Continuing down the road to the sea, you'll see some signs advertising **rooms** (ΔΩΜΑΤΙΑ, *dhomatia*)—the Greek version of B&Bs, and a great value for cheap sleeps. If you look young and desperate enough, someone might offer you a room as you pass.

• *Continue down to the water, walk out on to the concrete pier, and look around at...*

Kardamyli's Waterfront

Until a few generations ago, no roads connected Kardamyli to the rest of civilization. This pier was the main way into and out of the area, providing a link to the big city of Kalamata, and bustling with trade and passengers. The old smokestack (up the coast, to the right as you face the water) marks the site of a once-thriving olive-oil factory. The oil was shipped out from this pier. (The factory has been deserted since the 1950s, and much of the original equipment is rusty but intact. Some townspeople would like to turn it into a museum.)

Between the 1950s and the 1970s, the ever-improving network of roads made this port obsolete. Today only two professional fishermen work out of Kardamyli, and bring their catch right here to the pier to sell to locals, tourists, and restaurateurs. The little diving board is a favorite for kids. The small harbor across the bay has only a few boats. But Kardamyli still thrives, and most of its traditional lifestyles remain intact...thanks in part to respectful visitors like you.

Above the harbor, the Mirginos Tower completes the ring of fortifications that starts at the other end of town at Old Kardamyli. The terraces climbing the hillside made the steep incline farmable (you'll see endless such terraces if you do the loop trip around the Mani Peninsula). The little island offshore (Miropi) holds the barely visible ruins of an old church.

• *Our walk is finished. You can backtrack to any of the shops or activities (Old Kardamyli, hikes, beaches) that interest you. For a drink or bite right now, you have some handy nearby options (described later under "Eating in Kardamyli"): With the water to your back, to your left is Tikla Café, with mod decor, drinks and light food, and a loaner laptop for Internet access. Beyond it, through the trees, is Lela's Taverna.*

Sights in Kardamyli

Old Kardamyli

The fortified compound of Old Kardamyli perches just above today's modern town. On the ancient Mani Peninsula, "old" is

relative—this settlement, marked by a fortified tower, was established by the first families (who were forced into the hills in the Middle Ages by pirates) to return to flat ground at the end of the 17th century. After sitting in ruins for centuries, the complex has recently been partially restored and converted into a fine little museum about the Mani Peninsula and its traditional architecture. It's worth the 10-minute hike through an olive grove to poke around the fortified cluster and visit the museum.

Getting There: The trail to Old Kardamyli begins just behind the monument to the heroes along the main street (see my self-guided walk, earlier). From here, it's an up-and-down 10-minute walk—just follow the cobbled path, lined with lampposts, through the olive grove. As you approach the site, behind the ruined building on the right is an old cistern once used to draw and carry water back home. Curl around the right side of Old Kardamyli to hike right up into the complex.

Sights in Old Kardamyli: Passing through the archway, on the right you'll see the **Church of St. Spiridon** (c. 1750). Though it's not open to visitors, the exterior is interesting for its bell tower and its (typical-in-Greece) use of fragments of older buildings in its construction (such as the Byzantine marble frames that surround the door and windows). Over the window and door, notice the crowned, double-headed eagle, a symbol of the Byzantine Empire and the Orthodox Christian Church.

Now head toward the tower complex itself. The **Mourtzinos Tower,** not yet open to the public, was built by the powerful Troupakis family at

the beginning of the 18th century. It's named after the leader of the Troupakis clan during the War of Independence, who was known for his scowling face *(mourtzinos)*.

Attached to the tower, the former **Troupakis residence** now houses a multilevel museum (€2, Tue-Sun 8:30-15:00, closed Mon). Poke into all the little doors to see exhibits about the Maniots' terraces, cisterns, beekeeping, agricultural production, salt pans, and quarries. On the top floor, you can learn about the different sub-regions of the Mani. This tower complex is one of seven being converted to museums (many still under renovation) throughout the Mani.

Nearby: The cute little blue-and-white church just uphill from the complex, **Agia Sophia** (see photo on next page), marks the beginning of a cobbled path that leads up, up, up to the distant church on the hilltop (also called Agia Sophia). High above on the bluff was the site of the acropolis of Homeric-era Kardamyli. You can do the whole strenuous loop up to the church, then walk around to the adjacent village of Petrovouni (see "Hiking," later). Or, for just a taste, hike about five minutes up the cobbled trail to find two graves burrowed into a rock (on the right, behind the green gate). These are supposedly the **graves of Castor and**

Pollux, the "Gemini twins" of mythology. These brothers of Helen of Troy had different fathers. When Castor died, Pollux—who was immortal because he was fathered by Zeus—asked his dad to join the brothers together in immortality. Zeus agreed and turned them into the Gemini constellation. These brothers—so famous for their affection for one other—remain in close proximity even in death: Notice the connecting passage at the back of the graves.

KARDAMYLI

Beaches

Many visitors come to Kardamyli to enjoy the beach. Most simply head for nearby **Ritsa Beach,** a pleasant pebbly stretch that

begins just beyond the village church. While you can swim anywhere along its length, most beach bums prefer the far end, which has smaller pebbles and is more comfortable for swimming (an enjoyable

10-minute walk from the town center). The beach is bookended by twin restaurants with outdoor seating. Locals claim that the water's warm enough for swimming year-round, except in March, when it's chilled by snowmelt run-off from the mountains.

If you have a car and want to get out of town, two more good sand/fine gravel beaches lie to the south, near the hamlet of Neo Proastio on the way to Stoupa: **Foneas Beach** (a cove flanked by picturesque big rocks) and **Delfinia Beach.** The resort town of **Stoupa** also has some good sandy beaches and a promenade perfect for strolling.

Hiking

Hiking vies with beach fun as Kardamyli's biggest attraction. Especially in spring and fall, visitors head away from the sea to explore the network of color-coded trails that scramble up the surrounding hills. Many of these follow the ancient *kalderimi* (cobbled

KARDAMYLI

paths) that until fairly recently were the only way of traveling between villages. Ask your hotel for a map that explains the routes and codes; for serious hikes, buy a more detailed hiking map. As the hikes tend to be strenuous— uphill and over uneven terrain— wear good shoes and bring along

water and snacks (some walks do pass through villages where you can buy food and drinks).

The most popular destinations sit on the hillsides just behind Kardamyli: the hilltop church of **Agia Sophia** and the village of **Petrovouni.** You can hike to either one, or (with more time and stamina) do a loop trip that includes both. Consider this plan: Start by visiting Old Kardamyli, then continue past the smaller, blue-and-white Agia Sophia church and the ancient graves of Castor and Pollux (described earlier) to the higher church of Agia Sophia. Then, if your stamina holds, follow the path around to Petrovouni, from which you can head back down into Kardamyli. The paths are very steep (there's about a 650-foot elevation gain from Kardamyli to Petrovouni), and the round-trip takes about three hours at a good pace with few breaks (follow the yellow-and-black markings). Other trips lead farther into the hills, to the remote village of **Exohori.**

Sleeping in Kardamyli

Most of Kardamyli's accommodations cater to British, European, and Australian tourists who stay for a week or more. Rather than traditional hotels, you'll find mostly "apartments" with kitchenettes, along with simpler and cheaper rooms *(dhomatia)*. While some places do offer breakfast, most charge extra, assuming that you'll make your own in your kitchenette, or get a pastry and a coffee at a bakery or café. If you do want breakfast, be sure to tell your host the day before (they'll likely buy fresh bread for you in the morning).

In the Town
$$$ Hotel Anniska and **Hotel Liakoto** ("Sunny Place") rent nicely appointed, luxurious-feeling apartments with kitchenettes. The Anniska has 22 apartments that share an inviting lounge and delightful sea view terrace (studio-€85 July-mid-Sept, €75 off-season; one-bedroom apartment-€115, €90 off-season; optional breakfast-€7.50, air-con, free Internet access, free Wi-Fi in some rooms, tel. 27210-73601). The Liakoto's 25 apartments clus-

Sleep Code

(€1 = about $1.40, country code: 30)
S = Single, **D** = Double/Twin, **T** = Triple, **Q** = Quad, **b** = bathroom, **s** = shower only. Unless otherwise noted, breakfast is included and credit cards are accepted.

To help you easily sort through these listings, I've divided the rooms into three categories, based on the price for a standard double room with bath:

$$$ Higher Priced—Most rooms €80 or more.
$$ Moderately Priced—Most rooms between €50-80.
$ Lower Priced—Most rooms €50 or less.

Prices can change without notice; verify the hotel's current rates online or by email. For other updates, see www .ricksteves.com/update.

ter around a swimming-pool courtyard oasis, and many have sea views that turn golden at sunset (€10 more than Anniska's rates, tel. 27210-73600). Both hotels are run by friendly British-Australian-Greek couple Ilia and Gerry (fax 27210-73000, www .anniska-liakoto.com, anniska@otenet.gr).

$$$ Hotel Esperides has 19 rooms and apartments with kitchenettes, all surrounding a pleasant garden veranda just a few steps up from the main road. You'll enjoy a friendly welcome and lots of travel advice (studio-€90 Aug, €80 July, €70 April-June and Sept-Oct, €45 Nov-March; one-bedroom apartment-€120 Aug, €110 July, €90 April-June and Sept-Oct, €60 Nov-March; book early for best deals, breakfast-€9, air-con, free Wi-Fi, arrange arrival time in advance since reception isn't open 24 hours, tel. 27210-73173, fax 27210-73176, www.hotelesperides.com, info@hotelesperides.com).

$$$ Antonia's Apartments has two old-fashioned apartments and two newer ones a bit farther from the town center, above the beach at the Kalamata end of town. The veranda has great views of the town, beach, and mountains (Db-€85-90 Aug, €75 May-July, €65-70 Sept-March, air-con, reserve through local guide Elias Polimeneas: tel. 27210-73453, mobile 69469-98416, antoniasapartments@yahoo.gr).

$$ Gorgones Studios (Οι Γοργόνες, a.k.a. Les Sirènes) has 10 well-priced rooms over a recommended restaurant. The rooms are simple, but all have kitchenettes and balconies overlooking Kardamyli's little harbor (Db-€50-60 July-Aug, €40-45 off-season, price depends on demand; air-con, free Wi-Fi, good windows block out most of the dining noise, tel. 27210-73469, mobile 69323-34855, fax 27210-73373, Haralambea family).

$ Dhomatia: You'll see signs advertising rooms (ΔΩΜΑΤΙΑ) all over town. The rooms are generally quite simple, with kitchenettes but no breakfast. English can be limited, and values can vary. If you're in a pinch, check out a few, pick the best, and don't be afraid to haggle. Here are the best cheap rooms I found (both speak English): Warm and welcoming **Olympia Koymanakou** rents five rooms on the cobbled lane just down the road from the pharmacy (Sb-€30 July-Aug, €25 off-season; Db-€45 July-Aug, €30 off-season; air-con, shared kitchen, Paraleia street, tel. 27210-73623). **Markeas Stavoros,** who runs a gift shop on the main drag, rents four rooms along a dirt lane a block behind the main street (Db-€35 July-Aug, €30 off-season, air-con, free Wi-Fi, tel. 27210-73672).

Just Outside Kardamyli

These enjoyable retreats sit a bit farther from Kardamyli's main street. While walkable, they're more enjoyable if you have a car (especially the Kalamitsi).

$$$ Vardia Hotel is a stony retreat huddled on a hilltop just above town. All of its 18 rooms have balconies overlooking town, and a steep, stony path leads from the hotel's grand-view veranda directly to Old Kardamyli (studio-€85 July-Aug, €75 off-season; one-bedroom apartment-€120 July-Aug, €105 off-season; two-bedroom apartment-€170 July-Aug, €140 off-season; breakfast-€10, air-con, free Internet access and Wi-Fi, tel. 27210-73777, fax 27210-73156, mobile 69783-83404, www.vardia-hotel.gr, info@vardia-hotel.gr).

$$$ Kalamitsi Hotel is a charming enclave hovering above its own bay, beach, and olive grove a two-minute drive down the road from Kardamyli (toward Areopoli). In addition to 20 rooms in the main building, it has 15 bungalows that bunny-hop across its plateau (Sb-€90 July-mid-Sept, €70 off-season; Db-€110 July-mid-Sept, €90 off-season; suite-€160 July-mid-Sept, €130 off-season; bungalows-€120 July-mid-Sept, €100 off-season; breakfast-€10, dinner-€20, air-con, free Wi-Fi, tel. 27210-73131, fax 27210-73135, www.kalamitsi-hotel.gr, info@kalamitsi-hotel.gr).

Eating in Kardamyli

While many tourist-resort towns are notorious for bad food, Kardamyli prides itself on pleasing a huge group of return visitors, who come here on holiday year after year. Consequently, quality is high and value is good. When you ask locals where to dine, they shrug and say, "Anywhere is good"...and you sense it's

not just empty town pride talking. As you dine, notice the digni-
fied European visitors conversing quietly around you...and try to
imitate them.

Lela's Taverna is a Kardamyli institution and a sentimen-
tal favorite. Lela, the black-clad matriarch of a prominent clan,

is one of the great characters
of the village. She'll jabber
at you kindly in Greek as
though you understand every
word...and, in a way, you do.
In a land where "everybody's
grandma is the best cook,"
ancient Lela is appreciated
for how she gives her *tzatziki*
a fun kick, and for the special
way she marinates her olives. Her restaurant enjoys a fine seafront
setting above the rocks, illuminated by rustic lights with gourd
lampshades. Grab a table on the terrace or along the wall, and
choose from the chalkboard list of daily specials (€3-5 starters,
€6-10 main dishes, March-Oct daily 18:00-23:00, closed Nov-Feb,
well-signed from main road—take side street toward water from
pharmacy, tel. 27210-73541).

Kastro Taverna is a gourmet's delight. It sits just outside of
town toward Kalamata, a long walk or quick drive from the town
center. The trek is worth it—the chef uses local products for his
daily specials, including meat and produce from his farm in the hills
above town. A highlight is the *keftedes* (meatballs) in a savory tomato
sauce. Choose between the cozy fireplace interior and the broad
veranda with distant sea views (€3-6 starters, €7-10 main dishes,
daily 19:00-24:00, weekends only in winter, tel. 27210-73951).

Tikla Café sits just above the town pier, with great water
views and a stony-mod interior. While it's technically a bar/café,
you can order from a short menu of excellent, updated Greek
cuisine. The free Internet access (Wi-Fi, or borrow their laptop)
and inviting covered terrace round out this place's appeal (€5-7 salads and savory pies, €3-4 Continental breakfast, €12 two-person
American breakfast, daily 9:30 until late, next to pier, tel. 27210-
73223).

Harilaos (ΧΑΡΙΛΑΟΣ)—the restaurant below Gorgones
Studios—is another good waterfront option. Sit inside, or out on
the shady covered terrace, where you can watch boats bob in the
harbor. Maria brags that they buy their seafood fresh from the
fishermen who put in at the port below (€4-7 starters, €6-9 main
dishes, €8-15 seafood, daily 8:00-24:00, tel. 27210-73469).

Tis Eftichias (ΤΗΣ ΕΥΤΥΧΙΑΣ)—also known as "Secret
Garden"—is a fish joint on the main street with an untouristy

dining room and (true to its name) a delightful garden hiding out back. Owner Stavros prides himself on providing fresh fish—even if he has to drive around the Mani to find it (€3-5 appetizers, €7-8 main dishes, €8-14 seafood plates, daily 11:00-24:00 except closed Mon off-season, right on the main street, tel. 27210-73930).

Taverna Perivolis, run by a Greek-Australian family, lacks a view but offers good value. Check out their list of daily specials, including *pastitsio* (Greek lasagna) and freshly grilled meat (€5-7 starters, €7-10 main dishes, daily 19:00-24:00 except likely closed Mon off-season, tel. 27210-73713). To reach the taverna (between the water and the main road), follow signs from the main road to Hotel Anniska, turn left at the crossroads, and look for it on the left after 50 yards (across the street from the old deserted factory).

Taverna Dioskouroi has a great location on the headland overlooking Kardamyli's adorable little harbor, just south of the village on the road to Stoupa (€3-9 starters, €6-12 main dishes, daily specials, live music at sunset up to three nights per week, April-Oct daily 9:00-24:00, closed off-season, on the right 200 yards south of the village, tel. 27210-73236).

Cafés: Kardamyli enjoys a wide range of delightful cafés with traditional/chic decor and basic food; several line the main drag. Most of these have indoor and outdoor seating, and serve drinks as well as light food, including breakfast.

Picnics: The bakery on the main street has many temptations. Two grocery stores at the entrance to town can help you flesh out your meal (both open long hours daily).

Kardamyli Connections

Kardamyli's biggest disadvantage is its tricky-to-reach position on the far-flung Mani Peninsula. The nearest major city (with good bus connections to the rest of Greece) is Kalamata, about 24 twisty miles to the north. Kardamyli is connected to **Kalamata** by bus (4/day Mon-Fri, 3/day Sat-Sun, 1 hour; in Kardamyli, catch bus at main square). Kalamata bus information: tel. 27210-28581, www.kardamili-greece.com.

Route Tips for Drivers

The Mani Peninsula's mountains make driving slow going. The most straightforward approach to Kardamyli is from the city of Kalamata: As you enter Kalamata, follow signs reading *Port* or *Seafront.* Once past the port, keep driving in the same direction, with the water on your right. The road to Kardamyli is badly signed—you might see directions in Greek for *Καρδαμύλη* (Kardamyli) or *Μάνη* (Mani)—but as long as you keep the water on your right, you'll end up on the highway. (If you're here after the A7/E65 national road has been completed—likely sometime in 2012—you can bypass Kalamata entirely.) Heading south from Kalamata, you'll twist over a suddenly remote-feeling set of mountains, and emerge overlooking a grand bay with views over Kardamyli.

After going through Kardamyli, the road continues south, passing through the resort of Stoupa before climbing back up over mountains and around a dramatic bay to the regional capital of Areopoli.

From Areopoli, you can head east to Gythio, and then continue north to reach civilization (Sparta); or head south for a loop of the Mani on lesser roads. For all the details on the Mani loop, see the self-guided driving tour below.

The Mani Peninsula

The Mani Peninsula is where the rustic charm of Greece is most apparent. For many travelers, this peninsula is the rural slice of

Greek coast-and-mountains that they came to this country to see. The region's dramatic history (see sidebar on pages 324-325) has left behind a landscape that's at once eerily stark and remarkably scenic. While mountains edged with abandoned terraces hint that farming was once more extensive, olives have been the only Mani export for the last two centuries. Empty, ghostly hill towns cling, barnacle-like, onto distant ridges, still fortified against centuries-old threats. Cisterns that once caught rainwater to sustain hardy communities are now mucky green puddles that would turn a goat's stomach. The farther south you go, the bleaker conditions become. And yet, many Mani towns feature sumptuous old fresco-slathered churches...pockets of brightness that survive in this otherwise parched land.

Self-Guided Driving Tour

The Mani Peninsula

This region is difficult to fully experience without a car. To really delve into this rustic corner of Greece, follow this loop drive from Kardamyli. To hit all the places described below in one day, you'll need to get an early start and keep up a brisk pace. If you're aiming to reach the Pyrgos Dirou Caves before closing time, skip some of the earlier stops (I'd cut the out-of-the-way Kastania detour) or do

MANI PENINSULA

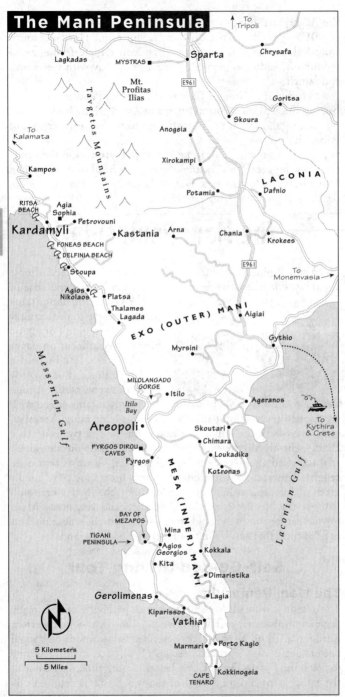

The Mani Peninsula

To Tripoli

Lagkadas

MYSTRAS

Sparta

Chrysafa

Mt. Profitas Ilias

E961

Goritsa

Taygetos Mountains

Anogeia

Skoura

To Kalamata

Xirokampi

LACONIA

Kampos

Potamia

Dafnio

RITSA BEACH

Agia Sophia

Petrovouni

Arna

Chania

Krokees

Kardamyli

Kastania

FONEAS BEACH

DELFINIA BEACH

E961

Stoupa

To Monemvasia

Agios Nikolaos

Platsa

Thalames

Lagada

EXO (OUTER) MANI

Aigiai

Messenian Gulf

Myrsini

Gythio

MILOLANGADO GORGE

Itilo

Itilo Bay

Ageranos

To Kythira & Crete

Areopoli

Skoutari

PYRGOS DIROU CAVES

Chimara

Pyrgos

Loukadika

MESA (INNER) MANI

Kotronas

Laconian Gulf

BAY OF MEZAPOS

Mina

TIGANI PENINSULA

Agios Georgios

Kokkala

Kita

Dimaristika

Gerolimenas

Lagia

Kiparissos

Vathia

Marmari

Porto Kagio

CAPE TENARO

Kokkinogeia

5 Kilometers

5 Miles

N

the caves just after Areopoli, then backtrack to follow the rest of the loop.

If you prefer a later start or a more relaxed day, skip either the caves (giving you more time to hike the ancient ruins on Cape Tenaro) or the cape (so that you'll have time to enjoy the caves' stalagmites and get a welcome break from the heat).

The light inside old churches can be very dim—if you have a flashlight, bring it along to illuminate the frescoes. Along the way, be prepared for stunning coastal vistas equal to California's Big Sur or the French Riviera. But keep a firm grip on the wheel—there are hairpin curves, missing guardrails, and blind corners in ancient stone villages. Take your time and pull over frequently to soak it all in.

• *Head south from Kardamyli on the main road. After a few miles, you'll pass the attractive little resort town of* **Stoupa**. *While Kardamyli turns its back to the sea, Stoupa embraces it—with a fine sandy beach arcing right through its center. (Stoupa also works as a separate jaunt from Kardamyli.)*

Just after Stoupa, keep an eye out for the turn-off (on the left) for our first stop, Kastania (Καστανια). Because Kastania is a time-consuming detour from the main road, you might want to skip it for now—if you're rushed, consider making it a separate side-trip from Kardamyli.

To reach Kastania from the main road, head uphill, passing through two other villages along the way. Keep going, following the well-traveled blacktop.

Kastania

Wedged in a gorge, the village of Kastania offers a rare opportunity to explore a traditional Mani village that's completely off the tourist track. While it feels sleepy today, Kastania was once a local powerhouse. During the 19th-century Greek War of Independence, it boasted no less than 400 "guns" (as Maniots called their menfolk), gathered under a warlord whose imposing family tower still stands over the town square. The town also had many churches, some of which still feature remarkably well-preserved old frescoes. The chance to poke around an authentic mountain town, and to stop in at one of the churches, is a unique Mani treat. (Unfortunately, the churches are often closed. If you come across one that doesn't look open, try the door. If it's locked, and you see people nearby, ask if they know how to

MANI PENINSULA

History of the Mani Peninsula

The Mani feels as wild as its history. The region was supposedly first developed around 200 B.C. by breakaway Spartans (from the famously warlike city to the north). Spartan stubbornness persisted in the Mani character for centuries—and made Maniots slow to adopt Christianity. In the 10th century, St. Nikon finally converted the Maniots, and a flurry of Byzantine church-building followed.

Most coastal Mani towns (including Kardamyli) were slowly deserted in the Middle Ages, as marauding pirate ships forced people to flee into the hills. There they hid out in villages tucked in the folds of the mountains, far from the coast. (Later, in the 18th century, the construction of protective tower houses allowed Maniots to tentatively begin to return to their coastal settlements.)

Fertile land here was at an absolute premium and hotly contested. In the 17th and 18th centuries, this hostile corner of Greece was known to travelers as the "land of evil counsel" *(Kalavoulia)*, because of its reputation for robbery and piracy—a more reliable way to survive than trying to eke out an honest living by farming. Maniots banded together in clans, whose leaders built the characteristic tower settlements *(kapitanias)* that are a feature of the region. Each *kapitania* controlled its own little city-statelet of land. Some larger towns were occupied by several, rival *kapitanias*. Honor was prized even more than arable land, and each clan leader had a chip on his shoulder the size of a big slab of feta cheese. Vendettas and violent bickering between clans— about control of territory, or sometimes simply respect—became epidemic. If Greece had a Tombstone and an O.K. Corral, this is where they'd be.

get inside—sometimes there's a key hidden somewhere close by.)

As you drive into Kastania, appreciate its strategically hidden location: You don't even see the town until you're right on top of it. As you enter the town, you'll pass the first of many Byzantine churches on the left—this one dedicated to St. John (Ag. Ioannis). Beyond the church, squeeze past the buildings and turn right onto what seems to be an alley. It's actually the link to the main square, which is watched over by the Church of the Assumption and the town's tower house (built by the local Dourakis clan and now mostly ruined, but may be renovated to become one of seven planned Mani museum towers). Park your car wherever you can near the square, and poke into one of the very traditional cafés on

When they weren't fighting each other, the Maniots banded together to fight off foreign invaders. Locals brag that the feisty Mani—still clinging to the stubborn militarism of the ancient Spartans—remained the only corner of Greece not fully under the thumb of the Ottoman Turks. During nearly four centuries of Turkish rule, the sultan struck a compromise to appoint more or less Ottoman-friendly Maniots as regional governors. After a failed Greek uprising against the Turks in the late 18th century, Greeks from all over the country flooded into the Mani to escape harsh Ottoman reprisals. As the population boomed, competition for the sparse natural resources grew even fiercer.

Perhaps not surprisingly, the hot tempers of the Maniots made the peninsula the crucible for Greek independence. On March 17, 1821, Maniot Petros Mavromichalis—the Ottoman-appointed governor *(bey)*—led a spirited rebellion against his Turkish superiors. Mavromichalis succeeded in taking Kalamata six days later, and the War of Independence was underway. What began in the remote hills of the Mani quickly engulfed the rest of Greece, and by 1829 the Ottomans were history and Greece was free.

Looking around today at the barren landscape of the Mani Peninsula, which now barely supports 5,000 people, it's hard to believe that 200 years ago it sustained a population of almost 60,000. Over time, that number was depleted by blood feuds, which raged into the early 20th century, and by the end of Ottoman rule in the early 19th century and the devastating Greek Civil War of the mid-20th century. These sparked population shifts out of the region, as Maniots sought easier lifestyles elsewhere in Greece, or set out for the promise of faraway lands, primarily America, the UK, and Australia. But these days, as the Mani emerges as a prime tourist destination, many Maniot emigrants are returning home—bringing back with them an array of accents from around the world.

MANI PENINSULA

the square for a coffee. The one at the top of the square is a real time-warp, where old-timers gather around simple tables, smoking and chatting.

For a sturdy uphill walk, leave your car at the square and hike up. Along a rustic lane near the old cistern is the **Church of St. Peter** (Ag. Petros), which dates from around 1200 and appears to be cobbled together using bits and pieces of antiquity. If it's open, go inside—it's richly adorned with frescoes that have told Bible stories to this community since the 14th century. While the lighting may be jerry-rigged and a destructive mold has hastened the aging of its precious art, the spiritual wonder of the place remains intact. (Enjoy it before some archaeologist scrapes off what's left of these frescoes and sends them to a museum in Athens.) The olive-oil lamp burns 24 hours a day, tended by a caretaker family. Even if the church is closed, stop to enjoy the views over town from this perch.

• *Back in your car, backtrack to the main road and turn left (south). Continue driving...*

From Stoupa to Areopoli

As you drive, keep an eye out for some typical roadside fixtures. On rooftops, look for **solar panels** attached to cylindrical tanks—an efficient way to heat water in this sunny climate. You might also see little **miniature churches** set on pedestals at the side of the road, marking the sites of traffic accidents. Most of these are "votive churches," erected as a "thank-you" gesture to God by someone who was spared in an accident. Little churches with a photograph of a person, however, are memorials to someone killed in an accident.

Heading south, you'll pass another fine beach town, **Agios Nikolaos** (St. Nicholas). Then the road begins to curve up the mountain, passing through **Platsa** (with the interesting church of St. John/Ag. Ioannis). If the church is open, poke inside to see the ceiling fresco with Jesus surrounded by zodiac symbols—a reminder of the way early Christians incorporated pre-Christian mythology. Higher up, the village of **Thalames**—its square shaded by a giant plane tree—is known for its olive-oil production (several shops on the square sell it). Then, in **Lagada,** watch (on the left) for the remarkably well-preserved Byzantine church, lavishly decorated with terra-cotta designs.

As you ascend ever higher, notice how the landscape fades from green to brown. From here on out, the Mani becomes characteristically arid. You'll also begin to see **terraces** etched into the mountainsides...a reminder of how hard Maniots had to work to earn a living from this inhospitable land. They'd scrape together whatever arable soil they could into these little patches to grow olive trees and wheat. Some of the larger stone walls surrounding the terraces demarcate property boundaries.

Soon you cross the "state line" that separates the Exo (Outer) Mani from the Mesa (Inner) Mani—its southern tip and most striking area.

As you reach the lip of the dramatic Milolangado Gorge, the town of **Itilo** (EE-tee-loh) comes into view. Like Kardamyli, this town was mentioned in Homer's *Iliad*. The fortifications on the southern side of the gorge belong to Kelefa Castle, built by the

Ottomans in 1670 in a short-lived attempt to control the rebellious Maniots. Enjoy the views before heading down to Itilo Bay, where you'll pass the settlements of Neo ("New") Itilo and Limeni (birthplace of the war hero Petros Mavromichalis, whom we'll meet shortly). From the bayside road, adventure-seekers enjoy hiking the 3.5 miles up into the gorge itself.

• *Continuing up the other side of the gorge, and then cresting the top, you'll shortly arrive in...*

Areopoli

Areopoli (ah-reh-OH-poh-lee)—named after Ares, the ancient god of war—is the de facto capital of the Inner Mani. Less charming but more lived-in than other Mani towns, Areopoli is the region's commercial center.

As you arrive from Itilo, signs direct you to the town center and its modern main square, **Plateia Athanaton** (where you should be able to find a place to park). Dominating the square is a statue of Petros Mavromichalis (1765-1848). This local-boy-done-good was selected to rule the region by the Ottoman overlords, who assumed they could corrupt him with money and power. But they underestimated his strong sense of Mani honor. On March 17, 1821, Mavromichalis gathered a ragtag Maniot army here in Areopoli and marched north to Kalamata, launching the War of Independence. Mavromichalis looks every inch a warrior, clutching a mighty curved sword, pistol tucked into his waistband.

The square hosts a lively market on Saturday mornings. At other times, everything else of interest is to be found about 500 yards west of here, around the old main square, **Plateia 17 Martiou.** To get there, follow cobbled Kapetan Matapan downhill. You'll emerge at the spot where Petros mustered his men for the march to Kalamata, a moment commemorated by a plaque on the northern wall. The square is dominated by the 18th-century Church of Taxiarhes ("Archangels"), sporting an impressive four-story bell tower. The well-preserved carvings above the main door (around the left side) show the archangels Gabriel and Michael, flanked by the saints Georgios and Dimitrios on horseback. Nearby is a private war museum of rough artillery. Just behind the church (*ΑΡΟΤΟΠΟΙΕΙΟ* sign, near the well), find the rustic bakery run by Milia, who wood-fires bread and savory pies.

With your back to the war museum's doorway, take the path straight in front of you, skirting around the ruins of the war tower of Petros Mavromichalis. Follow this alley as it winds its way next to a church. At the end of the alley, jog left, then right. On this second alley are the Church of St. John and the Pikoulakis Tower—home to the **Mani Museum of Religion,** which explains the religious history of the Mani people (free, Tue-Sun 8:30-15:00, closed Mon, tel. 27330-29531).

• *Leaving Areopoli, make a choice about whether and when you want to visit the Pyrgos Dirou Caves (described next). If you visit the caves now, you can do the rest of the Mani driving loop at a leisurely pace. Or, to avoid about 20 minutes of backtracking, you could do the rest of the loop now and visit the caves on your way back up to Areopoli—but you might need to rush to reach the caves before they close.*

To **see the caves now,** *continue south of Areopoli and follow the signs for* Gerolimenas/Γερολιμενας *at the fork (to the right), then follow the "Getting There" instructions in the next section. Later you can backtrack to Areopoli to do the full Mani loop.*

If you're **skipping the caves**—*or plan to swing by them later—follow signs toward* Kotronas/Κότρωνας *just south of Areopoli (take the left turn at the fork). Pick up this tour at "The Eastern Mani," on the next page.*

▲Pyrgos Dirou Caves
(a.k.a. Diros Caves and Vlychada Cave)

These remarkable cave formations—discovered by locals in 1900—rank among Europe's best. After you've boarded a little boat, your guide poles you along underground canals, calling out (usually in Greek only) the creative names for each of the spectacular formations..."Hercules' columns," "palm forest," "golden rain," "crystal lily," and so on. They range from stout stalactites and stalagmites, to delicate hair-like formations—many of them surprisingly colorful, thanks to reddish iron deposits. In some

MANI PENINSULA

places, the water below you is 100 feet deep...you're actually floating near the ceiling of a vast, flooded cavern. (Life preservers are provided, as are helmets that you'll need as you hunch over to get through narrow passages. Stay away if you're at all claustrophobic.) After your three-quarter-mile boat trip, you return to dry land and walk another quarter-mile for up-close views of even more limestone formations.

Cost and Hours: €12, daily June-Sept 8:30-17:30, Oct-May 8:30-15:00— these are last entry times, tel. 27330-52222. Because this is a very popular attraction, you might be in for a wait during the busy summer months. Buy your ticket at the gate, then walk five minutes down to the cave entrance to wait for your appointed entry time. Figure about an hour total to tour the caves (not counting wait time). The temperature in the caves is always between 60 and 65 degrees Fahrenheit—bring a sweater.

Museum: If you have more time and interest after your cave visit, consider paying an additional €2 to tour the little museum near the entrance, showing off Neolithic artifacts found in the caves (Tue-Sun 8:30-15:00, closed Mon).

Getting There: The caves are about six miles south of Areopoli. The cave entry is along a small bay, which you reach by driving through the town of Pyrgos, then twisting down by the water. If you're approaching from the north (Areopoli), follow signs to *Pyrgos*; the turn-off for the caves is marked with a blue sign in the center of town. If you go past Pyrgos and reach the turn-off sign for Γκλεζι, you've gone too far—backtrack into Pyrgos.

The Eastern Mani

To experience the Mani's most rugged and remote-feeling area, cross over the spine of the peninsula to the eastern coast. The few tourists you encounter melt away the farther south you drive, until it's just you, sheer limestone cliffs, fortified ghost towns, olive trees

twisting up to embrace the sky with a kiss of sage-green leaves, and tumbling surf. Here the terrain seems even more desolate than what you've seen so far (if that's possible).

After taking the left turn for **Kotronas**/Κότρωνας just south of Areopoli, you'll head overland through stark scenery. Cresting the hills at **Chimara/ Χιμαρα,** you'll begin to glimpse the Mani's east coast. At **Loukadika/Λουκαδικα,** bear right (south) along the main road toward **Kokkala/Κοκκαλα,** and you'll soon find yourself traversing the top of a cliff above the best stretch of scenery on the Mani. Heading south, you'll see more and more fortified towers climbing up the rocky hillsides. Imagine that each of these towers represents the many ruthless vendettas that were fought here.

Approaching **Dimaristika/Διμαριστικα,** notice the three tower settlements that dot the hill at three different levels. It's easy to imagine why the Ottomans never took this land—the villages could see them coming by ship from miles away and bombard them with cannonballs. And if the Ottomans managed to make landfall, they'd have to climb up, up, up to overtake the forts. It wasn't worth the trouble.

The village of **Lagia/Λαγια** was supposedly the site of the last Mani vendetta, a minor scuffle in the 1930s. The town seems almost abandoned today, but most of these houses are owned by Maniots who now live in Athens and come back for the holidays. On the square (along the main road through town) is a monument honoring Panagiotis Vlahakos, a villager who died in a 1996 conflict over a small Aegean island (called Imia in Greek, or Kardak in Turkish) claimed by both Greece and Turkey. While the Ottomans left this country close to two centuries ago, Greek-Turkish relations are still a raw nerve.

• *Leaving Lagia, continue straight ahead. After about five minutes, you'll reach a fork. If you're ready to head back around to the western Mani coast, take the right turn (and skip down to the "Vathia" section of this tour). But to reach the most distant corner of mainland Greece, Cape Tenaro, bear left toward the long list of Greek names (including Kokkinogeia/Κοκκινόγεια). Switchback your way tightly down toward the sea, always following signs for Kokkinogeia/Κοκκινόγεια; after passing through Marmari/Μαρμαρι, continue straight toward Tenaro/Ταίναρο. If highway signs are missing, look for smaller hiking-route signs that mark the* Tenaro Archaeological Site.

Cape Tenaro (a.k.a. Cape Matapan): Greece's "Land's End"

Drive out to the tip of the rocky promontory known as the "Sanctuary of the Dead." As the farthest point of the known world, this was where the ancient Greeks believed that the souls of the deceased came to enter the underworld. An underwater cave here was thought to belong to Hades, god of the underworld. It was also the site of a temple and oracle devoted to Poseidon, the god of the sea. Today visitors can still explore the scant, unexcavated ruins of an ancient town that was called Tenaron (mentioned in the *Iliad*). An inviting restaurant also offers a good opportunity for a break.

Just below the parking lot are the ruins of an early Christian church, likely constructed using giant blocks scavenged from the temple. To visit the poorly marked ruins, walk down from the parking lot toward the water, then bear right around the far side of the bay. You'll soon be able to pick out the footprints of ancient

Greek and Roman structures. Hiding behind one of these low walls, about a 15-minute walk around the bay, is a surprisingly intact floor mosaic from a Roman villa, just sitting out in the open. If you've got time to kill and are up for a long hike, you can trudge another 30 minutes one-way out to a lighthouse at the end of the world. A busy shipping channel lies just offshore; you can count the vessels heading east to Athens or west to the upper Mediterranean.

• *Retrace your tracks back to civilization. When you get back to your car, try tuning into Egyptian stations on the radio. Reaching the main road, turn left and head back up the west coast of the Mani (toward Vathia/Βαθειά). Soon you'll be treated to views of the classic Mani ghost town...*

Vathia

The most characteristic of all the Mani tower villages, Vathia is Vendetta-ville—it seems everyone here barricaded themselves in forts. The more towers a town had, the more dangerous it was—and

it's hard to imagine cramming more towers into a single town than they did in Vathia. Built on a rocky spur, Vathia was an extreme example of what can happen when neighbors don't get along. The 80-some houses were split north/south into two rival camps, which existed in a state of near-permanent hostility. Now Vathia is mostly uninhabited. Park your car and go for a stroll among the town's haunting ruins. Once-intimidating towers are now held together with boards and steel cables.

• *Driving north, you'll pass through the larger town of Kiparissos—*
originally Kenipolis ("New City"), which was settled by those who left
ancient Tenaron—then turn off to reach the town center and port of...

Gerolimenas

Gerolimenas (yeh-roh-LEE-meh-nahs, roughly "sacred port"), nestled at the back of a deep sheltered bay, is a cute fishing town kept

alive by tourism. The waterfront is lined with cafés and
restaurants, and the water is
good for a swim—making
it an all-around enjoyable
place to take a break and
watch the surf.

• *Continue back out to the*
*main road, toward **Kita**. This*
town was the setting for the Mani's final major feud in 1870—which
raged for weeks until the Greek army arrived, artillery in tow, to enforce
a truce.

If you're in a hurry, you can skip the next stop. But if you're enjoy-
ing all the little detours, a left turn at the village of Agios Georgios
(toward Μέζαπος/Mezapo/Beach) leads down to the...

Bay of Mezapos

At the cove at Mezapos (MEH-zah-pohs), carved out of limestone by the surf, boats bob picturesquely in the protective harbor,

watched over by an extremely
sleepy hamlet. Mezapos was once
a notorious haven for pirates. It's
easy to see why, if you look across
the bay to see the long, naturally
fortified peninsula aptly named
Tigani ("frying pan"). This was
once thought to be the site of the
Frankish castle of Maina (roughly

"clenched fist"), the namesake of the Mani—though historians are
increasingly convinced that it was instead Kelefa Castle at Itilo.

• *Continuing north, you'll first pass the village of Pyrgos—with an*
opportunity to turn off for the excellent Pyrgos Dirou Caves (described
earlier)—then arrive back at Areopoli. From here, retrace your steps
around Itilo Bay back to Kardamyli; or, if you're continuing onward,
head east just beyond Areopoli to reach Monemvasia.

MONEMVASIA

MONEMBAΣΊΑ / Μονεμβασία

Monemvasia (moh-nehm-VAH-see-ah), a gigantic rock that rockets improbably up from the blue-green deep just a few hundred yards offshore, is a time-warp to the medieval Peloponnese. Its little Lower Town hamlet hides on the seaward side of the giant Rock, tethered to the mainland only by a skinny spit of land. This remarkably romantic walled town—with the remains of an even bigger Upper Town scattered along the rock's peak high above—is a living museum of Byzantine, Ottoman, and Venetian history dating back to the 13th century. Summiting Monemvasia is a key experience on any Peloponnesian visit.

Monemvasia means "single entry"—and the only way to get here is to cross the narrow causeway. At the mainland end of the causeway is the nondescript town of Gefyra (YEH-fee-rah), a smattering of hotels, restaurants, shops, and other modern amenities that offer a 21st-century escape from the Rock.

Planning Your Time

It takes only a few hours to "do" Monemvasia—a stroll through the Lower Town, a hike to the Upper Town, and you've seen it all. Consider seeing Monemvasia as a side-trip (it's an hour's drive from Gythio, or about 2.5 hours from Kardamyli), or on the way between destinations. You'll probably pass through Sparta to get here (Sparta's not worth stopping in, but it is worth knowing about—see "Sparta" sidebar, later). Spending the night in Monemvasia—especially on the Rock—allows you to linger on the floodlight cobbles, and makes the long trip down here more worthwhile. Unfortunately, Monemvasia is poorly served by public transportation—bus connections to most other Peloponnesian destinations involve at least a transfer in Sparta.

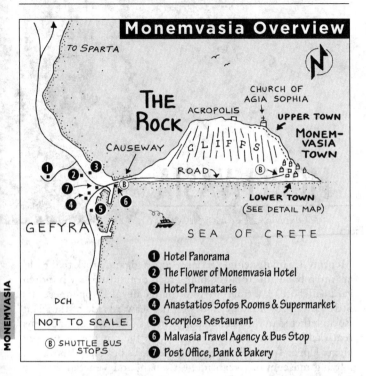

Monemvasia Overview

TO SPARTA

THE ROCK

ACROPOLIS

CHURCH OF AGIA SOPHIA

UPPER TOWN

MONEM-VASIA TOWN

CAUSEWAY

C L I F F S

ROAD

B

LOWER TOWN
(SEE DETAIL MAP)

GEFYRA

DCH

NOT TO SCALE

B SHUTTLE BUS STOPS

SEA OF CRETE

1 Hotel Panorama
2 The Flower of Monemvasia Hotel
3 Hotel Pramataris
4 Anastatios Sofos Rooms & Supermarket
5 Scorpios Restaurant
6 Malvasia Travel Agency & Bus Stop
7 Post Office, Bank & Bakery

Orientation to Monemvasia

Monemvasia is moored to the mainland at the village of Gefyra, where most of its services are located (though neither Monemvasia nor Gefyra has a TI). The road into Gefyra from Sparta becomes the main street, where you'll find—clustered where the road bends left toward the Rock—the post office, a bank with an ATM, and an excellent bakery (with a supermarket just up the street). The Malvasia Travel Agency, which sells bus tickets and serves as the town's bus stop, is on the main street, where it meets the causeway (tel. 27320-61752).

After passing through Gefyra, the main road leads to the causeway across to the Rock (Vraxos). The hamlet of Monemvasia itself, which locals call To Kastro ("The Castle"), is around behind the Rock. To Kastro is divided into the Lower Town (with houses, hotels, and restaurants) and the ruins of the Upper Town high above.

Arrival in Monemvasia

A road runs around the base of the Rock from the causeway to Monemvasia's Lower Town. To get from Gefyra on the mainland to the Lower Town, you have three options: walk (across the

Monemvasia's History

Mighty Monemvasia, a Gibraltar-like rock with a Crusader-style stone town at its base, has ruins scattered all across its Masada-like plateau summit.

Monemvasia's Upper Town was founded in the sixth century A.D. by refugees fleeing Slavic raids into the Peloponnese. Gradually the settlement spread down the hill and, thanks to its uniquely well-defended position, became a powerful town. In the declining days of the Byzantine Empire (1262-1460), when nearby Mystras was its ecclesiastical base, Monemvasia was its main city and one of the great commercial centers of the Byzantine world, with a population of more than 40,000. It was known for its Malvasia wine, a lightly fortified red that was prized at the royal courts of Europe. Over the next several centuries, highly strategic Monemvasia changed hands again and again—mostly back and forth between the Venetians and the Ottomans. While most of the buildings that survive today date from the second period of Venetian rule (1690-1715), foundations and architectural elements from each chapter survive.

By the 18th century, Monemvasia slipped into decline... until it was rediscovered by tourists in the 1970s. Today, Monemvasia is a leading destination both for international visitors and for wealthy Athenians, who are converting its old houses into weekend retreats.

causeway, then around the Rock, about 20 minutes); drive (park along the road near the entry to the Lower Town); or take a shuttle bus (runs regularly between the Gefyra end of the causeway and the Lower Town, marked *public bus*, €1/ride).

Helpful Hints

Name Variation: In English, the town's name can also be spelled Monemvassia, Monembasia, or Monembacia.

Addresses: Locals don't bother with street numbers, or even names—both Monemvasia and Gefyra are small enough that everyone just knows where everything is. If you can't find something, just ask around.

Boat Trips: Monemvasia Cruise runs various glass-bottom boat trips in the area, including a basic €6 sightseeing circle around the Rock for views of Monemvasia from the water (mobile 69771-73516).

Self-Guided Walk

Welcome to Monemvasia

There's only one thing to see in Monemvasia: the Rock, divided between the Lower Town and the Upper Town. Because it's also a real village, Monemvasia is free to enter and open all the time.

Lower Town

Begin outside the 17th-century **main gate,** designed by the Ottomans who were occupying the town at the time (and knew a thing or two about designing—and breaching—gates like this one). The only public WCs are to the right, in front of the gate.

Look up to the cliff and down to the sea, appreciating how successfully the crenellated wall protected this mighty little nugget of Byzantine power. There are only four entrances: two on this side, one on the opposite side, and one from the sea. Combine that with the ridiculously easy-to-defend little causeway (once a drawbridge), and the perfect bird's-eye view from the top of the Rock (ideal for spotting would-be invaders from miles and miles away), and Monemvasia was a tough nut to crack.

Enter the gate. (The stairway inside leads up to a terrace with a monument noting the fact that the 20th-century poet Yiannis Ritsos—beloved by Greeks but unknown abroad—spent much of his life here.) Inside the gate, notice that it jogs, preventing you from even getting a peek at the town until you emerge on the other side—another defensive measure. And then...

Bam! You're at the start of Monemvasia's narrow, cobbled **main street.** Bear uphill (left) at the fork, through a gauntlet of

tourist shops, hotel offices (renting rooms in buildings scattered all over town), and cafés with inviting terraces stretching toward the sea. Elsewhere in town, doors and windows are small, but here—on what's always been the main commercial drag—the wide, arched windows come with big built-in counters for displaying wares. Enjoy this atmospheric lane, window-shopping cafés, and restaurants for later (see "Eating in Monemvasia").

The lane leads to the town's

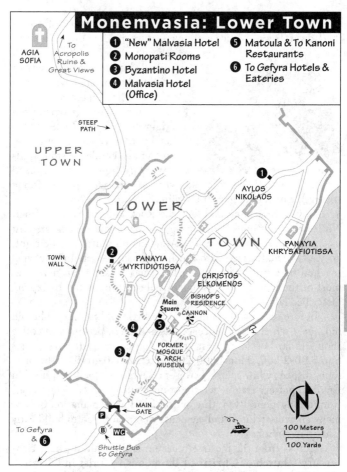

MONEMVASIA

main square, Plateia Dsami—literally "Mosque Square," a very rare-in-Greece tip of the hat to Ottoman rule. The namesake mosque still stands (the blocky building with the small red dome, on the right). In the middle of the square, notice two symbols of the town: a cannon (Monemvasia was nothing if not well-defended) and a well. Monemvasia is honeycombed with cisterns for catching rainwater...the one thing that a city clinging to a rock floating in the sea needs to survive. Virtually every house—in both the Upper and Lower Towns—had its own cellar cistern.

Walk to the edge of this square and survey the rooftops of the **Lower Town**. Notice a unique feature of Monemvasia houses:

sharply angled rooflines, which allowed built-in tile gutters to carefully channel water into those cellar cisterns. Houses are built of stone quarried from right here on the Rock—a very efficient way to get building materials. While the stone walls of many houses are exposed today, historically most houses were covered with plaster (some still are), which once gave the skyline Santorini-like soft edges.

Now turn around and face the Rock and the **Upper Town**. Notice the stoutly walled, zigzagging path that climbs the cliff face...yes, waaaay up there. Halfway up and a little to the right, notice the small cave burrowed into the cliff—a humble chapel reached by a precarious footpath. You can see from here that most of the Upper Town is in ruins...but it sure is fun to explore (described later).

Before leaving the square, do a little sightseeing. The old mosque—which has also served as a church, prison, and coffee shop—today hosts a modest **archaeological museum** (free, Tue-Sun 8:00-20:00, Mon 13:00-20:00, tel. 27320-61403). The one-room display, while sparse, is well-presented and well-described in English: pottery fragments, the stone chancel screen (iconostasis) from a long-gone Byzantine church, and an explanation of how many ancient architectural elements were scavenged to build early Christian churches.

Across from the mosque/museum is the whitewashed, 11th-century **Church of Christos Elkomenos** ("Christ in Chains").

While this was originally a Byzantine church, the Venetians substantially expanded it: Notice the elaborately carved lintel above the entrance, a sure sign of Venetian influence. The peacock relief above the lintel was added after independence (1820s), as was the bell tower. If it's open (generally daily 9:00-14:00 & 16:00-20:00), step into the tidy white interior for a serene visit to an Orthodox church. If you're so moved, drop a coin in the box, light a candle, and say a prayer. Hiding behind the marble iconostasis is a small reminder of the church's humble Byzantine origins: old amphitheater-like

Sparta

Sparta—where mothers famously told their sons to "come home with your shield...or on it"—is a classic example of how little a militaristic society leaves as a legacy for the future.

Nothing has been excavated of the ancient city that everybody wants to see, the Sparta that dominated Greek affairs in the sixth and fifth centuries B.C. and was re-created in the hit movie *300*.

The various excavation sites around town go down no further than the level of Roman Sparta, which was built on the foundations of the classical city from the first century B.C. The main feature of the excavations is an impressive Roman theater, but much of its stone seating was removed and used in the defensive wall built around the city's acropolis in the fourth century A.D.

One reason why so little remains is that the town was abandoned in the 13th century, and its buildings dismantled for reuse in the construction of nearby Mystras. Sparta was re-established in 1834 on the initiative of King Otto and his Bavarian court, whose classical education had given them a strong appreciation of Sparta's place in history. Otto ordered his planners to create a city of wide boulevards and parks; today Sparta looks more like 19th-century Bavaria than the home of King Leonidas. For more on Sparta, see the Greek History and Mythology chapter.

stone risers where bishops once stood.

While it's a little town today, Monemvasia was important enough historically to be a bishopric. Back outside, to the right

as you face the church, notice the entrance to the bishop's former residence—with the Venetian coat of arms (the winged lion of St. Mark) above the door. You'll also see that the church is attached by an archway to a small chapel.

Before huffing up to the Upper Town, poke around the Lower Town's twisty lanes. Through the archway to the right of the church, steps lead down through a maze of steeply cobbled streets to the sea wall. A gate at the center of the wall leads out to a rocky platform with ladders into the sea for swimmers.

As you explore, keep a few things in mind: It all looks medieval and quaint today, but the streets of Monemvasia are a textbook of architectural influences: Byzantine, Venetian, and Ottoman. Wandering the streets of the Lower Town, you might

notice pointed archways or large lintels (stones over windows), which are distinctively Venetian; or occasional tulip-shaped windows (curling on top with a little peak in the middle), which are unmistakably Turkish. Notice the many arched passageways spanning narrow lanes—the only way a crowded, walled town could grow. Quite a few houses are still in ruins, but with Monemvasia's touristic currency on the rise, many of these are now being excavated and rebuilt. Because the town is protected by the Greek government, restoration requires navigating a lot of red tape and giving painstaking attention to historical accuracy.

There are more than two dozen other churches in the Lower Town, and each significant site is numbered and explained by posted information (and guidebooks sold locally)...but there's no need to get bogged down by those details. Just have fun with the perfect medieval streetscapes awaiting discovery around each turn.

When you're ready to climb the Rock, be sure you're prepared: Wear good shoes and bring sun protection (there's very little shade up there) and water (there are no shops up top, but you can buy water at gift shops along the Lower Town's main drag). Then make your way to the top of town and huff up the steep path to the...

Upper Town

The ruins of the Upper Town are spread across a broad, rolling plateau at the summit of the Rock. Unlike the well-preserved Lower Town, virtually none of the Upper Town has survived intact. The last resident left the plateau nearly a century ago—probably after finally getting sick and tired of trudging up and down the path—and the plateau is now a wasteland of ruined old buildings, engulfed by a sea of shrubs and wildflowers that seem to sprout from the rocks. As you explore up

here, watch your step—sudden cliffs and open cisterns could bring your vacation to a sudden and tragic end.

Nearing the top of the trail, curl through yet another defensive gateway, then emerge at the edge of the plateau. While most of the buildings here are ruined, there are a few things to seek out. Major items are well-marked with directional signs, but you could miss the big picture by playing archaeologist. The best way to enjoy top of the Rock is to let your inner child take over for a king- or queen-of-the-castle scramble across the ramparts and ruins.

First, head more or less straight up along the path toward the 12th-century Byzantine **Church of Agia Sophia.** Thanks to recent

erosion, the church hangs precariously (and scenically) close to the edge of a sheer cliff. Like so many buildings here, the church has elements from various eras of history: a Byzantine core, with Ottoman elements (most now gone), and a triple-arched loggia grafted onto the front in the 16th century by the Venetians. The interior (usually closed to visitors, thanks to vandalism) was whitewashed when it was converted into a mosque under Turkish rule, but fragments of original frescoes survive. The whole thing was restored in the 1950s.

From here, you can climb higher up the hill for good views back down onto the church. If you want to lengthen your hike, you

can climb all the way to the acropolis, the fortification near the peak of the Rock (visible from here). Or, for an easier walk, head downhill to the crenellated watchtower area out toward the sea; this spot has the best views back up to the church.

As you explore the site, remember that this was regarded as the mightiest fortress in Byzantine Greece. Not surprisingly, it was never captured in battle—only by a protracted, starve-

'em-out siege. Monemvasia's Achilles' heel was its dependence on the mainland for food. While some basic supplies were cultivated atop the Rock, it wasn't enough to sustain the entire town for very long.

Back at the entrance gateway, consider heading right along the wall (as you face the Lower Town and water) for good views back down onto the Lower Town. If you continue farther along this path, you'll reach an old Turkish house, and then the granddaddy of all the town's cisterns: a cavernous vaulted hall.

Our tour of the Rock is finished. When you're done enjoying

the views and the evocative ruins, head back down the way you came up...and treat yourself to a drink on a seafront terrace.

Sleeping in Monemvasia

Monemvasia accommodations come with a big price hike in July and August. Rooms are tight during these summer months, and on weekends year-round (as it's a popular getaway for Greeks and visitors alike). Outside those times, you can usually get a deal. But because of this wild fluctuation, you might see some variation from the rates I've listed.

On the Rock

Sleeping in Monemvasia's old Lower Town is romantic and appealing, if remote-feeling. Various hotels rent rooms scattered through old buildings. All of them have decor that mixes new and old, with some old-fashioned Monemvasia flourishes (such as low platform beds, tight bathrooms, head-banging archways, and stone shower enclosures without curtains). Keep in mind that Monemvasia is a honeycomb of cobblestone alleys and stairs. Luggage with wheels won't work here. If you stay on the Rock, be prepared to carry your luggage to your hotel (drivers might want to cram essentials into a day pack).

$$$ "New" Malvasia Hotel—the shiny new extension of the old Malvasia Hotel (described later)—has 20 well-appointed but still traditional rooms in several small buildings at the far end of the Lower Town (Db-€85-120 depending on view and balcony—the cheapest rooms are a great value, air-con, pay Wi-Fi in lobby, tel. 27320-63007, fax 27320-63009, www.malvasia-hotel.gr, info @malvasia-hotel.gr).

$$ Monopati Rooms, well-run by Swiss-French Isabelle, is a delightful little compound renting one two-bedroom apartment (July-Aug: Db-€85, Tb-€100; Sept-Oct and March-June: Db-€70, Tb-€85) and one little stand-alone, two-bedroom cottage for up to five people (July-Aug: €130 for 2 people, €160 for 3 or more; Sept-Oct and March-June: €110 for 2 people, €140 for 3 or more) in a sleepy perch near the top of the Lower Town (kitchenettes, breakfast-€6; 4-night minimum July-Aug, otherwise 2-night minimum; closed Nov-Feb, air-con, free Internet access and Wi-Fi in lobby, tel. & fax 27320-61772, mobile 69748-32818, www.byzantine -escapade.com, info@byzantine-escapade.com).

$$ Byzantino Hotel rents 25 overpriced but tastefully old-fashioned rooms in the Lower Town (Db-€60-80 with no view, €80-120 with sea view, €100-135 with sea view and balcony, breakfast-€5, air-con, free Wi-Fi in lobby, rooms rented from central office, tel. 27320-61254, tel. & fax 27320-61351, www.hotel

---

Sleep Code

(€1 = about $1.40, country code: 30)
S = Single, **D** = Double/Twin, **T** = Triple, **Q** = Quad, **b** = bathroom,
s = shower only.

　　To help you easily sort through these listings, I've divided the rooms into three categories, based on the price for a standard double room with bath:

$$$ Higher Priced—Most rooms €100 or more.
$$ Moderately Priced—Most rooms between €70-100.
$ Lower Priced—Most rooms €70 or less.

　　Prices can change without notice; verify the hotel's current rates online or by email. For other updates, see www .ricksteves.com/update.

---

byzantino.com, friendly Tina). Avoid the pricey rooms in their Lazareto Hotel, which are halfway between the Lower Town and the mainland.

$ Malvasia Hotel—related to but separate from "New" Malvasia Hotel (described earlier)—is a collection of 50 rustic but atmospheric, and very affordable, rooms in four different buildings (Db-€50-75 depending on size and view, 4-person apartment with kitchen but no breakfast-€75, air-con, tel. 27320-61323, fax 27320-61722, malvasia@otenet.gr).

In Gefyra

While it lacks the romance—and prices aren't even that much lower—sleeping in the mainland town of Gefyra lets you stay in modern civilization within walking distance of sleepy, time-warp Monemvasia.

$$ Hotel Panorama is the best deal in town, well-run by friendly Angelos and Rena Panos. It's at the top of Gefyra, an uphill 10-minute hike from the main street, which means it's quiet and comes with great views. The 27 rooms—all with balconies— are comfortable and new-feeling, and the café/lounge/breakfast room is an enjoyable place to relax (Sb-€65; Db-€80, or €90 with sea view; Tb-€95, or €110 with sea view; family rooms, air-con, no elevator, free Internet access and Wi-Fi, tel. 27320-61198, fax 27320-62098, www.panoramahotel-monemvasia.gr, info @panoramahotel-monemvasia.gr).

$$ The Flower of Monemvasia is a pleasant family-run hotel with 21 rooms right along the main road, a short walk from the causeway (Sb-€50-80, Db-€60-100, soft rates—much cheaper outside of summer, also has pricier suites, air-con, no elevator, free

Wi-Fi, tel. 27320-61395, fax 27320-61391, www.flower-hotel.gr, info@flower-hotel.gr). Ask about their good restaurant To Liotrivi, in a restored olive-oil mill a 15-minute drive outside town (also rents rooms).

$ Hotel Pramataris offers 22 good-value rooms on the main street as you enter town, across the street from The Flower of Monemvasia. Most rooms have views of the Rock (Db-€60 May-Sept, €50 Oct-April; air-con, no elevator, free Internet access and Wi-Fi, tel. 27320-61833, fax 27320-61075, www.pramatarishotel .gr, hotelpr@hol.gr).

$ Anastatios Sofos rents seven cheap, barebones rooms along the main road (Db-€50 July-Aug, otherwise €40; no breakfast, air-con, tel. 27320-61202, speaks just enough English).

Eating in Monemvasia

On the Rock

Both of these eateries are along the main pedestrian artery of Monemvasia's Lower Town, just before the main square.

Matoula (Ματούλα), with its delightful vine-shaded terrace looking out to sea, is the most appealing of the restaurants on the Rock. Try the local specialty, *barbounia* (red mullet), or ask owner Venetia about the daily specials (€4 starters, €7-9 main dishes, seafood splurges, daily 12:00-24:00, tel. 27320-61660).

To Kanoni ("The Cannon"), next door to Matoula, is another good choice, with a cozy interior and a scenic upper veranda (€4-7 starters, €8-16 main dishes, pricier seafood dishes, daily 8:00-23:00, tel. 27320-61387).

In Gefyra

A collection of interchangeable eateries cluster like barnacles at the Gefyra end of the causeway. In good weather, it's pointless to eat anywhere here without a view of the Rock. I like to walk along the water (to the right as you face the Rock) and survey the options. I've eaten well at **Scorpios,** about halfway around the bay, with rustic white tables under a blue canopy, castaway ambience, and my favorite views of the Rock (€3-6  starters, €5-11 main dishes, daily 12:00-24:00, tel. 27320-62090).

Picnics: The bakery on Gefyra's main street (near the post office) is excellent, and the supermarket just up the side-street from there will help you round out your moveable feast for the top of the Rock. While you can buy basic drinks and snacks in Monemvasia's

Lower Town, there's no grocery store there—do your shopping in Gefyra.

Monemvasia Connections

Monemvasia is not particularly well-connected by bus. Virtually every connection requires a change in **Sparta** (4/day, 2 hours, €9), including to **Gythio** (4/day, 3 hours, €13), **Areopoli** on the Mani Peninsula (4/day, 3.5 hours, €16), and **Nafplio** (1/day, 4.5 hours, transfers in Sparta and Tripoli). To **Athens,** there's one direct bus daily, but it leaves early in the morning (at 5:15 in 2010, 5 hours, €27). The others change in Sparta (3/day, 6 hours total). There's no real bus station in Monemvasia, so buses stop across the street from the Malvasia Travel Agency, just before the causeway; you can buy tickets at the travel agency (recommended a day in advance in busy times) or onboard the bus.

BEYOND ATHENS & THE PELOPONNESE

DELPHI

ΔΕΛΦΟΊ / Δελφοί

Perched high on the southern slopes of Mt. Parnassos, and overlooking the gleaming waters of the Gulf of Corinth, Delphi (Greeks pronounce it "dell-FEE," not "DELL-fye") is without doubt the most spectacular of Greece's ancient sites.

Back then, Delphi was famous throughout the known world as the home of a prophetess known as the oracle (a.k.a. the Pythia or sibyl). As the mouthpiece of Apollo on earth, she told fortunes for pilgrims who came from far and wide seeking her advice on everything from affairs of state to wars to matrimonial problems. Delphi's fame grew, and its religious festivals blossomed into the Pythian Games, an athletic contest that was second only to the Olympics.

Today Delphi offers visitors several worthwhile sights. The archaeological site contains the ruins of the Sanctuary of Apollo. Next door is the great Archaeological Museum, where statues and treasures found on the site help bring the ruins to life. And a short walk from the site are still more ruins—including the Kastalian Spring and the photogenic Sanctuary of Athena, taking you back to Delphi's prehistoric origins.

Though Delphi can be done as a day trip from Athens, it's more relaxed as an overnight stop, allowing you to enjoy the pleasant modern town and craggy mountainside setting (suitably awesome for the mysterious oracle). Though the town is crammed with tourists, it still feels laid-back, offering sweeping vistas of the valley below and the Gulf of Corinth in the

Delphi Overview

PHAEDRIADES ROCKS

SANCTUARY OF APOLLO (SEE DETAIL MAP)

STADIUM

STADIUM

KASTALIAN SPRING

TO ITEA & PATRA

MUSEUM OF DELPHIC FESTIVALS

BUS STATION

GYMNASIUM

TO ATHENS

PAVLOU

FILELLINON

FRID.

APOLLONOS ST.

ARCHAEOLOGICAL MUSEUM

SANCTUARY OF ATHENA (THOLOS)

DELPHI TOWN

200 YARDS
200 METERS

→ ONE-WAY STREET

❶ Hotel Leto
❷ Hotel Acropole
❸ Pitho Rooms
❹ Tholos Hotel
❺ Hermes Hotel

❻ Sibylla Hotel
❼ Taverna Vakchos
❽ To Patriko Mas
❾ Taverna Dion
❿ Taverna Gargadouas

distance. (It's hard to find a hotel or restaurant that doesn't boast grand views.) Especially after a stay in bustling Athens, Delphi is an appealing place to let your pulse slow.

Orientation to Delphi

Visitors flock from all over Greece to walk the Sacred Way at Delphi. Many don't bother to spend the night. But the town, a half-mile west of the archaeological site and museum, is a charm-

ing place in its own right. Delphi, sometimes spelled Delfi or Delfoi in English (pop. 2,300), was custom-built to accommodate the hordes of tourists. The main street, Vasileos Pavlou-Friderikis, is a tight string of hotels, cafés, restaurants, and souvenir shops. Two other streets run roughly parallel to this main drag at different levels (Apollonos is one block uphill/north, and Filellinon is one block downhill/south), connected periodically by steep stairways. The three streets converge at the eastern end of the town.

Tourist Information

Delphi's modest TI has a display of old photographs that show how the ancient site looked in 1892—back when humble houses sat on the ruins and before the archaeologists moved in to clear things out (generally open Mon-Fri 7:30-14:30, closed Sat-Sun, along the upper street near the sanctuary end of the village at Apollonos 11, tel. 22653-51300).

When the TI is closed, an **exhibition hall** on the lower level of the same building remains open to show off temporary exhibits (mostly about the excavations) and dispense basic tourist information (Mon-Fri 8:00-20:00, Sat 8:00-14:00 & 16:00-20:00, Sun 16:00-20:00 in summer, closed Sun in winter, may stay open daily until 22:00 or 23:00 in summer, enter from the main street, Pavlou-Friderikis 12). On the porch in front of this office is a model of the Sanctuary of Apollo in ancient times.

Arrival in Delphi

Delphi is three hours north of Athens, and is reachable by bus or by car.

By Bus: Buses to Delphi depart Athens from Terminal B (described on page 218) about every three hours, including at 7:30, 10:30, and 13:00 (plus later buses). Buses back to Athens depart from Delphi about every three hours, including at 13:30, 16:00, and 18:00 (the last bus, except Sun at 21:00). The trip costs €13.60 each way (no round-trip tickets sold). Most buses have air-conditioning but no WC, and make a café rest stop en route. The drive takes you past Thiva (ancient Thebes) and has nice views of Mt. Parnassos as you approach.

Upon arrival at the Delphi bus station, consider buying your return ticket, since buses can fill up. It's a 20-minute walk to the archaeological site. From the bus station (at the west end of town), walk back through town on the main street, staying at the same elevation as the bus station. Leaving town at the other end, continue another 10 minutes along the highway to the Archaeological Museum, then the site (both on your left, east of town).

Many Athens-based companies offer convenient one-day **package tours** to Delphi, which include transportation, a guided tour, and lunch. Ask at your Athens hotel for details.

By Car: For tips on getting to Delphi by car, see "Route Tips for Drivers" at the end of this chapter. Drivers can park at the site for free, or anywhere in town where the street doesn't have a double-yellow line.

Helpful Hints

Services: The main drag, Pavlou-Friderikis, has just about everything you might need, including a **post office** (at the east end,

Delphi: From Legend to History

Delphi's origins are lost in the mists of time and obscured by many different, sometimes conflicting, legends.

The ancients believed that Delphi was the center of the world. Its position was determined by Zeus himself, who released two eagles from the opposite ends of the world and noted where they met.

It was here that a priestess (the sibyl) worshipped Gaia, the mother of the gods. A serpent called the Pythia, or Python, guarded the ravine of the Kastalian Spring. Apollo, the god of the sun and music, arrived in the guise of a dolphin (*delfini*, hence Delphi) and killed the Pythian snake. The sibyl became known as the oracle or Pythia, and she and the place now served Apollo.

Historically speaking, the site was probably the home of a prophetess as early as Mycenaean times (1400 B.C.). The worship of Apollo grew, and the place gained fame for the oracle and for its religious festivals. Every four years, athletes and spectators gathered here to worship Apollo with music and athletic competitions: the Pythian Games, which soon rivaled the Olympics. The sanctuary of Apollo reached the height of its prestige between the sixth and fourth centuries B.C., by which time Delphi so dominated Greek life that no leader would make a major decision without first sending emissaries here to consult the oracle. The sanctuary was deemed too important to be under the control of any one city-state, so its autonomy was guaranteed by a federation of Greek cities.

Even when Greece was conquered by the Macedonians (Alexander the Great) and Romans, the sanctuary was preserved and the conquerors continued to consult the oracle. For a thousand years, Apollo spoke to mortals through his prophetess, until A.D. 394, when Christians shut down the pagan site.

Mon-Fri 7:30-14:00, closed Sat-Sun), **ATMs,** and several cafés and shops advertising **Internet access.**

Local Guide: Penny Kolomvotsou is a great guide who can resurrect the ruins at Delphi (reasonable prices, tel. 22650-83171, mobile 694-464-4427, kpagona@hotmail.com).

Tourist Train: A handy, free train makes it easy to get around town (May-Sept only, departs from east end of town, near the big hotel). In the morning (8:00-13:00), it goes to the Sanctuary of Apollo, museum, and other ancient sites east of town. In the evening (departs from big hotel at 20:15), it loops once through the upper reaches of the town itself. If you see it coming and want to hop on, flag it down.

Weather: Delphi is in the mountains and can be considerably cooler and rainier than Athens. Check the forecast (ask at your hotel) and dress accordingly, especially off-season.

Sights in Delphi

Delphi's most important sights are its archaeological site (with the Sanctuary of Apollo) and the adjacent Archaeological Museum. Nearby are the Kastalian Spring, the gymnasium, and the Sanctuary of Athena. The Museum of Delphic Festivals is in Delphi town.

Planning Your Time: Allow 1.5 hours for the archaeological site (hiking to the stadium alone is nearly a half-hour round-trip) and another 45-60 minutes for the museum. By foot, allow another hour or so to visit the other sites to the east of the Sanctuary of Apollo (though you can see two of them, distantly, from in front of the site). Note that you can do the archaeological site and the museum in either order. I recommend doing the site first. You'll have more energy for the climb (there's a 700-foot elevation gain from the entrance to the stadium), and later, when you tour the museum, you can more easily imagine the original context of the items on display. Crowds and weather might help you decide. If it's hot or raining, do the museum first to hedge your bets for better conditions for the site.

▲▲▲The Sanctuary of Apollo

Ancient Delphi was not a city, but a sanctuary—a place of worship centered on the Temple of Apollo, where the oracle prophesied. Surrounding the temple are what remains of grand monuments built by grateful pilgrims. And the Pythian Games produced what are perhaps the best-preserved theater and stadium in Greece.

Cost and Hours: €6, €9 combo-ticket includes Archaeological Museum; April-Oct Tue-Sun 8:00-20:00, Mon 13:30-20:00; Nov-March Mon-Sat 8:00-18:00, Sun 8:30-15:00; off-season hours can change without notice—best to visit before 14:00; last entry 20 minutes before closing. Tel. 22650-82312, www.culture.gr.

Sudden Closures: The stadium at the top of the site closes occasionally after heavy rains (to keep visitors safe from possible rock slides), and even the Temple of Apollo may close on rare occasions. If the temple is a must-see attraction for you, call before coming to confirm it's open.

Getting There: The archaeological site is a half-mile east of the modern town of Delphi. When you reach the museum, continue along a path to the site's ticket office.

Services: A WC and a café (with a wide selection of slushee drinks, and little else) are located outside the museum. There are also WCs inside the archaeological site: one just above the entrance

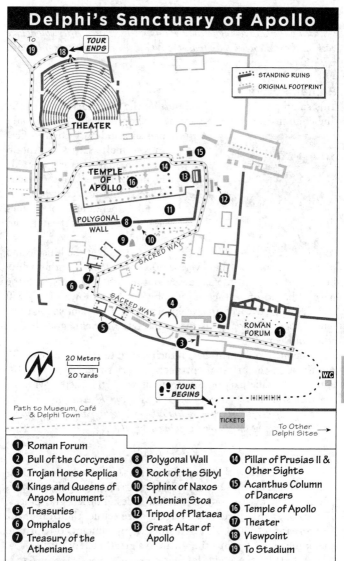

Delphi's Sanctuary of Apollo

Legend:
- STANDING RUINS
- ORIGINAL FOOTPRINT

Map labels:
- TOUR ENDS
- To ❶⑨
- ⑱ VIEWPOINT
- ⑰ THEATER
- ⑮
- TEMPLE OF APOLLO ⑯ ⑭ ⑬
- ⑫
- POLYGONAL WALL ⑧ ⑪
- ⑨ ⑩
- SACRED WAY
- ⑦
- ⑥
- SACRED WAY
- ④
- ⑤
- ② ROMAN FORUM ①
- ③
- 20 Meters
- 20 Yards
- TOUR BEGINS
- Path to Museum, Café & Delphi Town
- TICKETS
- To Other Delphi Sites
- WC
- DELPHI

Tour list:
1. Roman Forum
2. Bull of the Corcyreans
3. Trojan Horse Replica
4. Kings and Queens of Argos Monument
5. Treasuries
6. Omphalos
7. Treasury of the Athenians
8. Polygonal Wall
9. Rock of the Sibyl
10. Sphinx of Naxos
11. Athenian Stoa
12. Tripod of Plataea
13. Great Altar of Apollo
14. Pillar of Prusias II & Other Sights
15. Acanthus Column of Dancers
16. Temple of Apollo
17. Theater
18. Viewpoint
19. To Stadium

and another on the upper path between the theater and the stadium. No food or drink is allowed inside the site.

◆ Self-Guided Tour: Looking up at the sheer rock face, you see the ruins clinging to a steep slope. From here, you ascend a switchback trail that winds up, up, up: through the ruins to the Temple of Apollo, the theater, and the stadium, 700 feet up from the road. Every pilgrim who visited the oracle had to make this

same steep climb.
• *Start up the path, going to the right up a set of stairs. After you double back on the switchback path (past the WCs), you enter a rectangular area with 10 gray columns, marking the...*

Roman Forum

This small public space stood outside the sanctuary's main gate. The columns supported an arcade of shops. Here pilgrims could

pick up handy last-minute offerings—small statues of Apollo were popular—before proceeding to their date with the oracle. At festival times, crowds of pilgrims gathered here for parades up to the temple, theater, and stadium.

Gaze up at the hillside and picture the ruins as they were 2,000 years ago: gleaming white buildings with red roofs, golden statues atop columns, and the natural backdrop of these sheer gray-red rocks towering up 750 feet. It must have been an awe-inspiring sight for humble pilgrims, who'd traveled here to discover what fate the fickle gods had in store for them.

The men (only men) began their ascent to the oracle by walking through the original entrance gate, between 10-foot walls, entering the sanctuary on the street known as the Sacred Way.
• *A wall enclosed the sanctuary, forming a rough rectangle, with the Temple of Apollo in the center. Climb the four steps, passing through the walls and into the sanctuary, walking along the...*

Sacred Way

The road is lined with ruins of once-glorious statues and monuments financed by satisfied pilgrims grateful for the oracle's advice. Immediately to the right is a pedestal of red-gray blocks, 17 feet long. This once held a huge bronze statue, the **Bull of the Corcyreans** (c. 580 B.C.), a gift from the inhabitants of Corfu to thank the oracle for directing them to a great catch of tuna fish.

A half-dozen steps farther along (left side) was an even bigger statue, a colossal bronze replica of the **Trojan Horse.**

Just beyond that (right side) is a semicircle 40 feet across, which was once lined with 10 statues of the legendary **Kings and Queens of Argos,** including Perseus,

Danae, and Hercules.

Next comes a row of so-called **Treasuries** (left side), small buildings that housed precious gifts to the gods. These buildings and their contents were paid for by city-states and kings to thank the oracle and the gods for giving them success (especially in war). From the outside they looked like mini-temples, with columns, pediments, statues, and friezes. Inside they held gold, jewels, bronze dinnerware, ivory statues, necklaces, and so on. The friezes and metopes from the Sikyonian and Siphnian Treasuries are now in the museum.

• *At the corner where the path turns to go uphill is a cone-shaped stone called an...*

Omphalos

The ancients believed that Delphi was the center of the world and marked that spot with a strange cone-shaped monument called

an omphalos (navel). The omphalos was also a symbolic tombstone for the Python that Apollo slew.

Several omphalos stones were erected at different places around the sanctuary. The original was kept inside the Temple of Apollo. A copy graced the temple's entrance (it's now in the on-site museum). Another copy stood here along the Sacred Way, where this modern replica is today.

As the center of the world, Delphi was also the starting point for history. From here, the oracle could predict the course of human destiny.

• *Rounding the bend and gazing uphill, you'll face the...*

Treasury of the Athenians

The Athenians built this temple to commemorate their victory over the Persians at the Battle of Marathon in 490 B.C. The tiny inscriptions on the blocks honor Athenian citizens with praise and

laurel-leaf wreaths, the symbol of victory at Delphi's Pythian Games. When the ruins were rebuilt (1904-1906), the restorers determined which block went where by matching up pieces of the inscriptions.

The structure's ceremonial entrance (east end) has two Doric columns of expensive marble from Paros. They support six metopes (reconstructed; the originals are in the museum) that feature the Greeks battling the legendary Amazon women—symbolizing the Greek victory over the barbaric Persians at Marathon.

• *Follow the path as it continues uphill. By now, you have a great view to the left of the...*

Polygonal Wall and Other Ancient Features

The retaining wall (sixth century B.C.) supports the terrace with the Temple of Apollo. It runs across the hillside for some 250 feet at heights of up to 12 feet. It has survived in almost perfect condition because of the way that the stones were fitted together (without mortar). This created a "living" wall, able to absorb the many earthquakes for which the region is renowned (earthquakes caused the other buildings here to crumble).

Near the wall, just above the Treasury of the Athenians, the 10-foot **Rock of the Sibyl** hearkens back to the murky prehistoric

origins of this place as a sacred site. According to legend, the oracle's predecessor—called the sibyl (priestess)—sat atop this rock to deliver her prophecies, back when the area was sacred to Gaia, the mother of the gods.

Just behind that rock, near the stubby white column (walk up the path to get a better view), is a pile of rocks with a black slab pedestal. This was once a 35-foot-tall pillar holding the statue of the **Sphinx of Naxos** (c. 570-560 B.C., now in the museum). Inhabitants of the isle of Naxos used their best marble for this gift to the oracle, guaranteeing them access to her advice even during busy times.

A few more steps up, the three white, fluted, Ionic columns along the wall belonged to the **Athenian Stoa,** a 100-foot-long open-air porch. Here the Athenians displayed captured shields,

ships' prows, and booty from their naval victory over Persia at the decisive Battle of Salamis (480 B.C.). It was the oracle of Delphi who gave Athens the key to victory. As the Persian army swarmed over Greece, the oracle prophesied that the city of Athens would be saved by a "wooden wall." The puzzled Athenians eventually  interpreted the oracle's riddle as meaning not a city wall, but a fleet of wooden ships. They abandoned Athens to the Persian invaders, then routed them at sea. Once the enemy was driven out, Greece's cities ceremonially relit their sacred flames from the hearth *(hestia)* of Delphi's temple.

• *Continue up the Sacred Way and follow it as it turns left, up the hill. As you ascend, along the right-hand side you'll pass a square, gray-block pedestal that once supported a big column. This monument, the **Tripod of Plataea**, was built to thank the oracle for victory in the Battle of Plataea (479 B.C., fought near Thebes), which finally drove the Persians out. The monument's 26-foot bronze column of three intertwined snakes was carried off by the Romans to their chariot-racing track in Constantinople (modern Istanbul), where tourists now snap photos of what's left of it.*

At the top of the path, turn left and face the six Doric columns and ramp that mark the entrance to the Temple of Apollo. In the courtyard in front of the temple are the ruins of several sights.

The Temple Courtyard

Take in the temple and imagine the scene 2,000 years ago as pilgrims gathered here at the culmination of their long journey. They'd come seeking guidance from the gods at a crucial juncture in their lives. Here in the courtyard they prepared themselves before entering the temple to face the awe-inspiring oracle.

Opposite the temple entrance, pilgrims and temple priests offered sacrifices at the (partially restored) **Great Altar of Apollo.** Worshippers would enter the rectangular enclosure (only two of the three walls stand today), originally made of black marble with white trim. Inside they'd sacrifice an animal to Apollo—goats were especially popular. One hundred bulls (a hecatomb) were sacrificed to open every Pythian Games.

To the right of the temple (as you face it) once stood several sights that dazzled visitors. Imagine a 50-foot **Statue of Apollo Sitalkas** towering over the courtyard, where only a humble rectangular base remains today. Next to it is the still-impressive, 20-foot-tall, rectangular **Pillar of Prusias II.** Atop this was a statue of a second-century king on horseback who traveled here from Turkey to consult the oracle. The **three round column stubs** once held ceremonial tripods. Behind them rose the tall **Acanthus Column of Dancers,** three girls supporting a tripod (now in the museum).

• *But these sights paled in comparison to the...*

The Oracle

The oracle (a.k.a. the Pythia or sibyl) was a priestess of Apollo who acted as a seer or fortune-teller by "channeling" the god's spirit.

The oracle was always female, ever since the days when Delphi was devoted to mother-goddess worship. She was usually an older empty-nester from the village with a good reputation, who left her husband and family behind to live within the sanctuary walls. Most oracles were not well-educated. They did not become famous, and we don't know any of them by name. The women themselves were not the focus—rather, they were anonymous vessels for the words of Apollo, as interpreted by the priests.

In the early days, there was just one oracle, who only prophesied on special auspicious days of the year. At Delphi's peak, the demand for fortunes was such that two or three oracles worked shifts every day. The oracle purified herself in the Kastalian Spring. She dressed in white, like a virgin, even if she wasn't, and carried a laurel branch (we call it a "bay laurel"), a symbol of Apollo. Why the oracle sat on a tripod—a ritual cauldron on three legs—no one knows for sure. (For more on tripods, see page 297.)

The oracle presumably prophesied in a kind of trance, letting the spirit of Apollo possess her body and speaking in the first person as if she were the god himself. Many think she was high on intoxicating vapors that rose up from the natural chasm in the inner sanctum floor. Science has found no evidence of the supposed chasm within the temple walls, though ravines and springs nearby do emit psychotropic gases. Another explanation is that the trance came from the oracle eating or inhaling burned laurel leaves. Whether brought on by drugs, fakery, hysteria, or Apollo

Temple of Apollo

This structure—which in its day must have towered over the rest of the site—was the centerpiece of the whole sanctuary. It was dedicated to the god who ruled the hillside, and it housed the oracle who spoke in his name. This was the third and largest temple built on this site (completed 330 B.C.), replacing earlier versions destroyed by earthquake and fire. It was largely funded by Philip of Macedon and dedicated in the time of Alexander the Great.

The temple was gleaming white, ringed with columns, with a triangular pediment over the entrance and a roof studded with

himself, the oracle's ultimate message was tightly controlled by the priests.

The oracle addressed all kinds of questions. Travelers came to Delphi before starting long journeys. Rulers came to plan wars. Explorers wanted advice on how to get newfound colonies off to a good start. Philosophers asked the oracle to weigh in on ethical dilemmas. Priests sought divine approval of new rituals and cults. Ordinary people came because their marriages were on the rocks or simply to have their fortunes told.

Apollo was considered a god of peace, order, and personal virtue, in contrast with the other temperamental gods of the Greek pantheon. As the priestess of Apollo, the oracle could address moral questions and religious affairs. And since Delphi was considered the center of the world, the words of the oracle were the source of fate and the fortunes of men.

Many famous people (before you) have made the pilgrimage to Delphi. A young Socrates came here and was so inspired by the phrase "Know Thyself" (inscribed on the Temple of Apollo) that he pursued the path of self-knowledge...and changed the course of history. The oracle was visited by foreign kings such as Midas (of the golden-touch legend) and the ancient billionaire Croesus (of "rich-as" fame). The historian Plutarch (c. 46-120 A.D.) served here as a priest in the temple, interpreting the oracle's utterances. Roman Emperor Nero visited, participated in the Pythian Games, and was warned by the oracle about his impending assassination. Alexander the Great asked the oracle whether he'd be successful in conquering the world. When the oracle hemmed and hawed, Alexander grabbed her by the hair and wouldn't let go. The helpless oracle cried, "You're unstoppable." Alexander said, "I have my answer."

DELPHI

statues. Above the entrance, the pediment statues showed Apollo arriving in Delphi in a four-horse chariot (now in the museum). The six huge Doric columns that stand near the entrance today (reassembled in 1904) were complemented by 15 columns along each side. (Sections from a toppled column lie on the hillside below the temple's left side, near the Polygonal Wall, giving an idea of the temple's scale; to see this, backtrack down the hill to find the path that runs below the temple.) Though the temple was all white, it was actually constructed with a darker local limestone. The columns were coated with a stucco of powdered marble to achieve the white color. Only the pediments and other decorations were made from costly white marble shipped in from the isle of Paros.

Adopt the attitude of an ancient pilgrim, and imagine yourself preparing to meet the oracle. First, you'd bathe with the priests at the Kastalian Spring in the ravine east of the sanctuary. You'd parade ceremonially to the temple, up the same Sacred Way tourists walk today. At the Great Altar, you'd offer a sacrifice, likely of goat (a loaf of bread was the minimum cover charge). Now you could enter the temple with the priests (Head 'em up, pilgrim), climbing the ramp and passing through the columns. Inscribed at the entrance were popular proverbs, including "Know Thyself," "Nothing in Excess," and "Stuff Happens."

Inside, the temple was cloudy with the incense of burning laurel leaves. You'd see the large golden statue of Apollo and the original omphalos stone, announcing that you'd arrived at the center of the world. After offering a second sacrifice on the hearth of the eternal flame, it was time to meet the oracle.

The priests would lead you into the back chamber of the *cella*—the *adyton,* or holy of holies. There, amid the incense, was the oracle—an older woman, dressed in white, seated in the bowl of a tripod. The tripod was suspended over a hole in the floor of the temple, exposing a natural ravine where a spring bubbled up. While you waited, the priests presented your question to the oracle. She answered—sometimes crying out, sometimes muttering gibberish and foaming at the mouth. The mysterious riddles she gave as answers were legendary. The priests would step in to interpret the oracle's meaning, rendering it in a vague, haiku-like poem.

Then you were ushered out of the temple, either enlightened or confused by the riddle. For many pilgrims—like Socrates, who spent much of his life pondering the oracle's words—a visit to Delphi was only the beginning of their life's journey.

• *Uphill, to the right of the Temple of Apollo, stands Delphi's stone theater. The various routes all lead up (just follow the signs)—I'll meet you there.*

DELPHI

Theater

One of Greece's best-preserved theaters (fourth century B.C.) was built to host song contests honoring Apollo, the god of music. With 35 rows of white stone quarried from Mt. Parnassos, it could seat 5,000. The action took place on the semi-circular area (60 feet across, surrounded by a drainage ditch) known as the orchestra. As at most ancient theaters, the theater would have been closed off along the street, creating a back-

drop for the stage. This structure also served as the grand entryway for spectators. The *Bronze Charioteer* statue (now in the museum) likely stood outside the theater's entrance, in the middle of the road, greeting playgoers. The theater was designed so that most spectators could look over the backdrop, taking in stunning views of the valley below even as they watched the onstage action.

The theater's original and main purpose was to host not plays, but song contests—a kind of "Panhellenic Idol" competition that was part of the Pythian Games. Every four years, singer-songwriters from all over the Greek-speaking world gathered here to perform hymns in honor of Apollo, the god of music. They sang accompanied by flute or by lyre—a strummed autoharp, which was Apollo's chosen instrument.

Over time, the song competition expanded into athletic contests (held at the stadium), as well as other events in dance and drama. The opening and closing ceremonies of the Pythian Games were held here. One of the games' central features was a play that re-enacted the dramatic moment when Apollo slew the Python and founded Delphi...not unlike the bombastic pageantry that opens and closes today's Olympic Games.

• *A steep path continues uphill to a stunning...*

View from Above the Theater

With craggy Mt. Parnassos at your back, the sanctuary beneath you, and a panoramic view of the valley in the distance, you can appreciate why the ancients found this place sacred.

We're 1,800 feet above sea level on Mt. Parnassos (8,062 feet). In winter, Greeks go skiing at nearby resorts. The jagged rocks and sheer cliffs of Mt. Parnassos are made of gray limestone, laced with red-orange bauxite, which is mined nearby. The cliffs have striations of sedimentary rocks that have been folded upward at all angles by seismic activity. The region is crisscrossed with faults (one runs right under the temple), pocked with sinkholes, and carved with ravines.

Two large sections of rock that jut out from the cliff (to the left) are known as the Phaedriades Rocks, or "Shining Ones," because of how they reflect sunlight. At the foot of one of the rocks lies the sanctuary. Between the two rocks (east of the sanctuary) is the gaping ravine of the Kastalian Spring.

Looking down on the entire sanctuary, you can make out its shape—a rough rectangle (640 feet by 442 feet—about twice as big as a football field) enclosed by a wall, stretching from the top of the theater down to the Roman Forum. Trace the temple's floor plan: You'd enter where the columns are, pass through the

Delphi's Decline and Rediscovery

After reaching a peak during the Classical Age, the oracle's importance slowly declined. In Hellenistic times, traditional religions like Apollo-worship were eclipsed by secular philosophy and foreign gods. By the third century B.C., the oracle was handling more lonely-hearts advice than affairs of state. The Romans alternated between preserving Delphi (as Hadrian did) and looting its treasuries and statues. Nero famously stole 500 statues for his home in Rome (A.D. 66), and Constantine used Delphi's monument to decorate his new capital. As Rome crumbled, barbarians did their damage. Finally, in A.D. 394, the Christian Emperor Theodosius I closed down the sanctuary, together with all the other great pagan worship centers.

The site was covered by landslides and by the village of Kastri until 1892, when the villagers were relocated to the modern village of Delphi, about a half-mile to the west. Excavation began, the site was opened to tourists, and its remaining treasures were eventually put on display in the museum.

DELPHI

lobby *(pronaos)*, into the main hall *(cella)*, and continue into the back portion *(adyton)*, where the oracle sat (they say) above a natural chasm.

In the distance, looking south, is the valley of the Pleistos River, green with olive trees. Beyond that (though not visible from this spot) are the turquoise waters of the Gulf of Corinth.

• *If you're winded, you can make your way back down now. But you've come so far already—why not keep going? Hike another 10 minutes up the steep path to the...*

Stadium

Every four years, athletes and spectators from across Greece gathered here to watch the same kinds of sports as at the ancient Olympics. The Pythian Games (founded at least by 582 B.C.) were second only to the (older, bigger) Olympic Games in prestige. They were one of four Panhellenic Games on the athletics calendar (Olympia, Corinth, Nemea, and Delphi).

The exceptionally well-preserved stadium was built in the fifth century B.C. It was remodeled in the second century A.D. by the wealthy Herodes Atticus, who also built a theater in Athens

and a fountain in Olympia (the Nymphaeum). There was stone seating for nearly 7,000, which was cushier than Olympia's grassy-bank stadium. Among the seats on the north side, you can still make out the midfield row of judges' seats. The track—580 feet long by 84 feet wide—is slightly shorter than the one at Olympia. The main entrance was at the east end—the thick pillars once supported a three-arched entry. The starting lines (one at either end, depending on the length of the race) are still here, and you can see the post-holes for the wooden starting blocks.

The Pythian Games lasted about a week and were held in the middle of a three-month truce among warring Greeks that allowed people to train and travel safely. Winners were awarded a wreath of laurel leaves (as opposed to the olive leaves at the Olympic Games) because Apollo always wore a laurel leaf wreath. For more on the types of events held here during the games, see the Olympia chapter.

• *The museum is located 200 yards west of the Sanctuary of Apollo. Before heading in that direction, you might consider venturing a little farther out of town to reach the Kastalian Spring, gymnasium, and/or Sanctuary of Athena (all described later, under "Other Delphi Sights").*

DELPHI

▲▲▲Archaeological Museum

Delphi's compact-but-impressive museum houses a collection of ancient sculpture matched only by the National Archaeological and Acropolis museums in Athens.

Cost and Hours: €6 for museum, €9 combo-ticket includes archaeological site, same hours as Sanctuary of Apollo, tel. 22650-82312, www.culture.gr.

❍ **Self-Guided Tour:** Follow the one-way route, looking for the following highlights. Everything is well-described in English.

• *Show your ticket and head into the...*

First Room: This room holds the earliest traces of civilization at Delphi. Near the entry, find French architect Albert Tournaire's romantic rendering of how the Sanctuary of Apollo would have looked at its ancient peak. Also in this room is a giant bronze cauldron, which was once adorned with

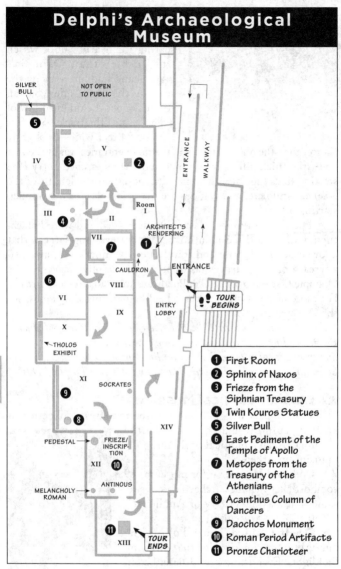

Delphi's Archaeological Museum

SILVER BULL

NOT OPEN TO PUBLIC

⑤

IV

③

V

②

III

④

II

Room I

VII

⑦

ARCHITECT'S RENDERING

①

CAULDRON

ENTRANCE

VIII

⑥

VI

IX

ENTRY LOBBY

ENTRANCE

👣🔊 TOUR BEGINS

X

THOLOS EXHIBIT

XI

SOCRATES

XIV

⑨

⑧

PEDESTAL

FRIEZE/INSCRIP-TION

XII

⑩

MELANCHOLY ROMAN

ANTINOUS

⑪

XIII

TOUR ENDS

WALKWAY

ENTRANCE

DELPHI

1 First Room
2 Sphinx of Naxos
3 Frieze from the Siphnian Treasury
4 Twin Kouros Statues
5 Silver Bull
6 East Pediment of the Temple of Apollo
7 Metopes from the Treasury of the Athenians
8 Acanthus Column of Dancers
9 Daochos Monument
10 Roman Period Artifacts
11 Bronze Charioteer

grotesque griffin heads.

• *Proceed into the next room, then turn right to find the...*

Sphinx of Naxos (c. 570-560 B.C.): This marble beast—a winged lion with a female face and Archaic smile (see photo on next page)—was once brightly painted, standing atop a 40-foot Ionic column in the sanctuary. The myth of the sphinx is Egyptian in origin, but she made a splash in Greek lore when she posed a

famous riddle to Oedipus at the gates of Thebes: "What walks on four legs in the morning, two at noon, and three at night?" Oedipus solved it: It's a man— who crawls in infancy, walks in adulthood, and uses a cane in old age.

• *Across the room, find the...*

Frieze from the Siphnian Treasury: This shows how elaborate the now-ruined treasuries in the sanctuary must have been. The east frieze (left wall) shows Greeks and Trojans duking it out. The gods to the left of the battle are rooting for the Trojans, with the Greek gods to the right. The north frieze (back wall) features scenes from the epic battle between the Greek gods and older race of giants.

• *Backtrack into the previous room, then turn right. You're face-to-face with...*

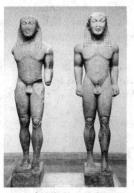

Twin Kouros Statues (c. 600-580 B.C.): These statues have the typical features of the Archaic period: placid smiles, stable poses facing the front, braided dreadlocks, and geometrical anatomy. These sturdy, seven-foot-tall athletes are the legendary twins of Argos, who yoked themselves to their mother's chariot and pulled her five miles so she wouldn't be late for the female Games (the Heraia). The twins were rewarded with death-by-blissful-sleep.

• *In the small room behind the twins (to the right) is what's left of a...*

Silver Bull: These silver-and-gold plates are the surviving fragments of a life-size bull from the sixth century B.C. The plates once covered a wooden statue of a bull. This bull and the other objects in the room were buried in ancient times (perhaps for safekeeping), and were discovered in the 20th century in a pit along the Sacred Way near the Treasury of the Athenians.

• *In the room after the twins, find the...*

East Pediment of the Temple of Apollo: This is what greeted visitors as they stood before the temple entrance. Though it's mostly fragments today, in the center you can make out some of the four horses that pulled Apollo in his chariot. To the right, a lion jumps on an animal's back and takes it down.

• *Continue into the next room, then turn left to find the...*

Metopes from the Treasury of the Athenians (510-480 B.C.): These carvings from the sanctuary's small surviving treasury

DELPHI

include (among other themes) six of the Twelve Labors of Hercules. In the most intact carving (directly to the left as you enter), Hercules is the one with curly hair and beard, inscrutable Archaic smile, and lion skin tied preppie-style around his neck.

• *Proceed through the next three rooms (the third of which has an exhibit with some pieces from the round tholos, at the Sanctuary of Athena). You'll wind up in a room with two monuments from the era of Alexander the Great, which once stood side by side in the sanctuary.*

Acanthus Column of Dancers: This giant leafy sculpture sat atop a 40-foot column to the right of the Temple of Apollo (on the same level as the theater). The three dancing girls originally carried a bronze tripod on their shoulders. Scholars now believe that this tripod supported the omphalos—the gigantic pinecone, which represented the "navel" of the world. The **omphalos** stone, now resting next to the column, is not "the" original stone marking the center of the earth, but it's a very old Roman-era copy. Nearby is the bottom of the column, which appears to be sprouting out of the ground.

• *Then as now, next to the column stand statues from the...*

Daochos Monument (c. 336-332 B.C.): Out of the nine original statues (count the footprints), today seven survive (OK, six—one is just a sandal). They have the relaxed poses and realistic detail of Hellenism. Daochos (center, wearing a heavy cloak) was a tetrarch under Alexander the Great. His family flanks him, including two of the three sons who were famous athletes, all of whom won laurel crowns at the same Pythian Games. Nude Agelaos (also in the center, armless with sinuous *contrapposto*) won running contests in Delphi. Aghias (to the right, with two partial arms and genitals) swept all four Panhellenic Games in *pangration*, a brutal sport that combined wrestling and boxing with few holds barred.

• *Across the room and facing these gents, notice the sculpture of bearded, balding Socrates, who was inspired by the mystery of this place. The next room features artifacts from the...*

Roman Period (191 B.C.-A.D. 394): The Romans made Delphi their own in 191 B.C. and left their mark. On the left are the frieze from the theater, and (high on the wall) an inscription from the proud Emperor Domitian, crowing that he had repaired the Temple of Apollo.

Across the room is the top of a pedestal erected by the arrogant King Perseus in anticipation of a military victory. Instead, the king was soundly defeated by Aemilius Paulus, who topped the pedestal with his own victory statue—and adorned it with a frieze of scenes depicting Perseus' defeat.

At the end of the room are two noteworthy sculptures. The small, lightly bearded head dubbed the "Melancholy Roman" (likely Titus Quinticus Flamininus, who proclaimed autonomy for the Greek state in 197 B.C.) demonstrates a masterful sense of emotion. Standing next to him is a full-size nude statue (minus its forearms) of Emperor Hadrian's young lover, Antinous. The handsome, curly-haired youth from Asia Minor (today's Turkey) drowned in the Nile in 130 B.C. A heartbroken Hadrian declared Antinous a god and erected statues of him everywhere, making him one of the most recognizable people from the

ancient world. Notice the small holes around his head, which were used to affix a bronze laurel wreath. Next to the sculpture, find the photo of excited archaeologists unearthing this strikingly intact specimen.

• *The grand finale is the museum's star exhibit, the...*

Bronze Charioteer: This young charioteer has just finished his victory lap, having won the Pythian Games of 474 B.C. Standing ramrod straight, he holds the reins lightly in his right hand, while his (missing) left hand was raised, modestly acknowledging the crowd.

This surviving statue was part of an original 3-D ensemble that greeted playgoers at the entrance to the theater. His (missing) chariot was (prob-

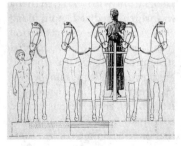

ably) pulled by four (mostly missing) horses, tended by a (missing) stable boy. Nearby, a case displays scant surviving chunks of the cart, the horse, and the stable boy's arm.

The statue is life-size (5'11") and lifelike. His fluted robe has straps around the waist and shoulders to keep it from ballooning out in the wind. He has a rounded face, full lips, awestruck eyes (of inset stones and enamel), and curly hair tied with the victor's headband.

The most striking thing is that—having just won an intense and dangerous contest—his face and attitude are calm and humble. The statue was cast when Greece was emerging from the horrors of the Persian invasion. The victorious charioteer expresses the sense of wonderment felt as Greece finally left the battle behind, gazed into the future, and rode triumphantly into the Golden Age.

As you exit the museum, examine the small model (in the lobby) of the sanctuary as it appeared in ancient times.

Other Delphi Sights

The first three listings below are associated with the Sanctuary of Apollo, are located along the main road beyond (to the east of) the site, and are free to enter. I've listed them in order, from nearest to farthest (you can walk to any of them, or you can simply view the gymnasium and the Sanctuary of Athena from the road in front of the site and museum). The last sight is at the very top of the town of Delphi, a steep walk or short drive up from the main drag.

Kastalian Spring—On the left side of the road, 800 yards past the archaeological site (around the jutting cliff), a spring bubbles forth from the ravine between the two Phaedriades rocks. It was here that Apollo slew the Python, taking over the area from the mother of the gods. Pilgrims washed here before consulting the oracle, and the water was used to ritually purify the oracle, the priests, and the Temple of Apollo. Today you can visit two ruined fountains (made of stone, with courtyards and benches to accommodate pilgrims) that tapped the ancient sacred spring. (Beware of Pythons.) Because of rock slides, the ravine is sometimes closed to visitors—but you can still see and hear the gurgling spring water.

Gymnasium—On the right side of the road, look for running tracks and a circular pool, where athletes trained for the Pythian Games.

Sanctuary of Athena—Farther along (also on the right side of the road) is a cluster of ruined temples. Because of the area's long association with Gaia, Athena was worshipped at Delphi along with Apollo. The star attraction is the *tholos* (c. 380 B.C.), a round structure whose exact purpose is unknown. While presumably less important than the Sanctuary of Apollo, its three reconstructed columns (of 20 Doric originals that once held up a conical roof)

DELPHI

have become the most-photographed spot in all of Delphi.

Museum of Delphic Festivals—Perched high on the hill above the town of Delphi, this old mansion explains the quest of beloved poet and local resident Angelos Sikelianos to create a new "Delphic Festivals" tradition in the 1920s. There's not much to see, aside from photos, costumes, and props of the event—which was held twice (in 1927 and 1930)—and some artifacts from Sikelianos' life. It's only worthwhile as an excuse for a strenuous hike (or quick drive) above town to grand vistas (€1, Thu-Mon 9:00-14:30, closed Tue-Wed, tel. 22650-82175).

Sleeping in Delphi

Spending the night in Delphi is a pleasant (and much cheaper) alternative to busy Athens. The town is squeezed full of hotels, which makes competition fierce and rates very soft—hoteliers don't need much of an excuse to offer a discount in slow times. When I've given a price range, it's based on demand (busiest April-May and Sept-Oct).

$$$ Hotel Leto is a class act with 22 smartly renovated rooms right in the heart of town (Sb-€45-60, Db-€60-85, air-con, mini-fridge, elevator, pay Internet access, free Wi-Fi, Apollonos 15, tel. 22650-82302, fax 22650-82303, www.leto-delphi.gr, info @leto-delphi.gr).

$$$ Hotel Acropole is a big but welcoming group-oriented hotel along the lower road. It's quieter and has better vistas than my other listings. Some of the 42 rooms feature view terraces for no extra charge; try to request one when you reserve (Sb-€64,

DELPHI

Sleep Code

(€1 = about $1.40, country code: 30)

S = Single, **D** = Double/Twin, **T** = Triple, **Q** = Quad, **b** = bathroom, **s** = shower only. Unless otherwise noted, credit cards are accepted and breakfast is included.

To help you easily sort through these listings, I've divided the rooms into three categories, based on the price for a standard double room with bath:

$$$ Higher Priced—Most rooms €60 or more.
$$ Moderately Priced—Most rooms between €35-60.
$ Lower Priced—Most rooms €35 or less.

Prices can change without notice; verify the hotel's current rates online or by email. For other updates, see www .ricksteves.com/update.

Db-€75, family suite with fireplace-€170, soft rates, 10 percent discount with this book, air-con, mini-fridge, elevator, pay Internet access, free Wi-Fi, 13 Filellinon, tel. 22650-82675, fax 22650-83171, www.delphi.com.gr, delphi@delphi.com.gr).

$$ Pitho Rooms ("Python") has eight good rooms above a gift shop on the main street. Your conscientious hosts, George and Vicky, pride themselves on offering a good value; they'll make you feel like part of the family (Sb-€40, Db-€50, Tb-€70, Qb-€75, air-con, no elevator, free Wi-Fi, Pavlou-Friderikis 40A, tel. 22650-82850, www.pithorooms.gr, pitho_rooms@yahoo.gr).

$$ Tholos Hotel has 20 clutter-free, quasi-Scandinavian rooms on the upper street, some with view balconies (Sb-€30-35, Db-€40-50, skip breakfast and save €5/person, air-con, no elevator, Apollonos 31, tel. & fax 22650-82268, www.tholoshotel.com, hotel_tholos@yahoo.gr).

$$ Hermes Hotel explodes with polished wood, cut glass, artwork, and even some fashionable mannequins in its public areas, but the 36 rooms are a bit drab in comparison (Sb-€40, Db-€50-60, ask for a room with a balcony, air-con, mini-fridge, elevator, free Wi-Fi, Pavlou-Friderikis 37, tel. 22650-82318).

$ Sibylla Hotel rents eight simple rooms at youth-hostel prices without a hint of youth-hostel grunge. No breakfast, no elevator, no air-conditioning...just good value (Sb-€24-26, Db-€28-34, mini-fridge, free Wi-Fi, Pavlou-Friderikis 9, tel. 22650-82335, fax 22650-83221, www.sibylla-hotel.gr, info@sibylla-hotel.gr, Christopoulos family).

Eating in Delphi

Delphi's eateries tend to cater to tour groups, with vast dining rooms and long tables stretching to distant valley-and-gulf views. The following restaurants distinguish themselves by offering high quality and good value. The first two are along the upper road (Apollonos), while the others cluster along the main road near the bus station. Look for the regional specialty, fried *formaela* cheese (spritz it with fresh lemon juice, then dig in).

Taverna Vakchos is homey and woody, with down-home, family-run charm. The focus is on tasty traditional dishes, such as *kokoras kokkinisto* (rooster cooked in red wine) and baked lamb with lemon sauce. For dessert, try the locally produced, farm-fresh yogurt with honey or grapes (€3-6 starters, €4-7 pastas, €7-14 main dishes, daily 12:00-16:00 & 18:30-22:30, Apollonos 31, tel. 22650-83186).

To Patriko Mas ("Our Family's Home") is a bit more upscale, with a classy stone-and-wood interior and a striking outdoor terrace clinging to the cliff face (€3-6 starters, €6-9 salads, €8-15 main dishes plus some splurges, daily 11:30-16:00 & 18:30-24:00, Pavlou-Friderikis 69, tel. 22650-82150, Konsta family).

Taverna Dion serves standard Greek fare at reasonable prices and specializes in grilled meats (€4-6 starters, €5-7 salads, €6-10 main dishes, Apollonos 30, tel. 22650-82790).

Taverna Gargadouas is proud *not* to cater to tour groups (it's too small). This simple taverna has a blaring TV in the corner and locals mixed in with the tourists, all here for affordable, unpretentious, traditional cuisine (€3-6 starters, €5-10 main dishes, €11-13 fixed-price meals, dinner only, next to bus station on main drag, tel. 22650-82488).

Picnics: Grocery stores and bakeries are well-marked along the main street. While picnics are not allowed inside the archaeological site, you could choose a perch along the road overlooking the vast valley.

Delphi Connections

By Bus

Delphi's one disadvantage is its distance from the other attractions described in this book (bus info tel. 22650-82317). Delphi is well-connected by bus to **Athens** (6/day—about every 3 hours, first bus from Athens to Delphi departs at 7:30, last bus from Delphi to Athens departs around 18:00—or 21:00 on Sun, 3-hour trip, €13.60 one-way). But connecting to the **Peloponnese** is long and complicated. For destinations in the eastern Peloponnese (such as **Nafplio**), it's best to go via Athens (see Athens bus connections on page 216). To the western Peloponnese, you'll connect through **Patra** (only one convenient bus per day from Delphi, departs around 13:15, arrives Patra 17:00, €13.60 one-way). From Patra, you can continue on to **Olympia** (via Pyrgos) or **Kardamyli** (via Kalamata). Either one is a very long trip, and the Delphi-Kardamyli trip can't be done in one day. For details on connections from Patra, see page 304.

Route Tips for Drivers

From Athens to Delphi: Head north (toward *Lamia/Λαμία*) on national road 1/expressway E75 (there are two toll booths). Take the second exit for ΘΕΒΑ/*Theba/Thiva*, which is also marked for *Livadia/Λιβαδειά*. From the turn-off, signs lead you (on road 3, then road 48) all the way to *Delphi/Δελφοί*.

From Delphi to the Peloponnese: As with the bus, for sights in the eastern Peloponnese (such as **Nafplio** or **Monemvasia**), it's faster to backtrack through Athens. (See page 219 for driving tips.)

To reach the western Peloponnese (such as **Olympia** or **Kardamyli/Mani Peninsula**), first follow the twisting road from

Delphi down toward Itea (Ιτέα) on the Gulf of Corinth, then follow signs toward *Galaxidi/Γαλαξίδι* and trace that body of water on a magnificently scenic, two-hour westward drive along road E65 (toward *Nafpaktos/Ναύπακτος*). Take your time and use the pullouts to enjoy the views. In Antirrio, follow signs for *Patra/Πάτρα* across the Rio-Antirrio suspension bridge (€12.20 toll) to the town of Rio. You'll enter the Peloponnese just north of the big port city of Patra (Πάτρα, described on page 302); ideally, skirt this city and head south another 1.5 hours along road E55 toward *Pyrgos/Πύργος*—be sure to get on the faster highway, with a green sign, instead of the slower regional road. (Note that attempting to "shortcut" through the middle of the Peloponnese takes you on some very twisty and slow mountain roads—avoid them unless you value scenery more than time.)

Once at Pyrgos, you can head east/inland to Ancient Olympia (Αρχαία Ολυμπία, well-marked with brown signs); or continue south to Kiparissia and Pilos, then eastward to Kalamata/*Καλαμάτα* (about two hours beyond Pyrgos; note that the Kalamata turnoff, just before Kiparissia, is not well-marked). From Kalamata, continue south another hour to Kardamyli.

DELPHI

GREEK ISLANDS

For many people, Greece is synonymous with islands. If you need a vacation from your busy mainland Greek vacation, the islands exert an irresistible pull.

Explore a tight, twisty maze of whitewashed cubic houses with vibrant trim. Dig your toes into the hot sand while basking

under a beach umbrella. Go for a dip in the crystal-clear, bathwater-warm Aegean. Nurse an iced coffee along a bustling harborfront, watching fishermen clean their catch while cuddly kittens greedily beg below. Dive into a succulent Greek salad at a rustic taverna, and chat with the big personality whose family has owned the place for generations, all while watching the sun gradually descend into the sea. Putter along remote-feeling roads across the spine of the island on a rented ATV, then drop down on a twisty lane to a desert-isle cove with an inviting beach. For all of these reasons, and more, the Greek islands live up to their worldwide acclaim.

While I appreciate a healthy dose of restorative island time, I prefer to spend my Greek vacation sightseeing and visiting its amazing wealth of ancient sights. That's why I cover just a few of Greece's islands (Hydra, Mykonos, and Santorini), and have instead focused this book on the bustling capital of Athens and Greece's "heartland," the Peloponnese, where (compared to the islands) I find the prices much lower, the people friendlier, and the opportunities to peel back layers of history more exciting. Still, if you want to sunbathe, swim, shop, eat, hike, sleep until noon, or

dance the night away to a thumping disco beat, the Greek islands definitely fit the bill.

Greece's Island Groups

Greece's roughly 6,000 islands and islets (227 of which are inhabited) are scattered far and wide across the eastern Mediterranean. Most are in the Aegean Sea (south and east of mainland Greece), while a few are in the Ionian Sea (west of the mainland). The islands are divided into distinct clusters:

The **Ionian Islands,** closer to Albania and Italy than to Athens, are Greece's northwest gateway to the Adriatic and the rest of Europe—they've had more foreign invaders and rulers (from Venice, France, Britain, Russia, Austria, and so on) than anywhere else in the country. The main island is  Corfu (Kerkyra in Greek), with a bustling, architecturally eclectic main town and a lush, green islandscape dotted with attractions and beaches.

The **Saronic Gulf Islands** (Argosaronikos), conveniently wedged between the Peloponnese and Athens, ooze charm and are particularly handy to visit from most of the other destinations in this book. They offer an enticing representative sample of the Greek island experience without requiring a lot of effort to get there. I've selected my favorite, **Hydra**, to cover here.

The **Sporades Islands,** due east of Athens, are dominated by the giant Evia island, which is attached to the mainland by a bridge. Thickly forested and less touristed by international visitors, the Sporades are a popular and handy weekend getaway for Athenians.

The **Cycladic Islands** (or simply **Cyclades**)—a bit farther south, between Athens and Crete—are the prototypical "Greek islands," boasting chalk-white houses with colorful windowsills and doorways; rocky, sun-parched landscapes; delightful beaches; old-fashioned white windmills topped with tufts of grass like unkempt hair; and an almost overwhelming crush of international visitors. I've covered the two best and most famous of the Cyclades in this book: **Mykonos** and **Santorini,** as well as the archaeological site of **Delos** (one of the most important locales of the ancient world) near Mykonos.

The **Dodecanese Islands,** at the sunny southeastern end of the Greek lands, are more rustic and less developed than the Cyclades. Their proximity to Turkey and historic ties to Venice give them a hybrid Turkish-Venetian flavor (though the population is mostly ethnic Greek, these islands merged with Greece only after World War II). Rhodes, with an appealing and very real-feeling Old Town, is the biggest of these islands.

GREEK ISLANDS

The **North Aegean Islands,** relatively untrampled and remote-feeling, lie roughly between Turkey and Thessaloniki (at the northern end of mainland Greece). The southernmost of these, Samos, is a particularly handy springboard for Turkey, as it's very close to the Turkish port city of Kuşadası (near the remarkable ancient site of Ephesus).

Crete is Greece's biggest island and practically a mini-state of its own (in fact, from 1897 to 1913 it was an autonomous state within the Ottoman Empire).

While many of Greece's smaller islands merit a day or two of fun in the sun, Crete could occupy even a busy traveler for a week or more. Historically, Crete was home to the Minoans—the earliest advanced European civilization, peaking around 1950 B.C., centuries before "the ancient Greeks" of Athens. While Crete's modern main city, Iraklio, is drab and uninviting, the rest of the island offers an engaging diversity of attractions: Minoan ruins, scenic mountains, enticing beaches, characteristic rustic villages, and dramatic caves and gorges (including the famous Samaria Gorge).

Choosing an Island

For this book, I've chosen to cover three of the most popular escapes. **Hydra** is my favorite, thanks to its speedy connections to Athens and the Peloponnese, its relaxing car-free ambience, and its charming harbor that invites you to just linger. Arguably the two most popular Greek islands are Mykonos and Santorini, both in the Cyclades and both relatively well-connected to Athens. **Mykonos** is an adorable, windmill-topped fishing village slathered in white and thronged by a hard-partying international crowd, enjoying its many beaches and side-tripping to the ruins on nearby Delos. **Santorini** is the most geologically interesting of all the Greek islands, and arguably the most picturesque, with idyllic villages perched on the rim of a collapsed and flooded volcano crater.

If you're choosing just one island, Hydra is a simple round-trip from Athens's port (Piraeus) and your closest foray into Greek island living. Farther-flung Mykonos and Santorini can be easily connected in a loop (they are linked to Piraeus, and to each other, by various boats and cheap flights). If your travels take you to islands beyond these three, pick up another guidebook to supplement the information here. In most cases, that perfect time-passed Greek island you hope to discover already has been—many times over. But it can still be satisfying to simply island-hop to determine your favorite.

As you explore, you'll discover that, while each Greek island has its own personality and claims to fame, most offer the same basic ingredients: a charming fishing village, once humble and poor, now a finely tuned machine for catering to (and collecting money from) a steady stream of tourists; a rugged interior with relatively little agriculture or industry, and rough roads connecting coastal coves; appealing beaches with rentable umbrellas and lounge chairs, presided over by tavernas and hotels; maybe a few dusty museums (with very short hours) collecting ancient artifacts or bits and pieces of local folklore; and occasionally a good or even great ancient site to tour.

Many islands have a main town, which is sometimes named for the island itself, or might be called Chora or Hora (Χώρα), which literally means "Village." This is generally the hub for transportation, both to other islands (port for passenger ferries and cruise ships) and within the island (bus station and taxi stand). Some islands—such as Rhodes, Corfu, and Crete—have large cities as their capitals.

Getting Around the Greek Islands

Greece's islands are connected to Athens' port (Piraeus) and to each other by a variety of ferries, ranging from hulking, slow-

moving car ferries to sleek, speedy catamarans. The faster the boat, the more you'll pay. Travelers who have the luxury of a relaxed itinerary might actually prefer to make their way gradually.

Because individual routes can be run by several different companies and boat schedules are often in flux, it's smart to do some preliminary research before your trip. A few helpful sites cover a range of companies (including www.openseas.gr, www.danae.gr/ferries-Greece.asp, and www.greekferries.gr). But be aware that ferry companies often post only their current schedule—if you're cruising the Web in January, you won't find sailing times for June. In Greece, local TIs, travel agents, and hoteliers can usually give you a basic rundown of your options (though beware that some travel agents might only tell you about the companies for which they sell tickets). For more tips on schedules, tickets, and specific connections from Piraeus, see page 210.

To save time, consider flying. Airlines that connect Athens to the islands at a reasonable cost include Olympic Airlines (tel. 210-356-9111, toll-free tel. 801-114-4444, www.olympicairlines.com), Aegean Airlines (tel. 210-626-1000, toll-free tel. 801-112-0000, www.aegeanair.com), and Sky Express (tel. 28102-23500, www.skyexpress.gr).

Understandably, the Greek islands are a major destination for cruise ships: With several enticing islands in close proximity, and big ports handy to captivating sights, Greece is made-to-order for cruising. If you're coming on a cruise, your challenge is that you'll arrive in town at precisely the same time as 2,000 other visitors—all hoping to fit the maximum amount of sightseeing, shopping, or beach time in a limited window of time. While there's little you can do to mitigate the crowds, getting as early a start as possible—and exploring the back lanes and beaches when the main drag gets too congested—can help. If you're not cruising, it's smart to be aware of when ships are scheduled to show up. If you're planning to visit outlying sights or beaches, do it when the ships are in port... by the time you return to town in the afternoon, the cruise-ship passengers will be loading up to leave again.

Accommodations

Greek-island accommodations range from basic (the rustic *dhomatia* rented by the elderly black-clad woman who meets backpackers at each arriving ferry) to plush (the chic designer hotel with spectacular views). Even out-of-the-way islands get heavy tourist traffic in the summer, so options abound. Some travelers just show up on the boat and are greeted by locals offering cheap beds; this can be a great way to find accommodations, but be very clear on the location before you agree.

At the busiest times (July-Sept, peaking in early to mid-Aug), visitors can outnumber beds; to get your choice of accommodations, consider booking ahead at these times. Also during these times, expect to pay (sometimes wildly) inflated prices; in the most popular destinations, such as Mykonos and Santorini, prices for even budget hotels can more than double during peak weeks. Other prices—such as scooter rentals and restaurant menus—also tend to increase when demand is high. Ideally visit just before or after these busy times, for the best combination of still-good weather, fewer crowds, and more reasonable prices.

Whenever you visit, enjoy your time here and simply give yourself over to the Greek islands. With a few exceptions, the "sights" (museums and ruins) are not worth going out of your way for—you're here to relax on the beach and explore the charming towns. Make the most of it.

HYDRA

ΎΔΡΑ / Ύδρα

Hydra (pronounced EE-drah, not HIGH-drah)—less than a two-hour boat ride from Athens' port, Piraeus—is a glamorous getaway that combines practical convenience with idyllic Greek island ambience. After the noise of Athens, Hydra's traffic-free tranquility is a delight. Donkeys rather than cars, the shady awnings of well-worn cafés, and memorable seaside views all combine to make it clear...you've found your Greek isle.

The island's main town, also called Hydra, is one of Greece's prettiest. Its busy but quaint harbor—bobbing with rustic fishing boats and luxury yachts—is surrounded by a ring of rocky hills and blanketed with whitewashed homes. From the harbor, a fleet of zippy water taxis whisk you to isolated beaches and tavernas. Hydra is an easy blend of stray cats, hardworking donkeys, welcoming Hydriots (as locals are called), and lazy tourists on "island time."

One of the island's greatest attractions is its total absence of cars and motorbikes. Sure-footed beasts of burden—laden with

everything from sandbags and bathtubs to bottled water—climb stepped lanes. While Hydra is generally quiet, dawn teaches visitors the exact meaning of "cockcrow." The end of night is marked with much more than a distant cock-a-doodle-doo; it's a dissonant chorus of cat fights, burro honks, and what sounds like roll call at an asylum for crazed roosters. After the animal population gets all that out of its system, the island slumbers a little longer.

Little Hydra—which has produced more than its share of

Hydra's Hystory

While it seems tiny and low-key, overachieving Hydra holds a privileged place in Greek history. The fate of Hydriots has always been tied to the sea, which locals have harnessed to their advantage time after time.

Many Hydriot merchants became wealthy running the British blockade of French ports during the Napoleonic Wars. Hydra enjoyed its glory days in the late 18th and early 19th centuries, when the island was famous for its shipbuilders. Hydra's prosperity earned it the nickname "Little England." As rebellion swept Greece, the island flourished as a safe haven for those fleeing Ottoman oppression.

When the Greeks launched their War of Independence in 1821, Hydra emerged as a leading naval power. The harbor, with its twin forts and plenty of cannons, housed and protected the fleet of 130 ships. Hydriots of note from this period include the naval officer Andreas Miaoulis, who led the "firebrands" and their deadly "fireships," which succeeded in decimating the Ottoman navy (see page 386); and Lazaros Kountouriotis, a wealthy shipping magnate who donated his fleet to the cause (see page 391).

Greece won its independence, but at a great cost to Hydra, which lost many of its merchant-turned-military ships to the fighting...sending the island into a deep economic funk. During those lean post-war years, Hydriots again found salvation in the sea, farming the sponges that lived below the surface (sponge-divers here pioneered the use of diving suits). Gathering sponges kick-started the local economy and kept Hydra afloat.

In 1956, Sophia Loren came here to play an Hydriot sponge-diver in the film *Boy on a Dolphin,* propelling the little island onto the international stage. And the movie's plot—in which a precious ancient sculpture is at risk of falling into the hands of a greedy art collector instead of being returned to the Greek government—still resonates with today's Greeks, who want to reclaim their heritage for the Acropolis Museum.

Thanks largely to the film, by the 1960s Hydra had become a favorite retreat for celebrities, well-heeled tourists, and artists and writers, who still draw inspiration from the idyllic surroundings. Canadian songwriter Leonard Cohen lived here for a time—and was inspired to compose his beloved song "Bird on the Wire" after observing just that here on Hydra. Today visitors only have to count the yachts to figure out that Hydra's economy is still based on the sea.

Hydra Island

SARONIC GULF — TO POROS & PIRAEUS — CAPE ZOURVA — MANDRAKI BAY — TO ERMIONI, METOCHI & SPETSES — KAMINIA — VLYCHOS — HYDRA TOWN — LIMNIONIZA — BISTI — MOLOS — NISIZA — AG. NIKOLAOS — DCH

1 MILE / 1 KM

•••• HYDROFOIL/CATAMARAN
···· WATER TAXI
--- TRAILS
🏖 BEACHES

military heroes, influential aristocrats, and political leaders—is packed with history. Rusted old cannons are scattered about town; black, pitted anchors decorate squares; and small museums hold engaging artifacts. But most visitors enjoy simply being on vacation here. Loiter around the harbor. Go on a photo safari for donkeys and kittens. Take a walk along the coast or up into the hills. Head for an inviting beach, near or far, to sunbathe and swim. Hang out past your bedtime in a cocktail bar. Hydra's the kind of place that makes you want to buy a bottle of ouzo and toss your itinerary into the sea.

Planning Your Time

While Hydra can be done as a long day trip from Athens, it's better to spend two nights (or more) to take full advantage of the island's many dining options, and to give yourself a whole day to relax.

To get your bearings, take my brief self-guided walk as soon as you arrive. While the walk gives you the historic context of the town, it also points out practical stops that will make your stay more efficient and enjoyable (and finishes at a wonderful little bakery). You'll still have ample time for your choice of activities—dipping into a museum that tickles your curiosity, enjoying a drink at a café, going for a hike into the hills, walking along the water to nearby villages and beaches, or catching a shuttle boat or water taxi for a spin around the island.

Orientation to Hydra

Remember, Hydra is the name of both the island and its main town (home to about 90 percent of the island's 3,000 residents). Hydra town climbs up the hill in every direction from the port.

HYDRA

Branching off from the broad café-lined walkway at the bottom of the harbor are four major streets. In order from the boat dock, these are called Tompazi, Oikonomou, Miaouli, and Lignou. Not that street names mean much in this town—locals ignore addresses, and few lanes are labeled. Though the island is small, Hydra's streets twist defiantly to and fro. If seeking a specific location, use the map in this chapter or ask a local. (Note that, like our map, most maps of Hydra show the harbor—which is actually to the north—at the bottom.) Expect to get lost in Hydra...and enjoy it when you do.

Consider venturing beyond Hydra town to settlements and beaches elsewhere on the island. The most accessible is the tiny seaside hamlet of Kaminia, which lies just over the headland west of the harbor (with a good restaurant—see "Eating in Hydra," later).

Tourist Information

Hydra has no TI. The Hydreoniki Travel Agency across from the hydrofoil/catamaran dock can help with information on transportation (tel. 22980-54007, www.hydreoniki.gr); or you can visit the Hellenic Seaways ticket office near the Alpha Bank, down the alley from the harbor by the bakery. For urgent questions, the municipal office facing the harbor between the fort and the museum is friendly (generally open Mon-Fri 9:00-14:00). Useful websites include www.hydradirect.com and www.hydra.com.gr.

Arrival on Hydra

All catamarans and hydrofoils dock in the heart of Hydra town's harbor (along its eastern edge). All of my recommended accommo-

dations are within a 10-minute walk (and located on the map on pages 384-385). At the port, you can hire a donkey to carry your bags (€10-15, establish the price up front). If you ask, better hotels will often meet you at the boat and help with your bags.

Getting Around Hydra

As there are no cars, your options are by foot, donkey, or boat. You'll walk everywhere in town. While you can hike to neighboring beaches, it's fun to hop a **shuttle boat** (€2.50 to Vlychos with boats leaving on the half-hour, catch shuttles in front of the clock tower) or take a **water taxi** (much more expensive unless you're a small group—same rate for one person or eight). You'll see the red taxi boats stacked and waiting near the donkeys on the harborfront. Sample taxi fares: €10 to Kaminia, €14 to Mandraki Bay (there's a fare board lashed to the pole by the taxi dock, with the English translation hiding on the back side). To get back to town via water taxi, call 22980-53690.

Helpful Hints

Internet Access: Flamingo Internet Café—which has no sign and looks like a big grocery store—is 50 yards from the harbor, on Tompazi (€3/30-minute minimum, daily 12:00-23:00, right side of the street, tel. 22980-53485).

Post Office: The post office (Mon-Fri 7:30-14:00, closed Sat-Sun) faces the outdoor market (just inland from the harbor).

Bookshop: Hydra's no-name bookshop—which sells maps, books about Hydra, and a few books in English (mostly translations of Greek literature)—is just up from the harbor on the stepped lane called Lignou (Mon-Sat 10:00-13:00 & 17:00-19:00, closed Sun).

Drinking Water: While the island's name means "water" in ancient Greek, that was a long time ago. Today there's no natural water source on Hydra (other than private cisterns). Water is barged in daily. No one drinks the tap water here— cheap bottled water is sold everywhere.

Self-Guided Walk

Hydra's Harbor

Hydra clusters around its wide harbor, squeezed full of fishing boats, pleasure craft, luxury yachts, and the occasional Athens-bound hydrofoil or catamaran. Get the lay of the land with this lazy 30-minute stroll.

• *Begin at the tip of the port (to the right, as you face the sea). Climb the stairs (by the cactus) to the cannon-studded turret. From here, you have a fine...*

View of the Harbor

The harbor is the heart and soul of Hydra. Looking at the arid, barren mountains rising up along the spine of the island, it's clear that not much grows here—so the Hydriots have always turned to the sea for survival. As islanders grew wealthy from the sea trade, prominent local merchant families built the grand mansions that rise up between the modest whitewashed houses blanketing the

HYDRA

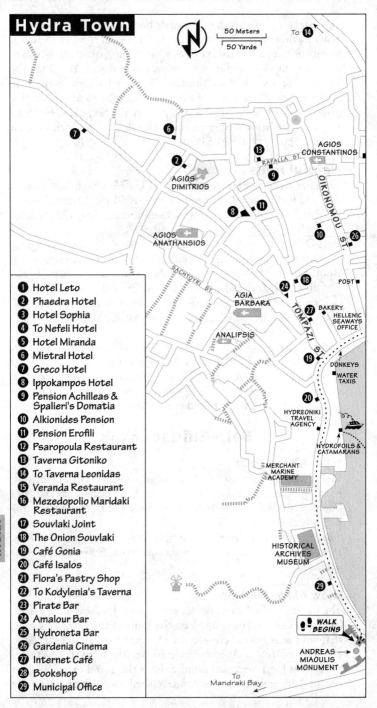

Hydra Town

50 Meters
50 Yards

To ⑭

1. Hotel Leto
2. Phaedra Hotel
3. Hotel Sophia
4. To Nefeli Hotel
5. Hotel Miranda
6. Mistral Hotel
7. Greco Hotel
8. Ippokampos Hotel
9. Pension Achilleas & Spalieri's Domatia
10. Alkionides Pension
11. Pension Erofili
12. Psaropoula Restaurant
13. Taverna Gitoniko
14. To Taverna Leonidas
15. Veranda Restaurant
16. Mezedopolio Maridaki Restaurant
17. Souvlaki Joint
18. The Onion Souvlaki
19. Café Gonia
20. Café Isalos
21. Flora's Pastry Shop
22. To Kodylenia's Taverna
23. Pirate Bar
24. Amalour Bar
25. Hydroneta Bar
26. Gardenia Cinema
27. Internet Café
28. Bookshop
29. Municipal Office

HYDRA

AGIOS CONSTANTINOS
RAFALLA ST.
AGIOS DIMITRIOS
OIKONOMOU ST.
AGIOS ANATHANSIOS
SACHTOYRI ST.
POST
AGIA BARBARA
TOMPAZI ST.
BAKERY
HELLENIC SEAWAYS OFFICE
ANALIPSIS
DONKEYS
WATER TAXIS
HYDREONIKI TRAVEL AGENCY
HYDROFOILS & CATAMARANS
MERCHANT MARINE ACADEMY
HISTORICAL ARCHIVES MUSEUM
WALK BEGINS
ANDREAS MIAOULIS MONUMENT
To Mandraki Bay

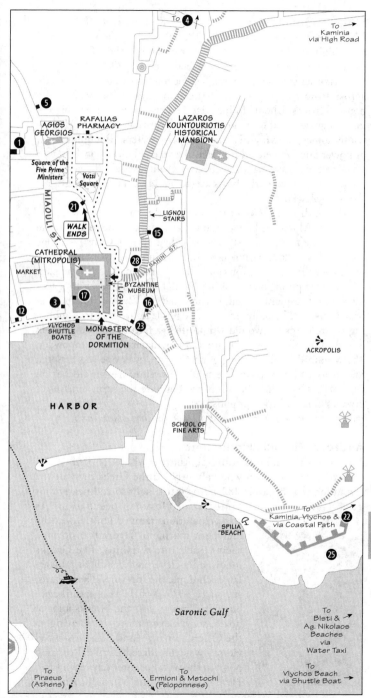

To **4**

To
Kaminia
via High Road

5

1

AGIOS
GEORGIOS

RAFALIAS
PHARMACY

LAZAROS
KOUNTOURIOTIS
HISTORICAL
MANSION

Square of the
Five Prime
Ministers

Votsi
Square

21

WALK
ENDS

LIGNOU
STAIRS

MIAOULI ST.

15

SAHINI ST.

CATHEDRAL
(MITROPOLIS)

28

MARKET

12

3

17

LIGNOU

BYZANTINE
MUSEUM

16

VLYCHOS
SHUTTLE
BOATS

MONASTERY
OF THE
DORMITION

23

ACROPOLIS

HARBOR

SCHOOL OF
FINE ARTS

To
Kaminia, Vlychos &
via Coastal Path

22

SPILIA
"BEACH"

25

Saronic Gulf

To
Bisti &
Ag. Nikolaos
Beaches
via
Water Taxi

To Piraeus
(Athens)

To
Ermioni & Metochi
(Peloponnese)

To
Vlychos Beach
via Shuttle Boat

HYDRA

hillsides. One of these—the Lazaros Kountouriotis Historical Mansion—is open to the public (the yellow mansion with the red roof, high on the hill across the harbor and to the left, with the small, red bell tower nearby; described later).

Another mansion, the rough stone four-story building directly across from the port (behind the imposing zigzag wall), now houses Hydra's School of Fine Arts. Artists—Greek and foreign—have long swooned over the gorgeous light that saturates Hydra's white homes, brown cliffs, and turquoise waters. The unique mix of power and art here adds to the charm of Hydra. Locals like to imagine Hydra as an ancient theater: The houses are the audience, the port is the stage, the boats are actors...and the Saronic Gulf is the scenic backdrop.

Look directly across the mouth of the harbor, to the opposite point. Along the base of the walkway, under the seafront café tables, is the town's closest "beach," called Spilia ("Cave")—a concrete pad with ladders luring swimmers into the cool blue. For a more appealing option, you can follow the paved, mostly level path around this point to the fishing hamlet of Kaminia (with a scenic seafood restaurant) and, beyond that, to Vlychos (for the best beach around). Visually trace the ridgeline above that trail, noticing the remains of two old windmills—a fixture on many Greek islands, used for grinding grain and raw materials for gunpowder. The windmills' sails are long gone, but the lower one was restored for use as a film prop (for the Sophia Loren film—see sidebar on page 380). Crowning the hill high above are the scant remains of Hydra's humble little acropolis.

• *Turn your attention to the centerpiece of this viewpoint, the...*

Andreas Miaoulis Monument

The guy at the helm is Admiral Andreas Miaoulis (1768-1835), an Hydriot sea captain who valiantly led the Greek navy in the revolution that began in 1821. This war sought to end nearly four

centuries of Ottoman occupation. As war preparations ramped up, the wealthy merchant marine of Hydra transformed their vessels into warships. The Greeks innovated a clever and deadly naval warfare technique: the "fireship." (For details, see page 391.) While this kamikaze-burning strategy cost the Greeks a lot of boats, it was even more devastating to the Ottoman navy—and Miaoulis' naval victory was considered a crucial turning point in the war. For three days each June, Hydra celebrates the Miaoulia Festival, when they set fire to an old ship to commemorate the burning of the Ottoman fleet.

On the monument, the cross that hangs from the steering column represents the eventual triumph of the Christian Greeks over the Muslim Ottomans. Miaoulis' bones are actually inside the stone pedestal under the statue. The three flags above honor the EU, Greece, and Hydra.

• *Head back down the stairs and begin walking along the harborfront.*

Along the Harbor

After passing the municipal office and the port authority, you reach the stout stone mansion that houses the **Historical Archives Museum.** This small but good collection (described later, under "Sights in Hydra") does its best to get visitors excited about Hydra's history. The gap after the museum is filled with monuments honoring Hydriot heroes. The green plaque in the pillar is a gift from Argentina, to honor an Hydriot aristocrat who fought in the Argentinean war for independence. The next building is the Merchant Marine Academy, where Hydra continues to churn out sailors—many of whom often hang around out front. (During the WWII occupation of Greece, this building was used as a Nazi base.) Next, the row of covered metal benches marks the embarkation point for the hydrofoils ("Flying Dolphins") and catamarans ("Flying Cats") that connect Hydra to Athens and other Greek islands (for those of us who lack yachts of our own).

Notice the three flags—specifically the **flag of Hydra** (which you'll see all over town)—flapping in the breeze. Dating from the uprising against the Ottomans, it's loaded with symbolism: the outline of the island of Hydra topped with a cross, a flag with a warrior's helmet, and an anchor—all watched over by the protective eye of God. The inscription, Η ΤΑΝ Η ΕΠΙ ΤΑΣ, means "with it or on it," and evokes the admonition of the warlike Spartans when sending their sons into battle with their huge shields: Come back "with it," victorious and carrying your shield; or "on it," dead, with your shield serving as a stretcher to carry your body home.

When you reach the corner of the harbor, you'll likely see **donkeys and mules** shooing flies as they wait to plod into town with visitors' luggage lashed to their backs. The donkeys are not just a touristy gimmick, but a lifestyle choice: Hydriots have decided not to allow any motorized vehicles on their island, keeping this place quiet and tranquil, and cutting down on pollution (unless you count dung). This means that, aside from a few garbage trucks, these beasts of burden are the only way to get around. It's not unusual to see one with a major appliance strapped to its back, as it gingerly navigates the steps up to the top of town. Locals dress their burros up with rugs, beads, and charms. Behind each mule-train toils a human pooper-scooper. On Hydra, a traffic jam looks like a farm show. And instead of the testosterone-fueled revving of moped engines, Hydra's soundtrack features the occasional, distant whinnying of a donkey echoing over the rooftops.

In the same corner as the donkeys is the dock for the feisty fleet of red **water taxis.** These zip constantly from here to remote points around the island.

The recommended **Café Gonia** ("Corner Café") nearby is a fun place to nurse a drink while watching the action here at the liveliest spot in town.

Hang a right and continue along the bottom of the harbor, noting the **six streets** that lead into town from here. At this corner (next to the Alpha Bank) is Tompazi, which quickly becomes a twisty warren of lanes with many hotels. Next is a tiny dead-end lane leading to a good bakery. Skinny Oikonomou Street, between the two banks, leads to shops and the open-air movie theater. A few steps farther, another narrow lane leads to the post office, public WC, and Hydra's ramshackle little outdoor market (mornings only). The next road, Miaouli, feels like Hydra's "Main Street," bustling with tavernas and a popular souvlaki joint. And the final street, Lignou, is next to the monastery at the far corner of the port. We'll venture up this lane at the end of this walk.

As you explore this harborfront area, window-shop the **cafés** and choose one to return to later. Overhead, notice the ingenious rope system the seafaring Hydriots have rigged up, so that they can quickly draw a canopy over the seating area—like unfurling the sails on a ship—in the event of rain...or, more common here, overpowering sunshine. While you sip your drink, you can watch simple fishing boats squeeze between the luxury yachts to put in and unload their catch...eyed hungrily by scrawny cats.

Shuttle boats line up in front of the clock tower. They offer cheap rides to points around the island—a service much appreciated by the owners of Hydra's many remote cafés and tavernas (but which angers the water-taxi drivers).

You'll also spot plenty of **jewelry shops** along here. Hydra is known for its jewelry. A few shops sell the handiwork of Hydriot designers and artists (such as Zoe and Elena Votsi), which you'd be hard-pressed to find anywhere but here.

• *At the end of the harbor stands a symbol of Hydra, the clock tower of the...*

Monastery of the Dormition

Hydra's ecclesiastical center is dedicated to the Dormition of the Virgin. "Dormition"—loosely translated as "falling asleep"—is a

pleasant Greek euphemism for death. While Roman Catholic views differ, Orthodox Christians believe Mary died a human death, then (like her son) was resurrected three days later, before being assumed into heaven.

Go through the archway under the tower, and you'll emerge into what was, until 1832, an active monastery. The double-decker arcade of cells circling the courtyard was once the monks' living quarters; it now houses the offices of the city government and mayor.

The monastery's church, which doubles as Hydra's *mitropolis* (cathedral), is free to enter. Stepping inside, it's clear that this was a wealthy community— compare the marble iconostasis, silver chandelier, gorgeous *Pantocrator* dome decoration, rich icons, and frescoes with the humbler decor you'll see at small-town churches elsewhere in Greece. Just inside the door (to the left), the icon of the Virgin and Child is believed to work miracles. Notice the many votive rings and necklaces draping it as a thank-you for prayers answered.

Back in the courtyard, you'll see war memorials and monuments to beloved Hydriots. The humble Byzantine Museum (up the stairs across the courtyard) displays a few rooms of glittering icons, vestments, and other ecclesiastical paraphernalia (€2, some English labels but not much information, generally Tue-Sun 10:00-14:00, closed Mon).

• *Return to the harborfront, then head inland (under the church's smaller bell tower) up Lignou Street. After a few steps, at the butcher's shop, you find a fork. The right branch climbs some steps to the upper reaches of town, including the Lazaros Kountouriotis Historical Mansion (described later), and eventually leads over the headland and down to the village of Kaminia. But let's take the left branch, to the orange-tree-filled square.*

Upper Town Squares

Tidy **Votsi Square** has a chess set, cannon, and lots of cats. Hydriots love their cats, which have a similar temperament: tender, relaxed, but secretly vigilant and fiercely independent. At the bottom of the square (on the left) is Flora's Pastry Shop, where we'll finish our stroll.

For now, keep walking about 100 feet above the square until the lane hits the old-time **Rafalias Pharmacy.** The pharmacy is an institution in town, and Vangelis Rafalias has kept it just as his grandfather did. He welcomes the browsing public, so take a look. Just inside the window (far right) is a photo of Jackie Onassis visiting Hydra. (If you like to dance, Rafalias runs tango classes each summer in the big garden behind his pharmacy.)

Facing the pharmacy, one lane leads to the right, heading uphill to the site of the original town, which was positioned inland to be safely away from marauding pirates. We'll head in the other direction, left, to the little **Square of the Five Prime Ministers.** The monument, with five medallions flanked by cannons, celebrates the five Hydriots who were chosen for Greece's highest office in the nearly two centuries since independence. It's an impressive civic contribution from a little island town, and perhaps due to Hydra's seafaring wealth and its proximity to the Greek capitals (Nafplio, then Athens). From here, narrow, stepped, cobblestone lanes invite exploration of Hydra's quiet side.

But for now, continue left and downhill, back to Votsi Square. The recommended **Flora's Pastry Shop** (daily 7:00-24:00) is at the bottom of the square, on the right. Treat yourself to a homemade ice cream or baklava. Or, for something more traditional, try the local favorite—*galaktoboureko* (gha-lahk-toh-boo-re-KOH), which is cinnamon-sprinkled egg custard baked between layers of phyllo.

Sights in Hydra

▲**Historical Archives Museum**—This fine little museum, in an old mansion right along the port, shows off a small, strangely fascinating collection of Hydra's history and has good English descriptions throughout.

Cost and Hours: €5, includes temporary art exhibit on ground floor, March-Oct daily 9:00-16:00 & 19:30-21:30, closed Nov-Feb, along the eastern side of the harbor near the hydrofoil/catamaran dock, tel. 22980-52355, www.iamy.gr.

◗ **Self-Guided Tour:** The core of the exhibit is upstairs. At the top of the stairs, look straight ahead for a tattered, yellowed **old map** by Rigas Feraios from 1797. Depicting a hypothetical and generously defined "Hellenic Republic," it claims virtually the entire Balkan Peninsula (from the Aegean to the Danube) for Greece. The map features historical and cultural tidbits of the time (such as drawings of coins from various eras), making it a treasure trove for historians. Drawn at a time when the Greeks had been oppressed by the Ottomans for centuries, the map—with 1,200 copies printed and distributed—helped to rally support for what would become a successful revolution starting in 1821.

The stairwell to the top floor is lined with portraits of **"firebrands"**—sailors (many of them Hydriots) who burned the Ottoman fleet during the war. They were considered the "body and soul" of the Greek navy in 1821. To learn more about their techniques, head behind the map and veer left into a long, narrow room; in its center, find the **model of a "fireship"** used for these attacks. These vessels were loaded with barrels of gunpowder, with large ventilation passages cut into the deck and hull. Suspended from the masts were giant, barbed, fishing-lure-like hooks. (Two actual hooks flank the model.) After ramming an enemy ship and dropping the hooks into its deck to attach the two vessels, the Greek crew would light the fuse and escape in a little dinghy... leaving their ship behind to become a giant firetrap, engulfing the Ottoman vessel in flames. Also in this room are nautical maps and models and paintings of other Hydriot vessels.

Continuing into the biggest room (immediately behind the old map), you'll see a Greek urn in the center containing the actual, embalmed **heart** of local hero Andreas Miaoulis. On the walls are portraits of V.I.H.s—very important Hydriots. Rounding out the collection is a small room of **weapons.**

Lazaros Kountouriotis Historical Mansion—Because of Hydra's merchant-marine prosperity, the town has many fine aristocratic mansions...but only this one is open to the public. Lazaros Kountouriotis (koon-doo-ree-OH-tees, 1769-1852) was a wealthy Hydriot shipping magnate who helped fund the Greek War of Independence. He donated 120 of his commercial ships to be turned into warships, representing three-quarters of the Greek navy. Today Kountouriotis is revered as a local and national hero, and his mansion offers a glimpse into the lifestyles of the 18th-century Greek rich and famous.

The main building of Kountouriotis' former estate is a fine example of aristocratic Hydriot architecture of the late 18th century, combining elements of Northern Greek, Saronic Gulf

Island, and Italian architecture. The house has barely changed since its heyday. You'll enter on the second floor, with several period-decorated rooms. These reception rooms have beautiful wood-paneled ceilings, and are furnished with all the finery of the period. Included is the states-man's favorite armchair, where you can imagine him spending many hours pondering the shape of the emerging Greek nation. Then you'll head upstairs to see a collection of traditional costumes and jewelry from throughout Greece, labeled in English. The lower floor displays the art of the local Byzantinos family: father Pericles (hazy, Post-Impressionistic landscapes and portraits) and son Constantinos (dark sketches and boldly colorful modern paintings).

Cost and Hours: €4, April-Oct daily 10:00-14:00 & 18:00-21:00, closed Nov-March, on the hillside above town, signposted off the stepped Lignou Street, tel. 22980-52421.

Beaches

Although Hydra's beaches are nothing to get excited about, there's no shortage of places to swim. There's one beach in Hydra town—the rest are reachable by foot, shuttle boat, or water taxi. Three decent beaches within a pleasant, easy walk of Hydra are Mandraki Bay, Kaminia Castello, and Vlychos. Distant beaches on the southwestern tip of the island (Bisti and Ag. Nikolaos) really get you away from it all, but are best reached by boat.

Spilia—The only spot to swim in town is Spilia ("Cave"), at the western entrance to Hydra harbor. There you'll find steps that lead down to a series of small concrete platforms with ladders into the sea—but no showers or changing rooms. (While Spilia appears to belong to the adjacent café, anyone is welcome to swim here.)

Mandraki Bay—This reasonable pebble beach is near the main coastal path to the east of Hydra (30-minute walk from the eastern end of the harbor, regular shuttle boat from Hydra). It's dominated by the Hotel Miramare, which rents windsurfing boards and other water-sports equipment, but you don't need to be a hotel guest to use the beach.

Kaminia Castello Beach—To the west of town is the delightful little harbor of Kaminia (15-minute walk). Just beyond that, you'll find a new restaurant and bar called Castello above the small Kaminia Castello Beach. While handy, the beach is bullied by the musical taste of the kids who run the bar and is often crowded with lots of families. For walking directions, see "Walks," later.

Vlychos Beach—Located past Kaminia, this is my favorite. Like a little tropical colony, 20 thatched umbrellas mark a quiet stretch of pebbly beach. You'll pay €3 for a lounge chair and €3 for an umbrella. There are showers, a café, and the Marina Taverna for a meal (daily 12:00-24:00, tel. 22980-52496). A shuttle boat zips from Hydra to Vlychos twice an hour (leaving Hydra on the half-hour, until 20:00, €2.50). The 40-minute walk from Hydra to Vlychos is great (described next).

Walks

From Hydra to Kaminia and Vlychos—The walk from Hydra town to the cute cove of Kaminia and the excellent beach at Vlychos (both described earlier) is one of my favorites. While the walk leads to two beaches, it's perfectly pleasant whether or not you're taking a dip.

For the easy approach, simply follow the mostly level coastal path that runs west from Hydra town to the villages of Kaminia and Vlychos. As you curve out of Hydra, you'll pass the town's best-preserved windmill, which was reconstructed for the 1957 Sophia Loren film *Boy on a Dolphin*. Look for a plaque at the wind-mill honoring the film that attracted many celebrities to Hydra.

After about 15 minutes, you'll find yourself in delightful **Kaminia,** where two dozen tough little fishing boats jostle within a breakwater. With cafés, a tiny beach, and a good taverna (see page 399), this is a wonderful place to watch island life go by.

Continue through Kaminia where the donkey path climbs a cliff, passing Kaminia Castello Beach. Soon you're all alone with great sea views. Ten minutes or so later, you round a bluff, descend into a ravine, cross an Ottoman-style bridge with an evocative single-pointed arch, and drop into **Vlychos,** with its welcoming little beach.

From Vlychos, a different, high trail leads back into Hydra (30 minutes, lit at night).

The Hydra-Kaminia High Road: For an alternate route to Kaminia, find your way up Hydra's maze of stepped lanes that lace the hills just west and south of town. Here, shabby homes enjoy grand views, tethering off-duty burros seems unnecessary, and island life trudges on, oblivious to tourism. Feel your way up and over the headland, then descend into Kaminia. Along the way, look for dry, paved riverbeds, primed for the flash floods that fill village cisterns each winter. (You can also climb all the way up to the remains of Hydra's humble acropolis, topping the hill due west of the harbor.)

More Walks and Hikes—Beyond walking to a nearby beach, Hydra is popular for its network of ancient paths that link the island's outlying settlements, churches, and monasteries. Most of the paths are well maintained and clearly marked, but serious hikers should pick up a copy of Anavasi's excellent 1:25,000 map of Hydra (€5, sold locally). If you do venture into the hills, wear sturdy shoes, sunscreen, and a hat, and take your own water and picnic supplies.

HYDRA

Nightlife in Hydra

Locals, proud of the extravagant yachts that flock to the island, like to tell of movie stars who make regular visits. But the island is so quiet that, by midnight, all the high-rollers seem to be back onboard watching movies.

And yet, there are plenty of options to keep visitors busy. People enjoy watching a film at the town's outdoor cinema or nursing a drink along the harborfront—there are plenty of mellow cocktail bars proudly serving "Paradise in a Glass" for €8.

Pirate Bar is run by a hardworking family serving drinks and light bites all day long from a prime spot on the water, at the little lane just past Lignou. The son, Zeus, runs the night shift and is famous for his Lychee Martini. This is a mellow, trendy spot to be at late at night (tel. 22980-52711).

Amalour Bar, run by Alexandros and his gang of good-looking bald guys, is "the place to fall in love" (or just enjoy wonderful music and good drinks). There's no sea view here—just cool music played at the right volume inside, and tables outside tumbling down a cobbled lane. It's easy jazz until midnight, and then harder music (€6 cocktails during the 20:00-23:00 nightly "happy hour," just up Tompazi Street from the harbor, mobile 697-746-1357).

Hydroneta Bar, catering to a younger crowd with younger music, offers great sea views from under the "Sofia Loren windmill," with a bunch of romantic tables nestled within the ramparts and cannons (tel. 22980-54166). Reach it by walking along the coastline past Spilia Beach and through the Sunset Restaurant. This and the neighboring Spilia cocktail bar charge €10 for cocktails and are the most touristy of Hydra's nightlife choices.

Gardenia Cinema is part of a great Greek summer tradition: watching movies in the open air. Hydra's delightful outdoor theater is right in the center of town on Oikonomou Street; it shows movies in the original language on summer weekends (€8, May-Sept Fri-Sun at 21:00 and 23:00).

Sleeping in Hydra

Hydra has ample high-quality accommodations. Unfortunately, the prices are also high—more expensive than anywhere on the Peloponnese, and rivaling those in Athens. Prices max out in the summer (June-Sept), and I've generally listed these top rates.

Sleep Code

(€1 = about $1.40, country code: 30)
S = Single, **D** = Double/Twin, **T** = Triple, **Q** = Quad, **b** = bathroom,
s = shower only. Unless otherwise noted, breakfast is included,
credit cards are accepted, and the staff speaks English.

To help you easily sort through these listings, I've divided
the rooms into three categories, based on the price for a
standard double room with bath:

$$$ Higher Priced—Most rooms €110 or more.
 $$ Moderately Priced—Most rooms between €65-110.
  $ Lower Priced—Most rooms €65 or less.

Prices can change without notice; verify the hotel's
current rates online or by email. For other updates, see www
.ricksteves.com/update.

Outside of these times, most accommodations offer discounts (even
if not noted here)—always ask. Longer stays might also garner you
a deal. If you're stuck, the boat ticket offices on the harborfront
might be able to help you find a room. If you arrive with no reservation and sniff around, you can generally find a rough little place
with soft prices renting doubles for around €50. Some cheaper
hotels don't provide breakfast, in which case you can eat for around
€5 at various cafés around town. Communication can be challenging at a few of the cheaper places (as noted). If there's an elevator
anywhere in town, I didn't see it (though no hotel has more than
three stories). Because the town has a labyrinthine street plan and
most people ignore street names, I list no addresses, so use the map
on pages 384-385. Most accommodations in Hydra close down for
the winter (typically Nov-Feb, sometimes longer). The lack of local
spring water means that Hydra's very hard water is shipped in from
wetter islands, which can make showering or doing laundry—and
rinsing out stubborn suds—an odd frustration. When I'm here in
the summer, I take several showers a day to cool off, but I don't
bother washing my hair.

Splurges with Character

$$$ Hotel Leto is the island's closest thing to a business-class
hotel, offering great service with a professional vibe, 21 elegantly
decorated rooms, and inviting public spaces (Db-€165-185, air-con,
free Wi-Fi, tel. 22980-53385, fax 22980-53806, www.letohydra.gr,
letoydra@otenet.gr, Kari).

$$$ Phaedra Hotel rents seven spacious, beautifully deco-
rated, and well-cared-for rooms. Delightfully helpful owner Hilda

takes pride in her hotel, and it shows (Sb-€120, standard Db-€135, superior Db with balcony-€160, apartment-€180 for four, family suites, prices soft off-season, open year-round, air-con, free Wi-Fi, tel. 22980-53330, mobile 697-221-3111, www.phaedrahotel.com, info@phaedrahotel.com).

$$$ Hotel Sophia is a plush little boutique hotel right above the harbor restaurant strip. It's been family-run since 1934; today English-speaking sisters Angela and Vasiliki are at the helm. The six thoughtfully appointed rooms are stony-chic, with heavy beams, tiny bathrooms, and good windows that manage to block out most of the noise. All the rooms have access to a little balcony, giving you a royal box seat overlooking all the harbor action (Db-€80-140 depending on the room, 10 percent discount with this book if paying cash and staying at least two nights, air-con, free Wi-Fi, tel. 22980-52313, www.hotelsophia.gr, hydra@hotelsophia.gr).

$$$ Nefeli Hotel is a place apart, providing an idyllic refuge high above the town. For the seclusion-seeking traveler, the steep 10-minute hike to get to this villa is a blessing (for €15, mule driver Giorgos can bring your bags up from the harbor on his donkey). There are nine thoughtfully appointed rooms, and the hotel's generous terraces and patios have stay-awhile lounge chairs, backgammon sets, yoga mats, and classic sunset views. With their warm expat welcome, Aussie Brett and Brit-Greek Alexandra create an ambience that forges friendships (Db-€75-130 depending on room and season, two-night minimum, air-con, free Wi-Fi, lots of helpful information, tel. 22980-53297, www.hotelnefeli.eu, info @hotelnefeli.eu).

Mid-Range Values

$$ Hotel Miranda is an early 19th-century sea captain's house with 14 rooms, a fine terrace, and classic style (Sb-€80, Db-€100, superior Db with view-€160, air-con, free Wi-Fi, tel. 22980-52230, fax 22980-53510, www.mirandahotel.gr, mirandahydra@hol.gr).

$$ Mistral Hotel is a well-run, basic place offering 17 rooms in a comfortable, modern stone building with a central lounge and breezy courtyard. It's a fine value at the very quiet, top part of town (Db-€100, big Db with view-€150, air-con, free Wi-Fi, tel. 22980-52509, www.hotelmistral.gr, info@hotelmistral.gr, Theo and Jenny).

$$ Greco Hotel, run by Maria Keramidas, rents 19 rooms set around a lovely garden where you're served a homemade breakfast. The front yard is a shady place to just relax and do nothing (Db-€75-110 depending on season and day, air-con, free Wi-Fi, tel. 22980-53200, www.grecohotel.gr, info@grecohotel.gr).

$$ Ippokampos Hotel has 16 basic rooms around a cocktailbar courtyard (Sb-€80, Db-€80-100, prices very soft, air-con, free

Wi-Fi, bar closes at 23:00, tel. 22980-53453, fax 22980-52501, www.ippokampos.com, ippo@ippokampos.com, owner Sotiris).

$$ Pension Achilleas rents 13 small but pleasant and nicely maintained rooms in an old mansion with a relaxing courtyard terrace (Sb-€55, Db-€75, Tb-€85, prices soft off-season, cash only, air-con, tel. 22980-52050, fax 22980-53227, www.achilleas-hydra.com, kofitsas@otenet.gr, Dina speaks only a little English).

Best Cheap Beds

$ Spalieri's Domatia has three rooms in a cheery home. The units, while simple, are spacious and air-conditioned. There's a community kitchen where you enjoy a self-serve breakfast, plus a welcoming garden courtyard. Staying with the Spalieri family provides a homier experience than at most other places in town (Db-€60-70, Qb-€100, next to Pension Achilleas, tel. 22980-52894, mobile 694-414-1977, spalstef@ath.forthnet.gr, minimal English).

$ Alkionides Pension provides perhaps the best lodging value in town. It has 10 tidy rooms buried in Hydra's back lanes, around a beautiful and relaxing courtyard (Db-€60, Tb-€80, apartment-€100, breakfast-€7, air-con, free Wi-Fi, tel. & fax 22980-54055, mobile 697-741-0460, www.alkionidespension.com, info@alkionidespension.com, Kofitsas family).

$ Pension Erofili is a reliable budget standby, renting 12 basic rooms facing a skinny courtyard in the heart of town (Db-€55—this special price with this book in 2011, Tb-€65, apartment-€90, rates soft in slow times, breakfast-€7, air-con, free Internet access and Wi-Fi, tel. & fax 22980-54049, mobile 697-768-8487, www.pensionerofili.gr, info@pensionerofili.gr, George and Irene).

Eating in Hydra

There are dozens of places to eat, offering everything from humble gyros to slick modern-Mediterranean cuisine. Harbor views come with higher prices, while places farther inland typically offer better value.

In Hydra Town

Psaropoula Restaurant fills the best spot in town, right on the harborfront, with rustic blue tables. While its interior is boring, its outside tables let you enjoy the strolling scene and almost bob with the tied-up yachts. Hydriots appreciate the classic Greek cuisine, and the prices are very fair—about what you'd pay without the prime location. Check out their big display case just inside to see what's cooking (€3-6 starters, €7-13 seafood starters, €8-12 main dishes, €15-25 seafood dishes, daily 12:00-23:00, tel. 22980-52630).

Taverna Gitoniko, better known as "Manolis and Christina" for its warm and kindly owners, is a Hydra institution. Offering wonderful hospitality, delicious food, and delightful rooftop-garden seating, this tricky-to-find taverna is worth seeking out for a memorable meal. Christina is a great cook—everything is good here. Order a selection of creative first courses (consider their delicious, smoky eggplant salad) and check their daily specials (€4-6 starters, €6-9 main dishes, seafood splurges, daily 12:00-16:00 & 18:30-24:00, closed Nov-Feb, Spilios Haramis, tel. 22980-53615).

Taverna Leonidas feels like a cross between a history museum and a friendly local home. It's been around so long it doesn't need (and doesn't have) a sign. The island's oldest taverna was the hangout for sponge-divers a century ago. Today, former New Yorkers Leonidas and Panagiota, who returned to Hydra in 1993 to take over the family business, feed guests as if they're family. Reservations are required: Call before their 10:00 shopping trip (or the day before) to order your  main dish. They prepare and cook up a great meal, including starters and dessert (sweets or fruit), for €15-17 per person (depends on the number of drinks). You'll enjoy their exuberant hospitality and traditional, rustic cooking, while appreciating the time-warp decor and rustic kitchen (daily 19:00-24:00, tel. 22980-53097). They're above town: Hike up Miaouli Street, passing Hotel Miranda, then a small church; as you curve right, watch for it on the right. Look for a lime-green door in the big white wall with a terrace, facing a staircase with blue flowerpots.

Veranda Restaurant, halfway up the steps on Sahini lane (off of Lignou), fills a terrace with fine views over the town and harbor. It's great on a summer evening; enjoy a cold drink before selecting from a menu that offers pasta served a dozen different ways and a creative assortment of salads (€8-11 seafood starters, €8-12 pastas, €10-15 traditional main dishes, €15-20 seafood dishes, better-than-average wine list, daily 18:00-24:30, upstairs with entry on Sahini, tel. 22980-52259, Andreas).

Mezedopolio Maridaki overlooks the harbor, up a set of stairs across from the Pirate Bar. A bit posh and modern, it caters more to locals than to tourists, focusing—as its name implies—on *mezedes,* or small dishes (the sardines are great). While pricey, portions are actually big, and three *mezedes* will easily and economically fill two people. Vasilias is known for his homemade *tsipouro,* the local grappa or firewater. It's worth reserving a view table (daily 11:00-24:00, tel. 22980-53046, mobile 697-741-3204).

HYDRA

Tavernas on Miaouli Street: Hydra's "Main Street" leading up from the port (to the left of the church bell tower) is crammed with appealing little tavernas that jostle for your attention with outdoor seating and good local food.

Souvlaki: For a quick and cheap (€2.50) meal, souvlaki is your best bet. The **hole-in-the-wall joint** on Miaouli (50 yards off the harbor, across from Hotel Sofia) serves the best in town to eat in or take away. They have a long and enticing list of variations. For a more civilized, sit-down souvlaki experience, drop by **The Onion Souvlaki,** a cute eatery filling a charming corner up Tompazi Street, next to the Amalour Bar.

Cafés on the Harbor: **Café Gonia** stakes out the best spot and serves the best Greek coffee. Nursing your drink here, you can enjoy the scene—drivers rolling their pushcarts, donkeys sneezing, taxi-boat drivers haggling, big boats coming and going—on Hydra's busiest corner. Nearby, **Café Isalos,** with a fun menu of light bites, is better for a meal (€6 sandwiches, €12 pizzas, good €3 iced coffees). In the early evening, watch for yachts trying to dock; some are driven by pros and others aren't—providing a comedic scene of naval inexperience.

Dessert: **Flora's Pastry Shop** is a hardworking little bakery cranking out the best pastries and homemade ice cream on the island. Flora has delightful tables that overlook a park on Lignou Street, just behind the monastery. She sells all the traditional local sweets, including honey treats such as baklava (two for €1). Many of her ingredients come from her farm on the nearby island of Dokos (daily 7:00-24:00).

Eating near Hydra, in Kaminia

A great way to cap your Hydra day is to follow the coastal path to the rustic and picturesque village of Kaminia, which hides behind the headland from Hydra. Kaminia's pocket-sized harbor

shelters the community's fishing boats. Here, with a glass of ouzo and some munchies, as the sun slowly sinks into the sea and boats become silhouettes, you can drink to the beauties of a Greek isle escape. Consider combining a late-afternoon stroll (along the seafront promenade) or hike (over the headland) with dinner. (For tips, see page 393.)

Kodylenia's Taverna is perched on a bluff just over the Kaminia harbor. With my favorite irresistible dinner views on Hydra, this scenic spot lets you watch the sun dip gently into the Saronic Gulf, with Kaminia's adorable port in the foreground.

Owner Dimitris takes his own boat out early in the morning to buy the day's best catch directly from the fishermen. For meals, you can sit out on the shady covered side terrace above the harbor. For drinks, sit out front on the porch. Relax and take in a sea busy with water taxis, hydrofoils that connect this oasis with Athens, old freighters—like castles of rust—lumbering slowly along the horizon, and cruise ships anchored as if they haven't moved in weeks (€3-7 starters, €9-14 meat dishes—visit their display case and see what's cooking, for a seafood meal figure €15-60 per person depending on what you order, daily 11:00-24:00, closed Dec-Feb, tel. 22980-53520).

Hydra Connections

The standard way to get to Hydra is on a Hellenic Seaways high-speed hydrofoil, called a "Flying Dolphin," or the slightly larger catamaran, called a "Flying Cat."  The boats leave frequently from the heart of Hydra's harbor, making it easy to connect to the mainland or other islands. While travel agencies will tell you to be at the port 30 minutes before departure, locals simply show up minutes before and walk on.

From Hydra by Hydrofoil or Catamaran to: Piraeus near Athens (9/day June-Sept, 7/day Easter-May and Oct, 4/day Nov-Easter, 1.75 hours, €25), **Ermioni** on the Peloponnese southeast of Nafplio (a.k.a. "Hermioni"; 4/day in summer, 2-3/day in winter, 20 minutes, €10), **Spetses** (6-7/day in summer, 3-4/day in winter, 30 minutes, €12), **Porto Heli** (5/day in summer, 2-3/day in winter, 45 minutes, €17), **Poros** (4-5/day year-round, 30 minutes, €14). "Summer" and "winter" seasons can vary, but summer is roughly Easter through October.

Tickets: You can buy tickets for the same price at virtually any travel agency in Greece, or at the Hellenic Seaways office in Hydra (just down an alley near the Alpha Bank; open anytime boats are running, tel. 22980-54007 or 22980-53812, www.hsw.gr). Because these boats are virtually the only game in town, it's wise to book well in advance—they can sell out during summer weekends. (It's especially important to book ahead for Sunday afternoon and evening boats to Piraeus, as they're packed with Athenians headed home after a weekend getaway.)

Book your tickets once you're comfortable locking in to a specific time or date. You can reserve a ticket on the Hellenic Seaways website and then pick it up at a travel agency, a Hellenic

Seaways ticket office, or at an automated machine at Piraeus. Or buy a ticket in person soon after you arrive in Greece. You can cancel or change your ticket (at any travel agency) up to 24 hours before departure in peak season, or three hours before departure off-season.

Possible Delays or Cancellations: Because the boats are relatively small (a Flying Dolphin holds about 150 passengers; a Flying Cat carries 200) and fast-moving, they can be affected by high winds and other inclement weather. Occasionally, departures are cancelled and they'll contact you to rebook. (For this reason, it's essential to provide a telephone number—at a minimum, your pre-boat-trip hotel—when you book.) Usually you can go later in the day, but it's possible (though rare) to get stranded overnight. Even if the sea is rocky, the ships may still run—but the ride can be very rough. If you're prone to seasickness, be prepared.

Emergency Alternative: If your boat is cancelled and you have a plane to catch in Athens, you could potentially hire a water taxi to zip you across to the mainland, and then take a taxi all the way to Athens—but this costs upwards of €200.

From Hydra to Metochi (for Drivers): The Freedom Boat is a recently added service connecting Hydra to a parking lot immediately across the water on the Peloponnesian mainland at Metochi, about 10 miles east of Ermioni (€6.50, about 8/day in summer, 4/day in winter, 12 minutes, mobile 694-424-2141, www.hydralines .gr). If traveling with a rental car on the Peloponnese, you could park here and day-trip over, saving lots of money over the Piraeus-Hydra ferry fare.

MYKONOS

ΜΥΚΟΝΟΣ / Μυκονοσ

Mykonos (MEE-koh-nohs) is the very picture of the perfect Greek island town: a humble seafront village crouched behind a sandy harbor, thickly layered with blinding-white stucco, bright-blue trim, and bursting-purple bougainvilleas. (Thank goodness for all that color, since otherwise this island—one of Greece's driest—would be various shades of dull-brown.) On a ridge over town stretches a trademark row of five windmills, overlooking a tidy embankment so pretty they call it "Little Venice."

Mykonos' more recent status as a fashionable, jet-set destination and a mecca for gay holiday-makers also gives it a certain hip cachet. These days, weary fisherfolk and tacky trinket stalls share the lanes with top-end fashion boutiques. Prices are stunningly high here, and the island is crammed full of fellow vacationers, particularly in August (try to come in spring or fall, if you can). But the Mykonians have taken all of the changes in stride. Fishermen still hang out on the benches by the harbor—always wearing their traditional caps (Mykonian men are famous among Greeks for their baldness). The natives generally seem appreciative rather than corrupted by all the attention. On my last visit, I overheard a young tourist gushing to her mommy, "Boy, people sure are friendly here!"

While Mykonos has some museums, they merely provide an excuse to get out of the sun for a few minutes. The real attraction here is poking around the Old Town streets: shopping, dining, clubbing, or—best of all—simply strolling. The

core of town is literally a maze, designed by the Mykonians centuries ago to discourage would-be invaders from finding their way. That tactic also works on today's tourists. But I can think of few places where getting lost is so enjoyable.

If you manage to break free, wander up to the windmills for the view, or take a bus (or rent a scooter or ATV) to reach one of the many enticing sandy beaches around the island. Near Mykonos, accessible by an easy boat trip, is the island of Delos—one of the Greek islands' top ancient sites. Delos hosts the remains of what was one of the most important places in the ancient Greek world: the temples honoring the birthplace of the twin gods Apollo and Artemis (it later became a bustling shipping community). Delos was a pilgrimage site for believers who came from all over to worship this "birthplace of light." Judging by the present-day sun-worshippers who scramble for the best patch of sand on Mykonos each summer, things haven't changed much around here.

Planning Your Time

Mykonos, a delightful place to be on vacation, merits at least a full day and two overnights. The easiest plan is to simply explore the Old Town lanes; the restless can dip into a museum or two, but they're all skippable. If you want to get out of town, you can tour the archaeological site at Delos (easy 30-minute boat trip each way, figure 3-4 hours round-trip total) or head for the beaches. As Mykonos has better beaches and less interesting in-town sights than many other Greek isles, I find it the perfect place to squeeze in some quality beach time.

Be warned that the island can be painfully crowded in peak season, roughly July through mid-September, peaking in August. During this time, hotel prices skyrocket, and the beaches (and everything else) are uncomfortably packed with people.

Orientation to Mykonos

Mykonos' main town is called Chora (or Hora, Χώρα; roughly "Village"), and that's how you'll generally see it signed. For ease, I refer to it as "Mykonos town."

Mykonos town is the main point of entry for the island. The Old Town clusters around the south end of the Old Port (some inter-island boats depart from the north end of the Old Port). Arcing in front of the Old Town is the sandy harbor; at the east end is Taxi Square (a hub for taxis and other services) and, beyond that, the Remezzo bus station and the Old Port; at the west end of the harbor is the pier for Delos ferries and cruise-ship tenders, and beyond that, the Little Venice quarter and the windmill ridge. Squeezed between the harbor and the main road (passing above

town on the gentle hill) is a tight maze of whitewashed lanes.

While some streets have names, others don't, and in any case, locals never use those names—they just know where things are. If you can't find something, just ask.

Tourist Information

Though there is a TI building (at the corner of the Old Port), the space hasn't been occupied in a while. To fill the void, local hotels, travel agencies, and other friendly locals can answer basic questions. Look for the promotional but helpful red *Mykonos Guidebook* (free around town).

Arrival in Mykonos

By Boat: Travelers coming by boat arrive in one of three places: at the New Port, a mile north of the Old Town (passenger ships to/from Piraeus and many cruise ships); at the Old Port, just north of the Old Town (Flying Cat catamarans to the other Cycladic islands, including Santorini); or at the pier jutting out from the Old Town's sandy harbor (tenders from some cruise ships).

From the **New Port,** you have several options for getting to the Old Town: Take a taxi (€5-6); ride a public bus (2/hour, €1.40); or, if arriving on a cruise, take the cruise line's shuttle bus (often free). Either type of bus takes you to the Old Port. Alternatively, you could do the dreary 20- to 25-minute walk along the coast into town (turn right, follow the water, and just keep going—you can see the gaggle of white houses across the bay).

To reach the Old Town from the **Old Port,** walk five minutes past a stretch of beach, then down a cozy shop-lined lane to Taxi Square and the main harborfront.

If your cruise ship is tendered, you'll disembark at the **pier** extending out from the heart of town. Just walk down the pier and you're at the harbor (there's a public pay WC on the right, along the water).

By Plane: Mykonos is well-connected by air to Athens, but also (thanks to its worldwide popularity as a vacation spot) to many other European cities (www.mykonos-airport.com). Mykonos' small airport sits just two miles outside of town, easily connected by a short taxi ride (€5-10). There are also sporadic public buses, but the taxi is so cheap I wouldn't bother with the bus unless there happens to be one there when you arrive. Some hotels can arrange airport transfers.

Getting Around Mykonos

Mykonos is a fun and easy island to explore, with several very different but equally inviting beach coves within a short drive.

By Taxi: The square at the southeast corner of the Old Port, nicknamed Taxi Square, is where you can catch a taxi to points around the island. Fares are reasonable; figure around €10 one-way to most beaches listed in this chapter (except Super Paradise, which is more like €15). Rather than paying the taxi to wait for you at the beach, hail or call a fresh one when you're ready to leave (tel. 22890-23700); you can also ask a taverna at the beach to call for you.

By Bus: Mykonos' bus network is well-designed for connecting travelers to its many fine beaches. Buses are frequent, though they might leave you a short walk from the beach itself. And since this is a party island, they run late into the night in peak season.

There are three bus stations in Mykonos town. For tourists, the most useful is the **Fabrika** station, with buses to nearby destinations, including the beaches I've described in this chapter. The Fabrika station is at the south end of town (away from the harbor), where several Old Town streets funnel gradually uphill to the main road that passes above. Two other stations are virtually next to each other at the northeast edge of the Old Town (from Taxi Square, head along the port with the water to your left): The **Old Port** station along the water is for buses to the New Port; a block uphill, the **Remezzo** station serves buses to the eastern half of the island (the large town of Ano Mera, plus the smaller towns of Kalafati and Elia). For specific bus connections, see "Mykonos Connections," page 415.

By Motorized Scooter or All-Terrain Vehicle (ATV): On Greek islands, tourists are notorious for renting a scooter or ATV, overestimating their abilities to control a machine they've never driven before, and denting someone's fender or leaving a strip of knee or elbow skin on the pavement...or worse. That said, and keeping in mind the risks inherent in renting wheels here, it can be an affordable, efficient, and memorably fun way to connect distant beaches. If I were renting a scooter or ATV on a Greek isle, I'd do it here, where the roads are not too heavily trafficked (you'll pass more fellow scooters and ATVs than cars), and idyllic beaches are a short ride away.

Travel agencies all over town rent both types of wheels for reasonable all-day rates (€15-20/day for a scooter or ATV, ATVs with reverse gear cost about €5 more). Two people can ride one machine, but both should ask for helmets (while you'll see many riders without them, it's stupidly risky not to wear one, and most rental agencies are happy to loan you one). The paperwork is quick and casual (they'll take a credit-card imprint as a deposit, you'll fill up whatever gas you use before you return it, and insurance... what's that?).

Once on the road, be especially careful around turns, where centrifugal forces make it suddenly more difficult to steer. Be aware that even distances that appear short can take time to reach on a slow-moving ATV; figure 15-20 minutes from Mykonos town to any of the beaches I list in this chapter (Super Paradise is the farthest). Note: You'll see ads for renting a "bike," but this refers to motorized scooters—the island is hilly and arid enough to make actual bicycling undesirable for all but the most serious cyclists.

By Car: You can also rent a car for as little as €40 per day, depending on demand; look for car-rental signs at several agencies around town.

Helpful Hints

Hours: I don't list specific hours for shops or restaurants, as these vary with demand. In peak season, they're open long hours daily, but when the tourists disappear, so do the opening hours.

English Bookstore: The **International Press Newsstand,** just off the harbor at the Taxi Square end, stocks a good selection of international (including English-language) paperbacks, magazines, and newspapers (daily, Kampani 5, tel. 22890-23316).

Services: You'll find travel agencies, ATMs, launderettes, Internet cafés, pay phones, and other helpful services scattered around the Old Town. For the highest concentration of services, head for the area around the Fabrika bus station, at the south end of the Old Town (near where it meets the main road; also pay WC, tattoo parlor).

Sights in Mykonos

▲▲**Old Town**—Mykonos' Old Town seems made for exploring. Each picture-perfect lane is slathered with a thick, bulbous layer

of stucco, giving the place a marshmallow-village vibe. All that white is the perfect contrast to the bright-blue sky and the vivid trim. Sometimes described as "cubist" for its irregular jostle of angular rooflines, Mykonos' townscape is a photographer's delight. Enjoy getting lost, then found again. Try wandering aimlessly for a while—you'll be amazed at how quickly you find yourself going in circles. To get your bearings, look at a map and notice that three "main" roads (still barely wide enough for a moped) form a U-shaped circuit facing the harbor: Kouzi Georgouli, Enoplon Dynameon, and Matogianni.

Or just relax along the sandy **harbor.** The pier for excursion

boats to Delos (described later) sticks straight out; nearby is an impossibly picturesque white chapel with sky-blue trim. Nurse an iced coffee or beer at a rustic café table and watch the tide of tourists wash over local village life. Glancing offshore,

you'll see humble fishing boats bobbing in the foreground, with

2,000-passenger cruise ships looming in the distance. Along the sandy harbor, fisherfolk sort and clean their catch at the marble table (while stray cats gather below), old-timers toss a fishing line into the water, kids skip rocks and rent ponies for a ride on the sand, and shutterbug tourists flock around the resident pelican, Petros. (Ever since a local fisherman found an ailing pelican and nursed it back to health half a century ago, these odd birds have been the town's mascots.)

The piazza known as **Taxi Square,** at the

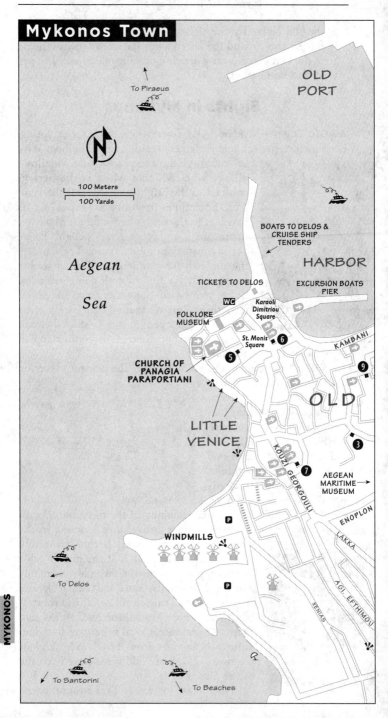

Mykonos Town

OLD PORT

To Piraeus

100 Meters
100 Yards

BOATS TO DELOS &
CRUISE SHIP
TENDERS

Aegean

Sea

HARBOR

TICKETS TO DELOS

EXCURSION BOATS
PIER

WC

Karaoli
Dimitriou
Square

FOLKLORE
MUSEUM

St. Monis
Square   ⑥

⑤

**CHURCH OF
PANAGIA
PARAPORTIANI**

KAMBANI

⑨

OLD

**LITTLE
VENICE**

KOUZI GEORGOULI

⑦

③

AEGEAN
MARITIME
MUSEUM

ENOPLON

LAKKA

WINDMILLS

P

P

AGI EFTHIMOU

XENIAS

To Delos

To Santorini

To Beaches

MYKONOS

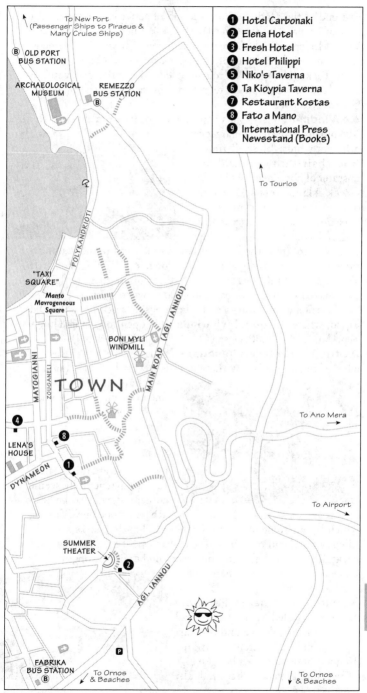

1 Hotel Carbonaki
2 Elena Hotel
3 Fresh Hotel
4 Hotel Philippi
5 Niko's Taverna
6 Ta Kioypia Taverna
7 Restaurant Kostas
8 Fato a Mano
9 International Press Newsstand (Books)

To New Port
(Passenger Ships to Piraeus &
Many Cruise Ships)

B OLD PORT
BUS STATION

ARCHAEOLOGICAL
MUSEUM

REMEZZO
B BUS STATION

To Tourlos

"TAXI
SQUARE"

Manto
Mavrogeneous
Square

BONI MYLI
WINDMILL

POLYKANDRIOTI

MAIN ROAD (AGI. IANNOU)

MATOGIANNI

ZOUGANELI

T O W N

To Ano Mera

4

LENA'S
HOUSE

8

1

DYNAMEON

To Airport

SUMMER
THEATER

2

AGI. IANNOU

FABRIKA
BUS STATION
B

P

To Ornos
& Beaches

To Ornos
& Beaches

MYKONOS

east end of the sandy harbor, is a hub of activity monitored by a bust of Manto Mavrogenous (1796-1848), a heroine of the Greek War of Independence. A wealthy aristocrat of Mykonian heritage, she spent her fortune supplying Greek forces in a battle against their Turkish rulers. Mavrogenous ended her life destitute on the island of Paros, never regretting the sacrifices she made for Greece's freedom.

▲▲**Windmills**—Mykonos is infamous for its wind. In fact, the Mykonians have special names for different winds: "the bell-ringer," "the chair-thrower," and "the unseater of horsemen." As in many Greek island towns, Mykonos' old-fashioned windmills harnessed this natural power in order to grind grain to supply its ships.

Five of them (plus the bases of two more) stand proudly along a ridge called Kato Myloi at the top of town, overlooking the Little Venice area. While there's nothing to see inside these buildings, they make for a fine photo op and great views over town.

To enter a windmill, head to the opposite (east) end of the Old Town, where the **Boni Myli windmill** is open to visitors (June-Sept daily 16:00-18:00, closed Oct-May, tel. 22890-22591).

▲**Little Venice (Mikri Venetia)**—Along the bay at the western edge of town, just below the windmills, wealthy local shipping merchants built a row of fine mansions, with brightly painted wooden balconies, that seem to rise from the deep. While "Little Venice" is a bit of a misnomer (where are the canals?), this is a particularly scenic corner of town. At the head of this area, a stately Catholic church (the only one on Mykonos, which boasts some 400 little Orthodox chapels) marks a square filled with restaurant tables. The embankment here is lined with cocktail bars and cafés, crowded every night with throngs of visitors enjoying the island's best spot to watch the sunset.

▲**Church of Panagia Paraportiani**—Huddled at the tip of land between Little Venice and the harbor, this unusual church is a striking architectural oddity—a hodgepodge of five small chapels that gradually

merged together, then were draped in a thick layer of whitewashed stucco. While it's a much-touted landmark (and one of the island's most-photographed spots), there's little to see beyond the initial, otherworldly appearance. One of the chapel interiors is open most days, where a local woman sells votive candles and fills the small space with the rich aroma of incense.

Archaeological Museum—Perched on a bluff at the south end of the Old Port, this museum displays artifacts from Rinia, which became the burial isle for Delos when residents of that sacred island's cemeteries were relocated by the Athenians in the sixth century B.C. (see sidebar on page 419). One room shows off intricately carved stone grave markers, called steles. The rest of the collection consists of sparsely described cases full of vases, jewelry, statue fragments, and other artifacts. There's relatively little to see, and it's difficult to appreciate—interesting only to armchair archaeologists (€2, Tue-Sun 8:30-15:00, closed Mon, tel. 22890-22325).

Aegean Maritime Museum—This tight but endearing collection traces the story of the local mercantile shipping industry. A desert isle of history in a sea of tourist kitsch, this little place takes its subject very seriously. In its four rooms, you'll find amphora jugs, model ships, a collection of stamps celebrating seafaring, and more. Don't miss the tranquil garden, which displays the actual, original lighthouse from the island's Cape Armenistis, as well as replicas of ancient sailors' gravestones. The good English descriptions offer a fine history lesson for those willing to read them (€4, April-Oct daily 10:30-13:00 & 18:30-21:00, closed Nov-March, Enoplon Dynameon 10, tel. 22890-22700).

Lena's House—Adjacent to the Maritime Museum (and part of the Folklore Museum), this is a typical middle-class Mykonian house dating from the late 19th century, complete with original furnishings and artwork (€2, April-Oct Mon-Sat 18:30-21:30, closed Sun and Nov-March, tel. 22890-22591).

Mykonos Folklore Museum—Housed in a typically Cycladic former sea captain's residence just up the bluff from the harbor, this museum displays a random mix of traditional folk items from around the island, as well as a typical kitchen and bedroom (free, April-Oct Mon-Sat 17:30-20:30, Sun 18:30-20:30, closed Nov-March, tel. 22890-22591).

Beaches

Mykonos' array of beaches rivals that of any Greek island. Each beach seems to specialize in a different niche: family-friendly or party; straight, gay, or mixed; nude or clothed; and so on.

(Keep in mind that in Greece, even "family-friendly" beaches have topless sunbathers.) Get local advice to find the one that suits your beach-bum preferences, or choose from one of the options listed here (all of my suggestions are within a 15- to 20-minute bus or scooter/ATV ride of town).

To connect the beaches, you'll drive steeply up and down over the dusty, dirty, desolate spine of this arid island. You can also connect many of these beaches (including Psarou, Platis Gialos, Paradise, and Super Paradise) by regular shuttle boat.

All of these beaches have comfortable lounge chairs with umbrellas out on the sand. Figure around €10-15 for two chairs that share an umbrella (or half that for one chair). Just take a seat—they'll come by to collect money. Be warned that in peak season (July and especially Aug), all beaches are very crowded, and it can be difficult to find an available seat.

Mykonos' beaches are lined with cafés and tavernas, with typical Greek-island menus...sometimes functional, sometimes surprisingly good. These can offer a welcome break from the sun.

Agios Ioannis—My favorite beach, this remote-feeling patch of sand tucked behind a mountain ridge best gives you the feel-

ing of being on a castaway isle. You'll enjoy views across to the important isle of Delos. From Mykonos town, go to Ornos, then head toward Kapari; on your way down the hill, turn off on the left at the low-profile beach signs (one directs you to Πύλη, one of the restaurants on the beach). You'll drop down the road to an idyllic Robinson Crusoe spot where two restaurants (Puli and Hippie Fish) share a sandy beach. I ate well at **Puli** (Πύλη), with big portions and fresh, tasty Greek classics (daily, tel. 22890-26660).

For the even more secluded **Kapari** beach, continue down the road past the Agios Ioannis turnoff, then swing right at the white church.

Ornos—Easy to reach since it's in a sizeable town in the middle of the island, this very family-friendly beach is also one of the more functional (and least memorable) of those I list. The whole place has an unpretentious charm.

Psarou and Platis Gialos— These two beaches, along the next cove to the east of Ornos, are much more densely developed. At each one, a tight line of hotels arcs along the top of a crowded patch of sand. Psarou is considered a somewhat exclusive, favorite retreat of celebrities, while Platis Gialos (see photo at bottom of previous page) feels more geared toward families (the far end from the bus stop/parking is less claustrophobic).

Paradise—This famous "meat-market" beach is a magnet for partiers in the Aegean, and even more of a destination than the other beaches listed here. Located at the southern tip of the island, Paradise (a.k.a. Kalamopodi) is presided over by hotels that run party-oriented bars for young beachgoers—perfect if you want to dance in the sand all night to the throbbing beat with like-minded backpackers from around the world. As you approach, the last stretch is through thick, high grasses, giving the place an air of secrecy; then you'll pass long rows of lockers before popping out at the party.

The next cove over hosts **Super Paradise** (Plintri) beach, which has eclipsed the original as the premier party beach on the island.

Sleeping in Mykonos

Mykonos is an expensive place to overnight—especially in peak season (roughly mid-July through mid-Aug, sometimes extend-

ing all the way to mid-Sept). During these premium times, even "budget" hotels dramatically increase their rates...which means you should lower your value-for-money expectations. If you can come just before or after this busy period, you can save more than half. In this party town, nighttime noise—dance clubs, people carousing in the streets, and so on—is epidemic; plan to wear earplugs, and if you're a light sleeper, try requesting their quietest room. I've tried to recommend places on streets that are less raucous than the norm, but they're also very central, so no promises. These places are quite similar in quality, location, and amenities. They all have mod white decor to match the lanes out front, as well as air-conditioning and free Wi-Fi for guests.

$$ Hotel Carbonaki is a family-run hotel near the top of town, with 21 nicely appointed rooms around an oasis courtyard with a Jacuzzi (late July-mid-Aug: Sb-€130, Db-€168; early July and late Aug: Sb-€110, Db-€132; June and most of Sept: Sb-€88, Db-€105; late Sept-May: Sb-€55, Db-€66; breakfast-€10, Panachrantou 23, tel. 22890-24124, www.carbonaki.gr,

Sleep Code

(€1 = about $1.40, country code: 30)
S = Single, **D** = Double/Twin, **T** = Triple, **Q** = Quad, **b** = bathroom,
s = shower only. Unless otherwise noted, breakfast is included,
credit cards are accepted, and the staff speaks English.

To help you easily sort through these listings, I've divided
the rooms into two categories, based on the price for a
standard double room with bath during the peak season:

$$ **Higher Priced**—Most rooms €130 or more.
$ **Lower Priced**—Most rooms less than €130.

Prices can change without notice; verify the hotel's
current rates online or by email. For other updates, see www
.ricksteves.com/update.

info@carbonaki.gr, Theodore and the Rousounelos family).

$$ Elena Hotel has 30 modern rooms and a mazelike floor plan (July-mid-Sept: Db-€140; late May-June: Db-€120; mid-Sept-late May: Db-€100; €20-30 more for sea-view room, Rohari street, tel. 22890-23457, www.elena-hotel.gr, info@elena-hotel.gr).

$$ Fresh Hotel's public areas have trendy pizzazz, though the 13 rooms feel a bit cheaper than the others listed here (July-Aug: Db-€150; off-season: Db-€70-90; some noise from adjacent restaurant, Kalogera 31, tel. 22890-24670, www.hotelfresh mykonos.com, info@mariosmykonos.com).

$ Hotel Philippi has 14 rooms huddled around a garden in the heart of the Old Town (July-mid-Sept: Db-€125; June and late Sept: Db-€75; April-May and Oct: Db-€55; rates flex with demand, no breakfast, closed Nov-March, Kalogera 25, tel. 22890-22294, chriko@otenet.gr).

Eating in Mykonos

The twisting streets of the Old Town are lined with tourist-oriented restaurants. Don't look for good values here—Mykonos is expensive. Little distinguishes one place from another; simply choose the spot with the menu and ambience that appeal to you: with a sea view, out on a busy pedestrian lane, or in a charming garden courtyard.

Along the Harbor: While the many tavernas and cafés that face the sandy

harbor are touristy and overpriced, it's hard to argue with
their appeal. Consider enjoying
an iced coffee or frappé—if not
a full meal—from this comfortable perch, which offers
the best people-watching (and
sometimes cat- and pelican-
watching) in town.

Tavernas near St. Monis
Square: Three rollicking tavernas with huge outdoor terraces surround this stepped square with a red-domed church, just a block
above the harbor. Like the harborfront places, these are not necessarily the best values in town, but the atmosphere is appealing (figure
€4-8 starters, €8-20 main dishes, all open long hours daily). **Niko's**
Taverna has an avid following (tel. 22890-24320), though locals
prefer the food at **Ta Kioypia** (Τα Κιούπια, tel. 22890-22866).

Deeper in the Old Town: **Restaurant Kostas** has reasonable
prices and unpretentious food on a charming little square facing
a characteristic chapel (€4-10 starters, €9-20 main dishes, open
daily, 5 Metropoleos, tel. 22890-23326). **Fato a Mano**—tucked
away from the busiest part of the tourist zone, but still lively—
offers a modern (rather than rustic) vibe and well-regarded food
(€7-14 starters, €12-22 main dishes, daily 11:00-late, Meletopoulou
Square, tel. 22890-26256).

Mykonos Connections

By Bus

From Mykonos town, buses connect to other parts of the island,
including many fine beaches: **Ornos/Ag. Ioannis** (1-2/hour),
Paradise (2/hour), **Platis Gialos** (2/hour), **Paraga** (hourly).
Schedules are posted at stops. Rides costs €1.40 (or €1.70 at night,
24:15-6:00); because tickets aren't always as readily sold at other
points on the island, get a return ticket when buying your out-
bound ticket in Mykonos town.

By Boat

To Piraeus (Athens): Daily, 3.5 hours on high-speed catamaran
(Hellenic Seaways, tel. 210-419-9000, www.hsw.gr; or Aegean
Speed Lines, tel. 210-969-0950, www.aegeanspeedlines.gr); or 5.5
hours on regular boat (Blue Star Ferries, tel. 210-891-9010, www
.bluestarferries.com; or Hellenic Seaways); these boats leave from
the New Port, about a mile north of town (buses: 2/hour, €1.40;
€5-6 taxi).

To Other Islands: The Flying Cat catamaran leaves from

the Old Port April through October daily at 14:55 (except the second Wed of each month) and heads for **Paros** (50 minutes), **Ios** (2 hours), **Santorini** (3 hours), and **Crete** (5 hours; operated by Hellenic Seaways, listed above).

Near Mykonos: Delos

Popular as Mykonos is today, it was just another island centuries ago, and the main attraction was next door: the island of Delos, worth ▲▲. In antiquity, Delos lived several lives: as one of the Mediterranean's most important religious sites, as the "Fort Knox" of Greek city-states, and as one of the ancient world's busiest commercial ports. Its importance ranked right up there with Athens, Delphi, or Olympia.

Today the island has no residents, and only ruins and a humble museum remain. Highlights of your visit include the much-photographed lion statues, some nice floor mosaics, and a windswept setting pockmarked with foundations that hint at Delos' glorious history.

Orientation

Cost: €5.

Hours: The site is closed (and boats do not run) on Mondays; on all other days, it's open from the arrival of the first boat to the departure of the last boat (i.e., 9:30-15:00 in summer).

Warning: Delos is an uninhabited island with virtually no shade and only a small museum and café. Bring good shoes, sun protection, and plenty of water.

Getting There: Delos is reachable only by a 30-minute boat trip. Boats depart Mykonos from the pier extending straight out from the Old Town; you can buy the €15 round-trip ticket at the little kiosk at the base of the pier. In peak season, boats go in each direction three times a day (Tue-Sun, generally departing Mykonos at 9:00, 10:00, and 11:00, and returning from Delos at 12:15, 13:30, and 15:00; no boats Mon); however, the specific times can change significantly depending on weather and cruise-ship arrivals and departures. This means you can have less than an hour to as much as six hours on the island.

Tours: Travel agencies in town sell package excursions that include

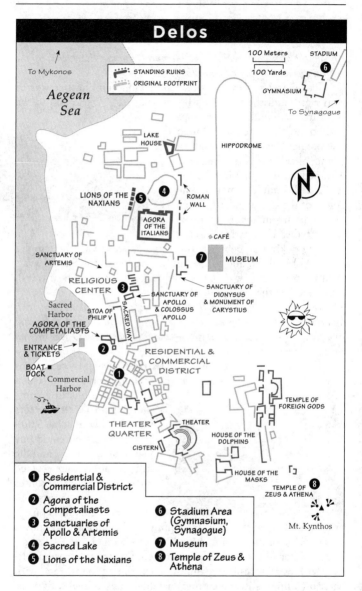

Delos

STANDING RUINS
ORIGINAL FOOTPRINT

To Mykonos

Aegean Sea

100 Meters
100 Yards

STADIUM 6

GYMNASIUM

To Synagogue

LAKE HOUSE

HIPPODROME

LIONS OF THE NAXIANS 5

4

ROMAN WALL

N

AGORA OF THE ITALIANS

CAFÉ

SANCTUARY OF ARTEMIS

7 MUSEUM

RELIGIOUS CENTER

3

SANCTUARY OF APOLLO & COLOSSUS APOLLO

SANCTUARY OF DIONYSUS & MONUMENT OF CARYSTIUS

Sacred Harbor

STOA OF PHILIP V

SACRED WAY

AGORA OF THE COMPETALIASTS

ENTRANCE & TICKETS

2

BOAT DOCK

Commercial Harbor

1

RESIDENTIAL & COMMERCIAL DISTRICT

TEMPLE OF FOREIGN GODS

THEATER QUARTER

THEATER

HOUSE OF THE DOLPHINS

CISTERN

HOUSE OF THE MASKS

TEMPLE OF ZEUS & ATHENA 8

Mt. Kynthos

1 Residential & Commercial District
2 Agora of the Competaliasts
3 Sanctuaries of Apollo & Artemis
4 Sacred Lake
5 Lions of the Naxians
6 Stadium Area (Gymnasium, Synagogue)
7 Museum
8 Temple of Zeus & Athena

the boat, museum entry, and a guided tour (ask at any travel agency). Local guides also meet arriving boats and show around small, impromptu groups (€10 for a one-hour quickie overview tour—you'll need more time to actually hike around the site and see the museum).

Length of This Tour: Most visitors find that two to three hours on the island is plenty to wander the site and see the museum.

The Tour Begins

• *From the boat dock, walk to the entrance, buy your ticket, pick up the helpful included map, and enter the gate.*

Pause and survey the site. The commercial harbor was to your right, and the sacred harbor to your left. Ahead and to the right are the foundations of shops and homes that once constituted one of the Aegean's finest cities. Standing above those ruins is Mount Kynthos, its hillsides littered with temple remains. The Agora of the Competaliasts—one of the main squares in town—is straight ahead (with the museum

building poking up behind). The religious area (with the temples of Apollo) is ahead and to the left, at the end of the Sacred Way. And far to the left was the Sacred Lake (now a patch of trees), overlooked by the iconic row of lions.

• *Start by wandering through the long rows of foundations on your right. You can circle back to these at the end—after summiting the mountain and winding down past the theater—but it's a good idea to poke around now in case you run out of steam later.*

Residential and Commercial District: Most of these remains were either homes or shops. In the second century B.C. (when

Delos was a bustling commercial port), the streets were lined with some 3,000 shops where you could buy just about anything, and the hillsides above were covered with the elaborate homes of wealthy merchants and shippers. Delos was considered to be the most important commercial center in the known world. (One of its major commodities was human flesh—it was a major center in the ancient slave trade.) The city was cosmopolitan, with 30,000 residents and distinct ethnic groups, each with their own linguistic and cultural neighborhood (Greeks, Syrians, Beirutis, Italians, etc.). Remains of these same neighborhoods can still be seen today.

Poke into some of the **house foundations.** Homes were generally organized around a central courtyard, above a giant cistern (underground water storage system). Look for fragments of elaborate mosaic floors (intact portions are on display inside the museum), as well as marble structures that once decorated the

The Rise and Fall of Delos

Delos enters history 3,000 years ago as a sacred place where a number of gods were worshipped. Blessed with a prime location (midway between the mainland of Greece and Asia Minor—today's Turkey—and in the center of the Greek islands), but cursed with no natural resources, the barren island survived as a religious destination for pilgrims bringing offerings to the gods.

According to myth, the philandering Zeus impregnated the mortal Leto. Zeus' furious wife Hera banished Leto from the earth, but Zeus implored his brother Poseidon to create a refuge for her by raising up the underwater world of "Invisible" (Greek *Adelos*) to create an island that was "Visible" *(Delos)*. Here, Leto gave birth to twins—Apollo (god of the sun) and Artemis (goddess of the moon). Their human followers built temples in their honor (ninth century B.C.), and pilgrims flocked here with offerings.

As Athens began to assert control over the Aegean (sixth century B.C.), it made sure that spiritually influential Delos stayed politically neutral. The Athenians ordered a "catharsis" (purification) of the island, removing dead bodies from the cemeteries. Later, they also decreed that no one could be born or die there—that is, there were to be no permanent residents. The Delians were relocated to an adjacent, larger island called Rinia. Ostensibly, this was to keep Delos pure for the gods, but in reality it removed any danger of rivals influencing the island's native population.

Because of its neutral status and central location, Delos was chosen in 478 B.C. as the natural meeting place for the powerful Delian League—an alliance of Greek city-states formed to battle the Persians and to promote trade. The combined wealth of the league was stored here in the fabulously rich bank of Delos. But all that changed in 454 B.C., when Pericles moved the treasury to Athens, and Delos reverted to being a pilgrimage site.

Centuries later, under the Romans, Delos' course changed dramatically once more. Thanks to its strategic location, the island was granted the right to operate as a free port (167 B.C.). Almost overnight, it became one of the biggest shipping centers in the known world, complete with a town of 30,000 inhabitants.

Then, in 88 B.C., soldiers from the Kingdom of Pontus, an enemy of Rome, attacked and looted the town, slaughtering 20,000 of its citizens. Delos never really recovered. Plagued by pirate attacks and shifting trade routes, Delos faded into history. Its once-great buildings were left to decay and waste away. In 1872, French archaeologists arrived (so far, scientists have excavated about one-fifth of the site), and Delos' cultural treasures were revealed to the modern world.

DELOS

place. The city even had a surprisingly advanced sewer system. Because wood was rare on the arid Cycladic Islands, most buildings were constructed from dry-stone walls; wood was a status symbol, used only by the wealthiest to show off. Delos had some of the biggest homes of ancient Greece, not necessarily because of wealth, but because they could build big here without fear of the devastating earthquakes that plagued other locations. The Greeks attributed this to divine intervention, but modern seismologists have found that Delos sits away from major fault lines.

• *Now circle back to the agora that's near the boat dock. This is the...*

Agora of the Competaliasts: This was the main market square of the Roman merchants who worshipped the deities called *lares compitales,* who kept watch over the crossroads. This is not *the* agora, but one of many agoras (marketplaces) on Delos—a reminder that several different communities coexisted in this worldly trading city.

• *From this agora, the Sacred Way leads off to the left. Follow the same path ancient pilgrims walked as they approached the temples of Apollo. Along the left side of the road runs the long ledge of the pediment from the **Stoa of Philip V** (what we see here as the "bottom" actually ran along the top of the building). At the end of the Sacred Way is the...*

Religious Center: The **Sanctuary of Apollo,** and beyond that, the **Sanctuary of Artemis,** both consisted of several temples and other ceremonial buildings. Unfortunately, these once-great buildings are in near-total ruin. In its day, Apollo's sanctuary had three large, stern Doric temples lined with columns. The biggest temple was nearly 100 feet long. The nearby Porinos Naos served as the treasury of the Delian League. Other treasuries once held untold riches—offerings to the gods brought by devout pilgrims.

Next to one of the Apollo temple foundations is a giant marble pedestal that once held the **Colossus Apollo** statue. The 35-foot statue (seventh century B.C.) was a gift from the Naxians and was carved from a single block of marble. It's long gone now, but a few bits of its fingers are on display in the museum.

• *Beyond the Sanctuary, pass the foundations of the spacious **Agora of the Italians** on the way to the former...*

Sacred Lake: This was supposedly the source of Zeus' seed. When Leto was about to give birth to Zeus' children (according to the "Hymn to Delian Apollo," attributed to Homer), she cried out: "Delos, if you would be willing to be the abode of my son Apollo and make him a rich temple, your people will be well-fed

by strangers bringing offerings. For truly your own soil is not rich."
The Sacred Lake was drained by French archaeologists to prevent
the spread of bacterial disease.

• *Overlooking the lake are the famous...*

Lions of the Naxians: This row of seven sphinx-like lion statues (originally there were 12) is the main, iconic image of this site.

These are replicas, but five of the
original statues (seventh century
B.C.) are in the museum. One of
the originals was stolen by the
Venetians, "repaired" with an
awkwardly too-big head, and
still stands in front of Venice's
Arsenal building.

• *Walk through the oval-shaped
Sacred Lakebed and hike up
toward the museum. Just before the museum, a path leads to the left far
into the distance, where you could detour to find the remains of the gymnasium, stadium, and the Jewish synagogue. Delos'* **stadium** *was where
Olympics-style games were held every five years. Like the more famous
games at Olympia and Delphi, these were essentially religious festivals
to the gods, particularly Dionysus. Pilgrims from across the Greek world
gathered to celebrate with sports, song contests, theatrical performances,
and general merrymaking.*

Make your way to the...

Museum: This scantily described collection includes statuary,
vases, mosaic floors, and other items. Inside the door is a model

of the site in its heyday. While
most of the site's best pieces are
in the National Archaeological
Museum in Athens, a few highlights remain, including five of
the original Lions of the Naxians
(in a room of their own) and the
fingers of Colossus Apollo.

For more body parts of other
gods, exit the museum and go straight ahead to the **Monument of
Carystius** (once part of the Sanctuary of Dionysus), with its large
penis-on-a-pillar statues.

• *If you have the energy, turn left (with your back to the museum) and
hike up the hill toward more remains of houses and temples. Hardy
travelers can huff all the way up to...*

Mount Kynthos: At 370 feet, the island's highest point feels
even taller on a hot day. To ancient Greeks, this conical peak
looked like the spot from which Poseidon had pulled this mysterious isle up from the deep. Up here are the remains of the **Temple**

of Zeus and Athena. As you observe the chain of islands dramatically swirling around Delos, you can understand why most experts believe that the Cycladic Islands got their name from the way they circle (or cycle around) this oh-so-important islet.

• *Head back downhill, toward the theater and harbor. On your way down, you'll pass the* **House of the Dolphins,** *with mosaics of cupids riding dolphins, and the* **House of the Masks,** *with a beautiful mosaic of a tambourine-playing Dionysus riding a leopard. As you return to the boat, you'll pass by the remains of a giant* **cistern** *and the 5,500-seat* **theater**...*starring a 360-degree view of the Cycladic Islands.*

SANTORINI

ΣΑΝΤΟΡΊΝΗ / Σαντορίνη;
a.k.a. Thira (ΘΗΡΑ / Θηρα)

If Santorini were only an island, it would already be one of the Mediterranean's most dramatic: a flooded caldera (collapsed volcanic crater) with a long, steep, multicolored arc of cliffs, thrusting up a thousand feet above sea level. Sometimes called "The Devil's Isle," this unique place has captured visitors' imaginations for millennia and might have inspired the tales of Atlantis. But the otherworldly appeal of Santorini (sahn-toh-REE-nee) doesn't end with its setting. Perched along the ridgeline is a gaggle of perfectly placed whitewashed villages, punctuated with azure domes, that make this, undeniably, one of Greece's most scenic spots. If this place didn't exist, some brilliant fantasy painter would have to conjure it up.

The island's main town, Fira (Φηρα, FEE-rah)—with Santorini's handiest services and best museum—is scenically situated, but is more functional than it is charming. Fira is not quite what you imagine when you think of "Santorini." If those chalk-white houses and vivid domes are what you came to see, don't linger in Fira—head to the northern tip of the island, to the town of Oia (Οια, EE-ah). Oia is the famous, idyllic white village smothering a steep cliff that tumbles down to the sea. Strolling through

Oia is like spinning a postcard rack—it's tempting to see the town entirely through your camera's viewfinder.

Not surprisingly, Santorini is hugely popular and can be very crowded—and expensive—in peak season (roughly July through mid-September, peaking in the first half of

August). Tourism—virtually the only surviving industry here—has made the island wealthy. It's one of the few places in Greece where the population isn't aging (as young people don't have to move away to find satisfying work). Fortunately, it's not difficult to break away from the main tourist rut and discover some scenic lanes of your own. In both Fira and Oia, the cliffside streets are strewn with countless cafés, all of them touting "sunset views"... the end of the day is a main attraction here.

Santorini Overview

The five islands that make up Santorini (a Venetian bastardization of "Santa Irene," after a local church) are known to Greeks as Thira (Θηρα, THEE-rah). Most of the settlement is on the 15-mile-long main island, also called Thira. The west side of Thira is a sheer drop-off (i.e., into the mouth of the former volcano), while the east side tapers more gradually to the water (the former volcano's base).

The primary tourist towns are on the steep, western side of Thira: The town of Fira is the island's capital and transportation hub, but the main attraction is Oia, a village six miles to the north-west. The relatively level east and south areas have the ancient sites and best beaches.

Planning Your Time

Santorini deserves at least two nights and a full day divided between Oia and Fira. While Fira is the handiest home base (with the best transportation connections and services), to really get away from it all, hang your hat in Oia.

If your time on Santorini is short, make a beeline (by bus or taxi) to Oia to get your fill of classic Santorini views; if possible, time your visit to coincide with sunset. You can fill any additional time in Fira, where the only worthwhile sight is the manage-able, well-presented Museum of Prehistoric Thira. It's also fun to explore some of the steep lanes below Fira's Orthodox cathedral.

On a longer visit, venture to other points on the island—ancient sites, red- and black-sand beaches, and maybe a boat trip to the active volcano crater and hot springs in the middle of the caldera.

Arrival in Santorini

By Boat

Boats arrive in one of two places on Santorini: Passenger ferries and catamarans come to the New Port at Athinios, about five miles south of Fira; cruise ships usually tender passengers to the Old Port, directly below Fira.

By Passenger Boat at the New Port (Athinios): From the Athinios port, a serpentine road climbs up the hill. Buses and taxis

Santorini Island

- **····** EXCURSION/ SHUTTLE BOAT
- **—** ROADS
- **---** TRAILS
- ℞ BEACHES

TO MYKONOS & PIRAEUS

OIA
FINIKIA
RIVA
THIRASIA
IMEROVIGLI
FIROSTEFANI
MANALOS
CABLE CAR
FIRA
NEA KAMENI
OLD PORT
MONOLITHOS
HOT SPRINGS
SEA DIAMOND SHIPWRECK
PALEA KAMENI
ATHINIOS PORT
AIRPORT
AKROTIRI TOWN
PIRGOS
KAMARI
ANCIENT THIRA
AKROTIRI RUINS
EMPORIO
PERISSA
TO CRETE

AEGEAN SEA

3 KM
2 MILES

DCH

meet arriving boats to take new arrivals into Fira, where you can connect to other points on the island. As these buses can be very crowded in peak season, don't dawdle—get on the bus as quickly as possible.

Visible from the road above Athinios, the roped-off area in the bay is the site of the *Sea Diamond* shipwreck—a cruise ship that sunk here in 2007; all but two of the 1,195 passengers were rescued.

For boat connections from Athinios, see page 442.

By Cruise Ship at the Old Port (below Fira): Cruise ships generally anchor in the caldera below Fira, then tender passengers to the Old Port. Portside, you'll find some car-rental offices and companies selling boat excursions to the little volcanic islands in the middle of the caldera.

From the port, there are three different ways to reach Fira's town center on the cliff above: Take a cable car, hike up, or ride a donkey. The **cable car** is the easiest option (€4 each way, daily 7:00-21:00, every 20 minutes or more with demand, 3-minute ride to the top). But, because the cable car is small (six cars take 6 passengers each, maximum 36 people at a time), you might be in for a long wait if you arrive on a big ship. **Hiking** up the 587 steps is very steep and demanding, and you'll share the steps with

When Santorini Blew Its Top

Coming to Santorini—by boat or by plane—your eyes can't help but trace the telltale arc of the island, a sure sign that you're about to set foot on what was once a volatile volcano.

Situated atop an edgy stack of tectonic plates, Santorini was created by volcanic activity that lasted more than two million years. The island once had a tidy conical shape, but around 1630 B.C., it exploded in what geologists call the "Minoan eruption"—one of the largest in human history. It blew out 24 cubic miles of volcanic material—at least four times the amount ejected by the huge 1883 explosion of Krakatoa (in today's Indonesia).

It appears that the volcano gave Santorini's inhabitants ample warning before erupting (via a major earthquake and later, an initial small eruption).  No human skeletons and few valuable items from that time period have been found here—suggesting that islanders had time to pack up and evacuate. Good thing. Soon afterward, large amounts of ash and pumice blasted out of the crater, and superheated pyroclastic flows (à la Mount St. Helens) swept down the island's slopes. Eventually, the emptied-out volcano collapsed under its own weight, forming the flooded caldera (meaning "cauldron") that we see today.

The volcano's collapse displaced enough seawater to send a huge tsunami screaming south toward Crete, less than 70 miles away. Archaeologists speculate that the tsunami (and perhaps earthquakes near the same time) caused severe hardship, even-

fragrant, messy donkeys. You can pay €5 to ride up on a **donkey,** but the stench and the bumpy ride make this far less romantic than it sounds.

Once at the **top** (the cable-car and donkey trail converge near the same point), you have several options for exploring the town: If you head straight up the stairs, you'll find (to the left) the Catholic cathedral and nearby folk museum, and (to the right) the less appealing of the town's two archaeological museums. If you turn right onto Gold Street (true to its name, lined with jewelry and tourist-trinket shops), you'll eventually reach the Orthodox cathedral, some recommended eateries and accommodations, and Santorini's best tually leading to the downfall of the Minoan civilization.

The volcano isn't done yet. Two little islets in the middle of the caldera emerged from the bay quite recently (by geological standards)—Palea Kameni ("Old Burnt Island") in 197 B.C., and Nea Kameni ("New Burnt Island") in A.D. 1707. To this day, these islets go through periods where they sputter and steam, and earthquakes continue to wrack the entire archipelago (including a devastating one in 1956). The last small eruption (on Nea Kameni) occurred in 1950, and steam and sulfur dioxide are sometimes emitted at the current active crater. Today, the hot springs on Palea Kameni are a popular tourist attraction.

Although the historic eruption devastated the island, it also created its remarkable shape and left behind a unique ecosys-tem and agricultural tradition (see sidebar on page 436). The volcanic soil was also the basis for a local industry. The upper layer of pumice and volcanic ash left by the eruption was quarried, pulverized, and mixed with lime to create a remarkably strong concrete (produced, until recently, in the big, deserted, blocky building on the cliff near Fira—visible from the bay below). Santorini is the country's sole source of this type of material.

Strolling on scenic, seismic Santorini, you're on special ground...carved out more than four millennia ago by one very big bang.

museum (the Museum of Prehistoric Thira). Or, if you want to escape some of the crowds and browse the scenic veil of cafés that cascade down the cliff, head toward the water, go left down the stairs just past Kastro Café, turn off onto the road, and explore to your heart's content.

Note that cruise-ship **excursions** are more likely to tender passengers to the New Port at Athinios (described earlier), where chartered buses wait to take you to your destination. After your excursion, the bus drops you off in Fira, where you can take the cable car (or donkey or hike) down to the return tenders below.

By Plane

Santorini's airport sits along the flat area on the east (back) side of the island, about four miles from Fira. It's connected to Fira by taxi (€10) or bus (€1.40, 10/day, 15 minutes).

Getting Around Santorini

By Bus: Fira is the bus hub for the island. The bus station is a block off the main road, near the south end of town (just downhill from the Orthodox cathedral and Museum of Prehistoric Thira). Buy tickets and get information at the kiosk at the far end of the lot. In peak season, buses can be extremely crowded. For bus connections, see "Fira Connections," page 436.

By Taxi: Just around the corner from Fira's bus station, along the main road, is a taxi stand (figure roughly €15 to Oia, €10 to Athinios port, €10 to Kamari's beaches, €15 to Akrotiri, and €15 to Perissa). You can also call for a taxi (tel. 22860-22555 or 22860-23951).

Fira

The island's main town, Fira, is a practical transit hub with an extraordinary setting. Sitting at a cliff-clinging café terrace and sipping an iced coffee gives you the chance to watch thousands of cruise-ship passengers flood into town each morning (via the cable-car and donkey trail), then recede in the afternoon. All of this built-in business has made Fira a bit greedy; its so-called Gold Street, starting at the cable-car station, is lined with aggressive jewelry salespeople and restaurants with great views, high prices, and low quality.

But if you can ignore the tackiness in this part of town, you'll discover that Fira has a charm of its own—particularly in the cozy labyrinth of streets that burrow between its main traffic street and the cliff edge, and on the steeply switchbacked lanes that zig-zag down the side of the cliff. Fira also has a pair of cathedrals (Orthodox and Catholic), a variety of interesting museums (including the excellent Museum of Prehistoric Thira), and a handy array of services (Internet cafés, launderettes, and so on).

Remember that Fira is not the setting of all those famous Santorini photos—those are taken in Oia (described later).

Orientation to Fira

The core of Fira is squeezed between the cliff and the main road through town, called 25 Martou. This street—with a taxi stand, TI (sometimes open), various scooter/ATV/car-rental places, Internet

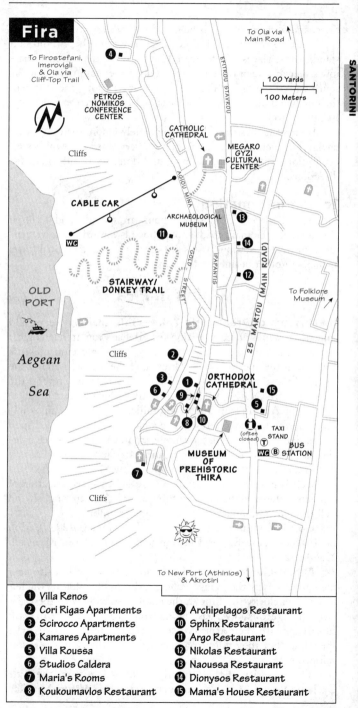

Fira

To Firostefani,
Imerovigli
& Oia via
Cliff-Top Trail

To Oia via
Main Road

PETROS
NOMIKOS
CONFERENCE
CENTER

CATHOLIC
CATHEDRAL

MEGARO
GYZI
CULTURAL
CENTER

100 Yards

100 Meters

Cliffs

EFITROU STAVROU

CABLE CAR

AGIOU MINA

WC

ARCHAEOLOGICAL
MUSEUM

11

13

14

STAIRWAY/
DONKEY TRAIL

"GOLD" STREET

IPAPANTIS

12

OLD
PORT

To Folklore
Museum

Aegean

Sea

Cliffs

2

3

6

1

9

8

ORTHODOX
CATHEDRAL

25 MARTOU (MAIN ROAD)

15

10

5

(often
closed)

TAXI
STAND

WC

BUS
STATION

7

MUSEUM
OF
PREHISTORIC
THIRA

Cliffs

To New Port (Athinios)
& Akrotiri

1	Villa Renos	**9**	Archipelagos Restaurant
2	Cori Rigas Apartments	**10**	Sphinx Restaurant
3	Scirocco Apartments	**11**	Argo Restaurant
4	Kamares Apartments	**12**	Nikolas Restaurant
5	Villa Roussa	**13**	Naoussa Restaurant
6	Studios Caldera	**14**	Dionysos Restaurant
7	Maria's Rooms	**15**	Mama's House Restaurant
8	Koukoumavlos Restaurant		

cafés, and other services—is busy and fairly dingy. The bus station is a block off this drag (around the corner from the TI and taxi stand). Most places of interest to visitors are in the cluster of narrow streets between the bus station (along the main road near the south end of town) and the cable-car station (along the cliff near the north end of town)—a distance you can easily cover in about a 10-minute walk.

If street names exist, locals completely ignore them. Making navigation even more confusing, it's a very vertical town—especially along the cliff. Use a map, and don't be afraid to ask for directions.

Tourist Information

Fira has the island's TI kiosk, but hours are sporadic and it's often closed (along the main road, about 50 yards toward the town center from the bus station). If it's not open, try asking at local travel agencies or other businesses for help.

Sights in Fira

▲▲Museum of Prehistoric Thira—This small but very good collection, while no competition for Greece's top archaeological museums, is Santorini's best. The manageable museum presents items from the ancient site at Akrotiri, at the southern end of the island. This settlement was the largest city outside Crete in the Minoan world, dating back to the earliest documented civilization on the Aegean (third to second millennium B.C.)—impossibly ancient, even to the ancients. The people who lived here fled soon before Santorini blew its top (likely around 1630 B.C.—see sidebar, earlier), leaving behind intriguing artifacts of a civilization that disappeared from the earth not long after. While the Akrotiri site itself is indefinitely closed (see page 441), its best selection of artifacts is viewable here. Everything is described in English and well-presented in modern, air-conditioned comfort.

Cost and Hours: €3; Easter-Oct Tue-Sun 8:00-20:00, Mon 13:30-20:00; Nov-Easter Tue-Sun 8:00-15:00, closed Mon; tel. 22860-23217.

❷ Self-Guided Tour: The model of the Akrotiri site near the entrance puts the items in context. From here, follow the letters counterclockwise through the exhibit, starting with the Early Cycladic figures and vessels, dating from 2700-2300 B.C. The stiff figurines, with their arms crossed, perplex archaeologists, who speculate that they might represent the Mother Goddess worshipped here.

The majority of the museum's pieces date from the Late Cycladic Period (mid-17th century B.C.), when Akrotiri peaked just before its residents fled the erupting volcano. While they took valuable items (such as jewelry) with them, they left behind easily replaceable everyday objects and, of course, immovable items such as wall frescoes. These "left behind" items form the core of the collection.

Primitive cooking pots, clay ovens, and barbeque grills, along with bronze vases, daggers, tongs, and fishing hooks offer clues

to the mysterious Minoan lifestyle. The Minoans were traders rather than warriors, so many items reflect their seafaring heritage. The stack of metal weights illustrates the evolution of standardization during early trading. Also look for the three **large containers,** each one marked differently to suggest their contents—for example, a vessel that held water was decorated with reeds (aquatic plants).

The museum's highlights are the vibrantly colorful, two-dimensional **wall frescoes.** In keeping with the artistic style of Crete (the home of the Minoans), men appear brown, and the

women, white. (If you've been to the National Archaeological Museum in Athens, you might recognize this style of fresco from that museum's collection, which includes wall paintings of antelopes, swallows, and young men boxing, all from this same Akrotiri site—see page 441.) The wall frescoes from the House of the Ladies show exquisitely dressed women. In one, an older woman leans over and appears to be touching the arm of another (now-

missing) woman and holding a dress in her right hand. Farther along, you'll see a fragment of another wall fresco showing blue monkeys. Because monkeys are not indigenous to Greece, these

images offer more evidence that the Minoans traveled far and wide, and interacted with exotic cultures.

Between these frescos, the **vessels** (such as beautiful vases decorated with dolphins and lilies) give us a glimpse of everyday life back then. Look for the ritual vessel shaped like a boar's head.

In the final display case (near the exit) is an exquisite miniature **golden**

ibex—one of the few items of great value that was left behind by fleeing islanders.

Orthodox Cathedral of Candelmas (Panagia Ypapantis)— This modern cathedral, which caps Fira like a white crown, has a grandly painted interior that's worth a look. The cliff-hanging lanes just in front are some of Fira's most enjoyable (and least crowded) to explore.

Archaeological Museum—This museum pales in comparison to the Museum of Prehistoric Thira. Its dusty cases are crammed with sparsely described jugs, statues, and other artifacts from ancient Thira (in contrast to the older Minoan pieces from Akrotiri). Skip it unless you're an archaeologist (€3, Tue-Sun 8:30-15:00, closed Mon, just up the street from the top cable-car station).

Catholic Cathedral—Directly up the stairs from the top cable-

car station, this cathedral is the heart of the island's Catholic community—a remnant of the island's past Venetian rule. Compare this rare Catholic cathedral to the giant Orthodox cathedral at the other end of town: Inside this one are pews, few wall paintings, and none of the tall, skinny candles that are a mainstay of Orthodox worship. Next door is a Dominican monastery and church.

Megaro Gyzi Cultural Center—Hiding in the alleys behind the Catholic cathedral, this modest but endearing local history museum celebrates Santorini life. You'll see photographs of the town from the early to mid-20th century (including scenes before and after the devastating 1956 earthquake), an archive of historic manuscripts and documents, modern paintings of Santorini, and samples of the various types of volcanic rock found on the island. Find the circa-1870 clipping from a London newspaper article about "Santorin," complete with a picture of a smoldering islet in the caldera. Linger over the evocative etchings of traditional Santorini lifestyles. (€3, May-Oct Mon-Sat 10:00-16:00, closed Sun and Nov-April, tel. 22860-23077, www.megarogyzi.gr.)

Petros Nomikos Conference Center—This burnt-orange building, capping a cliff at the northern end of town, features replicas of all the famous frescoes that have been excavated at the ancient Minoan site of Akrotiri. This made-for-tour-groups collection makes it easy to see the full sweep of

Santorini's remarkable prehistoric art in one place. But, after all, these *are* copies—if you're already visiting Fira's Museum of Prehistoric Thira and the National Archaeological Museum in Athens, you'll be able to view the originals in person...making this collection pointless (€4, May-Oct daily 10:00-19:00, closed Nov-April, www.therafoundation.org).

Folklore Museum of Santorini—This collection of folkloric bits and pieces, housed in a restored 19th-century cave house in the Kodochori neighborhood (at the northeast edge of town), illuminates the way of life that has evolved on this chunk of volcanic rock. Exhibits include winemaking, traditional crafts, historical archives, and a small chapel (€3, April-Oct daily 10:00-14:00 & 18:00-20:00, closed Nov-March, tel. 22860-22792).

Hike to Oia—With a few hours to spare, you can venture out on one of Greece's most scenic hikes. While the main road connecting Fira to Oia is drab and dusty, a wonderful cliff-top trail links the two towns, offering fantastic views most of the way. From Fira, head north through the adjoining villages of Firostefani and Imerovigli, then continue along the lip of the crater all the way to Oia. It's long (about five miles, plan on at least 3.5 hours one-way), fairly strenuous (with lots of ups and downs), and offers virtually no shade in hot weather, so don't attempt it unless you're in good shape and have the right gear (good shoes, water, food, sun protection). Get an early start. You can catch a bus or taxi back to Fira when you're done.

Sleeping in Fira

For a true getaway with maximum views and charm, sleep in Oia (recommendations on page 440). But Fira has its own share of breathtaking views, and is handier since it's the bus hub for the island. The best view accommodations (including Villa Renos and Maria's place) are on the steeply angled streets just below the cathedral. On this popular island, rates skyrocket in peak season (July-Sept).

$$$ **Villa Renos,** a class act well-run by Petros and Zina Matekas and their son Vassilis, has nine well-appointed rooms just below the cathedral, on a series of terraces facing the caldera (July-Sept: Sb-€210, Db-€270; May-June and early Oct: Sb-€200, Db-€245; April and late Oct: Sb-€150, Db-€195; March and Nov: Sb-€120, Db-€165; closed Dec-Feb, pricier deluxe rooms, air-con, free Wi-Fi, tel. 22860-22369, www.villarenos.gr, hrenos@ote net.gr).

$$$ **Scirocco Apartments,** run by a Greek-German couple (Eleftherios and Anja Sirigos), rents straightforward, traditionally decorated studios, apartments, and cave houses similarly sprawling

Sleep Code

(€1 = about $1.40, country code: 30)
S = Single, **D** = Double/Twin, **T** = Triple, **Q** = Quad, **b** = bathroom,
s = shower only. Unless otherwise noted, breakfast is included,
credit cards are accepted, and the staff speaks English.

To help you easily sort through these listings, I've divided
the rooms into three categories, based on the price for a
standard double room with bath:

$$$ Higher Priced—Most rooms €100 or more.
$$ Moderately Priced—Most rooms between €70-100.
$ Lower Priced—Most rooms €70 or less.

Prices can change without notice; verify the hotel's
current rates online or by email. For other updates, see www
.ricksteves.com/update.

down the cliff (late July-late Sept: Db-€125-175; May-late July and
late Sept-mid-Oct: Db-€98-155; April and late Oct: Db-€75-130;
more for additional people and larger units, closed Nov-March,
air-con, free Wi-Fi, balconies, swimming pool, tel. 22860-22855,
mobile 697-986-2943).

Several other similar caldera-view places are along the cliff,
including **$$$ Cori Rigas Apartments** (just below Villa Renos,
www.rigas-apartments.gr) and **$$$ Kamares Apartments** (at the
north/Oia end of town, www.kamares-apartments.gr).

$$ Villa Roussa offers 12 basic but comfortable budget rooms
tucked away in a dreary modern building behind the taxi stand
along the main road. Well-run by Peter Pelikanos, it's a humble
but well-located budget option (Db-€65-75 in July-Aug, €40-55 in
June and Sept, €35-45 in Oct-May, prices fluctuate with demand,
no breakfast but shared kitchen, air-con, free Wi-Fi, free trans-
fer from port or airport, tel. 22860-23220, www.villaroussa.gr,
villarousa@gmail.com). Peter also runs **$$$ Studios Caldera**—
situated near the bottom of town—with seven rooms with classic
cliff views and much higher prices (Db-€150 in July-Aug, €120 in
June and Sept, €70-90 off-season, tel. 22860-25166, www.caldera
studios.com, st.caldera@otenet.gr).

$ Maria rents two small, basic rooms with views of the
caldera, tucked on a lane between several other places with the
same views charging double or triple. Her spectacular panoramic
terrace is just as inviting as the big-money places. She has no
email or website, but speaks just enough English to make a reservation by phone. As the only really cheap caldera-view lodging in town, her place is understandably popular—book ahead

(Db-€70 in July-Aug, €60 off-season, tel. 22860-25143, mobile 697-325-4461).

Eating in Fira

You have two choices: expensive with a view overlooking the caldera, or much cheaper at a more typical Greek taverna. In general, places that are closest to the cable car lure in cruise passengers with great views, but—since they know cruisers are only in town for a few hours—have little incentive to put out good food. Natives and lingering travelers tend to dine at the places a 5- to 10-minute walk farther from the cable car.

With a Caldera View, under the Orthodox Cathedral

The streets just under the Orthodox cathedral (the gigantic white-domed building at the south end of town) are lined with several expensive, trendy eateries with good food...you're paying a premium for the high-rent location (€10-15 starters, €20-30 main dishes, all open long hours daily). **Koukoumavlos** is particularly well-regarded (tel. 22860-23807); **Archipelagos** specializes in Greek standards and pasta (tel. 22860-23673); and **Sphinx** has a broader Mediterranean menu that includes quite a bit of Italian (tel. 22860-23823). The steep streets below these restaurants are filled mostly with hotels, but many turn their breakfast terraces into cafés; exploring this area to find your favorite perch for a cup of coffee is a fun activity.

Argo, which serves traditional Greek food specializing in fish, is also along the cliffs but a bit closer to the cable car. Reserve ahead for the upper deck, with the best caldera views (€4-12 starters, €10-18 main dishes, open long hours daily, along the donkey path just below Gold Street, tel. 22860-22594).

In the Old Town

Deeper in the Old Town is a pedestrian street lined with several good choices (all open long hours daily). Like most Fira streets, it's nameless, located one block toward the cliff from the main road, a block north of the main square. Along here, the following three choices are most enticing: **Nikolas** oozes a family-run taverna vibe, with one big room crammed with tables overseen by the namesake patriarch; the menu consists of stick-to-your-ribs Greek classics (€3-5 starters, €7-14 main dishes, tel. 22860-24550). **Naoussa** is a family-friendly place churning out big plates of sloppy Greek food (€4-9 starters, €8-15 main dishes, tel. 22860-24869). **Dionysos** feels more trendy, with a vast terrace (€4-8 starters, €7-20 main dishes, tel. 22860-23845).

Island Cuisine in a Desert

Santorini has an unusual approach to cuisine, dictated (like all facets of life here) by its volcanic geology. Most produce on the island is never watered...which is even more surprising when you think that Santorini—and the neighboring island of Anafi—are the only places in Europe technically classified as having a desert climate. But the island's very steep cliffs trap passing clouds, so most mornings, there's a fine layer of dew covering the ground—just enough to keep plants growing. Residents claim that this approach, along with the volcanic soil, makes their produce taste particularly sweet. Santorini specialties include grapes, tomatoes, eggplant, and cucumbers.

You'll find the predictable Greek classics on most menus, but also look for some local dishes. A Santorinian salad uses the island's cherry tomatoes and cucumbers; tomato croquettes are also popular. *Fava* is a chickpea spread similar to hummus. Because the main settlements of Santorini are perched on the tops of cliffs—with challenging access to the sea—fish isn't as integral to the cuisine as on other islands.

While Greece isn't particularly acclaimed for its wines, Santorini's are well-respected. The discovery of ancient grape seeds at Akrotiri proved that the winemaking tradition here dates back more than 3,500 years. Today, local grapes are mostly Assyrtiko, one of the best Greek varietals; they produce a dry white wine with citrus notes. The growing vines are twisted into a round basket shape called *ampelies*, with the grapes tucked inside to protect them from the strong sunlight and fierce winds. The shape also helps retain moisture from nighttime fog on this otherwise arid isle. Connoisseurs say that the *terroir* created by Santorini's porous volcanic soil gives the wine a special flavor. Two of the most renowned Santorini wines are Vinsanto (sweet dessert wine made from a blend of sun-dried grapes) and Nykteri (dry white wine produced in one day; the name means "night work"). Several shops in Fira or Oia have wine-tasting opportunities, and you can visit a countryside winery if you're interested.

Mama's House, set a few steps down from the main road next to the taxi stand and TI, is another good budget choice with unpretentious Greek fare (€3-7 starters, €8-12 main dishes, daily 8:00-24:00, tel. 22860-21577).

Fira Connections

From Fira by Bus to: Oia (2/hour—generally departs at top and bottom of each hour, 25 minutes, €1.40), **Athinios** and the **New Port** (5-7/day, coordinated to meet boats, 20 minutes, €2;

for boat connections from Athinios, see page 424), **airport** (10/ day, 15 minutes, €1.40), **Kamari** and its nearby beaches (2/hour, 10 minutes, €1.40), **Akrotiri** with its red-sand beaches and (likely closed) archaeological site (nearly hourly, 30 minutes, €1.70), and **Perissa** with its black-sand beaches and access to the Ancient Thira archaeological site (2/hour, 30 minutes, €2). Bus information: tel. 22860-25462, www.ktel-santorini.gr.

Oia

Oia (remember, it's EE-ah, not OY-ah; sometimes spelled "Ia" in English) is the classic, too-pretty-to-be-true place you imag-

ine when someone says "Greek islands." This idyllic ensemble of whitewashed houses and blue domes is delicately draped over a steep slope at the top of a cliff. And in their wisdom, the locals have positioned their town just right for enjoying a sunset over the caldera. On a blue-sky day or

at sunset, there's no better place in Greece to go on a photo safari. In fact, if you can't snap a postcard-quality photo here, it's time to retire your camera.

Oia wasn't always this alluring. In fact, half a century ago it was in ruins—devastated by the earthquake on July 9, 1956. When rebuilding, natives seized the opportunity to make their town even more picture-perfect than before—and it paid off. While far from undiscovered, Oia is the kind of place that you don't mind sharing with boatloads of tourists. And if you break away from its main streets, you can find narrow, winding lanes that take you far from the crowds.

Getting There

To reach Oia from the island's transport hub at Fira, you'll have to take the bus (2/hour, generally departs Fira on the top and bottom of each hour, 25 minutes, €1.40) or a taxi (about €15 one-way).

Orientation to Oia

Oia lines up along its cliff. The main pedestrian drag, which traces the rim of the cliff, is called Nikolaou Nomikou. Oia's steep sea- ward side is smothered with accommodations and restaurants, while the flat landward side is more functional. The town is effec- tively traffic-free except for the main road, which sneaks up on Oia

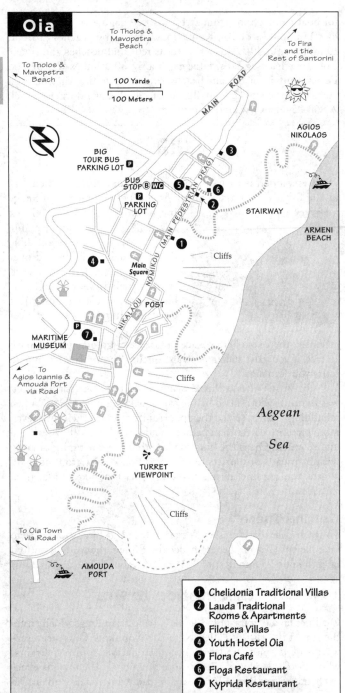

Oia

SANTORINI

To Tholos & Mavopetra Beach

To Fira and the Rest of Santorini

To Tholos & Mavopetra Beach

MAIN ROAD

100 Yards
100 Meters

AGIOS NIKOLAOS

BIG TOUR BUS PARKING LOT **P**

BUS STOP **B** **WC**

P PARKING LOT

5
6
2
3

ARMENI BEACH

STAIRWAY

NOMIKOU (MAIN PEDESTRIAN DRAG)

1

4 ■

Main Square

Cliffs

NIKALAOU

POST

Cliffs

MARITIME MUSEUM

P **7** ■

To Agios Ioannis & Amouda Port via Road

Aegean

Sea

Cliffs

TURRET VIEWPOINT

Cliffs

To Ola Town via Road

AMOUDA PORT

1 Chelidonia Traditional Villas
2 Lauda Traditional Rooms & Apartments
3 Filotera Villas
4 Youth Hostel Oia
5 Flora Café
6 Floga Restaurant
7 Kyprida Restaurant

from behind, opening onto a parking lot and the town's bus stop. From here, just walk a few short, nondescript blocks toward the cliff and its million-dollar views.

Sights in Oia

▲▲▲**Oia Photo Safari**—The main sight here is the town itself, and the best advice is to just get lost with your camera cocked. Shoot the classic, blue-domed postcard views, but also wander around to find your own angle on the town. At the far tip of Oia, venture down, then up, to reach the old turret-like viewpoint, facing the windmills on the horizon and affording a breathtaking 360-degree view.

Why all the whitewash? For one thing, white reflects (rather than absorbs) the powerful heat of the sun. White is the color of

lime—the mineral, not the fruit—mixed with water, which makes a good antiseptic (islanders used it to paint their houses, so it would naturally disinfect the rainwater that was collected on rooftops). Later, white evolved into an aesthetic choice...and a patriotic one: During the

400-year Ottoman occupation, Greeks were not allowed to fly their blue-and-white flag. But here in Oia—with its white houses, blue domes, and the blue sea and sky—the whole village was one big, defiant banner for Greece.

The most interesting houses are the ones burrowed into the side of the rock wall. These "cliff houses," surrounded by air-filled pumice, are ideally insulated—staying cool in summer and warm in winter. While cliff houses were once the poorest dwellings in town, today only millionaires can afford to own them (and most are rented out as very pricey accommodations).

▲▲▲**Oia Sunset**—The best place on Santorini to enjoy the sunset, Oia becomes even more crowded when the sun goes down. Shutterbugs jockey for position on the town's best viewpoints, and all that white captures the swirling colors of the sky for a fleeting moment. Many travelers plan their day around being here at sunset.

Maritime Museum—Every Greek island seems to have its own maritime museum, and Oia hosts Santorini's. With two floors of old nautical objects and basic English labels, the collection includes roomfuls of old ship paintings, letters and documents, model ships, and well-endowed mastheads. It's the only museum in town, but it's nothing to jump ship for, unless you're a sailor or need a place to get out of the sun (€3, Wed-Mon 10:00-14:00 & 17:00-20:00, closed Tue, well-signposted a block off the main clifftop drag, tel. 22860-71156).

Sleeping in Oia

(€1 = about $1.40, country code: 30)
Several interchangeable places rent out appealing "cliff houses" just down from the main cliffside road. They range from smaller rooms or studios for two people, to larger units sleeping four or more. While expensive, these provide an unforgettable experience. For budget travelers, Oia also has a fine youth hostel.

$$$ Chelidonia Traditional Villas, run by friendly Greek-Austrian couple Triantaphyllos and Erika Pitsikali, rents 10 traditional apartments burrowed into the cliff face right in the heart of town. Promising "panorama and privacy," this place lets you be a temporary troglodyte (studio-€160-180, villa-€185-210, suite-€230-250, no breakfast but kitchen in units, free Wi-Fi, tel. 22860-71287, www.chelidonia.com, erika@chelidonia.com).

$$$ Lauda Traditional Rooms and Apartments offers 16 units scattered along the cliffside facing the caldera. The furnishings are basic, but there's a swimming pool, and all come with a terrace or balcony (apartments-€190 for up to 4 people, €220 for 5 people, no breakfast but kitchen in units, cash only, free Wi-Fi, tel. 22860-71204, www.lauda-santorini.com).

$$$ Filotera Villas, family-run by Nikolas, is similar to the two listed above, with five small white houses and a swimming pool and Jacuzzi (July-Sept: €180-280; May-June: €160-230; April and Oct: €140-210; price depends on size, closed Nov-March, breakfast-€7.30 or use kitchen in unit, air-con, free Wi-Fi, tel. 22860-71110, www.filoteravillas.gr, filotera@otenet.gr).

$ Youth Hostel Oia is a well-run place tucked a few blocks back from the cliff edge. It rents 75 beds in institutional-feeling rooms around a tranquil courtyard with a fountain (4-, 6-, or 12-bed rooms, all mixed dorms, €17/bed in high season, €15/bed in shoulder season, includes breakfast, pay Internet access, laundry, reception open 8:30-14:00 & 17:00-22:00, closed Oct-April, a block straight ahead from the bus stop, tel. 22860-71465, www.santorinihostel.gr).

Eating in Oia

Dining with a view is a no-brainer here—it's worth the too-high prices to enjoy caldera views with your meal or drink. The cliffside places are pretty interchangeable, but if you can't make up your mind, consider one of these.

Flora Café is an affordable alternative to the budget-busting places along the cliff. Set along the main drag (at the Fira end of town), it offers a great view and serves up affordable, unpretentious fare in a casual pizzeria setting (€4-8 small dishes, €8-10 bigger meals, daily 9:00-late, tel. 22860-71424).

Floga dishes up traditional Greek food with a modern spin, a few steps below the main drag (and below Flora Café) at the Fira end of town (€8-12 starters, €11-19 main dishes, daily specials, open long hours daily, tel. 22860-71152).

Kyprida Restaurant, serving traditional Cypriot cuisine, is set a couple of blocks back from the cliff edge, but its top terrace still has a fine sunset view (€5-9 starters, €11-20 main dishes, daily 12:00-late, tel. 22860-71979).

More Sights on Santorini

The island of Santorini has several other worthwhile side-trips, doable by car, bus, or taxi.

Beaches—The volcanic composition of the island has created some unusual opportunities for beach bums. There are volcanic black-sand beaches near **Kamari** (tidy and more upscale-feeling) and **Perissa** (more popular with backpackers)—both on the east coast, but separated from each other by a mountain. Red-sand beaches are near the town of **Akrotiri** (facing away from the caldera along the southern arc of the island).

Ancient Sites—Santorini has two major archaeological sites: the Minoan site near Akrotiri (the town at the southern tip of the island) and the Archaic site at Ancient Thira (high on a bluff on the east coast, between Perissa and Kamari). As both of these (especially Akrotiri) have a history of unexpected closures, carefully confirm in town that they're open before making the trip there.

Near **Akrotiri** is the site of an important archaeological excavation from the Minoan period (whose citizens fled just before the massive 1630 B.C. eruption). But the site closed in 2005 after the roof of the visitor's center collapsed, killing one person. Authorities are implementing new safety measures and keep saying they might reopen it "next year" (year after year). Even if it's closed, you can still see the most interesting items discovered here—including some wonderful wall frescoes—on display at Fira's Museum of Prehistoric Thira (see page 430).

The site at **Ancient Thira,** dramatically situated on a mountaintop between Perissa and Kamari, dates from a more recent civilization. It was settled post-volcano by Dorians from Sparta, likely in the ninth century B.C., and continued to thrive through the Hellenistic, Roman, and Byzantine periods. Open to visitors every day but Monday, this place is less distinctive than the Akrotiri site and is only worth a visit by archaeology completists. If you've toured other Greek ruins from this era—in Athens, Delphi, Olympia, Epidavros, etc.—you'll see nothing new here. You can reach the Ancient Thira site from Kamari, which has regular bus excursions; hardy hikers could also huff up from Perissa on a very twisty serpentine path.

Volcanic Islets and Other Caldera Trips—A popular excursion is to sail from the Old Port below Fira out to the active volcanic islets in the middle of the caldera. The quickest trips include only a hike to the crater on **Nea Kameni** (€13); longer tours also include a visit to swim in the hot springs on **Palea Kameni** (€18), as well as other towns and villages (€25). The "sunset tour" includes a visit to the volcano and hot springs, followed by a boat trip under the cliffs of Oia for the sunset with a glass of wine (€35, 5 hours). Bus tours are also available. Various travel agencies around Santorini sell these trips—look for ads locally.

Santorini Connections

Remember, the New Port is a 20-minute bus ride away from Fira, and buses can be very crowded in summer.

By Boat from the New Port (Athinios): Santorini is connected daily to **Piraeus** (Athens) by a wide range of slower ferries (8-9 hours; Blue Star Ferries, tel. 210-891-9800, www.bluestar ferries.com; and ANEK Lines, tel. 210-419-7420, www.anek.gr) and faster catamarans (5.25 hours; SeaJets, tel. 210-412-1800, www .seajets.gr; and Aegean Speed Lines, tel. 210-969-0950, www .aegeanspeedlines.gr). The Flying Cat catamaran runs daily from April through October (except the second Wed of each month) to **Mykonos** (3 hours) and other Cycladic Islands, as well as to **Crete** (1.25 hours; Hellenic Seaways, tel. 210-419-9000, www.hsw.gr).

GREEK HISTORY AND MYTHOLOGY

Our lives today would be quite different if it weren't for a few thousand Greeks who lived in the small city of Athens about 450 years before Christ was born. Democracy, theater, literature, mathematics, science, philosophy, and art all flourished in Athens during its 50-year "Golden Age"—a cultural boom time that set the tone for the rest of Western history to follow.

Greece's history since Classical times may be of less value to the casual tourist, but it's fascinating nonetheless. From pagan to Christian to Muslim, to the freedom-fighters of the 19th century and the refugees of the 20th century, Greece today is the product of many different peoples, religions, and cultures.

The Pre-Greek World:
The Minoans (2000-1450 B.C.)

Classical Greece didn't just pop out of nowhere. Cursed with rocky soil, isolated by a rugged landscape, and scattered by invasions, the Greeks took centuries to unify. Greek civilization was built on the advances of earlier civilizations: Minoans, Mycenaeans, Dorians, and Ionians—the stew of peoples that eventually cooked up Greece.

A safe, isolated location on the island of Crete (a 12-hour boat ride south of Athens), combined with impressive business savvy, enabled the Minoans to dominate the pre-Greek world. Unlike most early peoples, they were traders, not fighters. With a large merchant fleet, they exported wine, olive oil, pottery, and well-crafted jewelry, then returned home with the wealth of the Mediterranean.

Today we know them by the colorful frescoes they left behind on the walls of prosperous, unfortified homes and palaces.

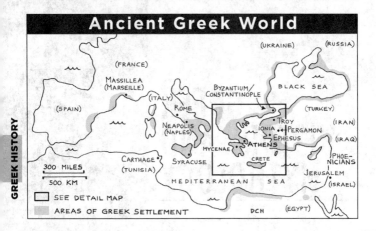

Ancient Greek World

Surviving frescoes show happy people engaged in everyday life: ladies harvesting saffron, athletes leaping over bulls, and charming landscapes with animals.

The later Greeks would inherit the Minoans' business skills, social equality, love of art for art's sake, and faith in rational thought over brute military strength. Some scholars hail the Minoans as the first truly "European" civilization.

In about 1450 B.C., the Minoan civilization suddenly collapsed, and no one knows why (volcano? invasions?). Physically and economically weakened, they were easily overrun and absorbed by a tribe of warlike people from the mainland—the Mycenaeans.

Minoan Sights

• Frescoes from Akrotiri on the island of Santorini, in the National Archaeological Museum in Athens, and the Museum of Prehistoric Thira in Fira

Mycenae (1600-1200 B.C.)

After the fall of the Minoans, the Greek mainland was dominated by the Mycenaeans (my-seh-NEE-uhns), a fusion of local tribes centered in the city of Mycenae (my-SEE-nee). Culturally, they were the anti-Minoans—warriors not traders, chieftains not bureaucrats. Their ruins at the capital of Mycenae (about two hours by bus southwest of Athens, or a half-hour's drive north of Nafplio) tell the story. Buildings are fortress-like, the city has thick defensive walls, and statues are stiff and crude. Early Greeks called Mycenaean architecture "cyclopean," because they believed that only giants could have built with such colossal blocks. Mycenaean kings were elaborately buried in cemeteries and tombs built like subterranean stone igloos, loaded with jewels, swords, and precious objects that fill museums today.

The Mycenaeans dominated Greece during the era of the legends of the Trojan War. Whether or not there's any historical truth to the legends, Mycenae has become associated with the tales of Agamemnon, Clytemnestra, and the invasion of Troy.

Around 1200 B.C., the Mycenaeans—like the Minoans before them—mysteriously disappeared, plunging Greece into its next, "dark" phase.

GREEK HISTORY

Mycenaean Sights

• The citadel at Mycenae, with its Lion Gate, Grave Circle A, palace, and *tholos* tombs
• Mask of Agamemnon and other artifacts at the National Archaeological Museum in Athens
• Dendra Panoply, a 15th-century B.C. suit of bronze armor in the Nafplio Archaeological Museum

The Greek Dark Ages (1200-800 B.C.)

Whatever the reason, once-powerful Mycenaean cities became deserted, writing was lost, roads crumbled, trade decreased, and

bandits preyed on helpless villagers. Dark Age graves contain little gold, jewelry, or fine pottery. Divided by mountains into pockets of isolated, semi-barbaric, warring tribes, the Greeks took centuries to unify and get their civilization back on track.

It was during this time that legends passed down over generations were eventually compiled (in the ninth century B.C.) by a blind, talented, perhaps nonexistent man that tradition calls Homer. His long poem, the *Iliad*, describes the battles and struggles of the early Greeks (perhaps the Mycenaeans) as they conquered Troy. The *Odyssey* tells of the weary soldiers' long, torturous trip back home. The Greeks saw these epics as perfect metaphors for their own struggles to unify and build a stable homeland. The stories helped shape a collective self-image.

Dark Age Sights

• The Kastalian Spring and omphalos monuments at Delphi

Greek Mythology

The following were the stars among a large cast of characters—gods, beasts, and heroes—who scampered through the Greek mindscape, mingled with mortals, and inspired so much classical art and literature.

The Gods

The major Greek gods (the Olympians) lived atop Mount Olympus, presided over by Zeus, king of the gods (and father of many of them). Each god had a distinct personality, unique set of talents, and area of responsibility over the affairs of the world (they specialized). Though they were immortal and super-powerful, these gods were not remote, idealized deities; instead, like characters in a celestial soap opera, they displayed the full range of human foibles: petty jealousies, destructive passions, broken hearts, and god-sized temper tantrums. They also regularly interacted with humans—falling in love with them, seducing them, toying with them, and punishing them. The Romans were so impressed by the Greek lineup of immortals that they borrowed them, but gave them new names (shown in parentheses below).

Zeus (Jupiter): Papa Zeus liked the ladies, and often turned himself into some earthly form (a bull, a cloud, or a swan) to hustle unsuspecting mortal females. Statues depict him wearing a beard and sometimes carrying a spear. He is also symbolized by a thunderbolt or an eagle.

Hera (Juno): The beautiful queen of the gods was the long-suffering wife of philandering Zeus. She was also—whether ironically or fittingly—the goddess of marriage.

Hades (Pluto): The king of the underworld and lord of the dead is depicted as sad, with a staff.

Poseidon (Neptune): The god of the sea, he was also responsible for earthquakes, earning him the nickname "Earth Shaker." He is often shown holding a trident.

Apollo: The ruler of the Sun, he drives the Sun's flaming chariot across the sky each day, and represents light and truth. He is also the god of music and poetry.

Hermes (Mercury): The messenger of the gods sports a helmet and shoes with wings. He delivers a lot of flowers in his current incarnation as a corporate logo.

Ares (Mars): The god of war (and Aphrodite's boyfriend), he dresses for battle and carries a spear.

Dionysus (Bacchus): The god of wine and college frats holds grapes and wears a toga and laurel wreath.

Athena (Minerva): The virginal goddess of wisdom was born from the head of Zeus, and is depicted carrying a spear. Athens is named for her and the Parthenon was built in her honor.

Artemis (Diana): The goddess of the Moon and hunting, she was the twin sister of Apollo. She carries a bow and arrow.

Aphrodite (Venus): The goddess of love and beauty, she was born of the sea. This good-looking lady was married to the crippled god Hephaistos, but was two-timing him with Ares.

Eros (Cupid): The god of desire is depicted as a young man or baby with wings, wielding a bow and arrows.

Hestia (Vesta): Modestly dressed, veiled goddess of the home and hearth, she oversaw domestic life.

Hephaistos (Vulcan): Poor cuckolded Hephaistos was lame and ugly, but useful. Blacksmith to the gods, he was the god of the forge, fire, and craftsmen.

Demeter (Ceres): Goddess of the seasons, the harvest, and fertility, she is shown holding a tuft of grain.

The Beasts

Pan (Faun): Happy Pan, with a body that's half man (on top) and half goat, was the god of shepherds and played a flute.

Centaur: This race of creatures, human on top and horse below, was said to be wise.

Satyr: Like Pan, satyrs were top-half man, bottom-half goat. And they were horny.

Griffin: With the head and wings of an eagle and the body of a lion, griffins were formidable.

Harpy: Creatures with the head of a woman and the body of a bird, harpies were known for stealing.

Medusa: With writhing snakes instead of hair, she had a face that turned people to stone. She was slain by Perseus.

Pegasus: The winged horse was the son of Poseidon and Medusa.

Cyclops: A race of one-eyed giants, they were known for their immense strength.

Minotaur: This beast with the head of a bull lived in the labyrinth at Knossos, the palace on Crete.

The Heroes

Hercules: This son of Zeus was born to a mortal woman. The strongest man in the world performed many feats of strength and tested negative for steroids. To make Hercules atone for killing his family in a fit of madness, the gods forced him to perform Twelve Labors, which included slaying various fierce beasts and doing other chores. He often wore a lion's skin.

Amazons: A race of powerful female warriors. Classical art often depicts them doing battle with the Greeks.

Prometheus: He defied the gods, stealing fire from them and giving it to humans. As punishment, he was chained to a rock, where an eagle feasted daily on his innards.

Jason: He sailed with his Argonauts in search of the Golden Fleece.

Perseus: He killed Medusa and rescued Andromeda from a serpent.

Theseus: He killed the Minotaur in the labyrinth on Crete.

Trojan War Heroes: This gang of greats includes Achilles, Ajax, Hector, Paris, Agamemnon, and the gorgeous Helen of Troy.

Heart of Greek Ancient World

Archaic Period (800-500 B.C.)

Tradition holds that in 776 B.C., Greek-speaking people from all over the mainland and islands halted their wars and gathered in Olympia to compete in the first Olympic Games. Bound by a common language and religion, Greece's scattered tribes began settling down.

Living on islands and in valleys, the Greek-speaking people were divided by geography from their neighbors. They naturally

formed governments around a single city (or polis) rather than as a unified empire. Petty warfare between city-states was practically a sport.

Slowly, the city-states unified, making alliances with each other, establishing colonies in Italy and France, and absorbing culture from the more sophisticated Egyptians (style of statues) and Phoenicians (alphabet). Scarcely two centuries later, Greece would be an integrated community and the center of the civilized world.

Statues from Archaic times are crude, as stiff as the rock they're carved from. Rather than individuals, they are generic people: called either kore (girl) or kouros (boy). With perfectly round heads, symmetrical pecs, and a navel in the center, these sturdy statues reflect the order and stability the troubled Greeks were striving for.

By the sixth century B.C., Greece's many small city-states had coalesced around two power centers: oppressive, no-frills, and militaristic Sparta; and its polar opposite, the democratic, luxury-loving, and business-friendly Athens.

Archaic Sights

• Dipylon Vase (National Archaeological Museum in Athens) and other geometric vases in various museums
• Kouros and kore statues (National Archaeological Museum in Athens, Acropolis Museum in Athens, Archaeological Museum in Delphi)
• The Olympic Stadium and Temple of Hera in Olympia
• Statue of the *Sphinx of Naxos* at Delphi
• *Lions of the Naxians* statues on the island of Delos

Pre-Golden Age: The Rise of Athens and the Persian Wars (500-450 B.C.)

In 490 B.C., an enormous army of Persians under King Darius I swept into Greece to punish the city of Athens, which had dared

to challenge his authority over Greek-speaking Ionia (in today's western Turkey). A few thousand plucky Athenians raced to head off the Persians in a crucial bottleneck valley, at the Battle of Marathon. Though outnumbered three to one, the crafty Greeks lined up and made a wall of shields (a phalanx) and pushed the Persians back. An excited Greek soldier ran the 26.2 miles from the city of Marathon to Athens, gasped the good news...and died.

In 480 B.C., Persia attacked again. This time, all of Greece put aside its petty differences to fight the common enemy as an alliance of city-states. King Leonidas of Sparta and his 300 Spartans made an Alamo-like last stand at Thermopylae that delayed the invasion. Meanwhile, Athenians abandoned their city and fled, leaving Athens (and much of the lower mainland) to be looted. But the Athenians rallied to win a crucial naval victory at the Battle of Salamis, followed by a land victory at the Battle of Plataea, driving out the Persians.

Athens was hailed as Greece's protector and policeman, and the various city-states cemented their alliance (the Delian League) by pooling their defense funds, with Athens as the caretaker. Athens signed a 30-year peace treaty with Sparta...and the Golden Age began.

Pre-Golden Age Sights

• Severe-style statues, such as the *Artemision Bronze* (Athens' National Archaeological Museum) and *Bronze Charioteer* (Olympia)
• Olympia's Temple of Zeus and the Bronze Helmet of Miltiades

Golden Age Athens (450-400 B.C.)

Historians generally call Greece's cultural flowering the "Classical Period" (approximately 500-323 B.C.), with the choice cut being the two-generation span (450-400 B.C.) called the "Golden Age." After the Persian War, the Athenians set about rebuilding their city (with funds from the Delian League). Grand public buildings and temples were decorated with painting and sculpture. Ancient Athens was a typical city-state, population  80,000, gathered around its Acropolis ("high town"), which was the religious center and fort of last defense. Below was the Agora, or marketplace, the economic and social center. Blessed with a harbor and good farmland, Athens prospered, exporting cash crops (wine and olive oil, pottery and other crafts) to neighboring cities and importing the best craftsmen, thinkers, and souvlaki. Amphitheaters hosted drama, music, and poetry festivals. The marketplace bustled with goods from all over the Mediterranean. Upwardly mobile Greeks flocked to Athens. The incredible advances in art, architecture, politics, science, and philosophy set the pace for all of Western civilization to follow. And all this from a Greek town smaller than Muncie, Indiana.

Athens' leader, a charismatic nobleman named Pericles, set out to democratize Athens. As with many city-states, Athens' government had morphed from rule by king, to a council of nobles, to rule by "tyrants" in troubled times, and finally to rule by the people. In Golden Age Athens, every landowning man had a vote in the Assembly of citizens. It was a direct democracy (not a representative democracy, where you elect others to serve), in which every man was expected to fill his duties of voting, community projects, and military service. Of course, Athens' "democracy" excluded women, slaves, freed slaves, and anyone not born in Athens.

A Who's Who of Classical Age Greeks

Socrates (c. 469-399 B.C.) questioned the status quo, angered authorities, and took his own life rather than change his teachings.

Plato (c. 424-348 B.C.) was Socrates' follower (and note-taker), and focused on elucidating non-material, timeless, mathematical ideas.

Aristotle (c. 384-322 B.C.) was Plato's follower, and championed the empirical sciences, emphasizing the importance of the physical world as a means of knowledge.

Pericles (c. 495-429 B.C.) was a charismatic nobleman who promoted democracy.

Pythagoras (c. 580-500 B.C.) gave us $a^2 + b^2 = c^2$.

Euclid (c. 335-270 B.C.) laid out geometry as we know it.

Diogenes (c. 412-323 B.C.) lived homeless in the Agora, turning from materialism to concentrate on ethical living.

Aristophanes (c. 446-386 B.C.), **Sophocles** (c. 496-406 B.C.), and **Euripides** (c. 480-406 B.C.) wrote comedies and tragedies that are still performed today.

Hippocrates (c. 460-370 B.C.) made medicine a hard science. He rejected superstition and considered disease a result of natural—rather than supernatural—causes.

Pheidias (c. 480-430 B.C.) designed the statuary of the Parthenon and several monumental statues.

Praxiteles (c. 400-330 B.C.) sculpted lifelike yet beautiful human figures.

Perhaps the greatest Greek invention was the very idea that nature is orderly and man is good—a rational creature who can solve problems. Their concept of the "Golden Mean" reveals the value they placed in balance, order, and harmony in art and in life. At school, both the mind and the body were trained.

Philosophers debated many of the questions that still occupy the human mind. Socrates questioned traditional, superstitious beliefs. His motto, "Know thyself," epitomizes Greek curiosity about who we are and what we know for sure. Branded a threat to Athens' youth, Socrates committed suicide rather than compromise his ideals. His follower Plato wrote down many of Socrates' words. Plato taught that the physical world is only a pale reflection of true reality (the way a shadow on the wall is a poor version of the 3-D, full-color world we see). The greater reality is the unseen, mathematical orderliness that underlies the fleeting physical world. Plato's pupil Aristotle, an avid biologist, emphasized study of the physical world rather than the intangible one. Both Plato and Aristotle founded schools that would attract Europe's great minds for centuries. And their ideas would resurface much later, after Europe experienced a resurgence of humanism and critical thought.

Greeks worshipped a pantheon of gods, viewed as supernatural humans (with human emotions) who controlled the forces of nature. Greek temples housed a statue of a god or goddess. Since the people worshipped outside, the temple exterior was the important part and the interior was small and simple. Generally, only priests were allowed to go inside, where they'd present your offering to the god's statue in the hope that the god would grant your wish.

Most temples had similar features. They were rectangular, surrounded by rows of columns, and topped by slanted roofs. Rather than single-piece columns, the Greeks usually built them of stacked slices of stone (drums), each with a plug to keep it in line. Columns sat on a base, and were topped with a capital. The triangle-shaped roof formed a gable—typically filled with statues—called the pediment. A typical pediment might feature a sculpted gang of gods doing their divine mischief. Beneath the pediment was a line of carved reliefs called metopes. Under the eaves, a set of sculpted low-relief panels—called the frieze—often ran around the building.

Classical Greek architecture evolved through three orders: Doric (columns topped with simple and stocky capitals), Ionic (rolled capitals), and Corinthian (leafy, ornate capitals). As a memory aid, remember that the orders gain syllables as they evolve: Doric, Ionic, Corinthian.

Classical art is known for its symmetry, harmony, and simplicity. It shows the Greeks' love of rationality, order, and balance. The Greeks of this era featured the human body in all its naked splendor. The anatomy is accurate, and the poses are relaxed and natural. Greek sculptors learned to capture people in motion, and to show them from different angles, not just face-on. The classic

DORIC   IONIC   CORINTHIAN

Greek pose—called *contrapposto,* or counter-poise—has a person resting weight on one leg while the other is relaxed or moving slightly. This pose captures a balance between timeless stability and fleeting motion that the Greeks found beautiful. It's also a balance between down-to-earth humans (with human flaws and quirks) and the idealized perfection of a Greek god.

Golden Age Sights
• The Acropolis in Athens, with the Parthenon, Erechtheion, Propylaea, Temple of Athena Nike, and Theater of Dionysus
• The Agora, Athens' main square—crossed by the Panathenaic Way and frequented by all the Golden Age greats
• Temple of Hephaistos, in the Agora
• Sanctuary of Apollo at Delphi
• Workshop of Pheidias at Olympia

Late Classical Period—The Decline of Athens (400-323 B.C.)
Many Greek city-states came to resent the tribute money they were obliged to send to Athens, supposedly to protect them from an

invasion that never came. Rallying behind Sparta, they ganged up on Athens. The Peloponnesian War, lasting a generation, toppled Athens (404 B.C.), drained Greece, and ended the Golden Age. Still more wars followed, including struggles between Sparta and Thebes. In 338 B.C., Athens, Sparta, and all the rest of the city-states were conquered by powerful Greek-speaking invaders from the north: the Macedonians.

Late Classical Sights
• *Bronze Statue of a Youth* at Athens' National Archaeological Museum
• *Statue of Hermes,* perhaps by Praxiteles, in Olympia

Hellenism (323-146 B.C.)
"Hellenism," from the Greek word for "Greek," refers to the era when Greece's political importance declined but Greek culture was spread through the Mediterranean and Asia by Alexander the Great.

After King Philip of Macedonia conquered Greece, he was succeeded by his 20-year-old son, Alexander (356-323 B.C.). Alexander had been tutored by the Greek philosopher Aristotle, who got the future king hooked on Greek culture. According to

GREEK HISTORY

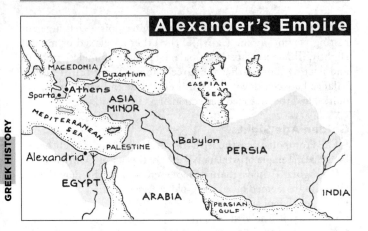

Alexander's Empire

legend, Alexander went to bed each night with two things under his pillow: a dagger and a copy of the *Iliad*. Alexander loved Greek high culture, but was also pragmatic about the importance of military power.

In 334 B.C., Alexander and a well-trained army of 40,000 headed east. Their busy itinerary included conquering today's Turkey, Palestine, Egypt (where he was declared a living god), Iraq, and Iran, and moving into India. Alexander was a daring general, a benevolent conqueror, and a good administrator. As he conquered, he founded new cities on the Greek model, spread the Greek language, and opened Greek schools. After eight years on the road, an exhausted Alexander died at the age of 32, but by then he had created the largest empire ever. (What have you accomplished lately?)

Hellenistic art reflects the changes in Greek society. Rather than noble, idealized gods, the Hellenistic artists gave us real people with real emotions, shown warts-and-all. Some are candid snapshots of everyday life, like a boy stooped over to pull a

thorn from his foot. Others show people in extreme moments, as they struggle to overcome life's obstacles. We see the thrill of victory and the agony of defeat. Arms flail, muscles strain, eyes bulge. Clothes and hair are whipped by the wind. Figures are frozen in motion, in wild, unbalanced poses that dramatize their inner thoughts.

For two centuries, much of the Mediterranean and Asia—the entire known civilized world—was dominated by Greek rulers and Greek culture.

Hellenistic Sights
• Stoa of Attalos, in Athens' Agora, built by a Grecophile from Pergamon
• Statues of the *Horse and Jockey, Fighting Gaul,* and others in Athens' National Archaeological Museum
• Head of Alexander the Great in Athens' Acropolis Museum
• Theater (and site) of Epidavros
• Philippeion temple in Olympia

Roman Greece (146 B.C.-A.D. 476)
At the same time that Alexander was conquering the East, a new superpower was rising in the West: Rome. Eventually, Rome's

legions conquered Greece (146 B.C.) and the Hellenized Mediterranean (31 B.C.). Culturally, however, the Greeks conquered the Romans.

Roman governors ruled cosmopolitan Greek-speaking cities, adopting the Greek gods, art styles, and fashions. Greek-style temple facades, with their columns and pediments, were pasted on the front of (Roman-arch) temples as a veneer of sophistication. Greek statues dotted Roman villas and public buildings. Pretentious Romans sprinkled their Latin conversation with Greek phrases as they enjoyed the plays of Sophocles and Aristophanes. Many a Greek slave was more cultured than his master, reduced to the role of warning his boss not to wear a plaid toga with polka-dot sandals.

Athens was a major city in the cosmopolitan Roman world. Paul—a Jewish Christian with Roman citizenship—came to Athens (A.D. 49) to spread the Christian message from atop Mars Hill. The Bible makes it clear (Acts 17) that the sophisticated Athenians were not impressed.

Athens, with its prestigious monuments, was well-preserved under the Romans, but as Rome began to collapse, it became less able to protect and provide for Greece. In A.D. 267, Athens suffered a horrendous invasion by barbarian Herulians, who left much of the city in ashes. Other barbarian invasions followed.

In A.D. 476, even the city of Rome fell to invaders. As Christianity established itself, Greece's pagan sanctuaries were closed. For a thousand years, Athens had carried the torch of pagan and secular learning. But in A.D. 529, the Christian/Roman/Byzantine Emperor Justinian closed Athens' famous schools of philosophy...and the "ancient" world came to an end.

Greek culture would live on, resurfacing throughout Western history and eventually influencing medieval Christians,

Renaissance sculptors, and even the Neoclassical architects who designed Washington, DC, in the Greek style.

Roman Sights
- Roman Forum (and Tower of the Winds) in Athens
- Temple of Olympian Zeus and Arch of Hadrian in Athens
- Odeon of Agrippa and Statue of Hadrian, in Athens' Agora
- Hadrian's Library (near Monastiraki) in Athens
- Temple of Roma and Monument of Agrippa, on the Acropolis in Athens
- Odeon of Herodes Atticus (built by a wealthy ethnic-Greek/Roman-citizen) in Athens
- Mars Hill (the rock where the Christian Apostle Paul preached to the pagans) in Athens
- Nymphaeum in Olympia
- Many Greek buildings and artworks that were renovated in Roman times

Byzantine Greece (323-1453 A.D.)
With the fall of Rome in Western Europe, Greece came under the sway of the Byzantine Empire—namely, the eastern half of the ancient Roman Empire that *didn't* "fall" in A.D. 476. Byzantium remained Christian and enlightened for another thousand years, with Greek (not Latin) as the common language. The empire's capital was Constantinople (modern Istanbul), founded in A.D. 330 by Roman Emperor Constantine to help man-

age the fading Roman Empire. For the next thousand years, Greece's cultural orientation would face east.

Though ostensibly protected by the Byzantine emperor in Constantinople, Greece suffered several centuries of invasions (A.D. 600-900) by various Slavic barbarians. The Orthodox Church served as a rallying point, and the invaders were eventually driven out or assimilated.

After A.D. 1000, Greece's economic prosperity returned—farms produced, the population grew, and cities engaged in trade—and Athens entered a second, more modest, Golden Age (c. 1000-1200). Greece reconnected with the rest of Western Europe during the Crusades, when Western soldiers traveled through Greek ports on their way to Jerusalem. This revived East–West trade, which was brokered by Venetian merchants, who were granted trading rights to establish ports in Greek territory.

This Golden Age is when many of Athens' venerable Orthodox

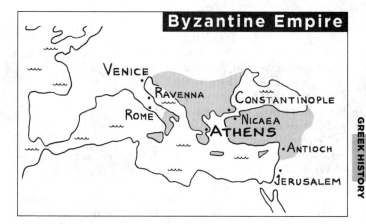

churches were built. Christian pilgrims from across the Byzantine Empire flocked to Athens to visit the famous church housed within the (still-intact) Parthenon. Byzantine mosaics, featuring realistic plants, animals, and people, were exported to the West.

The Byzantine Empire—and, by extension, Greece—were weakened by the disastrous Fourth Crusade (1204), in which greedy Crusaders looted their fellow Christian city of Constantinople. Following this, Western Crusaders occupied and ruled many parts of Greece, including Athens, and Byzantine Christians battled Crusading Christians at Monemvasia. Meanwhile, the Ottomans were whittling away at the empire's fringes. In 1453, Constantinople fell to the Ottoman Turks.

Byzantine-Era Sights
• Athens' old Orthodox churches, including the Church of Kapnikarea (on Ermou street), Agios Eleftherios (next to the cathedral), and Holy Apostles (in the Agora)
• Byzantine and Christian Museum in Athens
• Icons of the Eastern Orthodox Church
• Monemvasia fortress

Islamic/Ottoman Greece (1453-1821)
Under the Ottomans, Greece was ruled by Islamic Turks from their capital of Constantinople. Like many other temples-turned-churches, Athens' Parthenon (still intact) became a mosque, and a minaret was built alongside it.

Greek Christians had several choices for surviving the new regime. Some converted to Islam and learned Turkish, while others faked their conversion and remained closet Christians. Some moved to the boonies, outside the reach of Ottoman administrators. Many of Greece's best and brightest headed to Western

Europe, helping to ignite the Renaissance (which, fittingly, revived the Classical achievements of ancient Athens). Most Greeks just stayed put, paid the "Christian tax," and lived in peace alongside the Ottomans. The Ottomans were (relatively) benevolent rulers, and the Greek language and Orthodox Christianity both survived.

Greece found itself between the powerful Ottomans and powerful merchants of Venice. This made Greece a center for East–West trade, but also a battleground. Venetian traders (backed by their military) occupied and fortified a number of Greek seaports, in order to carry on trade throughout the Ottoman Empire. In 1687, the Venetians attacked Ottoman-controlled Athens. The Ottomans hunkered down on the Acropolis, storing their gunpowder in the Parthenon. A Venetian cannonball hit the Parthenon, destroying it and creating the ruin we see today. Venetian looters plundered the rubble and carried off statues as souvenirs.

Ottoman-Era Sights
• Benaki Museum of Islamic Art in Athens
• The Tzami, a former mosque on Monastiraki Square in Athens
• Venetian fortresses (including those in Nafplio) established in Byzantine times

Greek Independence and Neoclassicism (1800s)

After centuries of neglect, Greece's Classical heritage was rediscovered, both by the Greeks and by the rest of Europe. Neoclassicism was all the rage in Europe, where the ancient Greek style was used to decorate homes, and create paintings and statues. In 1801-1805,

the British Lord Elgin plundered half of the Parthenon's statues and reliefs, carrying them home for Londoners to marvel at.

Greeks rediscovered a sense of their national heritage, and envisioned a day when they could rule themselves as a modern democracy. In 1821, the Greeks rose up against rule from Constantinople. It started with pockets of resistance by guerrilla Klepht warriors from the mountains, escalating into acts of large-scale massacres on both sides. The Greeks' struggle became a cause célèbre in Europe, attracting Romantic liberals from England and France to take up arms. The poet Lord Byron died in Greece (of a fever) while fighting for Greece.

At one point the rebels gained control of the Peloponnese and declared Greek independence. The Greeks even sank the flagship of the Ottoman fleet in 1822, earning international respect for their nascent rebellion. But tribal rivalries prevented the Greeks from preserving their gains. With Egyptian reinforcements, the Ottomans successfully invaded the Peloponnese and captured several cities. An Egyptian army in Europe was too much to take for Britain, France, and Russia, who intervened with their navies and saved Greek independence.

By 1829, the Greeks had their freedom, a constitution, and—for the first time—a unified state of "Greece," based in Nafplio. But after its first president, Ioannis Kapodistrias, was assassinated in 1831, the budding democracy was forced by Europe's crowned heads to accept a monarch: 17-year-old King Otto from Bavaria (crowned in 1832). In 1834, historic Athens was chosen as the new capital, despite the fact that it was then a humble village of a few thousand inhabitants.

Over the next century, Greece achieved a constitution (or *syntagma*, celebrated by Syntagma Square in Athens, as well as Nafplio and many other cities) and steered the monarchy toward modern democracy. Athens was rebuilt in the Neoclassical style. Greek engineers (along with foreigners) built the Corinth Canal. The Greek nation expanded, as Greek-speaking territories were captured from the Ottomans or ceded to Greece by European powers. In 1896, Greece celebrated its revival by hosting the first modern Olympic Games.

19th-Century Neoclassical Sights

• Syntagma Square, Parliament, and the evzone at the Tomb of the Unknown Soldier, in Athens
• National Garden in Athens
• Zappeion exhibition hall in Athens
• Athens' Panathenaic Stadium (ancient stadium renovated for the first modern Olympics in 1896)
• Cathedral in Athens
• Museum of Greek Folk Art (17th-19th centuries) in Athens
• Corinth Canal

20th Century

Two world wars and the Greek Civil War caused great turmoil in Greece. During World War I, Greece remained uncommitted until the final years, when it joined the Allies (Britain, France, Italy, Russia, and the US) against Germany.

World War I scrambled the balance of power in the Balkans. Greece was given control of parts of western Turkey, where many ethnic Greeks lived. The Turks, having thrown out their Ottoman rulers, now rose up to evict the Greeks, sparking the Greco-Turkish War (1919-1922) and massacres on both sides. To settle the conflict, a million ethnic Greeks living in Turkish lands were shipped to Greece, while Greece sent hundreds of thousands of their ethnic Turks to Turkey. In 1923, hordes of desperate refugees poured into Athens, and the population doubled overnight. Many later immigrated to the US, Canada, and Australia. Today there are more than three million Greek Americans living in the US.

In World War II, Greece sided firmly with the Allies, heroically repulsing Mussolini's 1940 invasion. But Adolf Hitler finished the job, invading and occupying Greece for four brutal years of repression and hunger.

Making the situation worse, the Greek Resistance movement (battling the Nazis) was itself divided. It broke out into a full-fledged civil war (1944-1949) between Western-backed patriots and Marxist patriots.

World War II and the Greek Civil War left Greece with hundreds of thousands dead, desperately poor, and bitterly divided. Thanks to America's Marshall Plan (and tourism), the economy recovered in the 1950s and '60s, and Greece joined the NATO alliance. Along with modernization came some of Europe's worst pollution, which eroded the ancient monuments.

Politically, Greece would remain split between the extreme right (the ruling monarchy, military, and the rich) and the extreme left (communists, students, and workers), without much room in the middle. The repressive royalist regime was backed heavily by the United States, which made Greece the first battleground in the Cold War (the Truman Doctrine). By the 1960s, when the rest of Europe was undergoing rapid social change, the Greek government was still trying to control its society with arrests and assassinations. When the royalists began losing control, a CIA-backed coup put the military in charge (1967-1974). They outlawed everything from long hair and miniskirts to Socrates and the theme song from *Zorba the Greek* (because its composer was accused of being a communist).

For Greece, 1974 was a watershed year. In the midst of political turmoil, Turkey invaded the Greek-friendly island of Cyprus (sparking yet more decades of bad blood between Turkey and Greece). The surprise attack caught the Greek military junta off guard, and they resigned in disgrace. A new government was elected with a new constitution. Guided by two strong (sometimes antagonistic) leaders—Andreas Papandreou and Constantine Karamanlis—Greece inched slowly from right-wing repression toward open democracy. Greece of the 1970s and '80s would suffer more than its share of assassinations and terrorist acts. But the economy grew, and Greece joined the European Union (1981) and adopted the euro (2002).

20th-Century Sights

- National War Museum in Athens
- Central Market in Athens
- Greek flag atop the Acropolis in Athens (reminder of resistance leaders who flew it there during the Nazi occupation in World War II)

GREEK HISTORY

Greece Today

The Greek political landscape is still dominated by two figures named Papandreou and Karamanlis—they're the son and nephew of the earlier political giants. The two main political parties are the

center-right New Democracy party (ND) and the center-left Panhellenic Socialist Movement (PASOK). Some longstanding political debates are over the economy, Greece's high military spending, the draft, excessive privileges for the Greek Orthodox faith, governmental corruption, and the national debt.

Relations with Turkey—its next-door neighbor across the Aegean pond—remain strained. Control of Cyprus (and a couple of other small islands) is a sore point, though the conflict has softened considerably since Cyprus joined the EU. The current status quo is founded on a complex agreement, which involves sharing power between the island's Greek-speakers (80 percent) and Turkish-speakers (20 percent). Greece also bickers with Turkey over undersea oil rights and the extent of offshore waters. However, Greece and Turkey have been brought closer together by recent disasters—the 1999 and 2003 Turkish earthquakes—that inspired the two nations to work together to provide humanitarian relief.

After adopting the euro, the Greek economy boomed. EU subsidies flowed in for major infrastructure projects, such as highways and high-speed rail. As host of the 2004 Summer Olympics, Athens cleaned up its city and installed a new airport and Metro.

But the worldwide recession that started in 2008 hit Greece hard. Suddenly, international investors dumped Greek bonds, since the national debt—estimated at nearly $400 billion—was

GREEK HISTORY

larger than the country's gross domestic product (for more on the economic crisis in Greece, see page 39). After his election in 2009, Prime Minister George Papandreou asked the parliament to adopt an austerity budget, which cut deficits but caused high unemployment, a shrinking economy, and massive strikes. Greece became the poster boy for nations that spend too much and earn too little, but thanks to a $137 billion rescue package from the EU and the International Monetary Fund, the country avoided bankruptcy and has been given a second chance. Given that their language and culture have survived for more than two millennia—despite being conquered by Romans, Turks, and Nazis—Greeks seem confident that they'll survive this, too.

Greece Today Sights

- Ermou street pedestrian zone in Athens
- Renovated Monastiraki Square in Athens
- Acropolis Museum in Athens
- Athens' Metro and airport
- 2004 Olympic Games sights, including new stadium, in Athens

APPENDIX

Contents

Tourist Information

The Greek national tourist office **in the US** can be a wealth of information. Before your trip, request or download any specific information you may want (such as city maps and schedules of upcoming festivals). Call 212/421-5777 or visit www.visitgreece.gr. Other useful websites include www.culture.gr (Greek Ministry of Culture, with information on major archaeological sites and museums), www.breathtakingathens.com (City of Athens Tourism), and www.athensguide.com (guide to Athens by travel writer Matt Barrett).

In Greece, most tourist offices are run by the national tourism organization. Unfortunately, these are uniformly unreliable, but can give you a free map, a few local tips, and some help with bus connections. Occasionally you'll find a much better locally run office (such as in Patra). While they can be hit-or-miss, the tourist information office is generally your best first stop in any new town. Try to arrive, or at least telephone, before it closes. Have a list of questions ready, and pick up maps, brochures, and walking-tour information. In Greece, they are often marked *EOT* (for the Greek phrase "Greek Tourism Organization"). In this book, I refer to a tourist information office as a **TI.**

Note that many small towns (such as Hydra, Monemvasia, and Kardamyli) do not have a TI. In these cases, your hotel can be the best source of information.

Communicating

Telephones

Smart travelers use the telephone to reserve or reconfirm rooms, get tourist information, reserve restaurants, confirm tour times, or phone home. This section covers dialing instructions, phone cards, and types of phones (for more in-depth information, see www .ricksteves.com/phoning). The Greek phone company is known by its initials: OTE.

How to Dial

Calling from the US to Europe, or vice versa, is simple—once you break the code. The European calling chart in this chapter will walk you through it.

Dialing Domestically Within Greece

Greece has a direct-dial phone system (no area codes). To call anywhere within Greece, just dial the number. For example, the number of one of my recommended hotels in Athens is 210-324-9737. That's the number you dial whether you're calling it from the Athens train station or from Nafplio.

Dialing Internationally to or from Greece

If you want to make an international call, follow these steps:

• Dial the international access code (00 if you're calling from Greece, 011 from the US or Canada).

• Then dial the country code of the country you're calling (30 for Greece, or 1 for the US or Canada).

• Then dial the local number.

Calling from the US to Greece: To call an Athens hotel from the US, dial 011 (the US international access code), 30 (Greece's country code), then the hotel's phone number (e.g., 210-324-9737).

Calling from any European Country to the US: To call my office in Edmonds, Washington, from Greece, I dial 00 (Europe's international access code), 1 (the US country code), 425 (Edmonds' area code), and 771-8303.

Note: You might see a + in front of a European number. When dialing the number, replace the + with the international access code of the country you're calling from (00 from Europe, 011 from the US or Canada).

Public Phones and Hotel-Room Phones

To make calls from public phones in Greece, you'll need a prepaid phone card. There are two different kinds of phone cards: insertable and international. Either type of phone card works only in Greece. If you have a still-lively card at the end of your trip, give it to another traveler.

Insertable Phone Cards: These cards—called *Telekarta* (ΤΗΛΕΚΑΡΤΑ)—are the best way to make a call from public pay phones; there are no coin phones. Buy these cards at TIs, tobacco shops, newsstand kiosks, post offices, and train stations. They are sold in denominations of €4 and €10. To use the card, physically insert it into a slot in the pay phone. While you can use these cards to call anywhere in the world, they're only a good deal for making quick local calls from a phone booth. Call 134 if you need help with your *telekarta*. Be aware that with the prevalence of mobile phones, public phones in Greece are getting harder to find and are often in disrepair.

International Phone Cards: These are the cheapest way to make international calls from anywhere in Europe (generally around 25-50 cents per minute; they also work for local calls). You can use international phone cards from the phone in your hotel room (ask at the front desk if there are any fees for toll-free calls), but some may not work if you're calling from a Greek pay phone (Smile+Web, the card sold by the Greek phone system, will work from any pay phone; see www.smileandweb.gr).

These cards are found at small newsstand kiosks, electronics stores, and hole-in-the-wall long-distance shops. Ask the clerk which of the various brands has the best rates for calls to America. Because cards are occasionally duds, avoid the higher denominations. Before buying a card, make sure the access number you dial is toll-free, not a local number (or else you'll be paying for a local call *and* deducting time from your calling card).

To use a card, scratch off the back to reveal your code, dial the access phone number, and follow the prompts. If the prompts are in Greek, wait to see if the announcement also follows in English. If not, experiment: Dial your code, followed by the pound sign (#), then the number, then the pound sign again, and so on, until it works.

Remember that you don't need the actual card to use a card

European Calling Chart

Just smile and dial, using this key:
AC = Area Code, LN = Local Number.

European Country	Calling long distance within...	Calling from the US or Canada to...	Calling from a European country to...
Austria	AC + LN	011 + 43 + AC (without the initial zero) + LN	00 + 43 + AC (without the initial zero) + LN
Belgium	LN	011 + 32 + LN (without initial zero)	00 + 32 + LN (without initial zero)
Bosnia-Herzegovina	AC + LN	011 + 387 + AC (without initial zero) + LN	00 + 387 + AC (without initial zero) + LN
Britain	AC + LN	011 + 44 + AC (without initial zero) + LN	00 + 44 + AC (without initial zero) + LN
Croatia	AC + LN	011 + 385 + AC (without initial zero) + LN	00 + 385 + AC (without initial zero) + LN
Czech Republic	LN	011 + 420 + LN	00 + 420 + LN
Denmark	LN	011 + 45 + LN	00 + 45 + LN
Estonia	LN	011 + 372 + LN	00 + 372 + LN
Finland	AC + LN	011 + 358 + AC (without initial zero) + LN	999 (or other 900 number) + 358 + AC (without initial zero) + LN
France	LN	011 + 33 + LN (without initial zero)	00 + 33 + LN (without initial zero)
Germany	AC + LN	011 + 49 + AC (without initial zero) + LN	00 + 49 + AC (without initial zero) + LN
Gibraltar	LN	011 + 350 + LN	00 + 350 + LN
Greece	LN	011 + 30 + LN	00 + 30 + LN
Hungary	06 + AC + LN	011 + 36 + AC + LN	00 + 36 + AC + LN
Ireland	AC + LN	011 + 353 + AC (without initial zero) + LN	00 + 353 + AC (without initial zero) + LN

European Country	Calling long distance within ...	Calling from the US or Canada to ...	Calling from a European country to ...
Italy	LN	011 + 39 + LN	00 + 39 + LN
Montenegro	AC + LN	011 + 382 + AC (without initial zero) + LN	00 + 382 + AC (without initial zero) + LN
Morocco	LN	011 + 212 + LN (without initial zero)	00 + 212 + LN (without initial zero)
Netherlands	AC + LN	011 + 31 + AC (without initial zero) + LN	00 + 31 + AC (without initial zero) + LN
Norway	LN	011 + 47 + LN	00 + 47 + LN
Poland	LN	011 + 48 + LN (without initial zero)	00 + 48 + LN (without initial zero)
Portugal	LN	011 + 351 + LN	00 + 351 + LN
Slovakia	AC + LN	011 + 421 + AC (without initial zero) + LN	00 + 421 + AC (without initial zero) + LN
Slovenia	AC + LN	011 + 386 + AC (without initial zero) + LN	00 + 386 + AC (without initial zero) + LN
Spain	LN	011 + 34 + LN	00 + 34 + LN
Sweden	AC + LN	011 + 46 + AC (without initial zero) + LN	00 + 46 + AC (without initial zero) + LN
Switzerland	LN	011 + 41 + LN (without initial zero)	00 + 41 + LN (without initial zero)
Turkey	AC (if there's no initial zero, add one) + LN	011 + 90 + AC (without initial zero) + LN	00 + 90 + AC (without initial zero) + LN

APPENDIX

- The instructions above apply whether you're calling a land line or mobile phone.
- The international access codes (the first numbers you dial when making an international call) are 011 if you're calling from the US or Canada, or 00 if you're calling from virtually anywhere in Europe (except Finland, where it's 999 or another 900 number, depending on the phone service you're using).
- To call the US or Canada from Europe, dial 00, then 1 (the country code for the US and Canada), then the area code and number. In short, 00 + 1 + AC + LN = Hi, Mom!

account, so it's sharable. You can write down the access number and code in your notebook and share it with friends.

Hotel-Room Phones: Calling from the phone in your room can be cheap for local calls (ask for rates at the front desk first), but is often a rip-off for long-distance calls, unless you use an international phone card (explained earlier). Some hotels charge a fee for dialing supposedly "toll-free" numbers, such as the one for your international phone card—ask before you dial. Incoming calls are free, making this a cheap way for friends and family to stay in touch (provided they have a good long-distance plan for calls to Europe—and a list of your hotels' phone numbers).

US Calling Cards: These cards, such as the ones offered by AT&T, Verizon, or Sprint, are the worst option. You'll nearly always save a lot of money by using a locally purchased phone card instead.

Mobile Phones

Many travelers enjoy the convenience of using a mobile phone to make calls.

Using Your Mobile Phone: Your US mobile phone works in Greece if it's GSM-enabled, tri-band or quad-band, and on a calling plan that includes international calls. Phones from T-Mobile and AT&T, which use the same GSM technology that Europe does, are more likely to work overseas than Verizon or Sprint phones (if you're not sure, ask your service provider). Most US providers charge $1.29 per minute while roaming internationally to make or receive calls, and 20-50 cents to send or receive text messages. Contact your provider before you leave to be sure international roaming is allowed and to ask them about rates.

You'll pay cheaper rates if your phone is electronically "unlocked" (ask your provider about this); then, in Greece, you can simply buy a tiny **SIM card,** which gives you a Greek phone number. SIM cards are available at mobile-phone stores and most newsstand kiosks for about €5. I've used the Germanos (ΓΕΡΜΑΜΟΣ) electronics stores, which have staff who speak English, to help me switch my US mobile phone to a Greek number. They're all over Greece, including at the Athens airport.

When you buy a SIM card, you may need to show ID, such as your passport. Insert the SIM card in your phone (usually in a slot behind the battery), and it'll work like a Greek mobile phone. When buying a SIM card and calling credit, always ask about fees for domestic and international calls, roaming charges, and how to check your credit balance and buy more time. To call home, save money by using an international calling card (described earlier).

Many **smartphones,** such as the iPhone or BlackBerry, work in Europe—but beware of sky-high fees, especially for data downloading (checking email, browsing the Internet, watching streaming videos, and so on). Ask your provider in advance how to avoid unwittingly roaming your way to a huge bill. Some applications allow for cheap or free smartphone calls over a Wi-Fi connection (see "Calling over the Internet," later).

Using a Greek Mobile Phone: In Greece, mobile phones run about $70-90 (for the most basic models) and come without contracts. These phones are loaded with prepaid calling time that you can recharge as you use up the minutes. As long as you're not "roaming" outside the phone's home country, incoming calls are free. If you're traveling to multiple countries within Europe, make sure the phone is "unlocked," so that you can swap out its SIM card for a new one in other countries. For more information on mobile phones, see www.ricksteves.com/phones.

Calling over the Internet

Some things that seem too good to be true...actually are true. If you're traveling with a laptop, you can make calls using VoIP (Voice over Internet Protocol). With VoIP, two computers act as the phones, and the Internet-based calls are free (or you can pay a few cents to call from your computer to a telephone). If both computers have webcams, you can even see each other while you chat. The major providers are Skype (www.skype.com), followed by Google Talk (www.google.com/talk). It's not essential to have a laptop to use VoIP; some smartphones allow you to make VoIP calls over a Wi-Fi connection.

Useful Phone Numbers

Emergency Needs
Police: 100
Tourist Police: 171 (English-speaking)
Ambulance or Fire: 176 or 199

Directory Assistance
Operator/Directory Assistance for Athens: 11880
Operator/Directory Assistance for Rest of Greece: 132
Operator/Directory Assistance for International Calls: 139

Embassies
US Embassy: tel. 210-720-2419 during office hours; for after-hours emergency help, call 210-729-4301 or 210-729-4444; consular section open Mon-Fri 8:30-17:00, closed last Wed of each month, closed Sat-Sun (Vassilissis Sofias 91, Metro line 3/blue: Megaro Moussikis, http://athens.usembassy.gov).
Canadian Embassy: tel. 210-727-3400, for after-hours emergency help call Canada collect at tel. 1-613-996-8885, open Mon-Fri

8:00-12:30, closed Sat-Sun (Ioannou Ghennadiou 4, www.canada international.gc.ca/greece-grece).

Travel Advisories
US Department of State: US tel. 202/647-5225 (www.travel.state .gov)
Canadian Department of Foreign Affairs: Canadian tel. 800-267-6788 (www.dfait-maeci.gc.ca)
US Centers for Disease Control and Prevention: US tel. 800-CDC-INFO (800-232-4636, www.cdc.gov/travel)

Internet Access and Wi-Fi

It's useful to get online periodically as you travel—to confirm trip plans, check train or bus schedules, get weather forecasts, catch up on email, blog or post photos from your trip, or call folks back home (explained earlier, under "Calling over the Internet").

Some hotels offer a dedicated computer in the lobby with Internet access for guests. If you ask politely, smaller places may sometimes let you sit at their desk for a few minutes just to check your email.

With a laptop, netbook, or other Wi-Fi–enabled device, it's easy to get online if your hotel has Wi-Fi (wireless Internet access, sometimes called "WLAN" in Europe)—when you check in, ask them for the network name and password. Other hotels have a port in your room for connecting your laptop with a cable (if you don't carry a cable, ask to borrow one from the front desk). Some hotels offer Wi-Fi or cable Internet access for free; others charge by the minute or hour. A cellular modem—which lets your laptop access the Internet over a mobile phone network—provides more extensive coverage, but is much more expensive than Wi-Fi.

If your hotel doesn't have access, your hotelier can direct you to the nearest place to get online. You'll find plenty of cafés that offer Wi-Fi to customers.

Mail

Get stamps at the neighborhood post office, newsstands within fancy hotels, and some mini-marts and card shops. You can arrange for mail delivery to your hotel (allow 10 days for a letter to arrive), but phoning and emailing are so easy that I've dispensed with mail stops altogether.

Transportation

By Car or by Bus?

For connecting most of the destinations in this book (except the islands of Hydra, Mykonos, and Santorini), you have two options:

rental car or public bus. (Train service is minimal and not worth your while.)

A **rental car** allows you to come and go on your own schedule, and make a beeline between destinations. Outside of congested Athens, roads are uncrowded, and parking is often free. However, driving in Greece can be stressful, as Greek drivers tackle the roads with a kind of anything-goes, Wild West abandon. And it's more expensive than the bus. But if you're a confident driver, the convenience of driving in Greece trumps the hassles of bus transport.

Greece's network of public **buses,** run by KTEL (ΚΤΕΛ in Greek), will affordably get you most anywhere you want to go. Unfortunately, it's not user-friendly. Particularly outside of Athens, the frequency can be sparse and schedules are hard to nail down. You'd need to allow plenty of time, expect delays, and pack lots of patience to visit all of my recommended destinations. For more information on buses, see page 477.

Car Rental

If you're **renting a car** in Greece, you'll need to bring your driver's license. You're also technically required to have an International Driving Permit, which is a translation of your driver's license (sold at your local AAA office for $15 plus the cost of two passport-type photos; see www.aaa.com). While that's the letter of the law, I've often rented cars in Greece without having—or being asked to show—this permit.

Research car rentals before you go. It's cheaper to arrange most car rentals from the US. Most of the major US rental agencies have offices in Athens. For a friendly local car-rental company, consider Swift/Avanti (see page 218; www.greektravel.com/swift or www.avanti.com.gr). Comparison-shop on the Web to find the best deal. It can be cheaper to use a consolidator, such as Auto Europe (www.autoeurope.com) or Europe by Car (www.ebctravel.com), but by using a middleman, you risk trading customer service for lower prices; if you have a problem with the rental company, you can't count on the consolidator to intervene on your behalf.

For the best deal, rent by the week with unlimited mileage. If you want to save money on gas, ask for a diesel car. I normally rent a small, inexpensive model with a stick-shift. Almost all rentals are manual by default, so if you need an automatic, you must request one at least a month in advance and specifically request an automatic. You'll pay about 40 percent more to rent a car with an automatic instead of a manual transmission. Because of the size of Greek roads (and Greek parking spaces), it's a good idea to rent a small vehicle.

Figure about $100 per day for a short-term rental of just a few days, or less per day for longer stretches. Be warned that dropping

Driving in Greece

To Meteora

To Igoumenitsa

165m • 4.5h

140m
3.75h

Delphi

80m • 2h

To Corfu
& Italy

Ag. Nikolaos

Patra

Aigio

85m • 2h

To
Kefallonia

60m • 1.5h

Chlemoútsi

To
Zakynthos

PELOPONNESE
(PELOPONNISOS)

Pyrgos

20m
.5h

Olympia

75m • 2.5h

50m • 1h

35m • .75h

40m • 1h

Tripoli

75m • 2h

60m • 1.5h

35m • 1h

35m • 1.5h

Sparta

Kalamata

*Messenian
Gulf*

24m
1h

25m • .75h

Kardamyli

30m • .75h

Gythio

*Ionian
Sea*

15m
.5h

Areopoli

**MANI
PENINSULA**

25m • .75h

*Laconian
Gulf*

10 Kilometers

Vathia

10 Miles

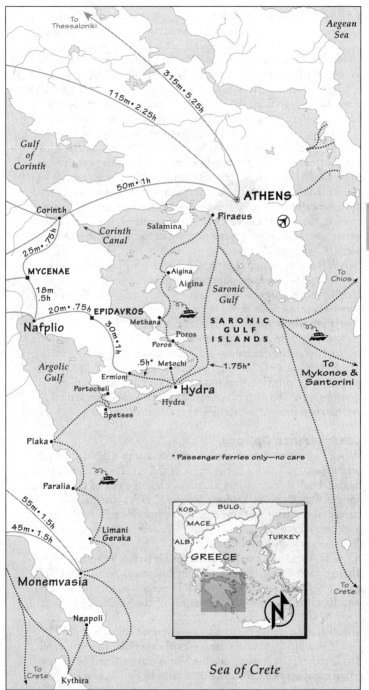

APPENDIX

a car off in a different country—say, picking up in Athens and dropping in Istanbul—can be prohibitively expensive (it depends on distance, but the extra fee averages a few hundred dollars).

You can sometimes get a GPS unit with your rental car or leased vehicle for an additional fee (around $15/day; be sure it's set to English and has all the maps you need before you drive off). Or, if you have a portable GPS device at home, consider taking it with you to Europe (buy and upload European maps before your trip).

As a rule, always tell your car-rental company up front exactly which countries you'll be entering. Some companies levy extra insurance fees for trips taken with certain types of cars (such as BMWs, Mercedes, and convertibles) in certain countries. Double-check with your rental agent that you have all the documentation you need before you drive off (especially if you're crossing borders into non-Schengen countries, such as Turkey, where you might need to present proof of insurance). For more on borders, see page 11.

When you pick up the car, check it thoroughly and make sure any damage is noted on your rental agreement. Find out how your car's lights, turn signals, wipers, and gas cap function. Be sure you know whether it takes diesel or unleaded fuel.

If you drop your car off early or keep it longer, you'll be credited or charged at a fair, prorated price. But always keep your receipts in case any questions arise about your billing.

Returning a car in a big city can be tricky; get precise details on the car drop-off location and hours. Note that rental offices may close from midday Saturday until Monday. When you return the car, make sure the agent verifies its condition with you.

Car Insurance Options

When you rent a car, you are liable for a very high deductible, sometimes equal to the entire value of the car. You can limit your financial risk in case of an accident by choosing one of these three options: Buy Collision Damage Waiver (CDW) coverage from the car-rental company, get coverage through your credit card (free, if your card automatically includes zero-deductible coverage), or buy coverage through Travel Guard.

CDW includes a very high deductible (typically $1,000-1,500). Though each rental company has its own variation, basic CDW costs $15-25 a day (figure roughly 25 percent extra) and reduces your liability, but does not eliminate it. When you pick up the car, you'll be offered the chance to "buy down" the deductible to zero (for an additional $15-30/day; this is often called "super CDW").

If you opt instead for **credit-card coverage,** there's a catch. You'll technically have to decline all coverage offered by the car-rental company, which means they can place a hold on your card (which can be up to the full value of the car). In case of damage, it can be time-consuming to resolve the charges with your credit-card company. Before you decide on this option, quiz your credit-card company about how it works and ask them to explain the worst-case scenario.

Finally, you can buy CDW insurance from **Travel Guard** ($9/day plus a one-time $3 service fee covers you up to $35,000, $250 deductible, US tel. 800-826-4919, www.travelguard.com). It's valid nearly everywhere in Europe, except the Republic of Ireland, and some Italian car-rental companies refuse to honor it. Oddly, residents of Washington state and Texas aren't allowed to buy this coverage.

For more on car-rental insurance, see www.ricksteves.com/cdw.

Driving in Greece

Statistically, Greece is one of the most dangerous European countries to drive in. Traffic regulations that are severely enforced back home are treated as mere suggestions here. Even at major intersections in large towns, you might not see stop signs or traffic lights; drivers simply help each other figure out who goes next. And yet, like so many seemingly chaotic things in Greece, somehow it works quite smoothly. Still...drive defensively. Greeks are typically polite and patient with other drivers (though they won't hesitate to pass you, if they feel you're going too slow).

Navigation: The driving directions in this book are intended to be used with a good local map. Pick up a Michelin map in the US or buy one of the good road maps available in Greece (the Road Editions maps are tops—www.road.gr). Study it before taking off, especially if you'll be driving solo. If you're traveling with a partner, you'll find that a competent copilot makes life much easier.

Since road numbers can be confusing and inconsistent, navigate by city names. Know the names of major cities en route to your destination. Often the signs will only point to the next major town, even if your final destination is a big city. Almost all road signs are in Greek and in English, but you should know the name of your destination using the Greek alphabet—road sign transliteration can be confusing. Kardamyli, for example, can be spelled a number of different ways in English, and can appear as Kardamili or Kardhamili.

Road Rules: The speed limit, almost never posted, can be hard to ascertain on backcountry roads. Generally, speed limits in Greece are as follows: city—30 mph/50 kph; open roads—50 mph/80 kph; freeways—74 mph/100 kph. Making matters even more confusing, half of all Greek drivers seem to go double the speed limit, while the others go half the limit. As Greeks aren't shy about passing, cars stay in their lanes like rocks in an avalanche. On country roads and highways, the lanes are often a car-and-a-half wide, with wide shoulders, so passing is common—even when there's oncoming traffic in the other lane. Do as Greek drivers do on two-lane roads with wide shoulders—straddle the shoulder if someone wants to pass you.

Learn the universal road signs. Seat belts are required, and two beers under those belts are enough to land you in jail. Many European countries require headlights to be turned on at all times (even in broad daylight) and forbid drivers from talking on mobile phones without a hands-free headset. Ask your car-rental company about these rules, or check the US State Department website (www.travel.state.gov, click on "International Travel," then specify your country of choice and click "Traffic Safety and Road Conditions").

Tolls: Special highways called *Ethniki Odos,* the National Road, have tolls, which vary and must be paid in cash. This includes the road between Athens and the Peloponnese and part of the stretch between Athens and Delphi.

Fuel: Gasoline (*venzini,* βενζίνη) prices are around $8 a gallon for regular unleaded—labeled 95, less for diesel (*ntizel,* ντίζελ). Self-service gas stations are rare. Tell the attendant how much you want to spend and use cash. He's just there to pump gas, so don't expect him to wash your windshield or check your tires.

Road-Trip Tips: Set up your car for a fun road trip. Establish a cardboard-box munchies pantry. Buy a rack of liter boxes of juice for the trunk, and some Windex and a roll of paper towels for clearer sightseeing.

Parking and Safety: Choose parking places carefully. You'll rarely pay for parking, and parking laws are enforced only sporadically. If you're not certain, ask at your hotel (or another local) whether your space is legit. Keep your valuables in your hotel room, or, if you're between destinations, covered in your trunk. Leave nothing worth stealing in the car, especially overnight. If your car's a hatchback, take the trunk cover off at night so thieves can look in without breaking in. Try to make your car look locally owned by hiding the "tourist-owned" rental-company decals and putting a local newspaper in your front or back window. While you should avoid parking lots with twinkly asphalt, thieves break car windows anywhere, even at stoplights.

Drive carefully. If you're involved in an accident, expect a monumental headache—you will be blamed. You may be stopped for a routine check by the police (keep your seat belt buckled and be sure your car insurance form is up-to-date). Small towns come with speed traps and corruption. Tickets, especially for foreigners, are issued and paid for on the spot. Insist on a receipt, so the money is less likely to end up in the cop's pocket.

Buses

While Greek buses are cheap—about €8 per 100 kilometers—and the fleet is clean, modern, and air-conditioned, the bus system can be frustrating, particularly for journeys that don't originate in Athens.

Athens has frequent bus service to popular destinations such as Delphi, Nafplio, and the port town of Piraeus, but smaller destinations on the Peloponnese are connected by only one or two buses a day.

All buses are run by a central company (KTEL, or KTEΛ in Greek), but the local offices don't cooperate with each other—each one sets its own schedules, and they often don't coordinate well. Specific bus schedules can be very difficult to pin down, even for buses leaving from the town you're in. (And forget about getting bus schedules for other Greek towns.) Local TIs often don't have the information you need. Don't hesitate to ask your hotelier for help—they're used to it.

KTEL has no helpful website or information office for the entire Greek bus system, but there is a list of local phone numbers at www.ktelbus.com (you'll need to know the name of the province where you are traveling). The KTEL Athens site, www.ktalattikis .gr, is in Greek only, but Matt Barrett's website has schedules for long-distance buses from and to Athens (www.athensguide.com). Or try this helpful, unofficial website in English: http://livingin greece.gr/2008/06/13/ktel-buses-of-greece.

Particularly on the Peloponnese, where your journeys will likely require a transfer (or multiple transfers), you frequently won't be able to get the information for the full route from the bus station at your starting point. For example, to go from Nafplio to Monemvasia, you'll change at Tripoli, then Sparta. The Nafplio bus station can give you details for the leg to Tripoli, but can't tell

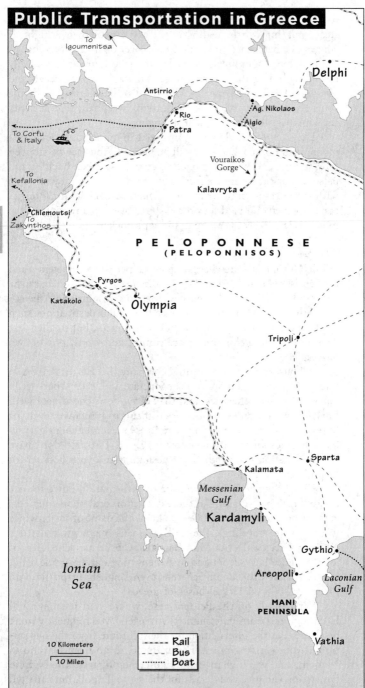

Public Transportation in Greece

To Igoumenitsa

Delphi

Antirrio

Ag. Nikolaos

Rio

Aigio

Patra

To Corfu & Italy

Vouraikos Gorge

To Kefallonia

Kalavryta

Chlemoutsi

To Zakynthos

PELOPONNESE
(PELOPONNISOS)

Pyrgos

Katakolo

Olympia

Tripoli

Sparta

Kalamata

Messenian Gulf

Kardamyli

Gythio

Areopoli

Laconian Gulf

Ionian Sea

MANI PENINSULA

Vathia

10 Kilometers

10 Miles

- - - - - Rail
- - - - Bus
· · · · · · Boat

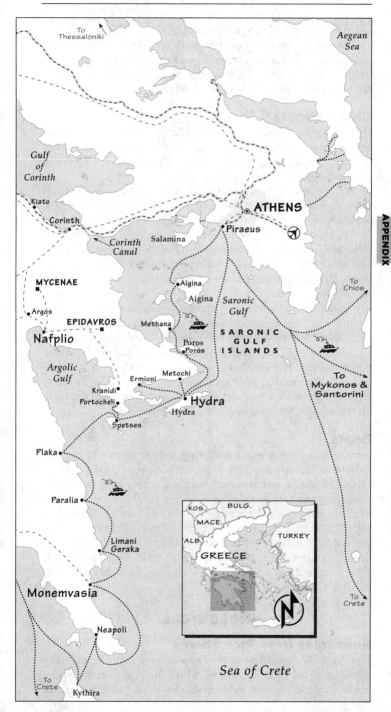

you anything about the other two legs.

Before you get on a bus, ask the ticket-seller and the conductor explicitly if there are transfers—as they might not volunteer these details otherwise. Then pay attention (and maybe even follow the route on a map) to be sure you don't miss your change.

Cheap Flights

If you're visiting other countries in Europe, consider intra-European airlines. While buses (or—outside of Greece—trains) are still the best way to connect places that are close together, a flight can save both time and money on long journeys.

One of the best websites for comparing inexpensive flights is www.skyscanner.net. Other comparison search engines include www.wegolo.com and www.whichbudget.com.

For flights within Greece, the country's national carrier is **Olympic** (www.olympicairlines.com). For flights between Athens and other cities in Europe, also try **Aegeanair** (www.aegeanair .com), **Brussels Airlines** (www.brusselsairlines.com), and **easyJet** (www.easyjet.com).

Buy tickets in advance. Although you can usually book right up until the flight departs, the cheap seats will often have sold out long before, leaving the most expensive seats for latecomers.

Be aware of the potential drawbacks of flying on the cheap: nonrefundable and nonchangeable tickets, minimal or nonexistent customer service, additional charges for everything, treks to airports far outside town, and pricey baggage fees. Read the small print—especially baggage policies—before you book.

Boats

Greece has been a great seafaring nation since the days of Odysseus. The only destinations in this book accessible by boat are Hydra, Mykonos, and Santorini, but if you're venturing beyond my coverage, you have a world of possibilities. In addition to the many ferries to the islands departing from Athens' port of Piraeus (see page 210), there are also boats to Cyprus. On the Peloponnese, you can sail from Patra to the islands of Corfu, Kefalonia, and Ithaki, as well as three towns in Italy (see page 304). Any Greek travel agency can sell you a boat ticket for no extra fee—they're experts on all of your options.

Resources

Resources from Rick Steves

Rick Steves' Greece: Athens & the Peloponnese is one of many books in my series on European travel, which includes country guidebooks, city and regional guidebooks, Snapshot guides (excerpted

chapters from my country guides), Pocket guides (full-color little books on big cities), and my budget-travel skills handbook, *Rick Steves' Europe Through the Back Door*. My phrase books—for German, French, Italian, Spanish, and Portuguese—are practical and budget-oriented. My other books include *Europe 101* (a crash course on art and history, newly expanded and in full color) and *Travel as a Political Act* (a travelogue sprinkled with tips for bringing home a global perspective). For a complete list of my books, see the inside of the last page of this book.

Video: My TV series, *Rick Steves' Europe*, covers European destinations in 100 shows, with four shows on Greece. To watch episodes, visit www.hulu.com/rick-steves-europe; for scripts and other details, see www.ricksteves.com/tv.

Audio: My weekly public radio show, *Travel with Rick Steves*, features interviews with travel experts from around the world. I've also produced free, self-guided audio tours of the top sights and a city walk in Athens. This audio content is available for free at Rick Steves Audio Europe, an extensive online library organized by destination. Choose whatever interests you, and download it for free to your iPod, smartphone, or computer at www.rick steves.com/audioeurope or iTunes. Rick Steves Audio Europe is also available as a free app for your iPhone, BlackBerry, or Android.

Maps

The black-and-white maps in this book, designed by my well-traveled staff, are concise and simple. The maps are intended to help you locate recommended places and get to local TIs, where you can pick up more in-depth maps of cities or regions (usually free). Better maps are sold at newsstands and bookstores all over Greece. Before you buy a map, look at it to be sure it has the level of detail you want. The Greek-produced maps by Road Editions are best (www.road.gr).

Other Guidebooks

Especially if you'll be traveling beyond my recommended destinations, $40 for extra maps and books is money well-spent.

The following books are worthwhile, though most are not updated annually; check the publication date before you buy.

Begin Your Trip at www.ricksteves.com

At our travel website, you'll find a wealth of free information on European destinations, including fresh monthly news and helpful tips from thousands of fellow travelers. You'll also find my latest guidebook updates (www.ricksteves.com/update) and my travel blog.

Our **online Travel Store** offers travel bags and accessories specially designed to help you travel smarter and lighter. These include my popular carry-on bags (roll-aboard and rucksack versions), money belts, totes, toiletries kits, adapters, other accessories, and a wide selection of guidebooks, journals, planning maps, and DVDs.

Choosing the right **railpass** for your trip—amidst hundreds of options—can drive you nutty. We'll help you choose the best pass for your needs, plus give you a bunch of free extras.

Rick Steves' Europe Through the Back Door travel company offers **tours** with more than three dozen itineraries and 400 departures reaching the best destinations in this book... and beyond. We offer a 14-day tour of Athens and the Heart of Greece. You'll enjoy great guides, a fun bunch of travel partners (with small groups of generally around 24-28), and plenty of room to spread out in a big, comfy bus. You'll find European adventures to fit every vacation length. For all the details, and to get our Tour Catalog and a free Rick Steves Tour Experience DVD (filmed on location during an actual tour), visit www.ricksteves.com or call the Tour Department at 425/608-4217.

Historians like the green Michelin guides and the Cadogan series; both have books on Greece. Others go for the well-illustrated Eyewitness guides (titles include *Athens and the Mainland* and *The Greek Islands*). The Lonely Planet series (which has books on Athens, Crete, and the Greek Islands) is well-researched and geared for a mature audience. Students and vagabonds enjoy *Let's Go: Greece* (updated annually) for its coverage of hosteling, nightlife, and the student scene.

Recommended Books and Movies

To learn more about Greece past and present, check out a few of these books and films.

Nonfiction

There's no shortage of great books about Greek history. *A Traveller's History of Greece* (Boatswain and Nicolson) is a compact, well-written account from the earliest times to the present. Fernand Braudel's *The Mediterranean in the Ancient World* is another marvelous overview. If you'd like a large-format book with many illustrations, your best bet is *The Cambridge Illustrated History of Ancient Greece* (Cartledge). For the standard text on ancient Greece by a leading scholar (still quite accessible), try *The Greeks* (Kitto). Readers who want to understand the relevance of Greek ancient culture to today should get Thomas Cahill's *Sailing the Wine Dark Sea: Why the Greeks Matter*.

Edith Hamilton's *The Greek Way* and *Mythology* are classic tomes on classic myths and cultures. For more about ancient war and its warriors, *Persian Fire* (Holland) is an excellent history of the fifth-century B.C. Persian conflict. Histories by Paul Cartledge cover *Alexander the Great* and *The Spartans*. Novelist Mary Renault (see "Fiction," later) also wrote non-fiction about the period, including *The Nature of Alexander*.

A Concise History of Greece (Clogg) is an excellent overview from the 18th century to modern times. *Inside Hitler's Greece* (Mazower) is a shocking account of the Nazi occupation of Greece and lays the background for the subsequent civil war. *Eleni* (Gage) is a riveting account by the author of his quest to uncover the truth behind his mother's assassination during that civil war. Though written in 1958, Patrick Leigh Fermor's *Mani: Travels in the Southern Peloponnese* is the definitive book on the "forgotten" side of the peninsula.

Classics: The classics may be slow-going, but they open a window to the Greek mind and soul. The dialogues of Plato *(Apology, Republic)* capture the words of Socrates from Golden Age times. The comedies of Aristophanes and the tragedies of Sophocles, Euripides, and Aeschylus explore the great issues of life and death.

Plutarch's *Lives* is an epic attempt to chronicle the ancient world through biography.

Memoirs: Henry Miller's *Colossus of Maroussi* is a sometimes graphic account of his down-and-out sojourn in Greece in the late 1930s. Patricia Storace's controversial *Dinner with Persephone* is more than a memoir about living in Athens—it's one writer's critical look at modern Greek culture and family life. On the lighter side, *The Summer of My Greek Taverna* (Stone) is an American expat's take on running a bar on the island of Patmos.

Fiction

Western literature begins with Homer. *The Iliad* is the classic account of the Trojan War; *The Odyssey* follows Odysseus on his return from that war. Some of the best translations are by Richmond Lattimore, Robert Fitzgerald, and Robert Fagles.

Historical novels about Greece abound, and no one wrote them better than Mary Renault. Try any of her books on Alexander the Great *(The Persian Boy, Fire from Heaven, Funeral Games)*, her re-imagining of the Theseus myth *(The King Must Die, The Bull from the Sea)*, or her account of a 400 B.C. actor *(The Mask of Apollo)*. *Gates of Fire* (Pressfield) re-creates the Battle of Thermopylae, where 300 Spartans held back the Persian army—for a while. *The Walled Orchard* (Holt) is an amusing and well-researched pseudo-autobiography of the comic playwright Eupolis.

Perhaps the most famous modern Greek writer is Nikos Kazantzakis. His *Zorba the Greek* shows how a wily old rogue can teach life's lessons to a withdrawn intellectual. His controversial *The Last Temptation of Christ* has a main character who is very human. Another favorite is Panos Karnezis, whose *Little Infamies* is a fine collection of short stories done in a magical realism style. Apostolos Doxiadis is a mathematician and author who writes in Greek and then translates his own works into English. His popular *Uncle Petros and Goldbach's Conjecture* is the tale of a Greek genius obsessed with trying to prove one of mathematics' great theories.

British author Louis de Bernières wrote a best seller—*Corelli's Mandolin*, later made into a movie—about ill-fated lovers on a war-torn Greek island. Another best seller, *Middlesex*, by Greek-American author Jeffrey Eugenides, explores the Greek immigrant experience in the US—as well as sexual identity. John Fowles' classic *The Magus* describes an Englishman's psychological games with a wealthy recluse on a Greek island. The Parthenon plays a pivotal role in the lives of Pericles' mistress, Aspasia, and Lord Elgin's wife, Mary, in *Stealing Athena* by Karen Essex. Mystery fans like to follow Paul Johnston's books about the Scots-Greek private investigator Alex Mavros, such as *The Last Red Death* and *A Deeper Shade of Blue*.

Books for Kids

These good non-fiction books help introduce Greece to young readers. *The Changing Face of Greece* (Osler) weaves first-person accounts from modern Greeks with a summary of today's challenges. *Ancient Civilizations: Greece* (Bargallo) offers a capsule history. For an illustrated primer on Greek mythology, try *The Random House Book of Greek Myths*. Kids can put themselves in the sandals of a young Grecian in *If I Were a Kid in Ancient Greece* (Cobblestone Publishing), and make traditional foods, build a model temple, and put on a play with *Ancient Greece! 40 Hands-On Activities* (Hart). *Greece in Spectacular Cross-Section* (Biesty) will fascinate kids and grown-ups alike with its cut-away diagrams recreating ancient sites. Miroslav Sasek's classic 1966 picture-book, *This is Greece*, was reissued in 2009.

Films

Hollywood loves ancient Greek history and myths: The audience already knows the characters, and there are no copyrights. A recent flood of "sword-and-sandal" epics includes *Alexander the Great* (2004), with Colin Farrell as the military genius who conquered the known world; *Troy* (2004), starring Brad Pitt as the petulant warrior Achilles; *300* (2006), a highly fictional and stylized account of the Battle of Thermopylae based on a graphic novel; and a 3-D version of the myth of Perseus—*Clash of the Titans* (2010). The earlier Hollywood version of *Clash of the Titans* (1981) has an all-star cast featuring Laurence Olivier, Claire Bloom, and Maggie Smith. There's also plenty of star power in *The Trojan Women* (1971)—Euripides' classic tragedy of Troy's female aristocracy in chains—which features Katharine Hepburn, Vanessa Redgrave, and Irene Pappas.

For Greece's WWII experience, try *The Guns of Navarone* (1961), where a team of soldiers tries to take out a German artillery battery. Another war film, *Captain Corelli's Mandolin* (2001), is the love story of an Italian officer and a Greek woman. *My Family & Other Animals* (2005) follows the adventures of an English family relocated to Greece in 1939.

Life in post-war Greece was illustrated in several movies starring Melina Mercouri (who later became Greece's Minister of Culture). She played a beautiful woman with a shady background in *Stella* (1955) and *Never on Sunday* (1960). *Zorba the Greek* (1964) shows how Greek culture can free even the most uptight Englishman. *Z* (1969) is a thriller about the assassination of a crusading politician—and the rise of the Greek junta—in the 1960s. *My Big Fat Greek Wedding* (2002) is a hilarious comedy about marrying into a Greek-American family. Finally, the ABBA musical *Mamma Mia!* (2008) may do for Greece what *The Sound of Music* did for Austria and *Lord of the Rings* did for New Zealand—hordes of fans now want to see the film's locations in the mainland region of Pelion and on the islands of Skiathos and Skopelos.

NOVA's informative *Secrets of the Parthenon* episode (2008) is available to watch on hulu.com.

Holidays and Festivals

This list includes many—but not all—big festivals in major cities, plus national holidays. Before planning a trip around a festival, make sure you verify its dates by checking the festival's website or contacting the Greek National Tourist Organization in the US (tel. 212/421-5777, www.visitgreece.gr). Many sights and banks close down on national holidays—keep this in mind when planning your itinerary.

Here are some major holidays:

Jan 1	New Year's Day
Jan 6	Epiphany
Mid-Jan-March	Carnival Season (Apokreo), famous in Patra, peaks on the last Sunday before Lent
March 2	"Clean Monday" (Kathari Deftera, the first day of Lent in the Orthodox church; March 7 in 2011, Feb 27 in 2012)
March 25	Greek Independence Day
Easter Weekend	Orthodox Good Friday through Easter Monday (April 22-25 in 2011, April 13-16 in 2012)
May 1	Labor Day
June	Miaoulia Festival, Hydra
June	Nafplio Festival, classical music, Nafplio
June-Aug	Athens & Epidavros Festival (music, opera, dance, and theater at the Odeon of Herodes Atticus beneath the Acropolis in Athens; drama and music at the Theater of Epidavros)
July-August	Ancient Olympia International Festival (music, dance, and theater at the site of the ancient Olympics)
Aug 15	Assumption
Sept	Athens International Film Festival
Oct 28	Ohi Day (Anniversary of the "No"; commemorates rejection of Mussolini's WWII ultimatum)
Dec 25	Christmas
Dec 26	"Second Day" of Christmas

Conversions and Climate

Numbers and Stumblers

- Europeans write a few of their numbers differently than we do. 1 = 1, 4 = 4, 7 = 7.
- In Europe, dates appear as day/month/year, so Christmas is 25/12/12.
- Commas are decimal points and decimals commas. A dollar and a half is 1,50, and there are 5.280 feet in a mile.
- When counting with fingers, start with your thumb. If you hold up your first finger to request one item, you'll probably get two.
- What Americans call the second floor of a building is the first floor in Europe.
- On escalators and moving sidewalks, Europeans keep the left "lane" open for passing. Keep to the right.

Metric Conversions (approximate)

A kilogram is 2.2 pounds, and 1 liter is about a quart, or almost four to a gallon. A kilometer is six-tenths of a mile. I figure kilometers to miles by cutting them in half and adding back 10 percent of the original (120 km: 60 + 12 = 72 miles, 300 km: 150 + 30 = 180 miles).

1 foot = 0.3 meter	1 square yard = 0.8 square meter
1 yard = 0.9 meter	1 square mile = 2.6 square kilometers
1 mile = 1.6 kilometers	1 ounce = 28 grams
1 centimeter = 0.4 inch	1 quart = 0.95 liter
1 meter = 39.4 inches	1 kilogram = 2.2 pounds
1 kilometer = 0.62 mile	32°F = 0°C

Clothing Sizes

When shopping for clothing, use these US-to-European comparisons as general guidelines (but note that no conversion is perfect).

- Women's dresses and blouses: Add 30
  (US size 10 = European size 40)
- Men's suits and jackets: Add 10
  (US size 40 regular = European size 50)
- Men's shirts: Multiply by 2 and add about 8
  (US size 15 collar = European size 38)
- Women's shoes: Add about 30
  (US size 8 = European size 38-39)
- Men's shoes: Add 32-34
  (US size 9 = European size 41; US size 11 = European size 45)

Climate

The first line is Athens' average daily temperature; the second line, the average daily low. The third line shows the average number of days without rain. For more detailed weather statistics for destinations throughout Greece (as well as the rest of the world), check www.worldclimate.com.

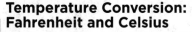

J	F	M	A	M	J	J	A	S	O	N	D
56°	57°	60°	66°	75°	83°	88°	88°	82°	73°	66°	59°
44°	45°	47°	53°	60°	68°	73°	72°	67°	59°	53°	48°
24	22	26	27	28	28	30	30	28	27	24	24

Temperature Conversion: Fahrenheit and Celsius

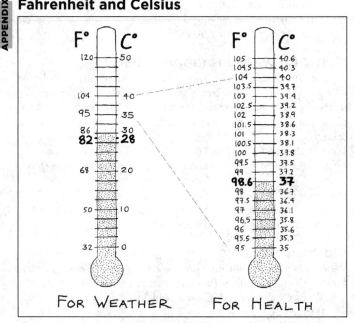

FOR WEATHER   FOR HEALTH

Greece takes its temperature using the Celsius scale, while we opt for Fahrenheit. For a rough conversion from Celsius to Fahrenheit, double the number and add 30. For weather, remember that 28°C is 82°F—perfect. For health, 37°C is just right.

Essential Packing Checklist

Whether you're traveling for five days or five weeks, here's what you'll need to bring. Remember to pack light to enjoy the sweet freedom of true mobility. Happy travels!

- ❑ 5 shirts
- ❑ 1 sweater or lightweight fleece jacket
- ❑ 2 pairs pants
- ❑ 1 pair shorts
- ❑ 1 swimsuit (women only—men can use shorts)
- ❑ 5 pairs underwear and socks
- ❑ 1 pair shoes
- ❑ 1 rainproof jacket
- ❑ Tie or scarf
- ❑ Money belt
- ❑ Money—your mix of:
  - ❑ Debit card for ATM withdrawals
  - ❑ Credit card
  - ❑ Hard cash in US dollars (in easy-to-exchange $20 bills)
- ❑ Documents (and back-up photocopies):
  - ❑ Passport
  - ❑ Printout of airline e-ticket
  - ❑ Driver's license
  - ❑ Student ID and hostel card
  - ❑ Railpass/car rental voucher
  - ❑ Insurance details
- ❑ Daypack
- ❑ Sealable plastic baggies
- ❑ Camera and related gear
- ❑ Empty water bottle
- ❑ Wristwatch and alarm clock
- ❑ Earplugs
- ❑ First-aid kit
- ❑ Medicine (labeled)
- ❑ Extra glasses/contacts and prescriptions
- ❑ Sunscreen and sunglasses
- ❑ Toiletries kit
- ❑ Soap
- ❑ Laundry soap (if liquid and carry-on, limit to 3 oz.)
- ❑ Clothesline
- ❑ Small towel
- ❑ Sewing kit
- ❑ Travel information
- ❑ Necessary map(s)
- ❑ Address list (email and mailing addresses)
- ❑ Postcards and photos from home
- ❑ Notepad and pen
- ❑ Journal

If you plan to carry on your luggage, note that all liquids must be in three-ounce or smaller containers and fit within a single quart-size baggie. For details, see www.tsa.gov/travelers.

Hotel Reservation

To: _____   _____
            hotel   *email or fax*

From:_____   _____
            name   *email or fax*

Today's date: _____ /_____ /_____
                       day   *month*   *year*

Dear Hotel _____ ,
Please make this reservation for me:

Name: _____

Total # of people: _____   # of rooms: _____   # of nights: _____

Arriving: _____ /_____ /_____   My time of arrival (24-hr clock): _____
                day *month* *year*   (I will telephone if I will be late)

Departing: _____ /_____ /_____
                  day *month* *year*

Room(s): Single____   Double ____   Twin ____   Triple ____   Quad____

With: Toilet ____   Shower ____   Bath ____   Sink only ____

Special needs: View____   Quiet____   Cheapest ____   Ground Floor____

Please email or fax confirmation of my reservation, along with the type of
room reserved and the price. Please also inform me of your cancellation
policy. After I hear from you, I will quickly send my credit-card information
as a deposit to hold the room. Thank you.

_____
Name

_____
Address

_____
City   *State*   *Zip Code*   *Country*

*Before hoteliers can make your reservation, they want to know the informa-
tion listed above. You can use this form as the basis for your email, or you can
photocopy this page, fill in the information, and send it as a fax (also available
online at www.ricksteves.com/reservation).*

Greek Survival Phrases

Knowing a few phrases of Greek can help if you're traveling off the beaten path. Just learning the pleasantries (such as please and thank you) will improve your connections with locals, even in the bigger cities.

Because Greek words can be transliterated differently in English, I've also included the Greek spellings. Note that in Greek, a semicolon is used the same way we use a question mark.

Hello. (formal)	**Gia sas.** Γειά σας.	yah sahs
Hi. / Bye. (informal)	**Gia.** Γειά.	yah
Good morning.	**Kali mera.** Καλή μέρα.	kah-**lee meh**-rah
Good afternoon.	**Kali spera.** Καλή σπέρα.	kah-**lee speh**-rah
Do you speak English?	**Milate anglika?** Μιλάτε αγγλικά;	mee-**lah**-teh ahn-glee-**kah**
Yes. / No.	**Ne. / Ohi.** Ναι. / Όχι.	neh / **oh**-hee
I understand.	**Katalaveno.** Καταλαβαίνω.	kah-tah-lah-**veh**-noh
I don't understand.	**Den katalaveno.** Δεν καταλαβαίνω.	dehn kah-tah-lah-**veh**-noh
Please. (Also: You're welcome.)	**Parakalo.** Παρακαλώ.	pah-rah-kah-**loh**
Thank you (very much).	**Efharisto (poli).** Ευχαριστώ (πολύ).	ehf-hah-ree-**stoh** (poh-**lee**)
Excuse me. (Also: I'm sorry.)	**Sygnomi.** Συγνώμη.	seeg-**noh**-mee
(No) problem.	**(Kanena) problima.** (Κανένα) πρόβλημα.	(kah-**neh**-nah) proh**v**-lee-mah
Good.	**Orea.** Ωραία.	oh-**reh**-ah
Goodbye.	**Antio.** Αντίο.	ahd-**yoh** (think "adieu")
Good night.	**Kali nikta.** Καλή νύχτα.	kah-**lee neek**-tah
one / two	**ena / dio** ένα / δύο	**eh**-nah / **dee**-oh
three / four	**tria / tessera** τρία /τέσσερα	**tree**-ah / **teh**-seh-rah
five / six	**pente / exi** πέντε / έξι	**peh**-deh / **ehk**-see
seven / eight	**efta / ohto** εφτά / οχτώ	ehf-**tah** / oh-**toh**
nine / ten	**ennia / deka** εννιά / δέκα	ehn-**yah** / **deh**-kah
hundred / thousand	**ekato / hilia** εκατό / χίλια	eh-kah-**toh** / **heel**-yah
How much?	**Poso kani?** Πόσο κάνει;	**poh**-soh **kah**-nee
euro	**evro** ευρώ	ev-**roh**
Write it?	**Grapsete to?** Γράψετε το;	**grahp**-seh-teh toh

English	Greek	Pronunciation
Is it free?	**Ine dorean?** Είναι δωρεάν;	ee-neh doh-ree-**ahn**
Is it included?	**Perilamvanete?** Περιλαμβάνεται;	peh-ree-lahm-**vah**-neh-teh
Where can I find / buy...?	**Pou boro na vro /** **agoraso...?** Που μπορώ να βρω / αγοράσω...;	poo boh-**roh** nah vroh / ah-goh-**rah**-soh
I'd like / We'd like...	**Tha ithela /** **Tha thelame...** Θα ήθελα / Θα θέλαμε...	thah ee-**theh**-lah / thah **theh**-lah-meh
...a room.	**...ena dhomatio.** ...ένα δωμάτιο.	eh-nah doh-**mah**-tee-oh
...a ticket to ___.	**...ena isitirio** **gia ___.** ...ένα εισιτήριο για ___.	eh-nah ee-see-**tee**-ree-oh yah ___
Is it possible?	**Ginete?** Γίνεται;	yee-neh-teh
Where is...?	**Pou ine...?** Που είναι...;	poo ee-neh
...the bus station	**...o stathmos ton** **leoforion** ...ο σταθμός των λεωφορίων	oh stahth-mohs tohn leh-oh-foh-**ree**-ohn
...the train station	**...o stathmos tou trenou** ...ο σταθμός του τρένου	oh stahth-mohs too treh-noo
...the tourist information office	**...to grafeio** **enimerosis** **touriston** ...το γραφείο ενημέρωσης τουριστών	too grah-**fee**-oh eh-nee-**meh**-roh-sis too-ree-**stohn**
...the toilet	**...toualeta** ...τουαλέτα	twah-**leh**-tah
men	**andres** άντρες	**ahn**-drehs
women	**gynekes** γυναικες	yee-**neh**-kehs
left / right	**dexia / aristera** δεξιά / αριστερά	dehk-see-**ah** / ah-ree-steh-**rah**
straight	**efthia** ευθεία	ehf-**thee**-ah
At what time...	**Ti ora...** Τι ώρα...	tee **oh**-rah
...does this open / close?	**...anigete / klinete?** ...ανοίγετε / κλείνετε;	ah-**nee**-yeh-teh / **klee**-neh-teh
Just a moment.	**Ena lepto.** Ένα λεπτό.	eh-nah lep-**toh**
now / soon / later	**tora / se ligo /** **argotera** τώρα / σε λίγο / αργότερα	**toh**-rah / seh **lee**-goh / ar-**goh**-teh-rah
today / tomorrow	**simera / avrio** σήμερα / αύριο	**see**-meh-rah / **ahv**-ree-oh

In the Restaurant

I'd like to reserve...	**Tha ithela na kliso**... Θα ήθελα να κλείσω...	thah **ee**-theh-lah nah **klee**-soh
We'd like to reserve...	**Tha thelame na klisoume...** Θα θέλαμε να κλείσουμε...	thah **theh**-lah-meh nah **klee**-soo-meh
...a table for one / two.	**...ena trapezi gia enan / dio.** ...ένα τραπέζι για έναν / δύο.	**eh**-nah trah-**peh**-zee yah **eh**-nahn / **dee**-oh
non-smoking	**mi kapnizon** μη καπνίζων	mee kahp-**nee**-zohn
Is this table free?	**Ine eleftero afto to trapezi?** Είναι ελεύθερο αυτό το τραπέζι;	ee-neh eh-**lef**-teh-roh ahf-**toh** toh trah-**peh**-zee
The menu (in English), please.	**Ton katalogo (sta anglika) parakalo.** Τον κατάλογο (στα αγγλικά) παρακαλώ.	tohn kah-**tah**-loh-goh (stah ahn-glee-**kah**) pah-rah-kah-**loh**
service (not) included	**to servis (den) perilamvanete** το σέρβις (δεν) περιλαμβάνεται	toh **sehr**-vees (dehn) peh-ree-lahm-**vah**-neh-teh
cover charge	**kouver** κουβέρ	koo-**vehr**
"to go"	**gia exo** για έξω	yah **ehk**-soh
with / without	**me / horis** με / χωρίς	meh / hoh-**rees**
and / or	**ke / i** και / ή	keh / ee
fixed-price meal	**menu** μενού	meh-**noo**
specialty of the house	**i specialite tou magaziou** η σπεσιαλιτέ του μαγαζιού	ee speh-see-ah-lee-**teh** too mah-gah-zee-**oo**
half-portion	**misi merida** μισή μερίδα	mee-**see** meh-**ree**-dah
daily special	**to piato tis meras** το πιάτο της μέρας	toh pee-**ah**-toh tees meh-rahs
appetizers	**proto piato** πρώτο πιάτο	**proh**-toh pee-**ah**-toh
bread	**psomi** ψωμί	psoh-**mee**
cheese	**tiri** τυρί	tee-**ree**
sandwich	**sandwich** or **toast** σάντουιτς, τόστ	"sandwich," "toast"
soup	**soupa** σούπα	soo-**pah**
salad	**salata** σαλάτα	sah-**lah**-tah
meat	**kreas** κρέας	**kray**-ahs

APPENDIX

poultry / chicken	**poulerika / kotopoulo** πουλερικα / κοτόπουλο	poo-leh-ree-**kah** / koh-**toh**-poo-loh
fish /seafood	**psari / psarika** ψάρι / ψαρικά	psah-ree / psah-ree-**kah**
shellfish	**thalassina** θαλασσινά	thah-lah-see-**nah**
fruit	**frouta** φρούτα	froo-tah
vegetables	**lahanika** λαχανικά	lah-hah-nee-**kah**
dessert	**gliko** γλυκό	lee-**koh**
(tap) water	**nero (tis vrisis)** νερο (της βρύσης)	neh-**roh** (tees **vree**-sees)
mineral water	**metalliko nero** μεταλλικό νερό	meh-tah-lee-**koh** neh-**roh**
milk	**gala** γάλα	**gah**-lah
(orange) juice	**himos (portokali)** χυμός (πορτοκάλι)	hee-**mohs** (por-toh-**kah**-lee)
coffee	**kafes** καφές	kah-**fehs**
tea	**tsai** τσάι	**chah**-ee
wine (spoken)	**krasi** κρασί	krah-**see**
wine (printed on label)	**inos** οίνος	**ee**-nohs
red / white	**kokkino / aspro** κόκκινο / άσπρο	**koh**-kee-noh / **ah**-sproh

sweet / dry /
  semi-dry
	**gliko / ksiro /
	  imixiro**
	γλυκό / ξηρό /
	ημίξηρο
		lee-**koh** / ksee-**roh** /
		  ee-**meek**-see-roh

glass / bottle	**potiri / boukali** ποτήρι /μπουκάλι	poh-**tee**-ree / boo-**kah**-lee
beer	**bira** μπύρα	**bee**-rah
Here you are. (when given food)	**Oriste.** Ορίστε.	oh-**ree**-steh
Enjoy your meal!	**Kali orexi!** Καλή όρεξη!	kah-**lee** oh-**rehk**-see
(To your) health! (like "Cheers!")	**(Stin i) gia mas!** (Στην υ) γειά μας!	(stee nee) yah mahs
Another.	**Allo ena.** Άλλο ένα.	**ah**-loh **eh**-nah

Bill, please.	**Ton logariasmo
	  parakalo.**
	Τον λογαριασμό
	παρακαλώ.
		tohn loh-gah-ree-ahs-**moh**
		  pah-rah-kah-**loh**

tip	**bourbouar** μπουρμπουάρ	boor-boo-**ar**
Very good!	**Poli oreo!** Πολύ ωραίο!	poh-**lee** oh-**ray**-oh
Delicious!	**Poli nostimo!** Πολύ νόστιμο!	poh-**lee** **nohs**-tee-moh

INDEX

INDEX

MAP INDEX

Audio Europe

RICK STEVES AUDIO EUROPE

Free mobile app (and podcast)

With the **Rick Steves Audio Europe** app, your iPhone or smartphone becomes a powerful travel tool.

This exciting app organizes Rick's entire audio library by country—giving you a playlist of all his audio walking tours, radio interviews, and travel tips for wherever you're going in Europe.

Let the experts Rick interviews enrich your understanding. Let Rick's self-guided tours amplify your guidebook. With Rick in your ear, Europe gets even better.

Thanks Facebook fans for submitting photos while on location! From top: John Kuijper in Florence, Brenda Mamer with her mother in Rome, Angel Capobianco in London, and Alyssa Passey with her friend in Paris.

Find out more at ricksteves.com/audioeurope

Join a Rick Steves tour

Enjoy Europe's warmest welcome...

with the flexibility and friendship of a small group
getting to know Rick's favorite places and people.
It all starts with our free tour catalog and DVD.

Great guides, small groups, no grumps.

tours.ricksteves.com

Start your trip at

Free information and great gear to

▸ Plan Your Trip

Browse thousands of articles and a wealth of money-saving tips for planning your dream trip. You'll find up-to-date information on Europe's best destinations, packing smart, getting around, finding rooms, staying healthy, avoiding scams and more.

▸ Eurail Passes

Find out, step-by-step, if a railpass makes sense for your trip—and how to avoid buying more than you need. Get a bunch of free extras!

▸ Graffiti Wall & Travelers' Helpline

Learn, ask, share—our online community of savvy travelers is a great resource for first-time travelers to Europe, as well as seasoned pros.

Rick Steves' Europe Through the Back Door, Inc.

ricksteves.com

turn your travel dreams into affordable reality

▶ Free Audio Tours & Travel Newsletter

Get your nose out of this guide book and focus on what you'll be seeing with Rick's free audio tours of the greatest sights in Paris, London, Rome, Florence and Venice.

Subscribe to our free Travel News e-newsletter, and get monthly articles from Rick on what's happening in Europe.

▶ Great Gear from Rick's Travel Store

Pack light and right—on a budget—with Rick's custom-designed carry-on bags, roll-aboards, day packs, travel accessories, guidebooks, journals, maps and DVDs of his TV shows.

130 Fourth Avenue North, PO Box 2009 • Edmonds, WA 98020 USA
Phone: (425) 771-8303 • Fax: (425) 771-0833 • www.ricksteves.com

Rick Steves

www.ricksteves.com

EUROPE GUIDES

Best of Europe
Eastern Europe
Europe Through the Back Door

COUNTRY GUIDES

Croatia & Slovenia
England
France
Germany
Great Britain
Ireland
Italy
Portugal
Scandinavia
Spain
Switzerland

CITY & REGIONAL GUIDES

Amsterdam, Bruges & Brussels
Budapest
Florence & Tuscany
Greece: Athens & the Peloponnese
Istanbul
London
Paris
Prague & the Czech Republic
Provence & the French Riviera
Rome
Venice
Vienna, Salzburg & Tirol

SNAPSHOT GUIDES

Barcelona
Berlin
Bruges & Brussels
Copenhagen & the Best of
   Denmark
Dublin
Dubrovnik
Hill Towns of Central Italy
Italy's Cinque Terre
Krakow, Warsaw & Gdansk
Lisbon
Madrid & Toledo
Munich, Bavaria & Salzburg
Naples & the Amalfi Coast
Northern Ireland
Norway
Scotland
Sevilla, Granada & Southern Spain
Stockholm

POCKET GUIDES

London
Paris
Rome

TRAVEL CULTURE

Europe 101
European Christmas
Postcards from Europe
Travel as a Political Act

Rick Steves guidebooks are published by Avalon Travel,
a member of the Perseus Books Group.

NOW AVAILABLE: eBOOKS, APPS, DVDs, & BLU-RAY

eBOOKS

Most guides available as eBooks from Amazon, Barnes & Noble, Borders, Apple iBook and Sony eReader, beginning January 2011

RICK STEVES' EUROPE DVDs

Austria & the Alps
Eastern Europe, Israel & Egypt
England & Wales
European Travel Skills & Specials
France
Germany, Benelux & More
Greece & Turkey
Iran
Ireland & Scotland
Italy's Cities
Italy's Countryside
Rick Steves' European Christmas
Scandinavia
Spain & Portugal

BLU-RAY

Celtic Charms
Eastern Europe Favorites
European Christmas
Italy Through the Back Door
Surprising Cities of Europe

PHRASE BOOKS & DICTIONARIES

French
French, Italian & German
German
Italian
Portuguese
Spanish

JOURNALS

Rick Steves' Pocket Travel Journal
Rick Steves' Travel Journal

APPS

Rick Steves' Ancient Rome Tour
Rick Steves' Historic Paris Walk
Rick Steves' Louvre Tour
Rick Steves' Orsay Museum Tour
Rick Steves' St. Peter's Basilica Tour
Rick Steves' Versailles

PLANNING MAPS

Britain, Ireland & London
Europe
France & Paris
Germany, Austria & Switzerland
Ireland
Italy
Spain & Portugal

Rick Steves books and DVDs are available at bookstores and through online booksellers.

Credits

To research and write this book, Rick relied on...

Writers

Cameron Hewitt

Cameron writes and edits guidebooks for Rick Steves. For this book, he explored Greece's evocative ancient sites, windswept seascapes, delightfully chaotic cities, and rollicking tavernas—along the way discovering a new favorite dessert *(kataifi)*. Cameron lives in Seattle with his wife Shawna.

Gene Openshaw

Gene is the co-author of 10 Rick Steves books. For this book, he wrote material on Greece's art, history, and contemporary culture. When not traveling, Gene enjoys composing music, recovering from his 1973 trip to Europe with Rick, and living everyday life with his daughter.

Researcher

Tom Griffin

Tom fell in love with Greece many years ago, thanks to Homer, *The Magus*, and a crazy sojourn in a fishing village in Crete. Before joining the book department at Rick Steves, he was a magazine editor, newspaper reporter, and Berlitz teacher. He lives in Seattle with his wife Julie.

Acknowledgments

Efharisto poli to our tour-guide friends David Willett, Colin Clement, Colleen Murphy, and Julie and Reid Coen for their invaluable help in shaping this book. Their travel savvy, knowledge, and understanding of Greek culture—and their never-ending quest to find the perfect ruined temple, secluded beach, bottle of ouzo, and other Back Door experiences—gave this book a firm foundation. Also, many thanks to Kiki Tsagkarki-Rae for her help with the Greek survival phrases. *Stin i gia mas!*

Image Credits

Full-Page Images	**Photographer**
Parthenon, Acropolis, Athens	Cameron Hewitt
Vathia, Mani Peninsula, Peloponnese	Laura VanDeventer
Sanctuary of Athena, Delphi	Rick Steves

Rick Steves' Guidebook Series

Country Guides

Rick Steves' Best of Europe
Rick Steves' Croatia & Slovenia
Rick Steves' Eastern Europe
Rick Steves' England
Rick Steves' France
Rick Steves' Germany

Rick Steves' Great Britain
Rick Steves' Ireland
Rick Steves' Italy
Rick Steves' Portugal
Rick Steves' Scandinavia
Rick Steves' Spain
Rick Steves' Switzerland

City and Regional Guides

Rick Steves' Amsterdam, Bruges & Brussels
Rick Steves' Greece: Athens & the Peloponnese
Rick Steves' Budapest
Rick Steves' Florence & Tuscany
Rick Steves' Istanbul
Rick Steves' London

Rick Steves' Paris
Rick Steves' Prague & the Czech Republic
Rick Steves' Provence & the French Riviera
Rick Steves' Rome
Rick Steves' Venice
Rick Steves' Vienna, Salzburg & Tirol

Rick Steves' Phrase Books

French
French/Italian/German
German
Italian
Portuguese
Spanish

Snapshot Guides

Excerpted chapters from country guides, such as *Rick Steves' Snapshot Barcelona*, *Rick Steves' Snapshot Scotland*, and *Rick Steves' Snapshot Hill Towns of Central Italy*.

Pocket Guides (new in 2011)

Condensed, pocket-size, full-color guides to Europe's top cities: Paris, London, and Rome.

Other Books

Rick Steves' Europe 101: History and Art for the Traveler
Rick Steves' Europe Through the Back Door
Rick Steves' European Christmas
Rick Steves' Postcards from Europe
Rick Steves' Travel as a Political Act

Avalon Travel
a member of the Perseus Books Group
1700 Fourth Street
Berkeley, CA 94710, USA

Text © 2011 by Rick Steves. All rights reserved.
Maps © 2011 by Europe Through the Back Door. All rights reserved.
Photos are used by permission and are the property of the original copyright owners.
Printed in the U.S.A. by Worzalla
First printing March 2011
Portions of this book were originally published in *Rick Steves' Best of Europe* © 2006 by
Rick Steves and *Rick Steves' Europe Through the Back Door* © 2002, 2003, 2004, 2005, 2006,
2007, 2008 by Rick Steves.

ISBN 978-1-59880-772-1
ISSN 1947-4725

For the latest on Rick's lectures, books, tours, public-radio show, and public-television
series, contact Europe Through the Back Door, Box 2009, Edmonds, WA 98020, tel.
425/771-8303, fax 425/771-0833, www.ricksteves.com, rick@ricksteves.com.

Europe Through the Back Door Reviewing Editors: Cathy Lu, Jennifer Madison Davis,
    Cameron Hewitt
ETBD Editors: Gretchen Strauch, Tom Griffin, Cathy McDonald
ETBD Managing Editor: Risa Laib
Additional Writing: David Willett
Research Assistance: Tom Griffin
Avalon Travel Senior Editor & Series Manager: Madhu Prasher
Avalon Travel Project Editor: Kelly Lydick
Copy Editor: Naomi Adler-Dancis
Proofreader: Janet Walden
Indexer: Laura Welcome
Production & Typesetting: McGuire Barber Design
Cover Design: Kimberly Glyder Design
Graphic Content Director: Laura VanDeventer
Maps and Graphics: David C. Hoerlein, Laura VanDeventer, Lauren Mills, Brice Ticen,
    Pat O'Connor, Barb Geisler, Mike Morgenfeld
Photography: Rick Steves, Cameron Hewitt, Gene Openshaw, Tom Griffin, Laura
    VanDeventer, Carol Ries, David Willett
Front matter color photos: p. i, Greek Column Fragments © Laura VanDeventer; p. iv,
    Anafiotika Neighborhood, Athens © Laura VanDeventer, Vathia © David Willett; p. v,
    Gythio Harbor © Cameron Hewitt, Minoan Boxers, National Archaeological Museum,
    Athens © Cameron Hewitt, Church of Agia Sophia, Monemvasia © Rick Steves; p. viii,
    Old Kardamyli © Laura VanDeventer
Cover Photo: Acropolis including Library of Hadrian columns, Athens, Greece © Marco
    Simoni/Getty Images

*Although the author and publisher have made every effort to provide accurate, up-to-date
information, they accept no responsibility for loss, injury, bad souvlaki, or inconvenience sustained
by any person using this book.*